Founder of Modern Economics

OXFORD STUDIES IN THE HISTORY OF ECONOMICS

Series Editor: Steven G. Medema, University of Colorado, Denver

This series publishes leading-edge scholarship by historians of economics and social science, drawing upon approaches from intellectual history, the history of ideas, and the history of the natural and social sciences. It embraces the history of economic thinking from ancient times to the present, the evolution of the discipline itself, the relationship of economics to other fields of inquiry, and the diffusion of economic ideas within the discipline and to the policy realm and broader publics. This enlarged scope affords the possibility of looking anew at the intellectual, social, and professional forces that have surrounded and conditioned economics' continued development.

Founder of Modern Economics: Paul A. Samuelson

Volume 1: Becoming Samuelson, 1915–1948

ROGER E. BACKHOUSE

OXFORD
UNIVERSITY PRESS

(4

OXFORD
UNIVERSITY PRESS

Oxford University Press is a department of the University of Oxford. It furthers
the University's objective of excellence in research, scholarship, and education
by publishing worldwide. Oxford is a registered trade mark of Oxford University
Press in the UK and certain other countries.

Published in the United States of America by Oxford University Press
198 Madison Avenue, New York, NY 10016, United States of America.

Library of Congress Cataloging-in-Publication Data
Names: Backhouse, Roger, 1951– author.
Title: Founder of modern economics : Paul A. Samuelson / Roger E. Backhouse.
Other titles: Becoming Samuelson, 1915–48.
Description: New York, NY : Oxford University Press, [2017]– | Series: Oxford
studies in the history of economics | Includes bibliographical references
and index. Contents: Volume 1. Becoming Samuelson, 1915–48 —
Identifiers: LCCN 2016036634 | ISBN 9780190664091 (vol. 1)
Subjects: LCSH: Samuelson, Paul A. (Paul Anthony), 1915–2009. |
Economists—United States—Biography. | Economics—United States.
Classification: LCC HB119.S25 B33 2017 | DDC 330.092 [B] —dc23
LC record available at https://lccn.loc.gov/2016036634

9 8 7 6 5 4 3 2 1
Printed by Edwards Brothers Malloy, United States of America

CONTENTS

LIST OF FIGURES

LIST OF TABLES

PREFACE AND ACKNOWLEDGMENTS

T O ECONOMISTS OF a certain age, a biography of Paul Samuelson requires no justification. He was a towering figure in economics, but little is known about him other than his publications and the reputation of his department at Massachusetts Institute of Technology (MIT). As with most economists, his life is, for the most part, of little interest, containing few of the dramatic events and none of the scandals that hold the attention of the nonspecialist reader. Unlike, for example, the scientists J. D. Bernal or J. Robert Oppenheimer, there is no life of action, intrigue, communism, or sexual exploits to entertain. He married young and his marriage lasted until his wife's death. Apart from government consultancy and joining a scientific laboratory for a period during the Second World War, Samuelson sat in his office doing economics, went to seminars and conferences discussing economics, advised politicians about economics, wrote about economics in the press, and even sat at home with his children on his lap, thinking about economics. He could have fun outside economics (the book mentions some occasions remembered by his many friends) and he was a keen tennis player, but economics was never far from his mind. His life is of interest only insofar as it is relevant to his economics. There is thus ample reason for this being an intellectual biography—the story of the evolution of his ideas—rather than a full life.

Moreover, even if it were desirable to write a detailed account of Samuelson's life, it would not be possible. Any biography is constrained by the source material. Few subjects leave materials that are sufficient to answer every question the biographer wants to ask of them, and Samuelson is no exception. His papers, filling 155 boxes, with over 70 boxes of correspondence alone, are extensive but not comprehensive. His activities as a student are not documented in detail: his correspondence indicates that he kept his student notes at least until the late 1940s, but they appear not to have survived. The boxes of unpublished papers include some student essays, but these can surely be only a fraction of the ones he wrote. His transcripts indicate only those courses he attended for credit, leaving us in ignorance of the many that he audited. No records survive of how and where he met many of the teachers he claims to have known well. Information is also patchy on the courses he taught. Such student notes as exist suggest that in the early years he told students what to read and that written reading lists may never have existed. The report written at the end of his first externally funded research project is missing, making it necessary to speculate as to what it achieved (or, much more likely, failed to achieve). Records of his submissions to journals, and hence what referees thought of them, are incomplete because neither he nor the journal offices have kept records. The publication history of *Foundations of Economic Analysis* is well documented in the archives of Harvard University Press, but the early history of his textbook is less clear: McGraw-Hill's archives, if they still exist, have not been located. There is also the problem of no written traces of most of his interactions with friends, teachers, and colleagues. He left nothing resembling an engagement diary.

Samuelson was forever telling stories about his life, frequently bringing them into accounts of people he had known, but these stories were not systematic. They focused on the events that supported his self-image as a self-taught prodigy who fell in love with economics at first sight. He enjoyed reminiscing about the past, especially the golden years of Harvard economics, and celebrating the achievements of his teachers and friends, often hailed as if they were Greek or Roman gods. Later in his life, Samuelson embarked on an autobiography but abandoned it, writing about little beyond his early life. Autobiography loses interest, he wrote, when success arrives, a point he dated to 1940, when he was just twenty-five years old. Even his account of his Harvard years did little more than reproduce material from an article he had previously published. These recollections are invaluable in filling out the archival record, but they need to be treated with caution. He was generally reluctant to provide details beyond what was needed to back up the claims he wanted to make. For example, when asked about his mathematical education, he listed areas of mathematics on which he had attended lectures but was deliberately vague on who had taught him and when. As far as he was concerned, the questioner appeared to be doubting his claim to be essentially self-taught in mathematics. Details have to be teased out of a variety of sources, and even then they are incomplete.

There is the further problem that there are places where Samuelson was clearly saying things for effect and the absence of alternative sources makes it impossible to disentangle the facts from the points he wanted to make. His account of his first encounter with Harold Burbank was intended to make the point that he was bold and confident, standing up to an anti-Semitic department chair whom he despised. Some readers will wonder whether his account of this meeting is plausible. If Samuelson behaved as he did, then surely he would have given an anti-Semite ample excuse to refuse him admission to Harvard. In many cases I have simply reported Samuelson's accounts, leaving it to the reader to decide for herself whether they should be read as factual reports of events or as autobiographical accounts that reveal Samuelson's personality and attitudes without necessarily telling us what an impartial spectator would have seen. This procedure does mean that in a few places this biography becomes autobiography; but these instances of autobiography are no more than glimpses, and in the book as a whole they are placed within a context that is not one provided by its subject.

Though structured around the life of one economist, the story told here offers an account of the overlapping communities of economists to which Samuelson belonged: the University of Chicago, Harvard University, Massachusetts Institute of Technology (MIT), and wartime Washington. Parts of this book are therefore, by design, as much a picture of the people with whom he interacted and the ideas to which he was been exposed as of Samuelson himself. The reason for this emphasis is to explain the context in which Samuelson developed his ideas, revealing connections with the past that might otherwise not be apparent to anyone viewing Samuelson's writings in the context of what happened subsequently. The work of economists such as Aaron Director, Frank Knight, Jacob Viner, Paul Douglas, Leonard Crum, Joseph Schumpeter, Edwin Bidwell Wilson, Gottfried Haberler, Wassily Leontief, Alvin Hansen and Lawrence Klein is important both to understand Samuelson and to understand the transition of which he was a part. Because some of them are little known, or known by their later work, their ideas have to be described in some detail.

This emphasis is central to my reading of Samuelson as a transitional figure linking what has been described as a pluralist interwar economics with the narrower, more theoretical, mathematical, "neoclassical" economics that emerged after the Second World War. It is also important in providing a picture of that transition, which can be seen by comparing Samuelson's own approach to economics with that of his teachers. Though he was not single-handedly responsible for the transition—it would be absurd to suggest that—his work and that of the growing community of his friends and colleagues embodied the new approach to economics. The story of an individual that I present here is at the same time a story of a succession of overlapping communities of economists in a period that saw dramatic changes in the subject.

Samuelson's biography poses organizational problems, for there is more than one thread running through his intellectual development and these different threads overlap. There are some clear chronological breaks—notably his moves from Chicago to Harvard in 1935 and from Harvard to MIT in 1940 (the latter was a less decisive break; Chicago to Cambridge is nearly a thousand miles; from Harvard to MIT is close to two miles and he continued to live very close to Harvard). For his student years, the rhythm of the academic year makes it possible to adopt a roughly chronological structure, but once he moved to MIT and into government service, this rhythm disappears. It becomes necessary to depart from strict chronology in order to avoid jumping back and forth between different themes. An earlier draft was strictly chronological, and though it may have shown how Samuelson juggled many activities simultaneously, it was baffling for readers trying to follow the development of his ideas.

Samuelson's personality and the social networks in which he became involved are essential to understanding his intellectual development and the position he came to hold within American economics. However, for all that he liked to be the center of attention—and he did—he was private. It is impossible to reconstruct a day-to-day account of his activities and his interactions with family and friends. Occasional glimpses are given in his correspondence, and these are brought into the narrative as much as possible, but no more than this is attempted. The place where this probably matters most is his relationship with Marion Crawford, whom he married in 1938. Such evidence as there is suggests that her role in his early work was substantial and may have gone beyond what it has been possible to document here.

Many economists reading this book will expect me to relate Samuelson's early work to what he did later in his life. Clearly, the book would never have been written had he not gone on to become a significant figure in the profession, and it is impossible to forget what happened to him after 1948. However, I have tried as far as possible to put aside what I know of his subsequent career and to read as little as possible of his later writings into his early work. Given Samuelson rarely missed a chance to talk about himself or to praise his friends, this exposes me to the danger that readers who are more familiar with some of his later writings than I have chosen to be will find in them pieces of evidence that I would have taken into account had I known about them. However, though I have drawn upon his later writings where I knew there was material relevant to his early life, I decided that this was a price worth paying. Samuelson once praised a biography of Abraham Lincoln because it was written as if you did not know what was going to happen next; I have tried to do something similar.

Even if Samuelson was, as he claimed, born to be an economist, quickly falling in love with the subject, the mature economist did not emerge fully formed. The young Samuelson was not a pure "neoclassical" economist, but combined mathematical theory with ideas thoroughly rooted in the more pragmatic, empirical, less abstract economics of the interwar period, much of which goes under the label of "institutionalism." It is possible that I have gone too far in trying to recover someone whose economics was less "orthodox" than it is generally assumed to be, but I see this as a risk that must be taken in order to allow the young Samuelson to be heard over the mature Samuelson who is well known today. Where Samuelson did change his mind significantly after 1948, that is a matter for the next volume.

I would never have embarked on this project without the support of the Leverhulme Trust, which awarded me a Major Research Fellowship, freeing me from all teaching and administrative duties, for the three academic years from 2011 through 2014. I am grateful both to the Trust and to colleagues in the Department of Economics at the University of Birmingham for their support. After that, my main debt is to the archivists at Duke University—Will Hansen, Elizabeth Dunn, and their colleagues—who have been helpful beyond the call of duty as I have worked my way systematically through Samuelson's papers and materials from many of the other collections housed there. I have also spent much time in the archives of Harvard University and MIT, where the staff have enabled me to access invaluable materials. I also wish to thank the archivists at the National Archives and Records Administration (NARA) (College Park, Maryland, and Waltham, Massachusetts), Yale University, Cornell University, University of Wisconsin–Madison, and Columbia University. Michael Aronson assisted me with access to papers archived at Harvard University Press. Assistance in obtaining archival materials has also been provided by Olav Bjerkholt, Juan Carvajalino, Beatrice Cherrier, Bud Collier, Luca Fiorito, David Laidler, David Levy, David Mitch, Tamotsu Nishizawa, Maxime Demarais-Tremblay, and Donald Winch. Andrew and Reiko Fry translated relevant parts of Tsuru's autobiography from Japanese.

I am also greatly indebted to some of those closest to Samuelson. At the start of the project, Robert Solow was generous with his time and since then has read and offered advice on many chapters. I also benefited from conversations with Robert Bishop, Peter Diamond, and James Poterba and from email exchanges with Kenneth Arrow, William Baumol, Henry Manne, Flo Conway and Jim Siegelman. I owe Janice Murray an enormous debt both for her assistance and for her work in organizing Samuelson's papers before they were archived at Duke. She has helped me correct many mistakes. Family members, notably Marnie Crawford Samuelson and Anita Summers, provided advice and information.

Steven Medema, Perry Mehrling, Mary Morgan, and Roy Weintraub were of assistance in formulating the project and supporting me in the early stages, and Roy's organization of a conference on the history of economics at MIT brought together many people who have been helpful. Friends at the Center for the History of Political Economy at Duke University have been very supportive, providing a critical audience for several papers. Kevin and Catherine Hoover provided accommodation that made staying away from home to work in the archives much more congenial than it would otherwise have been, with journeys to and from the campus providing occasions for Kevin pushing me to think more carefully about some of the material I was uncovering. Kevin also read an entire draft, an onerous task given that it was much rougher than this one, pointing out countless mistakes and instances of poor writing. Beatrice Cherrier, working on the history of MIT economics, has been a continuous source of assistance, as has Yann Giraud, working on Samuelson's textbook. Material on Samuelson's work for the Bowman Committee and on his work with Rupert Maclaurin draws on two papers written jointly with Harro Maas. Probably the biggest debt (I qualify that only because I owe so much to others) is to Steven Medema, who read virtually every chapter soon after it was written, alerting me to problems with the writing and providing endless ideas on questions to ask. He also provided a detailed critique of the entire manuscript, correcting details, raising new questions, and prompting me to structure the material in a more comprehensible way and then provided comments on a second draft. Perry Mehrling has contributed much to my understanding of Alvin Hansen and his relationship to Samuelson, and Juan Carvajalino has shared valuable ideas on E. B. Wilson and Samuelson from his PhD thesis. Roy Weintraub has provided assistance helping me think about both mathematical economics and how to handle Samuelson's Jewish identity. I have also benefited from comments of anonymous readers of the manuscript and from those attending seminars and conferences where material from from book has been presented. However, I have not taken all the advice I have been offered. Much as I would like to take credit for anything that is good in the book and pass the buck for anything that is not, responsibility for any errors remains my own. Last, but definitely not least, my wife Ann has had to live with my obsession with Samuelson for the past five years, and has the prospect of a few more to come.

I am grateful to Robert C. Merton for permission to quote from Samuelson's papers; the Institute of Economic Research, Hitotsubashi University, for permission to quote from the papers of Shigeto Tsuru; the Special Collections Research Center, University of Chicago Library, for permission to quote from the Robert Hutchins papers; Harvard University for permission to quote from material held in the Harvard University Archives; and the MIT Archives for permission to quote from materials they hold.

The manuscript was prepared using Scrivener, which made writing the text incomparably easier than if I had been forced to use a conventional word processor. DevonThink, a database program for the Mac, was invaluable for processing the tens of thousands of photographs taken in the archives, converting each of them to a PDF, and searching them. Referencing was handled with Sente, which I used to catalog manuscripts as well as publications.

INTRODUCTION: PAUL SAMUELSON
AND MODERN ECONOMICS

O N DECEMBER 28, 1947, in the Knickerbocker Hotel in Chicago, the president of the American Economic Association (AEA), Paul H. Douglas, who was shortly to leave academic life for a long career in the U.S. Senate, presented the association's first John Bates Clark medal to Paul Samuelson. This medal, which was to be awarded biennially to the economist under the age of forty who was judged to have made the greatest contribution to economics, marked him among the rising generation of American economists. Douglas described Samuelson as having made "extraordinarily penetrating contributions to the theory of employment, production, distribution, and value," a long list to which he could have added the theory of the consumer, the theory of international trade, and welfare economics.[1] Three months earlier, Harvard University Press had published a book based on Samuelson's PhD thesis, written in 1940 when he was only 25; the book's title, *Foundations of Economic Analysis*, revealed the extent of his ambition: to provide a framework within which all economic analysis could subsequently be undertaken. Five months after the award, Samuelson's ambition to reshape the discipline was confirmed when McGraw-Hill published the textbook *Economics: An Introductory Analysis*, which virtually swept the board in teaching economics in American colleges and universities and made Samuelson a fortune.

Over the following thirty years it became clear that Samuelson's ambitions had been realized. By 1970, the techniques he had developed in *Foundations* had become central to the graduate curriculum and his introductory textbook had entered its eighth edition, having dominated the market for many years. His presence at Massachusetts Institute of Technology

(MIT) had been instrumental in turning a department focused on teaching elementary economics to engineering students into one of the world's leading economics departments.[a] Samuelson had also become a prominent commentator on economic events, writing regularly for major newspapers, with many of his articles syndicated worldwide. He had been an economic advisor to President John F. Kennedy and was known as one of the leading American proponents of the Keynesian economics that dominated debates over economic policy in what came to be known as a golden age. In 1970, he became the first American to be awarded the Nobel Memorial Prize in Economic Science "for the scientific work through which he has developed static and dynamic economic theory and actively contributed to raising the level of analysis in economic science."[b] Excepting those who felt themselves more deserving, the vast majority of economists would have supported this judgment. "Samuelson" had become an institution in world economics.

When he received the John Bates Clark medal, Samuelson was only thirty-two years old. Though he was still in the early stages of an immensely productive career, this award, together with the publication of his two books and his appointment as a full professor at MIT, mark the end of the period in which his vision of economics and his position within economics were established. This phase of his career, which had begun in 1932 when he first encountered economics as an undergraduate at the University of Chicago and which ended in 1948, is the subject of this book. Economics changed dramatically during this sixteen-year period. The most well known of these changes is the "Keynesian revolution," which involved the emergence of a new way of thinking about both economic theory and the conduct of economic policy, closely tied to a revolution in national accounting.[c] This period also saw the transformation of mathematical economics and the analysis of economic data using formal statistical methods ("econometrics") from being the concern of a tiny minority of economists to occupying a well-established place in

---

a. A survey in 1964 ranked MIT's economics department second only to Harvard, with department chairs and junior scholars ranking it equal to Harvard. It was considered to have the most attractive graduate program in the country. MIT had not even figured in the equivalent survey in 1957 (Cartter 1966, pp. 34–35).

b. The first prize, in 1969, had gone to two European economists, Ragnar Frisch and Jan Tinbergen, born in 1895 and 1903, respectively, for work on dynamic statistical models, most of which was undertaken in the 1930s. See http://www.nobelprize.org/nobel_prizes/economic-sciences/laureates/1970/samuelson-facts.html; accessed September 25, 2015.

c. The concept of national income, or gross national product (GNP), now a routine part of economic discourse, was not defined until the 1930s, and the wider system of national accounts, of which GNP forms a part, was not formally laid down until the 1940s.

the discipline. American economics changed from being a pluralistic discipline in which there was no dominant theoretical framework and in which there was a divide between "institutionalists," who sought to ground their thinking firmly in data, and "neoclassical economists," who saw a greater role for abstract mathematical theory, to one in which "neoclassical economics" dominated.[2] Samuelson was such an important player in these developments that to understand his intellectual development is to understand some of the most important developments in this period of dramatic change. This book, therefore, is a story about both Samuelson and the transition in economics in which he played a major role.

PART I | The Early Years,
1915–1935

CHAPTER 1 | Childhood

Russian-Polish Origins

Paul Anthony Samuelson was born on May 15, 1915, in the office above his parents' drugstore, at the intersection of 17th and Broadway, in Gary, Indiana.[1] His parents were Jewish immigrants from Suwalki, a much-contested land not far from the Baltic that had at various times been part of East Prussia (and hence Germany), Poland, and Russia. Much of their family history is unknown, even his parents' exact ages. His father acquired the name Frank Samuelson on arrival in the United States at Ellis Island, and when Paul learned that the family name did not go back to the Middle Ages, he "developed a Freudian lack of interest in all things European." He knew none of his grandparents but this never concerned him. "If somewhere in Europe progenitors of my genes still lived up until about 1925, I cannot ever recall experiencing curiosity or interest."[2] What he knew about his family was learned only much later when he sought things to talk about with his mother, then a widow in her eighties. The name Samuelson was chosen because it was the one favored by a relative, "Uncle Jimmy," who had landed at Ellis Island a few years before Frank.[3]

What he did know (or at least believed he knew) was that his mother, Ella Lypski, born on March 19 between 1885 and 1888, came from the district's capital, Suwalki, and his father, then Ephraim, was born in 1886 and lived in a small village, Ratzki, on what was then, in the 1880s, the East Prussian frontier.[a] This location on the border was so that Ephraim's

a. Paul spelled it Rotzk, but Ratzki appears to be the correct name.

father could run a horse-trading business in East Prussia, even though he could not get the necessary permit to live there. This geographical difference, though amounting to little more than fifteen miles, was enough to make Ella, whom Paul thought harbored pretensions about the her family's status, very conscious of the difference in class between the two of them. Ella's father, Meyer Lypski, a wheat merchant, had three daughters from his first marriage (Eva, and two others) and six children by his second wife (née Epstein): Fanny (b. 1888), Ella, Alfred (1887), Frank (1891), Norman, and Sarah (1894).[4] Ella's mother and Frank's were sisters, making them first cousins.

As was typical of Eastern Europeans of this generation, many members of the family moved to the United States in search of economic opportunity. Paul's great-grandfather had gone there alone before the Civil War, eventually returning with some savings. Paul conjectured that these savings may have been the origin of Ella's sense of her family's superiority, though she preferred to talk of being descended from princes, "via Spain." Eva left Russia for the United States in 1885, and ended up the wife of the manager of the general store in Hankinson,[5] North Dakota. Paul's father, Frank, appears to have left, as a teenager, in 1904,[6] going first to New York City and then to Chicago along with some relatives. His motives were, of course, economic, but additional motives were provided by his not wanting to be conscripted into the Russian army, and what Paul described as "his resentments for the surliness and worse on the part of majority neighbors of the Polish Catholic faith."[7]

Ella had met and fallen in love with Frank before he left Russia, romantically taking the view that his blue eyes made up for the lower social status of his family, and she decided to follow him to America.[8] In her father's grain business, it was common to resort to borrowing to build up inventories when there had been losses, and learning that her father was about to go into debt again, Ella demanded the small amount of money needed to pay for her passage to New York. Her plan was to join Eva in North Dakota, to improve her English, and then to move near to Frank, who was then in pharmacy college in Chicago. This plan worked. She attended school in Hankinson, starting alongside the ten- and eleven-year-olds, including her mortified cousin Hazel, in fifth grade, even though she was by then close to twenty.[9] Three weeks later, however, she progressed to seventh- and eighth-grade classes. Then, having finished her education, she moved to Chicago and resumed her relationship with Frank, working in two giant Chicago department stores, an example later followed by her younger sister, Sophie. At the time of the 1910 Census, she and Frank were living in Chicago in a household that included half a dozen members of the extended family.[b]

By 1912, Frank had completed his pharmacy training and had acquired a drugstore in Chicago, raising the possibility of marriage to Ella. However, because they were first cousins, this was illegal under Illinois law, so they had to elope to Kenosha, Wisconsin, where the law was more relaxed. They did not remain in Chicago because Ella's eldest brother, Frank, also a pharmacist and a good businessman, told the couple about a pharmacist, Mr. Kline, in Gary who wanted to move to Chicago so that he could train as a doctor. He would be willing to trade his business in the center of Gary for one that was nearer to Rush Medical School. This turned out to be a good exchange for both sides: Mr. Kline became Dr. Kline and apparently had a successful practice, and it gave Frank and Ella a prosperous business in the heart of a town that was to boom two years later.

The reason for Gary's prosperity during Paul's earliest years was the First World War, which even before the United States became a combatant in 1917 raised the demand for steel. High demand for steel resulted in high wages and working hours in a town dominated by US Steel: $1 an hour, with twelve-hour days and seven-day weeks meant that steelworkers could earn $84 a week, which was an excellent income for the time. With such overtime rates, people could not afford to take time off, so if they had a stomach ache, bronchial infection, back pain, or other ailments, they would turn to the pharmacist for diagnosis. Paul recounted how his father would then prescribe calomel (now known to be toxic but then used as a laxative), aspirin, or rubbing alcohol he had himself prepared. Given the high profit margins on home-prepared medicines, the business was a gold mine. Frank, who could speak a variety of Eastern European languages, was able to take advantage of this opportunity by serving the large immigrant workforce. However, having become rich, Frank lost no time in leaving the pharmacy, after which he was helped by his "brilliant" brother-in-law Alfred in losing his wealth through a series of bad investments. Of the five brothers and brothers-in-law, all pharmacists, only Paul's uncle Frank, the least intellectual of the five, had any success as an investor.

Marriage was followed, nine months later, by the birth of Harold and then, two and a half years later, by Paul. Though prospering, the family may have lived in a crowded apartment behind the store, and the office above was that of Dr. Antonio Georgi.[10] Paul later described him as "A great man

---

b. They include Ella's sisters Fannie and Sarah, her brothers Alfred and Frank Lypski (who had emigrated in 1905, a year after Frank), and Fannie's husband, Jacob Steine, a cousin of Frank Samuelson. It is tempting to speculate that Steine was previously Epstein.

with the knife, he could cure everything but the common cold by surgery. I am lucky to have escaped with only my tonsils and my adenoids unintact. He was a short and excitable man, with a handsome face."[c] He played a role in the success of Frank and Ella's pharmacy, giving them the prescription business from his medical practice and the dispensary at his Mount Angelus Hospital, and it was he who delivered Paul on May 15, 1915, in his office. He sought to name the baby Antonio, after himself. In the end, so they thought, a compromise was reached, whereby he was named after Dr. Georgi's son, Paul, and given the middle name Anthony. It was only a quarter of a century later, shortly before Pearl Harbor, when Paul was sent his official birth certificate in anticipation of the draft, that he discovered that Dr. Georgi had had the last word, registering him as Paul Antonio Samuelson.[11]

Farm and Pharmacy

Paul's parents lived in Gary, but his earliest years, from seventeen months to five or six years, were divided equally between living at home and living on a farm with a couple who behaved as foster parents. In November 1916, he went to live with the Gordons, whom he came to know as Aunt Frieda and Uncle Sam, on their 100-acre farm between Valparaiso and Hobart. They were family friends his parents had met at the funeral of a produce buyer.[12] Later in life he spoke of his resentment about being abandoned by his parents in this way for reasons he never understood. However, he could also write that aside from the sadness when his parents left after a visit, the years were happy ones. Sixty years later he wrote that his memories of the farm were "fresh and dear to me,"[13] regarding the Gordons as many people regard grandparents. It was Aunty Frieda who allowed him, at the age of four, to cut off the long curls that his mother and relatives loved, but that he hated, giving him for the first time a boy's haircut. Of the couple, Frieda was twenty years younger and the one Paul thought the most intellectual. In the longest of his unpublished autobiographies, he described his time on the farm as his "Hoosier idyll,"[14] though in another he talked of it more ambiguously as "exile to Arcadia."[15]

> When people hear of these early years they are somewhat aghast. And when I came as an adult to look back on those days it did occur to me

---

c. Paul compared Dr. Georgi's appearance with the Italian economist Piero Sraffa, whose photograph is at https://en.wikipedia.org/wiki/Piero_Sraffa.

to marvel that all worked out so well. (Freud and Jung would no doubt sneer at this complacent repression.) At the time it all seemed part of the natural order of things. I could remember no time earlier than when I arrived, nursing bottle in hand, and was immediately weaned by disapproving Aunt Frieda. I learned later it was all a matter of one dollar a day: and that included board, room, and love.[16]

The Gordons had a working farm with, so Paul remembered, ten dairy cows, four horses, hogs, chickens, and fowl. It was in the days before mechanization, indoor plumbing, running water, or electricity, though Paul argued that life there was not that primitive.[17] His own life, given that he had few chores to perform, was that of a "gentleman farmer."[18]

We had no indoor heating either. A cast iron kitchen stove, stoked by both kindling wood or soft coal, did radiate some warmth and did heat its storage-tank water used for laundering and cooking. In addition, inside the living room below a second floor heat register, was a stove just like those in sixteenth century paintings. It was freezing cold when I threw off my blankets and spread the clothes I would wear over the register above the downstairs stove. No wonder that we wore heavy, scratchy winter underwear and layers of sweaters and coats.

Our main water supply came from the huge windmill that every midwest farm had. . . . A supplementary hand pump in the kitchen drew up from a cistern soft rain water used to fill the one weekly tub of bath water. If there were five of us in the house, only the lucky first one got clean—clean water to bathe in. . . . Nor did we have electricity in those pre–Roosevelt New Deal days. Candles, lanterns, and kerosene lamps provided light—inadequate light—so naturally we went to bed early and read only between dawn and dusk. Seven years later my family brought us a one-tube battery radio. Then on the great Thanksgiving weekend we could hear live the big annual Army vs. Navy football match.

We did have a telephone! In fact two phones: the Bell System phone and a local Buckeye or Keystone phone that hardly ever got used. You had to turn a crank to hear and be heard. Each phone was one of a multi-party line; ours was one of an eight-party group. Eavesdropping was fair game. Each of us could overhear any conversation so that you came to know your neighbors well—maybe too well. And sometimes when you wanted to call a neighbor, your friendly central operator would inform you that she was shopping in Valparaiso.

Gasoline tractors had not yet come to pull our ploughs and other farm equipment. Pete and Tom, our sturdy geldings, serviced the buggy for Aunt Frieda. They pulled our various wagons. Never, never did we plough the snow on our gravel roads; that would have made unmovable the sleigh wagons whose wheels had been removed for all of the winter.

Valparaiso, Indiana was a bare five miles from our Wheeler, Indiana [,] township. It was the Porter County seat and shopping center. To get there, Uncle Sam or a hired hand would have to harness up Pete for Aunt Frieda and me. Then it would take hours—not minutes—to get to the town square with its hitching posts at the central square. (As I witnessed the gradual replacement of horse power by gasoline-fueled machinery, every five years the hitching posts would become less and less. Ultimately they disappeared altogether.)

His earliest political memories date from the farm, where the Gordons posted a picture of Warren Harding on the door during his 1920 campaign, and he remembers being there when news of Harding's death came in the summer of 1923. However, his most vivid memories were inevitably of the animals and events on the farm.

I remember Babe the white collie. Pete (who pulled our horse and buggy), Tom (who was one-eyed and we believed had fought in the war), Mollie a gray mare whom I hoped would have colts (not realizing that the horse was on the way out). We used to hitch up for the ride to Wheeler, either through the back fields or over the Pennsy bridge. A much longer trip for a little boy was a buggy ride all the way to Valpo [Valparaiso], or more rarely, to Hobart.... For a small boy, the walk of a quarter of a mile up and down hill to get the mail was an adventure. I remember reading the Prairie Farmer by lamplight, and how cosy the room seemed as the windows became mirrors on account of the dark outside....

In the morning one shivered while dressing over a register that drew a little heat upstairs from the coal-burning stove in the not much used living room. The warm range in the kitchen provided the real heat, both for cooking and living. I recall bringing in kindling wood; but I suppose coal was the main ingredient. I also recall going to the windmill pump to fetch a pail of water. One of the worst traumas of my infancy was when we once changed the pump from automatic windmill to hand pumping. One had to take out a bolt from two holes that held together two adjoining[19] pieces of the piston. I was told to hold the lower part during the maneuver. But it got away from me, and the top of the handpump sank into the well, probably having to be recovered by a professional. I was very ashamed of myself. In the winter, sometimes I was the only child on the farm. Then I had Aunt Frieda's undivided attention. Bliss! One year I must have had scarlet fever and was in quarantine. Through the windows of the El-shaped downstairs I could see others who weren't allowed to come in to visit me. At night I remember the eerie sound of the Pennsy and Nickel Plate train whistles. On summer afternoons the wind in the silver poplar lulled one to sleep. I remember when we built a new cistern near the willow tree that Lester [Uncle Sam's son] had planted.[20]

He also remembered some of the people he got to know and even claimed to remember some of the conversations he had with them.

Lester was our handsome hero, blond with a touch of red in his hair. He was away at medical school most of the time. But his picture in tuxedo was on the parlor organ. I remember when the organ used to work. It seems to me that Lester learned to chew tobacco one summer; I was too chicken even to try. Do I recall that Lester went with a girl called Alma for a while, someone who lived across the bridge in the general direction of Valpo?

Miss Ruth and Miss Bradley [his teachers] I of course remember. With their Model T Ford, which carried them to distant places each summer. Actually, my time was before the consolidated school bus. . . . I promised I would take Aunt Frieda around the world. I never lived up to that promise. I do remember her funeral and that of Uncle Sam. I remember threshing time. The apple tree I used to climb and sit in toward the road. We used to peek at the girls taking their weekly baths in the wash tubs; what a thrill! Even better than watching the bull service the cow.[21]

In the same letter he wrote that the Gordon schoolhouse, built up the road by Uncle Sam, was the first he ever attended, and that he still had a brick from it (it was one room and had privies). However, Miss (Ethel) Ruth, one of his teachers, replied by saying that his memory was wrong. Paul might have played there, but he had never been a pupil. She remembered him clearly, writing,

You were ahead of the other children and I had to give you extra work to keep you busy and not bored. Your mother told me before you started to school, "Don't let him sit with his elbow on his desk and his head in his hand." But with 40 pupils and 2 grades I just couldn't give you my undivided attention.[22]

Moreover, his talents were not merely academic. "Don't you remember," she wrote, "the whole evening's musical program of 'The Three Bears,' put on by the Wheeler 1st and 2nd graders? You were The Baby Bear, the star of the show and your family and friends came from Gary and Chicago to show their pride in you. You had a number of solos as well as speaking parts."[23] Paul, however, thought that she had confused him with his younger brother, Robert, born in 1922, who went through the same experience.[24] Robert, however, went for shorter periods, possibly only for summer vacations, and never felt the same resentment as Paul was later to feel.[25]

Paul never could explain why his family chose to send him and his brothers to the Gordons. They were well off, so it was not for financial reasons. His only explanation was that his mother was a career woman who chafed at domestic chores. However, his recollections also contain suggestions that his father's health might not have been perfect. In Frank's youth, whereas his brothers had been accomplished horsemen, he had been sedentary, due possibly to rheumatic fever. However, for all his resentments, Paul could write that "It was all part of a wonderful world" that was "not really gone, because it is so vividly remembered."

The other part of Paul's early childhood was the Gary pharmacy that his family owned until they gave it up in 1923, the year after his younger brother Robert was born. They spent the summer of 1923 in "the Shack" on the Gordons' farm before moving to Chicago. In 1925–26 they lived in Miami Beach, in Florida, losing money when a large hurricane caused the real estate bubble to burst.[26] The 1930 Census found them still living in Chicago, along with another relative, Herman Samuelson.[27] There, his mother ran a restaurant called Plantation Chicken Barbecue, which Paul found surprising as he did not consider his mother to be a good cook.[28] At some point his father fell ill and became virtually an invalid. This peripatetic childhood resulted in Paul's having a pre-university education involving eight schools. He recalled later that he did not find this a problem—to the contrary, he appreciated the variety it provided.

Education, however, took place at home as well as at school, notably in his father's drugstore. In one of the very few places in which Paul discussed his father, he wrote:

> It was exciting for me to own a drug store. You could get free Hershey bars and cherry cokes. I saw the soda fountain come into the American

pharmacy and, later, I saw it go out. I was all admiration to see how neatly my father could wrap a bottle of castor oil or a prescription for codeine. (I knew I could never excel in a calling that called for precision folding.) It was fascinating to type on the old Oliver typewriter that was used for prescriptions. Mortar and pestle were in constant use back in those early times when druggists prepared their prescriptions from scratch. Long before the time when the subject of algebra was to come up in Freshman high-school math class, Dad taught me cute tricks for solving simultaneous equations. (8 ounces of alcohol at 70°F added to 12 ounces of water at 73°F would give a liquid at 72°F; and even trickier methods were everyday fare for the practising professionals.) I also can remember the long hours of boredom, during which Norman would read the French novels of Anatole France or pore over a few days, old issue of *Le Monde*.[29,d]

Thus while it may have been Ethel Ruth, his first-grade teacher in Wheeler, who taught him "to read, write and figure," a significant element of his mathematics education came at home.[30] However, despite his parents' language skills—his father spoke Polish and Russian and could make himself understood in "Croatian, Serbian, Slovenian, Slavonian, Rutterian, Czech, Slovakian, and Lithuanian," a collection that they lumped together under the label "Slavish," and his mother had learned Latin and French, as well as Russian, Polish, and Yiddish—Paul resisted learning other languages.[31,e] Being bookish, he frequented the Carnegie Library in Gary, a magnificent stone building complete with pillars in the classical style, opened in 1912, where he read "old, end-of-the-19th-century popular books." This education including getting frightened by Alice's changes in height.[32] He attributes his failure to notice the impending arrival of his younger brother to being immersed in the world of books. However, though his father did possess a copy of Adam Smith's *Wealth of Nations*, Paul never ventured up to that shelf.

Paul would have been conscious of his family's Jewish identity from an early age. Many of those who frequented his father's pharmacy would have been Jews, and the list of names of his contemporaries in high school suggests that many of his school friends were Jewish. Very unusual for their generation, his parents did not practice their family's religion. Jewish ceremonies

---

d. While his father's pharmacy may not have acquired one earlier, many pharmacies had soda fountains in the nineteenth century.

e. It is not clear what Rutterian refers to.

were not, therefore, part of his upbringing. Until much later in life, when he addressed the topic of anti-Semitism at Harvard and its absence at Chicago, he was virtually silent on the subject. He deduced from the bookshelves that his father was an atheist.

Hyde Park High

Paul paid tribute to the high school systems in both Gary, where he was allowed to skip grades, moving from class to class, and Chicago. From 1928 to December 1931, he attended Hyde Park School, only a short distance from the University of Chicago, where he encountered teachers from whom he claimed to have learned much. In 1982, unable to attend a reunion, Paul sent a note that read, "All I am or ever hope to be I owe to Hiram Benjamin Loomis and Beulah Shoesmith."[33] Hiram Loomis had been Principal of Hyde Park School since 1905, leaving only when he reached the mandatory retirement age of seventy, in 1933. When Paul arrived he was sixty-five, with twenty-three years' service in the school, and a figure to be reckoned with, well known in the local community. He had insisted that his teachers be in the school for seven periods a day, stopping them from drawing their salaries and disappearing after lunch to take second jobs.[34] He had also tried hard to stop secret societies from playing a role in the school, having once called for the re-election of all officers when he found they were members of such societies. In the fall of 1928, just before Paul arrived, he had insisted that any student holding an office or honor had to swear before a notary that he "never had, does not, and does not expect to belong to any secret society, while in Hyde Park School."[35]

In Paul's junior year, a reporter painted a picture of life at the school based on what he had heard milling around among students at lunchtime. Seventy-five percent of them went outside the school for lunch. One group of girls discussed the money they could make from taxi dances, and he noted that many a quarter was diverted from lunch to buying from neighboring stores some obscene postcards such as war veterans would remember having seen in Europe. Yet not all was bad:

> We noticed a lot of the students wandering over into Jackson Park. A few of them stole away to slyly hold hands on an obscure park bench, but the majority simply walked about, with one eye on a wrist watch to keep tab on the time. Many, many, high powered automobiles drove off with boys and girls in their teens at the wheel. Three or four girls

had smart appearing roadsters with older men in the driver's seat call for them.

A school skip, that's a dance you know, was in progress in the gym. The postures were about the same seen in any well conducted dance hall. There was very little pairing off after the dance—a group of girls went their way as did the boys.[36]

The reporter concluded that one of the advantages of a public school was that "students rub elbows with one another and develop character in a way that cannot be taught in books. No better, no worse than any other school, Hyde Park High."

However, though the paper's portrait of the school was not unflattering, Principal Loomis was not happy, and the following week, in a letter to the editor, he responded to the allegation that some students might be buying obscene postcards by expressing his willingness to cooperate with the police to stop their sale, asking the journalist to help identify the offending stores. He observed that objectionable books were being sold—translations of French and Italian "classics."[37] In the same issue, a number of students defended the school, complaining that the journalist had insulted the 95 percent of students who did not engage in these activities. Interestingly, one of them observed that Hyde Park was a district where parents could afford a few luxuries, such as the cars the reporter had seen. These reports make it clear that Loomis presided over a school that attempted to maintain a high moral tone in a district that was not suffering as much as many from the ravages of the Depression. This was no doubt particularly significant given that the Chicago school system, mismanaged for many years, faced financial problems; from December 1929 onward, teachers worked days for which they went unpaid. Some were reduced to breaking point by their contact with the children of poor and unemployed families. By May 1932, shortly after Paul left Hyde Park, the city owed its teachers, on average, $1,400 each.[38] Paul may have attended a public school, but he was spared the worst effects of the Depression. What is not apparent from these reports, though it can be inferred from the lists of names and photographs in the yearbooks, is that the school had a significant number of students of Jewish origin.

Described as the "Grand Old Man" of Hyde Park School, Loomis was praised by his assistant as strongly as he was by Paul:

Mr. Loomis's everlasting kindness, his patience, his fair decisions, and his charmingly modern mind, have endeared him to the thousands of teachers, former pupils, and to those other thousands who have known him through the school. Mr. Loomis is retiring only because he has reached the retirement age—he will be 70 this summer. No question was too trivial for him, and no interruption ever bothered or vexed him. He was invariably kind to the shabbiest student with the lowest grades, as he was to the district superintendent. And one last memory is of him standing out in Jackson Park near the baseball diamond, his curly white hair and "Vandyke" shining in the bright sun, umpiring a baseball game with all the joy and excitement of any of the pupils, and with the skill of a big leaguer. His three sons and two daughters are all graduates of the school.[39]

Even allowing for the hyperbole that one would expect on the occasion of someone's retirement, this strongly suggests that Loomis may have contributed significantly to Paul's education.

After the principal, the other teacher Paul picked out for praise was Beulah I. Shoesmith, another long-serving teacher at Hyde Park School, having taught mathematics since 1910.[40] A graduate of the University of Chicago, she established a national reputation in mathematics education. She began the school's participation in mathematics contests, and the school won the Wilson Junior College contest, a Chicago-wide mathematics tournament, for eighteen consecutive years.[41] In school, she was known as Beulah "Isosceles" Shoesmith, on account of her having regularly set her new class in plane geometry a difficult problem that only the best students could solve, involving an isosceles triangle.[42] Princeton physicist Jay Orear has written that when she taught him, the school trained around ten students to compete in mathematics tournaments and that they always won the top three prizes, something that was effectively impossible to achieve by chance.[43] To support interest in mathematics, she argued for the creation of mathematics clubs, making her case in an article that was still cited almost a decade after its publication:

> Miss Beulah I. Shoesmith, of the Hyde Park High School, Chicago, Illinois, in an article on mathematics clubs reports that the study of algebraic fallacies in her club created such an interest that pupils outside the club asked to be allowed to visit the club meetings; and that so much enthusiasm was aroused over the working out of original proofs for the Pythagorean Theorem by the advanced pupils, that the plane geometry students began to inquire when they would be allowed to study this entertaining theorem. Such lively interest as is reported from these clubs is the need of every high school mathematics department.[44]

The problem to which mathematics clubs provided the solution was the need to offer greater variety than was possible in the classroom. In her article, she explained:

> In addition to the problem of arousing the dull or the indifferent pupil from his lethargy there is the difficulty of keeping the brighter and more original at concert pitch, so that while we are attempting to create interest we may not kill that which already existed. While more intensive work on the subject in hand may be assigned for extra credit to these more ambitious pupils and other devices may be used to retain their interest, still it is a lamentable fact that the amount of uniformity necessary in classroom work makes it difficult to bring out the capacity of the individual pupil. Yet we owe it to the excellent student to hold his interest and by opening up to him new fields of thought inspire him to the development of mathematical power of which he may be unconscious. The mathematics club is at least a partial solution of this difficulty and the work of such a club reacts favorably on the attitude toward mathematics throughout the school.[45]

She clearly maintained this concern for brighter students while Paul was there, for shortly after he left Hyde Park, she presented a paper to the National Council of Teachers of Mathematics, titled "What Do We Owe to the Brighter Pupil?"[46]

At Hyde Park School there were two mathematics clubs, entry to which was based on course grades. For younger students there was the Euclidian Club, and for seniors it was the Pythagorean Club, which she described in the following terms:

> When the possibility of organizing a small club was proposed these pupils were very enthusiastic. From the high-school student's point of view it was of course imperative that the club be equipped at the outset with constitution, a name, and a pin. Regular program meetings, usually an hour and a half in length, are held every two weeks at the close of the school day. The president, usually a Senior mathematics student, presides at the meeting. The program committee confers with the mathematics faculty in regard to the subject-matter of each program and urges club members to propose problems and topics of special interest which they may wish to hear discussed. At each meeting programs for the next meeting are distributed so that members may be informed two weeks in advance of the topics which will be up for consideration. A committee on proofs passes on the validity of

original solutions and sees to it that these are written up in permanent form and preserved.[47]

Shoesmith retired from Hyde Park School in 1945, teaching at the Illinois Institute of Technology for five years more. On her death in 1959, she left an estate of just over $1 million, designating $50,000 to fund a scholarship at the University of Chicago.[48] Paul was at Hyde Park School during the stock market boom and the Great Crash of 1929, taking a strong interest in what was happening. He recalled helping Shoesmith to pick out stocks, "Hupp motors and some other losers."[49] He was not alone in being surprised to learn that she had left so much money, for her success contrasted with the demeanor of someone he remembered as wearing the same dress every day.[50] Shoesmith taught him algebra and geometry, followed by "advanced courses in Solid Geometry and College Algebra."[51] Paul recalled that he skipped trigonometry on the grounds that the old-fashioned version taught there was too boring. A trigonometry class, did, however, feature in a short story he wrote that appeared in *The Scroll*, a magazine produced by the Hyde Park School Story Scribblers' Society.[52] It was a dialogue in which one student was telling another about falling in love with one girl in summer camp, and then with someone who was in their trigonometry class, and needing to be told by his friend to be more realistic. Though he clearly performed well, Paul later claimed to have been something of an underachiever, because it was not the "done thing" to be seen to work too hard. This perhaps explains why, though he was a member of the Euclidian Club in 1929, he appears, on the evidence of his yearbook, not to have got into the Pythagorean Club.

For all his praise for the Gary school system, he considered the move to Chicago, and to Hyde Park High, to have been very significant. He noted that had his parents not moved away from Gary when he was eight, "I could be a spot-welder; or a master printer; while at the same time contributing at the frontier of Shakespearean studies."[53] He dated his success in mathematics and physics from his time at Hyde Park School and attributed it to Shoesmith's teaching. The hours spent in the Gary library, and with his family's books, reading the nineteenth-century literary classics were, he seems to be saying, being left behind.

The evidence from his school yearbook and his Chicago transcript (which records his high school credits) suggests a more complicated story of someone who, though interested in mathematics, was still inclined to the humanities. He took more than the required year of algebra, attending virtually all the mathematics courses that the school offered (two courses in algebra and courses in plane and solid geometry), and there is no reason to question the influence that Shoesmith had on him. However, there is no evidence that he took any particular interest in science at Hyde Park High, for he took only a semester's general science and did not take any of the more specialized science courses offered (which covered botany, zoology, physics, chemistry, and astronomy). In contrast, he took two and a half years of history, well in excess of the required one year. His choice of subjects to study gives no hint of his later interest in the natural sciences, which was aroused only at the University of Chicago. Social studies and economics were offered at Hyde Park High, but Paul took neither of them.

The picture of someone inclined to the humanities is reinforced by his other activities. For three years he was a member of the school's literary club, The Story Scribblers' Society, entry to which was based on a writing contest, and he was also on the staff of the school's literary magazine, *The Scroll*. He was also involved with *The Weekly*, the school newspaper, accounting for his half-credit in journalism. Paul referred to this in a letter he wrote to Norman Davidson, an eminent chemist who was two years behind him at Hyde Park.

> I believe that you were two years behind me at Hyde Park High.... I remember this because retiring editors of the school newspaper conducted kind of an I.Q. Competition to select new members. Having the usual dollop of arrogance of smart nerds, I was surprised and interested to learn that there were other bright guys. (As Barnum didn't quite say, "There's one born every minute.") It is a story on me rather than you.[54]

Paul was in Sigma Epsilon, the school's honor society, for all four years at Hyde Park School. In his final year, though he did not get into the Pythagorean Club, he was in the English honor society. This is not the picture of a mathematical prodigy, but of a student who loved reading and writing; he was to approach economics not from science but from the humanities. He was involved in some sport—the yearbook lists him as being in track for three years and in basketball and fencing in his senior year—and as with over half the school, he was in the Civil Industrial Club, a service organization.

Childhood Reflections

Paul's own accounts of his childhood contain much self-reflection. Clearly, his childhood was something he felt important, for he repeatedly referred to Freud's claim that personality is formed between the ages of two and six, explaining the importance he attached to his experience on the farm. Yet it was a story that he found difficult to write, for otherwise it is hard to see why there should be so many unfinished accounts of his early life, each with a slightly different emphasis.[f]

There is a disarming sense of modesty and frankness in many of Paul's accounts of his life, admitting to several failings. He claims to have acquired a belief in evolution very early on, and he ascribed his intelligence to genetics: "I began as an out-and-out believer in heredity. My brothers and I were smart kids. My cousins all weighed in above the average."[55] He was congenitally smart and made no secret of it, at one point noting that in the early 1950s he was prescribed some medication that dulled his mind, giving him for the first time an insight into "how the other half lives." His most frequently used self-description was "precocious,"[56] but though this is often associated with early signs of brilliance, Paul did not see it that way. "Being an early developer in I.Q. is not a serious matter: all academics, even the pedestrian permanent assistant professors, are proficient in solving puzzles at high speed—which is what I.Q. tests mostly measure."[57] Having a high I.Q. did not enable him to draw the conclusion that his mother was pregnant until the night before the birth of his younger brother. He could clearly respect dimensions of intelligence that were different from puzzle solving and academic work, such as the more practical skills of his parents and those he encountered on the farm.

Though he had no idea that he would become an economist, Paul remembers himself as being aware of economic issues and events that supported his later Keynesian views. His remark that he could see the Keynesian multiplier at work when he was on the farm is clearly a later interpretation, but he claims that he was aware at an early age of wartime prosperity as a result of high grain and steel prices, and of the sharp postwar recession that preceded the longer boom of the 1920s.[58] He recalled an argument with his parents, presumably in the early 1930s, in which his mother retorted, "Don't you know, son, that times are really prosperous only during war?"—a view that accurately reflected the experience of those years.[59] His family's misadventures in Florida when he was ten made him acutely aware of property speculation and bubbles that eventually burst. Even though he had no commitment to pharmacy, Paul's father had been more successful as a pharmacist than as

f. One of these was written shortly after receiving an honorary degree from Valparaiso University in 1987 (aged 72). He had revisited Gary, only to find that the family drugstore and the Carnegie Library where he had spent so many hours had both been demolished. It is likely that his "Brief history of the Samuelsons" dated from the late 1970s, when his mother recounted their family history.

a property speculator. Discussions on the stock market with his high school teacher Beulah Shoesmith were another sign of Paul's interest in finance, a branch of economics in which he would later specialize.

Paul's recollections of his past provide some clues to his parents' politics. He comments that his father was a "*progressive* Republican," with emphasis on progressive. In 1924, his father voted, so Paul recalled, for "'Old Bob' La Follette, of the Independent Progressive Party." Stemming from immigrant stock, Frank had an aversion to inequality and thought that the democratic process should be used to reduce the inequalities brought about by the market.[60] His father was enthusiastic about the sermons of Father Charles Coughlin. Coughlin was a Catholic priest whose sermons were, from 1926 to 1940, broadcast weekly over the radio, becoming very popular during the Depression years, when he moved from religion to economics. He was an advocate of social justice through implementing radical monetary reforms. Though an enthusiastic supporter of Franklin Roosevelt in 1932 (with the slogan "Roosevelt or Ruin"), by 1936 Coughlin had turned against him on grounds that the reforms he was introducing were insufficiently radical. However, Coughlin's attacks on bankers moved in a direction that was widely considered anti-Semitic, causing Frank Samuelson to become disenchanted. His mother was presumably no conservative, if Paul could describe her as an early feminine activist. However, the main characteristic that he picked out when describing Ella was her certainty that she was right. He suggested that his own eclecticism was a reaction against this. On the farm, the Gordons were supporters of Warren Harding, and Paul clearly attached political significance to their gift of a celluloid elephant.

The "serious" dimension of his precocity was not intelligence but boundless self-confidence. "Why did I think for a moment," he wrote, "that I could be a great baseball announcer? Or, God help me, that I could even be a better ball player if only I 'really' set my mind to it?"[61] Part of the answer, he suggested, might lie in his being regarded as "cute." This was something he hated: his mother would lovingly comb his long curls, which were not cut until he was four. When "cooing aunts lusted orally for [his] locks," Paul snarled back "I'll trade you even."[62] However, he drew the conclusion that

> Being "cute" must have contributed to my precocity.... [W]hen asked to "recite" I never needed any coaxing. At the age of three I drew a laugh when I announced, "And now I'll give you my encore."[63]

He went on to describe this cuteness as "pseudo-pulchritude" that did not outlast puberty. Thus he never possessed "IT." He wrote, "No Radcliffe College class ever asked for an old shirt of mine to be torn into fair shares for division among its many co-ed members.[64] (That happened to Russ Nixon, a pal in the Harvard graduate school.)"[65] Paul also gave his parents some of the credit for his self-confidence—nurture was important as well as nature. He never doubted that he was favored, and that even his elder brother Harold put up with this. Harold's lack of resentment was illustrated by the story of how one long-serving maid regularly asked Harold to run errands because she mistakenly thought he was the younger brother. Paul attributed the maid's mistake not to his size or physique but to his habit of being forever immersed in books. This may have contributed to the distance that developed between Paul and his brothers, for his younger brother Robert became closer to Harold than Paul was to either.

Those who knew Paul were well aware that he bitterly resented being left on the farm. This may be one reason why he "psychologically left the den of the nuclear family," immersing himself in books before he had physically left home. When drafting an autobiography, Paul projected this resentment on to having been deceived, not on to having been forcibly separated from his parents. He admitted to the pain of learning that his parents, after one of their visits, had departed while he was in a barn seeing to the horses, though he described the pain as momentary. In another account of deception he describes being told, on a visit to Dr. Georgi, that he was going simply for an examination of his tonsils. Having been dragged screaming to Dr. Georgi's new hospital, he had to be forced on to the operating table where, as the ether cap was put over his face, he cried "You've lied to me. You've cheated me."[66] At the age of seventy-two he said that he still resented this more than he resented being sent away from home during what he described as "the endless months of my infancy." He was critical of his family's "pragmatic" attitude to truth, not simply in relation to the facts of life (which he learned from observing bulls and cows on the farm) but also more seriously in relation to adoption and step-parents. Paul's cousin Stanley, with whom he was very close, their ages differing by a mere ten days and who also spent time on the farm, was the son of his Aunt Sophie and her first husband, Fred Mendelsohn, but after their divorce and her remarriage to David Ratner, he was given the name Ratner and "brainwashed" into believing that David Ratner was his true father. Paul claims to have been an embarrassment to his parents when, because of his precocious memory, he had once asked his cousin, "Stanley, which father do you mean? This one? Or the World War I soldier father?"[67] Paul was silenced and twenty years later, when Stanley registered for the draft, he experienced the shock of discovering that his father was really his stepfather.

Though he did not express it this way, Paul's story can be seen as typically American. Paul's reaction, on learning that his family name did not go back further than his father, was simply to dismiss his European roots as irrelevant: arrival in America marked a new beginning. Such an attitude chimes with the metaphor of new birth, which Paul used repeatedly to describe the most important new stages in his life. This characteristically American sense that breaking with the past can be liberating is perhaps another factor behind his immense self-confidence.[68] It could also be linked to the peripatetic experience of his early childhood, which he presented in a positive light. His "chauvinistic" resistance to learning languages other than English can possibly be linked to this lack of interest in Europe, though he noted that in taking this position he failed to appreciate that his family's prosperity rested on his father's being able to speak the languages of Gary's Eastern European immigrants.

Paul repeatedly described himself as self-taught, through hours spent in libraries.[69] This habit had started early. At the age of seven, when his brother Robert was born, Paul was already "living mostly in a world of books." He remembered that "It was Curley [his older brother, Harold] who spent hours on the floor playing with the cute new addition; I merely turn my book pages with benevolent but absent-minded and distant approbation."[70]

Paul's story involved mobility—the family's migration and its progress through moving from one city to another in search of opportunities—but he found moving difficult. Having found a new home, he wanted to stay there. His subsequent move from Chicago to Harvard was forced. Moving from Harvard to MIT was a move he made very reluctantly, even though it did not require his either leaving home or losing contact with his friends at Harvard. His wife's family were to provide the home he had missed through being sent to the farm and from which he had cut himself off by immersing himself in his books.

CHAPTER 2

The University of Chicago, 1932

Encountering Social Science

From Hyde Park School, Samuelson went, almost inevitably, to the University of Chicago, which was to play an important role not just in his career but also in his self-image as an economist. It was as an undergraduate there that he made the decision to become an economist and to approach the subject using mathematics. He also credits the University of Chicago with having introduced him to the natural sciences—subjects that he had studied only briefly at Hyde Park School. However, the University of Chicago had an importance beyond that, for he argued repeatedly it had trained him in the traditional economics that was to be undermined by the Keynesian revolution into which he was swept up a few years later, at Harvard. He claimed to have known, from the inside, what it was like to be as a "classical" monetary theorist; though he had turned away from the ideas taken up by Milton Friedman, his fellow columnist at *Newsweek* in the 1960s and 1970s, he understood the tradition in which Friedman's thinking was rooted.

In the 1930s, the University of Chicago was one of the main centers of social science research in the United States, and in the curriculum Samuelson followed for the first two years, economics was taught as part of the social sciences. The economic system was presented not as something distinct—not as being about an isolated, abstract entity called "the economy"—but as part of a reflection on the workings of society as a whole. He was introduced to an anthropological perspective on human existence. Though this was not something to which Samuelson drew attention, his training in the social sciences, which was unlike that received by most modern economists, helps explain the way he was to tackle economic problems. It was an important part of his intellectual development. We can be sure that he took non-economics seriously because, aside from his getting straight As and receiving a prize in political science, his commitment to studying economics came late—at one point he even thought of becoming a sociologist.

It never occurred to Samuelson to attend any university other than Chicago, even if his family's finances had allowed it, and they probably did not. He lived at home throughout his undergraduate career, Hyde Park School had a scheme that allowed its high-performing students to move on to the University of Chicago in the middle of their senior year. His first class was thus in January 1932, an event so significant that he repeatedly described it as a second birth—as a new stage in his life. "At 8:00 A.M. on a cold 1932 January 2nd I entered into heaven. My heaven. I walked into a Chicago lecture room. And I stepped out a different person."[1] The professor whose lecture had this effect was not an economist, but a sociologist, Louis Wirth, lecturing on Malthus's theory of population growth.[a] The topic appealed to Samuelson because it involved a good story and enabled him to use his high school mathematics. Unlike many who took up economics during the Great Depression, he did not claim to have been motivated by a desire to understand or solve the problem of unemployment.

Starting his university career with a lecture that showed him how he could apply mathematics to social problems was one of the benefits Samuelson attributed to his mid-year start. The timing of his arrival and his consciousness of the fact that he would be competing with students who had started four months earlier had the further benefit of transforming him from being an underachiever into someone who worked hard and sought to get as much out of his courses as he could. Commuting from home and missing out on the social events at the beginning of the academic year that would have introduced him to his contemporaries did not matter.

Samuelson arrived in the first year of the new undergraduate program instituted by Robert Hutchins, the university's president since 1929. It required all students to take a multidisciplinary program for the first two years of their BA degree. Samuelson had no great enthusiasm for the

---

a. Thomas Robert Malthus, whose *Essay on the Principle of Population*, first published in 1798, had developed the theory in which population has a tendency to expand faster than the supply of food and needs to be kept in check by various mechanisms that he classified into misery and vice. His ideas have been used to explain the problems faced by poor countries. See Winch 2013.

philosophy of Mortimer Adler, which was the basis for the new curriculum, or for the Hundred Great Books program, but he was enthusiastic about the requirement that students take courses in physical science, biological science, social sciences, and the humanities. He believed he had benefited greatly from taking an excellent course in biology and an up-to-date course in natural science, subjects he had chosen not to study in depth in high school. Many outsiders were brought in to teach, and he was able to listen to some world-famous lecturers. Hutchins had been able to achieve so much, in the depths of the Great Depression, through financial support from the Rockefeller Foundation, though according to some this was at the cost of the university's assets. However, according to Samuelson, another factor behind Chicago's greatness in this period was that though Chicago suffered, like all universities, from anti-Semitism, it was far less marked there than elsewhere. The result was that it placed Chicago in what Samuelson described as a monopoly position in relation to the hiring of Jews, a position it lost when anti-Semitism declined elsewhere. Samuelson illustrated the position at Chicago with the story of a sports coach who immediately fired one of his assistants who had made an anti-Semitic remark.[2]

> In my undergraduate time, a Chicago coach was reported to have said aloud (there is no other way to say something): "There are getting to be too many Jews around here." When this was reported to the head-coach Amos Alonzo Stagg, Stagg called in the accused. "Did you say that?" "Yes, in a thoughtless moment I did say those words." "Well then, as of this hour, you are fired. Collect your pay and sweat garb and go."[3]

The significance of this incident lay in its rarity. Another incident that he learned from a classmate, Jacob Mosak, testified to the openness of their teachers.

> In the 1920s when Frank Knight, Jacob Viner and other Chicago economists decided to recruit Henry Schultz, protegé of H. L. Moore and an early econometrician, they were told: "But President Max Mason does not like Jews." "Well, let him veto the appointment then. We think he's the best man for the post."

There was anti-Semitism in Chicago, but Samuelson clearly did not consider it a major issue in that most non-Jews were not anti-Semitic "in any *significant sense.*"[4]

However, the main benefit Samuelson believed he derived from his late start was that, while he got to take Hutchins's new interdisciplinary program, he had missed what he dismissively called "economics for poets" taught by Harry Gideonse in the first semester and was required to take a second-semester beginners' economics course intended for juniors and seniors who had not experienced the new regime. Samuelson thus experienced both the new interdisciplinary program and a traditional introductory economics course.

The Humanities

As a student who had given much of his time at high school to literature and writing, Samuelson must have been excited by the introductory humanities course that he had to take in the first year. This covered the "intellectual, emotional, and artistic values in life" through a historical account of Western civilization from ancient Greece to the modern world; architectural, artistic, literary, and intellectual creations were placed within the evolution of political organization and socioeconomic institutions, giving the course a social-science flavor.

Guidance on how to approach the course material began with religion, explaining that it was being treated simply as an element of human culture, an approach Samuelson would surely have found congenial given his lack of a religious upbringing, before listing the main questions philosophers had asked and the answers that had been proposed. They were advised that historical context was never far away: "the reader who assumes that everything should be written as it is written in the twentieth century cannot be very sound in his literary judgment."[5] For example, it would be wrong to criticize Sophocles for using choruses in his tragedies when he should be praised for "minimizing and modifying" their role.

Samuelson missed the part of the course dealing with the ancient world, so his first lectures would have been on the breakup of the Roman Empire and its replacement by Byzantine, Moslem, and "Western Roman–Teutonic" cultures. Lectures on these three topics provided the background for a discussion group in which the text was taken from Augustine's *Confessions*. The course then covered political history up to 1250, and the major institutions of medieval society—feudalism, the church, and the town, discussion being of the *Song of Roland*. After this it turned to theology, philosophy, mysticism, education, the arts, and literature. The same framework was followed for the Renaissance and the Reformation. The third quarter began with the Enlightenment, seeing its culmination in the French Revolution. The eighteenth-century intellectual synthesis that characterized the Enlightenment proved temporary, in part because of developments in science, in part due to the political changes brought about by the French Revolution, and in part because of the industrial revolution. It was at this point, in covering the period 1815–1870, that the course first turned to the United States, with lectures on American philosophy, architecture, literature, religion, and science.

A significant feature of this part of the course, given Samuelson's developing interest in the idea of science, was that it provided a context for the emergence of the social sciences. With Galileo and Newton, nature came to be seen as a system of mathematical laws, and it was believed that these laws could be discovered through reason: "reason was the admirable essence both of Nature and of Man."[6] Any doubts about these propositions were dispelled by Descartes and Newton, who "by the exercise of reason in alliance with observation and experiment had brought all nature within the boundaries of a single mathematical formula."[7] Whether or not he noted the point at the time, he was being exposed to the idea that would dominate his work on economics: that mathematics could unify seemingly disparate fields of knowledge.

The displacement of tradition and theology by reason was the context in which the social sciences emerged.

> The new thinking habits established in connection with the study of Nature were bound before long to influence the ... Social Sciences. If law and order, reduced to an impressively simple pattern, obtained throughout the physical universe, why did they not obtain also in human society?[8]

Why was it, people asked, that if nature was rational, the affairs of mankind were characterized by "irregularity, caprice, injustice, inequality, in sum, the most distressing denial of reason at every point?" The intellectuals applied reason to make the case of reform, not concerned with whether this led to the downfall of the old order and the transfer of power to their own (middle) class.

Given the need for gold to finance war in an age when raising credit was difficult, the first doctrine to emerge was mercantilism, supporting restrictions on trade that were intended to increase the supply of precious metals and promote national self-sufficiency. However, mercantilism failed to meet the needs of the middle class, which "possessed in constantly increasing measure the courage, enterprise, and capital necessary to take advantage of the economic opportunities of an expanding world."[9] It was "contrary to the simplicity of nature," which favored the doctrine of laissez-faire expounded by Adam Smith. Samuelson's teachers clearly sided with laissez-faire, endorsing the idea that businessmen were rugged individualists. However, following

Smith, they pointed out that businessmen turned to the state for protection when laissez-faire did not suit them. In the nineteenth century, the individualist philosophy of laissez-faire remained powerful but had to be modified to respond to the "glaring defects" of unrestrained individualism: state intervention increased and there were moves toward equalizing incomes. Liberalism, arising to counter socialism, was presented as one of the few transforming factors affecting the contemporary world, alongside science and the industrial revolution. Asserting that people should be allowed to govern themselves, liberalism was always "a compound of political and economic considerations" and offered an ideal toward which it was thought society should move.

The culmination of the course was the United States, "our own throbbingly vital country," the culture of which was also to be analyzed using the genetic method.[10] By this point in the course, Samuelson's teachers claimed, students had been "provided with a set of spiritual values enabling us to bring a tutored understanding to bear upon the religion, the philosophy, the art, and the literature by means of which our own countrymen offer the latest version of man's eternal hopes, despairs, and dreams—eternal in their essence but ever changing in their fragile, iridescent forms."[11] After reviewing American literature since the Revolution, tracing various strains of optimism and pessimism against the background of industrialization and economic change, the course ended with an account of pragmatism, presented as neither optimistic nor pessimistic but aiming to be objective, and abandoning any search for certainty and finality in philosophy. Thus, even in his humanities course, Samuelson was being exposed to a clear vision of science and a pragmatic political philosophy centered on laissez-faire that implied an important role for the social sciences.

Introduction to the Social Sciences

The January 2 lecture that Samuelson considered to mark his second birth was the first of four lectures on "The Industrial Revolution and Social Change" in the introductory social science course. Starting with a quotation from John Dewey, "Change is the primary social fact as surely as motion is the primary physical fact," these lectures began with talk of technological change and population. Wirth's lecture on Malthus was part of a discussion of how people settled down to live in a world where resources were limited. The course then proceeded to explore relations between technology, the relations of humans to their habitat, and social change. These lectures led into almost a whole month (no fewer than twelve lectures) on "The Transition from Folk Society to Industrial Society." Cultures were seen as complete systems, each one unique and encompassing economic activity, language, and social organization. The industrial revolution marked not just an economic change but also the passing of folk society. This change involved the rise of commerce and the world economy, a move from relationships governed by social status to ones based on contract, a weakening of community control, and the rise of interest groups. Quoting the British economic historians John and Barbara Hammond, whose book *The Rise of Modern Industry* they were recommended to purchase, students were required to discuss the proposition that "the Industrial Revolution destroyed a great body of significant custom. Large numbers of men and women lost their chief shelter, for in the eighteenth century custom was the shield of the poor, as the law was the weapon of the rich."[12] This age saw the rise of nationalism and individualism and the emergence of new social movements: the women's movement, the labor movement, abolitionism, and various democratic and revolutionary movements.

The industrial revolution ushered in what was called "Modern Industrial Society." Here there was a return to Malthus and population growth, though with the addition of "eugenics and differential fertility." The syllabus does not make it clear what position was taken on eugenics, widely accepted during this period and not yet tainted by association with Nazi doctrines. The course covered two features of modern society, urbanization and the professionalization of life, as well as social institutions—the family, the education system, and religion; the quarter ended with lectures on "The New Social Control" and "Social Research and Social Planning," following on from discussions, in the immediately preceding lectures, of race, social unrest, and problems of social adjustment. Cultural heterogeneity made social control difficult, but it was implemented at different levels and through different mechanisms: custom, the law, education, propaganda, prestige, public opinion, and "the crowd." The final lecture then tackled the problem of how the social sciences could be brought to bear on policy, discussing the nature of science, as technical and instrumental, in relation to the problems of prediction in social life. This was a prelude to the coverage of politics in the third quarter.

The methodological message underlying the course was that society, whether in its economic, social, or political aspects, needed to be understood in terms of evolving habits and customs. This was reinforced by the books that students were required to read alongside the "indispensable" readings reproduced along with the syllabus: *Middletown*, by Robert and

Helen Lynd (1929); *The Mind of Primitive Man*, by Franz Boas (1911); and *Folkways*, by William Graham Sumner (1906). However, beneath all of this was industrialization, explaining both the frequency with which the Hammonds were cited and why the first quarter had mostly been devoted to economic history. Samuelson had missed this, but given his belief that he needed to work hard to catch up with the other students, his need to pass an examination, the frequency of references to the industrial revolution in the lectures he was hearing, and that the material was printed in his course syllabus, he must have studied recommended reading on the nature of social problems and on comparing the natural and social sciences. The discussion of institutions, as habits of mind, would have been central to the material he was having to cover in the second quarter. He would seem likely also to have pondered the readings that raised questions about the naïve application of statistical methods to social problems. It is hard not to connect his later attitude toward economic statistics to the articles he was required to read. In one of them, on whether sociology was a science, he will have read:

> I am not—far from it—arguing against what is called the quantitative method in the social sciences. The further it can go the better, the surer, our knowledge will become. I am arguing against the naive assumptions which accompany a too inclusive confidence in the use of statistics. . . . What we are really seeking to understand are systems of relationship, not series of quantities. With the quantitative method must go hand in hand the method of logical analysis and synthesis.[13]

This view, endorsed by one of the teachers to whom he was closest at Harvard, was consistent with the stance he eventually took toward quantitative work in economics. He was also assigned readings from a textbook on English economic history by Abbott Usher, whose course he was to take at Harvard a few years later. These chapters, along with readings from the Hammonds, R. H. Tawney, Adam Smith, and Karl Marx, covered both the social and the economic implications of the industrial revolution. He was getting the message that the economic and the social could not be separated.

Over seventy years later, Samuelson acknowledged the importance of one of the books prescribed for this course—Sumner's *Folkways*. Sumner's book prepared him for the distinction between propositions pertaining to science and ones that relied on values on which individuals might legitimately differ. Referring to the argument made by Lionel Robbins concerning scientific and nonscientific propositions, he observed:

Yes. But, you see, most economists resisted Robbins, because they thought there was nothing left by way of policy prescription, although Robbins never quite said that. He said: "As a scientist, I cannot tell you this. But, as a voter, I can tell you which way I would go." This view can be traced back to David Hume, who was a great reductionist. I was ripe for that, because when I was an undergraduate student at the University of Chicago and studying sociology, I had to read William Sumner's *Folkways*. Sumner was a very conservative economist at Yale, but he was a great sociologist. He studied all cultures and showed how what was right in one culture was wrong in another and you could not prove by the methods of science which of them was correct.[14]

The separation of facts from values was certainly taught in this the course, but it did not come only from Sumner's book. The idea that something was right in one culture but wrong in another pervaded the syllabus. *The Mind of Primitive Man* and *Middletown* would have clearly shown how modern American society differed from the "primitive" ones analyzed by Boas. Sumner provided a criterion, closely related to the pragmatism taught in the humanities course, by which to judge mores and customs: "Bad mores are those which are not well fitted to the conditions and needs of the society at the time."[15]

It is interesting that Samuelson considered Sumner to have been a "very conservative economist" but a "great sociologist," for Sumner's sociology provided the basis for his conservatism. Sumner's main thesis was that social mores changed slowly and that societies were not organized on rational principles. Mores that were "understood, regular, and undisputed" made for social stability, and even inhabitants of slave societies could live together in peace and harmony if they adhered to traditional and customary ways.[16] Social chaos, such as occurred in the French Revolution, could result from attempts to replace traditional customs with ones based on a rational ideal imposed on society by the ruling authorities.[17] Perhaps, in remembering Sumner as a great sociologist, Samuelson was expressing some sympathy for the idea that social customs should change only slowly. It is also possible that he later projected ideas he took from the course onto his reading of Sumner's book.

The argument that scientific and ethical judgments needed to be kept separate was discussed explicitly in the course, in which the writings of John Dewey featured strongly. Samuelson will have read the article, reprinted in the syllabus, in which Joseph Spengler challenged the claims that a "real scientist" was concerned only with quantification and prediction, and that "No scientist dares, as a *scientist*, to express a judgment as to what is good and bad."[18] This would have been reinforced by the textbook he was using on his parallel course in economics, which expressed the view that "it is not the peculiar function of economics, or of any other science, to determine what is good and what is bad."[19] Though economists generally associate such ideas with Lionel Robbins, Samuelson will have heard this through Spengler, who cited not Robbins (whose essay had yet to appear when Samuelson began the course) but the sociologist Pitirim Sorokin and the nineteenth-century American economist Francis Walker. Spengler also expressed the view that "social science differs categorically from physical science. . . . No amount of pretended exactitude or assumed impersonalism can transform social science into physical science. The social scientist, therefore, is condemned to be an artist who must rely on common sense instead of upon an esoteric methodology, who must be governed not only by the standards of the laboratory but even more by those of common sense and common decency. He cannot even act *as if* he were a physical scientist."[20] This was a view that Samuelson, who thought a lot about science, would later reject.

First Encounter with Economics

The course Samuelson took to substitute for what he had missed in the first quarter was The Economic Order (Econ 102 and 108), which he described as an old-fashioned course that was being phased out.[21] The teacher, Aaron Director, who had been appointed to the Chicago faculty in 1930, was a specialist in labor economics who came from a Russian family that owned a flour mill, but whose members had immigrated to Portland, Oregon, in 1914. In Oregon they faced overt discrimination, both against Russians (branded Bolsheviks) and against Jews. Director had spells working as a migrant laborer in coal mines and textiles, and had visited England to study the education of adult workers. As a student at Yale, he had, with painter Mark Rothko, edited an iconoclastic weekly paper with socialist and progressive sympathies that sought to challenge the complacency and prejudice they encountered there.[22] This educational mission motivated a spell at Portland Labor College, in the two years before he moved to Chicago to work with Paul Douglas, with whom he wrote *The Problem of Unemployment* (1931).[b]

---

b. This is the Paul Douglas who was to present Samuelson with the Clark Medal fifteen
    years later, and whose ideas are discussed in more detail in chapter 5 of this volume.

This book was written as a survey of the unemployment problem that could serve as the foundation for an ongoing research project on a topic that had come to dominate the political agenda. As such most of the book involved analyzing the problem and identifying research that needed to be undertaken, rather than the politically more contentious issue of proposing policies. Its five hundred factually and statistically dense pages, drawing on the experiences of several countries, covered seasonal, technological, and cyclical unemployment, as well as discussing the placement of labor and unemployment insurance. Yet the book was far from neutral in its tone. At the end of a chapter reviewing the extent of unemployment and its costs, Douglas and Director concluded that the fear created by mass unemployment probably reduced rather than improved efficiency, implying that policies to reduce unemployment would not reduce incentives to work. They proposed no fewer than nineteen ways in which action could be taken to provide a more efficient public employment service, and offered a plan for unemployment insurance, countering the objections raised concerning such schemes. They also expressed the belief that public-works schemes could not only reduce fluctuations in unemployment but could also reduce its average level. Monetary policy could also help, through stabilizing prices. Douglas and Director had no radical new theory to offer, but they were arguing a clear case for government intervention to reduce unemployment.

This was the Director who taught Samuelson the economics he had missed through his late start.[c] The textbook they used was *Modern Economic Society,* by Sumner Slichter (1931), possibly the most well known economist of the day on account of his lecturing and his writing for *Harpers* and *New Republic*. Samuelson remembered Director as using the book but not speaking well of it. This could have been because Slichter was slightly more skeptical about the possibilities for government intervention than Director was at that point, or it could have been that he was impatient with the institutional detail contained in the book's nine hundred pages. Given what Samuelson was learning in his other courses, he should have appreciated Slichter's claim that economic arrangements in different countries had developed so differently that it was no longer possible to have a single theory to fit them all.[23]

---

c. Director, of course, dramatically changed his views on the role of the state in economic life. Douglas believed this change began in 1932 as he came under the influence of Frank Knight and Henry Simons (Van Horn 2010a, p. 265). If Douglas was right about the change beginning during 1932, it seems unlikely that his position had changed significantly by January.

This was the first economics textbook that Samuelson had to study carefully, and it was one that he remembered for many years.

Like Samuelson's teachers in the general courses on humanities and social sciences, Slichter began with the industrial revolution. Technological advance had transformed production to an extent unimaginable in 1800, but despite this, economic problems were far from being solved. Indeed, some problems had arisen because of industrialization. The problems of poverty and provision for old age were not solved, and even under normal circumstances, industry failed to work at full capacity. He wrote,

> When we observe modern industry failing to give steady employment and to produce to capacity, even when millions of people urgently need more goods; unnecessarily killing and maiming thousands of men each year; wasting irreplaceable natural resources simply because it is more profitable under existing economic arrangements to waste them than to conserve them; employing thousands of experts for the purpose of making men desire certain things, not because they are good for men to use, but because they are profitable for business enterprises to sell; denying to wage earners an opportunity to participate in making the rules under which they work; . . . [making man] a slave to his creations, dominated by industry instead of making it serve his ends.[24]

From this, Slichter concluded,

> How to make industry more of a tool and less of a tyrant, how to prevent the process of making a living from interfering with the opportunity and the capacity of men to live a good life . . . these are the supreme economic problems.[25]

The economic problem was framed, as in his other courses, as that of the social control of industry: industry was failing and needed to be controlled so that it could work in the interests of society.[d] Many of Slichter's "constructive suggestions" were directed at remedying defects in the free enterprise system: the provision of better market information, more accurate cost accounting, improving the regulation of public utilities and increasing their number, and reducing the uncertainty facing business. Other suggestions reflected a progressive outlook, such as raising inheritance taxes, redistributing income in response to needs, giving labor and consumers a greater role in directing industry, and greater planning of the economy.

---

d. This was a common theme in the 1930s. See Backhouse 2015b.

The theoretical content of the book was, by modern standards, minimal. There was a diagrammatic treatment of supply and demand, and numerical examples to illustrate how costs might change with output, but beyond that the argument never strayed far from describing American industry. The interdependence of markets was explained using concrete examples. Director, however, exposed Samuelson to more abstract treatments of economics, one of the more unorthodox readings he assigned being the chapter on "The Arithmetic of Pricing" in Gustav Cassel's *The Theory of Social Economy* (1923), something mentioned nowhere in Slichter's text.[26] Here, in place of the American economy, was a self-contained economy in which production has already taken place, leaving a fixed stock of goods to be exchanged between producers and consumers. For each good, Cassel wrote down demand functions, according to which demand for each good depended on prices of all goods in the system. Assuming demand for each good equaled supply, the result was a set of equations, where the number of equations was equal to the number of goods and hence prices in the system.

Cassel then took account of production, assuming that production of each good required specified amounts of each of the primary factors of production (labor, raw materials, and capital goods already in existence). He obtained an equation linking the price of each good to its cost of production, this depending on the prices of the factors of production. Solving these sets of equations could give the values of all the prices (of goods and factors of production) and the quantities used and produced. Cassel's chapter covered the same problem, of the interdependence between markets, in a far more abstract way than Slichter in his discussion of free enterprise.

In later life, Samuelson attached great importance to Director's having introduced him to Cassel's work, arguing that it was because of this that he first took a serious interest in mathematics.

> Director, oddly, recommended to me the brief section in *The Theory of Social Economy* on mathematical general equilibrium that Cassel had cribbed from Walras. I was amazed and delighted. So I hurriedly took the basic courses in university mathematics. By that time my economics explorations were running ahead of assigned course textbooks in mathematics.[27]

However, while it is possible that Director may have introduced him to Cassel at this point—it would have fitted as providing a more formal account of the operation of free markets than Slichter provided and it involved no more than simple mathematics—Samuelson's transcript suggests that the decision to study mathematics, and possibly even the decision to major in economics, came much later.[e]

In the third quarter, Lloyd Mints took over from Director.[28] Mints was a specialist in monetary economics who had joined Chicago in 1919, and had taught the course on economic organization until 1927.[29] His having taught the course for so long may explain his choice of a long-established textbook, *Outline of Economics* (1931), the main author of which, Richard T. Ely, had been one of the founders of the American Economic Association in 1885. The textbook had been extensively revised and the latest edition contained chapters revised, if not written, by the economist widely considered to be one of America's leading economic theorists: Allyn Young. Mints did not use the whole book—850 pages would have been too much in a quarter—but did use the chapters on money, banking, and the business cycle.[30] Given that he later took Mints's course on money and banking, the main significance of this lies in Samuelson's early exposure to one of the economists whom Milton Friedman would cite as responsible for establishing the Chicago tradition in monetary economics, of which Samuelson was to become very critical.[f]

Samuelson may have taken this more traditional course in economics in place of the material he had missed through his late arrival, but it was not his only exposure to the subject. Economic ideas were present even in the course on the humanities. There, and in the social science course, economics was presented as dealing with one aspect of the social system, meaning there was no sharp separation between economics and the other social sciences. He was obtaining a broad education in the humanities and the social sciences, as part of which he was forced to think extensively about what it meant to be a scientist, auditing additional courses and attending special lectures at the university. He was on track to become a social scientist and had not yet made the decision to become an economist. At the end of the year he won a prize, not for anything he did in economics but for a political science essay.[g]

---

e. Equally, it is possible that Samuelson misremembered and that Director had introduced him to Cassel's general equilibrium system in a course on labor problems, discussed in chapter 4 this volume.

f. See chapter 5 this volume.

g. The Civil Government Prize. Samuelson's essay appears not to have been preserved.

| Natural and Social Sciences,
1932–1933

The Natural Sciences

Samuelson attached great importance to the courses in the biological and physical sciences that he took in his sophomore year. As with his social science course the previous year, the General Introductory Course in the Biological Sciences, taught by Merle Coulter, which Samuelson described as an excellent survey course,[1] began with a discussion of the scientific method. He was taught that the method of science was "essentially empirical and based on observations of phenomena," that "the rationalness of reality" was implicitly assumed, and that the goal of scientific research was to establish cause-and-effect relationships.[2] Observation came first, followed by analysis, but biology was only just moving into this latter stage. He was also introduced to the idea that equilibrium could be fundamental to science. "Dynamic equilibrium" was central to biology because it was used to define the notion of an animal, the basic unit of life. There was no sharp distinction between life and "non-life," an animal being "something that happens":

> Each living unit is a pseudo-isolated system in dynamic equilibrium. Through this individual passes a steady stream of matter and energy which undergo changes in their passage. This flow of substance is controlled by the organization of the system so as to maintain itself as a unit despite profound replacements within it. Other systems in dynamic equilibrium show in essence all the properties of living things. It is

almost impossible, for example, to distinguish a candle flame from a living organism by any definition in words. Into each come oxygen (respiration) and substances (food) which are broken down (digested), taken into the structure, and finally oxidized (metabolism), yielding energy for purposes of maintaining the organization and wastes which are removed (excreted).[3]

Equilibrium, a concept that Samuelson would later use to unify economics, was being applied as a general framework within which to understand the whole of the living world. The bulk of the course involved explaining the significant groups of living organisms, drawing attention to some of the cases where delineating boundaries was difficult, and identifying the differences between higher and lower organisms. This part of the syllabus ended with prehistoric humans and an evolutionary account of race. The latter focused on visible characteristics, explicitly denying that race and nationality were connected, and denying that there was any such thing as an Aryan race. Biology had implications for the analysis of society.

After this classification of types of life, living organisms were analyzed as "running machines," explaining how they functioned, emphasizing biochemical processes. The syllabus explained that there would be no attempt "to cover comprehensively the fields of human physiology in health and disease," but a few topics would be covered "with a moderate degree of penetration."[4] One of those topics was blood pressure, which covered the causes of hypertension, or raised blood pressure.[5] This was of particular relevance to Samuelson because in his freshman year he had been found to suffer from hypertension and was banned from involvement in intramural sports.[6] His father had the same problem and, though still alive, he was in poor health. Given that it was then untreatable, his father's condition will have contributed to his anxiety about the problem.

Students were warned of the danger of reifying concepts, whether "mind," "consciousness," or the "self." "Ideas" are not stored—they are not "immaterial, spiritual things hiding in the subconscious" or like "old letters, waiting to be re-read."[7] What persists is the effects of previous sensory experiences on the nervous system. "One may as well assert," it was claimed, "that the actual music is *in* a phonograph record and is released by the needle as to assume that ideas exist as entities in some hypothetical, immaterial mind or soul."[8] This led to a clear lesson:

> The reification of abstractions has been the source of considerable confusion and error in psychological thought. The criticism to the effect that psychology first lost its *soul*, then its *mind*, and finally its

consciousness, is literally true of these terms are regarded as rounds denoting independently existing entities or forces.

This injunction may have been in a course on biological sciences and its conclusions for the social sciences other than psychology may not have been drawn out, but it would not have been difficult for a bright student to see the implications for the study of human behavior in other contexts.

The course ended by covering genetics, eugenics, and ecology, the last of which, like the parallel course on the physical sciences, meant that it finished with geography. The section on genetics was the most mathematical part of the course, involving statistics and the curve of a normal distribution. Samuelson remembered that "His [Coulter's] discourse on simple Mendel genetics led, it appeared to a Gaussian distribution when the number of genetic attributes grew from 2, 3, . ., to N = infinity."[9] However, the explicit mathematical content was minimal, with barely an equation to be seen in the syllabus. Samuelson later remembered this as having been his first introduction to the normal distribution for which he had been prepared by attending a lecture by the sociologist William F. Ogburn, which he had attended with a girl he described simply as "a short-term date." Forgetting to mention his assumption of a normal distribution, Ogburn had claimed that two-thirds of observations would be within x standard deviations of the mean, a claim that Samuelson believed he could disprove. He found, on his own, a copy of *Fundamentals of Statistics* (1925), by Louis Thurstone, a professor in the Department of Psychology, which presumably helped him think more deeply about the problem that Coulter was discussing in very simple terms. Though he had not yet seen the overall importance of mathematics, this shows that he was already following up on the mathematical elements in the lectures he was attending.

Genetics led Coulter into a discussion of eugenics, "defined roughly as human genetics."[10] Though the focus was on understanding heredity, one aim of eugenics was to control human evolution by controlling reproduction. Eugenicists advocated a program involving sterilization of "hereditary defectives," subsidies to the fit, caution in admitting "hereditarily inferior types of immigrants," and the dissemination of information on heredity. Whatever Samuelson's reaction, it is worth noting that he was exposed to Coulter's arguments in favor of such measures, which "could surely do no harm and might do an immense amount of good." Coulter supported his position by referring the students to Edward East's *Heredity and Human Affairs* (1927)—a book that he expected them to "read liberally": the importance of the topic to the modern citizen justified such a long assignment.[11]

The assignment of this racist text shows the clear difference between what was acceptable then and what is now.

Though East recognized the great variety within racial groups, he argued that there were significant differences between races: "the negro averages about two grades lower than the English, the Scotch a fraction of a grade above, and the Athenians of the time of Pericles two grades above."[12] Though recognizing that comparisons had to be made "with great caution," East concluded that

> One who makes a thorough study of the available evidence, however, cannot avoid concluding that the intelligence level of the negro is far below that of the white, though not significantly different from the lowest of the white subgroups. The range of averages in the white subgroups extends as far above the general average as that of the negro does below it.[13]

On average, Jews and Nordics were "great races" in that they produced more than their share of exceptional individuals. However, the price of this was a larger number of "simpletons":

> They have left their mark on every science, on every art. *But it is not the race that counts, it is the individual.* The genetic basis of genius being what it is, the race producing exceptional segregates on one side of the curve must also produce exceptional segregates on the other side of the curve. The presence of genius entails the presence of simpletons in the ordinary course of human affairs.[14]

Under a strict eugenic regime, where breeding was controlled, this would not be true. "Race suicide," involving degeneration of the population, could be avoided. In this book, the conclusions of which were endorsed by his teacher as capable of doing no harm, science was being used to support a racist ideology and widely held prejudices. Remarks in other parts of the course suggest that Coulter did not share East's belief that there were substantial differences between races, but he nonetheless recommended the book sufficiently strongly that it is hard to believe that Samuelson did not read it.

In the parallel course on the physical sciences, taught by Harvey Lemon, an experimental physicist who was soon to publish a textbook titled *From Galileo to Cosmic Rays: A New Look at Physics* (1934), and Hermann I. Schlesinger, an inorganic chemist who had taught at Chicago since 1907, astronomy was used as a route into physics and then into chemistry. After a lecture on the uniformity of nature, students were introduced to the night sky and what it meant to think of the earth as an astronomical body. Lectures in the Adler Planetarium, established only two years earlier—the first planetarium in America—served to make the material more concrete. Discussions of more abstract physics (matter and force, energy and work, the mechanics of fluids) were covered as they arose. After covering celestial bodies, from the sun to the galaxy, the course turned to the composition of matter: molecules, then atoms, electricity, magnetism, radioactivity, atomic structure, sound, and spectroscopy.

From spectroscopy it was a short step into chemical change, combustion, and a range of topics in chemistry that ended with the carbon cycle (providing a link with the biological sciences course). It was only at this point, after fifty-six lectures, that the course turned to mathematics, with lectures on arithmetic and algebra; geometry, trigonometry and analytic geometry; and calculus. Mathematics was explained in relation to the problems requiring its use, brought together in a chapter, "Mathematics and Life." Mathematics lay beneath the calendar, the motions of the solar system, maps, physics, chemistry, the medical and statistical sciences, transport and communication, civil engineering and architecture. The social sciences were not mentioned. In the following lecture, a presentation of geometry gave rise to some general statements about the role of mathematics that are of interest in view of Samuelson's later work.

THE STRUCTURE OF A MATHEMATICAL SCIENCE

The structure consists of definitions and axioms designed to correspond with experience, and the theorems which can be deduced from them by the laws of mathematical logic. In order for a theory to be useful in the interpretation of natural phenomena the superstructure of theorems must be in accord with experimental data as well as the axiomatic basis. The purposes of such a theory are the correlation of results which may otherwise seem heterogeneous and unrelated in character, and the logical prediction of results which might be difficult or impossible to discover experimentally.[15]

The point about mathematics being a means of bringing heterogeneous data under the same theory was then repeated specifically in relation to physics.[16] The course ended by going into geology, its relation to life, meteorology, climate and the weather, and mapping. In relating the distribution of mankind across the earth to geology, it was linking physics to the biological and social sciences.

Samuelson was to remember this course and Harvey Lemon more than half a century later. Though he did not say this, its message that mathematics could unify seemingly different fields, and that useful theorems needed to be in accordance with data, was to find strong echoes in his economics. However, the specific point that he noted when, in 1996, he wrote to Caltech chemist Norman Davidson, with whom he had taken a calculus course at Chicago, was that it was in Lemon's course that he had first encountered the Le Chatelier Principle, an idea that was to be important in his subsequent work.[a] Samuelson wrote of Lemon, "I didn't like his teleology. I preferred this [the principle of Le Chatelier] as a prosaic corollary to Jacobi's theorem on determinants, which is just as applicable to economics as it is to chemistry."[17] It is not clear what he meant by Lemon's "teleology," but perhaps it was the progression from the universe to the place of mankind on the earth that Lemon might have discussed in relation to Coulter's evolutionary theories. Samuelson was correct that he had encountered the principle in Lemon's course, but his account of his response to it does not ring true; for in the same letter as the one from which the previous quotation is taken, he confessed that at that point he had not seen the importance of mathematics: "You know the brutal truth: that, late in life as an aging *wunderkind*, a good fairy whispered to me that math was a skeleton key to solve age old problems in economics." If he had not yet seen the significance of mathematics for his future work, and had yet to take the introductory calculus course, it is hard to believe that, for all his teachers' statements about the unifying power of mathematics, he would have seen that a principle in chemistry, that was not even described algebraically, was a more general theorem in mathematics. He simply had not studied enough mathematics to be thinking in these terms.

The Social Sciences—How to Think

Though a major function of the second-year course in the social sciences was to prepare students going on to further work in the field, it focused on what were claimed to be "major social problems of the day," though this time the order of the different social sciences was changed.[18] The first quarter tackled urbanization; the second, the role of the national government (particularly contentious given Franklin Roosevelt's aggressive use of government powers to try to deal with the Great Depression); and the third quarter, the general problem of economic interdependence—a more theoretical concern, though given topicality by what was happening in the world economy.

---

a. For an explanation, see chapter 14 this volume.

Most of the items on the "whole volume" reading list, emphasized by being made available as a rental set, focused on critical thinking. First on the list was *Straight and Crooked Thinking*.[19] The aim of this book was to expose dishonest tricks used to make an argument appear more persuasive than it should be. Words could be chosen because of their emotional appeal ("pig-headed" rather than "firm"); jumps could be made from propositions true of some people to assumptions they were true of all; one could show that some-one is wrong on a trivial point and conclude that his or her main argument is wrong; one could present two extreme positions and assume that the mean must be correct. The book sought to expose "tabloid thinking," the pitfalls in drawing analogies between different situations, and the perils of vagueness. In an appendix, flagged in the syllabus as a crucial part of the book, no fewer than thirty-four illegitimate types of argument were cited. It was a book in logic, though more practical than normal textbooks in logic. Thouless[20] likened it to flypaper, writing, "if we have a plague of flies in the house we buy fly-papers and not a treatise on the zoological classification of *Musca domestica.*" The point was vividly illustrated with an imaginary but highly plausible conversation in which virtually every statement involved crooked thinking.

"Straight thinking" was exemplified by science. "The scientist," Thouless[21] argued, "weighs, measures, and calculates without any use of emotional phraseology, guided only by a simple creed of the universality of cause and effect." The result was that science, by leading to new experiments, increases knowledge and makes it possible to control our environment: "blind forces" can be replaced by "our own intelligent and conscious control." The idea that disease should be brought under control was widely accepted, and Thouless argued that similar methods should be used to cure social ills such as trade depressions and international conflicts. "The man who brings a scientific atti-tude of mind to the analysis of a dispute between his own country and another is labelled a 'traitor.' ... When we suggest that poverty is an evil whose causes must be discovered and, at all costs, removed, we are told that the life of societies follows unchangeable economic laws with which it is dangerous to tamper."[22] The argument was flawed, for although an automobile obeyed mechanical laws, it could nonetheless be driven to a chosen destination. If controlling social phenomena was dangerous, the remedy was not to leave them uncontrolled but to understand the laws behind them. His conclusion amounted to a powerful argument for the social science that Gideonse and his colleagues were offering.

We can solve the problems of war and poverty if we approach them in the same scientific spirit as we have now learned to apply to disease, sure that every effect has a cause, and that impartial scientific investigation will reveal those causes and that sufficiently determined effort will remove them.

A really educated democracy, distrustful of emotional phraseology and all the rest of the stock-in-trade of the exploiters of crooked thinking,... could take conscious control of our social development and destroy these plagues of our civilization—war, poverty, crime— if it were determined that nothing should stand in the way of their removal—no old traditions and none of the ancient privileges which are called "rights" by their holders. That would be a beneficent revolution which we can have if we are willing to trust our own intelligences sufficiently boldly and if we want it badly enough. But the revolution must start in our own minds.[23]

What began almost as a textbook in practical logic ended with a bold statement of political faith allied with a belief in the power of social science to bring about a political revolution.

The first task the students were set attests to the importance attached to this book. The whole book was listed as "indispensable reading," and students were asked to keep a "fallacies notebook" in which they recorded examples of crooked thinking, found either in the press or in course readings, together with their own explanation of why the reasoning was false. This had to be shown to their instructor at least once a quarter.

The message that becoming a social scientist involved learning to apply a critical, scientific attitude to social problems was reinforced with other reading. They were directed to read *The Autobiography of Lincoln Steffens* (1931) for its first-hand reports of social movements, especially ones arising in large cities; and *Prospects of Industrial Civilization* (1923)—by Bertrand Russell, "one of the outstanding philosophers of our time," and Dora Russell—on account of the critical attitude it displayed toward industrial civilization. The Russells' suggestions for a way out of these problems were described as incidental to its critical analysis. Different ways in which people might be trained to be citizens were covered in *The Making of Citizens* (1931) by Charles Merriam, a professor of political science at Chicago since 1920. In line with Thouless's thinking, Merriam was concerned with both unconscious and conscious ways in which citizens' ideas were shaped.

The theme of revealing unconscious barriers to clear analysis of social problems was covered explicitly in Norman Angell's *The Unseen Assassins* (1932). Like Steffens, Angell was a journalist, though he had just served two years as a Labour Party Member of the British Parliament. He was famous worldwide for his book *The Great Illusion* (1910), which had challenged the ability of war to resolve economic issues; and in 1933 he was awarded the Nobel Peace Prize. *The Unseen Assassins* challenged notions of nationalism, patriotism, and imperialism, arguing as in his earlier book for a more rational organization of world affairs. A major focus of the book was on educating ordinary voters who, he argued at length, could never master the technical details of economic and social problems: they were far too complex and yet it was impossible simply to rely on experts, for the experts were divided. Angell's contention was that, though "John Smith" could never become an expert, he could nonetheless reach sensible conclusions by drawing on knowledge he already possessed but to which he was blind. For example, arguments about retribution against Germany could be undermined by recognizing the obvious fact that, though Germany might be referred to as "she," nations were not individuals but, rather, collections of people with different goals and interests. Such recognition was sufficient to undermine notions of punishment. Many disasters, including the First World War, could have been avoided if ordinary people had not been driven, through false conceptions, to hold the "suspicions, hatreds, insane passions, and cupidities" that they did.[24] Angell thus took an optimistic view of what could be achieved by opening the eyes of ordinary people.

The rental set also included two books specifically on economics, presumably intended to support the theme of economic interdependence to be covered in the third quarter, the first of which was *Recovery: The Second Effort* (1932), by the British economist Arthur Salter. Salter argued that although unemployment was the most obvious contemporary problem, it concealed deeper problems. The purpose of his book was to provide comprehensive coverage of what he called the "immediate distress," encompassing money, gold, finance, reparations and war debts, trade policy, industrial organization, government regulation and control, and political security, on the grounds that anything less would be "partial and misleading."[25] The root cause of postwar problems was the dislocation of the world economic system brought about by the First World War. There had been a remarkable recovery by 1925, but because the defects of the system had not been addressed, there was now need for another recovery. Theoretical ideas were introduced in the context of working out solutions to urgent policy problems.[b]

In the nineteenth century, the laissez-faire system had achieved much: an outburst of scientific invention and rising living standards. It was an

---

b. During the Second World War, a major focus of Samuelson's research was the aftermath of the First World War, to which he had been introduced here.

automatic, self-regulating system governing the flows of goods and money throughout the world. It was so successful that few realized "how miraculous was the self-adjusting quality of this individualistic, competitive, free, unregulated, unplanned and unplanning system; and upon what a fortuitous combination of conditions, precarious and temporary, its success was dependent."[26] Government had intervened to respond to defects in the system, with the result that the world now found itself with a system intermediate between laissez-faire and planning, each of which had its own defects. The task facing policymakers was to design a new system that transcended both laissez-faire and planning.

Though the book focused on immediate policy problems, it held out clear methodological lessons. The first of these was that economic problems were much more complicated than they appeared to be, thereby undermining simple solutions that might be found in popular writing. This message was reinforced in another text in the rental set, *The Control of Wages* (1928) by Walton Hamilton and Stacy May, the message of which was that even in the context of something so apparently simple as wages, the interdependence of different markets meant that careful analysis was needed. In the course of his analysis of current problems, Salter also covered important theoretical ideas—competition, the business cycle, speculation—introducing the idea that theory was important for understanding concrete problems. This message was reinforced by one of the optional readings listed to support the students' preparation of their "fallacies notebooks": "It May Be So in Theory," by James Bonar.[27] In this chapter, Bonar attacked the notion that theory and practice were opposed. Theory was, he argued, essential, and if theory did not work in practice, that meant that the theory must be wrong. The maxim espoused by many so-called practical men that "The proof of the pudding is in the eating of it" did not justify popular disbelief in abstraction.[28] Bonar went on to argue for the method adopted by the nineteenth-century classics.

> In Political Economy we are making an endeavour after a Science. Is our endeavour fruitless?
>
> Must we be content with a register of facts? The right answer seems to be that the motives and actions of men in regard to economy in society undoubtedly yield general principles; they present certain broad uniformities that have a greater persistence and regularity than exist in any other group of social facts. This is proved by practice in the sense of being inferred from the known character of the great masses of civilized men. The onlooker sees these uniformities; to be

an economist, he takes permission to look at them (in the first place) separately as if they were the only causes at work. This detachment of them is his offence in the eyes of the "practical" men. It is the method described as essential to economic investigation by J. S. Mill, Senior, Cairnes, Bagehot, and [Neville] Keynes, the last summing up the whole case sanely and wisely. It is the method dictated (to use a figure) by the facts of human nature.[29]

Whatever stance his teachers took toward Bonar's position (it must never be forgotten that their aim was to expose students to contrasting views), Samuelson was exposed at an early stage in his training to strong arguments for abstract theorizing in the social sciences, paralleling the arguments he was encountering in his physical sciences course, but these arguments were all firmly rooted in contemporary problems.

Social Science—The Syllabus

Urban civilization was the topic for the first quarter both because it was seen as "a laboratory for the study of human nature and social life" and also because the city was an integral element in the growth of modern civilization—the move from a folk society to an industrial society that had featured strongly in the introductory course.[30] The latter point emerges strongly from the discussion topics the students were assigned at the end of the first week.

FOR DISCUSSION

"What his house is to the peasant, the city is to civilized man. . . . It is a quite certain, but never fully recognized, fact that all great cultures are city-born. . . . World-history is the history of city men."—Oswald Spengler, *The Decline of the West*

"The growth of cities, the world over, has been the most conspicuous social phenomenon of the past hundred years."—W. B. Munro, *Municipal Government and Administration*[31]

The course progressed through the structure of cities, their social organization, and human behavior in cities. The last covered "urban personality," which included typical urban institutions, work (and lack of work) and income, delinquency, and crime, as well as various problems relating to cities (social disorganization, communication, housing, religion, education, and recreation). They were required to discuss, among other quotations, the romantic poet Shelley's remark that "Hell is a city much like London."[32] The quarter concluded with social control: zoning and planning, the city and the country, the city of the future, and research and reform (the muckraking period being discussed here). The city was presented "as a social laboratory from the point of view of the Sociologist."[33]

In the second quarter, warning students to assume neither that the United States was superior to Europe nor vice versa, the course turned to politics, offering a detailed comparative study of the political, legal, and administrative systems of the United States, Britain, Germany, France, and Switzerland. This was followed by lectures on British and French empires, the Soviet Union, Italian corporatism, Japan's absolute monarchy, Latin American republics, and recent political developments in Central and Eastern European countries. The quarter ended by looking at European education. What is clear from the syllabus is that Samuelson would have emerged from the course with a comprehensive and detailed knowledge of how different countries were governed.

The third quarter, on the "interdependent economic relations of men," focused on the need for coordination and the means by which it might be achieved.[34] In the year that Samuelson took this course, the Great Depression was at its worst, with high unemployment (giving him the excuse to spend the summer on the beach, because there was no hope at all of getting work) and the progressive disintegration of the world's economic system into a number of trading blocks. After a historical account of interdependence from the industrial revolution to the present day, various methods of coordinating economic activity were discussed: custom, central planning, and the market. Students were recommended to read material on the Soviet system and on scientific management. Before turning to what was probably seen as the heart of the course, students were introduced to the institutions of a market economy. This covered private enterprise and ownership, specialization, business organization, labor organization, speculative production, and credit. Only then was the operation of the price system discussed.

The six lectures on "How Price in the Market Organizes Economic Activity" were, unlike any previous section of the course, on theory. They were more abstract than previous material—so much so that the sections on the price system, supply and demand, and the pricing of productive services were followed by "The Problem of the 'Application' of Economic Theory": (a) the measurement of prices, demand, and supply; and (b) the statistical method in economics.

Though economics has a long history of supply and demand analyses, the statistical estimation of demand and supply curves was then very much a minority activity. It was much more common to defend economic theory by appealing to introspection or psychological theory, but in Henry Schultz, Chicago had one of the major exponents of this approach. However, the topic for discussion was not any remark made by Schultz but, rather, a long paragraph by the physicist Max Planck.

How can practical laws be derived by considering phenomena the cause of which has, provisionally, to be left unexplained? Like the social sciences, physics has learnt to appreciate the great importance of a method completely different from the purely causal, and has applied it since the middle of the last century with continually increasing success. This is the statistical method, and the newest advances in theoretical physics have been bound up in its development. Instead of seeing, without tangible results, the dynamical laws at present completely unknown to us, which govern a solitary occurrence, observations of a large number of isolated occurrences of a definite kind are collected and an average or mean value obtained. For the calculation of these mean values certain empirical rules are available, according to the special circumstances of the case. These rules permit the prediction of future occurrences, not with absolute certainty, but with a probability which is often practically equivalent to certainty. Though a method which is fundamentally an expedient appears unsuited and unsympathetic to the scientific needs of many workers, who desire principally an elucidation of causal relations, yet it has become absolutely indispensable in practical physics. A renunciation of it would involve the abandonment of the most important of the recent advance of physical science. —Max Planck, *A Survey of Physical Theory*.[35]

The authority of one of the world's most eminent physicists was clearly being used to argue for what was still a highly controversial stance in economics. It was consistent with the motto, attributed to the British physicist and engineer William Thomson, Lord Kelvin, that adorned the recently built Social Sciences Building:

"WHEN YOU CANNOT MEASURE ❀ YOUR KNOWLEDGE IS ❀ MEAGER ❀ AND ❀ UNSATISFACTORY ❀" Lord Kelvin[c]

---

c. The flowers stand for the decorative motifs that are placed within the quotation as it is carved on the Social Sciences Building and which have been shown to denote words that

Though some Chicago economists agreed with the sentiment—the quotation had been organized by the sociologist William Ogburn, one of whose lectures Samuelson had heard earlier that year—others did not. Frank Knight and Jacob Viner both disagreed with it; moreover, it represented a view that had been opposed in a highly influential book published the previous year by Lionel Robbins (1932), who questioned whether statistically estimated demand curves were useful.[d] Given such disagreements within the social science faculty, the discussion surrounding the Planck quotation must have been lively.

The problem of economic interdependence almost inevitably led to problems of international trade, the lectures covering tariffs and protection, international monetary problems, migration, and the economic causes of war, all immensely topical subjects in 1932. The course ended with no fewer than six lectures on "the general problem of human welfare in a system based on pecuniary exchange." The first topic under this heading, "Social Cost and Profit vs. Individual Cost and Profit," is reminiscent of the welfare economics associated with the Cambridge (UK) professor A. C. Pigou, whose *Economics of Welfare* (1920), then in its fourth edition, has come to be seen as the leading treatment of the subject. However, the syllabus suggests a different approach was taken, inquiring about "human costs of industry" and "human utility of consumption."[36] Such language resonates more with romantic critics of orthodox economics and John Ruskin than with Cambridge economics. It is notable that the "indispensable reading" included several chapters from John A. Hobson's *Work and Wealth: A Human Valuation* (1914), in which Ruskinian arguments about the merits of different activities were used to drive a wedge between "economic" and "human" costs. The work of the Cambridge economists Alfred Marshall and Pigou is conspicuous by its absence.[e] To support the claim that consumption guides production—a claim that could have been supported with orthodox supply and demand theory—the course drew on Slichter's *Modern Economic Society* (1931), the textbook Samuelson had used with Director the previous year.

---

had to be omitted to make the quotation fit the available space. The full story of this inscription is told in Merton et al. 1984.

d. Viner is reputed to have amended it to "When you can measure it, when you can express it in numbers, your knowledge is still of a meagre and unsatisfactory kind," and Knight is reputed to have added, "and when you cannot measure, measure anyway." See Merton et al. 1984.

e. Given what does appear in the reading list, it seems unlikely that such material was omitted simply because it was thought too technical for students at this level.

In the assigned chapters, Slichter stressed consumers' ignorance about the products they were buying, marketing, and the need for consumer protection. This brought the students back to questions of long-range planning, discussed at the start of the course, though here they were referred not to discussions of Soviet central planning but to an article in the *New Republic* by the Columbia economist John Maurice Clark, the son of John Bates Clark, the latter commonly seen as one of the great figures in American economics at the end of the nineteenth century.[f]

J. M. Clark's "Long Range Planning for the Regularization of Industry," published in January 1932, the year of Franklin Roosevelt's first presidential election victory, was directed at the problem facing the United States three years into the Great Depression, with output still falling. Clark started from the assumption that everyone agreed something was wrong with the way private enterprise was operating and that action needed to be taken. Rejecting Soviet planning as unsuitable for a democracy, he sought a path between that and laissez-faire, arguing for the establishment of a planning board composed of experts who would collect data and issue advice. It would tackle the problems of sick industries (ones with chronic excess capacity), technological unemployment (unemployment caused by the failure of industry to re-employ workers displaced by machinery), and the business cycle. Clark sought to avoid price controls and limitations on production (tried by Roosevelt early in his administration), arguing for labor market reform, spending on public works, and use of public finance to stabilize rather than destabilize the level of economic activity. Underlying his approach was a plea for a scientific approach to the problem.

> The main hope of results lies in the combination of scientific fact-finding directed to uncovering the cause of instability, a standing organization [composed of experts] devoted to the problem, and representation of all the interests involved, which between them have a far larger stake in stabilization policies than single business enterprises feel. No one of these alone would be sufficient, but from the combination of all of them some results may fairly be expected.[37]

A letter Samuelson wrote to Clark in 1946 makes it clear that, though he was eventually to come around to Clark's views, as an undergraduate Samuelson became critical of attempts to manage spending and control the business cycle.[38] The course he took with Director the previous year may have

---

f. Samuelson thus had an unorthodox introduction to welfare economics, a field on which he was to leave a distinctive mark. See chapter 22 this volume.

encouraged him to assume a skeptical position toward planning. If so, he would have been critical of the position taken by Gideonse.[g] Samuelson's dismissal of Gideonse's introductory course, which he disparagingly called "economics for poets," would have been an apt summary of the Ruskin-inspired welfare economics that Gideonse taught in the course that Samuelson did take. Given that he did not see the relevance of mathematics to economics until the following year, it is plausible that at this stage he may not have grasped the significance for economics of Planck's arguments about statistics, along with Clark's support for stabilization policy. If so, these were both views on which he was to undergo a profound change of mind.

Social Economic Organization

Whether or not Samuelson reacted negatively to the line Gideonse was taking in the lectures, this course was significant as being the first place in his program where he was exposed to the work of Frank Hyndman Knight (1885–1972). Samuelson provided an affectionate portrait of the professor he described as a "Cracker-barrel Socrates."

> A profound philosopher and a superb economic technician, he was also the village atheist and a sage of the Will Rogers vintage. These days professors tend to come from Exeter Academy or the Bronx High School of Science. Knight was of that turn-of-the-century generation who—like Karl and Arthur Compton and Wesley Mitchell—came off the farm.
>
> He used to say in his squeaky voice that he became an economist because his feet hurt him following the plow. Perhaps nearer the truth was the fact that when he was a graduate student at Cornell, he was given an ultimatum: "Stop talking so much, or leave the philosophy department." This gave Knight no choice but to gravitate down to economics. (It also made him an authority on the laws of talk, as in his dictum: "Sociology is the science of talk, and there is only one law in sociology. Bad talk drives out good.")[39,h]

The fruit of Knight's time at Cornell and the basis for his reputation as an economist was a book, *Risk, Uncertainty and Profit* (1921), a revised version

---

g. Gideonse's teachers at Columbia had included Wesley Mitchell (an enthusiast for Hobson's welfare economics) and J. M. Clark.

h. Knight's law of talk was a variant of Gresham's Law, named after the sixteenth-century Thomas Gresham, that bad money (coins with a low silver content) drives out good

of the PhD thesis he had submitted in 1916. In this he had connected profit to uncertainty, arguing that, in the absence of uncertainty, profits would be zero. However, the required reading for the course was not this book, but four chapters Knight had written while at Iowa, printed in the syllabus under the heading of "Social Economic Organization" and taking up well over half the pages devoted to readings. Samuelson was later to acknowledge the similarity between the view of economics presented in his own textbook and the view Knight had proposed in these readings.[40]

In these chapters, Knight began with the problem of economic organization, a topic that arose because economic activity required many people to cooperate in performing different tasks.

> The problem of organization, which sets the problem of economic science, deals with the concrete means or mechanism for dividing the general function of making a living for the people into parts and bringing about the performance of these parts in due proportion and harmony.[41]

Performing this task required that five functions be performed if the economic system was to work successfully: fixing the standards or values that determine consumption; organizing production; distributing resources among individuals; providing for economic progress; and adjusting consumption-to-production within very short periods (accommodating temporary shortages or gluts). Knight explained why organized production would be more efficient than if each person lived in isolation, but like many writers from Adam Smith onward, recognized that the division of labor could have harmful effects.

Taking up a theme that had been developed at length in the previous year's course, Knight outlined different types of economic system (caste, autocracy, anarchy, and democratic socialism) before turning to the system with which he was most concerned: the price system. This achieved organization without planning.

> No one ever worked out a plan for such a system, or willed its existence; there is no plan of it anywhere, either on paper or in anybody's mind, and no one directs its operations. Yet in a fairly tolerable way, "it works," and grows and changes. We have an amazingly elaborate division of labor, yet each person finds his place in the scheme.[42]

(coins with their full silver content), on the grounds that if they have both, people will choose to spend the bad money and to hoard the good money.

One can understand Knight's taking this view in the mid-1920s, but it would be interesting to know how Samuelson and his fellow students reacted to the claim that the price system "worked" in 1932–33, when the place of many people was in dole lines. A few pages later, Knight explained that in the real world, the system did not work as well as theory suggested. "Much conscious social interference" was needed to counteract monopolies. A further problem was that pecuniary demand did not measure "the real human importance of products": "desires may be manufactured by fraud or corruption of tastes, and at best it cannot be assumed that what people individually want is uniformly what is best for them or for society."[43] The significance Samuelson attached to these remarks will have depended on whether he read them as minor qualifications to an argument about the virtues of free enterprise, or as substantial points relating to welfare analysis, perhaps drawing out implications of the ethics he had encountered in Hobson's writings the previous year.

Knight then proceeded to outline what is often described as a broadly "Austrian" view of economic activity.[i] That is, the aim of economic activity is the satisfaction of wants, which can be achieved either directly, through producing goods such as food and housing, or indirectly, through producing machinery and factories that can be used to produce consumption goods. In the course of this, Knight presented the circular flow diagram that Samuelson was later to make central to his introductory macroeconomics teaching— Knight's "Wheel of Wealth," reproduced here as figure 3.1.[j] In the 1920s, economists did not distinguish macroeconomics and microeconomics, and Knight was no exception to this rule. He used the Wheel of Wealth to make the point that the price system involved people making their living by selling their "productive power" to businesses, using the income they receive to buy the goods and services they consume. It was a simplification because it ignored the fact that much business activity involves providing for future consumption and because the distinction between people and businesses is not clear-cut. The flow of money in the diagram represents "total social income," which has different meanings at different points in its "circular flow." (Knight used the phrase that Samuelson would later use to describe the

---

i. It is termed Austrian because it is a perspective that can be traced back to Carl Menger, an economist who worked in Austria in the late nineteenth century. In *Risk, Uncertainty and Profit*, Knight had cited the followers of Menger as being almost the only economists to have tackled the problem of profit.

j. Knight was not the first to draw such a diagram. On the history of the diagram, see Backhouse and Giraud 2010. On Samuelson's use of the idea, see chapter 27 this volume.

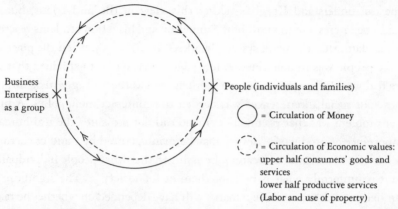

Business Enterprises as a group ✕

✕ People (individuals and families)

◯ = Circulation of Money

⌒ = Circulation of Economic values:
upper half consumers' goods and
services
lower half productive services
(Labor and use of property)

FIGURE 3.1 Knight's "Wheel of Wealth."

process.) It measured personal incomes, the aggregate cost of living, the cost
of production, and business income.

The remaining two chapters provided a conventional account of supply
and demand—an excellent summary of the theories of Alfred Marshall, in the
1920s still the world's preeminent economist—and an analysis of income distribution. The most remarkable aspect of this account is that it was entirely
verbal, without even the diagrams that had become standard in the three
decades since Marshall's textbook. The main principle underlying the theory
of distribution was marginal productivity.

Several features of Knight's chapters are of interest in relation to
Samuelson's later work. Though Knight did not hesitate to talk in terms
of "utility" and "marginal utility," he made it clear that it was the "relative
utility" of one commodity in relation to others that determined demand:
that *levels* of utility did not matter.[44] He reiterated the point made earlier
that "the preferences of individuals, reflected in their price offers, do not
always represent what is 'best' for the individuals themselves."[45] The notion
that Samuelson was later to make his own—that preferences are revealed
by consumers' decisions—was taken for granted by Knight in the course of
questioning the significance of those preferences. He drew a clear distinction
between the analysis of welfare, resting on ethical judgments, and consumers' preferences. Knight also pointed out the existence of externalities—the
problem that one person's actions may directly affect someone else. The free
enterprise system might direct resources into uses where they had the "greatest social usefulness," but there were many exceptions.

Knight also argued that there was no clear distinction between monopoly
and competition, the point taken up by another of Allyn Young's doctoral

students, Edward Chamberlin, who was to be one of Samuelson's teachers at Harvard. "Ultimately all commodities compete with each other for the consumers' money," Knight wrote, goods differing in the *degree* (a word that Knight emphasized when he first used it) to which they could be distinguished from each other.[46] Notwithstanding this qualification, Knight could write about the "evils" involved in monopoly.[47]

In contrast, Knight had nothing but praise for speculators who performed the important social function of ensuring uniform prices across time and space, buying when (or where) prices are low and selling when (or where) prices are high.

> Most of the popular abuse of speculators is due to failure to understand the function they perform, and especially the failure to see that they can only make money by doing what is to the interest of producers and consumers alike to have them do.[48]

No doubt drawing on the experience of farm prices gained in Iowa, Knight claimed that speculators did not make excessive gains. To the contrary, speculative middlemen dealing in agricultural markets lost more than they gained, the reason being that they were playing a game much like gambling, and for similar psychological reasons they tended to overreach themselves. No, the real evils of speculation were "due to 'manipulation' through misrepresentation of facts by fraudulent reports and the like, and to the operations of ignorant persons whose mere gambling on the market often produces serious effects."[49] Given the dramatic change in his family's fortune through its involvement in Florida property speculation, Samuelson would no doubt have seen this as more than a theoretical problem.

A significant feature of Knight's discussion of distribution was that though his theory was traditional in linking the rate of interest to the supply of capital (saving) and demand for capital (investment), he questioned the extent to which saving reflected the choices of optimizing agents. The conventional view was that saving depended on peoples' attitude toward the future: their preference for consumption now rather than in the future. Knight challenged this:

> To some extent this is perhaps true. But the motives underlying saving are very complex and uncertain. One thing is obvious; the great bulk of the social supply of capital comes and must come from saving by persons who do not consume or expect to consume their saving at any time, but die and leave it behind them. It hardly seems real to refer to the motives for leaving an estate after death as a comparison between

present and future goods. Other arguments still further weaken the view of psychological discounting [of the future] as a main cause affecting the interest rate, but they cannot be given here.[50]

Samuelson was later to use similar arguments in his own work on capital theory.

Commitment to Social Science

Samuelson's program was completed with a sequence of three courses on the history of the United States, from the arrival of Columbus in the Caribbean to events of the twentieth century. Taught by William Thomas Hutchinson, an authority on American constitutional history and historical methods, the course focused on the political and constitutional history of the country. He also took a noncredit course Hippology and Equitation, part of the university's Military Science program.[k]

Toward the end of his sophomore year, Samuelson began to keep a diary in which he made occasional entries reflecting on both his personal life and bigger issues on his mind.[l] Perhaps significantly, its first word is "Science."

> Science is essentially the establishing of Cause and Effect relation-ships. This knowledge can be utilized in controlling causes to pro-duce desired effects. It is the realm of philosophy to decide what these objectives shall be, and that of science to achieve those decided upon.[51]

This was the view to which he had been exposed at the start of the Biological Sciences course, and which would have been reinforced by his reading of Thouless's *Straight and Crooked Thinking*. Samuelson noted in his diary that there was a division of labor between philosophy and economics, the former deciding on objectives and the latter on how they should be achieved. He then reflected on the motivation for pursuing a career in science.

> But men do not become scientists chiefly to benefit society—rather because there is a certain "aesthetic" pleasure in the solving of prob-lems. It is a battle of wits to find explanations of facts, observed uniformities, etc.[52]

---

k. The study of horses and horsemanship.

l. In two years there were but nineteen entries.

Given that many of his generation, coming to economics during the Great Depression, did so because they wanted to do something about unemployment and the social problems with which they were surrounded, it is hard not to see this statement as autobiographical. He told a story about himself to make the point.

> To illustrate this. Once Dr. Carlson, the physiologist, was discussing with me after class the hydrodynamics of the blood system. We were outside in sub-zero weather, and not till the end of our conversation did I notice that my nose was frozen.
>
> Now is there anything admirable about this? No, I was not engaged in the pursuit of truth, or attempting to widen the vistas of human thought. It was merely a puzzle which I was engaged in solving, and because of my absorption in it, I did not notice the cold. Just so must Lord Sandwich have felt when, engaged in "breaking the bank," he refused to leave the gaming table and took his meals in the then novel, but now common, form of "sandwiches."[53]

He concluded that scientists were merely "tinkerers who have been closed with an air of mysticism and awe by the admiring public."

Elsewhere, he preferred to say he came to economics by accident or to imply that he was lured into it by the theorems lying around waiting to be discovered.[54] Referring to Director's course in his freshman year, he wrote,

> Even if I had had Mr. Squeers for a teacher, the first drink from the economic textbooks of Slichter and Ely would have been like the Prince's kiss to Sleeping Beauty.
>
> I was too young to know fear. It was as if, like a bird dog bred to point at hunt, my DNA was born to manipulate supply and demand curves. How could those upper-class fellow students be making heavy weather of what was so transparently simple?[55]
>
> To my surprise I could outstrive in class discussions those older members of the class who did not find economic theory to be as easy as I did. One tends to like what one does well. You are very lucky if early on you discover a research field that you like to do and that you are best fitted for.

This self-centered attitude, divorced from considerations of society, was to change in the 1940s when, under the tutelage of Alvin Hansen and knowing that many of his friends were having to fight, he became politically engaged—but that was a decade away.

Samuelson's second diary entry, on April 29, 1933, contained a clear economic opinion.

> I object to the system of laissez-faire, not so much because it doesn't accomplish what it is supposed to do (which it doesn't) but chiefly because even if it worked perfectly, it would require an eternal vigilance by men over their economic interest, and preoccupation with material things—all of which I personally do not like.[56]

Such a view was no doubt developed through his reading of Knight, who unlike many academic critics of socialist planning did so on ethical grounds rather than because it was inefficient. It certainly shows that he had absorbed the message coming from Gideonse and from Knight's text that laissez-faire was not perfect. However, this remark about laissez-faire was not followed up in the diary. Instead, five days later, citing the famous Oxford Union debate,[57] he reflected on cowardice, clearly siding with the Oxford students against critics who accused them of being cowards by voting not to go to war. The remaining three entries in 1933 were exercises in poetry.

It was in this year that Samuelson committed to entering the Division of Social Sciences, his transfer from the College to the Division being made on March 10. In June he obtained As in all the courses he had taken, entitling him to the College Certificate that permitted him to proceed to more specialized courses the following year. He claims there was one point during this year that he briefly toyed with the idea of becoming a sociologist. However, even if he was thinking of becoming an economist, at this point in his studies he was still being trained not as an economist but as a general social scientist. It would be another year before his specialization as an economist would be confirmed; before then, he had to take courses in all the main social science disciplines. Given Chicago's preeminence in the social sciences at this time, this meant that he would be exposed to some of the leading social scientists of the day—in anthropology, sociology, and political science, as well as in economics.

CHAPTER 4 | Social Scientist to Mathematical
Economist, 1933–1934

Fledgling Social Scientist

Samuelson entered the Division of Social Sciences to be equipped with a
broad training in the social sciences. In his first term he took subjects in
anthropology, education, English composition, and sociology, of which he
later picked out anthropology and sociology as two subjects he found interesting. The Introduction to Anthropology was taught by Fay-Cooper Cole, a
student of the leading anthropologist Franz Boas, who had founded Chicago's
anthropology department in 1929.[1] Cole's importance was sufficient for the
writer of his obituary in *Science* to describe him as the "architect of anthropology."[2] Though his earlier work had been on cultures in Indonesia and
Malaya, in the 1930s he was turning to the archeology of the midwestern
United States. Samuelson was therefore being taught by someone at the top
of his field and with broad interests in the subject. The course he taught covered themes Samuelson had already studied at length, with a particular focus
on race. Cole's stance on race, shown in an article he had written two years
before, was that scientific analysis indicated that many of the scare stories
circulating about interbreeding and the superiority of one race over another
could readily be disproven by scientific analysis.[3] There was a need for great
statesmanship and tolerance in dealing with problems of race, but although
the mixing of races would create "more of a hybrid people," there was no
reason to fear for the America of the future.

Samuelson's teachers in sociology, the subject in which he had briefly thought about specializing, also went on to be eminent figures in their field. Leonard Cottrell, who worked as a probation officer for part of his career, took the statistical methods used to predict the success or failure of parole and applied them to marriage. He was also concerned with the philosophical problem of reconciling such statistical predictions with the fact that people were making conscious choices.[4] Though it was Cottrell who taught the course in the autumn term, when Samuelson took it, in other terms the course was taught by Herbert Blumer, a student of George Herbert Meade and a major figure in the development of the theory of symbolic interactionism.[a] As an article by Blumer, "Science without Concepts" (1931), shows, they were both concerned with developing rigorous methods and with questioning the uncritical accumulation of concepts that were not rooted in evidence. The course was, according to the syllabus, "basic," covering the place of sociology within the social sciences, human nature, social contact and interaction, social change, and social progress as applied to problems of population, immigration, race, and crime. However, given the teachers' backgrounds and the students' prior training in the social sciences, it would have been surprising if there had not been considerable discussion of methods.

Samuelson's first term was completed by Education 201, a survey of the problems of the American education system, emphasizing secondary education, and a compulsory course on English composition, focusing on the topic of narrative. For this class he wrote an essay, "Rationalization," on the theme of a friend's suicide.

His social science education continued into the winter term, when he took a course in social history, Rise of New American and European Society, and two courses in political science—Introduction to Political Science and International Relations, both taught by Fred Lewis Schuman, an assistant professor who had been at Chicago since 1927 but had spent most of 1933 in Germany, seeing events unfold. The description of the International Relations course was couched in abstract terms. It dealt with "conflicts of nationality, imperialism, international trade, and foreign policy; elementary conceptions of international law; peaceful and hostile methods of international settlement, and the development of international organization."[5]

---

a. Symbolic interactionism is the idea that peoples' actions are based on what things mean to them and that those meanings are derived from social interaction. In one term Blumer was assisted by Wirth, who had taught Samuelson in the first year.

Though these were abstract problems, in January 1934, shortly after Hitler's rise to power, they were of more than academic interest, especially to a student of Jewish origins whose family roots lay in central Europe. The course must have been influenced by Schuman's own research, which included articles on American foreign policy and on the ethics and politics of international peace.[6] Moreover, in the year that Samuelson took his course, Schuman published a series of articles on the theory of German fascism, German foreign policy, and "The Third Reich's Road to War."[7] In the last of these, he predicted an "inevitable" war and "irremediable disaster."

> Should the pattern of diplomacy revert to type, the revisionist coalition led by Nazi Germany may be expected to be consummated before 1940. Should earlier conflict be averted, the second World War may be anticipated during the decade of 1940 to 1950.[8]

It is easy to imagine how such analysis could have sparked Samuelson's interest in a diplomatic career: given his habit of talking to teachers outside classes, he would surely have encountered them even if they had not been part of the formal syllabus. On February 28, after philosophical discussions of free will and determinism, and the idea that words were symbols (presumably an echo of the symbolic interactionism of his sociology teachers), he wrote in his diary:

> The idea occurred to me not long ago that I should carve out a career for myself in the Foreign Service as a diplomat. I sent away for the booklet on entrance requirements. It is by examination, and I think that with a year's study (and it might be worth the time), I could pass the exam sufficiently high to be admitted. Salaries start at $2,500 and there is prestige attached.[9]

However, reality soon sank in, for he continued, "However, with the depreciation of the dollar this is not so good. Moreover, right now the service is filled and there are no exams."[b] Becoming a diplomat was not a feasible option in the circumstances of 1933. This reasoning might conceal the realization that, as someone of Jewish descent who had attended neither a prestigious private school nor an Ivy League university, certain opportunities were largely closed to him.

---

b. The logic here is not clear, because prices were falling. Perhaps he was assuming that diplomats had to live abroad and were hurt by a low value of the dollar.

His diaries for 1934 mostly centered on his or his friends' girlfriends. However, on February 24, he was exploring a political stance.

But to turn to more important (oh yeah?) matters. For the last year or so I have been increasingly skeptical. In the field of politics, it seems to me that a rational analysis of the implications and consequences of any piece of legislation will make one increasingly hesitant about advocating it. Too often does one overemphasize the gains to be achieved, and underestimates the cost of those gains. "Wishful thinking" is particularly dangerous and prevalent in this field.

It seems that the more intelligently one examines a problem, the less dogmatic he becomes about answering it. Thus the sage tends toward inaction—discussion, approbation and deprecation. But in this world, men devise activity, whether it be wisely directed at achievable goals or not, and so the charlatans, fanatics, demagogues, crusaders, etc., become the leaders of the people, and the wise people write pamphlets deploring the act after it has been committed.

Why then do the people so blithely follow the moths again and again to the flame and get repeatedly burned? In the first place, it is kind to establish the fact that their following them caused them to be burned. And secondly, a new moth always comes along, and the great majority of people seem neither capable nor desirous of discriminating against moths.[10]

There was considerable skepticism here that led to an almost Burkean conservatism, suspicious of idealist promises to improve society. It supports claims he made, over fifty years later, to have been a conservative at Chicago. In a chapter reflecting on his life philosophy, he wrote, "I was taught at the University of Chicago that business freedoms and personal freedoms have to be strongly linked, as a matter both of brute empirical fact and of cogent deductive syllogism. For a long time I believed what I was taught."[11,c] In an unpublished autobiographical fragment, he wrote:

I was the proverbial tabula rasa as far as political economy was concerned: nothing to unlearn in that bloody sponge called my brain. Aaron Director's laissez-faire conservatism got first crack at me.

---

c. In this piece he went on to say that he had gradually acknowledged that this view did not fit the facts, explaining why Hayek's view that societies in which markets were not free would slide into serfdom was wrong.

I marvel that the worst virulences of that particular system got worked out of my system early.[12]

These claims, however, need to be qualified by the fact that Samuelson supported Roosevelt. He may have been a conservative, but it is not clear how deep his commitment was.

Aaron Director and Labor Problems

Any frustration Samuelson felt about the impossibility of following his interest in international relations with a diplomatic career must have been short-lived, for in the same quarter he took the course that was to move him decisively toward economics: Labor Problems, taught by Aaron Director. If the brief remarks in his diary are a guide, Samuelson was by this point becoming more skeptical about what government could achieve. This conservatism was based primarily on skepticism about whether reform, exemplified by the Progressives and Roosevelt's New Deal, would achieve its stated objectives. Such thinking would have been reinforced by Director, still a very young professor, whom Samuelson got to know very well, who had by now abandoned the radical views of his youth. Director was no longer working with Douglas, but was within the orbit of Knight.[d]

The course syllabus gave no clues about the position that would be taken toward labor, or the type of analysis that would be used. It offered

A general survey—analytical, causal, historical—of the main forces and factors which give rise to modern labor conditions and problems, and which must be taken into consideration in the attempted solution of specific labor problems, together with a brief discussion of social programs, organized labor and labor legislation.[13]

There was clearly a thorough explanation of the institutions of the labor market and also of "points of view and social programs;" beyond that there is little indication of the material covered.

However, what does survive is an essay that Samuelson wrote for this course and which, surprisingly, was later included, not just in his papers

---

d. Samuelson remembered taking the course a second time, with Douglas, so that he would know something about wages and unions. Had Director covered an idiosyncratic syllabus, or was Samuelson skeptical about Director's coverage of these problems? Either is possible.

but also in his publications list: "The Limitations of Collective Bargaining."[14] Aside from the odd sentence in his diary, it is his earliest surviving piece of economic writing. It adds support for his claim to have been an economic conservative at Chicago, for he attempts a sustained critique of the idea that collective bargaining, by trade unions, can be beneficial. Samuelson began with a statement of social philosophy.

> A few hundred years ago men believed that social conditions were the result of natural or divine laws, any interference with which was doomed to failure. More recently, however, arose the doctrine that society can be what we make it; that whatever is, is not necessarily right; that whatever has been, is not necessarily what should have been.
>
> This shift in belief from natural genesis to social telesis has been a powerful justification for volitional change. But in our reaction, often we have gone too far. Whereas the burden of proof should be upon those who contemplate innovations inasmuch as random change is bad in a complex, highly adjusted society, actually we seem to have come to value change for its own self.[15]

This was particularly true, he argued, in economic matters, where there was a tendency to assume that if conditions were not perfect, they would be improved, without thinking sufficiently carefully about what would actually result from the actions being pursued. This was Knight's reason for skepticism about reform. Free markets might be bad, but intervention might well make things worse.

Samuelson then quoted, at some length, the remarks of a "trade union theorist," John Mitchell, one-time president of the United Mine Workers of America, hailed in Spring Valley, Colorado, after a successful negotiation, as "the father of the eight-hour day."[16] In this passage, taken from *Organized Labor* (1903), Mitchell argued that bargaining power between workers and employers was very unequal, resulting in exploitation. This view, Samuelson claimed, was supported not just by "labor economists" such as Beatrice and Sidney Webb (British socialists, familiar to Samuelson from his introductory course) but also by "a large number of 'academic' economists, such as Adam Smith, the apostle, and more modern writers such as F. W. Taussig, J. B. Clark and even Alfred Marshall."[17]

Samuelson countered this by arguing that if there was free competition among both workers and employers, wages would not be driven down to subsistence. Employers would not pay more than the marginal product, but they would nonetheless need to pay more than any other employer would pay—otherwise the workers would go elsewhere. He cited Marshall in support of this argument that inequality in bargaining power did not matter, but where Marshall treated this as a theoretical point, Samuelson believed that it was a fact: "Any realistic appraisal of actualities in the labor market establishes a presumption that there is free competition amongst buyers for labor."[18] The problem, Samuelson argued, arose from the fact that people considered bargaining between an employer and an individual worker in isolation from the existence of other workers, reaching the mistaken conclusion that the wage was indeterminate. Those who believed that inequality in bargaining power led to exploitation did not understand the theory of free competition.

Given this, there were only two ways in which unions could raise wages. Collective bargaining might be able to get workers a share of monopoly profits, and in a growing economy they might be able to reduce the extent to which wages lagged behind productivity. Against this, Samuelson argued that unions would not be able to identify industries where workers were getting paid too little and that they would likely force wages too high. In addition, he argued that maintaining wages would tend to prolong depressions. Even if productivity were rising, it would not be beneficial for unions to raise wages because lower wages might result in faster expansion of the industry: "By prematurely raising wages, trade unions have forestalled a better allocation of resources and thus decreased the potential national income increase. Moreover, they have brought about a wage differential, and more inequality." He left no doubt that collective bargaining did great harm.

This essay, which exhibited flaws such as one would expect from an eighteen-year-old who had previously studied very little economics, offered a purely theoretical argument, confidently criticizing Adam Smith, Clark, Taussig, and Alfred Marshall for being inconsistent. Samuelson claimed that they had asserted there would be indeterminacy in the wage bargain that could be exploited by unions, even under free competition, a phrase Samuelson underlined both in his summary of their views and in building his own case against them. He denied that this was true. The essay shows evidence of wide reading. He had presumably read Mitchell's *Organized Labor*, the work of a committed trade unionist, as well as W. H. Hutt's (1930) contrary appraisal of collective bargaining and the relevant chapter of Marshall's *Principles of Economics* (1920). A handwritten footnote strongly suggests that he had read Joan Robinson's *Economics of Imperfect Competition* (1933a), even if he had not understood the implications of imperfect competition for his claims.[19] Samuelson also cited an article, "The Economics of Unionism," by Alvin Hansen (1922), to whom he would later become extremely close. He cited Hansen as his source for the list of techniques unions might use to maintain artificially high wages and it would seem likely that his discussion of wages and industrial growth owed something to his reading of this article. However, there is no evidence about whether he had engaged with Hansen's dynamic arguments about population growth or explored the link between biological differences among people and inequality of rewards in a free market economy.

Typically for a young tyro, Samuelson supported his arguments by claiming boldly that he was being scientific and that those whom he was criticizing were not. His closing paragraph reads,

> In reading the literature on collective bargaining, one is surprised by the constant tendency of writers to go to almost any extremes to justify trade unions. In an effort, perhaps, to show that economics is not a "dismal science," they make it appear as if economics is, indeed, no science at all. Almost unanimously they have joined with other wishful thinkers in the vast army of "Thobbers."[20]

A Thobber was someone who, as Samuelson learned from Henshaw Ward's *Thobbing* (1926), recommended reading on the previous year's social science course, preferred guesswork to investigation, and used pseudo-science as a shortcut to solutions. Unfortunately we do not know what Director made of this uncompromising dismissal of those who questioned the efficiency of freely competitive labor markets. All we know is that Samuelson's performance on the course was "Satisfactory."

Becoming a Mathematical Economist

In the spring quarter, 1934, immediately after the Labor Problems course, Samuelson took Math 104, Elementary Mathematical Analysis, a course also taken by freshmen. In later life he claimed to have signed up for this course immediately after encountering Cassel's theory of general equilibrium in Director's introductory economics course, but this memory is problematic.[e] It seems much more likely that he conflated the two courses he took with Director and that it was in Labor Problems that he took the decision to take the mathematics course. As Math 104 was a course for freshmen, he could clearly have taken it earlier had he chosen to do so. Had the regulations stopped him from taking the course for two years, he would surely not have praised the Hutchins curriculum in such glowing terms, for the frustration would have

---

e. See chapter 2 this volume.

been too great. It might have been in Labor Problems that Director exposed Samuelson to Cassel, or it could have been something else in the course that prompted his decision to study mathematics systematically.

One of the freshmen taking elementary mathematics was Norman Davidson, another graduate of Hyde Park School taught by Beulah Shoesmith, who was on his way to being a chemistry major and whose later research on DNA would become important for molecular biology and genetics. In 1996, Samuelson and Davidson were both awarded the Presidential Medal of Science by President Clinton and would meet in the Rose Garden. This prompted an exchange of letters. Samuelson, who had been out of touch with Davidson, aside from some interaction with him through the National Science Foundation, opened the correspondence by recalling their high school years: "I see that two of Beulah Shoesmith's pupils at Hyde Park High School are to receive the Medal of Science this year. And why not?"[21] Davidson had not remembered this, but recalled that they were classmates at the university.

> What I do have a very strong impression of is you as an Econ major and I as a Chem major were in the same introductory calculus class at Chicago, probably in 1933–1934, which was my first year and you had become convinced that the future of Economics would depend on mathematical analyses and formulations. Is this correct?[22]

Samuelson replied by explaining how he had come to see the importance of mathematics for economics.

> Since I am a grandson of Willard Gibbs—through my Harvard mentor Edwin Bidwell Wilson, who was Gibbs' last (and maybe essentially only) protege at Yale—I am considered in economics to be a physicist *manqué*. You know the brutal truth: that, late in life as an aging *wunderkind*, a good fairy whispered to me that math was a skeleton key to solve age old problems in economics. This must explain why I as a junior was in Professor Bliss's calculus class with you as a freshman. (Or was it Professor Barnard? When I went to him to show how I solved a famous problem in *duopoly* (two monopolized sellers), he said: "Oh, you could have used Lagrange multipliers." And presto, all mystery evaporated. I knew I wanted more of that good stuff. And like Oliver Twist, always it was a case of MORE.[23,f]

---

f. Elsewhere he recognizes that Irving Fisher was also a protégé of Gibbs, but he overlooks this here.

It is not clear whether this refers to the same incident as when he recalled discovering some results on asymmetric oligopoly, in ignorance of what economists had already done.[24,g]

If this memory is correct, it was a mathematician, Gilbert Bliss, chair of Chicago's mathematics department, who persuaded Samuelson to become a mathematical economist. If that is the case, the sequence of events seems to have been that attending Director's Labor Problems course in the winter quarter of 1934 made him realize the need to learn some mathematics, and so he took a course involving calculus in the spring. During that quarter he had the exchange he reported to Davidson, where their mathematics teacher put him on to the use of Lagrange multipliers, and he realized that he needed to know more mathematics, and thereafter he took as many mathematics courses as he could. Samuelson's last-minute decision to take mathematics, a course other students took much earlier in their careers, may have been the reason why, in the spring quarter, he took five courses, not the usual four. Of the remaining courses, which also included Introduction to Accounting, focused on double-entry bookkeeping, and Undergraduate Research, the most important was clearly Intermediate Economic Theory, taught in the spring quarter by Douglas. This was a course for students requiring a more systematic training in economic theory, being aimed at economics majors who had completed the other requirements for their degree and for graduate students with limited exposure to systematic economic theory.[25]

In the spring of 1934, Samuelson wrote a paper, "The Relationship Between Changes in Exchange Rates and General Prices," the only other surviving paper from his undergraduate years.[26] While it could have been written for Douglas's course in economic theory, it is also possible that it was written for the otherwise undocumented course Undergraduate Research. The context for the paper was Roosevelt's attempts, early in the New Deal, to combat the Depression by trying to raise prices, the devaluation of the dollar in January 1934 being one of the ways by which this would be achieved. Samuelson sought to establish whether devaluation would in fact raise domestic prices.

Samuelson tackled this problem using the theory of purchasing power parity, associated with the Swedish economist Gustav Cassel (to whose account of general equilibrium Director had previously introduced him).

---

g. Oligopoly is a situation where there is a small number of sellers in an industry, each of whom has to take account of how others will respond to his or her own actions.

According to this theory, exchange rate must equal the ratio of domestic to overseas prices, implying that devaluation must raise domestic prices by the same proportion. Samuelson explained the theory carefully before explaining that, though it held for internationally traded commodities, it was not true of goods that did not enter international trade, such as housing.

One of the interesting features about the essay is that it supports the argument with long quotations from Keynes's *Treatise on Money* (1971b). In these, Keynes denied that there was any justification for assuming that the cost of living in one country depended on the exchange rate, and any appearance to the contrary arose because wholesale price index numbers were biased toward internationally traded commodities. Samuelson also argued that the theory assumed all prices moved together, something that was not true. A good many problems, he wrote, "arise because of short-run deviations from long-run generalizations," supporting this with Keynes's famous remark, "*long run* is a misleading guide to current affairs. In the *long run* we are all dead. Economists set themselves too easy, too useless a task if in tempestuous seasons they can only tell us when the storm is long past, the ocean is flat again." This remark was taken not from the *Treatise* but from the *Tract on Monetary Reform* (1971a), suggesting that Samuelson had been reading significant parts of Keynes's work.[27,h] Given that Lloyd Mints used Keynes's *Treatise on Money* for his graduate teaching, it is tempting to speculate that he might have been the teacher for whom this essay was written, perhaps for the Undergraduate Research course.[28]

Given that Samuelson later believed that his Chicago teachers had no theory to explain how an increase in the money supply would stimulate the economy,[29] it is interesting to note what Samuelson himself wrote about this question while he was still under their influence.

> Moreover, it does not necessarily follow that the new equilibrium [following a change in the money supply] will be the same as the old one. It is an over-simplification to think that a monetary change moves all prices equally, just as the movement of the world leaves all places on the earth in the same relationships to each other. For monetary changes often initiate non-monetary changes.
>
> Furthermore, we must examine the mechanism by which price levels diffuse. Obviously, in two ways can an increase in the price of one

---

h. Nowadays Keynes's words are known by virtue of frequently being quoted, but in 1934 it would have been unlikely that Samuelson had picked it up from other sources. The *Tract* would have been a natural work for his teachers to recommend.

group of commodities affect the prices of other commodities: first, by changing the demand for the other commodities; secondly, by changing the supplies of the other commodities.[30]

He went on to explain how differences in elasticities of demand would cause prices of different commodities to change by different amounts; and how, on the supply side, "idle reserves of factors of production" and "immobility and 'unsubstitutability' of productive resources between various industries" would have similar effects. The result was that a new equilibrium might be "long delayed" and might be different from the original one. If Chicago monetary theory were as bad as Samuelson made out, then he knew things that his teachers did not.

Samuelson came closer to a quantity theory analysis when he allowed for the possibility that foreign prices would not remain constant in the face of a dollar devaluation: there would likely be retaliation, rendering any advantages only short term. There would be a rise in world prices only if devaluing the dollar increased the means of payment. The 40 percent devaluation that had taken place in January would not affect the world's money supply very much. However, by allowing a given quantity of gold to support a larger money supply, it raised the possibility of inflation:

> Perhaps the important thing about devaluation is that it permits a higher pyramid of money on a smaller base. In other words, it raises the lid on inflation, whether this is desirable or not, but it is not in itself inflationary. For just as the mythical Greek king could not stop the tide merely by command, so cannot the government merely by exhortation lift the price level.[31]

Samuelson thus concluded that though devaluation would not raise the price level much, it would "permit greater inflation in the future."[32]

From here, Samuelson's academic career was laid out, as shown in table 4.1. In order to major in economics, he was required to take Money and Banking, Economic History, Government Finance, and Statistics,[i] together with meeting language requirements, for which he studied French and German. He already knew Director, Mints, Douglas, and probably Knight, and in the coming year he would take courses with the other Chicago luminaries, Jacob Viner and Henry Simons. Of these, he was particularly attracted to Director, with whom he took no fewer than three courses, feeling honored to be invited

---

i. Samuelson remembered that Director used Mitchell's (1927). This implies that it was not a course in statistical theory but, rather, in the practical use of statistics.

TABLE 4.1 Final Year Program, 1934–35

Quarter	Economics	Mathematics	Other
Autumn 1934	230. Introduction to Money and Banking (Mints) 211. Statistics (Director)	102. College Algebra 103. Plane Analytic Geometry	
Winter 1935	220. Economic History of the U.S. (Wright) 301. Price and Distribution Theory (Viner)	215. Calculus, I	French
Spring 1935	260. Elements of Government Finance (Simons)	216. Calculus, II	French German
Summer 1935		217. Differential Equations	

to weekend in a shack that Director owned, with Knight, in the Indiana dunes and to meet his dog, Jude the Obscure.[33] As be became committed to economics, the other students in the department grew more prominent in his life. These included Jacob Mosak, his rival for prizes; Gregg Lewis, who graduated a year later; and graduate students Martin Bronfenbrenner, George Stigler, Allen Wallis, Albert Hart, and Milton Friedman. He cited two ways in which he got to know the graduate students. One was through his performance in the graduate theory course, alternately taught by Viner and Knight. This course was notorious as the hurdle students had to clear to progress through the graduate program. Viner was incisive and organized, Rose Friedman later wrote, whereas Knight was more philosophical, with the result that some students took the course from both of them. Samuelson took Viner's course for credit, but given that he states he did attend some lectures by Knight, it is possible that he also audited the course when Knight was teaching it.

In addition, employment elsewhere being impossible in the midst of the Depression, Samuelson was given work in the Economics Department:

> As I performed various make-work tasks for the department—dusting off the pictures of Böhm-Bawerk, Menger, and Mill in the departmental storage room which Stigler and Wallis had squatted in—we would gossip for hours over the inadequacies of our betters and the follies of princes who try to set right the evils of the marketplace.[34]

Stigler claimed that it was he who had introduced Samuelson to the joys of large determinants, showing him the notes he had taken in the course by Henry Schultz, and that Samuelson had told the story of how it was he (Stigler) and Wallis who had persuaded him to take advanced mathematics and become a mathematical economist.[35] Whether it was his fellow students or his mathematics teacher who persuaded him, Samuelson proceeded to take as much mathematics as he could fit into the final year of his program, with the courses in algebra, geometry, and calculus listed in table 4.1. After graduating he took a summer course in Differential Equations. He would leave Chicago having taken more mathematics courses than any other economics student.

Stigler and Wallis were also responsible for telling Samuelson that the American Economic Association was meeting in Palmer Hall, in Chicago, in December 1934 and that he should, as he put it, "pay the zoo a visit."[36] This was his first exposure to Joseph Schumpeter, who was to become important for him when he arrived at Harvard. Samuelson remembered Schumpeter, introduced by Arthur Marget, as speaking incomprehensibly in his German accent about business cycles in ways he had never encountered. "It was not love at first sight," Samuelson remembered, "but he did capture my interest."[37,j] Whatever the topic, Stigler was clearly not impressed, for Samuelson's account elicited the reply, "Isn't he the nut who believes the rate of interest to be zero in the stationary state?"—an idea that went against the claims of their hero, Knight. More revealing of the way Samuelson's interests were developing, he appears to have attended a session on statistical techniques, and when Stigler and Wallis asked him what he had learned, he was able to reply, "Harry Carver from Michigan Math Department suggested, 'to avoid the sample assumption of normality, permute the sample's measured properties with that universe's means properties,'" to which Wallis replied that it was the silliest idea he had ever heard.[38] This story, told against Wallis, who later made use of such methods, was likely embroidered with hindsight, for there was no Harry Carver on the program, though there was a session on sampling techniques and statistical methods.

Science and Politics

Though Samuelson had begun to immerse himself in economics and mathematics, he still followed what was going on in the wider university. On June 18,

---

j. This session was actually organized by the American Statistical Association, holding its meeting simultaneously with the American Economic Association (American Economic Association 1935).

1934, at the end of his junior year, his diary contained another discussion of science, focusing on the split he found at Chicago between two camps. On one side were Mortimer Adler and Hutchins, who argued for what Samuelson called an "absolutist" view, in which it is necessary to approach science with a preconceived hypothesis rather than "indulging in meaningless measurement, i.e. raw empiricism."[39] The other side was skeptical about whether one could know, in advance, what was significant, and it stressed the importance of measurement, as well as logical thinking. Samuelson's assessment was that there was no more than a difference of emphasis and "even that is not great." However, while the implications for scientific practice were not significant, the philosophical implications concerned absolutism and relativism, and whether there were an infinite number of hypotheses that could explain reality. This led into an argument against Hutchins's Great Books program—namely, that great thinkers do not necessarily provide the best exposition of their own thoughts; though he does not draw this conclusion, it is a clear argument for the use of textbooks rather than original works. Echoing the anti-materialism of just over a year earlier, he reflected that the problems of living, to which education should provide the answer, were only "in small part economic and vocational"; rather, they concerned "the finer acts of life—the forming of tastes, habits, attitudes, which contribute to more enjoyable living."[40]

Later in 1934, Samuelson discussed the scientific basis for psychoanalysis. In general, he claimed, people either endorsed psychoanalysis or condemned it completely. In contrast, what was needed was to test it using "scientific methods" such as control groups, statistical correlation, and quantitative comparisons.[41] It was also important to analyze Freud's work to distinguish between his hypotheses and his underlying assumptions, for this was the necessary prelude to testing the theory. His skepticism concerning the use of rationality to achieve desirable ends (a theme picked up from Knight or from Director, perhaps) was strengthened by news of events in Germany and stimulus coming from his reading of Lion Feuchtwanger's *The Oppermanns* (2001), published in German the previous year and in English in March 1934. It was a political novel about how events in Germany affected the lives of individuals, told through the story of a typical, fairly affluent Jewish family, and was aimed at alerting the world to the disaster that was engulfing Germany, from which Feuchtwanger himself had fled in 1932.

It is not clear what prompted Samuelson to read this book when he did, but during the previous month the American press contained reports of the Nazi seizure of Jewish businesses and the banning of Jewish publications, as well as of Jews escaping from Germany. On June 28, the *New York Times* reported that $704,000 had been raised in New York City toward a target of $1.2 million for the relief and resettlement of German Jews. It was clear that German Jews faced a crisis and that action needed to be taken. On July 2, Samuelson wrote in his diary,

All day I have been reading *The Oppermanns* by Leon [*sic*] Feuchtwanger. It is the story of a German Jewish family, and the vicissitudes thru which they went as a result of the coming to power of the anti-Semitic national socialists. The book is a remarkably restrained nomination of facts, written from the standpoint of a Jew, and I suppose a traditional humanitarian liberal.

He went on to reflect on his own feelings, suggesting that strong emotions were likely irrational, for rationality implied that one should have sympathy with any victims, not just with fellow Jews.

It has awakened in me a feeling of sympathy, and a moderate amount of emotion, but to a less degree than in the case, I think, of the average Jew. For altho' I recognize the suffering involved, I also realize that this suffering is not perilous to Jews, and to Germany [*sic*]. During the post-war years the Turks butchered a few hundred thousand Armenians, and people like my father deplored the fact, but were little touched by it. Now, however, that people with whom they have sentimental ties binding them are touched they immediately become emotionally disturbed, and thereby often irrational in behavior. All the above is no criticism of their being emotionally disturbed—it is merely an illustration of the nature of sympathy. In this case I share to some degree in the emotion, for which I offer no apology, but I also, at the same time, recognize the psychological origin of this emotion.[42]

Though his father was not religious, he felt a strong emotional connection with Jews in Europe that Samuelson dismissed as "sentimental" and a barrier to rational thought. He admitted that he felt some emotion, but rationalized it as psychological in origin. Emotion, he claimed, led to wishful thinking that might be counterproductive. How many of the people who advocate an economic boycott of German goods, he asked, had rationally tried to determine its probable effects, and was it even possible to ascertain this with certainty? This led him to question whether human behavior could be rational.

The whole business in Germany weakens further my faith in the possible use of rationality by human beings to secure the objectives which they consider desirable. Brutality, the use of force, the unleashing of hate, etc., on the part of some Germans, has evoked from previously tolerant men, answering feelings of hate, desire to use violence, etc.

Even Einstein, the embodiment of rationality, had fallen victim to this. "Previously," Samuelson wrote, "he held that no war was justified. Now because of his experience with the Nazis, he is willing to admit that in rare cases war may be justified. But each person always thinks that in his special case war is justified." These remarks are particularly striking, given that he was later to develop economic theory on the basis of rational choice: he is presenting rationality as an ideal that people can never attain.

He tried reading the history of an American family, Gertrude Stein's *The Making of Americans* (presumably the abridged edition that had just been published that year, 1934), but he was not impressed with the unconventional writing style for which the book is renowned, and he put it aside. The next day, on July 7, he returned to the issue of Jewish identity, explaining that his own ideas had changed back and forth.

> In my own mind, I have not been able to arrive at any conclusions or convictions concerning the "Jewish" question. At one time I was for "assimilation"; later after reading the "Island Within" I swung over more or less to the view of Lewisohn et al. Today I am in doubt.

This mention of *The Island Within* (1928), a novel about the experience of a Jewish family struggling as immigrants in a hostile America, shows both that Samuelson had been thinking about his Jewish identity and that he was doing so through reading literature. Ludwig Lewisohn came from a family that had converted to Christianity, but after being told that as a Jew he could never teach English in an American university, he returned to his family's Jewish heritage, becoming an outspoken opponent of assimilation. No doubt reflecting his social science training, Samuelson pointed out that though two cultures coming into close contact would eventually fuse, the question remained about how quickly this could happen.

> The question is: Can the Jews be assimilated? And at what costs can they be assimilated? To the first question I was about to answer "yes." But if we use "can" in the broader sense of the "will," then I am not so sure. Or, in the face of the past conflicts between the peoples, and the present attitudes, appearances, and cultures of the people, can they be assimilated?

Even to this question, I would answer a tentative affirmative. Given time and proximity, in this country at least, I believe that the Jews will gradually more and more become like Americans until finally they will be to a much greater degree than now indistinguishing. I state only what seems to me to be a probability, and I believe it despite the two thousand years of maintenance of differences between the groups. This fusion of culture (and incidentally, of blood) will progress to the extent that any factors which produce isolation are reduced.

After discussing the physiological and cultural differences, he went on from arguing that assimilation was possible to arguing that it was "necessary and inevitable," at least for the majority of Jews for whom Zionism was not an option.

We must now discuss the costs of assimilation. There are some who argue that it is at too great a cost, and therefore argue against it. But is there any choice open? Either the Jews must withdraw from non-Jewish society to a home of their own, or they must become more assimilated? For any other accommodations must be only temporary and fraught with peril to the Jews. Now, the question presents itself[:] [I]s there any possibility of the Jews to any great numbers, withdrawing from Western Society to such a place as Palestine? To me, this seems remote, and could only come about if all the Jews were forced to leave. For modern American Jews are more American than Jews, and would not willingly leave behind the institutions and life to which they are accustomed.

This is not to condemn Zionism. It is merely to point out that Zionism is only a solution for a small percentage of Jews. It is a refuge for the outcasts, the homeless, the persecuted. But it can be a homeland for them only as long as they are few in numbers. Modern Jewry is committed to the non-Jewish world by ties which in my opinion are unbreakable. They would not, and could not, migrate en masse to Palestine.

It is upon them, therefore, to reduce the barriers between them and the people amongst whom they live. This may be done only perhaps at the cost of friction and conflict at first, and loss in Jewish solidarity and peculiarly Jewish customs and individuality; but these costs are necessary and inevitable, for the Ghetto is disintegrating under modern conditions, whether we like it or not.

He was clearly speaking for himself when he asserted that modern American Jews were more American than they were Jews and that his father was being irrational in his emotional attachment to German Jews. In his attempt to be completely rational, a position he had previously argued to be unsustainable, he was implying that his primary identity was not with his family—that he was indeed an American with no ties to the past.

Turning Against Chicago Economics

Samuelson's later recollections of what he was taught at the University of Chicago were mixed. He praised the education he had received—both the Hutchins curriculum (though not the Great Books element) and his training in economic theory, the rigor of the latter equipping him much better than his contemporaries for what they were to encounter in Harvard's graduate program. He also formed long-lasting friendships with many of his teachers and other faculty members, notably Aaron Director, Paul Douglas, Frank Knight, Henry Simons, Lloyd Mints, and Jacob Viner. While a student at Harvard, he returned to visit them regularly, catching up on gossip about the place. But he became very critical of what they taught him about monetary economics and the business cycle: about the field that came to be known as macroeconomics. He referred to "the schoolmen," describing the department as "dogmatically conservative,"[1] and he claimed several times that he was taught nothing more than the simple quantity theory of money, in which the price level was proportional to the money supply.

> I took all the macroeconomic courses on offer by Chicago teachers: Mints, Simons, Director, and Douglas. Also in that period, I attended lectures and discussions on the Great Depression, involving Knight, Viner, Yntema, Mints, and Gideonse. Nothing beyond the sophisticated account by Dennis Robertson, in his famous *Cambridge*

Handbook on Money, of the Fisher-Marshall-Pigou MV = PQ paradigm can be found in my class notes and memories.[2]

In an unpublished note he was even stronger, adding Oskar Lange to those he had conversations with on returning to Chicago. He claimed that "With the exception of eclectic Jacob Viner, there were essentially *no* advances on 1911 Fisher or 1924 Keynes-Robertson."[3] They were taught that in an ideal world, in the long run, money did not matter: it was "neutral" in that changes in the money supply would have no effect beyond leading to higher prices.[a] It was recognized that "under dynamic conditions," before a new equilibrium was established, there might be effects on output, but these would be "relatively transient aberrations." However, these qualifications to the simple quantity theory tended to be taught in courses on applied topics, with the result that there was a disconnect between such discussions and the theory they studied.

> From 9 to 9:50 A.M. we presented a simple quantity theory of neutral money. There were then barely ten minutes to clear our palates for the 10 to 10:50 discussion of how an engineered increase in M would help the economy. In mid-America in the mid-1930s, we neoclassical economists tended to be mild inflationists, jackasses crying in the wilderness and resting our case essentially on sticky prices and costs, and on expectations.
>
> Returning to the 9 o'clock hour, we thought that real outputs and inputs and price ratios depended essentially in the longest run on real factors, such as tastes, technology, and endowments. The stock of money we called M.... An increase in M—usually we called it a doubling on the ground that after God created unity he created the second integer—would cause a proportional increase in all prices (tea, salt, female labor, land rent, share or bond prices) and values (expenditure on tea or land, share dividends, interest income, taxes).[4]

This memory was an important part of Samuelson's story of his own life: his precocity had enabled him, as a teenage undergraduate, to understand what pre-Keynesian monetary economics was really like—unlike those who had started only a little later than himself and had to use their imagination. He

---

a. Of course, as Samuelson had known when he wrote the international economics essay discussed in chapter 4 this volume, the Keynes of 1923 explicitly denied that one could live in the long run. This account does an injustice to Fisher's 1911 book.

argued that other economists who had tried to construct a picture of classical economics were "in the position of a man who, looking for a jackass, must say to himself, 'If I were a jackass, where would I go?'" In contrast, he wrote:

> Mine is the great advantage of having once been a jackass. From 2 January 1932 until an indeterminate date in 1937, I was a classical monetary theorist. I do not have to look for the tracks of the jackass embalmed in old journals and monographs. I merely have to lie down on the couch and recall in tranquillity, upon that inward eye which is the bliss of solitude, what it was that I believed between the ages of 17 and 22. This puts me in the same advantageous position that Pio Nono enjoyed at the time when the infallibility of the Pope was being enunciated. He could say, incontrovertibly, "Before I was Pope, I believed he was infallible. Now that I am Pope, I can feel it."[5]

In writing this he no doubt had in mind that he had arrived in Chicago before even Milton Friedman, three years older but who had arrived only as a graduate student in the autumn of 1932, and that he had stayed there longer.[6]

However, though Samuelson stuck by this picture of his Chicago teachers as being blinkered in their theorizing, he sometimes acknowledged that his teachers had gone beyond this. In the 1930s it was obvious, he claimed, that the pure classical theory, according to which money was neutral and there could be no deficiency of aggregate demand, was useless in explaining the Depression.

> I knew 100 people without jobs in 1931–1934 and 100 with jobs. The groups would never voluntarily change places: the latter felt very lucky. The former, about equal in ability, felt unlucky. That's not what happens when auction markets equate supply and demand.[b]

Samuelson credited Simons with having sensed the "liquidity trap"—the notion that there may be some rate of interest at which the public is willing to hold whatever money is issued, and hence a floor to the rate of interest. And he credited Viner with being eclectic and for being responsible for the

---

b. When Samuelson wrote these words he will have been aware that many economists with whom he disagreed on macroeconomics modeled unemployment as voluntary—as an optimal response to perceived wages and prices.

empirical research that substantiated the idea that people were willing to hoard money, making it hard for people to borrow.[7]

While there is no reason to doubt that he was taught the classical theory in which equilibrium in competitive markets results in a world in which prices are proportional to the money supply, it was an oversimplification of monetary economics as found at Chicago at this time: there were attempts to develop a theory in which expansion of the money supply would have effects on production and employment.[8] That Samuelson was aware of this at the time is shown by his international economics paper, in which he went through theoretical arguments about why a rise in the money supply would *not* raise prices proportionally.

Keynes's monetary economics was a significant part of his education. The closing paragraphs of that essay, about how reducing the fraction of the money supply backed by gold might be inflationary, links to what came to be known as the "Chicago Plan" for monetary reform, signed by several Chicago economists. Their main proposal was for "100% money."[9] If banks were required to hold reserves to back all their loans, it would be possible to separate the functions of commercial bank lending from the creation of money. The creation of money could become the sole responsibility of government, which could use it to counter depression.

This proposal, made in a pamphlet signed by a group of Chicago economists in 1933, though mostly written by Simons, was part of a much wider debate over monetary policy to stabilize the economy.[10] The previous year, a similar proposal had emerged from a conference organized by international relations specialist Quincy Wright and involving economists from Columbia and Harvard, as well as Viner, held in January 1932 and published in July.[11] The following year, Harvard's Lauchlin Currie made a similar proposal, and Simons incorporated the idea into another, more wide-ranging pamphlet, *A Positive Program for Laissez-Faire* (1934). Here, monetary proposals were accompanied by an extensive program of anti-monopoly policies designed to restore competition. The view that monopoly was an important cause of the Depression was widespread, but whereas other economists considered that the growth of big business was a feature of American capitalism that policymakers needed to take into account, Simons proposed to remove the problem. His vision of liberalism required a strong government to break up large firms in order to bring about a world in which competitive private enterprise could operate effectively.

A teacher who was rarely mentioned in Samuelson's recollections of Chicago monetary theory was Paul Douglas. He wrote *The Problem of*

Unemployment with Aaron Director, but whereas Director subsequently became more skeptical about labor unions, moving into the Knight circle, Douglas became stronger in his support for collective solutions. At the beginning of Samuelson's sophomore year, he produced *The Coming of a New Party* (1932), a book that began by arguing that, while individualism may have made sense in the early frontier society, American industry had changed and with it American society. Industry was much more hierarchical, and ownership more concentrated, with the result that opportunities for social mobility were much fewer. The notion, supported by Harvard's Thomas Nixon Carver, that workers would, through their savings, come to control industry was "almost a grotesque misunderstanding": the top 2 percent of the population controlled 70 percent of property.[12]

> The direction of industry is concentrated in the hands of a comparatively small number, while the major portion of the wealth and the surplus income is held by substantially the same group joined with a fringe of wealthy idlers. It is still not absolutely impossible for an individual "outsider" to break into the charmed circle, but this tends to become ever more difficult because of the great head start which the sons and daughters of the wealthy "insiders" increasingly possess.[13]

Thus, given that it was impossible for most people to rise to the top, the great majority of people should focus on improving their position as workmen and should combine with others to improve their collective situation. They should turn to trade unionism and political action. It was an attack on the individualism to which Director was turning. After outlining the needs of various groups of the population, Douglas turned to the political means by which these might be achieved.

Two years later, Douglas completed *The Theory of Wages* (1934), published when Samuelson was taking his intermediate economic theory course. This book, developed from work for which he had been awarded a prize in 1926, represented the culmination of a long research project, and included several other books on wages; it was completed with help from Director and Schultz, the latter having provided considerable assistance with the statistical work. Though it cited approvingly Joan Robinson's analysis of imperfect competition, and it argued that not all decisions were the outcome of rational behavior, its analysis rested on the theory of marginal productivity: the theory that, in competitive markets, the wage rate will equal the value of the output produced by employing an additional worker. Where Douglas went beyond previous work was in quantifying this, calculating the shares of labor, capital, and land in national income, the implications of economic growth for the distribution of income, and the implications of raising or lowering wages for the level of employment.[c]

It is not known how much of this book's contents Samuelson would have been exposed to, though it would seem unlikely that a course taught by Douglas with the aim of exposing students to systematic economic theory would not cover the very standard theoretical ideas on which it relied, or that Douglas could have failed to mention the idea that concepts such as elasticities of demand and supply could be quantified. However, Samuelson did acknowledge a debt to Schultz, then working on empirical demand analysis, as the economist who introduced him to the idea of operationalism. This notion was to become central to Samuelson's PhD thesis and his *Foundations of Economic Analysis* (1947a), interpreted as the idea that meaningful theorems were ones that were capable of being shown to be false.[d] In the preface to *The Theory of Wages*, Douglas also cited Bridgman in a context that is significant, given Samuelson's later commitment to the analysis of economic aggregates.[e]

Douglas was confronting the criticism that he erred in trying to explain the overall rate of wages when he should, instead, be seeking to explain wages for "an indefinite series of labor groups" and, similarly, the payments to different types of capital and land. His first response was that there was sufficient substitutability, or "transferability," between different types of labor and between different types of land (and capital was fairly homogeneous) that his approach made sense. In addition, it was legitimate to explain wages by starting with a theory of the basic rate of wages and then combining it with a theory of wage differentials that explained differences from the basic rate. He then turned to Bridgman:

> It would be almost impossible to measure the incremental productivities of this infinite series of sub-groups or to determine their supply curves. In view of the present inability to test the validity of this great sub-division of the factors, I can only consider this suggestion to be at present, in the words of Professor Bridgman, a non-operational concept. From the standpoint of scientific progress, we should primarily concern ourselves with problems which we can solve.[14]

---

c. An important analytical device in this work was what came to be known as the Cobb-Douglas production function, worked out with the assistance of Charles Cobb, a mathematician. Biddle 2012 provides a history of this function.

d. This is slightly different from Bridgman's definition. This is discussed in chapter 14 this volume.

e. As was mentioned elsewhere, Samuelson took Labor Problems with Douglas after having taken it with Director, making it very likely that he would have read this.

Not only does this remark defend aggregate analysis as being operational, it also suggests that Bridgman's operationalism, implicitly defined in terms of testability much as Samuelson was later to do, was well known to Chicago economists at this time. No citation or explanation of the remark was thought necessary. Given Samuelson's later attachment to the idea of being his intellectual grandson, it is interesting to note that Douglas went on to reinforce this point by citing a claim made by the physicist Willard Gibbs:

> It will be noticed that I have treated the marginal productivity and supply curves for labor and capital in society as a whole and not for particular industries and plants. This has been done in part because as Willard Gibbs once remarked "the whole is simpler than its parts" and because it has seemed to me to be the more significant problem.[15]

Douglas was citing Gibbs to justify looking at the economy as a whole without looking at the individuals of which it is made up, an approach Samuelson was to take when he turned to the problem of the business cycle.[f]

The Theory of Wages was a work for economists; its findings, such as its estimates of the responsiveness of labor demand to wage rates, might have policy relevance, but it did not directly address the problem of mass unemployment. However, halfway through Samuelson's final year in Chicago, Douglas did produce such a book, *Controlling Depressions* (1935).[16] This offered an eclectic survey of theories of the cycle. His analysis rested on a distinction between "initiating" and "cumulative" causes, the latter being most important.[g] If, for some reason, there was a downturn, there could arise a cumulative breakdown. When businesses cut back production, incomes of their workers and suppliers were reduced. Retail sales then fell, causing retailers to purchase less, producing an accelerated decline in production. Such a downturn could be initiated by a variety of factors. For example, structural factors such as the course of invention or population growth might cause a slowdown in the growth of consumption, which would lead (through the accelerator) to falling investment and hence to depression. Though he did not use the phrase, Douglas clearly saw aggregate demand, and hence monetary and fiscal policy, as playing a role. While it might be right to balance the budget over the

---

f. Using the terminology that became fashionable in the 1970s, Douglas was saying that macroeconomics did not need micro foundations.

g. This distinction was not uncommon in the business cycle literature. Its most famous supporter was Ragnar Frisch (1933), who distinguished between the "impulse" and "propagation" problems: between the shocks experienced by the system and the mechanisms whereby those shocks were propagated through the system.

entire business cycle, it was, Douglas claimed, perfectly proper for it to be unbalanced in depressions. It might be correct that "every past depression ha[d] sooner or later turned into the spring of revival," but this might take a very long time.[17] He criticized strongly the view that it was right to leave recovery to private enterprise.

> If we have been successful in muddling through all of these past depressions, say the apostles of laissez-faire, we will have similar luck with the present. Let us simply keep quiet and events will ultimately right themselves.... There are two answers to this optimistic appeal to history. The first is that even though we have frequently managed to get out of these depressions, it frequently took a long time to do so, with much accompanying misery.... The second answer is that if one studies these past depressions more closely, recovery in many cases may well have been more accidental than inevitable.... On several occasions the proximate and immediate cause of the pick-up was the apparently accidental coming of an external savior.[18]

These external saviors could be new inventions, stimulus from the rest of the world, or war.

Picking up a view that was widely held by economists at the time, Douglas questioned the health of the capitalist system, challenging the prevalence of theorizing about equilibrium.

> There are present in our present economic system latent tendencies which may, and more or less periodically do, result in a cumulative disequilibrium. This feature of our system has been too much ignored by the orthodox economists, who have tended to concentrate their attention upon the forces making for equilibrium in the field of prices, value, and the distribution of the national income among the factors of production. The economists have used up their vital energy in explaining how the economic system works. They have not devoted nearly as much attention to how it fails to work, or how it operates in a viciously cumulative fashion. The forces of equilibrium are real, but they are only half the story. There are also forces making for breakdown. And intellectual interest in or emotional enthusiasm for the smooth-running features of competitive capitalism should not blind us to the other side of the story.[19]

Samuelson may not have read these particular passages, but they show that, despite his portrayal of Chicago as a place of darkness, this view *was* represented among the teachers to whom he was close. He was later to confess that, as an undergraduate at Chicago, he had read related arguments in a book by a friend and former colleague of Douglas, John Maurice Clark; some of the ideas he had learned from the book proved very important to him, even though he was at the time very critical of them.[h] Samuelson was reading very widely and was encountering and reacting negatively to work toward which he would later be very sympathetic.

Economic Theory

Even if it had been Director who had introduced Samuelson to economics, and Douglas who had provided the more systematic coverage of economic theory that economics majors were required to encounter, it was Viner whose Economic Theory course he was to remember most clearly. Part of the reason was, no doubt, that it was his first formal exposure to a graduate course with fellow students who would go on to become prominent economists. This course moreover had a reputation, for it was used to sort out who was fit for graduate work and who was not. The first difficulty was getting into the course, which Samuelson managed to do so only on the strength of a letter from Douglas, who told Viner that he was "somewhat 'cantankerous' but a good bet."[20] Given that he allowed Samuelson into the class, Viner must, so Samuelson claimed, have been in an indulgent mood after a stint at the U.S. Treasury. It was a class that Samuelson recalled in great detail.[i]

> With about thirty-five other aspirants, who I recall included Martin Bronfenbrenner and Warren Scoville, we lined up around a huge seminar table in the basement of the then new Social Sciences Research building. Viner appeared, holding our names on index cards; and after a speedy inquisition, five of us were found wanting in previous preparation or motivation. But that was only the beginning.
>
> My impression of Viner never changed from that first glimpse. He was short and intense, like a bantam cock. His upper lip, usually bedewed by a bead of moisture, curled in what seemed half a smile. In my imperfect memory his hair was then red, and his complexion matched. His suit coats were on the short side and his posture was not

---

h. The letter in which he made this confession and the ideas of Clark that he referred to are discussed in chapter 24 this volume.

i. This account of Viner's course conforms with Rose Friedman's account (Friedman and Friedman 1999, p. 35).

that of a West Point cadet. How I remember anything about his person I do not know, since every eye in the room was fastened upon the diabolical deck of index cards in his hands through which he shuffled nervelessly. To be scrupulously honest, subsequent legend has contaminated my account. I was too innocent to be nervous. In contrast to the graduate students present, I had nothing at stake. But for them, their whole careers and professional futures were in jeopardy each time he riffled through the cards.

Viner was a student, *the* prize student of Frank Taussig, that master of the Socratic method. Taussig played on his classes as Pablo Casals plays on his 'cello. He knew which idiot would botch up Ricardo's trade-off between profit and the real wage; he knew which cantankerous student had to be kept out of the classroom verbal interaction lest he short-circuit the dialogue. Viner added one new ingredient: terror. Members of the seminar sat tensely around the table, and when the name of the victim was read off the cards, you could almost hear the sighs of relief and the slumping back into chairs of those who had won temporary respite. Indeed, the stakes were high. Three strikes and you were out, with no appeal possible to any higher court. And this was no joke. I remember an able graduate student who, having failed to give an acceptable answer on two previous occasions, was told by Viner: "Mr. ———, I am afraid you are not equal to yourself or this class." This man barely managed to retrieve his position at the final moment. If a graduate student was refused admittance to 301, the basic course in theory, he had no choice but to drop out or to transfer to the slums of political science or sociology. (Years later when I discussed with Jack Viner the legend of his ferocity, he said that the department had given him the function of screening the candidates for higher degrees. It was not work for which he was ill-equipped.[21]

Samuelson survived "Viner's ferocious manhandling of students, in which he not only reduced women to tears but on his good days drove returned paratroopers into hysteria and paralysis," so he recalled, because of his innocence.

I, nineteen-year-old innocent, walked unscathed through the inferno and naively pointed out errors in his blackboard diagramming. These acts of Christian kindness endeared me to the boys in the backroom of the graduate school: George Stigler, Allan Wallis, Albert Gaylord Hart, Milton Friedman, and the rest of the Knight Swiss guards.[22]

Five years earlier, a student had taken what Viner considered to be skimpy notes on the course and circulated them, something of which Viner did not approve.[23]

Samuelson remembered the course he took as being very different, in scope and coverage, from the one recorded in these notes. Samuelson remembered the first lecture as using the analogy of a well-balanced aquarium to explain the nature of a continuing equilibrium. "Before and since," he wrote, "I have heard much of the circular flow of Quesnay and Schumpeter and Walras, but I cannot recollect a similar treatment of this issue." François Quesnay, the eighteenth-century author of the *Tableau économique*, and Léon Walras, the nineteenth-century developer of general equilibrium theory, were pioneers in analyzing formally the interdependence of different sectors of the economy.[24,j] If "well balanced" referred to the equalization of water levels in different tanks, this was an analogy drawn from Irving Fisher, but if he had in mind balance between populations of different species of fish, then it was a much more Marshallian analogy.[k]

As in *Studies in the Theory of International Trade* (1937), published shortly afterward, Viner emphasized the historical development of the subject. The content was up to date, but it did not cover all the latest literature.

> Viner made clear at the beginning that he would not be covering the latest wrinkles in the theory of imperfect or monopolistic competition. However, since Viner himself, along with his student Theodore Yntema, had independently discovered the marginal cost–marginal revenue conditions for maximization of an imperfect competitor's profits, much of what was contained in the Chamberlin and Robinson treatises was adequately covered.[25]

Samuelson noted that Viner's course was the only place in his own curriculum where the latest analytical techniques, such as indifference curves and production possibility frontiers, were used. Indifference curves are a device for representing consumers' preferences. In the same way that a contour line on a map indicates places that are the same altitude, an indifference curve shows bundles of goods between which the consumer is indifferent: bundles of goods that have the same level of utility. If consumers' preferences can be

---

j. The general equilibrium system of Cassel, to which Director had introduced Samuelson, was a simplification of Walras's system. Walras was receiving increasing attention from economists in the 1930s. See Backhouse and Medema 2014.

k. Marshall famously favored biological analogies, such as likening the firms in an industry to the trees in a forest.

represented by a utility function, then indifference curves are simply a way to represent that function. "Well-behaved" indifference curves are illustrated in figure 9.2 later in this volume, along with a production possibility frontier (the solid curve) showing the maximum quantities of two goods that can be produced.

The use of indifference curves became fashionable in the 1930s, when two British economists, Roy Allen and John Hicks, realized that it was possible to use indifference curves to dispense with the concept of utility. To analyze behavior, it was necessary to know only the shape of individuals' indifference curves. It was not necessary to assign numbers to them; all that was necessary was to know whether one indifference curve represented a higher level of well-being than another, without any need to measure well-being. However, Samuelson's remark is hardly an indictment of the curriculum, since it was natural that novel techniques would appear first in the graduate theory course.

Viner's approach to economic theory involved a mixture of verbal and graphical analysis. It was his use of graphical analysis that earned Samuelson his legendary reputation for correcting Viner.

> After I left Chicago I learned that I was something of a legend myself in Viner's course of that year. Legends grow on legends. So let me set the record straight. The prosaic fact is that Viner had a custom of coming to class with complicated diagrams to be copied on the blackboard. Such transcriptions are notoriously subject to minor errors in which curves intersect on the wrong side of axes, and so forth. Fools rush in where angels fear to tread, and so it was left to the only undergraduate in the course to point out such occasional petty aberrations which detracted nothing from his evident erudition and keenness.[26]

The reason these incidents became magnified into legend was a previous incident concerning the drawing of one of the diagrams in an article on cost curves.[27] This involved drawing a series of U-shaped curves together with the "envelope" (a larger U-shaped curve) that contained them all. The draftsman explained that it was impossible to draw the envelope touching each of the other curves at their lowest points, as Viner had asked him to do: it was a mathematical impossibility. Samuelson wrote that Viner reported to the class that he had been wrong, mathematically and economically:

> "But," he said to me privately just as the class bell had rung, "although there seems to be some esoteric mathematical reason why the envelope cannot be drawn so that it passes smoothly through the declining

bottoms of the U-shaped cost curves, nevertheless I can do it!" "Yes," I replied impishly, "with a good thick pencil, you can do it."[28]

One reason for Samuelson's situation in relation to Viner was that, although he had not progressed far in his mathematical education, he had already taken three mathematics courses and was currently taking the first of two calculus courses. Thus, when Viner told the class that the prerequisite for the course should be knowledge of calculus, but that as he lacked the qualification he would waive it for the students, he was telling Samuelson something he already knew. Samuelson's knowledge of mathematics will already have contributed to his already substantial confidence in his engagements with Viner.

Science and Economics

It is not known when Samuelson had first met Knight, though a strong possibility is that it was on November 2, 1932, when Knight gave a talk for the National Student League with the title "The Case for Communism: From the Standpoint of an ex-Liberal."[29] Delivered less than a week before the presidential election that brought Roosevelt to power, Knight offered a denunciation of the political system. Politics was about talk that was a potent and devastating drug that could lead to insanity: "cheaper talk drives out of circulation that which is less cheap."[30] Talk had nothing to do with truth, a failing that affected the academy, too, where professors sought acclamation rather than veracity. Knight's lecture was full of anecdotes that would have greatly entertained a youthful audience, as in a story he told.

> I am reminded of an incident told me the other day by a college book man. He went, with another book man, to call on the President of one of our largest and greatest universities. The President turned to book man No.2, with whom he was more acquainted, and said: "I am very glad to see you men. You meet different classes of people; you see the college and university people and you meet up with business men and all classes in hotel lobbies and smoking compartments. Tell me what the people of America are really talking about." The book man responded without hesitation with a short monosyllable, which was not the word "*sex*," but that is the way I have to report it, and *that* is the more important point I wish to make.[31]

Knight went on to argue that certain words were acceptable in public discourse but others were not.

> For instance, "cow-dung" is not a particularly "bad" word ... but I must admit that I lack the courage merely to change the sex of the animal and use a different monosyllabic synonym for the substantive part of the expression.

People would not find one more shocking than the other, but they would pretend that they were. This was entirely right because social stability depends on public talk not meaning what it says. "Its first and most fundamental category must always be—'B.S.' But don't say it!"[32] It was nihilistic, dismissing the possibility of political processes involving serious thought; hence, the remark with which he opened his talk, that those who wanted change and wished to vote intelligently should vote Communist. A strong Communist vote might lead to the growth of a real conservative, aristocratic alternative. This ability to entertain students makes clear why Samuelson would describe Knight as a "cracker-barrel Socrates," but it is far from clear that he took much from Knight's skepticism except insofar as it contributed to his conservatism. He later summarized Knight's position as finding it difficult to choose between communism and fascism—a choice the despised Roosevelt, whom Samuelson had supported, rendered unnecessary.[33]

Knight was to repent of this talk, given when he was particularly depressed because of personal problems and the political situation, and he tried to withdraw printed copies from circulation, but his skepticism about the state of politics remained. He gave a series of public lectures in June–July 1934, with the title "Intelligence and the Crisis in Western Culture," in which many of the same themes recurred (though not the suggestion that people should vote Communist). Given his claim to have idolized Knight and his interest in both politics and economics, Samuelson would surely have attended. These lectures offered a historical perspective, contending that liberalism and democracy had worked in the nineteenth-century United States because of special circumstances. The vast resources made available by the movement of the frontier reduced the extent of competition between people: "With an essentially unlimited domain awaiting economic conquest, life ceased to be seriously competitive for individuals," for success in life could involve exploiting nature rather than other people.[34] But the situation changed with the closing of the frontier, the result being a resurgence of the state and of politics.

This belief that there were higher ends than those typically stressed by economics was an important theme in Knight's writing in the late 1920s and 1930s. Ten years before Samuelson's encounter with economics, Knight had explored the relation between "ethics and the economic interpretation."[35] Knight challenged the view of some economists that human wants and desires should be taken as scientific facts—data that the scientist should take as a given. Wants were continually changing, but whereas many writers were focusing on the manipulation of consumers by business, Knight saw the development of wants as an important part of human nature. People aim not to satisfy their existing wants but to develop better wants.

> Life is not fundamentally a striving for ends, for satisfactions, but rather for bases for further striving; desire is more fundamental to conduct than is achievement, or perhaps better, the true achievement is the refinement and elevation of the plane of desire, the cultivation of taste.[36]

Where did this leave economics? Knight argued that there was no basis on which to distinguish between "economic" and "non-economic" wants. Biologically determined needs did not explain human motivation, for people sought not life but a good life. Neither were instincts a suitable basis for scientific analysis.[1] This led Knight to the conclusion that "in so far as the ends are viewed as given, as data, then all activity is economic."[37] However, rather than conclude that economics should dominate inquiry, he saw its significance as very limited. "Economics" he wrote,

> treats of human conduct *in so far* as conduct is amenable to scientific treatment, in so far as it is controlled by definable conditions and can be reduced to law. But this, measured by the standard of material science, is not very far. *There are no data* for a science of conduct in a sense analogous to natural science. The data of conduct are provisional, shifting, and special to individual, unique situations in so high a degree that generalization is relatively fruitless. *For the time being*, an individual acts (more or less) *as if* his conduct were directed to the realization of some end.[38]

He illustrated that with the example of the chess player who "acts *as if* the supreme end in life were to capture his opponent's pieces," even though he did not believe this.

The result was that a science of conduct was possible only if its subject matter became so abstract that it said little about actual behavior. Evaluation

---

1. The first of these was an implicit attack on Alfred Marshall and the second an attack on Thorstein Veblen, two very influential economists in this period.

of motives was left to ethics, but this required standards by which to judge actions, and if this was to go beyond economics, it meant drawing on "something more than scientific data."[39] A scientific ethics was simply not possible.

In subsequent articles Knight developed this position. In "The Ethics of Competition," he argued that it was not possible to pass judgment on economic policy without starting from some set of values, or ethical criteria— "social policy must be based on social ideals."[40] He then went on to explore the standards of value implicit in what he called "the *laissez-faire* or individualistic social philosophy"—"the standards actually involved in making some familiar moral judgments in regard to the economic system."[41] This resulted in an argument that sounded very negative, for he was critical not only of Thorstein Veblen—the distinction between business and industry was without foundation and the idea that engineers should control the allocation of resources was "grotesque"—but also of liberal individualism.[42]

The starting point for Knight's critique of individualism was the claim that economic activity performed several functions simultaneously.

> Economic activity is *at the same time* a means of want-satisfaction, an agency for want- and character-formation, a field of creative self-expression, and a competitive sport. While men are "playing the game" of business, they are also molding their own and other personalities, and creating a civilization whose worthiness to endure cannot be a matter of indifference.[43]

He then proceeded to point to failings in each of these. The conditions necessary for perfect competition, the foundation on which the case for laissez-faire rested, were not met in real life. As the results produced by the economic system rested on tastes and purchasing power created by that system, it was impossible to impute to them ethical significance. "No one," Knight claimed, "contends that a bottle of old wine is ethically worth as much as a barrel of flour, or a fantastic evening wrap for some potentate's mistress as much as a substantial dwelling house."[44] The process of valuation was a "vicious" circle. Incomes went not to factors of production but to their owners, and the fact of ownership had no ethical validity. "The competitive system," Knight concluded, "falls far short of our highest ideals."[45] When he turned to production, he argued that there were values involved in the economic process itself; people value their social situation rather than consumption itself. There were conflicts between three ethical ideals: allocating goods in proportion to effort; efficient distribution of resources; and fairness. Furthermore, there could be no assumption that competition itself was morally desirable.

In these arguments, Knight drew on many themes that would have been familiar from the Hobsonian welfare economics to which Samuelson had been introduced in Gideonse's social science course. Like Hobson and utilitarians before him, Knight presumed a consensus on values, for his conclusions rested on values that be believed were "part of our culture"—"the common-sense ideals of absolute ethics in modern Christendom."[46] However, unlike Veblenian and Hobsonian critics of orthodox economics, Knight shied away from radical change, not because individualism was good but simply because "radical critics of competition as a general basis of the economic order generally underestimate egregiously the danger of doing vastly worse."[47] He justified his rejection of radical change by claiming that the problem was to find the right mixture of policies: "there is no question of the exclusive use or entire abolition of any of the fundamental methods of social organization, individualistic or socialistic. Economic and other activities will always be organized in all the possible ways, and the problem is to find the right proportions between individualism and socialism and the various varieties of each, and to use each in its proper place."

These two articles were chosen by four graduate students—Friedman, Stigler, Wallis, and Homer Jones—to begin a volume of Knight's essays, published in 1935 to mark his fiftieth birthday, *The Ethics of Competition and Other Essays*.[48] Though this was published after Samuelson had left Chicago (Knight's birthday was in November), he would certainly have thought very carefully about the essays it contained.[m] After these two pieces on ethics and welfare, a discussion of "Economic Psychology and the Value Problem" continued in the same vein. The purpose of knowledge was to predict and to control, and feelings could contribute to this only insofar as they could be linked to behavior: the only way to produce and manipulate feelings was "by means of established behavior sequences."[49] However, though he thought that science had to work exclusively in terms of relationships between observable behaviors (as in Samuelson's later theory of revealed preference), Knight dismissed the idea that this was all there was. "Much that the devotee of natural science methods," he wrote, "dismisses contemptuously as 'mere emotion' may turn out to have as strong a counterpart in ultimate reality as can be put forth by any human experience whatever."[50] Drawing an analogy with

m. Even if Samuelson's claim to have read everything Knight wrote is not taken literally (though there seems to be no reason not to do so), these articles, assembled into a book by his friends, would certainly have been among those that he had read.

mechanics, he pointed out that while physicists were uncomfortable with the notion of force, unobservable independently of the effects it produces, they used the notion freely. In discovering gravity, what Newton really discovered was that the same formula was applicable in apparently diverse cases.[51] Feelings and motivations were important, in part because there was more to life than simply economics. After citing Ruskin's dictum "There is no wealth but life," Knight argued that "in the connection and for the purpose of Ruskin's preaching, [it] is anything but nonsense. It is exactly what our over scientifically minded students of social problems need to be told, with all possible emphasis."[52]

A further chapter, "The Limitations of Scientific Method in Economics," reinforced this message. Knight offered a very precise and all-encompassing view of scientific economics:

> From a rational or scientific point of view, all practically real problems are problems in economics. The problem of life is to utilize resources "economically," to make them go as far as possible in the production of desired results. The general theory of economics is therefore simply the rationale of life.[53]

However, he then went on to say that this could not get us very far. It was the rationale of life, he claimed,

> In so far as it has any rationale! The first question in regard to scientific economics is this question of how far life is rational, how far its problems reduce to the form of using given means to achieve given ends. Now this, we shall contend, is not very far; the scientific view of life is a limited and partial view; life is at bottom an exploration of the field of values, an attempt to discover values, rather than on the basis of them to produce and enjoy them to the greatest possible extent.[54]

Knight worked into this argument about the limitations of the scientific method many more specific methodological observations. Economists frequently used the term "dynamics," but did so in ignorance of the way it was used in mechanics. Statics was about equilibrium, raising the question of whether forces in operation would tend to produce an equilibrium. Economists had ignored this problem, leaving "a fatal gap in the science." "The crying need of economic theory to-day," he contended, "is for a study of the 'laws of motion,' the *kinetics* of economic changes."[55] This was a theme that Samuelson was later to take up.

Samuelson's Debt to Chicago

The University of Chicago was very important for Samuelson's development as an economist. It was there that he decided to become an economist and that the way to do economics properly was to learn as much mathematics as he could. Beulah Shoesmith, his high school teacher, had clearly been important to him, but in view of the two and a half years when he showed little interest in the subject, it is justifiable to see his mathematical education proper as beginning in his junior year, when he belatedly took the university's introductory mathematics course. There is much that is unknown about Samuelson's time in Chicago, notably the nature and extent of his contacts outside the courses he took for credit. He mentioned contacts with some faculty members. For example, he claimed to have accosted Knight and Viner, when walking around campus, about why price should equal marginal cost (understood as a question in welfare economics), though his bracketing of them with Schumpeter at Harvard raises the question of whether this might be a stylized memory. He also recalled that the person who introduced him to Keynes was Eugene Staley, again someone who had not taught him, unless he had been a teaching assistant for Director or Mints. He claimed that it was not Director, but Harry Gideonse and Staley, who persuaded him to major in economics.[56] But beyond such memories, some of which have been recounted earlier, there is little evidence. Samuelson's reluctance to provide more detail may reflect problems with memory over several decades, but it also reflects his self-image as substantially self-taught and his desire to distance himself from Chicago economics. A diary entry, dated March 1935, toward the end of Viner's Economic Theory course, records:

> In the field of economics I have made many discoveries quite independently (I think), only to find that somebody else had already arrived at similar results. A discussion of variability of proportions in joint supply gave me a clue to the pricing of the factors of production by marginal productivity. At great length, by analytical geometry, I worked out the relationship between an average curve, only to find that in one step of calculus the same relationship could be stated. In the field of monetary theory, I worked out relationships between reserves and deposits, lack of liquidity of any assets for a system as a whole, etc. The reconciliation of economies of large scale production with Euler's theorem, I secured, by a redefinition of all indivisible changes of factors into one factor. Independently, I worked out a three dimensional ... picture of the supply from an industry and the special case of atomistic

competition. Many of the deeper problems of abstraction and equilibrium have occurred to me independently, e.g. the adequacy of the *composition of prices* notion of describing economic phenomena. The fruitfulness of arguments based upon (1) purchasing power; (2) the arbitrary division of a variable into two non-independent variables, where one is a catch-all into which everything is impounded by ceteris paribus, has always been questionable in my mind (Quantity theory/ Money, etc.).[57]

The significance of this lies in its being written at the time and not, like most of his recollections, many years later. It is consistent with his later claim to be "much of an autodidact in mathematics," despite admitting to taking six mathematics courses at Chicago, one at the University of Wisconsin–Madison, and auditing several more at Harvard.[58] The diary entry exhibits a pattern found in many of his later self-appraisals. Ostensibly it is modest, for he is arguing that he found nothing new, and that simultaneous discovery is universal. However, given that he is comparing his discoveries as a teenage undergraduate with the discovery of calculus by both Leibniz and Newton, he is being anything but modest. A similar point could be made about the remark: "It was as if, like a bird dog bred to point at hunt, my DNA was born to manipulate supply and demand curves."[59] He is modest in denying any merit in being a good economist, but he nonetheless sets himself apart from his fellow students whose DNA was less favorable.

However, for all that he liked to see himself as self-taught, it was important for him to be able to say that he had been taught under the *ancien régime* in economics. He repeatedly claimed the authority of someone who can remember a past that others know only as history.

> Sophie Tucker, the nightclub singer, used to say: "I've been rich. I've been poor. Believe me, rich is better." I can say: "Having been brainwashed by Jesuits with a lower case 'j', I've known nineteenth century economics and mid-twentieth century economics. Believe me, later is better in this case."[60]

To use the metaphor quoted earlier, there was an advantage to having been a jackass.

Viner's graduate course in economic theory was undoubtedly important to Samuelson, both as an exposure to more rigorous economics than he had previously encountered and because his performance in it became legendary. However, the economist he repeatedly cited as having been important to him was Knight, his "boyhood idol" and "god," by whom he had been "bewitched" and with whom he had been "besotted." He has said he read everything Knight had ever written, a claim he makes of no one else.[61] In stressing his former allegiance to Knight, Samuelson was establishing his authority to oppose the Chicago School of Friedman, Director, and Stigler, which traced its roots back to Knight. He had once been an insider and understood the basis on which their ideas rested.[n]

However, despite these reasons for Samuelson to emphasize his closeness to Knight and his subsequent distance, he would appear to have owed much to his teacher. It is easy to see how Knight's wit and skepticism would have been attractive to Samuelson, who developed some of the same characteristics. He was clearly attracted by Knight's liberalism, writing that his "priceless contribution" had been to draw attention to the market's merits at a time when faith in markets was at its nadir. Samuelson never backtracked on liberalism or support for the market, even though after encountering Hansen at Harvard, he reacted against Knight's skepticism toward the New Deal and attempts to improve society. A planned economy, Knight contended, was "simply a well-managed penitentiary," a position Samuelson later found to be too simplistic, making Knight a poor prophet of events after 1932.

Samuelson turned against Knight's politics, and in turning to mathematics and operationalism, he rejected important tenets of Knight's economics. He saw a much bigger role for science than Knight had countenanced. And yet Knight had exposed him to many of the ideas with which he was to grapple over the coming decade and a half. In the second edition of his textbook he acknowledged Knight's influence on the way he conceived the economic process and the way he defined economics.[62] Possibly more important, much of Samuelson's subsequent work can be seen as engaging with issues raised in Knight's writings. Samuelson's work on consumer theory, dynamics, and welfare economics tackled issues about which Knight had written in *The Ethics of Competition and Other Essays*. The approach to welfare economics Samuelson developed in the 1940s directly reflected Knight's view that one could not draw welfare conclusions without making ethical judgments. In following up Knight's emphasis on ethics, his view that there was more to life than economic value, and that real-world agents were not necessarily rational, Samuelson was picking up on aspects of Knight's thought that were "safe" because they were not taken up by subsequent generations of Chicago economists.

---

n. His position was analogous to that of free-market economists, such as Ronald Coase and James Buchanan, who emphasize that they were once socialists, until they saw the light.

Samuelson's relation to Knight over the fifteen years after he left Chicago was to be a complex one. He rejected much of what Knight stood for, eventually becoming so critical of him that Knight complained Samuelson seemed to consider it his duty to belittle him.[o] At the same time, he never stopped engaging with Knightian themes, often explicitly. Knight had left more of a mark on him than he realized, even though when he left Chicago and acquired new mentors, his work moved in new directions.

---

o. Referring to one of Samuelson's writings, Knight wrote, "It starts off with a long dialogue between Samuelson and me in which the main point on S's part seems to be to make disagreements where there are none, or in general to offer criticisms without content, and occasionally to throw in a slur, which he perhaps thinks are witticisms, (but I don't see how this is possible). . . . I am by no means the only one who has noticed, on various occasions, over the years, that Samuelson does not miss a chance, or a chance to make a chance, to get such 'criticisms' of me into print. He evidently thinks it part of his duty to the profession and the cause to belittle me and destroy what standing I may have as an economist." F. H. Knight, October 28, 1950, Letter to David McCord Wright, PASP 78 (Wright).

PART II | The Harvard Years,
1935–1940

CHAPTER 6 | # First Term at Harvard,
Autumn 1935

Arrival

On April 15, 1935, Jacob Viner wrote glowingly about Samuelson to the Social Science Research Council, supporting his application for an SSRC fellowship.

> Mr. Paul A. Samuelson, although an undergraduate, did distinctly better work than any other member of my graduate course in Economic Theory during the past Quarter. He is a sober, careful and extremely able student, equipped with extensive mathematical technique, zealous, original and independent, without the belligerences and the arrogance that so often marks young men with keen minds and the knowledge that they are superior in mental capacity to their classmates. Mr. Samuelson shows all the signs of having it in him to become a very distinguished economic theorist, and is, with one possible exception, the most promising undergraduate I have ever encountered since I began teaching some twenty years ago. I have only known him for some four months, but I do not think that this is too hasty a judgment.[1,a]

---

a. It is hard not to wonder about the identity of the student whom Viner thought might be more promising. The obvious name to come to mind is Milton Friedman, who had taken

Samuelson's application was successful, meaning that he was assured of a grant for as long as it took him to get a PhD. It carried an important condition: that he could not hold the grant at the university where he had undertaken his undergraduate study. He had to leave Chicago.

He discussed the choice of where to go with his teachers and fellow students. Allen Wallis and Milton Friedman urged him to go to Columbia to learn statistics from Harold Hotelling. So, too, did all his teachers, without exception.[2] This was the university to which many Jewish students went. In the end, he chose Harvard, not on account of its economists, though Edward Chamberlin was a significant attraction, but "in search of green ivy": he expected Harvard Yard to look like Dartmouth's Hanover common, surrounded by "white churches and spacious groves."[3] Confident that as a holder of such a prestigious award he would be accepted anywhere, he did not formally apply to become a research student: he simply went to Harvard.

Samuelson could have got to Cambridge on a Greyhound bus, but instead he decided to travel in style. The trip began with his first flight, in a Ford trimotor—a propeller-driven airplane with three motors—to Detroit. A boat then took him overnight to Buffalo, where he had what he described as his first culture shock on seeing older buildings.[b] The shock would have been less had he made the trip to the East more slowly. From Buffalo, the trip became much less comfortable. The first discomfort was on the bus, making the nineteen-hour journey through New York State: Buffalo, Rochester, Utica, Binghamton, the Catskill mountain range, and finally New York City. In New York, he had arranged to stay with two friends from Chicago who had a room in a hotel on 22nd Street and Broadway, right near the Flatiron building. Whereas others were inspired by the city's dynamism and its architecture, Samuelson was not: "New York's teeming masses, yearning to be free, depressed me then and still weigh down on me. I do get cold comfort from learning that the tallest skyscrapers are borne up by solid granite."[4] His friends were out when he arrived, so he left his two suitcases by the door and went down to the lobby clerk. Panic ensued when the clerk told him he should never have left his luggage unattended, and to pray it was still there. He claims that, being an atheist, his only prayer while rushing back was to Charles Darwin.

---

the price theory course a few years before, but he was an undergraduate at Rutgers, not Chicago.

b. His claim that he had not previously seen buildings more than twenty years old was clearly an exaggeration.

Samuelson recorded little about his two days in New York other than he learned that to be eligible for entry into Harvard, it was necessary to have evidence of immunity against smallpox. He had been vaccinated, and had the unmistakable mark on his arm to prove it, but getting a doctor's certificate to prove it relieved him of $50—as much as it would have cost to travel all the way from Chicago had he taken the Greyhound bus.

After his experience in New York, Samuelson was both relieved and excited to be on the Greyhound to Boston. He asked the driver to drop him at the YMCA, where he expected to be able to get a room. He had not taken account of the fact that, it being the beginning of term, they had been fully booked for weeks. The clerk wished him luck at the Athens Hotel, but he got the same answer there and was advised to try the men-only Technology Chambers, near the Huntington railroad tracks. Accosted by a prostitute on his way out of the Athens Hotel at 2:20 A.M., he had no choice but to try the Technology Chambers and luckily was able to find a room. Having found a room, he had only to register for classes at Harvard.

Registration at Harvard involved an encounter in which he claims to have alienated the department chair, Harold Hitchings Burbank, who was to become the focus of many resentments. Explaining that he had not applied in advance on the grounds that a paying SSRC Predoctoral Research Fellow could get in anywhere, and that he intended to "skim the cream" of Harvard on the grounds that he might not stay more than a year, Samuelson refused to take E. F. Gay's famous, but "sterile and dull," course in economic history, taking instead Edward Chamberlin's Monopolistic Competition and Allied Problems in Value Theory, intended for second-year graduate students. It was emphatically not, as Samuelson put it, "love at first sight." In his later reflections on his years at Harvard, he consistently characterized Burbank as anti-Semitic and as representing "everything in scholarly life for which I had utter contempt and abhorrence."[5] He was, however, accepted into the graduate program.[c]

In his first two years at Harvard, Samuelson was required to attend classes. In the first year, the core course was Ec.11, Economic Theory, the course made famous by Viner's teacher, Frank Taussig, but now taught by Joseph Schumpeter. In the first term, he also took Theory of Economic Statistics,

---

c. Samuelson's claim to have virtually dictated terms to Burbank raises questions. If there was a requirement to register in advance, why would an anti-Semitic head of department not have used Samuelson's failure to follow proper procedures as an excuse to exclude him? The same goes for Samuelson's claimed refusal to take required courses. His account does, however, make clear his contempt for Burbank.

taught by Leonard Crum.[6] Evidence of what Crum taught is not clear, other than that he used an old textbook, but given his work, it seems likely to have been a course focused on practical problems of data analysis and interpretation, mathematically not very demanding given the courses Samuelson had taken in Chicago.[7] Samuelson claimed that, at his initial meeting with Burbank, he argued his way out of taking this course, along with E. F. Gay's course, as mentioned earlier. However, he later wrote that Crum taught what was "not so much a course *on* statistics as *against* statistics," warning students that it was a powerful weapon that might explode in their hands, and he obtained an A+ in it.[8] What is more likely is that after taking the course in the first term, he managed to avoid taking the follow-up course in the second term, instead taking E. B. Wilson's Topics in Statistical Theory, which approached statistics in a way he found much more congenial. Samuelson also took Money and Banking with John Williams, who had a reputation as being the best lecturer in the department and whose courses were very popular, and Monopolistic Competition with Edward Chamberlin.[d]

Harvard in 1935

The Harvard to which Samuelson came that fall was in the throes of change. Its recently appointed president, James Bryant Conant, formerly a successful academic chemist, sought to reform the curriculum and to raise the academic standing of the university. Under his predecessors, Harvard had changed from a college primarily catering to the New England elite into a full-fledged university taking scholarship seriously. Conant wanted to take that further to create a meritocratic university, based on the assumption that talent was spread uniformly across the socioeconomic spectrum.[9] The faculty should be aiming to advance learning, not merely to preserve it. To achieve his goal of a university in which liberal education was linked to research, he sought to get rid of unpromising junior faculty and to appoint high-profile senior faculty, often from outside Harvard. This brought him into repeated conflict with faculty members and alumni who questioned his prioritizing of research over teaching. The Economics Department was one part of the university where such conflicts erupted.[e]

---

d. Mason (1982, p. 412) wrote of Williams: "He was an excellent lecturer ... the best the Department had to offer and his courses in money and banking and international trade were heavily attended."

e. See chapter 15 this volume.

In the years immediately before Samuelson's arrival, Harvard's Economics Department had changed significantly, with the departure of several senior faculty members. The most significant among these departures was that of Frank Taussig, a professor since 1892 and author of a leading textbook, *Principles of Economics* (1911, third edition 1921), who retired in 1935 at age seventy-five, having taught the compulsory theory course for forty years.[f] Prominent among the replacements were recruits from Europe, notably Joseph Schumpeter, easily Harvard's most eminent economist in the 1930s, and Wassily Leontief and Gottfried Haberler, all of whom, along with Edwin Bidwell Wilson in the Institute for Public Health but attached to the Economics Department, were to be very important for Samuelson.[10]

Harvard's main research activity during the 1920s had been for the Committee on Economic Research and the Harvard Economic Service, an organization that under Warren Persons had been responsible for producing economic forecasts—the Harvard barometer of business conditions. This committee acquired a solid reputation in the 1920s, selling its advice to businessmen. In 1929, their graphs of economic indicators (famously known as the A, B, and C curves) gave a clear warning of a downturn, but those writing the forecast could not believe what they were seeing and failed to warn their subscribers.[g] The Economic Service was discontinued in 1933, but it left a legacy. It established the *Review of Economic Statistics* (later the *Review of Economics and Statistics*), an academic journal focused on quantitative research initially bundled with subscriptions to the weekly Economic Service. It was taken over by the Economics Department as a second journal along with the long-established *Quarterly Journal of Economics*. Also, though Charles Bullock, the driving force behind the committee, had retired and, though Persons had left in 1928, two people recruited to work on the project stayed on as faculty members.

Edwin Frickey, appointed in 1917, focused on the problem, crucial to Persons's methods, of decomposing an economic series into trend and cycle. He was a regular contributor to the *Review of Economic Statistics*, with articles

---

f. Other notable retirements included Thomas Nixon Carver and Charles Bullock, all three having been appointed before 1914. For an account of Harvard during this period, see Mason 1982.

g. The A curve was believed to be a measure of speculation, including variables that changed early in the business cycle. The B curve was calculated from measures of physical production and commodity prices, and the C curve covered financial markets. These correspond to what are nowadays called leading, coincident, and lagging indicators. See Mason 1982, p. 417; Friedman 2014; Morgan 1990.

on stock prices and bank clearings, as well as on general fluctuations in economic activity. This work was characterized by meticulous analysis of statistical data and a determination to follow an inductive approach, driven only by the data, not by economic theory. One of Frickey's innovations was to argue that, in decomposing a series into trend and fluctuation, the investigator should make use of information about other data series—something that was possible because of the high correlation between them; that is, in estimating the trend for one price, account should be taken of developments in the economy as a whole. It was an approach very much in the spirit of the work that Wesley Mitchell was doing at the National Bureau of Economic Research: painstaking accumulation and analysis of economic statistics. When Frickey later assembled his articles into a single volume, it was favorably reviewed by Mitchell's collaborator, Arthur Burns, who praised it for innovations in statistical technique, for documenting the rhythmic fluctuations in economic activity, and for constructing important new series (for manufacturing output and employment, and of output in transport and communications).[11]

In 1925, Frickey had been joined on the Harvard Economic Service project by Leonard Crum, a Yale-trained mathematician. There was considerable overlap between their work, for Crum also investigated finance and the business cycle, and he worked on methods for calculating trends and analyzing seasonality, publishing analyses of business conditions in the *Review of Economic Statistics*. Crum was a co-author, with Bullock and Persons, of a review of the Harvard Economic Service's experience with its index of business conditions, explaining what they were trying to achieve and defending it against critics.[12] Five years later, he and Bullock—Persons having left Harvard—evaluated the performance of their forecasting methods in the light of the Depression by then approaching its lowest point. "If followed mechanically," they pointed out, "the chart would have given a satisfactory forecast even of the extraordinary developments late in 1929."[13] However, they had not interpreted the index mechanically and had supplemented it with "economic analysis."[14] Their overall conclusion was a defense of their performance.[15]

Even more prolific in his output, Crum's interests ranged more widely than Frickey's. In addition to his work on forecasting the cycle, he tackled other problems such as the relationship between business size and profitability, the validity of opinion polls, the reliability of examination results, and the apportioning of joint costs between activities within a business. He took issue with the claims made by Adolf Berle and Gardner Means (1932) about the concentration of economic power in the United States.[16] However, what is most notable is that, as would be expected of someone trained as a mathematician, his work exhibited a greater concern with statistical theory. He explored ways to measure the dispersion of an ordered series (such as time series, in which the order in which the observations appear is significant), the statistical implications of using the median rather than the mean in measuring seasonal variations in a series, and the relation between correlation and measures of the periodicity of a series. It is thus not surprising that he published a number of papers arguing for the importance of mathematics to students of business and economics. He later published, as a supplement to Harvard's *Quarterly Journal of Economics*, an elementary primer on the mathematics that economists and statisticians needed to do their work effectively, starting with graphs and moving through simple algebra to limits and differential equations.[17] He was most famous, Samuelson recalled, for his predictions that Roosevelt would lose the elections in both 1936 and 1940.[18]

The remaining "old guard" included Eli Monroe, appointed in 1914, a historian of economic thought, who was managing editor of the *Quarterly Journal of Economics* during Samuelson's time at Harvard; the economic historian Edwin Francis Gay, appointed in 1902; and Harold Burbank, the faculty member who, in his role as Head of Department, had interviewed Samuelson on his arrival. Appointed an instructor in 1912, Burbank had a significant influence on the department, frequently serving as its chairman, usually because no one else was anxious to take on the task. A specialist in public finance who published little, he was instrumental in recruiting Schumpeter. Mason remembered Burbank in the following words:

> My memories of "Burbie," as he was called by young and old alike, are of two quite different people. In the 1920s he was a fat, jolly, friendly man enthusiastically engaged in building up the tutorial system and immersed in undergraduate instruction. He offered a helping hand to young instructors who were not too frequently noticed by older members of the Department, and was always accessible to students. In his later years, he was a disappointed, disgruntled, reactionary figure who had influence in the Department mainly because of his willingness, even alacrity, in taking over the chairmanship, a job shunned by almost everyone else.[19]

During the 1920s, the Harvard department had developed the practice of allowing a number of its own students to stay on to join the faculty when they obtained their PhDs. These included John Williams (1921), Seymour Harris (1922), Edward Mason (1923), Edward Chamberlin (1927), and Overton Taylor (1928). Abbott Payson Usher, an economic historian who had studied with Gay, joined in 1922, after spending a dozen years elsewhere. Williams was a specialist in international finance, one of a remarkable series of PhD students supervised by Taussig, which also included Samuelson's Chicago teacher, Jacob Viner, who undertook studies of balance-of-payments adjustments in different countries. Williams combined being a successful teacher at Harvard with a career advising the Federal Reserve Bank of New York, becoming a vice president in 1936. Harris, who did not achieve tenure at Harvard until 1948, perhaps because he was Jewish,[20] spent many years editing the *Review of Economic Statistics*, and was to prove more receptive to Keynes than were many of his colleagues. Mason specialized in industrial organization and relationships between government and industry.

Samuelson dismissed Harvard's old guard as "sterile" and "lack[ing] enthusiasm for foreign high-falutin theorist newcomers not trained at Harvard."[21] It was, he claimed, the European émigrés (Schumpeter, Leontief, and Haberler) along with E. B. Wilson (whose many works lay outside the Economics Department) who were important for him. However, as this account shows, though Samuelson might not be enthusiastic about their work, the "old guard" was far from sterile, for it included people who were doing important applied work.[22] It would be impossible to guess from Samuelson's remarks that Wilson, whom Samuelson admired, respected the work of Frickey and Crum, and collaborated with them.[h] The explanation must be that although Samuelson would later engage in applied statistical work, as a twenty-year-old student taking courses in the Economics Department he was interested only in mathematical economic theory, an activity in which they simply did not engage, and this caused him to dismiss them out of hand.

Edward Chamberlin

When Samuelson arrived, the most well known member of this group was Edward Chamberlin. His reputation rested on a book based on a PhD thesis he had submitted to Harvard in 1927, published as *The Theory of Monopolistic Competition* (1933), which appeared in the same year as *The Economics of Imperfect Competition* (1933a), by the young Cambridge economist Joan Robinson. These two books came to be seen as establishing a new approach to the theory of value: the theory of how markets worked and of how prices were determined, of which the canonical statement was

---

h. See chapter 8 this volume.

to be found in Alfred Marshall's *Principles of Economics* (1920), widely used as a graduate textbook in economic theory. The received theory, associated above all with Marshall, was based on a distinction between two types of market. *Monopoly* meant that there was a single seller who could raise or lower the market price so as to achieve the combination of price and quantity sold that maximized profit. *Competition* involved markets in which there were too many sellers for any one of them to influence the market price and in which high profits would attract new sellers into the market, pushing prices down to the point where no one earned more than the "normal" rate of profit. Chamberlin's "monopolistic" and Robinson's "imperfect" competition covered the intermediate case in which each seller had some market power (as with monopoly), but in which high profits would attract new sellers into the industry (as with perfect competition). For his whole career, Chamberlin was concerned with differentiating his theory from Robinson's. Not only had his doctoral thesis been submitted before the controversy had even begun out of which Robinson's book emerged, but the two books were methodologically very different. Whereas Robinson's book was an exercise in abstract economic theory, Chamberlin had sought to create a realistic theory to account for companies' behavior in a world in which advertising led to product differentiation and where companies might respond to changes in market conditions not by changing their prices but by investing more in marketing.[23]

Though Chamberlin was considered the rising star of Harvard's department, Samuelson was not impressed with his course. It was not intended as a compliment when, later in life, he described Chamberlin, age thirty-five when he taught him and less than a decade after submitting his thesis, as having being at the zenith of his scholarly career.[24,i] He found Chamberlin disappointing, perhaps because it was an advanced course that he was taking a year earlier than was the norm and he had expected it to be more demanding. His memory was no doubt tinged with the belief that Chamberlin was among the more anti-Semitic members of the department.[25] However, Samuelson was able to make his mark, in his first term in Harvard, even in a course he did not recall with enthusiasm. A fellow student, Shigeto Tsuru (2001, p. 121) remembered an incident involving Samuelson and an eminent young visitor from the London School of Economics, Nicholas Kaldor.

---

i. The reason for this was no doubt Chamberlin's obsession with defending his youthful work.

It was the norm for many visiting foreign scholars to drop into this lecture, and one day, instead of Chamberlin, when Samuelson was presenting his own paper on "duopoly theory," Nicholas Kaldor came into the class. As soon as the discussion following the report had concluded, he walked towards the lectern proffering his hand in greeting with a "Congratulations, Professor Chamberlin. It was an excellent lecture." It was a perplexed Samuelson who was being offered the handshake, and he was at a loss as to how to respond. Kaldor, who realized his mistake immediately, turned towards the real Chamberlin and came up with a specious excuse saying he was expressing his gratitude for guiding such a brilliant student to this level. A few years later, I asked Kaldor about it, asking "Was it an act?" He only responded with a suppressed smile and "Why, of course!"

Twenty years later, when Chamberlin was on leave from Harvard, Samuelson agreed to teach this course as a visiting professor. Chamberlin provided him with the reading list he used, prompting Samuelson to remark that it had barely changed since he had taken the course.[26]

Samuelson's papers contain an undated and incomplete manuscript on the problem of oligopoly. This was almost certainly written for Chamberlin's course and could have been the paper that Samuelson was presenting in the incident described by Tsuru.[27] The problem of oligopoly arises when each member of a small group makes decisions independently of other members of the group, but where the outcome for each individual depends on the actions taken by the group as a whole. For example, there might be two car manufacturers (call them Ford and Nissan) serving a market, each one of which has to decide what price to set. If Ford decides to raise its price, the resulting change in its sales, and hence the profit made, will depend on whether Nissan decides to match the price rise or to leave its price unchanged and take advantage of the situation by selling more cars. The same is true for Nissan: its sales will depend on what Ford decides to do.

Samuelson's main point was that the problem of oligopoly, including the special case of duopoly (two agents interacting with each other), was indeterminate in that the specification of the problem did not make it possible to determine a unique solution: there was an infinite number of possible outcomes. In this respect, it was fundamentally different from problems of monopoly and competition as traditionally conceived, including Chamberlin's monopolistic competition. He wrote down an expression for what each agent was trying to maximize, but concluded that, except for special cases, "there can be no objectively correct judgment by any seller as to the form of this function."[28,j] For example, in a duopoly each seller could influence its rival's belief about how it would react to the rival's actions: the functions describing behavior were, Samuelson wrote, "essentially unstable and depend upon the past behavior of each seller, his 'bluff,' etc. And is no more stable or predictable than would be the result of the nigglings of two equally powerful bilateral monopolists."[29] He concluded,

> We must agree with Professor Chamberlin that in the absence of Uncertainty as to what one's rival is going to do we get deterministic solutions. But the whole purpose of our discussion has been to show that each seller must in general always be without certainty, for it should be clear that we can not have at least two free-wills in a system of interrelationships that we have described, and still have each know all the consequences of his own acts, which is the necessary condition for Certainty to be present.[30]

Samuelson attempted to be more general than the existing literature in at least three respects. He did not specify whether his oligopolists were choosing prices or quantities, thereby claiming that his statement of the problem was more general than those found in the previous literature.[k] He argued, in an appendix to the paper, that the problem of duopoly was equivalent to that of bilateral monopoly, implying that his theory covered both. And his argument ran in terms of "individuals," who need not be the firms or companies discussed by Chamberlin: he seems to have been consciously aiming for a more general theory of human interaction and not just a theory of how companies behaved . These individuals were assumed to be rational, causing Samuelson to write,

> *We mean by a determinate solution that set of values of the variable involved to which the individuals under discussion must eventually arrive at if they behave rationally*, being in full knowledge of the situation. When there are an infinite set of such values possible, we speak of the solution as being indeterminate.[31]

This definition, he claimed, was generally accepted, especially among mathematical economists.[32] He was seeking a general theory of the interaction

---

j. Individual $i = 1, \ldots n$ maximizes $Z_i = Z_i(q_1, q_2, \ldots q_i, \ldots q_n)$ where the q's are interdependent. In most cases, individual i is assumed to control q_i. As explained in the text, the q's could be prices or quantities.

k. He cited the early nineteenth-century mathematician Augustin Cournot, as well as Chamberlin, on this point.

between rational individuals, trying to focus on the general problem and avoid getting sidetracked by "the arithmetic of particular solutions" found in the existing literature.[33]

Though Samuelson was engaging directly and in detail with Chamberlin's work, he approached it from the perspective of Leon Walras and Wilfredo Pareto. One of the points he criticizes Chamberlin for is that of failing to see the problem of indeterminacy in the way that the turn-of-the-century economist, Pareto, with his mathematical training, did: in terms of having the wrong number of equations to determine the unknowns.[34] Given that it is possibly the earliest example of Samuelson's making an analogy with physics (something that was to become a habit), it is worth quoting the relevant paragraph in full:

> In the year 1887 two young scientists puttered in the basement of Ryerson Laboratory at the University of Chicago on an experiment the results of which were eventually to blast the Scientific Cosmos of the Victorian Age into confusion and chaos. What the Michelson-Morley experiment did to the Victorian Synthesis, the theory of Duopoly may be said to have done to equilibrium theory in economics. Just as Newtonian mechanics is still taught in most physics classes, we still teach in our economics classes the conventional Walrasian system in economics, but on the forefront of economic thought lies the shadow of duopoly.[35]

It was no doubt the enthusiasm of a recent graduate for his *alma mater* that led him to overlook the fact that the Michelson-Morley experiment—which raised doubts about the concept of aether, through which light waves would propagate as sound waves travel through the air, by establishing that light traveled at the same speed in all directions—was undertaken before Michelson had moved to Chicago and before the Ryserson Laboratory was set up. The passage shows the level at which Samuelson had set his ambitions: not simply to settle the theory of duopoly for good, but also to overthrow the standard theory of economic equilibrium, which he associated with Walrasian theory. Chamberlin, too, sought "a reorientation of the theory of value" (the subtitle of his book), but he did not associate the theory he was trying to change with Walras. It is interesting to note that John von Neumann and Oskar Morgenstern had similar ambitions with their *Theory of Games and Economic Behavior* (1944). Though Samuelson was not thinking in terms of game theory, which he had presumably not encountered at this point, and though he certainly did not use similar mathematics to von Neumann and Morgenstern, he was tackling problems that later came to be seen as lying in the domain of game theory.

Moreover, though Samuelson agreed with Chamberlin that the problem was determinate if there was no uncertainty about one's rival's behavior, Samuelson went further in arguing that there would always be uncertainty because this was a consequence of having more than one "free-will" operating in an interdependent system. Certainty was impossible. He also challenged the significance of Chamberlin's analysis (in chapter 5 of *The Theory of Monopolistic Competition*) of how monopolistically competitive markets respond to changes in demand. This is perhaps what Samuelson meant when he wrote that he was comparing chapter 3 (on duopoly and oligopoly) with chapter 5 (on product differentiation and the theory of value): he was using the first of these chapters to undermine the argument found in the second.[1]

The paper is also important because it shows that Samuelson was familiar with the content of parts of Pareto's major work on economics, which was not to be translated into English for another four decades. It seems most likely that he read it in French, something that would not have been difficult given that he had passed an examination in the subject and that Pareto's use of mathematics would have made reading much easier.[m] Given this, it seems safe to suggest that he would also have looked at Walras's *Elements d'économie politique pure*. He was simultaneously taking a course with Schumpeter, who would certainly have mentioned Walras, piquing Samuelson's interest.

Though Chamberlin's course was in the fall term, Samuelson wrote another paper for Chamberlin in the winter, presumably in December 1935 or January 1936. This built on the earlier paper, which it cited, but it was completely different in style.[36] That earlier paper tackled a problem that was perhaps too difficult for him to handle rigorously. It followed Chamberlin closely in the way it analyzed change, and it is perhaps not a coincidence that it tackled the one topic on which Chamberlin's book provided, in an appendix, an algebraic treatment. Samuelson's second paper abstracted from time and all other complications, providing a rigorous algebraic discussion of the simplest possible case, where a firm was maximizing the difference between revenue and cost, where these depended solely on output. Interactions between firms, advertising, product

---

1. A fourth section would have dealt with the relation of duopoly to reality and to conventional theory, through the contract curve, collective, agreements, leadership, and "Chamberlin's special theory of monopoly price." However, we do not know whether Samuelson ever wrote this.

m. Though he claims to have struggled with Pareto in Italian, he cites it as the "*Manuel*," not the "*Manuale*," implying he was using the French translation of this book.

differentiation, and other factors were assumed away so that he could derive the conditions under which profit would be maximized—that marginal cost equaled marginal revenue.[37] Perhaps because it was a criticism of those he saw as his rivals at Cambridge (UK), Chamberlin had noted "Good" in the margin at the point where Samuelson observed, "It is perhaps *a reflection on modern economists* that it should have received attention only after its presentation by means of involved (and practicably useless) Euclidian geometry (Cf. Robinson et al.)."[38] His target here, which Chamberlin would have appreciated, was Joan Robinson, whose *Economics of Imperfect Competition* spurned algebra (which she did not understand) and made extensive use of geometry.

Samuelson then introduced advertising, deriving the maximum conditions, this time using partial derivatives. This led to a discussion of the best way to represent a problem that now had three dimensions rather than two (price, output, and advertising expenditure). After rejecting the method of "contour lines, or so called lines of indifference," he opted to use the method of envelopes, on the grounds that it could equally be applied to an n dimensional problem. After drawing revenue curves to illustrate the effects of different levels of advertising, and drawing the envelope (the curve that showed revenue given the optimal level of advertising for each level of output), Samuelson showed how this problem could be reduced to one that was formally the same as the previous one, by replacing revenue with "net gross revenue"—revenue net of optimal advertising cost. Product differentiation could be handled in precisely the same way, this time by introducing "product quality" as a variable. Here, however, he went in another direction, in that product quality need not be a single variable but might involve a number of attributes, each of which could be chosen by the firm.

After this, Samuelson turned to joint production, where a firm produces more than one product using more than one factor of production, deriving optimum conditions that include the marginal productivities of different factors. This involved more variables but the required mathematics was no more complex than partial differentiation of a function of several variables. More complicated mathematics was required to handle the next generalization— production for sale to customers who are spread out over an area, incurring transport costs proportional to the quantity of goods sold and the distance over which they had to be transported.[n] It was at this point that he introduced the problem of indeterminacy, for if each firm serves a specific area,

---

n. To solve this problem it was necessary to introduce integral calculus and to describe space in terms of polar coordinates so as to reduce the dimensions involved.

then it must be in competition with those firms that produce in neighboring areas, implying oligopoly (competition between a small number of sellers). Because output would depend on the actions of competitors, "these interrelationships would *in general* be indeterminate," leading to the same conclusion as in duopoly, "that in the absence of the specification of given (arbitrary?) extra conditions as to these interrelationships, our result is indeterminate."[39] There was, he concluded, "no presumption in favor of a symmetrical or rational [*sic*] settling along the line [or over the area]."[40]

Finally, he turned to "the most difficult problem of all," that of time. Even this problem could, so long as there was no uncertainty, be simplified so that it fitted into the same framework, through discounting the net income expected at each point in the future to obtain a present value. What increased the mathematical complexity of the problem was that Samuelson assumed that net revenue depended on advertising, which meant that the firm had to decide how to set its advertising expenditure over time.

> In this case, before we know our quantity to be maximized, namely net value of assets, we must know the value of advertising expense at every instant of time, since, for every different *function* between E [advertising expenditure] and T [time], we get a different value of V [profit]. Thus we have here a *functional* instead of a function.... Our problem becomes one in the Calculus of Variations.[41]

At this point, Samuelson drew the paper to a close because he considered it long enough. Going further would require even more advanced mathematics, raising the problem that "to the trained mathematician the results would seem, I am afraid, more or less trivial," whereas "to the economist, 'almost entirely innocent of mathematics,' the results would be unintelligible."[42] What is interesting about this remark is that he was seeing himself as potentially addressing audiences of mathematicians and economists. He closed with remarks on the relationship of his analysis to reality. He had defended the most abstract part of the paper, on choice over time, by claiming that "the business man is constantly in every experiment and in every decision, going through a process exactly comparable to this mathematical one, except that he is always dealing with averages of finite intervals, over a total finite interval" (his mathematics assumed an infinite time horizon).[43] However, a page later, in his conclusions, he stressed the lack of realism in his analysis:

> In the real world, there are no economic men behaving under the simple conditions envisaged by our theories. Actually, decisions are made upon the basis of more or less hazardous guesses as to the nature of the

complex form and relationships of the infinite number of related and relevant "variables," and upon the basis of complex motivations. For this reason, our analysis, while internally consistent, does not present us with a picture of reality.[44]

To give a "true picture of the complexity of economic life," Samuelson claimed, the theory would have to be so cumbersome that it would constitute no more than an "extended description of a particular situation" that would have no explanatory power. For this reason, he continued, the analysis should be as formal as possible so that it did not lead to premature judgments about its relevance to policy.

Samuelson described the paper as comprising "fragmentary notes" on the grounds that he provided a series of disconnected models. He was, however, doing himself an injustice, for there was a clear logical development from one model to the next. Moreover, there was a unity to the paper, for it showed that all the problems could be analyzed in a similar way, and that results followed naturally from the mathematics. This was the reason why he neither claimed originality nor cited sources for all the theories.

> Moreover, little claim is made to originality in what follows since I am unable to trace the origins of many of the conclusions which I have presented, and since moreover, so many of the interesting propositions presented develop naturally from the mathematics so that they cannot rightly be attributed to any individual, but must be owned in common by all who even contemplate these problems.[45]

Aside from a question mark in the margin by a point he did not understand, and some trivial corrections to the language, Chamberlin's only comment, written on the front page, was "A very interesting paper. EHC." One wonders what Samuelson would have had to do on the course to have earned a straight A rather than the A- that Chamberlin gave him.[o]

Wassily Leontief

It might appear that there would have been considerable overlap between Chamberlin's course on Monopolistic Competition and Associated

---

o. Samuelson was later to describe Chamberlin as one of the most anti-Semitic members of the department, raising the question of whether Chamberlin's grading of his work contributed to this view.

Problems in Value Theory and a seminar titled Price Theory and Price Analysis (Ec. 18) that Samuelson also attended in 1935–36, seemingly not for credit.[p] This course had been established by Schumpeter soon after his arrival, to remedy the deficiency in Harvard's teaching of mathematical economics. However, Schumpeter was not a sufficiently good mathematician to be a success in teaching this course, and in 1935 it was taken over by a young assistant professor, Wassily Leontief, whose mathematical credentials were much stronger than Schumpeter's. Leontief's offering this course was no doubt also a result of Schumpeter's having to take over the main theory course that Taussig had taught for the previous half-century, and the extensive reallocations of teaching necessitated by the retirements of Carver and Bullock. This was not the first occasion that Samuelson had seen Leontief, for he remembered seeing him at the American Economic Association meeting in Chicago the year before (though there is no suggestion that they spoke on that occasion).

Quite understandably, reconstructions of Leontief's career normally focus on input–output analysis, which became the focus of his life's work. Its origins can be traced back to his youthful publication, "The Balance of the Economy of the USSR: A Methodological Analysis of the Work of the Central Statistical Administration."[46] The idea for examining the relations between different sectors of the economy can in turn be traced back to the linear models employed by Karl Marx, and from there to Quesnay's *Tableau économique*. When he taught Samuelson, Leontief was reporting on the first fruits of his project on constructing an input–output table for the United States.[47] He presented his task as implementing empirically the vision of interdependence that motivated Quesnay's *Tableau*: though the idea of general interdependence between the different parts of the economic system had become "the very foundation of economic analysis," that vision had not been implemented empirically. Economists still worked with hypothetical numerical examples because it was not yet possible to work with real data. "The proverbial boxes of theoretical assumptions," Leontief claimed, "are in this respect as empty as ever."[48]

National income analysis had gone part of the way toward filling this gap, but it remained at a highly aggregative level. Analyzing national income, treating the economy as a whole, lost an enormous amount of information, for

---

p. It is not clear exactly when he took this, for it is listed as being available in either term. His comment about its preparing him for Wilson's expositions of thermodynamics suggests it might have been in the fall of 1935. This might help account for the facility with which he used mathematics in his second paper for Chamberlin, discussed earlier.

it could say nothing about the relationships between industries. Leontief's first step was essentially a generalization of the national accounts to represent production and income for every sector of the economy. Of course, that raised the problem of how sectors should be defined, but in principle they should comprise businesses that produce similar outputs in similar ways. This required that the national accounts become a matrix, listing every sector's purchases from and sales to every other sector of the economy. The input–output coefficients that formed the heart of his system were the ratios of inputs to output in each sector.

For example, the production of $1 of steel required purchases of 43¢ from coal industry, 10¢ from the railways, and so on. Leontief addressed many of the technical problems involved, including how far to aggregate. For example, should "mining" be one sector, or should coal, iron ore, and bauxite be treated separately? Or, should coal be aggregated with petroleum under the heading of energy? The result was a table containing hundreds of such coefficients. Expressed this way, this is no more than an elaboration of the national accounts. What turned this into a theory was adding the assumption that the input–output coefficients were constants. The problem then became one of analyzing the properties of a set of linear equations relating inputs to outputs.

However, for the first decade of his career Leontief's work had not been so specialized as it later became, and he had worked on a variety of problems in economic theory.[49] Russian by birth, Leontief escaped from the USSR after graduating from the University of Leningrad, to spend three years studying for his PhD in Berlin, followed by three years at the University of Kiel (with a year advising the Ministry of Railways in China). In 1931, he moved to the United States, where, after a year at the National Bureau of Economic Research, he took up an instructorship at Harvard. In 1933 he was promoted to assistant professor. In the years before Samuelson's arrival, he was prolific, producing a string of papers linked by little more than their use of mathematical economic theory.[q]

In a paper published in May 1935, just before Samuelson's arrival, he turned to the business cycle, examining the relations between prices and quantities of pig iron and cotton (typically taken to represent investment

---

q. While at Kiel, he had published papers on industrial concentration (1977, chapter 2 [1927]) and on the problem of identifying supply and demand curves from price and quantity data (1929). The latter took him into debate with Elmer Working (Leontief 1932) and Ragnar Frisch (Leontief 1934a, 1934b). He combined indifference curves with Gottfried Haberler's concept of the production possibility frontier to produce a theory of

and consumption goods) over a series of business cycles.[50] Though a contribution toward understanding the mechanism of the business cycle, the analysis related to his earlier work on identifying demand and supply curves for individual commodities. In 1936, he published papers on monopolistic competition, aggregation and index numbers, and Keynes's *General Theory of Unemployment, Interest and Money* (1972; Leontief 1936a, 1936d, 1936b). This was the profile of an ambitious young researcher who applied his mathematical skills to many of the problems that were currently fashionable: supply and demand, the business cycle, market structure, and monetary economics.

What was common to all of this work was an interest in the interaction of economic theory and data. His 1925 article had been concerned with statistical methods used in the USSR and the appropriateness of different ways of measuring concepts such as output and income, tackling problems such as gross and net income, value added, and the treatment of intermediate goods. Much of the theoretical analysis involved linear inequalities and indifference curves, then less widely used than they became after the papers by Hicks and Allen in 1934, and he engaged with those who were working on the problem of relating theory to price and quantity data. He tackled directly the problem of aggregation, deriving conditions under which rigorous aggregation over commodities was possible; however, when he applied indifference curves to the problem of international trade, he was not sufficiently familiar with these ideas to see that aggregation posed theoretical problems for the type of analysis he was constructing.

Samuelson wrote that although Leontief's course was "camouflaged" by the title "price analysis," this did not fool him, and that it was a course in mathematical economics. "We were a small class," he wrote, "Abe Bergson, then a third-year graduate student, was one attendee. Another was Harvard honors senior, Sidney Alexander [later a colleague at MIT]. Maybe Shigeto Tsuru and Philip Bradley were auditors, as was Schumpeter occasionally."[51] Tsuru did indeed attend the course, he and Samuelson getting to know each other well because it was one of three courses they were attending together (the others being Schumpeter's and Chamberlin's).[52] As befitted

---

international trade (Leontief 1933), and he challenged the marginal productivity theory of wages proposed by Samuelson's Chicago teacher, Paul Douglas (1934), on the grounds that using a production function in which output depended solely on inputs of labor and capital did not make it possible to build a theory of the rate of interest, as well as the prices of individual capital goods (Leontief 1934c). Leontief's theory of international trade is explained further in chapter 9 this volume.

a seminar, the course was not based on a textbook or assigned reading, but on exercises. Given the importance Samuelson attached to the course, about which he wrote glowingly, it is worth noting in detail his memory of its contents, which would be familiar to any modern student who has covered consumer theory.[r]

Samuelson wrote about the class discovering normal and inferior goods and then, "the Holy Grail at the North Pole," the case of a so-called "Giffen good" where a rise in the price led to an *increase* in consumption, the opposite of the normal case.[53] Leontief made the students work these results out for themselves, using determinants: "We *proved* it by 2x2 determinants! Ah bliss."[54,s] Tsuru remembers that Samuelson achieved a particular rapport with Leontief:

> Leontief, who wasn't particularly eloquent, started to explain by drawing a diagram on the blackboard. When Leontief said, "At this point where two lines cross . . . " and was thinking for a moment, Samuelson said "That's where. . . ." Then, Leontief stopped him and said, "Yes, that's right, therefore. . . . " Often, lectures continued in such a way. There was a tacit understanding between them; however, other students were often left bemused.[55]

This is as much as we know about what Leontief taught in the year Samuelson took the course. However, we have more detailed evidence on what Leontief was teaching two years later, when Lloyd Metzler took it and made extensive notes.[56,t] The first thing to stand out is that Metzler's handwritten notes open with a statement that the law of diminishing utility is *nonoperational*, a word that Metzler underlined suggesting that

---

r. "Here is what we learned from late September to almost November Thanksgiving. (a) Specified two-good indifference contours, non-intersecting and 'convex to the origin.' (b) A negatively sloped budget line. (c) No indicator of *cardinal* utility at all. The commodity (numbered 2) on the vertical axis was specified to be numéraire good, so that P_1/P_2 determined the absolute slope of the budget line. (d) As this price ratio changed, the budget line pivoted around the intercept where it hit the vertical axis. (e) What could we *prove* about the signs of both $\partial q/\partial(P_1/P_2)$ and $\partial q_2/\partial(P_1/P_2)$? But first, (f), what might be true of the signs of the income elasticities or of $\partial q_2/\partial(P_1/P_2)$ when I/P_1 is defined as $(P_1/P_2)q_1 + q_2 = I/P_1$, the budget constraint?" (Samuelson 2004b, p. 5.)

s. Many students recall their time studying such problems as anything but blissful.

t. It is possible that what Leontief covered in 1937 reflects included results derived by Samuelson, who was then starting to publish articles on the subject. However, even if this is the case, it provides evidence on the way Leontief was thinking.

Leontief may have stressed the point, on the grounds that it cannot be inferred from the actions of individuals:

> Law of dim. utility is *non operational* (equil be inferred from actions of individuals. This law becomes operationally defined if we assume marg utility of one good (or of money) is constant. Thus an additional assumption is necessary (this is the assumption of independent utilities).[57]

If the marginal utility of one good can be assumed constant, or if the utilities of different goods were independent, Leontief continued, the theory became operational. In either case, an additional assumption was needed. This led into a discussion of the properties of demand functions: Would demand rise or fall when prices or income changed? Leontief stressed the difference between necessary and sufficient conditions, something that was important because it determined whether a point could be made by finding a single example or whether it required a general proof. Given that these notes were presumably made in the fall of 1937, they could well have reflected discussions in which Samuelson played a part and possibly a reading of Henry Schultz's work on demand.[58] However, the emphasis on the marginal utility of money and independence reflects what others, including Wilson, were doing before Samuelson's arrival. It establishes that Samuelson's early work on consumer theory had a very close fit with what his teachers were doing.

After starting with consumer theory, Leontief turned to problems of choice over time, time preference, and saving and investment, including Keynes and the classics (analyzed using a three-by-three matrix of coefficients). At this point, Leontief discussed alternative approaches to modeling, explaining that most empirical studies are of particular equilibrium, and that most general equilibrium studies are "macro economic" (interesting as an early use of the term) and some are "macro dynamic." Here, Leontief posed a choice. One option was to have a few variables and to model the dynamics. The other was to take account of many variables and to ignore problems related to time, such as lagged effects. Metzler then went on to make notes on Leontief's own approach, describing the input–output method. The two-by-two determinants that were such bliss for Samuelson were, at least in the year Metzler took the course, the prelude to analyzing much larger input–output models, for by December they were analyzing saving and investment using n-by-m matrices.

What this evidence shows is that, although Leontief might not assign readings from Hicks and Allen—the economists responsible for the modern theory of the consumer—the material was clearly up to date, in line with issues that were actively being discussed in the journals. It was a course in contemporary mathematical economics using what, by the standards of the time, were advanced mathematical techniques. Indifference curves were increasingly being used to analyze behavior without making the assumptions necessary for the notion of utility to have operational significance. The stress on operationalism presumably reflected ideas that were being widely discussed at Harvard among Percy Bridgman's colleagues, and it is notable that Leontief was using the term in precisely the sense that Samuelson was to use it in his discussions of revealed preference.

Thus, even though Samuelson could not have been exposed to all the ideas that Leontief included in his 1938 class (discussion of Keynes could not have been there), there is no reason to doubt his claim that Leontief prepared him for the lectures he was to take the following term from Wilson.

> No other course I ever took so profoundly set me on the way of my life career. It was, so to speak, slow motion, and all the better for that. It prepared me to master Edwin Bidwell Wilson's exposition of Willard Gibbs' thermodynamic analysis.[59]

Shigeto Tsuru and the Other Students

In all his accounts of these years, Samuelson emphasized that his fellow students were as important for his education as his teachers, usually recounting a long list of names. "Harvard made us," he wrote, "yes, but we made Harvard."[60] Samuelson's view about the importance of fellow students was shared by his friends. Tsuru cites approvingly Robert Triffin, a Belgian who was also studying economics, who claimed that he learned as much or more from "student colleagues of mine in the most brilliant class that Harvard probably ever had ... than from the professors whose classes I attended."[61] And it was not just Harvard teachers and students who mattered, for the presence of Schumpeter, Haberler, and Leontief, and later Hansen, attracted young scholars on Rockefeller scholarships to Harvard. These included Oskar Lange, Abba Lerner, Paul Baran, Erich Roll, Nicholas Kaldor, Fritz Machlup, Nicholas Georgescu-Roegen, Oskar Morgenstern, and Jacob Marschak. Samuelson recalled meeting many of these visitors at the homes of Haberler and his wife, Friedl.[62] According to Tsuru, "Almost every day, either at lunch or cocktail hours or late at night, was an occasion for heated discussion on the state of economic reasoning among us all."[63]

The cohort of which Samuelson was a member counted around twenty, almost half of whom were non-American. The only graduate of Harvard

College in the program was the Japanese student Shigeto Tsuru, who had the advantage of having attended some of the courses as an undergraduate. Samuelson and Tsuru got to know each other because they were attending many classes together, having decided, somewhat unusually, to try to pass "generals" in one year. This involved a *viva voce* examination that was the main hurdle before the PhD dissertation and which qualified students for an MA with no further work. As graduate students, Samuelson and Tsuru socialized together outside class regularly, playing squash and billiards, and attending burlesque shows at the Old Howard in Scully Square, in Boston. They often dined together with Triffin, in Adams Hall, where Triffin lived. Tsuru recalls, without giving the reason, that they were called "the three Musketeers." They were often joined by other students, including Arthur Schlesinger Jr.—the son of Harvard historian Arthur Schlesinger Sr.— who was studying history. Close, lifelong friendships developed among Samuelson, Tsuru, and Schlesinger.[64]

Tsuru, three years older than Samuelson, had attended high school in Japan, but in December 1930 he was expelled and arrested for radical political activity. His education in Japan was blocked. Unusual for a Japanese person at that time, while he had still been in middle school he had been given weekly English lessons from a native English speaker, which meant that his father was able to arrange for him to continue his education in the United States, where he went to Lawrence College in Appleton, Wisconsin. His choice of Wisconsin was motivated, at least in part, by the presence there of a German community, for he secretly harbored the intention of transferring to Germany at some point, for his German was better than his English. During his two years in Wisconsin, as well as working very hard to improve his English, he spent much time studying philosophy, becoming attracted to pragmatism, with its emphasis on "the *practical results* of alternative ideas." Many years later he noted that since then, it had become a habit "to relate any policy proposal to its probable concrete consequences."[65] He also published his first academic paper, an experiment that involved asking American subjects to identify the meaning of pairs of contrasting Japanese words (such as *bitter* and *sweet*) from their sounds.

It proved impossible to go to Germany, for the Reichstag fire in February 1933 and the rise of Hitler ruled out studying in a German university.[u] By then, he had greatly improved his command of English. He considered staying at Lawrence College, for it had two good economists, one of whom was

---

u. The Nazi Party was attacking socialists and communists, as well as Jews.

Harry Dexter White, who along with Jacob Viner and John Williams, was one of the cohort of international economists whose PhD had been supervised by Frank Taussig on the theory of balance-of-payments adjustment. It was, however, not White who persuaded Tsuru to move to Harvard, where Taussig was still teaching (though he was to retire in 1935), but his dean, who advised him that he should begin to focus on his main subject. So in 1933, he transferred to Harvard College with the intention of focusing on economics, where he completed his undergraduate education, graduating in 1935.[66] However, even at Harvard, he could not focus exclusively on economics, finding the philosophy of Alfred North Whitehead and the cultural history of Crane Brinton too alluring, and psychologist Gordon Allport persuaded him to do further experiments extending his theory about the Gestalt of meaning. He did, however, find time to sit in on Schumpeter's advanced economic theory lectures.

During the summer between graduating and starting the graduate program, Tsuru spent what seems to have been an idyllic summer relaxing at the lakes of Wisconsin, staying in summer houses owned by the families of two of his friends. One of these was Rosemary, the daughter of Alexander Wylie, U.S. Senator for Wisconsin, who had been in his class at Lawrence College. Rosemary invited one of her friends, Marion Crawford, to the house; it was here where Tsuru persuaded Marion, whom he thought very serious about her studies, to follow his example and move to Harvard for her junior year, though she would, of course, have to go to Radcliffe, the women's college. The challenge of moving was made easier because Rosemary, who was already engaged to a Harvard economics student, Phil Bradley, was also moving to Radcliffe, and for the first year they could share rooms. It was not until her second year at Harvard that she could move into a dormitory in the Radcliffe quadrangle.

Marion Crawford

Marion Estelle Crawford was the third of three children of Will and Edna Crawford. Her father was born on a farm in Wisconsin, and after a brief spell teaching, he become a bank teller. By 1915, when Marion was born, he was president of the First National Bank of Berlin, Wisconsin, working long hours. Her mother, ten years younger than her father, was ebullient and headstrong. Berlin, then a town of around 6,000 people, was a white Protestant community, with no African Americans and no more than one or two Jews. The Crawfords were linked to the Methodist church, though after her marriage Edna stopped attending church except for social events relating to her husband's death. Samuelson remembered that "Marion discharged her obligations by singing in the church choir, but sneaking out before the sermon and prayers. No one ever had less religion than Marion."[67]

Friends consistently remembered Marion as being simple and straightforward, untouched by the success Paul was later to achieve.[68] Lively and with a good sense of humor, calm and tolerant, she hated cant and was modest and, in Paul's mind, extraordinarily unambitious. She was athletic, and applied herself to tennis, the sport for which Paul was an enthusiast, learning to play well. Being good at mathematics, she thought at one point of studying physics. Marion provided the emotional security Paul needed. Though he dutifully visited his parents, on vacations it was her parents' home in Berlin where they spent more time, despite her parents' initial concerns about his being Jewish. Marion did not share her parents' prejudices—to the contrary, her mother's sense of social superiority was so strong that she reacted against it. Paul thought that this experience made her more aware than he was of the prejudice that surrounded them at Harvard and the merits of moving to MIT. The first summer after they met, they chose to attend summer school in Wisconsin, not Chicago.[v] Paul said much later that, when he left home, he did so for good, and he adopted Berlin as the hometown he didn't have.[69] Gary had been too big and in any case, he had spent much time on the farm, and Wheeler was too small.

Marion may have been lonely at first. Though Harvard accepted women, they were taught separately and subject to different regulations, such as having to leave the stacks in the Widener Library by 6 P.M., whereas men could stay there till 10 P.M. In addition she did not fit in socially; she was a Midwesterner who had never been out of the country, but had to listen to the other girls talking about their visits to France and Austria. She had friends in Rosemary and Phil, but became more distant when Phil became more conservative, something that clearly mattered to her. Then late in 1935, Tsuru introduced Paul and Marion to each other at Mary's Coffee shop on Church Street, just off Harvard Square, which Paul remembered as having good brownies. Samuelson summarized the way their relationship developed:

It was a case of "liking at first sight." Her quiet serenity was light years away from flirtatious coquetry. I was no accomplished Casanova.

---

v. See chapter 9 this volume.

Among the graduate school nerds, all that distinguished me was my superior Chicago preparation in economics and my brash ability to correct our teachers' quota of mistakes.

A couple of times we walked together along the Charles River on nice autumn days, chatting about how different New England folks were from Wisconsin and other midwesterners, and how unintelligible at first seemed the lecture dialects of Professors Schumpeter and Leontief.

Near where the Cambridge Tennis Club is, there used to be a little ice cream shop. We sat down for chocolate sundaes, then only 20¢ each. What then happened astonished Marion completely, and surprised me even more. It was so uncharacteristic. I leaned over and kissed her on the lips. It was unprovoked, uncharacteristic, and quite unplanned. (Most of my kissing in my previous 20 years had probably been at the stroke of midnight New Year's eve.)

Neither of us said anything. It had never happened. But liking at first sight had turned into love at second sight.

With increasing frequency we met for lunch, or for a movie or concert. Or just for walks in the incessant Boston rains. She would walk me back from the Radcliffe Quadrangle to the Cambridge Common. And I would trudge back all the way across the river to my sumptuous B-School suite, whistling Rogers & Hart or Gershwin all the way.

We became inseparable.[70]

Though still an undergraduate, Marion became part of the group of graduate students who socialized with Paul and Tsuru, and her relationship with Paul became increasingly close. Paul remembered having spent most of their days together, separating only at night when they retired to their respective residences. The following academic year, 1936–37, was Marion's final year at Radcliffe, during which Paul became one of the most regular male visitors to the university residence in which she lived. In addition to her required courses and writing her thesis, she audited Schumpeter's graduate theory course, which Paul had taken the year before.[71] Her honors thesis bore the title "A Mathematical Reconstruction of the Elasticity of Substitution" and was submitted in April 1937.[72] The elasticity of substitution was a concept used to measure the ease with which two factors of production (usually capital and labor) could be substituted for each other. It was first defined in a book, *The Theory of Wages* (1932), by the young British economist John Hicks, who used it to show how this parameter—seemingly a technical concept rooted in technology—determined how the distribution of income between wages and profits would change when the supply of either labor or capital changed. Marion's thesis reviewed what was known about the concept, drawing attention to differences in the way it had been used and arguing that Hicks's use of the concept could not bear the weight placed on it. She contrasted Joan Robinson's use of it to describe the situation of an individual company producing a single commodity as opposed to Hicks's use of it to describe an entire economy. There might be a formal similarity between the mathematics involved in the two cases, but they were not the same: "the difference," Marion argued, "lies in the text which must accompany any mathematical expression."[73] If we have a "rude and simple sort of economic system where really only one commodity is produced and consumed," then there is no problem with Hicks's use of the concept, for it becomes very similar to Robinson's. However, she argued that was not the case.

> Rather the "National Dividend" is thought of as being produced by heterogeneous productive agencies classified into two categories by dichotomy.[ʷ] In some sense the "National Dividend" must be thought of as a composite bundle of a great many different consumer's goods; but in just what sense Mr. Hicks does not think necessary to specify. It is in this omission, "in this implicit theorizing," that we may find the clue to all the misunderstanding which later arose, and which, as I shall later argue, vitiates Mr. Hicks' analysis.[74]

She proceeded to challenge the idea that it was meaningful to speak of a "production function" linking "National Dividend" to inputs of aggregate capital and aggregate labor.

> But if we wish to consider an economic system of any complexity at all, where there is more than one commodity and more than two factors of production, then the meaning of the "National Dividend" is extremely doubtful, as is even more so any functional relationship between it and two composite bundles of productive agencies, however demarcated.[75]

What Marion is doing here is challenging the idea that there is an exact parallel between the behavior of an individual company and the behavior of the nation as a whole. Not only does her thesis reveal that she understood

---

w. National Dividend is what is now called national income or national product, the most common measure of which is gross national product (GNP). The phrase "implicit theorizing," used in the last sentence, comes from Leontief 1937.

and was capable of criticizing some of the latest developments in economic theory, but it also shows that she had a level of competence in mathematics that placed her ahead of most economists of the day. Given that they were so close, it is inconceivable that she did not discuss these things with Paul, who may have suggested certain ideas to her, but it shows conclusively that she was able to engage closely with his work in economics.

Marion stayed on at Harvard after earning her AB, studying for an MA in economics, presumably taking many of the courses attended two years earlier by Paul, and then working as an assistant to Schumpeter and Seymour Harris. She was highly regarded. Wilson described her as "a grand economist," and Schumpeter apparently rated her as highly as Paul.[76] She assisted Harris in writing a book on the Social Security system, in the preface to which he wrote:

> Mrs. Samuelson contributed research assistance and editorial help. More than to anyone else, the author is indebted to her. Her clear, mathematically trained mind and her faculty of lucid expression have left their impression on this manuscript. Numerous pages are, indeed, her work.[77]

This acknowledgment went far beyond anything dictated by politeness. Paul's view was that she was smarter than Harris and kept taking things out of the book.

They were married in July 1938, in Cambridge. The match was, at least initially, welcomed by neither of their families, though for Marion's family he was the lesser of two evils, in that a Jew was less unwelcome than a Japanese. Paul wrote:

> Then too, differences in religious heritage had to be faced. I was the child of non-observing Jews. Marion's Methodist grandmother played organ and piano in church. Her own mother was drafted to similar duty. And until her grandmother died (in 1924), the Crawford children dutifully attended Sunday School. . . . Seventy years ago interfaith marriages were already on the way but not yet the torrent they were to become.[78]

The marriage of a Jew to a non-Jew also caused a stir in Harvard, though Paul explained that a further factor behind the reactions of the older generation was the economic situation.

> In those depression days 20-year-old academics didn't marry. Most of our Harvard professors had only one or two children or were childless. Jobs were short in those pre-war days of recovery from the Great Depression.

Schumpeter had the further objection that it was inappropriate for scholars to marry in what he considered the "sacred decade" of their twenties, though it has also been suggested that Schumpeter had been attracted to Marion.[79] Paul described him as being "very soft on her" for "he liked Aryan types" and she was tall and blonde.[80] However, by then Paul had a junior fellowship (see chapter 10 this volume), which gave him the income and security he needed. Their friends had no qualms about the event.

> The die was cast. On July 2, 1938 (at the bottom of the 1937-9 recession) we were married by the Cambridge Clerk across the street from Central square post office. The wild wedding party that evening in our studio Ware Street apartment spawned subsequent marriages by Abram and Rita Bergson and Shigeto and Masako Tsuru. In return for Shigeto's being our go-between, we assisted him in choosing Masako.[81]

The apartment into which they moved, on Ware Street, adjacent to Harvard Yard, became a place where the group of young economists held parties. One friend, Bob Bishop (later to be a colleague at MIT), recalled regular evenings when six or more of them played poker for very small stakes. This was an activity for which Marion left Paul behind, for according to Bishop, "it was usually a matter of whether Marion's winnings were enough to offset Paul's losses."[82] On occasion a group of around fifteen couples rented a hall, where they organized dances to recorded music.

Marion was very important to Paul. Not only did she provide him with the emotional security he needed, eventually taking responsibility for their growing family, but also in the early years of their relationship they worked together. Paul credits her with stimulating his interest in Social Security. One of his most important publications, on the theory of international trade, was a subject about which she had published an article and was written with her assistance. They also wrote a joint paper on population growth that was not published. Her undergraduate thesis shows that, though her mathematics probably did not keep up with Paul's, she knew enough to engage with what Paul was doing, and it touched on several problems that he would later write about himself. Like Paul, she was a supporter of Franklin Roosevelt.

| Joseph Alois Schumpeter

Economic Theory

When Samuelson arrived at Harvard, the star of its economics department was Joseph Schumpeter, a flamboyant Austrian economist recently recruited from the University of Bonn. He had arrived at Harvard, full time, in 1932, the result of a long attempt to recruit him. Born to a well-to-do German-speaking, Catholic family in 1883, in what is now the Czech Republic, Schumpeter's father died when he was four years old.[1] His mother, Johanna, chose to move to Graz, in Austria, believing that it would offer more opportunities for her and her son. When Schumpeter was nine, Johanna married an army officer thirty years her senior and moved to Vienna.

Though Schumpeter came from a German-speaking community that considered itself Austrian, he was viewed as an Easterner; he never felt he completely belonged. Coming to maturity in an aristocratic family in Vienna during the last years of the Hapsburg Empire, he lived through the cultural flowering of those years. In 1901, he entered the University of Vienna, graduating in 1906 in law, though he had discovered his interest and aptitude for economics, and having published three articles on statistics and one on the mathematical method in economics. His most important teacher was Eugen von Böhm-Bawerk, and Schumpeter was immersed in the controversies between the marginalism of his teachers, the German historical school of Berlin's Gustav Schmoller, and Marxism. His fellow students, who included Ludwig von Mises, Otto Bauer, Rudolf

Hilferding, and Emil Lederer, spanned the political spectrum from liberalism to Marxism.[a]

Not sure of how he could develop his career, and having expensive tastes that could not be satisfied on a regular academic salary, Schumpeter toured western Europe, visiting Britain. He loved the idea of becoming an English gentleman, visiting "good English clubs," and he famously claimed to have had an audience with Alfred Marshall at his home. Samuelson, however, was skeptical of this story, noting that Schumpeter was a great storyteller and that we have no evidence other than his own account of these events. "When Schumpeter told me he had champagne breakfast and rock pheasant with Edgeworth at All Soul's [College, Oxford]," he wrote, "I have to wonder about the assertion that it was Marshall who invited him to breakfast."[2] He married an English woman and, as he could practice law there, he moved to Cairo to support himself while writing the thesis (his Habilitation) that would give him the right to lecture at the university. The thesis was published in 1908.[3]

In this book, Schumpeter sought to reconcile the different continental schools of economics, much as Marshall had reconciled competing approaches to economics in Britain. If he could do this, he could bring to an end to what was termed the *Methodenstreit*, the battle over methods that divided German-speaking economics in the closing decades of the nineteenth century, after Austrian Carl Menger had published a critique of the historical school headed by Gustav Schmoller, in Berlin. Schumpeter argued that theory could provide a way to bridge the claims of different schools. Though Schumpeter clearly sided with Menger in attaching great importance to static theory and the subjective theory of value, he decisively rejected Menger's claim that the theory analyzed the "essence" of economic phenomena. It was no more than a device for organizing ideas that were to be tested against historical reality; in this sense, he was adopting an instrumentalist methodology. This fits with what Leontief describes as Schumpeter's "masterly exposition of the 'method of variation'—later popularized under the name of 'comparative statics.'"[4] The importance of comparative statics was to become central to Samuelson's main work in economic theory.[b]

On the basis of this book, Schumpeter obtained a position at the University of Czernowitz, in the far east of the Austrian Empire, in what is now

---

a. Liberalism is here used in the European sense, associated with an emphasis on individual freedom.

b. See chapter 14 this volume.

Ukraine.[c] There his wrote his *Theory of Economic Development* (1934[1911]).[5] From Czernowitz he moved to the University of Graz, once his hometown, becoming the youngest professor of economics in the Austrian Empire. In 1913, probably on the advice of the eminent American economist John Bates Clark, who had favorably reviewed Schumpeter's latest book, he was invited to spend two terms visiting Columbia University. During his U.S. visit he gave lectures at many universities, meeting as many influential economists as he could, including Taussig, with whom he established a crucial, lifelong friendship. His reputation was established.

Schumpeter spent the First World War teaching in Graz, and while there he became involved in politics. He tried but failed to enter government during the war, but in 1919, his university friend, Otto Bauer, became foreign minister and on Hilferding's advice, Schumpeter was appointed finance minister. He was a top minister in a socialist government despite being "a conservative who had no party affiliation and no independent power base."[6] His proposals for reconstructing the Austrian economy on the basis of opening up trade and importing capital came to nothing, and in office at the time of the Treaty of Versailles, he never forgot the effect of the Allied demands for reparations.

His tenure at the finance ministry did not last long; neither did a career as a private banker, which ended with the failure of the bank after which he was saddled with large debts. However, in 1925 he returned to scholarship, as he put it, after obtaining a position as Professor of Public Finance at the University of Bonn, for which he was supported by Gustav Stolper, the leading economic journalist in Vienna. Schumpeter was, Stolper argued, eminently well qualified for the position, but was being held back by his flamboyant, "un-Austrian," "un-Bourgeois" lifestyle, the attempt to support which was the reason for his unsuccessful venture into banking.[7] Success, however, turned to tragedy in 1926. Shortly after the death of the mother to whom he was devoted, Annie Reisinger—with whom Schumpeter had fallen in love and married, despite his family's disapproval of her low social status and the fact that the status of a previous marriage of his was not clear—died in childbirth, as did his prematurely born son. From being a *bon vivant* he became depressed, unable to bear his grief and for the rest of his life immersed himself in his academic work.

---

c. The *Methodenstreit*, as the controversy was called in German, had begun with in a dispute between the theoretical Carl Menger, based in Vienna, and the historical economist Gustav Schmoller, based in Berlin.

His connection with Harvard came shortly afterward. Taussig, his friend since 1913, persuaded him to become a visiting professor, and for five years he divided his time between Harvard and Bonn. When a suitable vacancy arose in 1928, Taussig, Burbank, and even Harvard's President Lowell tried to persuade Schumpeter to come permanently, and he eventually came in 1932. Recruiting him was a major coup for Harvard. This was the teacher who would provide Samuelson's first taste of economic theory at Harvard—a showman and brilliant economist, but stricken with personal insecurities that led him to follow a work schedule that threatened his health. Additionally, he had a desire for popularity that resulted in his going further than most professors in making himself available to students and in displaying a notorious liberality in grading. He lived with Taussig until, in 1936, he married an economic historian and specialist on Japan, Elizabeth Boody, who looked after him until his death in 1950.

Giving up an earlier attempt to write the book on money that had occupied him for several years, Schumpeter devoted himself to writing the book that was published in two volumes as *Business Cycles* (1939). Produced single-handedly, this compendium of economic history and statistical analysis sought to provide a comprehensive account of economic fluctuations. It was, however, eclipsed by the appearance of Keynes's *General Theory* (1936). It was Keynes's theoretical apparatus—oversimplified in the view of Schumpeter and his senior colleagues—that the graduate students wanted to discuss. They were not interested in the mixture of theory, statistics, and economic history in his book. Success came not with this book but with two others: *Capitalism, Socialism and Democracy* (1942), written much more quickly than the book on business cycles, and which he considered a potboiler; and *A History of Economic Analysis* (1954), unfinished at his death but brought to publication by his devoted Elizabeth Boody, assisted by several of his colleagues.

Samuelson's first encounter with Schumpeter had been on December 26, 1934, when Schumpeter had contributed to a session on the business cycle at a meeting of the American Statistical Association being held in Chicago.[8,d] On coming to Harvard, Samuelson's first encounter with Schumpeter was in Ec. 11, the main economic theory course for graduate students. Schumpeter was assisted by Paul Sweezy, who was to become one of America's most prominent Marxist economists.[e] This course was legendary not just because Taussig had taught it for so long but also because of the Socratic method he

---

d. See chapter 4 this volume.

e. Not to be confused with his brother, Alan, also at Harvard at this time.

had perfected. It had been the model for Viner's course that Samuelson had taken at Chicago, and Taussig's method was admired and copied by other teachers at Harvard who had at one time been through it.[9]

Taussig would ask a question, choosing a student who could be relied upon to give a suitably stupid answer, which would then be discussed by the entire class without the student's being told whether he or she (the class included women from Radcliffe) had given the correct answer. It was, Samuelson believed, not an effective method for teaching modern economic theory, but it was favored by Taussig because, as he once conceded to Samuelson over dinner, he had not kept up with developments in economic theory since the First World War, focusing instead on his specialism of international trade. Schumpeter was less effective than Taussig in teaching this way, but he held the students attention in other ways.

Whereas Taussig was "a rather austere gentleman of the old school," Schumpeter played the showman.

> After, and not before, the students had assembled for the class hour, in would walk Schumpeter, remove hat, gloves, and topcoat with sweeping gestures, and begin the day's business. Clothes were important to him: he wore a variety of well-tailored tweeds with carefully matched shirt, tie, hose, and handkerchief. My wife [Marion] used to keep track in that period of the cyclic reappearance of the seemingly infinite number of combinations in his wardrobe: the cycle was not simple and it was far from random.[10]

Another student, Robert Triffin, remembers Schumpeter talking about the mysteries of bilateral monopoly that had kept him awake the previous night while "playing with his gloves or his wallet."[11] He would lay out a problem and leave the class to argue among themselves, after which, "with a discrete yawn, he expressed amazement at how enthusiastic the combatants were, associating himself with the others' lack of interest in a problem so dry and uninteresting."[12] Some students would follow up the readings he posted on the blackboard, but he would turn the discussion around to other subjects. This affectation of lack of interest and the deliberate cultivation of a dilettantism, along with his love of skepticism and paradox, were part of the show whereby, according to Samuelson, he "somehow made the class itself seem witty, so that even earnest Radcliffe students felt themselves to be engaging in brilliant sortie and repartée."[13] Though it served to keep students' attention in the hour after lunch, this approach was, in Triffin's view, a challenge to the puritanism of Boston and New England society.

Samuelson praised the contents of the course for the range of both authors they were expected to read and the topics: "It involved readings in Marshall, Wicksell, Pigou, Böhm-Bawerk, Knight, and Wicksteed. In addition, much was made of Chamberlin, Robinson, and current journal articles by Hicks, Harrod, Sraffa, and others. Such advanced authors as Cournot, Edgeworth, and Hotelling were at least sampled."[14] Even though Chamberlin also discussed the subject in a separate course, Schumpeter covered the controversy over the theory of value that erupted in the 1920s and its outcome, the theory of monopolistic competition. Samuelson remembered the order of topics being the firm, the industry, monopolistic competition, general equilibrium, and the marginal productivity theory of income distribution, which covered the theory of capital. Welfare economics was scheduled, but Schumpeter did not manage to cover it. Samuelson's memory of the topics covered in Ec. 11 fits with the evidence from notes that another student, Wolfgang Stolper (son of the journalist Gustav Stolper, with whom Schumpeter had been associated), had made the previous year, when Schumpeter had shared the course with Taussig.[15]

Perhaps because Taussig had focused more on the nineteenth-century classics—Ricardo, Mill, and Marshall—Schumpeter began his part of the course with Marshall's demand curve, pointing out the different ways it could be derived: from a utility curve, from indifference curves, or as a statistical relationship. Stolper's notes suggest that there was an emphasis on diagrammatic treatments of theory, with the occasional equation but few if any algebraic proofs. Schumpeter spent much time on costs, covering both marginal productivity and income distribution and the literature arising out of the so-called cost controversy, comprising many articles from the *Economic Journal*, including the theory of imperfect competition, monopoly, and bilateral monopoly. The reading list included *The Theory of Wages, The Economics of Imperfect Competition,* and *The Theory of Monopolistic Competition.*[16] The syllabus covered material that would have been familiar to almost anyone trained in economics in the half century after the Second World War.

For some students, the course appeared very mathematical. Triffin, coming from a training in law, noted Schumpeter's "constant use of mathematics" and though he admired it, he was dumbfounded and convinced he was watching something in which he would never be able to participate.[17] More perceptively, Abram Bergson observed that Schumpeter, though he used mathematics, never appeared at home with it in the sense that he was not able to use it to generate new results. "I had," he said, "the impression that he was inspired by his conviction that this is the way economics would become a science—by the increased use of mathematics—and that he must be a champion for it."[18]

As a result Bergson found the course less useful and much less interesting than Leontief's. For Triffin, on the other hand, the course was important: it was his fascination with Schumpeter that persuaded him to stay at Harvard much longer than he had intended. Samuelson believed that Schumpeter was at his best in the classroom where he was not constrained by a script, as he was on formal occasions such as his Presidential Address to the American Economic Association. He told many stories, of which he had an immense number, and never repeated them.

When he taught Samuelson, Schumpeter was actively working on his *magnum opus, Business Cycles*. He was an enthusiast for mathematical economics, but as the book's subtitle made clear, it was an attempt to integrate theory, history, and statistics. Not even the theory was formulated mathematically. He talked in terms of a "model," but this was far from a mathematical model as the term was coming to be understood (a set of equations that determined the values of variables of interest) and was defined very loosely. The task of the economic theorist was not to derive explanatory hypotheses or theorems that could verified. It was primarily to derive concepts or analytical tools. Concepts might embody nothing more than methods by which they could be defined and measured, a definition reminiscent of Bridgman's operationalism. A "model" or "schema" was, for Schumpeter, a set of concepts or analytical tools framed to deal with a particular problem: "A set of such analytic tools, if framed to deal with phenomena which form a distinct process, we call a *model* or a *schema* of this process."[19]

This was the methodological basis for his work on business cycles. He analyzed the economic process through what he considered a complex interaction of theory and statistical and historical analysis. The conditions necessary for induction to be a valid method of reasoning were not satisfied, for a particular time series could always be explained in different ways, with the result that statistical data alone could never verify a theory. "There is," Schumpeter wrote, "along with Nonsense Induction, such a thing as Spurious Verification."[20]

> [N]o statistical finding can ever either prove or disprove a proposition which we have reason to believe by virtue of simpler and more fundamental facts. It cannot prove such a proposition, because one and the same behavior of a time series can analytically be accounted for in an indefinite number of ways. It cannot disprove the proposition, because a very real relation may be so overlaid by other influences acting on the statistical material under study as to become entirely lost in the numerical picture, without thereby losing its importance

for our understanding of the case.... Material exposed to so many disturbances as ours is, does not fulfill the logical requirements of the process of induction.[21]

He made it clear that this was the commonly accepted opinion among students of business cycle theory.

Despite his reputation for not pushing his own work and being willing to treat fairly those who did not agree with him, these methodological points are ones that he would have made in the course he co-taught with Haberler, and which Samuelson took in his second year.[22] Schumpeter would also have made the point found at the start of his book—namely, that to analyze the business cycle was to analyze the working of a capitalist economy. Cycles were, he claimed, the essence of the economic system as much as the beat of the heart was of a biological organism.[23] The analytical apparatus to which he turned was very similar to the one he had used almost thirty years earlier, in his *Theory of Economic Development*. This involved consideration of a normal business situation that could be analyzed in terms of general, or Walrasian equilibrium, disturbed by innovations and other events. The economy had to be analyzed at the level of the individual company or household, for though it was possible to talk about equilibrium at the level of aggregates—as was done in much business cycle theory—he considered such reasoning superficial. Analysis in terms of aggregates took no account of the industrial processes operating beneath the aggregates, and it was these processes that really mattered. In his book, Schumpeter's remarks were the prelude to a largely historical and statistical account of the cycle.

Schumpeter's *Business Cycles* was published in 1939. The methodology and the theoretical framework on which the book was based will have been familiar from his teaching, but even his students may have had to wait until its publication to see its full scale. Given that he was beginning to focus on business cycle theory, it seems virtually certain that Samuelson was one of the students who attended an evening seminar at which he talked about his book. As the evening progressed, it became clear that hardly anyone had read the book, and most of the discussion was about Keynes. Some of the students present said that it was the only occasion on which they had seen him genuinely furious; suffering from acute embarrassment, they afterwards wrote a letter of apology.[24] However, though the students may have realized that they should have been as willing to take Schumpeter's work as seriously as he took the views of those with whom he disagreed, they will have become aware during the year that some of the established economists who had read it were critical of it.

Schumpeter on Economic Science

Throughout his career, Schumpeter reflected on what it meant for economics to be scientific, these reflections culminating in his posthumous *History of Economic Analysis* (1954). The most fully developed statement of Schumpeter's approach to science came in his earliest book. In Leontief's opinion, this book contained the basis for Schumpeter's entire scientific worldview.[25] There, Schumpeter took an instrumentalist methodology, drawing on the positivism of Ernst Mach, then very widely discussed in Vienna, and Henri Poincaré.[26] The sole purpose of the hypotheses on which economic theories were based was to show the relationships between economic phenomena; they were not true in any absolute sense. Economic theory might seek to explain economic phenomena, but explanation was "nothing but a specification of the uniquely determined magnitude of the unknowns and the laws of their motion."[27] This was a point that Schumpeter emphasized repeatedly.

> [T]he expressions "explanation" and "description" are generally synonymous for us, or in other words, we do not want and cannot contribute anything other than description to the explanation and understanding of economic facts. . . . A theory constructs a scheme for facts; its aim is to give a brief representation to an immense amount of facts and to achieve as simply and completely as possible what we call understanding. . . . I want to talk not about the "cause" of phenomena but only about functional relationships between them. This brings greater precision. The concept of function is carefully elaborated by mathematics and has clear, unquestionable contents, but that is not the case with the concept of cause.[28]

This perspective led Schumpeter to be skeptical of providing psychological explanations for theoretical assumptions; he preferred the subjective theory of value, not because it could be justified using arguments from psychology, but because it fitted the economic facts better.[29]

Schumpeter's first book, with its instrumentalist approach to economic theory, though little known in the English-speaking world, was widely debated in Germany. The economist Oskar Morgenstern testified that it was read "avidly in Vienna, even long after the First World War," its freshness and vigor leading him to resolve to read everything its author wrote.[30] Many of the German-speaking economists who immigrated to the United States will therefore have been familiar with it. Moreover, Schumpeter still held many of these views very strongly. Triffin has recounted that Schumpeter made it clear in his lectures that economic theory was a method, not a dogma, and that it was important to avoid the "Ricardian sin" of claiming to demonstrate scientifically ideas that were no more than one's own political or social prejudices.[f] According to Triffin, Schumpeter drew an analogy between scientific theory and a flour mill: feeding into it different types of wheat would produce different types of flour. Just as the use of bad wheat would produce bad flour, so too could some economic doctrines be better than others. On taking over Ec. 11, Schumpeter's first act had, therefore, been to abolish the title, Schools of Political Economy, on the grounds that there should no more be schools of economics than there were schools of physics or chemistry. This emphasis on scientific precision coexisting with doctrinal pluralism clearly echoed the position he had taken in 1908.

After arriving at Harvard, Schumpeter continued to think systematically about the scientific method, his later views finding expression in his posthumously published *A History of Economic Analysis* (1954), on which he had been working since 1940.[31] In that book, Schumpeter argued that economics had progressed in fits and starts, experiencing repeated "classical situations" in which synthetic works usher in periods of consensus that are eventually shattered.[32] Underlying this was the view that scientific knowledge had to be understood in relation to the practitioners who created it.[g] Science was "tooled knowledge," produced by a community of professionals with shared problems and methods of inquiry. Schumpeter emphasized the importance of economic "analysis"—the product of conscious, systematic reasoning about economic problems.[33] Though he did not deny the importance of fact gathering, he focused on reasoning and hence on analytical rigor, consistent with his belief in the importance of mathematics in economics.

Economic analysis was, for Schumpeter, synonymous with economic science, covering economic history, statistics, and economic sociology, as well as economic theory. However, it was economic theory to which he attached the greatest importance. He tried to argue that economic theory

---

f. Schumpeter was later to criticize Keynes, as well as Ricardo, for the sin that he had mentioned in his lectures—for piling up assumptions until the conclusions they wanted followed inexorably from their assumptions, creating the illusion that the policies he supported had firmer foundations than was in fact the case (Schumpeter 1954, p. 1171; Triffin 1950, p. 415).

g. This view of science was rooted in the interdisciplinary Pareto Circle, discussed in chapter 21 this volume, which formed part of what Isaac (2012) has termed Harvard's interstitial academy. Schumpeter's view of how economics developed exhibits parallels with that found in Thomas Kuhn's *Structure of Scientific Revolutions* (1962), a book that arose out of the same environment (on Schumpeter and Kuhn, see Backhouse 1998b, chapter 14; on Kuhn and Harvard, see Isaac 2012).

could do more than simply generate explanatory hypotheses. Citing mathematician Henri Poincaré's argument that "tailors can cut suits as they please; but they try to cut them to please their customers," he argued that economic theories, though they might be framed in the light of observations, were "arbitrary creations of the analyst."[34] Economic theorists used this freedom to create tools—concepts, relations between concepts, and methods for handling them—that could then be used to solve problems. Economic theory was, as Joan Robinson had argued, "a box of tools."[h] The rationale for creating such tools was that economic problems shared important features, and much mental effort could be saved by analyzing them all at once: the "engine or organon of economic analysis ... functions *formally* in the same way, whatever the economic problem to which we may turn it."[35]

Schumpeter will have reinforced the view that Samuelson was to hear even more forcefully from Wilson that there was nothing specifically physical about the mathematics used in physics, even if it had been developed with physics in mind. It was simply mathematics, and it should be used in economics if it fit the problems economists were trying to solve. What economists must not do was pretend that the successful use of mathematical tools in physics gave them authority in economics—the sin that Hayek termed "scientism."[36] Most economists were not guilty of scientism, even if some of them had made near-meaningless programmatic statements that described only poorly what they were actually doing. It was true, Schumpeter admitted, that physical analogies were frequently used in the classroom, but this simply reflected human thought processes.

> It therefore seems as though the things we are accused of borrowing are merely the reflexes of the fact that all of us, physicists or economists, have only one type of brain to work with and that this brain acts in ways that are to some extent similar whatever the task it tackles.[37]

Schumpeter's belief that the future lay with mathematical economics is shown clearly in a letter he wrote to Haberler in March 1933, in which he compared himself with Moses: he knew that the Promised Land of a more exact economics required the use of mathematics, but he knew that he was too old to enter it. In contrast, Haberler was young enough to enter, and Schumpeter encouraged him to overcome his reluctance to engage in mathematical analysis. "Forgive my preaching," he wrote, "if we confine ourselves to telling each

---

h. Samuelson was very familiar with *The Economics of Imperfect Competition*, in which she made this point.

other that it is impossible, we shall never get beyond what is a rather uncomfortable transition stage. It is supreme courage that is wanted just now."[38] In the same terms, Schumpeter encouraged Samuelson, "Moses-like" to enter "the Promised Land of Pareto, Hotelling, Tinbergen and Frisch" through discovering and using new mathematical tools.[39]

Mathematics was important because it was a concomitant of the focus on the formal structure of economic theory that was necessary in order to show that seemingly inconsistent theories were, in fact, compatible with each other, thereby revealing the terminological humbug with which economists sought to differentiate their theories. This attitude toward economic theory, which fits well with the attitude Samuelson was to adopt, explains why Schumpeter was such an enthusiast for mathematical economic theory. Economics was quantitative because certain aspects of economics, notably prices, were inherently numerical and hence mathematics was required for many problems, for it was the only language for dealing with more than the most primitive quantitative arguments.[40] This did not mean that economics *had* to be mathematical, for there was much that could be done without its help: mathematics was not needed to study "the history of business organization, the cultural aspects of economic life, economic motive, the philosophy of private property, and so on."[41] History and sociology were essential.

However, despite his enthusiasm for mathematics, his attitude toward it was far from simple. As Bergson noted, Schumpeter was not a proficient mathematician, which was why he had been replaced after two years by Leontief as the lecturer on Ec. 8a (Mathematical Economics).[42] However, Haberler claimed that Schumpeter acquired great mathematical knowledge and that he was an effective expositor even of material that mathematical economists found difficult.[43] He used little mathematics in his own work in which economic theory was combined with history and sociology. This has been attributed to his reluctance to simplify and to focus on those details that were important for the purpose in hand, an attitude consistent with the terms in which he criticized Keynes.[44]

Similar remarks could be made concerning his attitude toward empirical work. His first publications, in 1905, had been in statistics—on population measurement and index numbers.[45] *Business Cycles*, the book on which he was working for much of the 1930s, was packed with statistics. However, rather than trying to test a specific model, his use of statistics resembled what one reviewer, Simon Kuznets, called "an intellectual diary" in which theoretical ideas were discussed alongside historical facts.[46] Jan Tinbergen, who in the 1930s was constructing macroeconometric models for the League of Nations, explained Schumpeter's attitude in terms of the distinction, introduced by Ragnar Frisch, between the mechanism that generates cycles and the exogenous shocks that keep fluctuations going. "Schumpeter," he wrote, "shows a scarcely-hidden preference for the shocks to be the 'true' 'causes' and tends to belittle the importance of the mechanism."[47] For example, Schumpeter focused on the innovations that disturbed equilibrium rather than on the mechanics of how innovations diffused through the economy. In contrast, for the most economists who came after him, the mechanism, amenable to mathematical modeling, was more important than the shocks.

The complexity of Schumpeter's attitude toward mathematics—something about which he had thought carefully since his first publication on the subject in 1906—was explained in a letter he wrote to Wilson in May 1937, after auditing his course. The economist, he wrote, should not try to copy arguments from physics, but should "learn from physics how to build up an argument."[48,i] Schumpeter believed that there were methods and procedures that, while not pure mathematics, were sufficiently general that they were applicable to many fields and should be taught to all students. He suggested that part of what Wilson was teaching, presumably including its discussions of thermodynamics and economics, could be developed into such a course.

Samuelson remembered having been very much influenced by what he described as Schumpeter's "off-the-cuff general methodological remarks," such as that "You never in economics kill a theory by a fact; you kill a theory by a better theory."[49] However, Schumpeter's influence may have gone deeper, for he would have exposed Samuelson to an instrumentalist, practice-oriented view of science that was consistent with what he was to learn from Wilson, and that would be reinforced by the scientists he would meet when he entered the Society of Fellows. Of particular interest is what Schumpeter might have taught about how individual behavior should be analyzed. Haberler has claimed that Schumpeter had changed his views on the so-called psychological method, in that "in his theory classes at Harvard and in conversation he often argued on 'psychological grounds,' using introspection in favor of cardinal utility or, occasionally, even for the possibility of inter-individual comparison of utility."[50] However, this remark needs to be treated with caution, given Schumpeter's penchant for taking competing positions seriously and given that utility measurement was widely debated by his colleagues. It is important to note that echoes of the instrumentalist

---

i. These remarks by Schumpeter are discussed in relation to Wilson's views on mathematics in chapter 8 this volume.

position on utility theory found in Schumpeter's *Das Wesen* (1908) can also be found in his posthumous *History of Economic Analysis* (1954). What is perhaps most significant here is less his intense dislike of utilitarianism than that he made a very clear distinction between utilitarianism as a normative system, in which all human values were reduced to utility, and utilitarianism as a system of social science. Thus, he wrote that "it is logically possible to despise utilitarianism, root and branch, both as a philosophy of life and as a political program and yet to accept it, as an engine of analysis, in all or some of the departments of the social sciences."[51] Though expressed very differently, this was an expression of the clear separation of welfare analysis and consumer theory that Samuelson was making when he started publishing. Also, as noted previously, Schumpeter was an early exponent of the method of comparative statics.

Schumpeter and Samuelson

Samuelson got to know Schumpeter well. Schumpeter was nominated as his "sponsor," required to report regularly to the SSRC on his progress,[52] and he kept in regular touch until shortly before Schumpeter's death on January 8, 1950. One reason why "Schumpy," as they called him, was popular with the graduate students was that he made time for them. He spent the afternoons in a coffee shop near the library, where students knew they could talk to him, and he had immense patience even for the weaker students, especially if they had some interesting idea but lacked the skills to work it out. He was also quite willing for the bright students, including Samuelson, to correct his mathematics—something that, according to some of those present, was a frequent occurrence. His willingness to learn by going to Wilson's lectures cannot have gone unnoticed by the students, even though few of them attended these courses. He regularly entertained graduate students and visitors to Harvard, over lunch and dinner, conversations often continuing into the night. "As the undisputed star of the Economics Department, . . . an inveterate showman who needed an audience, . . . being Joseph Schumpeter was just as important to him as being a great economist."[53]

Schumpeter continued to take a close interest in the development of Samuelson's career. At the December 1938 meeting of the American Economic Association, he included Samuelson's paper, "A Restatement of the Theory of Cost and Production with Emphasis on Its Operational Aspects," in a session that he chaired, alongside papers by Irving Fisher—protégé of Willard Gibbs and arguably the biggest name in mathematical economics—and Jacob

Marschak, then a Rockefeller-funded fellow visiting the United States, but who was to become director of the Cowles Commission, the major U.S. center for econometric research. After the session, Samuelson had to prepare an abstract for publication in the March issue of the *American Economic Review*. Schumpeter told him, in a letter sent while Samuelson was visiting with Marion's family in Wisconsin, "Your abstract *was* too short and conveyed what you really had to say just as inadequately as did your oral presentation, which entirely failed to impress the audience as I hoped it would."[54,j] However, given that time was short, he proposed that Samuelson leave it unchanged, even though he thought it was inadequate. The material in this paper was to become an important part of his thesis. When Samuelson came to submit a thesis, it is no surprise that Schumpeter, along with Wilson, was one of his examiners. They remained in touch even when Samuelson's interests had developed in other directions. Schumpeter continued to read everything Samuelson wrote, writing at one point, "I like to have a complete collection of Samuelsonia" and describing him as "one of the ablest economists of our time."[55] Their relationship is indicated by a remark made in 1943 that is much more significant coming from a German speaker used to more formal forms of address, "Don't professor me any more—let's drop that!"[56]

When Schumpeter became president of the American Economic Association, he invited Samuelson to join him on the program committee and to produce something to mark the centenary of Pareto's birth.[57] Their last meeting was at this AEA conference, talking about many things in a hotel bar before they, along with Haberler, were persuaded to join a colleague for dinner in his apartment. When their host fell asleep, and Haberler had made his excuses, Samuelson and Schumpeter were left alone, talking about all sorts of things, until they too decided to make an exit.

Dismissing what he was writing as "psychoanalytical babble," Samuelson wrote about the inner melancholy that lay beneath Schumpeter's elegant and confident exterior. He discussed his personal tragedy—the disappearance of the pre-1914 Hapsburg Empire whose high society was so important to Schumpeter and in whose rich culture he had been educated—and the conflicts brought about by the United States later fighting on the same side as the Soviet Union that he disliked so intensely and whose rise he feared. Schumpeter founded no school. Not only was he opposed to schools in economics, he was too much the showman and solo artist to be a leader. His

j. The letter was typed, but Schumpeter had underlined *was* with a pen, as though it was a point he had made before and which Samuelson had resisted.

love of aphorisms, many of which implied a cynicism about life, also worked against his creating a group who would loyally develop his ideas. He adopted an attitude of detachment toward his own work, never discussing it in class and being too eclectic in his appreciation of different types of work to engage in sustained controversy.[58]

He nevertheless inspired students. Samuelson wrote of Schumpeter's circle at Harvard as including a list of graduate students who were to become eminent in the profession.[k] After the war, Schumpeter continued to inspire students. Samuelson wrote that from his "perch three miles down the Charles River, I recognized that an Elizabethan Golden Age coincided with the late Age of Schumpeter."[l] When praising his friends and colleagues, Samuelson invariably resorted to hyperbole, but there seems little doubt that Schumpeter was very important to him—a conclusion reinforced by the fact that, unlike his tributes to other teachers, Samuelson's stated intellectual debts to Schumpeter are so nonspecific.

When Schumpeter, increasingly unhappy at Harvard, was on the verge of moving to Yale, Samuelson appears to have been instrumental in organizing a petition among the Harvard graduate students urging him to stay.[59]

> Each one of us has been stimulated by the breadth and vision of your thought. As no one else, you have always shown intense interest in our problems regardless of the field; and we have always had reason to be extremely grateful for your willingness to give us your time and energy. Our research has been greatly aided by your helpful criticism and generous encouragement. You have implanted in us a belief in the importance of a more exact and objective economic science and a desire to contribute to its development. Above all, you have been more than a teacher to us we have always been proud to think of you as a true friend. We feel that our departure would be an irreplaceable loss to us and to future Harvard students.[60]

The letter had, of course, to be sufficiently general that twenty-six students, working in a variety of fields, could sign it, but it is tempting to see the

---

k. Abram Bergson, Alice Bourneuf, Wolfgang Stolper (not to be confused with his father, Gustav Stolper), Richard Musgrave, Tsuru, Triffin, Sidney Alexander, Joe Bain, John Lintner, Lloyd Metzler, and Robert Bishop—together with Marion Crawford [Samuelson] and David Rockefeller.

l. Samuelson 2011b. Robert Solow, who was a graduate student at Harvard in the late 1940s, was less enthusiastic about Schumpeter. Samuelson may have failed to recognize that by this time Schumpeter had changed and was no longer the charismatic figure he was in the 1930s.

remark about encouraging "a more exact and objective economic science" as being either something that Schumpeter emphasized in his dealings with students or something that Samuelson picked out as particularly important. The letter went on to express the fear that the fields of theory and business cycles would collapse were Schumpeter to leave.

Samuelson would certainly have taken advantage of Schumpeter's generosity with his time, and their conversations no doubt ranged widely. It is hard to believe that they did not end up discussing Schumpeter's ideas about science: in addition to Samuelson's taking Schumpeter's courses in Economic Theory and Business Cycles, they were both among the four people taking Wilson's courses. It is little exaggeration to say that they were both obsessed with the idea that economics should be a science. The "operationalism" on which Samuelson drew in his *Foundations* (1947a) was not the same as the "instrumentalism" of Mach and Poincaré on which Schumpeter's early methodological work was based, but there was a strong resemblance. The same could be said about Schumpeter's skepticism of the "psychological method" and Samuelson's revealed-preference theory. It is possible that Samuelson tried to read Schumpeter's first book, though given that his German was limited, it is more likely that such ideas simply came up in conversation. Samuelson later wrote that he was surprised when, at the very end of his life, Schumpeter said that if one was faced with a choice between economic history or "mathematical econometrics," one should opt for the former. His surprise at this remark may show that Samuelson had not consciously absorbed the many qualifications Schumpeter made to his support for the use of mathematics in economics, even if his later work was to show that he had, at least partially, internalized the message.[m]

m. The last remark is based on the content of Samuelson's textbook (see chapters 25 and 27 this volume).

CHAPTER 8 | Edwin Bidwell Wilson

Wilson and Mathematical Statistics

Paul Samuelson took great pride in describing himself as the intellectual grandson of the great American physicist Josiah Willard Gibbs, on the grounds that he was a student of Edwin Bidwell Wilson, Gibbs's last protégé.[1] Gibbs's other protégé had been the eminent mathematical economist Irving Fisher, whose PhD thesis had been submitted to Yale in 1891. Wilson (1879–1964) was Professor of Vital Statistics in Harvard's Institute of Public Health and also a member of the Economics Department, teaching statistics and mathematical economics in alternate years. He had been trained as a mathematician at Yale and at the *École normale supérieure* in Paris before joining MIT's Mathematics Department in 1907. Wilson had been close to Gibbs in the last years of his life, from 1899 to 1902, and as a graduate student he was responsible for writing up Gibbs's lectures on vector calculus, in circulation since 1881, for publication as *Vector Analysis* (1901). This settled the notation that American physicists used for operations on vectors, as well as expounding the theory and some of its physical applications. However, in complete contrast to Gibbs, Wilson was loquacious and with a sharp wit and sometimes caustic tongue, and had no qualms about challenging authority. His mathematical interests were broad, covering geometry, algebra, and various applied fields.[2] In 1902, while a student at the *École normale supérieure*, he criticized David Hilbert's attempt to set out new foundations for geometry in a paper provocatively titled "The So-called Foundations of Geometry" (1903), which questioned the way Hilbert used set theory and logic. As with his later criticisms of theorems in set theory, Wilson's ideas were complicated, out of tune with modern developments in mathematics, and did not always survive well. His early output included what was, for more than a decade after its publication, the only modern American advanced calculus textbook.[3] In 1917, he was appointed Professor of Mathematical Physics, becoming head of the Physics Department. From 1920 to 1922, he was one of three academics who took over the running of MIT after the death of its president, Richard Maclaurin. He moved to Harvard in 1922. Working in many fields, publishing in mathematics, physics, aeronautical engineering, statistical theory, public health, and economics, and acquiring a knowledge of many other fields, he was managing editor of the *Proceedings of the National Academy of Sciences* from 1915 to 1964—almost half a century. He was described by Wesleyan University on the occasion of receiving an honorary degree as "the modern Renaissance man, taking all knowledge for his province."[4] As the only intelligent man known to Samuelson who enjoyed committee meetings, he was active in Harvard's administration, the National Academy of Sciences, and the Social Science Research Council, as well as many other bodies; he had contacts throughout the academic world and government.[5] He was an important figure in American science.[6]

The First World War was important for Wilson's career. Just before the war he had taught the theory of aerodynamics at MIT, and in 1916 his analysis of an aircraft's behavior when it encountered gusts of wind was included in a National Advisory Committee for Aeronautics Report to Congress. This work led to the publication of *Aeronautics* (1920). Samuelson described him as "a pioneer in writing down the stability conditions for the new-fangled aeroplane."[7] During the war, Wilson also developed an interest in statistics and public health, and after his move to Harvard he turned to mathematical statistics. In 1927, he arrived at an idea of confidence intervals that was very similar to that developed by Jerzy Neymann and Karl Pearson in the early 1930s, and which became one of the foundations of statistical inference. However, because he chose to work in the no-man's-land between sciences rather than develop any one discipline, his profile among statisticians was lower than it might have been. This may have been one reason, along with Henry Schultz's connection with Columbia, why Samuelson's teachers in Chicago had claimed that he would learn mathematical statistics only by going to Columbia to study with Harold Hotelling.

Samuelson's first formal contact with Wilson was in the course Topics in Statistical Theory in the spring term of his first year, shortly before he was scheduled to take his "generals." As its title suggests, this was a theoretical course and it appears to have covered some mathematical economics. But, whatever the balance between mathematical economics and statistics in the classroom, Samuelson learned from Wilson outside the classroom as well. He wrote that, as one of the good students, he was able to talk to Wilson for an hour after each lecture, and that their conversations covered "any and every subject."[8] It is most likely in these after-class conversations that Wilson taught Samuelson about thermodynamics. This way, Samuelson would have picked up more of Wilson's attitudes toward economics and different types of research than could have been conveyed in the more formal setting of the classroom.

Though it was a course in statistics, Wilson appears to have covered consumer theory in a way that was pertinent to the paper Samuelson was to write later that year, and which was to become his first academic article, as well as to papers he was to write over the next few years. On July 14, 1936, Wilson wrote to his colleague John Black that he had "bored the class dreadfully going so slowly over the first 12 pages of the Introduction to Mathematical Economics."[9,a] The reason he proceeded so slowly through what was a textbook in mathematical economics was that it had become clear to him that "some of our high-powered mathematical economists did not know their fundamental definitions and would read right over a pair of statements which were contradictory and assume that both were right." It can be no coincidence that the previous year, Wilson had published an article in the *Quarterly Journal of Economics* criticizing Bowley, the book's author, for making a mathematical error:

> such phraseology as: "There are certain simplifications if we suppose that the marginal utility of money be unaffected by the sale or purchase of a good, in other words, that the individuals have so much money that the particular deal does not sensibly affect its marginal utility" . . . seems to be of doubtful validity because the change of the marginal utility of money nowhere enters into the proof of the theorems but only its rate of change—a change may be infinitesimal while a rate of change is finite.[10]

What Wilson had done in this short article was to take a theorem in which Pareto had shown there would be an inverse relationship between a good and its price if the utility of each good was independent of all other goods being consumed and show that the same result could be proved under more general

---

a. The book he referred to here is *Mathematical Groundwork of Economics* (1924) by the British statistician and economist Arthur Bowley.

assumptions: it did not matter whether or not the utilities of goods other than the one whose price was changed were dependent upon each other or not. Moreover, and this was the point where Wilson believed Bowley to have made a mistake, the result did not rely on constancy of the marginal utility of money.

Given that he discussed Bowley in such a detail and that his paper had just been published in the department's journal, it is hard to believe that he did not expose Samuelson and his fellow students to the problem of what was necessary to derive results in consumer theory, and that he would have made clear to them the value of using advanced mathematics in providing rigorous proofs.[b]

Wilson's course was attended intermittently by Schumpeter, whose interest was apparently to learn techniques he could use to analyze the mass of data he had assembled for his *Business Cycles,* on which he was then working. Schumpeter proved an irregular attender at the course, and eventually had to drop out. In April he wrote apologetically to Wilson,

> I wish to write a line in explanation of the fact, which I greatly regret, that I have dropped sitting in on your course to which you generously admitted me and which I greatly enjoyed. As a matter of fact, I need your instruction very badly to fill the most shocking lacunae in my statistical armor, but work on my manuscript, which it is of the greatest importance to me to finish before the end of June or at all events in the summer, has been so slow as to send me into something like a panic.[11]

It is no surprise that Wilson replied Schumpeter with no need to apologize, going on to explain that his lectures were, in his opinion, "not of very great advantage to a person who works with actual statistical material."[12] In justifying this view, Wilson explained that the "modern mathematical methods" with which he was dealing had so far not proved themselves to be of real practical importance. In saying this, he was expressing the view of someone with great experience in practical statistical analysis.

If the techniques he was teaching had not proved their worth, what was the case for teaching them? Wilson's answer was the negative one, that it

---

b. Samuelson took Wilson's mathematical economics course in 1937. However, by this
   time, his first paper on consumer theory, tackling some of the problems Wilson had
   discussed in his paper, was published, and the idea on which his second paper rested had
   already occurred to him.

protected young mathematicians from being over-impressed with mathematical statistics.

> I regard the course as valuable to the young mathematician and economist chiefly because of the protection it affords him in dealing with the contributions of mathematical statisticians. . . . People [mathematicians] who have an over-elaborate technique . . . make a very great impression on those who don't have it and may in fact publish remarkable theorems which persons acquainted with the facts in detail believe are of no particular importance if valid.[13]

He went on to explain that, given what was happening in economics, the course was particularly important for graduate students.

> Now there is such a trend toward mathematical economics and mathematical statistics that unless our students working for the doctorate get further into mathematical statistics than may ever be necessary for them in their personal statistical work they won't have any adequate protection from the increasing number of persons who are using what is probably an excess of mathematics and they won't even be able in an all-around way to discuss their contributions. The educational value of the course for young people ought to be considerable.

Its value was, therefore, largely negative. This was, however, a situation that might change if the techniques he covered were in future to prove their worth.

The depth of Wilson's commitment to this view is indicated by the fact that it was more or less a corollary of critical remarks he had published a decade earlier, when writing in *Science* on the topic of statistical inference. Many statisticians, he wrote, did not take responsibility for making sure that the formulas they were using were appropriate to the problems they were tackling and would give the right results. "They seem," he wrote, "for some reason to believe that a mathematical formula is eternally true. Their attitude is Shamanistic. They go through with magic propitiatory rites, idolatrous of mathematics, ignorant of what it can and can not do for them."[14] It was not simply young scholars and those with limited training who were guilty: "I am not quite sure," Wilson continued, "that the high priests of this pure and undefiled science do not somewhat aid and abet the idolatory."

Why was this? It was because statistics had not yet developed to the point where its foundations were as secure as those other branches of mathematics, because the premises were not yet understood. As a result it was impossible to prove when particular methods would and would not work: it was necessary to work this out case by case. This was consistent with Wilson's view, expressed to the Harvard agricultural economist John Black, that the way to train students to engage in practical work was to employ them in a project in which they would "work in detail on a lengthy piece of statistical analysis." As an example he cited a project on Industrial and Related Agricultural Fluctuations, on which the department was about to embark.[15] While some prior statistical training would be required, their main training would come through doing the research.

Wilson's course was one he had designed himself, drawing on his own ideas and materials scattered throughout the literature. If he was covering his own work, then it would have included inference and confidence intervals. Wilson covered characteristic functions, a way of representing probability distributions that makes it easier to undertake certain types of analysis.[16] Though the course may have changed by then, correspondence with Lloyd Metzler indicates that two years later Wilson spent a lot of time on the problem of smoothing data.[17] The course was a rigorous introduction to important topics in mathematical statistics, but it was not a standard course. As Wilson explained to Schumpeter later in the summer, "The material is concentrated all over the literature and what I do is to get it together and discuss it with the class. It is almost impossible to give any decent assigned reading. I find it hard enough to dig the stuff out of the memoirs [journals] myself."[18]

This lack of a close fit with what they were studying elsewhere caused a problem for Harvard students, whose attendance was often irregular owing to the way the examination system was structured, for students were concerned more with passing their generals than with tackling courses like Wilson's. Samuelson, though he got an A-, was one of those students who failed to benefit from the course as much as Wilson thought he should have done. "The difficulty with him [Samuelson]," Wilson wrote, "was that he was so concerned about his 'generals' that he could not concentrate on the course as well as a man like Levine."[19] In addition, because other students were concentrating in mathematics, Samuelson did not get the top grade in the course.[20] He had, however, impressed Wilson enormously. Samuelson was "the most original and inquisitive of all the students";[21] he did not perform any better than the other students, but in Wilson's view, "he had the potentialities to be as good as anybody in the class."[22]

Mathematical Economics

A year later, in the spring of 1937, Samuelson audited Mathematical Economics, the other course Wilson taught for the Economics Department.

Schumpeter also attended this course and appears to have had more success in attending than the previous year, for at the end of it he wrote to Wilson to express his gratitude both for what he had learned from it and for the support Wilson had given "to a line of advance which at Harvard still has to fight for its existence."[23] His letter made it clear that Wilson had not been teaching the course in a conventional way. The approach Wilson was taking was, he claimed, "indispensable if economics and economic policy is ever to emerge from the stage of phraseology on the one hand, and of pedestrian fact-eliciting on the other." Schumpeter then went on to explain his view of the mathematics that young economists needed to learn, in a way that strongly implies he was echoing views Wilson had expressed in his course, for he urged Wilson to expand the first part of the course into its main content.

Schumpeter believed that it was important for economists to learn from physics how to build up an exact argument. This would involve the use of concepts that were intermediate between pure and applied mathematics: they were neither pure mathematics (dealing with abstract concepts) nor applied mathematics (relating to specific problems).

> [W]e can learn [from physics] to understand the relation of mathe-
> matics to the reality to which it is applied. Most important of all is the
> consideration that there are obviously a set of concepts and procedures
> which, although belonging not to the field of pure mathematics but to
> the field of more or less applied mathematics, are of so general a char-
> acter as to be applicable to an indefinite number of different fields.[24]

Given Wilson's belief that concepts such as friction and inertia had to be defined in relation to economics before mechanical and physical analogies could be used, this may have been the result of Wilson, in his lectures, criti-cizing what he saw as Schumpeter's overemphasis on theory.[25] When faced with difficult factual problems, it was important to learn to pay close atten-tion to how existing mathematical tools could be applied, and to develop new ones, rather than simply copying techniques from one discipline to another. This is entirely consistent with Samuelson's view of what he learned from Wilson about the relation between economics and physics: that there were similarities between the structures of economic problems and certain problems in physics. He could thus make use of these similarities to solve economic problems without implying that there was any deeper relation between the physical and the economic concepts.

The main example of this was the Le Chatelier Principle, the idea for which he attributed specifically to Wilson's lectures: "In particular,

I was struck by his statement that the fact that an increase in pressure is accompanied by a decrease in volume is not so much a theorem about a thermodynamic equilibrium system as it is a mathematical theorem about surfaces that are concave from below or about negative definite quadratic forms. Armed with this clue, I set out to make sense of the Le Chatelier principle."[26] He was to make the Le Chatelier Principle central to *Foundations* (1947a).[c] It should be noted that though accounts of it are often couched in terms of differential calculus, the principle is much more general and applies, as Samuelson argued, equally to systems in which discrete choices mean there is no smooth substitution between variables.

During the course Wilson asked Samuelson to present two lectures, afterward telling him that he had done "a beautiful job both with respect to the selection of his material which was mostly his own and with respect to the presentation of it."[27] Notes taken by Lloyd Metzler give an idea of how Wilson may have approached some of the material, but because they date from 1938 or 1939, care has to be taken not to attribute to Wilson material that he had learned from Samuelson in the intervening years.[28] The notes began with a discussion of consumer theory, assuming continuous, differentiable functions before proceeding in the next class to the discontinuous case. Here it is notable that an equation very similar to one that Samuelson was to use to sum up all that was known about consumer theory was described as the "J. Willard Gibbs condition."[d]

A week later, Wilson brought in thermodynamics, describing it as "a problem of constrained equil. since the system must always be *closed*—is similar to econ. in this respect."[29] Wilson then wrote down the maximization problems for thermodynamics and the consumer to show that, though there were similarities, they were not exactly the same. He even claimed that had Pareto been familiar with "the notion of *physical* equilibrium which was then prevalent in scientific work," he would have worked out equilibrium conditions using finite differences rather than with derivatives, for it was more general.[30] The notes went on to discuss integrability (deriving a utility function from demand functions) and the notion of a utility index.

---

c. See chapter 22 this volume.

d. Wilson's equation is $\Delta\xi\Delta x > 0$, where ξ denotes marginal utility and x quantity (it is possible that Metzler transcribed the inequality sign incorrectly). The equation to which Samuelson attached importance was $\Delta p\Delta x < 0$, where p is price.

Wilson's Attitude Toward Mathematics and Science

The skepticism that Wilson expressed about the practical value of mathematical statistics was firmly held and extended to mathematical economics. In July he wrote to Black, inquiring as to whether Black had read an article, just published in *The Atlantic*, by the writer and humorist Stephen Leacock (1936). Though widely known as a humorist, Leacock was also a social scientist; he had been trained at Chicago under Thorstein Veblen's supervision, where he obtained a PhD in political science that was the prelude to a long career as a political scientist and economist at McGill University in Montreal. Though his reputation among economists was not high, he was known to outsiders as an economist, and it was with that authority that he offered, in the article Wilson recommended to Black, what was clearly intended as a devastating criticism of mathematical economics.

Leacock's article, "Through a Glass, Darkly," was prompted by his reading of *The Economics of Stationary States* by A. C. Pigou, professor of economics at Cambridge, though Leacock dared identify neither him nor his university, for fear that he should be "crushed flat at once under the dead weight of prestige and authority" were he to do so.[31] He quoted a paragraph in which Pigou discussed the problem of comparing real incomes received by people who purchased different goods and therefore faced different sets of prices. It would now be considered a classic index number problem, though admittedly the language was somewhat labored. Leacock, however, did not merely point out that Pigou's writing was not as clear as one would wish; he also sought to use the paragraph as the basis for a savage assault on mathematical economics.

> As the last echo of the paragraph dies away, the readers are seen to lie as thickly mown down as the casualties of Vendémiaire. The volley has done its work. There will be no further resistance to the argument on the part of the general public. Theirs not to reason why, theirs but to do and die. They will learn to surrender their economic thought to the dictation of the élite. They are not to question where they do not understand.[32]

Convoluted technical language is being used for no purpose other than to assert the authority of the academic economist, for nothing is being said that could not be said more plainly. He continued,

> For the whole of the "plan" [Pigou's analysis] and its pretentious mathematics, when interpreted into plain talk, amounts to something so insignificant and so self-evident that it is within reach of the

simplest peasant who ever lived in Bœotia, or failed at Cambridge. It only means that different people with the same money would buy different things; one might buy roses, one cigars, and another concert tickets; and you couldn't very well compare them because the weight wouldn't mean anything, and the color wouldn't, nor the number.

Such mathematics, Leacock claimed, failed to aid thought and served no end other than "to turn economics into an esoteric science."

The mathematician is beckoning economics toward the seclusion of the dusty chamber of death, in the pyramid of scholasticism [in the darkness of which] lie mummified bodies of the learnings that were, that perished one by one in the dead mephitic air of scholasticism; of learning that had turned to formalism and lost its meaning, to body and lost its soul, to formula and lost its living force. Here lie, centuries old, the Scholarship of China, the Learning of Heliopolis, the Medicine that the Middle Ages killed, and the Reason that fell asleep as Formal Logic.

Leacock's argument has been explained at length because without this it is impossible to appreciate the significance of Wilson's observation in his letter to Black: that he had always had a great deal of sympathy with Leacock's point of view that mathematics should not be used in applied fields without good evidence that it advances our knowledge. Wilson was endorsing an article that, he accepted, would "make some of our mathematical economists pretty mad." The danger, he wrote, was that "[mathematics'] very elegance and precision would give us an entirely false opinion of the value of whatever conclusions we came to."[33,e]

Wilson then went on to explain why mathematics could be useful: conducting arguments in terms of symbolic logic made it much easier to check for redundant or inconsistent assumptions, something that was easy to introduce if one wrote in a "free literary style." However, he immediately qualified this by stating that it did not justify the "elaborate mathematical theories which some people are giving." It was fine to use such theories if one is doing no more than testing working hypotheses or clarifying ideas. However, he observed that they were then addressing only their colleagues and not the "general body of students." To use such methods was to do what Einstein was doing when "he put out his theory of generalized relativity with the statement that he did not suppose that there would be more than a dozen or

e. This was the occasion for the other remarks made to Black quoted earlier.

sixteen persons in the world who could fully understand them": ideas were being put forward to be criticized and tested, not to be used in applied work. To Metzler, he explained, after noting that he did not know how useful mathematical economics was likely to be to economists, it would provide them with "some protection against those mathematical economists who appear to prove something important when as a matter of fact they have not done so."[34] He thought statistics much more important.

This was a vision of the role of mathematics in economics that was in part Marshallian. Mathematics had an important role within the circle of specialists capable of reading it critically, but such economists were not the entire profession. Outside the narrow circle of economists who were sufficiently well trained in mathematics to read it critically, though Wilson wanted more mathematics to be used, he wanted that mathematics to be kept simple. Until they had acquired the necessary skills to use it properly, economists should not be exposed to elaborate mathematics, for it would be misunderstood and would carry unjustified authority, just as Leacock had pointed out. Unlike Marshall, who suggested burning the mathematics after results had been translated into English, Wilson favored the wider use of mathematics, but wanted the results of elaborate mathematics to be terms that would be interpreted correctly.

Wilson's attitude toward the scientific method was explored in correspondence with Wesley Mitchell, founder of the NBER and author of two major studies of the business cycle. In 1938, he told Mitchell that it was fortunate that he (Mitchell) was the only social scientist with any chance of being elected president of the American Academy of Arts and Sciences, because he had long operated "in a scientific manner both on the analytic and synthetic side." He likened Mitchell's approach to that of a naturalist classifying species:

> A naturalist doesn't recognize a bird or insect by a system of statistics. He does it by a process of diagnosis much like the way the physician recognises a disease. There are certain birds or insects which are so clearly differentiated from others that some one criteria will tell you what you want to know as far as classification is concerned ... but by and large the different species grade into each other just as different diseases do in such a way that it is by the consideration of a large number of non-compelling small bits of evidence that we come to a sound judgment as to how to classify.[35]

The social sciences were a complex field, and effort had to be put into its morphology. He then remarked on the methods required in the social sciences:

It isn't my idea that the methodology of the social sciences is any different from the methodology of the natural sciences. We need all the methodology of every kind that we can use whether in the social sciences or in the natural sciences. There may be special problems in the social sciences where the methodologies of physics are valuable but there certainly are many others where the methodologies of the systemic zoologist or the medical man have to be resorted to.

Wilson must have written to Mitchell again in a similar vein, for in October 1938, Mitchell wrote that his recent letter had given him "much spiritual comfort," for he agreed that economics needed a lot of taxonomic work.[36] The problem with economics was that "our taxonomists have spun their classifications so largely out of their head and have made so little use of their eyes." Their taxonomy was more like the classifications of geometry than botany, zoology, or paleontology.

Wilson was enthusiastic about Mitchell's work. Referring to an article Mitchell and Arthur Burns had written on business cycle indicators, he wrote that he considered it "very good as is the case in my judgment with all your work." After explaining that Harvard was blessed with an abundance of economic theorists, theory pervaded "nearly everything from the first course in economics on to the most advanced courses Schumpeter and Leontief give."[37] However, he considered this emphasis on theory a cause for concern.

I have no doubt that theory is important but if anything was discovered in the teaching of physics in the 19th century it was that one shouldn't teach students theory without giving them at the same time the means of getting personally familiar with the physical phenomena through experiment and further that theory unless based on a keen appreciation of physical realities was merely an exercise in pure mathematics which might even come to the point not only of getting no worthwhile results but of preventing people from thinking intensively about physical phenomena.

The problem was not with pure theory per se, but with the fact that theorists often failed to present evidence for their theories.[38] Thus, he wished Harvard had been able to recruit Mitchell.

Wilson was less complimentary toward Keynes, with whose work he had some familiarity. He had reviewed the *Treatise on Probability*, in which Keynes sought to provide an axiomatic foundation for probability theory.[39] Wilson's view was that Keynes had proposed axioms that were better than those suggested by anyone else, but further work was still needed, for they were not ideal.[40] In contrast, Wilson found *A Treatise on Money* incomprehensible because it was not based on any consistent set of assumptions.[41] By February 1937, a year after Keynes's *General Theory* had been published, Wilson had still not read it, but he did not expect to agree with it. He wrote to Alvin Hansen, then at Minnesota but shortly to arrive in Harvard, that he had read and enjoyed footnote 3 of his review in the *Journal of Political Economy*.[42] In this footnote, Hansen had quoted Keynes's description of a book by J. A. Hobson as "made much worse than a really stupid book could be, by exactly those characteristics of cleverness and intermittent reasonableness which have borne good fruit in the past," opining that the same could be said of the *General Theory*.[43] Keynes was, Wilson believed, someone whose own views were better than his statements about other people and other peoples' theories, an observation that prompted Wilson to reflect on a general problem with the social sciences: that social scientists needed to stop trying to be brilliant and sounding like natural scientists, and instead try to work out what was agreed by everyone.

> What we very badly need is an encyclopedia of the social sciences constructed like an encyclopedia of medicine or of physics to tell us chiefly what we do know in the sense that everybody agrees to it, that it has been amply demonstrated under the stated conditions. . . . I would like to know what is known. It mightn't be very much but if we had some propositions we could quote as we do the propositions of Euclid by reference to the standard compendium we save a lot of trouble in the long run.[44]

The social sciences contained too much speculation about what might be known in the future, something Keynes was prone to do, and too little agreement on established facts.[45]

One of the problems with Keynes, Wilson wrote to his former Harvard colleague and public finance specialist Charles Bullock, two years later, was that he believed "that he ha[d] a mathematical proof that spending and overspending are marvelous things for government to do," a proposition that ran counter to "the experience of the race."[46] Wilson immediately reiterated his point about the importance of experience, expressing the view that "experience would seem to be what counted rather than theory." In the case of public spending, experience led him to believe that, though things might be different for young nations, it could not be good for old nations to spend more than their income, "no matter what a brilliant economist may prove with the aid of assumptions that perhaps cannot be verified and by a long mathematical deduction which gets a fair distance away from the facts . . .

even if one starts with facts." Though in no way denigrating formal statistical inference, Wilson's talk of "experience" suggests a much broader, more elastic notion, possibly allowing what might be called "folk wisdom," as evidence alongside any propositions that could be proved formally. He seems to have shared Marshall's suspicion of long chains of reasoning, at least in cases where the assumptions were not based on firmly established facts.[f] This perspective enabled Wilson to be convinced that Keynes must be wrong, despite admitting that he had still not read the *General Theory* with care.

Samuelson and Wilson

However, for all that Schumpeter mattered to Samuelson, it is Wilson whose attitudes pervade Samuelson's work. His debt to Wilson cannot be overestimated. It was at Chicago that he had realized the importance of mathematics to economics; Schumpeter encouraged him to enter the Promised Land of mathematical economics, offering him continued guidance and advice, and Leontief had provided Samuelson with his first training in mathematical economics. But it was Wilson who, more than anyone else, set him on the path toward his PhD thesis and *Foundations of Economic Analysis* (1947a). Wilson taught him how to be rigorous in his mathematical analysis in a way that Schumpeter, or even Leontief, could never do and, equally important, shaped his conception of economic theory. Though there will have been an element of politeness involved, there is no reason to doubt what he wrote to Wilson on the occasion of his move to MIT:

> I have benefitted from your suggestions, perhaps more than from anyone else in recent years, and even chance remarks which you have let fall concerning Gibbs's thermodynamical systems have profoundly altered my views in corresponding fields of economics.[47]

Wilson's remarks concerning thermodynamics encouraged Samuelson to study the subject more deeply. Wilson also made it clear that the value of turning to physics was in learning to understand mathematical structures common to both disciplines, a view that would have been reinforced by reading works such as Bridgman's *The Nature of Physical Theory* (1936), published while Samuelson was attending Wilson's classes. Samuelson also learned from Wilson the importance of basing economic theory on a clear set of postulates

---

f. Ironically, Keynes held a similar view. See Hoover 2006.

and of analyzing the general case where functions were not necessarily smooth and differentiable. Wilson pushed Samuelson to analyze finite changes and, as Gibbs had done, to base conclusions on inequalities linked to generalized notions of convexity.[48] He thus pushed Samuelson away from relying too extensively on methods based on calculus. It also appears to have been Wilson who directed Samuelson to the types of mathematics he was to use extensively, recommending a textbook on numerical methods, *The Calculus of Observations* by Whittaker and Robinson (1926). This book covered many of the techniques on which Samuelson was later to work: interpolation, difference equations, determinants, linear equations, and statistical theory (linear regression and correlation analysis), with an emphasis on methods for obtaining numerical solutions.[49]

However, though Wilson pushed Samuelson to go beyond the calculus-based methods that had generally been associated with mathematical economics since the late nineteenth century, he remained an applied mathematician whose conception of mathematics had been formed by the turn of the century.[50] He sought precise arguments. He did not expose Samuelson to twentieth-century mathematics—to the methods that John von Neumann and other mathematicians were to apply to economic problems. He rejected the topology and existence proofs to which economists with a different mathematical training were to turn. Samuelson, too, was to find little use for topological methods, relying primarily on techniques for analyzing difference and differential equations and matrix methods for the analysis of systems of equations. Samuelson appears also to have picked up something of Wilson's skepticism of elaborate empirical methods. Like his mentor, he appreciated the data-intensive methods of economists such as Mitchell, in which as much importance was attached to the sources of the data as to the use of rigorous theory—this over the formal statistical modeling that was, from the 1940s, to become increasingly common in economics. However, this side of Samuelson's work was not to develop until after he had left Harvard.[g]

---

g. This will be discussed in part III of this volume.

CHAPTER 9 | Making Connections

"Generals" and Summer School in Madison

Samuelson's first year at Harvard was completed with his "generals."[a] If Wilson is to be believed, Samuelson, contrary to his claims about his boundless self-confidence, was anxious about this.[b] Part of the reason for his anxiety was probably that the content of the examination was a lottery, for it was an oral examination and the questions the candidate was asked depended on the examiners present. If one got Chamberlin, for example, there was only one topic that could come up—monopolistic competition—whereas if one had Monroe, the questions might never get past Adam Smith. In any event, the examination on May 18, 1936, went well, his examiners apparently being Schumpeter, Leontief, and Seymour Harris. At the end, Schumpeter, who had a strong sense of humor, is said to have turned to Leontief to ask, "Did we pass?"[c]

---

a. Harvard also had language requirements. He passed a reading examination in French on November 5, 1935, and on February 25, 1936, the university ruled that a reading test passed in Chicago satisfied the German requirements. M. L. Ballard, March 4, 1936, Letter to Miss Campbell, HUESR (PAS student folder).

b. See chapter 8 this volume.

c. This remark has been widely quoted, though it is often claimed that it was made at Samuelson's defense of his thesis in 1941. However, Leontief was not involved in that event. Moreover, it makes more sense in the context of his generals, when Samuelson was still only twenty-one and a year into his graduate study. The remark is consistent

Samuelson's ability to pass his generals a year earlier than usual was in part the result of his having a strong undergraduate education in economics. This meant that he could read widely in the Widener Library, where he acquired a desk in the stacks, and take his mathematics further. He wrote that "instead of spending hours trying to understand the Harvard lectures, I was free to attend optional mathematics courses on differential equations, numerical analyses, applied rational mechanics and classical thermodynamics."[1] On another occasion he wrote that he attended courses in "real variables, differential equations, Fourier analysis, and calculus of variations," again without specifying who taught him.[2,d] He referred to the usefulness of the calculus of variations, "taught by Bliss and Graves at Chicago and George Birkhoff and Hestenes at Harvard."[3] It is natural to deduce that he attended the course on the calculus of variations (Math 15) that Magnus Rudolph Hestenes, a young instructor who had recently obtained a PhD at Chicago, and who jointly authored an article on the subject with Birkhoff, taught in the second half of his first year.[e] Wilson will have known about the work of Birkhoff and Hastenes on this subject, because they had had an article published in the *Proceedings of the National Academy of Science*, which he edited, and which Samuelson later cited. Wilson could easily have suggested this course to him.[4]

Working out which other mathematics courses he took is more speculative because, when asked about his mathematical training, Samuelson liked to emphasize the extent to which he was self-taught. He could easily have attended Birkhoff's course on differential equations in the fall of 1936, and the course he took on thermodynamics was probably the one offered by Percy Bridgman (Physics 41a), also in the fall of 1936.[f] No one at Harvard taught a course on Fourier analysis while Samuelson was there, but there was a course

---

with what is known about Schumpeter's sense of humor. Robert Solow, who knew all the people involved, is among those who is convinced that the remark was genuinely made.

d. The non-mathematician should note simply that these are advanced mathematical techniques, familiar to many engineers but with which very few economists of the time would have been familiar.

e. Attending this would have provided justification for substituting Wilson's statistics course for the second half of Crum and Frickey's, for it was taught at precisely the same hours as the latter.

f. This course was offered only in alternate years, so it would not have been available in 1937. The only other course on thermodynamics was Heat and Elementary Thermodynamics, intended for undergraduates; but given Samuelson's self-confidence, his rapidly growing mathematical skills, and that Wilson had introduced him to the subject the previous spring, he would have opted for Bridgman's more advanced course.

in the subject offered at MIT, again in the fall of 1936. If he did attend this, it may have been one of his earliest contacts both with the institution he later made his own and with the mathematician behind much work in cybernetics, Norbert Wiener, who taught the course.[g]

There is, however, one part of Samuelson's mathematical education after Chicago that has been recorded. In 1936, after taking his generals, he spent part of the summer attending courses at the University of Wisconsin–Madison.

> [Marion's] plan was to go once again to the Wisconsin summer school in Madison. I then realized that my math needs required that I master Fourier analysis in Madison. I roomed in a fraternity house. She roomed in a nearby sorority house. Times were different then. (Example: It never entered my head that a male could go above the first floor in Whitman House, Marion's Radcliffe dorm on Walker Street. Autos, park benches, and dark movie houses had to suffice.)[5]

He neglected the additional factor—namely, that there would have been a matron or house mistress experienced in stopping men from reaching parts of the building they were not allowed to enter. Samuelson took courses in German, the theory of equations, and the theory of analytic functions (not Fourier analysis). The German course, also attended by Marion, was a "rapid reading course" in nineteenth- and twentieth-century literature, taught intensively, at 7:30 every morning from Monday to Friday. Taking this course after he had been exempted from the requirement to take an examination in German implies that it was a language he intended to use. Marion attended the German class with Paul, though each day, when they had finished doing German, Marion moved to a course in money and banking, while Paul turned to the Theory of Equations, taught by Margarete Wolf, one of the few American women to obtain a PhD in mathematics at this time.[h] The course description explained that it covered "systems of linear equations and determinants with applications." Margarete and her sister, Louise, had both obtained their doctorates at Wisconsin in 1935, with theses involving matrix algebra.[i] A paper written jointly with her sister and

---

g. Samuelson (1997c) reports having known Wiener since 1937 and of hearing him give lectures, but did not provide any more detail. In *Foundations* (1947a, p. 342), he mentions Wiener in the context of Fourier analysis.

h. Green and LaDuke 2009 managed to identify 228 women with PhDs in mathematics before 1940.

i. Margarete's results were published as "Symmetric Functions of Non-Commutative Elements" (Wolf 1936).

presented to the American Mathematical Society two years later dealt with the problem of deriving necessary and sufficient conditions for the existence of solutions to linear matrix equations and determining the number of solutions.[6] Though the course she taught may not have covered these topics, she was certainly working on problems that Samuelson would, had they got into them, have considered relevant to economics, given his exposure to Leontief the previous term.

After an hour with Wolf, Samuelson turned to the Theory of Functions of Complex Variables with Herman W. March. March, like Wilson, was an applied mathematician. He had worked as an assistant in astronomy, and for a year as an instructor in physics at Princeton, before taking a PhD in Munich in 1911. His research covered the flow of liquids and the deflection of plates under stress—both problems important in aeronautical engineering, one of the subjects on which Wilson had published. Significantly, this involved using experimental data to obtain numerical solutions for differential equations, illustrating—so the university's memorial notice argued—the unifying power of mathematics. When he entered his second year at Harvard, Samuelson had significantly increased his knowledge of mathematics.

Measuring Utility

It was during Samuelson's second year at Harvard that he made the transition from writing papers solely for his teachers to writing for publication: in February 1937, he had an article published in the British journal *The Review of Economic Studies* and in May, another in Harvard's *Quarterly Journal of Economics*. However, though he had passed his generals, he was still taking courses when he wrote these articles. Two courses he took that year, International Trade with Haberler, and Business Cycles and Economic Forecasting, which comprised lectures by Schumpeter in the first term and a seminar run jointly by Schumpeter and Haberler in the second term, introduced him to fields that were eventually to be transformed by his work. Public Finance with Burbank, which he described as a course *against* public finance rather than on it, and Recent Economic History, where *recent* meant since 1450, taught by Usher, were presumably taken solely to meet his course requirements.[j]

---

j. On his arrival at Harvard he had, he claimed, argued his way out of taking Gay's course in the subject; this was probably to meet a requirement to take economic history at some point.

The first of the two articles Samuelson wrote was "A Note on the Measurement of Utility."[7] He probably wrote this during the summer, after his generals and after attending summer school in Madison, making final revisions in the fall of 1936. It was well known that it is not generally possible to derive a unique measure of utility.[k] In this paper, Samuelson showed that if one considered an individual deciding how to spend money over time, and if one made some seemingly natural assumptions about behavior, it was possible to derive a unique measure of utility. He simplified the problem by considering an individual who starts with a given amount of money. The individual thus has to choose how much money to spend at each moment in time. Samuelson assumed that utility at any moment depends on consumption at that moment, and that future utility is discounted with a constant discount rate, reflecting the assumption that future consumption is less valuable than present consumption. Samuelson showed that, given this set of assumptions, if we know the time path of consumption chosen by the individual, it is possible to calculate what the utility function must be.[l]

However, though Samuelson showed that utility could be measured, he went on to point out that this measure of utility was subject to "serious limitations" that "almost certainly vitiate it even from a theoretical point of view."[8] His result rests on very special assumptions about utility—namely, that utility at any moment depends on consumption at that moment, and not on the whole time path of consumption. This was the "independence assumption" for which Wilson had criticized Pareto: it was completely arbitrary. Samuelson claimed that it would be more general to assume that utility depended on the time path of consumption throughout the individual's life, but such an assumption was not specific enough to lead anywhere useful: there were no a priori grounds for saying anything about how utility related to the time path of consumption, and given that it relied on more advanced mathematics, it was hardly a convenient simplification of the standard theory.[9]

Samuelson's mathematical analysis stopped abruptly at this point, and he adduced evidence that people do not behave in this way. As time passes,

---

k. If an individual maximizes some utility function (call it $U(x)$, where x is whatever affects the individual's well-being), then the functions $2U(x)$, $3U(x)$, etc. will also be maximized. More generally, any monotonic transformation of $U(.)$ will be consistent with exactly the same choices.

l. Subject to a constant of integration. The key feature of this problem is that the utility function is additively separable—the assumption that had concerned Wilson in his article on consumer theory.

people typically change their spending decisions, and recognizing that they may be tempted to spend rashly, they do things like set up irrevocable trusts and commit themselves to saving through life-insurance schemes. He claimed that the time path of consumption would depend on "socially determined" parameters: desire for prestige, life expectancy, the "life cycle of individual economic activity," and the institutional structure of industry and finance. His conclusion was that the entire analysis was inappropriate:

> Even to generalise concerning these can only be done in terms of a theory of "history" (in itself almost a contradiction in terms). In any case, this would seem to lie in the region which Marshall termed Economic Biology, where the powerful tools of mathematical abstraction will little serve our turn, and direct study of such institutional data would seem in order.[10]

This reference to "economic biology" is one that Schumpeter and Wilson would both have approved. However, this did not deter Samuelson from concluding that his mathematical analysis was useful and that utility *could* be measured. What he had shown is that utility measurement requires "Pareto's Postulate Two"—namely, that the individual can compare differences in utility—a corollary of his assumption that total utility was obtained by adding up utilities obtained at different points in time. This was precisely the issue that had concerned Wilson two years earlier, though he had tackled it in the context of demand for different commodities at a particular point in time.[11]

In the last paragraph of the article, Samuelson explained that the utility he was measuring did not measure the individual's welfare.

> In conclusion, any connection between utility as discussed here and any welfare concept is disavowed. The idea that the results of such a statistical investigation could have any influence upon ethical judgments of policy is one which deserves the impatience of modern economists.[12]

Given that he had not previously mentioned the problem of welfare, this short paragraph appears almost as an afterthought; perhaps it was added at the last minute when he realized that his paper might cause a misunderstanding without it, and it was too late to modify the main text. Despite the brevity with which it is expressed here, this point was one to which Samuelson attached great importance, for it was central to the approach to welfare economics he was to propose in *Foundations* (1947a) and to which he held throughout his career.

Gottfried Haberler

Gottfried Haberler was a key figure in some of the connections Samuelson was to make between different branches of economic theory. He had just arrived from Vienna, where he had taught since 1928. "When I first knew him," Samuelson wrote, "I was turning just old enough to vote [21] and he was 36 years of age. I can see his tall figure walking across the Harvard Yard, briefcase in hand: his broad forehead marked him as a professor and, except on the tennis court, he did not seem young to me. But then time stood still: I grew older; new generations of students strode the Harvard Yard; but Gottfried Haberler changed not at all."[13] Born in 1900, into what Samuelson called "the *grande bourgeoisie* of the Hapsburg Dual Empire meritocracy," to parents who came from professional families, Haberler had studied at the University of Vienna under Wieser and Mises, submitting his habilitation thesis in 1925.[m] This thesis, written to obtain his academic position, had been published as *Der Sinn der Inxexzahlen* [*The Meaning of Index Numbers*] (1927), a widely discussed topic in the early 1930s. He became a major figure in the fields of international trade and the business cycle. In 1931–32 he had been a visiting lecturer at Harvard, and during the year participated in a symposium at the University of Chicago sponsored by the Harris Foundation, with a lecture on "Money and the Business Cycle" (1932). The following year saw the publication of a book on international trade, the English edition of which came out in 1936, just at the time Samuelson was taking his course.[14] Before coming to Harvard, Haberler had worked at the League of Nations, drafting the first edition of *Prosperity and Depression* (1937b), a survey of business cycle theory.

Samuelson praised Haberler for being consistent and yet eclectic, cautious and yet open to new ideas. Comparing him with two other Austrian economists, he noted that he was more thoughtful than Ludwig von Mises, who "exploded rather than ruminated," or Schumpeter, who "sparkled," throwing out ideas and criticisms.[15] He was also catholic in his friendships, knowing all his fellow Austrian émigrés, supporting scholars who were unpopular because of their conservative views. Samuelson recalled that if Arthur Burns (Wesley Mitchell's one-time co-author) was "belittled in catty Cambridge conversations," Haberler would stand up for him.[16] Consistent with this eclecticism and with his Viennese background, Haberler kept up

---

m. His description of the Austro-Hungarian Empire as the "Dual Empire" is not strictly correct, as it was an empire and a kingdom.

with developments in logical positivism, relating these to the earlier methodological positions taken by Mises and Lionel Robbins, and he followed the methodological writings of Felix Kaufmann, Terence Hutchison, Percy Bridgman, and Arthur Eddington. Samuelson thus considered Haberler well informed on the latest developments in the philosophy of science.

The content of the course—very significant, as Samuelson was soon to write the first of his highly influential articles on the theory of international trade—can be inferred from two sources: Haberler's recently published *International Trade* (1936) and notes that Lloyd Metzler took on Haberler's course in the fall of 1938.[17,n] In his book, Haberler began by explaining why there was any need to consider international trade differently from any other market activity. His answer was that factors of production—land and labor—did not move freely from one country to another. There were physical barriers to the movement of labor, such as the costs of transport, but the barriers to capital flows were different: the political and legal uncertainties associated with investment in countries with different legal, political, and monetary systems. However, though the difference between domestic and international trade might be substantial, that difference was a matter of degree. It might be common to describe international trade as if countries were trading with each other, but purchases and sales of goods were undertaken by individuals, implying that, like domestic trade, it was influenced by consumers' preferences and companies' costs.[18] Thus Haberler observed that there was a need to apply the theory of imperfect competition and business cycle theory to problems of international trade.[19]

Like the book, Haberler's course started not, as was traditional, with the pure theory of trade, but with balance of payments and monetary problems, covering the workings of the gold standard and variable exchange rate systems, as well as the transfer problem: the mechanism whereby a transfer of money from one country to another (such as the reparations Germany had been required to pay to Allied governments after 1919) was translated into a transfer of goods. It was only halfway through the course that Haberler turned to the pure theory of trade, advising students to read recent articles by Leontief and Abba Lerner, a young economist from the London School of Economics (LSE), as well as the classic texts by Alfred Marshall.[20] "Pure theory," Metzler noted, "is concerned with welfare aspects of international

---

n. The structure of the latter corresponds closely to that of the book, suggesting that Haberler did significantly change his views on how the subject should be presented. The 1938 lectures cite some new material, notably Viner (1937) and Samuelson (1938f), but most of the references were ones Haberler would have known before writing the book.

trade."[21] It seeks to explain why trade takes place and what will be traded, and does so in terms of nonmonetary factors. Metzler then made the interesting note that "the more general a theory becomes, the more tautological it is and the less it says about the real world."[22] Haberler first analyzed trade using the theory of supply and demand (citing one of Samuelson's Chicago teachers, Henry Schultz, who had tried to measure demand curves) before criticizing it as a partial equilibrium theory—a theory that considers a single market in isolation.[23] He then went on to develop a general equilibrium theory, in which all markets are considered together, developing the theory of comparative costs—the standard explanation of trade—to include the case where production costs fall as production increases.

It had been widely assumed that comparative costs—the ratio of the costs of production of goods in two countries—did no more than establish the limits within which the relative prices of internationally traded goods must fall. It had been known, since the early nineteenth century, that international trade between two countries would be profitable only if, in the absence of trade, they faced different comparative costs, for it was price differences that created an incentive to trade. Haberler (1930) had noted that the cost of producing a commodity might rise as more of it was produced, which meant that each country's comparative costs would change as it altered its production to take advantage of international trade. For example, suppose that under autarky, producing an extra roll of cloth involved sacrificing 100 pounds of wheat, and that in the rest of the world the price of cloth was 150 pounds of wheat; comparative costs in that country and in the rest of the world would be different. However, if the country took advantage of its ability to produce cloth more cheaply than the rest of the world and increased its cloth production so that it could be exported in return for cheaper wheat, the cost of producing the cloth might rise to 150 pounds of wheat.[24] After trade, comparative costs would be the same in both countries and would be the same as relative prices.

Haberler represented this by a geometric device he called the "substitution curve." Given a country's resources, there was a maximum quantity of goods it could produce. The points where this frontier touches the axes gives the potential output if there is specialization. In between, the frontier is a straight line if there are constant costs and is convex if costs are rising (see figure 9.1). This did not explain the point at which production would take place, whether under autarky or with international trade, but it provided a framework for thinking about costs and the supply of goods. However, though later writers were to make the connection, Haberler did not use indifference curves to represent the demand side of the economy in his book; when

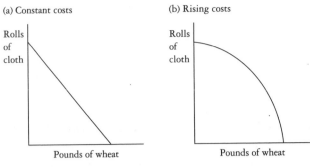

FIGURE 9.1 Haberler's substitution curve.

Note: The relative cost of wheat and cloth is indicated by the slope of the curve. As production of wheat rises and production of cloth falls, in case (a) the amount of cloth given up to obtain an additional pound of wheat does not change, whereas in case (b) it rises.

Source: Haberler 1930, pp. 357, 9; Haberler 1936, p. 176.

he wanted to look at the interaction of supply and demand, he used demand and supply curves. There is, therefore, no reason to doubt Samuelson's later memory that Haberler was resistant to the idea of using indifference curves in his lectures.

In December, Haberler turned to the work of Bertil Ohlin (1933), which Samuelson was to make famous as one of the creators of the "Heckscher-Ohlin" theory of international trade, claiming that Ohlin was the first person to integrate location theory with the supply of goods in international trade. In the course of discussing Ohlin, he considered the influence of international trade on factor prices, noting that the factors specific to exporting industries would rise in price and conversely would decline for those specific to importing industries. Labor, however, had "nothing to fear from foreign trade in the long run—if it is mobile!!!!!!!"[25] Metzler clearly noted the implication that immobile labor had much to fear in the short run.

Haberler's conclusion here was consistent with the position he took on trade policy in his book. Aware of the problems caused for the world economy by the widespread introduction of tariffs in response to the Great Depression of the 1930s, Haberler was a committed supporter of free trade, considering it important to counter popular arguments for protection. One of the arguments he thought it important to argue against was that tariffs could be used to maintain wages:

> [T]he *pauper-labour* argument is very popular in countries of high wages, especially the United States and England and her Dominions. The layman is impressed by the statement that the expansion of American industry could never have taken place, in face of the competition from

Asiatic and European countries where wages are half or less than half American wages, without the protection of the American tariff.[26]

This argument was wrong because trade in goods did not lead to equalization of wages unless labor moved from one country to another. He continued:

> Nevertheless, the implication that trade between countries in goods leads to an equalisation of *factor-prices*, and in particular of wages, is fundamentally false. An equalisation of wages comes about only if labour is mobile and can move from districts where wages are lower to districts where they are higher.[27]

The way to keep wages up was not protective tariffs on goods, but by prohibiting immigration. He described the use of tariffs to counteract other countries' lower costs, thereby ensuring "fair" competition, as a "stupid idea."[28] Wages were higher *because* American industry was more productive. This was a problem on which Samuelson was shortly to write one of his most highly cited articles.[29]

Inevitably, given events of the 1930s and his aim of viewing trade theory in relation to policy, Haberler also discussed tariffs as a way to cut unemployment. This took him into a discussion of different types of unemployment and issues such as the immobility of labor and wage flexibility, even covering Richard Kahn's theory of the multiplier and various ideas of Keynes. He conceded that tariffs could reduce unemployment, but there were good reasons to prefer other solutions. For example, in writing about unemployment in a particular branch of industry (perhaps having in mind Britain's problems with unemployment in industries such as textiles and shipbuilding), he concluded that the best solution was "to wait until the transition to full employment comes without any intervention, or possibly to assist the unemployed, for example by training them, to find jobs elsewhere."[30] The depth of his opposition to tariffs then came out more clearly in the following sentence: "But to use the dynamite of tariff increases against the less pleasant aspects of economic progress is to destroy economic progress itself." Haberler left no doubt as to his opposition to the use of tariffs.

Prosperity and Depression was considered by the United Nations to be a major study, a conference being convened in Geneva in June 1936 to discuss a draft of the book.[31] Haberler believed that progress could be made by coordinating the work of the many economists working on business cycles in Europe and the United States; sandwiched between the Geneva conference and a meeting of the Standing Committee of Business Cycle Institutes in Vienna had been another conference in Annecy, France, that was aimed at discussing the merits of encouraging cooperation on business cycle research.[32] The organization of the book makes Haberler's approach very clear. Part I, the first to be written, provided a survey of theories of the cycle, classified according to the causal mechanism involved: theories that explained the cycle as the result of monetary policy; "over-investment" theories that linked cycles to periods when investment was unsustainably high, owing to either monetary policy or an uneven pace of innovation; theories that focused on changes in costs of production in different sectors or the creation of excessive levels of debt; under-consumption theories that blamed crises on a shortage of consumer demand, possibly caused by profits being too high; "psychological theories" based on the assumption that business psychology, central to investment, lay beyond the scope of economic analysis; and theories that related the cycle to the harvest. Each theory, to quote Samuelson, was put "under the Haberlerian microscope."[33]

Haberler had started out as a supporter of the Mises-Hayek over-investment theory of the cycle according to which monetary expansion, driven by low interest rates, was the cause of the boom, and these low interest rates caused a structural imbalance in the economy that could be corrected only through a period of contraction. However, by around 1930 he had become critical of this view, mainly on the grounds that it was unable to explain why a downturn had to take place and, hence, why depressions were inevitable. This theory, he believed, might help explain the expansion phase of the cycle, but it could neither explain depressions nor shed light on how to combat them. Instead, he adopted an eclectic view. Though he did not relent on his complete dismissal of under-consumptionist theories, according to which excessive saving led to a shortage of aggregate demand, he accepted that there might sometimes be a shortage of demand for consumer goods, and even found some worthwhile points in Keynes's *General Theory*, which had appeared in February, a few months before the text of *Prosperity and Depression* was finalized.

It is inconceivable that these ideas would not have come up in the course Samuelson took: aside from having the imprimatur of the League of Nations, *Prosperity and Depression* was the latest major publication on business cycle theory, reflecting wide-ranging debates during the previous three years. Moreover, though it did not convince everyone (Hayek found many passages unsatisfactory, and Cambridge economists claimed that more space should have been given to Keynes's ideas), the book would have introduced students to the latest theoretical developments.

Three aspects of the book are worth noting. The first is that the problem of depression—clearly the most important "macroeconomic" issue facing economists in the 1930s—had to be considered in the context of the business cycle.[o] Thus, Haberler opened part II of *Prosperity and Depression* with the remark:

> There is complete unanimity among economists that the problem of the recurrence of periods of economic depression and the cognate problem of acute economic or financial crises cannot fruitfully be discussed in isolation from the major problem of which they form part—viz., the problem of the business or trade cycle; by which is meant, a wave-like movement affecting the economic system as a whole.[34]

While Haberler may have exaggerated the extent to which there was agreement on this (Keynes took a different stance in his *General Theory*), this point is worth stressing for it shows the perspective from which macroeconomic problems were generally addressed when Samuelson was a student. Thus it should be no surprise that, when he began to write his introductory textbook in 1945, the business cycle came first and the theory of employment later.[p]

The second, a point on which Haberler's critics mostly agreed, was that discussion of the cycle should be organized under four headings, each corresponding to a specific phase of the cycle: expansion; down-turn and crisis; contraction; and up-turn, or revival.[35] This was a way in which the problem of the cycle could be simplified, thereby isolating points on which no consensus could be reached. Haberler had hoped that disagreement would be confined to the causes of turning points, but this turned out not to be the case, for there was disagreement over whether contractions should or should not be seen as disequilibria.

The last point that merits attention is the importance Haberler paid to the notion of the accelerator, the principle that the level of investment is proportional to the growth rate of output, and hence fluctuates much more than output, a concept that was being widely discussed in the early 1930s.[q] Indeed, Hayek criticized him for attaching too much importance to the concept.[36] Given that his book provided a more detailed discussion of the accelerator

---

o. Quotation marks are used around macroeconomic to signal that this was not a term in common use at the time.

p. See chapter 25 this volume.

q. If there is a fixed relationship between the capital stock (buildings, plant and machinery, working capital) and the volume of production, it follows that investment (the increase in the capital stock) should be proportional to the change in output. Haberler cited John Maurice Clark, Simon Kuznets, A. C. Pigou, Roy Harrod, Wesley Clair Mitchell, Dennis Robertson, and Arthur Spiethoff as recent authors who had made use of the concept.

than his earlier draft, he clearly thought it important at the time he was teaching Samuelson, and the topic would have been comparatively fresh in his mind. Haberler's attitude to the interaction of the accelerator with the multiplier is shown by his response to Roy Harrod's *The Trade Cycle* (1936). This book, to which multiplier–accelerator interaction was central, appeared only while *Prosperity and Depression* was in press, but Haberler reviewed it in the *Journal of Political Economy*, where he remarked:[37]

> Mr. Harrod does not realize, or at least does not say, that this interaction of "Relation" [accelerator] and "Multiplier" is not a new invention, dating from the birthday of the word "Multiplier" (1931). It is in reality a common feature of almost all trade-cycle theory.[38]

He attributed the idea, though not the name, to Wicksell and his followers, John Maurice Clark and Sumner Slichter. He emphasized its compatibility with other theories of the cycle, and in an interesting footnote, he noted the importance of time lags to multiplier–accelerator interaction, criticizing Harrod for his aversion to using such lags.[39] When Samuelson began to write on the business cycle, though his immediate inspiration was Alvin Hansen, he was to adopt a stance very similar to Haberler's.

International Trade and Consumer Theory

Haberler's course was important for Samuelson for it provided problems to which he could apply the economic theory and the mathematics he was learning elsewhere. In particular, he was making connections between the mathematical economic theory he had learned from Wilson and problems that were raised by material he covered with Haberler. Early in 1937, he wrote a paper on one of the topics covered in Haberler's international trade course—the transfer problem, or the problem of how a payment from one country to another gets translated into flows of goods and services; the topical example of this was the reparations imposed on Germany after the First World War. Entitled "The Effects of a Unilateral Payment on the Terms of International Trade," it was completed in April 1937.

The classical theory, represented by Harvard's Frank Taussig, held that balance of payments adjustments came about through price changes. This was an important problem, and in the early 1920s, several of his students, including two of Samuelson's teachers, Jacob Viner and John Williams, had written dissertations on how such adjustments had taken place under the nineteenth-century gold standard. According to the quantity theory, under which prices depend on the quantity of money in circulation, a transfer of money from one country (call it Germany) to another (call it France) would lower German prices and raise French prices. This would have two effects. The first is that these price changes would worsen the terms of trade, for Germany would have to export more goods to pay for the same quantity of imports. The second effect is that, because German goods would now be cheaper—more competitive—German exports should rise and imports fall. The size of these changes would depend on elasticities of demand—on the responsiveness of exports and imports to changes in relative prices. This was crucial because, as Keynes had argued in his highly influential book *The Economic Consequences of the Peace* (1919), if elasticities of demand were low (as he believed they were), Germany would be unable to generate the export surplus it needed to reduce its foreign debts. This was a major reason for his argument that the Versailles settlement was unworkable: Germany could not pay, even if it wanted to. Bertil Ohlin challenged Keynes, arguing that this analysis neglected something important: demand for imports depended not only on prices but also on income: the transfer payment would reduce German income and raise French income.[40] Thus, even if elasticities of demand were zero, Ohlin claimed, German imports would fall and French imports would rise, producing the necessary adjustment.

In his paper, Samuelson challenged the claim that such income effects undermined the traditional (classical or neoclassical) theory of trade.[41] He aimed to show that even if economists had reached incorrect conclusions, this did not show that the theory itself was faulty: the conclusions were incorrect because theorists had been insufficiently rigorous in their reasoning. To provide the rigor necessary to settle the dispute, it was necessary to turn to algebra, because the complexity of the problem meant that "intuition fails, as do the usual graphical devices."[42] He solved the problem by seeing the similarity with the problem of barter between two individuals that he had encountered in Bowley's *Mathematical Groundwork of Economics* (1924), the textbook used by Wilson. Samuelson simplified the problem by assuming that there were two countries, each producing a fixed quantity of a single good (say, tea and coffee), which they then traded—assumptions that would have made sense to any trade theorist. He set the price of one good (say, coffee) equal to 1, so that the only remaining price measured the price of tea in terms of coffee. Assuming that the proportions of tea and coffee consumed in the two countries depended on this price, he was able to show that the five variables in his model (consumption of tea and coffee in each country, and the price of tea) would all depend on the transfer being made from one country to the other.

Using differential calculus, "elementary theorems on linear equations," and assumptions about consumer preferences, he was able to show that the effect of a change in transfer payments would depend on how consumption of tea and coffee responded to changes in income in each of the two countries—something on which economic theory had nothing to say. Thus, although he believed the conventional theory associated with Taussig and Viner was right, critics such as Ohlin were right to claim that adjustment to a transfer payment could take place even without any change in the terms of trade.[r]

Samuelson submitted the paper to Chicago's *Journal of Political Economy*, edited by Viner. It would appear that Viner was the paper's first reader and that Samuelson did not get it checked by his Harvard teachers first.[43] Perhaps he thought that Wilson, who would understand the mathematics, would not understand the trade theory, and that Haberler would not appreciate the mathematics or the use of indifference curves. Leontief would, however, have been an ideal reader, but there is no evidence that he saw it at this stage. Samuelson's sending the paper to Viner presumably indicates his self-confidence. However, Viner rejected the paper on the grounds that "no one would today seriously dispute the conclusions you draw, given your assumptions, and your article therefore does not really touch the issues which are still in controversy."[44] He did not consider Samuelson's claim that, though Leontief had proved a similar result, he had not done so in the context of a barter economy, sufficient to justify publication. Samuelson needed to be much clearer about the mistakes he claimed to be correcting. However, Viner's reaction was not entirely negative, for he said that he would consider publication if Samuelson could, without "an excessively elaborate array of mathematical and graphical material," prove that his results would hold even in the presence of domestic commodities (not entering into international trade) and where producers' and consumers' indifference curves do not have abnormal properties.

This unpublished paper shows the stage Samuelson had reached by the spring of 1937. He understood consumer theory well, and could apply it to the field of international trade. His problem was that, though he understood the transfer problem, he was not on top of the latest developments in the field. This is consistent with the complete absence of references (other than to Bowley) in the paper. Trade theorists such as Viner might not be studying the subject as rigorously as Samuelson thought they should be, but they attached

---

r. This account is a simplification in that it ignores the distinction between net and gross barter terms of trade, which Samuelson discussed in detail.

importance to issues that Samuelson had brushed aside when he simplified the problem so that he could solve it rigorously.

Samuelson's method in this paper was to take a literature that he believed was confused and apply to it mathematical techniques, including the linear algebra he had learned the previous summer in Wisconsin, that were not usually used. The topic he chose in this paper was one in which Harvard economists (Haberler, Leontief, Williams, and Taussig in retirement) were actively involved, and where his teachers were introducing him to the most advanced techniques being used. However, this advantage could not compensate for his not knowing the literature sufficiently well. Viner's marginal notes on the paper show that he completely understood Samuelson's mathematics, but despite understanding this, he was not persuaded that the paper was worth publishing.[s] Viner was also able to point out important limitations in Samuelson's economic analysis. Samuelson explained that he was engaged in a comparison of two different systems, with different transfer payments (what was later called "comparative statics"), whereas Viner argued that he should also consider how one got from one system to the other (dynamics). It was not simply conservatism and hostility to mathematics that caused Viner to find Samuelson's paper unconvincing.[45]

The unsuccessful paper on the transfer problem was not the only fruit of his attendance at Haberler's course, for a remark made by Haberler proved important in stimulating the theory of consumer behavior to which his name was soon to become firmly attached. Haberler's substitution curve (figure 9.1) depicted the supply side of an economy, showing the combinations of two goods that could be produced given available resources. To become a complete theory identifying a single point on the substitution curve, it was necessary to have a theory of demand, for which some economists, including his colleague Leontief, had turned to the device of indifference curves. That is, consumers will choose the point on the substitution curve that enables them to reach the highest possible indifference curve,

---

s. Samuelson differentiated a set of equations with respect to the transfer payment to obtain another set of equations that he described as linear. Viner queried this, but then crossed out his query, presumably realizing that, though had not said so, Samuelson was taking a linear approximation in the neighborhood of the equilibrium. When Samuelson observed, toward the end of the paper, that his results, which held strictly only in the neighborhood of the equilibrium, could easily be generalized by integration along a specified path, Viner noted that this was misleading. Even though Samuelson may have been the better mathematician, Viner could still follow the technical details of his mathematical arguments.

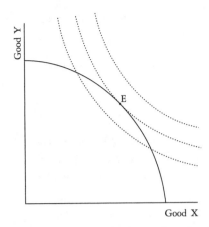

FIGURE 9.2 Equilibrium between consumption and production.
Note: Indifference curves are utility contour lines. If consumers prefer more of everything, contours farther from the origin are preferred to ones nearer the origin. The crucial assumption is that they have the curvature shown here.

denoted point E in figure 9.2. Because he could not accept that indifference curves had the shape shown in figure 9.2, Haberler had refused to take this last step, meaning he had no explanation of which point on the substitution curve would be chosen.

The problem with this approach is that, even if individuals' indifference curves are well behaved, there is no reason why a country—a collection of heterogeneous individuals—will have indifference curves with the required properties. There is no theoretically rigorous basis for treating a country as if it were an individual. Haberler not only shared such doubts but was a skeptic about the use of indifference curves in general, for he was doubtful that they had the properties needed to ensure an equilibrium.

Samuelson claimed that it was Haberler's skepticism that prompted him to work out a way to simplify the theory of the consumer by seeing the connection with index-number theory, on which Haberler had written his doctoral thesis. He wrote,

> My own work in this direction grew out of a remark made to me by Professor Haberler in his 1936 international trade seminar at Harvard. "How do you know indifference curves are concave?" My quick retort was "Well, if they're not, your whole theory of index numbers is worthless." Later I got to thinking about the implications of this answer (disregarding the fact that it is not worded quite accurately). Being then full of Professor Leontief's analysis of indifference curves, I suddenly realized that we could dispense with almost all notions

of utility: starting from a few logical axioms of demand consistency, I could derive the whole of the valid utility analysis as corollaries.[46]

Haberler's theory of index numbers was concerned with measuring the change in the cost of living when the prices of different goods change by different amounts.[47] The now standard solution is to use an average of all price changes weighted by the quantities of different goods purchased. However, if people respond to price changes by changing the quantities they consume (they will presumably be inclined to buy less of goods that have become more expensive in relation to other goods, and to buy more of goods that have become cheaper), the choice of weights is not clear: Is it better to use the quantities purchased before the price change (the Laspeyres price index), or the quantities purchased after the price change (the Paasche price index), or some other index altogether? Haberler's solution, taken from the British economist Francis Edgeworth, was to argue that if prices change, the "true" rise in the cost of living was the amount by which someone's income had to rise if he or she were to be indifferent about the situations with the old and new prices. He argued that the Laspeyres and Paasche price indices provided limits to the "true" cost of living. His results quickly became part of a large literature involving many leading economists.[48] Haberler's double condition required that the Laspeyres index be larger than the Paasche index. Haberler argued that, though this would not necessarily be true, it was likely to be true because, if the prices of certain goods fell relative to prices of other goods, consumption of those goods was likely to fall.[49] He was one of several economists deriving this result, though different economists derived it in different ways. For example, Roy Allen at the London School of Economics derived it using the assumption of convex indifference curves, the assumption to which Haberler took exception.[50]

This remark is important because it makes clear that, even though Samuelson was studying the theory of the consumer most rigorously with Wilson, he associated indifference curve analysis with Leontief. He was thinking actively about consumer theory, having already written one paper that was on its way to publication; Haberler's remark, made by a teacher whom Samuelson associated with his thesis on index numbers, made him realize that he could go further than others had gone in showing that the theory of the consumer could be derived simply from observations of consumer choices.[t] As with his work on international trade, Samuelson was making connections between material covered in different courses. However, even though he wrote, much later, that the theory of revealed

---

t. Samuelson's first paper, discussed in the first section of this chapter, was published in

preference was born in his exchange with Haberler, it was to be two years, during which much was to happen, before his articles on the subject came to fruition.[51]

The Theory of Capital

At the end of the academic year, Samuelson's second article was published, not on consumer theory but on "Some Aspects of the Pure Theory of Capital."[52] The theory of capital was a widely discussed topic in the 1930s, mainly because of its use by Friedrich Hayek to provide an explanation of the Great Depression.[53] Hayek, a prominent opponent of Keynes in 1930, blamed the business cycle on over-expansionary monetary policy, but he used a theory about capital and production to explain why a downturn would trigger dislocation and unemployment, rather than simply a fall in prices. His idea was that low interest rates during the boom would induce businesses to invest in excessively capital-intensive methods of production; when interest rates eventually rose and the downturn took place, business would find itself saddled with production processes that were no longer profitable and would shut them down. Depression and unemployment would persist because it would take time to organize new, less capital-intensive production processes that could be profitable at higher interest rates.

While Hayek was the main proponent of such views, taking a hard line on measures to alleviate the slump, this view was held by many others as well; traces of it can be found, to varying degrees, in both Hansen's and, as has already been seen, Schumpeter's analyses of the cycle. Significantly for Samuelson, the theory of capital was one of the subjects on which his Chicago idol, Frank Knight, had written extensively, challenging Hayek's claim that the capital stock could be represented by a single magnitude, the "period of production"—the average time between investing in a project and obtaining a return.[u] The theory of capital was also central to the theory of the rate of interest, about which Knight and Schumpeter took opposing positions.

February 1937, implying that it had probably been written before the exchange with Haberler took place, given that the pure theory of trade was covered at the end of the course.

u. An example of a "short" period of production would be using workers' shovels to build a canal. A longer process of production would involve first making mechanical diggers and then using these to dig the canal. An even longer process of production might involve designing and building machine tools that are used to make mechanical diggers,

Given that two of his most important teachers were arguing about the topic, Samuelson could hardly avoid becoming involved.

However, Samuelson did not get into the larger literature on the theory of capital, despite alluding to its existence. Instead, he tackled a more isolated problem in pure theory: the objectives that should be pursued by a single company undertaking investment. His starting point was not Hayek, or any of those who were using capital theory to argue about the business cycle, but an article by a relatively unknown economist just five years older than himself, Kenneth Boulding (1910–1993). Boulding was British, graduating from Oxford in 1931. After a year of graduate work in Oxford, he went to Chicago for two years on a Commonwealth Fellowship, spending the fall of 1933 at Harvard working with Schumpeter.[54] He met and engaged with Knight. Samuelson was there, but there is no reason to think they met.

Boulding's aim in "The Theory of a Single Investment" (1935) was to extend the theory of the company to decisions taking place over time. He pointed out that the theory of profit maximization could be applied to any activity defined by a single income account. This could be an entire company or an activity within a company; if there was a single account (even if a notional one) through which all receipts and payments passed, then this account could be treated as a single investment, to which the theory of profit maximization could be applied. Boulding abstracted from uncertainty and argued that the rational, farsighted investor should invest so as to maximize the internal rate of return on the investment. The internal rate of return was the rate of discount at which the present value of the inputs equals the present value of the outputs. Using this result, he derived dynamic equivalents of the static condition that marginal cost equals marginal revenue.[v]

Samuelson took up Boulding's device of the single investment account, but worked out the mathematics for more general assumptions. He assumed that the time path of income and expenditure flows might have any pattern

_____

which then dig out the canal. If interest rates are low, it may be more efficient and more profitable to adopt such longer processes, whereas with high interest rates, the cost of building the additional capital equipment (the machine tools and mechanical diggers) may mean that such methods are more expensive than simply using shovels to dig the canal.

v. The approach of maximizing present value is frequently, though not always, equivalent to the more common approach, adopted by Irving Fisher and Keynes, of equating the rate of return on an investment with the rate of interest.

rather than the simple case assumed by Boulding, that interest might be compounded continuously or at the end of each period, and that the rate of interest might vary over time. One result of this was that the internal rate of return might not exist or it might not be unique (there might be multiple rates of interest at which the net present value of the investment was zero). Samuelson then introduced the market rate of interest to argue that Boulding's conclusion, that the firm should maximize the internal rate of return, was incorrect. Instead,

> Given an interest rate at which all can lend or borrow ... each entrepreneur will select that value of the variable under control which maximizes the present value of the investment account, the present value being computed by capitalization of the income stream at the market rate of interest.[55]

This was, as he pointed out, a well-known result. Boulding, he claimed, had assumed rather than demonstrated his result.

What Samuelson was doing in this paper formed part of an emerging pattern. He was employing more advanced mathematics than was currently being used—mathematics he had learned from Wilson (he cited both Wilson's *Advanced Calculus* and the textbook by Whittaker and Robinson that Wilson had recommended)—and as a result he was able to analyze a more general case, thereby reducing what he believed to be confusion in the literature.[56] In other words, he was saying that Boulding had a good idea, but that it needed to be tackled using more advanced mathematical techniques. In taking on Boulding, he was tackling someone whose views had been criticized by Knight, and Samuelson may have had Knight in mind when noting that the internal rate of return might not be unique, even if it existed.[57] Moreover, though the paper focused on Boulding, Samuelson also took aim at a bigger target, John Maynard Keynes. *The General Theory* included a chapter on "own rates of interest." These were rates of interest calculated in terms of different commodities. In an appendix to his paper, Samuelson argued that Keynes's statements about own rates of interest were completely misconceived, for it made no difference which of these many rates were used; the investment policy that maximized the value of an investment in terms of money would maximize its value in terms of any other commodity. This was another example of Samuelson's removing confusion from the literature by raising the level of mathematical analysis being used. It also provides evidence of Samuelson's sympathy with Knight's ideas and his taking a critical stance toward Keynes.

Abram Bergson and Welfare Economics

Samuelson's friends among the graduate students included Abram Burk, only a year older than Samuelson but who had come to Harvard's graduate school in 1933 when Taussig was still teaching, at the same time as his brother had come to study physics. Descended from Russian Jewish immigrants, Gus Burk was uncomfortable having a name that did not immediately identify his ancestry, and so he and his brother agreed legally to change their surname to Bergson.[58] Samuelson was one of those to whom Abram turned for support. "Don't you suspect, Samuelson, that some will think I am trying to travel on the prestige of the great French philosopher, Henri Bergson?" he asked. Samuelson reassured him that there was virtually no chance of that.

Bergson and Samuelson took some courses together and their first publications appeared within a few months of each other, in October 1936 and February 1937, respectively.[59] These dealt with the measurement of utility. They both started with a method for measuring utility proposed by the Norwegian economist Ragnar Frisch, one of the major figures in the Econometric Society. They focused on different problems, but both reached the conclusion that there was no basis for assuming the utility function took a specific form—something that was essential for the method Frisch had proposed.

Bergson went further than Samuelson, who mentioned the idea only briefly and without explanation, in developing the concept that the theory of the consumer was tied up with index number theory. At Samuelson's suggestion, he paid great attention to the case of "expenditure proportionality," introduced in a survey of index number theory by Frisch that had been published in *Econometrica* the previous year.[60,w] Though Frisch attached much importance to this case, Bergson emphasized that it was very much a special case, for if it were true, the Laspeyres and Paasche index numbers, known to provide upper and lower limits for index numbers of real income, would be the same.[x] Bergson did not comment on the implications of utility—as the term was being used—for welfare, but given his claim that the values Frisch was saying could be computed could "in no sense be considered *measurements of real* money utility,"[61] he may not have thought it necessary to do so; if

---

w. Expenditure proportionality means that in order to keep utility at the same level, a set of price changes needs to be accompanied by the same rise in total expenditure, irrespective of whether people start out with high or low expenditure.

x. These index numbers are discussed earlier in this chapter. Bergson 1936, p. 42, n1.

Frisch's measure did not measure real money utility, then a fortiori it could not have welfare implications.

Samuelson's first article did not discuss welfare except for the final sentence, in which he observed that there was no connection at all between utility and welfare.[62] He made almost the same remark at the end of a paper that was published a year later:

> In closing I should like to state my personal opinion that nothing said here in the field of consumer's behavior affects in any way or touches upon at any point the problem of welfare economics, except in the sense of revealing the confusion in the traditional theory of these distinct subjects.[63]

It seems plausible to conjecture that these brief remarks were written in response to reactions to Bergson's article, published shortly before and probably written at much the same time.[y]

Implied in these remarks is a criticism of virtually all existing literature on welfare economics for confusing two completely different concepts. "Utility," as used in the theory of the consumer, was a device for analyzing how consumers behaved—for modeling the choices they made when confronted with prices and incomes. It was also taken to be a measure of how well off someone was, and hence relevant for the assessment of social welfare. It had been widely assumed that these two meanings were connected; this is clearest in classical utilitarianism, where social welfare is specifically assumed to be the sum of individuals' utilities. Modern writers avoided committing themselves to utilitarianism, with its suggestions of hedonism (that people were mechanical seekers of pleasure and avoiders of pain), but the connection between welfare and the consumer had not been abandoned. For example, the Cambridge economist A. C. Pigou, whose *Economics of Welfare* (1920) had by then been through four editions, and whose work dominated discussions of welfare in the English-speaking world in the 1920s, argued in terms of "satisfactions" rather than utilities; Pigou pointed to many limitations of the utilitarian criterion, but he still grounded his analysis of welfare on a theory of the consumer. The Italian economist Vilfredo Pareto, whose work was in vogue in Harvard in the 1930s, also refused to argue in terms of utility, preferring the term *ophelimité*. Though he was willing to distance himself even further than Pigou from an aggregative notion of welfare, he still saw a close

---

y. This remains a conjecture, for the precise timing of these articles, and the lags between submission and publication, are not known.

connection between utility and welfare.[z] So, too, did most of the literature on welfare economics with which Samuelson and Bergson were engaging.[aa] The main exception was Lionel Robbins's *Essay on the Nature and Significance of Economic Science* (1932), which proposed a definition of economic science so strict that it excluded scientific welfare economics altogether.

At some point in the 1936–37 academic year, Samuelson recalled, Bergson kept asking him, "What can Pareto mean by this 1898 use of the French singular when he speaks of 'the social optimum'?"[64] The problem was that Pareto referred to *a* social optimum, yet the conditions he proposed did not seem to define any unique point. Samuelson and Bergson concluded that Pareto's writings were ambiguous. Samuelson explained this in the following way:

> I had to read Pareto in the Italian original, and my command of Italian was very poor. Nevertheless, I had a feeling when I read the 1913 article—I say this with diffidence—that he may momentarily have had the notion of an imposed-from-outside social welfare function. . . . But I thought I detected in it also a positivistic real political function of certain elites in any society. Each one of these elites has different power, like the powers of father and mother, oldest son, younger sons in a family. If you try to get a demand function for the family, you must combine these different influences. Generally speaking, when you do that, you don't get an integrable function. To me, that was what Pareto was talking about in the 1913 article.[65]

The implication is that in 1937, Samuelson and Bergson believed that Pareto confused positive and normative conceptions of social welfare (that was certainly his view later on).[66]

Irrespective of whether the idea was in Pareto, the insight that lay behind such thinking was that there was a clear separation between ethical value judgments and empirical propositions, a point Knight had emphasized very strongly. As Samuelson put it in a memoir about Bergson, "In connection with ethical value judgments Bergson clarified how they

---

z. The interest of many Harvard academics in Pareto is discussed in chapter 10 this volume.

aa. There is a strand in the literature, associated with J. A. Hobson, to which Samuelson had been introduced at Chicago, that made this distinction (see chapter 3, this volume); however, Hobson spurned the idea, important to Bergson and Samuelson, that economics could be scientific, and introduced some very specific and controversial value judgments (see Backhouse 2009; Backhouse and Nishizawa 2010). This may explain why Samuelson, though he claimed to have read the entire literature on welfare economics, does not even hint at the existence of such work.

could be distinguishable from testable empirical relations, a problem inadequately grappled with by Lionel Robbins (1932), Bentham, J. S. Mill, Edgeworth, as well as Pareto, Myrdal, Lerner, Hicks, Kaldor, and Scitovsky."[67] Welfare, Bergson contended, was a normative judgement that had to rest on ethical judgments conceptually completely distinct from propositions about behavior—they were imposed from outside. Of course, they might include ethical judgments on the value of certain behaviors, but that was a different matter: the key point was that they were derived from some ethical system.

In his paper "A Reformulation of Certain Aspects of Welfare Economics," Bergson formulated the concept of a social welfare function.[bb] In its most general form, the social welfare function had virtually no content, for it stated that social welfare depended—in some unspecified way—on the quantities of goods consumed by each individual in the society, the amount of labor each individual devoted to producing each good, the amounts of nonlabor factors of production (e.g., land or natural resources) used in producing each good, and any other factors that might affect welfare. It was, however, useful, for Bergson could take the welfare criteria used by previous writers and work out what restrictions they implied on the form of the social welfare function. This enabled him to work out the value judgments these writers were implicitly making. The social welfare function was thus a device for thinking systematically about the previous literature on the subject.

This approach eventually became known as the Bergson-Samuelson social welfare function, for though Bergson's article was published first, Samuelson's account of the concept in his *Foundations* (1947a) is the one most economists came to read.[cc] Samuelson repeatedly denied credit for it, preferring to call it by names such as the "Bergson Ethical Normative Function."[68] "Mine," he wrote, "was the spectator's seat for Bergson's creative travail. I was the stone against which he honed his sharp axe—the semiabsorbing, semireflective surface against which he bounced off his ideas."[69] On another occasion he went slightly further in claiming that he was the "helpful midwife" who helped pull the baby out, denying emphatically that he was a co-author of the crucial paper.[70] What seems most likely, given Bergson's suggestion that Samuelson should have been a co-author, is that, formalizing a lesson Samuelson had encountered in Knight's work—the idea that in making judgments about

bb. This was published in February 1938 and probably written no later than the middle of 1937, perhaps in the summer after his courses were finished.

cc. See chapter 22 this volume.

welfare, it is *necessary* to introduce ethical judgments—the social welfare function was something they developed together.

In the 1950s, following Kenneth Arrow's *Social Choice and Individual Values* (1951), the term "social welfare function" came to be used in a different way, to represent a procedure for moving from a set of individual preferences to a social preference.[dd] Samuelson, however, consistently defended Bergson's and his own conception of the social welfare function, referring to Arrow's function as a constitutional function. This attitude may have been connected to his having discussed axiomatic treatments of constitution design with the mathematician George Birkhoff. In January 1940, referring to an earlier conversation, Birkhoff wrote to Samuelson:

> For a long time I have been interested in a critical analysis of the type of axiomatics which is generally implicit in economic reasoning and in reasoning such as I employed in my lecture on ethics. As a preliminary to this question, I would in particular like to talk to you about the systems for proportionate representation in Congress which *seems* to have been so thoroughly treated by Huntington.[71]

It seems safe to assume that the discussion Birkhoff sought took place, for when he gave another version of his lecture, on March 6, he acknowledged Samuelson's advice in a footnote.[72]

E. V. Huntington was another Harvard mathematician who had worked on providing axiomatic foundations for mathematical systems, and he had proposed a formula for allocating congressional representatives to different states so that the final allocation corresponded as closely as possible to each state's population.[73] This was one of the problems that Birkhoff examined in his lecture, which was concerned with formalizing problems involving ethical choices. His ethical measure, or moral satisfaction, was G—the total good achieved—and the problem was how to measure it. Different rules for allocating representatives to states involved minimizing different measures of the difference between the actual distribution and complete proportionality—in

---

dd. Suppose there are three states of the world: (A) an airport with two runways is built, (B) an airport with one runway is built, (C) no airport is built. Assume every individual can rank these three options in order of preference. Someone concerned only with being able to travel might have the ordering (A, B, C), whereas someone who attaches priority to climate change might opt for (C, B, A). The problem of social choice becomes that of how to move from the set of individual rankings to a social ranking. It could involve a voting system or a mechanism for identifying the person whose preferences will determine the outcome.

other words, different measures of G. In assessing these, Birkhoff invoked a number of conditions that a state's allocation should satisfy: (1) a state with a larger population should not have fewer representatives than one with a smaller population; (2) every state should receive at least the integral part of the exact number of representatives to which it is entitled; (3) if the number of representatives increases, no state should have its representation reduced; (4) it must not be possible to improve the allocation between any two states by transferring a representative from one state to another. The problem was that, although these seemed inherently reasonable, they were often mutually contradictory and a choice needed to be made between them.[74]

When Birkhoff wrote about the parallels with "the type of axiomatics which is generally implicit in economic reasoning," he presumably had in mind economists' discussions of welfare. The footnote where he acknowledges Samuelson suggests that they discussed Bentham's utilitarianism, saying that Samuelson drew Birkhoff's attention to Edgeworth's treatment of the topic in *Mathematical Psychics* (1881). Given that Birkhoff wrote Edgeworth's name as "Southworth," it is not clear how carefully he followed this up, but it suggests that he and Samuelson may have discussed whether what Birkhoff called Bentham's "semi-philosophical" treatment of ethics could be treated with greater mathematical rigor. Though Birkhoff was tackling the problem of welfare in a way that was consistent with Bergson's approach to welfare, and with Samuelson's repeated assertion that judgments about welfare had to be based on ethical judgments, this shows that Samuelson was exposed to the idea of providing an axiomatic foundation for political choices while still a junior fellow. As a result, when he encountered Kenneth Arrow's *Social Choice and Individual Values* (1951), he should immediately have understood the point that seemingly obvious postulates about welfare might be inconsistent with each other.[ee]

At the end of his second year at Harvard, Samuelson had reached the stage where the normal route would lead into writing a doctoral thesis, a task for which his ESRC grant would have given him sufficient financial support. He had by now significantly expanded his knowledge of mathematics and was using this to tackle the problems identified by his teachers, making connections between courses on outwardly disparate topics. Though he was still a student with much to learn from his teachers, applying mathematics without

---

ee. Their discussion of Birkhoff's lecture on ethics came after Samuelson's articles, though it is of course possible that they had, through discussions of Pareto, got onto such topics much earlier.

always having an economically interesting problem to solve, his mathematical knowledge was already beginning to mark him as separate from his contemporaries. One of his friends, Walter Salant, described him as being miles ahead of any other graduate student. However, his next move was not to write a doctoral thesis but to join Harvard's prestigious Society of Fellows, where he was to remain for the next three years.

| Simplifying Economic Theory

Harvard's Society of Fellows

In the middle of Samuelson's second year at Harvard, Wilson had written to Lawrence Henderson, describing Samuelson as "One of the most brilliant young men in political economy whom I have ever met," recommending him for appointment as a Junior Fellow in Harvard's Society of Fellows.[1] The Society of Fellows was the creation of Lawrence Lowell, just after he stepped down as president of Harvard, and Lawrence Henderson, professor of biological chemistry who had become head of the Fatigue Laboratory in the Graduate School of Business Administration and had developed a strong interest in sociology. They shared the view that PhD training was stifling the creativity of talented young scholars, who would flourish if, instead of undertaking formal training, they were given the freedom and the resources to pursue independent research. Graduate schools, Lowell believed, had "developed into a mass production of mediocrity."[2]

The Society of Fellows was the solution that they, together with Alfred North Whitehead, professor of philosophy, came up with. There was to be a group of around twenty-four junior fellows, each of whom would be appointed for three years, with the possibility of renewal for at most one further term; they would have few obligations other than to meet for dinner on Monday evenings and for lunch on Fridays. A condition of their appointment was that they were *not* allowed to register for a higher degree. These arrangements reflected a belief that creativity could best be nurtured in an environment in which young scholars engaged in dialogue with people from many disciplines. It was intended that, whether they remained at Harvard or moved elsewhere, having being elected to such distinguished company would make it unnecessary for junior fellows to have the union card of a PhD.[a] As mentors, they had nine senior fellows who joined them for dinner on Mondays. Of these, as much by force of personality as by any formal position, Henderson was the dominant influence. One of his associates wrote of him:

> Henderson's beard was red but his politics were vigorously conservative. His method in discussion is feebly imitated by the pile-driver. His passion was hottest when his logic was coldest. Yet if he felt a man had something in him, no one could be more patient than he in helping it come to light. He had the gift of taking a scholar's raw data, no matter how far they might be from his own field of biochemistry, and bringing out the pattern that lay in them.[3]

Though he had not yet (formally, at least) taught him economics—Samuelson had taken only his mathematical statistics course—Wilson believed Samuelson to be suitable for appointment as a junior fellow, telling Henderson: "I think he has had enough course instruction. I think he is a self-starter and might do an extraordinarily good job if he had the opportunities that would come with being chosen as a Junior Fellow."[4] Questions had presumably been raised concerning both his personality and, Wilson presumed, his being Jewish, but he argued that neither should be a barrier to his appointment.[5]

> Some people say Samuelson will be hard to place because of certain [doubts] about his personality and because I suppose he is Semitic. My own personal contacts with him lead me to believe that he is not objectionably Semitic. I personally think that his personality defects are of the sort often found in aggressive clear-thinking self-directing young men and that they auger well for a productive life. I don't believe they are so bad as to make it difficult to place him and I do believe that three years as a Junior Fellow might of a great deal to ameliorate such defects as he has.[6]

In using the phrase "not objectionably Semitic," Wilson was alluding to the distinction that was sometimes drawn between the cultured and wealthy

---

a. The Society was modeled on the Trinity College Prize Fellowships at Cambridge, with which Whitehead was familiar, and the Fondation Thiers, in Paris, which Henderson had visited in 1913.

Jews, such as the Rothschilds, who had long been established in the United States and were welcome at Harvard, and the more recent influx of Eastern European Jews, who were less welcome.[7] Their long conversations after class must have reassured Wilson that, despite his Eastern European origins, Samuelson would fit well into the cultured conversations that lay at the heart of Henderson's Society of Fellows. Such "personality defects" as Samuelson had were common in precisely the sort of bright young men Henderson was trying to recruit for the Society of Fellows. Wilson must have known that his view would carry weight with Henderson, for they knew each other well, with Wilson participating in Henderson's interdisciplinary sociology course.[b]

Wilson's support for Samuelson's becoming a junior fellow was echoed by Schumpeter, who described him as "the most gifted graduate we have had these many years," capable of discussing matters with all his professors on "the footing of perfect intellectual equality."[8] He had passed his generals "with the utmost ease" and had two "highly original" papers that were about to be published. Writing to the mathematician George Birkhoff, then a senior fellow, as well as to Henderson, Schumpeter then tackled the issue of Samuelson's mathematics, arguing that this provided a reason why the Society of Fellows should take him.

> He has the additional claim that, owing to the mathematical turn of his mind, he will not be very acceptable to the common run of economists and that, unless he gets that fellowship, he will be forced to deviate from the path he has cut out for himself and to accept injurious compromise.[9]

He was too mathematical to be acceptable to most economists and so needed the opportunity that a junior fellowship would give him.[c] Schumpeter then turned to the objection that, although the Society of Fellows included brilliant mathematicians, Samuelson's mathematics would not be attractive to them, either: "The Society I know is not very favorably disposed to economists and to theoretical economists of the mathematical type least of all." He countered this by arguing that even if Birkhoff and Henderson were skeptical about mathematical economics, this should be a reason to help "gifted young

---

b. This quotation raises the question of Wilson's anti-Semitism. This is discussed in relation to anti-Semitism at Harvard in the context of Samuelson's decision to leave Harvard for MIT, a decision in which Wilson played an important role. See chapter 15 this volume.

c. This is another issue that will be discussed further in the context of Samuelson's decision to leave Harvard.

men who devote their energies to the thorny task of making an exact science of economics."

Samuelson's application was accepted, and in the autumn of 1937, he joined the Society of Fellows. As a junior fellow, free of all responsibilities other than to pursue his research and to attend the weekly dinners, he was completely happy. It was, he wrote, lucky that no one offered him a permanent fellowship, for he would have accepted it.[10] It was a period, coinciding with that in which economists took up Keynes's *General Theory*, that he repeatedly described using lines from Wordsworth's *The Prelude*, "Bliss was it in that dawn to be alive / But to be young was very heaven!"[11] Writing in the third person, he reflected on this period:

> Before his SSRC fellowship gave out, he overcame the opposition of the Society of Fellows to economics and rode on the shoulders of Vilfredo Pareto into the sacred circle of Junior Fellows. The philosopher Willard van Orman Quine, the mathematician Garrett Birkhoff [son of George Birkhoff], the double-Nobel physicist John Bardeen, the chemists Bright Wilson and Robert Woodward, the polymath Harry T. Levin were his companions in arms in the Society of Fellows.[12]

Other junior fellows with whom he had close contact included the mathematicians Lynn Loomis and Stanislaw Ulam, physicist Ivan Getting, historian of science Henry Guerlac, and historian Arthur Schlesinger Jr.[d] In this environment, Samuelson wrote, "he hit his stride and began to turn out articles faster than the journals could absorb such quasi-mathematical stuff."[13] During his three years as a junior fellow, he published thirteen articles covering fields as diverse as consumer theory, production theory, the rate of interest, international trade, and business cycle theory; his confidence showed in reviews that dismissed the books in a few lines of criticism.[14]

Samuelson's appointment to the Society of Fellows, in September 1937, placed him at the heart of a community in which attempts were being made to establish new foundations for the human sciences. The central figure was Henderson who, in addition to his role in setting up the Society of Fellows, was involved in other elements in what historian Joel Isaac (2012, p. 60) has called "the interstitial academy," or "the Harvard complex," a network of institutions firmly rooted in Harvard's traditions but standing apart

---

d. Note that Bright Wilson, Garrett Birkhoff, and Willard Quine had ceased to be junior fellows in 1936, though they probably attended dinners, as former junior fellows were entitled to do. He remained in contact with all three.

from conventional departments.[15] The first of these was a seminar, Pareto and the Methods of Social Investigation, which began in 1932 and included Schumpeter among its members. In his biochemical research, Henderson had applied Willard Gibbs's ideas about chemical equilibrium to biochemistry and human biology. This work prompted Henderson to engage with a cluster of philosophical problems relating to scientific inquiry.[16] He invested heavily in the concepts of system and organization, recognizing that such manmade symbolic frameworks could be important elements of science, for without them the collection and interpretation of facts would not be possible.

During the 1920s Henderson's interest in scientific reasoning developed, and in 1926, he encountered the work of Pareto. What attracted him to Pareto was that he offered a set of concepts—nonlogical motivations that manifested themselves either as core values ("residues") or as verbal rationalizations ("derivations")—that could function as the concepts of temperature, pressure, and concentration functioned in chemical systems. Pareto's sociology offered a way to describe social phenomena in such a way that they could be analyzed as "dynamical, thermodynamical, physiological, and economic systems."[17]

The Society of Fellows was, along with his course Concrete Sociology (Soc. 23) and his work in the Fatigue Laboratory, the instrument through which he propagated his ideas. Several of Samuelson's contemporaries in the society had either worked with Henderson or were working in accordance with his views on organic systems (George Homans, Conrad Arensberg, William Whyte, James Miller). Charles Curtis and Crane Brinton, close associates of Henderson, were appointed senior fellows. Samuelson has stated that he rejected the ideas of this group, which came to be known as the Pareto Circle.

> My relation to the Pareto-Henderson-Homans-Curtis coterie at the Society of Fellows can be simply put. These turned out to be purely social. I went but once to the famous Henderson sociology seminar. That was either once too many or many too few. When I would want to talk about Gibbs to Henderson, he would prefer to enumerate the shortcomings of Franklin Delano Roosevelt. In 1937 it was a case of Henderson's being too old or Samuelson's being too young, or both. My guarded admiration for Pareto the economist has been great; but during the vogue for his sociology, I stayed out to lunch.[18]

However, though he might "stay out for lunch" as regards Paretian sociology, there remained the compulsory Monday evening dinners; he could ignore the Pareto seminar, but this did not mean he could ignore Henderson or his views on science. As has been noted, Henderson was forceful in putting forward his views and dominated the society—to the extent of choosing the wine served at dinner, being proud of the cellar comprising good French Burgundies and Alsatian wines he had collected, and crucially, setting the topics for conversation over dinner. He held forth on Pareto and scientific method, and circulated his lecture notes for Sociology 23 to all the junior fellows. "Henderson's preoccupations," it has been claimed, "were all but impossible for Junior Fellows to ignore."[19] When Samuelson came to leave Harvard, he wrote to Wilson that he had learned a great deal from conversations with people like Lowell, Whitehead, and Henderson.[20] Notwithstanding his rejection of Paretian sociology and the demands of politeness in writing to a friend of Henderson's, there is no reason not to take this remark at face value.[e]

Scientific Method

One reason for taking this remark seriously is that Henderson was expressing views that will have reinforced ideas about thermodynamics that Samuelson was also hearing from Wilson. Henderson was, like Wilson, an enthusiast for Gibbs. Dynamics and equilibrium, two concepts central to Samuelson's thinking, were also central to Henderson's system. Samuelson may have remembered Henderson's wanting to criticize Roosevelt when he wanted to talk about Gibbs, but the significance of this memory rests in the fact that he wanted to discuss Gibbs in the first place. It is also significant that, when asked about his attitude toward formalizing economic theory, Samuelson referred to Henderson: "He always emphasized, probably derivatively from Pareto but also from his own methodological work, that you can't be a pure empiricist; you've got to have a systematic way of thinking about things."[21] This was far from being an off-the-cuff remark: it expressed one of the central tenets of Henderson's scientific philosophy and would surely have been something Samuelson discussed with his mathematician and physicist friends (Birkhoff, Ulam, Bardeen, and Getting). Furthermore, the views on science that he will have heard from Schumpeter and Wilson will have prepared him for the practice-oriented view of science that was being developed under Henderson's influence in the Harvard complex in which the Society of Fellows was an in integral part.[22]

---

e. As is noted in chapter 22 this volume, Henderson was the first person whose work Samuelson cited in his *Foundations*.

Another figure in the Harvard complex was physicist Percy Bridgman (1862–1961), a teacher at Harvard since 1910, whose reputation rested on his experimental work on thermodynamics, for which he later (1946) received the Nobel Prize for physics. He attracted the attention of philosophers and students of other disciplines with *The Logic of Modern Physics* (1927), which put forward the method of "operational analysis." Samuelson remembered having been introduced to operationalism by Henry Schultz when he was an undergraduate in Chicago. However, the development and spread of operational analysis was most closely linked to Harvard, where it proved particularly influential in psychology, and the behaviorism advocated by B. F. Skinner (a junior fellow 1933–36) and others.[23] As was noted earlier, Samuelson, who was to make much use of operationalism, had probably attended Percy Bridgman's lectures in the autumn term of 1936. In any case, he could hardly have avoided Bridgman, who had close connections with those involved in the Society of Fellows.

Bridgman's starting point in *The Logic of Modern Physics* was the "truism" that "all our experimental knowledge and our understanding of nature is impossible apart from our own mental processes," and that his essay was based on observing what physicists were currently thinking.[24] A reconsideration of the fundamentals of physics was needed because physicists' ways of thinking had been challenged by recent developments, including both Einstein's theory of relativity and quantum mechanics, the latter developing so fast that Bridgman had to concede some of his material was already out of date. Physicists were working with ideas that could not easily be related to everyday experience, which necessitated a revision of how we thought about concepts. That is, concepts could no longer be defined in terms of their properties, but had to be defined in terms of operations: "In general we mean by any concept nothing more than a set of operations: *the concept is synonymous with the corresponding set of operations*."[25] These operations might be physical (as with physical concepts such as length) or mental (as with mathematical concepts such as continuity).

This view had clear implications. It meant all knowledge was relative to the operations involved. It meant questions were meaningless if it was not possible to find operations by which answers could be obtained. Thus, notions of absolute time and space were meaningless because they had no connection with reality, for any operations to measure them would of necessity be relative to those operations. Venturing beyond physics, Bridgman opined,

I believe that many of the questions asked about social and philosophical subjects will be found to be meaningless when examined from the point of view of operations. It would doubtless conduce greatly to clarity of thought if the operational mode of thinking were adopted in all fields of inquiry as well as the physical. Just as in the physical domain, so in other domains, one is making a significant statement about his subject in stating that a certain question is meaningless.[26]

Bridgman went on to argue that thinking in terms of operations had consequences for science, for it would simplify thinking, rendering earlier speculations "unreadable."[27] In developing his ideas, Bridgman paid much attention to "intuition," which was tied to his ideas about what it meant to explain something, and "models." Explanation involves reducing situations to ones that are consistent with our intuitions. At this time, neither the word "intuition" nor the word "model" was widely used in economics journals, but beginning in the 1940s, they came to be widely used by mathematical economists.

Bridgman's philosophy, derived from his own observations of what appeared to be successful in physics, fits with Henderson's craft-oriented view of the scientific method.[28] At the same time, Bridgman parted company with Henderson in ways that would have been attractive to scholars such as Samuelson, skeptical about the latter's leap into Paretian sociology. His focus on operations—he disliked the terms "operationalism" and "operationism," as implying something more esoteric than his "simple ideas"—placed concepts firmly in the arena of scientific practices and cautioned scientists against claiming more than their methods could demonstrate.[29] It also left room for creativity, for operations could never be fully specified, allowing for nonrational decisions by scientists. That is, scientific knowledge was not something that could be understood apart from human psychology. It was factors such as this that, Isaac contends, made Bridgman's views attractive to Harvard's psychologists, who were significantly under-represented in the Pareto Circle.[30] Coming from a different discipline, better established and with a more developed, if problematic, theoretical foundation, it is easy to see why Samuelson, who could have escaped it no more than he could have avoided Henderson's ideas, found the idea of operationalism attractive even if he was to define it rather differently from Bridgman.

Bridgman's operational methods were adopted by logical positivists and behavioral social scientists (notably Skinner), but were taken in directions different from those in which Bridgman himself wished to go. Bridgman held that there was an irreducibly individual, subjective element in all knowledge, and he was critical of attempts, whether by positivists or the Vienna

Circle,[f] to equate his operational method with their attempts to derive rules by which the objectivity of knowledge could be ensured: that was an impossible goal.[31] Given this ambiguity, we need to be careful in imputing to Samuelson a particular interpretation of operationalism, for though he was to make the idea central to his work, there is little evidence of how much he read and precisely what he made of it—though he was to recommend that his MIT students read Bridgman—or of personal interactions with Bridgman that might have colored his reading of his work. In any case, his understanding of operational analysis will have been mediated by his discussions with Wilson, Schumpeter, Henderson, and colleagues in the Society of Fellows, all of whom had strong views on scientific method.[g]

Consumer Theory

Samuelson regularly sent drafts of his papers on consumer theory to Wilson. In a letter to Wilson in January 1938, he thanked him for comments on a manuscript, presumably "The Empirical Implications of Utility Analysis," which was submitted to *Econometrica* about a month later.[32] Samuelson's letter shows that, encouraged by Wilson, he was pursuing "the Gibbs approach," by which he meant the analysis of finite differences, assuming "certain arithmetic inequalities" or concavity conditions to hold.[33] He had derived some results using more traditional, calculus-based methods, but conceded that his final theorem related only "to instantaneous rates of change and does not approach the generality of the Gibbs formulation which makes no continuity or differentiability assumptions." This was clearly something to which Wilson had objected, for Samuelson defended himself by saying that he had not followed the more general approach because he had been unable to develop a proof. However, though following the Gibbs approach very closely,

---

f. The Vienna Circle was a group of philosophers who, from 1924 to 1936, worked out what came to be known as logical empiricism, or logical positivism, and whose work proved very important in philosophy.

g. Isaac (2012, p. 108) describes Samuelson's interpretation as Popperian. However, there is no evidence that he had encountered the work of Karl Popper, and the Popperian pedigree of his use of operationalism is less clear if one remembers that Bridgman placed much emphasis on meaningfulness and that Samuelson was concerned with "pencil and paper" exercises that needed to be related to reality. This creates more ambiguity than Samuelson's focus on testability might suggest. In the next section, the suggestion is made that the link to Vienna might have come though Felix Kaufmann or Willard Quine rather than Popper.

he recognized that there was a difference between physical and economic systems: a physical system was in a "relative" minimum, whereas in an economic system, entrepreneurs and consumers were "sometimes" believed to be able to select "the actual absolute maximum or minimum out of a number of different relative maxima or minima."[h]

When the paper was submitted to *Econometrica*, the managing editor, Dickson Leavens, asked Wilson to referee it, a procedure that today would be considered to involve a conflict of interest but that was considered acceptable in the 1930s. Wilson replied that he was already familiar with the paper and that no purpose would be served by his reading it again. Though he conceded that it was the type of work for which it was very difficult to make sure there were no mistakes, Samuelson was "a very good man and careful," and Wilson thought that he had "done a thoroughly good job," recommending that Leavens accept the paper.[34] On the same day Wilson wrote to Samuelson to tell him of his recommendation, and shortly afterward Leavens sent the paper to Ragnar Frisch for approval and publication.[i]

There is evidence that while he was thinking about these problems, Samuelson was also thinking about thermodynamics and lessons that could be drawn for economic modeling. He read the *Textbook of Thermodynamics* (1937) by Sophus Epstein, a physicist at Caltech, and on November 29 he sent Wilson what he described as "a dangerous excursion . . . into a field about which I know very little."[35] The paper on a topic related to physics rather than economics was, Samuelson said, provoked both by remarks Wilson had made in his lectures, and by the "confusion and ambiguity" that he had found in

---

h. Imagine that the line in the following diagram represents a tube full of water, containing an air bubble that always moves upwards. If the bubble starts anywhere to the left of C, it will end up at point A; if it starts to the right of C, it will end up at B. In contrast to such physical systems, humans may be able to achieve B whatever their starting point. Nowadays it is more common to refer to local and global maxima or minima. A and B are local maxima, but only B is a global maximum.

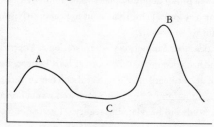

i. Those familiar with refereeing practices in modern economics, where taking two to three months to review a paper is considered normal, may react with disbelief to such speedy consideration of papers.

the work of someone who was, "as far as I can judge," a competent physicist. In reply, Wilson said that he considered Epstein to be a better mathematical physicist than Einstein, albeit not so original.[36] Samuelson's letter did not name the paper he sent Wilson, but it seems likely to have been a version of "The Le Chatelier Principle of Displaced Equilibrium."[37,j] The Le Chatelier Principle was to play an important role in his thesis.[k]

Samuelson's third article on consumer theory, "A Note on the Pure Theory of Consumer's Behaviour," which appeared in February 1938, offered a much more tightly focused argument than his first article had done. In it he argued that, starting with the work of Heinrich Gossen in the middle of the nineteenth century, the theory of consumer choice had involved the removal of more and more assumptions. All that remained in the modern theory of the consumer, represented by the work of his contemporaries John Hicks and Roy Allen, was the diminishing marginal rate of substitution—the assumption that indifference curves were convex to the origin.[38,l] What Samuelson appears to have noticed in the conversation with Haberler discussed in chapter 9 earlier was that, given certain seemingly reasonable assumptions, convexity of indifference curves can be demonstrated using methods familiar from the theory of index numbers. If convexity were the only substantive proposition in consumer theory, it followed that he had a complete theory of the consumer.

The way Samuelson presented his theory was by pointing out that, because economists no longer believed that utility theory provided a psychological explanation of behavior, it was not clear why they should accept indifference curve analysis: there was no explanation of where the diminishing rate of substitution came from. As a result of this lack of clarity, utility kept sneaking back in, for it provided the missing explanation. Instead of this, Samuelson proposed an alternative set of assumptions on which consumer theory could be based, showing that the last vestiges of utility theory could be eliminated without losing anything that mattered. It was even possible to get rid of indifference curves: if people wanted to use indifference curves, his theory could be read as providing the justification for doing so, but there was no need to do this.

---

j. The paper is undated, but the style of the typing indicates that it was written around this time. The main caveat is that the extant draft says he had been working on the problem for "many years," a phrase he might not have used less than three years after he had met Wilson, whom he credited with introducing him to the principle (Samuelson 1947a, p. 81).

k. It is discussed in chapter 14 this volume.

l. As in figure 9.2.

All that was necessary, Samuelson argued, was to make three assumptions about consumer behavior:

(1) When faced with his or her income and market prices, an individual will choose the same combination of goods.
(2) This combination will not change if all prices and income change in the same proportion.
(3) Individuals are consistent in that they will never choose bundle of goods x when a different bundle, x', is available if at a different set of prices and income, they choose x' when x is available.[m]

Samuelson defended this last assumption by claiming that to deny it would be to render invalid all preceding analysis of consumer behavior and the whole of the theory of index numbers. This was the meaning of his claim that his approach was "close to the modern theory of index numbers."[39]

Of the three postulates, the third was the most important, in that it could be used to derive properties of consumer demand functions. He did this using finite differences—at the level of generality that, to put it as Wilson's would have done, Willard Gibbs would have desired.[n] An early draft of the paper shows that Samuelson initially conducted the whole argument in terms of finite differences, and that the discussion of what would happen as these differences shrunk toward zero was added later.[40] Though he attached more importance to the case of finite differences: it was generally important to consider what happened when the changes in prices were smaller and smaller, shrinking toward zero, because it enabled him to derive all the results traditionally derived using continuously differentiable utility functions. However, though these results *could* be derived from utility maximization, Samuelson claimed that there was no benefit in doing so. There was one result that could not be derived from his assumptions, but he denied it was important.[o]

---

m. Though he did not use this terminology, confining himself to the language of choice, this amounts to saying that x' cannot be preferred to x if x is preferred to x'. Using such language would have taken him back toward indifference curve analysis. Samuelson's notation has been simplified by using a Latin rather than a Greek letter.

n. His result, $\sum_{i=1}^{n} \Delta x_i \Delta p_i < 0$, where x_i and p_i denote quantity and price of good i and n is the number of goods.

o. If demand were derived from maximization of a utility function (if demand functions were integrable), the matrix of cross-substitution effects (the effect of the price of good i on consumption of good j) would be symmetric. However, he was skeptical of attempts

In other words, he had derived every useful proposition that could be derived from the assumption that consumers were rational and consistent. The novelty of his results lay not in the result he derived, for another Harvard student, Nicholas Georgescu-Roegen, had previously derived this main equation, but in the method by which Samuelson had derived it: from observable choices made by consumers.

An issue to which economists had paid significant attention was complementarity—the possibility that demands for two products might move in the same direction in response to price changes.[p] Samuelson noted his lack of interest in the problem, observing that "in other isomorphic systems, e.g., the equations of analytic dynamics, of the Gibbs's system of thermodynamic equilibrium, it is not felt to be necessary to define similar measures."[41] This remark implied that the mathematical structure of the problem, not the economic significance of the system's components, determines which variables need to be defined. Neither analogy had been mentioned previously, and there was no explanation of why the isomorphism was significant; it was taken for granted. Complementarity had been important historically only because its analysis had led economists to see mistakes in Pareto's reasoning and to see that utility was not needed.[q]

Samuelson followed this with a methodological remark: "Woe to any who deny any one of the three postulates here!" he wrote, "It is hoped that the orientation given here is more directly based [than other approaches] upon those elements which must be taken as *data* by economic science."[42] This remark prompts two observations. He was suggesting that, though it was possible to see his work as an extension of traditional theory, he saw it as alternative. This was even clearer in the title of an early draft of the paper, "New Foundations for the Pure Theory of Consumer's Behavior."[43] It is tempting to think that the more bland title of the published version was the result of input from *Economica*, the editorial board of which included Friedrich Hayek

---

to test this. Some historians (Hands and Mirowski 1998b, 1998a) have attached much importance to Samuelson's having been at Chicago where Henry Schultz was attempting to test this proposition, but aside from Samuelson's claim that he learned about operationalism from Schultz, there is no evidence that he engaged with Schultz's work when he was there.

p. For example, a rise in the price of postage stamps might cause a fall in demand for both stamps and envelopes. People might write fewer letters or write shorter, lighter letters requiring less postage.

q. He cited no sources to substantiate this claim.

and Lionel Robbins, colleagues of Hicks and Allen.[r] More significantly, his claim that there were elements that "must" be taken as data by economic science suggests not operationalism, with its implication that scientific propositions should be testable, but Robbins's claim that economic theory could be derived from indisputable propositions.[44] The suggestion that disaster might befall anyone who entertained the possibility that consumers might be inconsistent reflects an ongoing tension in his work between his engagement with pure theory and his espousal of operationalism.

Later that year, Samuelson published an addendum to this paper in which, this time using the language of preference (people choose the bundle of goods they prefer out of those they can afford), he demonstrated that the third of his three postulates implied the first two.[45] The implication was that he had summarized all that could usefully be said about the theory of the consumer in one postulate that later came to be known as the weak axiom of revealed preference.[s]

In the papers he wrote, Samuelson argued merely that consumer theory could be analyzed "more directly" using a set of postulates that made no mention of utility.[46] In another paper, a version of which was presented to a meeting of the Econometric Society in Atlantic City in December 1937, before being published in *Econometrica* in October 1938, Samuelson started with the historical argument that the "moral, utilitarian, ethical connotations" had first been removed from the concept of utility, and that subsequently the "hedonistic, introspective, psychological elements" had also been eliminated. This was consistent with his two articles in *Economica*. However, here, instead of dispensing with the concept of utility, he asked what remained of it:

> Does not the whole utility analysis become meaningless in the operational sense of modern science? A meaningless theory according to this criterion is one which has no empirical implications by which it could conceivably be refuted under ideal empirical conditions.[47]

This was his first published use of the notion of operationalism. However, though he used the language of operationalism and knew Bridgman personally through the Society of Fellows and through his lectures, Samuelson's

---

r. As with many academic journals from this period, *Economica*'s records have not survived, making it impossible to tell who handled submissions or what the refereeing process involved.

s. Note that the name "revealed preference," by which this theory came to be known, had not yet been invented.

equating meaningfulness with refutability under ideal empirical conditions is closer to the language of the philosophers associated with the Vienna Circle. It may be significant that Samuelson backed up his view that many defenses of utility theory were circular and he implied nothing about observable behavior by citing an article by his friend Alan Sweezy, published in 1934. Sweezy argued not in terms of operationally significant propositions but "empirically significant laws," supporting it with a quotation from the philosopher Felix Kaufmann: "The principle of marginal utility is, therefore, neither an empirical assertion nor a tautology nor a synthetic judgment *a priori*, but a heuristic postulate."[48] Sweezy would have been very familiar with Kaufmann's work; not only did he cite several of his publications but he also had assisted him with the English of the article he quoted.[49] Though much less well known than Karl Popper, Kaufmann was a significant figure in bringing Vienna Circle ideas into economics.[50] Given Samuelson's close friendship with Sweezy and that Sweezy had published on the topic he was investigating, it is likely that they had discussed these ideas at some point. It is also possible that he discussed them with Quine.

Samuelson's starting point in this paper, the aim of which was to show that utility analysis contained "meaningful implications by which it could be refuted," was to indicate that all that was needed was an *ordinal* utility index—one that places alternative bundles of goods in an order from best to worst, without saying anything about how *much* better one bundle is than another. For example, it is possible to observe that someone considers a cappuccino better than a latte, but without being able to say they consider it twice as good, 10 percent better, or a hundred times better.[t] He started by proving that, so long as the ordering of different bundles of goods was not changed, the utility numbers could be changed without affecting the crucial conditions for utility maximization.[u] Having established this, he could resort to the theory outlined in his *Economica* paper, deriving a series of results relating to the properties of demand functions, both for individual consumers and the whole markets, where the demand function for each good depended on the prices of all goods, and not just the good's own price. Because prices,

---

t. It may be possible to say that they will pay twice as much for it, but this just shifts the problem to the value of money.

u. Formally, this means that if $U = \Phi(x_1, \ldots x_n)$ is a valid utility function (consistent with the individual's choices) where U is utility and the x's denote the quantities of goods consumed, and if $F(.)$ is any increasing function, then $U = F\left[\Phi(x_1, \ldots x_n)\right]$ will also be a valid utility function.

quantities of goods, and household incomes were all observable, his results satisfied the criterion of being operational.

Samuelson claimed that he derived all the results found in the previous literature, even in a recent paper by the Columbia economist Harold Hotelling, and some more besides. They went beyond the results in his *Economica* paper in that using an ordinal utility function enabled him to derive symmetry conditions (that the effect of the price of a cappuccino on the demand for lattes was the same as the effect of the price of lattes on the demand for cappuccinos) that could not otherwise have been obtained. This was the implication of traditional theory that he had dismissed as unimportant in his earlier paper. Perhaps it was because he was aware that he had previously dismissed it as unimportant that he defended his approach by claiming that he had shown how the use of mathematics made it easy to derive results, a conclusion most readers of *Econometrica* would have found congenial.

In parallel with this paper, Samuelson took up an argument made by Oskar Lange, a Polish economist who had recently immigrated to the United States and had become a professor at Chicago in 1938.[51] Lange conceded that observations of behavior could yield no more than an ordinal utility function. However, he argued that it was possible to get more information by asking people to compare *changes*. For example, a consumer could be asked whether he would prefer to have an extra muffin at breakfast or an extra sandwich for lunch. Lange claimed that, if we could do this, we would be able to obtain a cardinal measure of utility—one in which the numbers attached to a utility function were significant. With such a measure, differences in utility could be made as meaningful as differences in temperature.[v] Having a cardinal utility function rather than an ordinal one might be irrelevant for describing behavior, but it could be useful, Lange contended, for judgments about welfare.

Lange's argument provoked controversy as soon as it appeared, but Samuelson believed that Lange's critics had missed the main problems with the paper. Samuelson's first criticism involved reiterating the point he had made briefly in his previous articles— namely, that utility was completely irrelevant to the problem of welfare economics, which was about ethical judgments. Citing Bergson's paper on the subject, Samuelson argued that

---

v. Technically, a cardinal utility function is defined up to a linear transformation. If $U = \Phi(x_1, \ldots x_n)$ is a valid utility function, then all other valid utility functions can be expressed as $U = a + b\Phi(x_1, \ldots x_n)$ where a and b are constants. In the case of temperature, where degrees Fahrenheit (f) and degrees centigrade (c), $f = 32 + 1.8c$. This is more restrictive than the requirements for an ordinal utility function.

if one could rank the quantities of goods consumed by all individuals, it was possible to make judgments about welfare; having a cardinal measure of utility added "literally nothing."[52] His second criticism was that the discussion had got into a muddle over the conditions under which it was possible to represent preferences by a utility function. Assuming that consumers could rank differences in utility was irrelevant; the crucial additional assumption needed to get a utility function was transitivity—the assumption that if a consumer preferred A to B and preferred B to C, then she must prefer A to C. If preferences were transitive, they could be represented by a utility function.

Samuelson sent a copy of his paper to Lange, who replied in May 1938 that he agreed with Samuelson's claim that cardinality of the utility function was irrelevant for welfare economics.[53] He admitted that he had previously been wrong about this. As for the other criticism, Lange explained that he was not concerned with whether a utility function would exist (the integrability problem) but, rather, with whether, if it existed, it would be unique. The reason for his choice of assumptions was that he had wanted to show how earlier writers such as Pareto and Bowley had been inconsistent. This remark, and Lange's observation that, subject to seeing Samuelson's final draft, he might wish to publish a rejoinder, may be the reason why, when the paper was published in October, its concluding remark was, "I should like to express my agreement with Dr. Lange concerning the inconsistencies in the writings of the earlier mathematical economists."[54] He and Lange might disagree on technical matters, but they were at one in believing that mathematical analysis could cut through the confusions found in the previous literature.

In the fall of 1939, Samuelson sent Lange a draft paper on a topic closely related to the issues they had discussed the previous year. This was intended for a memorial volume for Henry Schultz, who had died in November 1938 in a motor vehicle accident. It seems likely that the paper had not been solicited by Lange because, after thanking Samuelson for sending him the paper, he explained that he did not know whether he would be able to include it in the volume. Not only was it a long paper but, more important, he did not yet know how many other contributions he was going to receive and hence whether the volume could go ahead. He asked whether Samuelson would mind waiting two or three weeks for a decision. In this paper, not published for nearly three years, Samuelson dealt with the problem of what it meant to assume that the marginal utility of income was constant. This was an assumption used by Alfred Marshall in the 1890s, both to derive downward-sloping demand curves from the assumption of diminishing marginal utility and to derive the "consumer's surplus" that formed the basis for his welfare economics.[w]

Inevitably, Samuelson showed his paper to Wilson, who had recently published on the subject. Wilson told him in December that he found it very interesting and hoped it would be published. In his own paper, Wilson had focused on the problem of "independent" goods—goods the utility of which does not depend on consumption of other goods.[55,x] He encouraged Samuelson to provide "more text and historical discussion" in order to reach "economists who are not really able mathematicians as you are."[56] This was important because Wilson thought there was a lot of confusion and because, though Walras's definition of independence had become standard, Hicks and Allen had introduced a new definition, and the relationship between the two definitions was not understood.

This was a particular problem when many economists constructed arguments verbally, without going into the underlying mathematics. Wilson even suggested that Samuelson might consider presenting the whole argument verbally, consigning the mathematics, which would frighten people, to an appendix, or at least placing the mathematics nearer the end. This was neither the first nor the last time that Wilson urged Samuelson to make more concessions to less mathematical readers.

Samuelson did not take his mentor's advice. The version that was eventually published, in 1942, in the memorial volume edited by Lange, contained a brief opening paragraph introducing the problem, but if this was a response to Wilson, it was little more than a token gesture.[57] All it said was that because much of the literature on consumer demand was based on the assumption that the marginal utility of income was constant, the literature contained many conclusions that were "of restricted validity" and that there were even "outright contradictions."[58] There was no attempt to explain at

---

w. If an extra loaf of bread is worth $5 to a consumer, but he has to pay only $2 to obtain it, there is a surplus of $3. If the bread were worth only $2, he would gain nothing from buying it; he would be indifferent to having the bread and having the $2 to spend on something else. If marginal utility—the value of an extra loaf to the consumer—is falling, then the first loaf consumed will be of more value than the second, and so on. Consumer's surplus is the surplus on all the loaves consumed. Unless the marginal utility of income (money) is constant, a utility of a $1 surplus on different loaves consumed will be different, and the measured surplus (a sum of money) will not correspond to a total of utility.

x. If goods are independent according to this definition, the utility function has the form $U = \Phi_1(x_1) + \Phi_2(x_2) + \ldots + \Phi_n(x_n)$ where the functions $\Phi_i(x_i)$ denote the utility functions of each good.

the outset what these doubtful results were or why they arose, even though his aim was to show that that previous literature was muddled. Samuelson's first result, after defining his terminology, was to show that the marginal utility of income depended on the choice of utility index; as the utility index was not unique, this undermined the concept. This led Samuelson to explain that the meaning of constant marginal utility of income—a term important to Marshall—was ambiguous: Was it constant when prices changed? Or was it when income changed?[y] As Wilson recognized in his letter to Samuelson, this list of guilty economists included Marshall.

Production and the Rate of Interest

Samuelson was also trying to clarify the other side of the theory of supply and demand—the theory of the firm and production. In December 1938, he had presented a paper on the theory of production at a meeting of the American Economic Association, despite Schumpeter's arguing that the paper was too short.[z] According to the abstract Samuelson wrote for the published summary of the session, he criticized economists for failing to provide a clear and correct account of the relationship between the production function and the cost curve, and for not deriving results of operational significance. He stated that the optimality conditions could provide "unambiguous, meaningful restrictions upon price-quantity behavior," but he did not explain what these were. His concluding remark was the claim, hardly controversial, that it is free entry that causes the company to earn zero profits, and that such a condition cannot be deduced from any "internal" equilibrium condition relating to the company.[59]

A year earlier, in December 1937, Samuelson had written to Knight, enclosing a paper he had written on what determined the rate of interest— a topic on which Knight had taken a strong stand.[60] Samuelson began by pointing out that when discussing competitive markets, economists usually

---

y. The first definition of a constant marginal utility of income (that the marginal utility of income would not change when the price of a good changed) was Marshall's. The second was that the marginal utility of some good—the good in terms of which other prices were measured, usually called "money"—was constant. Using each definition, along with other commonly made assumptions, Samuelson was able to derive unexpected and unwarranted implications, such as that the shares of income spent on each good never changed.

z. See chapter 7 this volume.

started by analyzing how individuals would behave, given the market price (the essence of a competitive market is that an individual has no power to influence the market price). Only after that did they analyze how the actions of all individuals taken together determined market price. He proposed to apply the same method to the theory of the rate of interest, bringing mathematics into a discussion of a controversial topic to which much of the previous literature employed purely verbal reasoning. However, although Samuelson had hoped that the paper would interest him, Knight was not impressed. Echoing the comments Viner had made six months earlier in relation to a different paper, Knight took the view that although the mathematics was correct, it added nothing significant to what was already known:

> Anyhow, the fact is that your paper rather leaves me cold! In considerable part ... it impresses me as symbolic restatements of fairly obvious relations always do; I find it "sound," and admit that symbolic formulations have some value in the way of definiteness and precision. But I can't see that the paper makes any important "contribution."[61]

Knight argued that "the high intellectual quality" of Samuelson's work was all the more reason for developing his ideas "to a point where they do achieve clarity and make a real contribution." For example, he thought Samuelson had not been clear where he referred to "total asset holdings" as a variable that adjusted so as to bring the system into equilibrium. Knight considered this misleading, because the sum of total assets was the outcome of the processes involving investment, disinvestment, and asset revaluation that he was analyzing, and should not be seen as a variable in the system. He wanted an approach that focused more on the actions of individuals and less on aggregates.

The one aspect of the paper that Knight liked was Samuelson's criticism of Keynes. Samuelson revised the paper and it was eventually published in February 1939 as "The Rate of Interest Under Ideal Conditions."[62] "Ideal conditions" meant the absence of any uncertainty. He accepted that uncertainty was the normal situation, and that it was impossible to define the conditions under which there could be perfect certainty, given that "the behavior of each individual forms the obstacle or *liaison* under which all other individuals act"; but he defended the assumption of perfect certainty "as an analytic device."[63] Given this assumption, he could draw on the theory of investment worked out in his earlier paper. Samuelson argued that the result was a more general theory of the relationship between investment and the rate of interest than those often used in the literature, because he made very general assumptions about production conditions. "It is," he wrote, "almost impossible to formulate a production function of wide applicability."[64] He also distinguished his theory of investment as differing from Keynes's marginal efficiency of capital, which he found problematic.[65,aa]

Samuelson then turned to consumers. He justified considering individuals and families separately, on grounds that in modern specialized life, thought patterns tended to be compartmentalized: "the same man thinks differently as an entrepreneur and [as] a consumer."[66] There was justification for this in that the existence of financial markets meant that, if entrepreneurs maximized the present value of their assets, this sum could then be spent in whatever way the individuals preferred. Samuelson rejected hedonistic theories that explained saving in terms of the disutility of abstaining from consumption, or in terms of the utility of consumption over time—a view that, originating in the early nineteenth century, had dominated economic thinking for a long time. He even argued that because, as Knight had pointed out, revenues from personal services cannot be capitalized and sold (people cannot sell themselves into slavery), "it serves no purpose to consider each family as owning its future discounted earnings."[67] The result was that consumption was determined by factors that were very different from those determining investment.[bb] That is, it depended primarily on the age structure of the population.

> Starting from a few elemental facts concerning our civilization, it is
> clear that individuals are born into families and remain dependent for
> a number of years. There follows a period of earning power during
> which income may be rising, falling, or remaining constant, and usu-
> ally a twilight period of decreased earnings or even no earnings. . . .
> Because of the break between generations and the growing tendency
> for each generation to keep its own books, except in the case of bring-
> ing up children, there is a considerable holding of assets by individuals
> in anticipation of a period of dependency.[68]

The purchase and liquidation of financial assets would not cancel each other out, and as a result there would be a need for families to hold a large quantity of assets, including life insurance policies, pension funds, and savings

---

aa. His argument was that it was not a true marginal concept. This was the second occasion
when his publication was critical of Keynes. His position in relation to Keynes will be
discussed in subsequent chapters.

bb. Note that Samuelson is assuming that people cannot borrow against their anticipated
future earnings, something that would now be considered normal (think of student loans
or, in a sense, a mortgage on a house).

accounts. The volume of asset holding would depend on the distribution of income. It was "probable" that the rate of interest—the factor traditionally thought to determine asset holding—was "only a minor element among many" in determining a demand for assets: "The cultural values of modern society are such that there would presumably be asset accumulation at any rate of interest."[69] People might, Samuelson argued, accumulate assets even if the rate of interest were negative. To explain how the behavior of entrepreneurs and consumers determined the rate of interest, Samuelson argued in terms of discrete periods, his exposition perhaps reflecting the approach adopted by John Hicks in his very recently published book *Value and Capital* (1939b), or his own reading of Swedish economists such as Erik Lindahl and Bertil Ohlin.

> I break time up into discrete periods and discuss the determination of the rate of interest in each. All rates of interest and all asset holding of previous periods are taken as *data* when considering any given period. Like a never-ending chain, the values of the variables of each period proceed from those of the previous, and in turn become the determinants of succeeding periods. This being so, *the interest rate which will be established in any period must be such as to equilibrate the total asset holding of all individuals (households, investors) and the total assets of all enterprises, optimally determined for each rate of interest.*[70]

In a footnote, he worked out the continuous-time case.

The discussion is interesting because it contains many ideas that were to become central to postwar economics: the "life-cycle" theory according to which households save to provide consumption in old age, and the idea Samuelson himself was to popularize as the overlapping-generations or consumption-loan model.[71] And yet, despite the presence of these ideas, he refused to accept some of the presuppositions of later theories, in that he rejected the idea of consumption being based on discounted future earnings and questioned whether households could be seen as maximizers. Rather than being an application of the theory of utility maximizing households, as was the case in his later work on the consumption-loan model, his analysis of overlapping generations was intended as an *alternative* to that theory. The paper provides evidence of the way his thinking was still framed, very strongly, by the views of his teachers—Knight as much as Wilson and Schumpeter. He was also, like his teachers, critical of Keynes. He went along with Keynes in arguing that the rate of interest would adjust so that people wanted to hold the stock of assets existing in each period, and in denying that equality of saving and investment could determine the rate of interest (saving and investment must be equal).[cc] However, beyond that, their theories were very different.

Samuelson adopted an explicitly dynamic framework; he abstracted from uncertainty; he focused on the total stock of assets rather than just money. Samuelson also differed from Keynes over the identity of investment and saving, for he defined investment to include not just the production of new capital goods but also the change in the value of existing assets. In arguing that trade in old capital goods would necessarily cancel out and could be ignored, Keynes had become trapped by "a subtle fallacy" analogous to Zeno's famous paradox of motion.[72,dd] This could well have been the passage that Knight enjoyed reading.

In this paper, as in his earlier paper on investment, Samuelson was using his mathematics to cut through the confusions that he thought abounded in less rigorous theorizing. The theory of capital was a major area of confusion, but by focusing on the value of assets, he believed that he had managed to build a theory in which investment was the outcome of maximizing behavior without defining anything called the "quantity of capital." The literature on measuring capital had, he claimed, concealed the difference between rising asset values and the real physical investment—something to which his analysis drew attention. However, as he was unwilling to make the assumptions necessary to model consumption formally (for example, as the solution to a maximization problem), his analysis of that side of the model remained purely verbal, and as a result the conclusions he could draw were limited.

Samuelson never wavered in his belief that, in all the areas of economics he was investigating, mathematics could be used to cut through confusions in the previous literature. He explained his position to his friend Tsuru:

> I think it is like trying to cut with a small knife through the brambles of a wood that have overgrown to the extent that one cannot move, in order to make a path big enough for people to pass. Economics is inundated with categories and system with complexity in direct proportion to the multiplying number of economists, but in the end, when the general notion and the reasoning are clarified and a thorough investigation is carried out, the theoretical framework is revealed as quite simple and has common features.[73]

---

cc. In itself this suggests that, like many economists at the time, he had not properly understood the *General Theory*, in which although realized saving and investment must be equal, planned saving and planned investment need not be.

dd. It is not clear that Samuelson's analogy makes sense here.

Samuelson's work on consumption and production was to be central to his doctoral thesis and a major part of his *Foundations of Economic Analysis*, the book that cemented his authority as a mathematical economist. However, though he was simplifying economic theory, cutting through the complications that others had introduced, these early papers reveal a young economist still finding his way, containing many remarks that imply skepticism of ideas that would later become standard assumptions in economic theory.

His first article showed that if individuals maximized the discounted sum of utilities, it would be possible to measure utility—but he went on to question the relevance of this, given evidence on actual behavior. His article on the rate of interest provided reasons for skepticism of using a theory based on utility maximization for analyzing what might be thought the natural subject matter for such a theory—saving and the rate of interest. He even added a footnote dismissing his earlier paper, describing it as "an intellectual curiosity, which served to treat to my own satisfaction the arbitrariness of the assumptions and the barrenness of the results."[74] He showed that utility analysis had empirical implications even though in another paper he had argued that these implications were of no consequence. The term "revealed preference," which came to define his approach to consumer theory, was introduced only in what was effectively an addendum to his earlier paper in *Economica,* where the main ideas had been presented in a form that turned out to be more complicated than strictly necessary. His approach to capital theory was conceived in terms that fitted with the work of Knight and Schumpeter. In short, he may have been simplifying the previous literature, but he had not yet cut free of the way questions were formulated in that literature.

There are also suggestions that his methodological position was still evolving. His first paper in *Economica* toyed with a traditional defense of his assumptions as indisputable, whereas a few months later he turned to operationalism—but he interpreted it in a way that echoed the Vienna Circle ideas with which two of his friends, Alan Sweezy and Quine, were engaging. His work in this period contained ideas that were to be of lifelong concern—operationalism, revealed preference, overlapping generations, and conceptions of capital—but his thinking about them was evolving as he turned out paper after paper.

There is no question that he was ambitious, very confident, and filled with a belief that the use of mathematics could dramatically change economic theory. A young scholar in a hurry, he was receiving the message consistently from his teachers, including Wilson, Schumpeter, and Knight, that he should take more time to present his ideas in such a way that more notice would be taken of them. On August 4, 1939, he acquired a further reason to be in a hurry when his father died, at age fifty-six. Samuelson was then only twenty-four, but having been living with the knowledge of his hypertension since his student days, and having had his activities restricted on account of this, he became anxious that he did not have long to live.

CHAPTER 11 | Collaboration

Population Dynamics

When Samuelson left Harvard, he had a reputation as a "cooperator."[a] He reported that this was because he had once co-authored an article with one of his friends, but his reputation rested on more than that. It was a tribute to the assistance he gave to the economics graduate students and his involvement in their work. He had got ahead of his friends in learning mathematics and in using it in economics, but it never caused him to disparage their work. To the contrary, he supported his friends, and during 1939–40, he went so far as to give them a series of lectures on mathematical economics.

His starting point was the notion of a function, which he stressed did not need to be numerical. He illustrated nonlinear functions using a simple physics example—the motion of a freely falling body. He used this to explain the idea of limits. Algebra, diagrams, and numerical examples were all used. The same techniques were then applied to cost curves and the supply curve of the profit-maximizing company, as well as the effect on output of imposing five different types of tax on a company. These were all essentially exercises in using differential calculus to analyze maximum positions.[1] Having started with just two variables, Samuelson then went through similar exercises with three variables—output was a function of land and labor. Deriving the condition for minimum cost, he showed how the second-order conditions could

---

a. See chapter 15 this volume.

be represented as a two-by-two determinant. He stated that the equivalent maximum and minimum conditions for three and four variables involved additional conditions relating to the signs of larger determinants.

These lectures show not only the trouble Samuelson took to assist his friends but also the gap that existed between his own mastery of these mathematical techniques and the much more limited mathematics of his colleagues—even those who, like Stolper, had successfully completed Harvard's graduate program. The material was elementary in comparison with his own work, but his fellow students needed to have it explained very carefully, with alternative explanations of important points and worked examples being provided. Though mathematics such as Samuelson was using would become commonplace in the 1950s, and would be universally required of graduate students (and many undergraduate majors) by the 1960s, such training was much more limited in 1940.

The example of Bergson shows that Samuelson could be generous in crediting his friends and in minimizing his own role, refusing to be acknowledged as a co-author of work with which he had been involved. One of his most important co-authors was Marion, with whom, at some point in 1938, he began work on the dynamics of population growth. This was a problem of interest both to Wilson (as professor of vital statistics) and, on account of its implications for the business cycle, to Hansen.[b] In February 1939, Samuelson sent a copy of a paper he and Marion had written to the statistician Alfred Lotka (1880–1949).[2] Lotka, born in what is now Poland and trained in mathematics and physics in Birmingham, England, applied thermodynamic ideas to biological evolution, seeing evolution as a physical law. Wilson had been one of those who reviewed Lotka's *Elements of Physical Biology* (1925), and the two remained in contact. Like Wilson, Lotka harbored a certain skepticism of sociology, once remarking to Wilson that while listening to a long-winded and platitudinous paper, he had drafted a definition: "Sociology is a pseudo-science which develops the faculty of speech at the expense of that of thought," though hoping that the field as a whole did not merit such an opinion.[3] By the time Samuelson got in contact with him, he was a statistician for the Metropolitan Life Insurance Company and was working on various aspects of population dynamics. Lotka drew Samuelson's attention to a substantial literature on the problem of population dynamics, including his own, and sent him a draft of a paper on "self-renewing aggregates" and the problem of "industrial replacement."[4]

---

b. Hansen is discussed in chapter 12 this volume.

The paper that Paul and Marion wrote together was titled "A Fundamental Function in Population Analysis."[5] Its starting point was the observation that a population was the sum of all births, weighted by the proportion of the population surviving to each age. Thus in 1938, the total population would comprise all births in 1900 multiplied by the proportion surviving to age 38, plus the number of births in 1901 multiplied by the proportion surviving to age 37, plus births in 1902 multiplied by the proportion surviving to age 36, and so on. The problem was that it would be useful to turn the problem round and, starting from knowledge of what the population was in each year, deduce how many births there must have been in each preceding year. Lotka had solved this problem, making special assumptions about the time path of the population, but his result was not completely general. Using some complicated mathematics, Paul and Marion derived what they called a replacement function: the pattern of births over time that would keep a population constant. That their inspiration may have come from physics is shown by a sentence deleted in the manuscript, "The analogy with the Heaviside step function of electric circuit theory obviously suggests itself."[6]

Paul and Marion stated that the replacement functions they were calculating could apply to either human populations or to stocks (populations) of industrial equipment. However, rather than discuss specific numbers, they derived two general theorems. The first was that if population growth were exponential (i.e., grew at a constant percentage rate) after a certain date, the number of births must asymptotically approach an exponential form (a constant growth rate), and the age distribution of the population would eventually stabilize. The second theorem generalized this result to the case where there were cyclical fluctuations in the population. As Paul explained to Lotka, this was motivated by their interest in business cycle theory.

Samuelson's correspondence with Lotka continued, and in March 1939, Lotka said that he thought Samuelson had not provided a good motivation for the statistical problem he was trying to solve.[7] In looking for the birth rate that would keep the population constant, Samuelson was assuming that when someone died, the person was immediately replaced by a newborn baby. This was not what happened with human populations where the birth rate depended on the age distribution of potential mothers. However, Samuelson's problem was relevant to the problem of industrial investment, where a worn-out capital good might immediately be replaced with a new one. This comment might have been the motivation for an unfinished paper Samuelson wrote, "A Note on the Net Reproductive Ratio and the Intrinsic Rate of Population Growth," in which he argued in terms of female births per female of any given age.[8] In this note he argued in terms of limits rather than precise values, one of the reasons being that the length of a generation was uncertain. Biology determined minimum and maximum ages for childbearing, and the length of a generation could be anywhere between those limits.

In the fall, Samuelson submitted a paper under his sole authorship, "The Structure of a Population Growing According to Any Prescribed Law,"[9] to the *Journal of the American Statistical Association*. This paper began by noting that while it was straightforward to deduce the behavior of a population from knowledge of births (and other assumptions), it was much harder to go in the other direction. Up until then, he claimed, the problem of finding the birth rate when one knew about the growth of the population had been solved only for certain special cases, such as when a population was growing exponentially (a constant percentage growth rate) or according to a logistic curve (in which the growth rate rises and falls in a specific pattern). Data for the 1930s had shown that the U.S. population growth no longer fitted a logistic curve, even though it had done so previously, and therefore another method was needed in order to find a basis for long-term forecasting. Wilson had, according to Samuelson, debunked demographers' infatuation with the logistic curve, which may explain his attempt to find an alternative way of modeling population dynamics.

Samuelson's method was to consider a simple case in which population began at zero and then suddenly rose to one, calculating the number of births (a fraction) needed to keep population at this new level.[c] It was then possible to analyze any time path of the population: "A population growing according to any law whatsoever can be regarded as made up of a sum of step functions, and the number of births at any time is equal to the sum of the replacements computed for each such step function."[10] No doubt responding to Lotka's criticisms of his earlier paper, Samuelson explained that his results assumed a simplified model of reproduction, in which all births occurred at the average age of confinement, assumed to be thirty. Whereas conventional estimates showed a slow decline in the rate of population growth, his own methods suggested that population growth was slowing down rapidly and that after 1960 it would begin falling.

The editor, Frederick Stephan, showed Samuelson's paper to Lotka, who then contacted Samuelson. Lotka pointed out that he had presented a paper on the same subject at the American Statistical Association

---

c. This is the Heaviside step function, taken from electrical circuit theory, mentioned previously.

meeting in December 1938, which had been published in June.[11] Lotka suggested that Paul might present a slightly different paper, drawing on his own (Lotka's) equation, to the forthcoming meeting of the American Statistical Association.[12] Samuelson was unable to take up Lotka's invitation, as he was not attending the AEA/ASA meeting that year, but he explained the motivation for his and Marion's work.[13] The reason they could not use Lotka's statistical methods was that they would not work when there were periodic fluctuations, as in business cycle data.[14] They had used a different technique, and "much to our gratification" this had led to the same type of equation as used by Lotka.[15,d] This letter shows the connection that Paul and Marion were trying to make between population growth and business cycle theory, using a type of mathematics very different from that involved in his more familiar multiplier–accelerator model.[e]

Labor Economics

Though Paul spent much of his time discussing ideas with fellow students and faculty members, only one joint paper was published while he was at Harvard. His work with Marion remained unpublished, and his work with Stolper on international trade was not published until 1941.[16] His co-author on the paper published in 1940 was Russ Nixon, a couple of years older than Paul and who had been an instructor at Harvard since 1936.[17] John F. Kennedy took pride in having been taught by Russ Nixon, telling John Kenneth Galbraith on one occasion, "Remember, I'm pretty good at this; I was a student of Russ Nixon."[18] Samuelson described him as "our class radical and Radcliffe students' pin-up boy."[19] He left Harvard in 1941, and by the end of the year had set up the Washington office of the left-wing United Electrical Workers Union. "I am sure J. Edgar Hoover has my name in his FBI files as a collaborator with Nixon," Samuelson wrote, "but I have not had the curiosity to use the Freedom of Information Act to learn the details."[20] (A recent freedom of information request revealed no FBI interest in his relationship with Nixon; the file was all about his relationship with another fellow student,

---

d. The technique they had used was Volterra integral equations. Lotka, who typically responded by explaining to Paul that something had been covered in his earlier work, said that while Paul's method had expositional advantages, he did not consider it more general.

e. See chapter 13 this volume.

Tsuru.) Not surprisingly, Nixon's thesis, submitted in 1940, had been on employability and the labor market.

Samuelson explained that he became involved in writing the paper "Estimates of Unemployment in the United States" with Nixon because he learned that "a third-party go-getter was elbowing Nixon out of a joint venture," and he sympathized with the underdog.[21] Friendship clearly provided an important motivation for Samuelson: they kept in touch when he was visiting Washington during the war, even though they were no longer working together. Though Samuelson claimed that as a theorist he was not destined to work on unemployment statistics, the topic fitted well with his growing interest in business cycle theory and Keynesian economics. The division of labor is not clear, but it is natural to assume that Samuelson played a significant role in the theoretical discussion that preceded their presentation of statistics for employment and unemployment.

The heart of the paper was their discussion of five measures of unemployment from 1929 to 1940 during the Great Depression. Taking into account statistical issues, such as the way different censuses treated unpaid family labor, they concluded that there was no uniquely correct measure of unemployment. However, though the paper was primarily an exercise in statistics, its main interest in relation to Samuelson's intellectual development lies in the theoretical arguments used to make sense of different ways in which unemployment could be measured. They started by defining full employment in terms of a short-run labor supply curve: "Employment is full when individuals work as much as they would be willing to work at a given real wage (or structure of real wages)."[22,f] Such a definition, though it might seem complicated, was essential in a world in which workers had different preferences and if one family member became unemployed, other family members tried to find employment. Employment might be less than full because the labor market was imperfect, perhaps because those who were unemployed held back from bidding down the wages received by those who were working, or because employers refused to hire workers at less than what they believed to be a "fair" wage.[23]

This was the conventional analysis. It rested on the tacit assumption that a cut in wages would reduce or eliminate unemployment, as implied by the theory of supply and demand in a competitive market, and it was at this point that they tackled the ideas of Keynes. Citing criticisms made by

---

f. The real wage is the money wage rate adjusted for changes in prices; it measures the quantity of goods and services that the wage rate will buy.

Leontief, they were skeptical of Keynes's argument that workers might suffer from an "optical illusion," whereby they resisted cuts in money wages but did not resist cuts in real wages brought about by prices rising faster than wages. They argued that, according to Keynes's own theory, employment and the real wage would change only if the interest rate, investment, or the propensity to consume were changed; it was thus possible to have a downward spiral of wages and prices without any change in employment. They were equally dismissive of Keynes's attempt to provide an alternative definition of full employment as the level of employment where rising effective demand caused wages to rise; wages often rise, they argued, when unemployment was still high. Noting that "an increase in unemployment is usually associated with declines in production and the real national income," they accepted that "fluctuations in these magnitudes are the result of fluctuations in the level of 'effective demand.' "[24] However, they were clear that this idea was not tied to any particular theory of the cycle; they did not see it as a specifically Keynesian idea.

A concept to which they attached particular importance was "disguised unemployment," on which they cited Joan Robinson.[25] When people lost their jobs, they might engage in subsistence farming or house-to-house selling, or they might accept lower-paid work than they were qualified to do. This was a significant problem in the United States, for agricultural statistics showed unpaid family workers and subsistence farmers as being employed, and their reclassification would raise the unemployment count by millions. The importance of agriculture was no doubt the reason why they had discussed the topic with Harvard's main agricultural economist, John Black, whom they thanked for many suggestions and several of whose papers they cited.

Their discussion of this point raised the question of where the boundary was between problems of microeconomic resource allocation and problems of the business cycle. "Some readers," they claimed, "may believe that problems of non-optimal allocation of resources belong in the field of welfare economics and value theory, and that consideration of such problems in connection with a study of unemployment is tantamount to permitting welfare economics to swallow up business cycle theory completely."[26] Against this, they countered,

> We would argue that the concept of disguised unemployment should not include all deviations from optimal allocation, *but only those which are due to cyclical variations in the level of effective demand.* The concept of disguised unemployment is peculiarly useful because it illustrates that

even in a perfectly organized labor market ... large fluctuations in the level of the national income and production would still be possible.[27]

Nixon and Samuelson were, like Keynes, making a clear separation between what would later be called microeconomics and macroeconomics. They also followed Keynes in arguing that the failure of Say's Law (the idea that supply creates its own demand and so there cannot therefore be a shortage of demand) is not simply the result of rigidities in the price system. However, their use of Keynesian ideas was selective, for they had clearly accepted some of the criticisms that their teachers, notably Leontief, had made of Keynes's *General Theory*.

It is also worth noting that this article is the first indication of how the war, which had broken out in Europe, though the United States was not yet fully involved, was beginning to affect thinking. British authors (including Keynes) were turning to a different concept of full employment—maximum labor resources or "national potential"—which, if used, would result in much higher estimates of unemployment. "It is paradoxical," they wrote, "that the true economic realities of scarcity and choice become apparent, even to the uninitiated, only in time of war, when the problem of effective demand becomes nonexistent and the monetary veil is pierced."[28] War had made people aware that, although the immediate problem was lack of demand, the basic economic problem remained that of scarce resources. This led Samuelson and Nixon to think of full employment as a ceiling that could never be reached.[29] They were thinking seriously about the supply side of the economy, and not just about aggregate demand.

Trade and Welfare

Though the social welfare function was Bergson's, in the following decade it was Samuelson who defended the underlying approach to welfare economics.[g] The first context for Samuelson's application of this approach was international trade. "Welfare Economics and International Trade" (1938f) opened with the observation that the theory of international trade had been developed in order to answer normative questions, and because the theory of welfare

---

g. Bergson's publications were focused on issues relating more directly to problems confronting the government agencies for which he was working during the war—price flexibility and the economics of the Soviet Union—and after the war he became a specialist on the latter.

economics was going through a period of controversy, it was appropriate to revisit the theory of international trade to see whether existing conclusions were valid in light of new ideas about welfare.

Samuelson's starting point was the position that formed the basis for Bergson's social welfare function: that welfare economics implied making ethical judgments.

> At the outset, it is understood of course that every discussion of welfare economics implies certain ethical assumptions. I do not propose, however, to discuss the philosophical grounds for holding or rejecting different ethical precepts or assumptions. Rather will the discussion be confined to the implications of different ethical assumptions and the necessary and sufficient presuppositions or the truth of various theorems.[30]

Though he wrote in terms of utility, he had in mind ordinal utility, which meant that it was impossible to measure the difference in utility between two situations. If utility functions served only to rank alternative combinations of goods in order of preference, and could not measure how good they were, then a fortiori they could not be used to compare the well-being of different individuals.

Samuelson simplified the argument by considering trade between two individuals, so that no aggregation problems arose within each of the parties engaging in the trade. This meant that he could represent each trader's behavior by a set of indifference curves. He made the assumption that if one trader preferred one outcome to another, this was better for that trader (the judgment that each individual is the judge of his or her own welfare). If both parties were better off, then this was an overall welfare gain. The problem was that if one of the two parties was made better off and the other worse off, it was impossible to know whether or not there was an overall increase in welfare, for there was no way to measure or add their utilities. This meant that, though he could show that some trade was better than no trade, he could not show that free trade was optimal; it was possible that moving from protection to free trade would benefit one person and harm another.

The following year he developed this argument, arguing that if the introduction of trade resulted in relative prices that were different from those prevailing with no trade, all parties to the trade would be better off than if the trade did not take place.[31] This was a familiar result, but Samuelson argued that writers often claimed it could be proved only under restrictive assumptions about production costs. In contrast, he claimed that all valid normative propositions about international trade could be derived from "the most general theories of equilibrium," without making any restrictive assumptions about costs other than those necessary to ensure there could be perfect competition.[32]

He then made what is often called the small-country assumption that the country being analyzed is too small to influence world prices—and he showed that, if all individuals were identical (removing the possibility that some would gain and others would lose), the introduction of international trade would increase welfare so long as world prices were different from those prevailing under autarky (where the prices at which goods are traded must equal world prices). His proof involved using techniques very similar to those employed in his first *Economica* article. He compared feasible bundles of goods with and without international trade, making the assumption that if, after some change in circumstances, people bought a different bundle of goods when they could have bought the same bundle as they bought before the change, then they must be better off. Such reasoning, closely related to the index number theory that had inspired it, was sufficient to prove his theorem. He noted that if any of the assumptions were removed, the proof would break down. One example he cited was that if production conditions varied between industries, with some industries facing increasing costs and others seeing falling costs, protection might sometimes be beneficial.[33]

Samuelson then turned to the case where individuals were not identical, conceding that it undermined the argument that everyone would benefit from the introduction of trade. However, rather than concede that nothing could be said, he turned to the idea of compensation, then being introduced into discussions of welfare. John Hicks and Nicholas Kaldor were arguing that there was an improvement in welfare if those who gained from a policy change could compensate any losers and still remain better off than before the change. Using similar reasoning, Samuelson argued that if trade were introduced, those who gained would be able to compensate those who lost and still remain better off themselves, implying that everyone could be made better off through trade. However, he refused to provide any measure of the gains from trade. Perhaps implicitly responding to John Hicks's attempts to reinstate the concept of consumers' surplus, Samuelson noted that "constructs such as consumers' surplus are in general inadmissible," and that in the special cases where they could be used, they were "perfectly arbitrary and conventional, adding nothing to the analysis."[h]

---

h. Consumers' surplus was a measure of welfare developed by Alfred Marshall, discussed in chapter 10 this volume. Samuelson 1939a, p. 205.

Thus, although his discussions are consistent with Bergson's social welfare function, Samuelson confined his welfare judgments essentially to the Pareto criterion: that if at least one person is better off and no one is worse off, then there is an overall improvement in welfare. As in his previous work, he emphasized the importance of formal reasoning. He attached less importance to the results he had derived (perhaps not surprisingly, as they were very weak) than to the fact that he had demonstrated them rigorously, "with little reliance on intuition."[34] The theorems, he continued, "are true consequences of the premises, and do not rest on *presumption* or *probability*." Addressing the relevance of such formal reasoning, he concluded his article by writing,

> Whether or not this [rigorous reasoning] should be done is, of course, a matter of taste.... For in pointing out the consequences of a set of abstract assumptions, one need not be committed unduly as to the relation between reality and these assumptions. On the other hand, in advancing a presumption in favour of an undeducible proposition, the suggestion is conveyed that the difficult task of interpreting reality has already been performed.[35]

His assumptions might be unrealistic, but this had the merit of making clear that no claims were being made about the real world. The implication was that although other economists—whose theories were based on more realistic assumptions—might seem to be saying something about the world, they were making claims that did not follow from their assumptions. The use of rigorous mathematics was revealing faults in existing theories.

Ironically, it was Marion who was the first to make use of these results that Paul had derived. In 1938, the *Quarterly Journal of Economics* carried an article by Karl Anderson of Bryn Mawr College, attacking those Australian economists who argued that Australia's historical circumstances justified the imposition of a protective tariff. A tariff on manufactured goods was claimed have two favorable effects: (1) it would divert labor from agriculture to manufacturing, thereby helping to maintain the prices of the agricultural products that Australia exported; (2) because labor was more important, in relation to land and to manufacturing rather than to agriculture, it would raise the income going to the laboring class. In contrast, Anderson contended that the income of every group would be maximized under free trade and that "there is nothing about the 'historical situation' of Australia to warrant the opinion that she can derive any kind of economic benefit from protection."[36]

At some point during 1939, Marion wrote a reply to Anderson, published in the November issue of the *Quarterly Journal of Economics*. She constructed a numerical example in which protection was shown to raise Australian consumption of both manufactured goods and primary products, and in which the income accruing to labor increased. Anderson's claim was wrong. A central argument in Marion's paper was that Paul had provided "a general analytical proof" of the conclusions she had reached; it could be shown that the only critical assumption was that Australia should be able to affect the prices of its exports by imposing a tariff.[37,i] Faced with her argument, Anderson conceded that his involved "a complete *non sequitur*" and did not try to defend it.[38] However, in his rejoinder he made the point that it was questionable whether one should talk about supply and demand curves in international trade; that is, it was impossible to devise units in which to measure goods traded that would give any meaning to supply and demand curves (or the notion of an elasticity of demand) such as she had used.

This latter remark prompted a reaction from Frank Graham, a Princeton economist who had published extensively on international trade, cited by Paul in "The Gains from International Trade" (1939a). Not unusual for that time, even though it was Marion whose name was on the journal article, Graham wrote to Paul, stating that he presumed she was his wife, as if that entitled him to ignore her. He noted that Anderson objected to the idea of constructing a demand function for a country, observing that he thought he had "disposed pretty thoroughly of that question" in two of his articles, but "the vitality of error makes the Phoenix look supremely mortal!"[39]

One point that is interesting about Marion's article is her use of Bergson's arguments about social welfare. Whereas Paul, in his article "The Gains from International Trade," presumably written before hers, argued that trade was beneficial if those who gained could compensate those who lost, Marion did not use such an argument. She cited Bergson in support of her claim that no one had ever demonstrated that equilibrium under pure competition represented the maximum of "some social magnitude."[40] She noted that government subsidies to the landowners who lost through protection might "modify" the situation, but she refrained from noting that if national income had risen, this meant the laborers could still be better off if the landowners were compensated. Given that she must have known and understood the argument, it seems possible she was more skeptical about that point than Paul was.

When Samuelson did eventually publish on this topic, his co-author was not Marion but Wolfgang Stolper, a fellow graduate student who lived close by. Samuelson remembered Stolper as being his first contact with continental

i. That the elasticity of demand for Australian imports was not infinite.

European culture, introducing him to Viennese waltzes and Lederhosen, and reacting indignantly when an ignorant waiter responded to a complaint about the temperature of some Chablis by adding an ice cube to the glass.[41] The cultured Stolper found it incredible that Samuelson would listen to the movements of a Beethoven symphony in the order 1, 4, 2, 3, because this minimized the number of times he had to get up to turn over the 78 RPM records on which they were recorded. Stolper and his wife married in the same year as Paul and Marion, and the two couples became close friends.

Samuelson's later memory of his early collaboration with Stolper was vivid.

> One day in the late 1930s, Stolper mentioned to me a curiosity: "Old Taussig . . . asserts that free trade raises American wages by drawing workers into the sectors of maximum comparative advantage. How do we square this with Ohlin's notion that the input America is most niggardly endowed with can have its return lowered by free trade in comparison with autarky?"
>
> The point was a new one to me. I said, "You've got something there. Work it out."
>
> He did. And in the course of his explorations we talked endlessly about the many ramifications of the problem. The analysis soon went beyond the point about free trade, which fell naturally into place after one had sorted out the issues.[42]

It was presumably this work that placed Samuelson in a position where he could provide the more general analysis to support the numerical example Marion used in her paper, even if he and Stolper had at that point not reached the point where either of them was prepared to publish on the subject. Perhaps he still remembered Viner's letter saying that mathematical arguments were more interesting if he could prove something that was not obvious.

Though it was Wolfgang Stolper and Paul Samuelson who were named as the authors of the paper that eventually emerged, "Protection and Real Wages" (1941), Marion was also involved in the writing. Stolper admitted that, as would have reflected the prejudices of the time, she typed the paper, though his memory that they "literally dictated alternate sentences to her" suggests that her role was probably much greater, involving at a minimum translation of their competing suggestions into something coherent.[43] What came to be known as "the Stolper-Samuelson theorem" made a sufficiently important contribution to the theory of international trade that, many years after Marion's death, a conference was convened to celebrate its fiftieth anniversary. On that occasion, Samuelson reflected, in terms that may reveal some guilt for not having made sufficient acknowledgment of her work at the time, "my unconscious mind must have benefited enormously in 1940–41 from knowledge of Marion's 1939 QJE findings."[44] The crucial point in the paper was that, though much traditional theory concealed this fact by applying a labor theory of value, international trade theory actually involved two factors of production—labor and land. Though it was the Stolper-Samuelson paper that made it explicit, the same point had been implicit in Marion's paper.

In their paper, worked out after Samuelson had left Harvard, they stated that economists had repeatedly tried to show the fallacy in the popular view that protective tariffs could raise either employment or real wages, However, though that popular view might be wrong, the literature contained few unambiguous results. By making additional assumptions, Stolper and Samuelson proved that, if labor was the scarce factor of production, protection could raise wages. Their starting point was to assume that there were two commodities (wheat and watches) and two factors of production (labor and capital). For each commodity there was a production function relating output to the inputs of capital and labor allocated to that sector, from which they could derive the conditions for optimal allocation of capital and labor between the two sectors. It was a model of the production side of the economy. Furthermore, demand conditions did not need to be specified, because they assumed that the relative price of wheat and watches was determined in international markets. They could then work out the effect of changes in this price ratio on the allocation of capital and labor within the economy, and hence on real wages. They concluded that "[i]nternational trade necessarily lowers the real wage of the scarce factor," a result that was true whether workers were assumed to consume wheat, watches, or a mixture of both.[45,j] This result would be true even if there were more than two commodities; however, it would not necessarily be true if there were more than two countries.

Their paper was submitted to the *American Economic Review*, where it was considered by Howard Ellis and Paul Homan, who provided the following assessment, on May 2, 1941:

> We both agree that the article is a brilliant theoretical performance, and since we wish to have from time to time good and substantial theoretical articles in the Review, we very much dislike to reject it. On the other hand, we agree that it is a very narrow study in formal theory, which adds practically nothing to the literature of the subject with which it is nominally concerned. Indeed, by your own admission

---

j. Though the term "wage" is mostly used to refer to labor income, in this sentence it is used as a generic term to refer to the income earned by any factor of production.

in the last pages, it is practically a complete "sell-out." It does not, in other words, have anything to say about any of the real situations with which the theory of international trade has to concern itself.[46]

Homan decided to return the paper despite it being "so good of its kind." He urged them to rewrite it so as to add "something relevant that really will have some bearing upon the practical problem that you introduce at the beginning and end of the article." He argued that there must be something that could be said even if it could not be reduced to the neat theoretical treatment they had used. This amounted to suggesting that they write a new paper on the same problem so, not surprisingly, they did not take his advice. Stolper and Samuelson then submitted it to the *Review of Economic Studies,* where the British economist Ursula Hicks accepted it for publication with the remark, "I do congratulate you on having found a new point in the theory of international trade."[47]

Though Hicks appreciated the paper, it seems likely that even she did not appreciate how significant the paper would prove to be. The paper laid the foundation on which much trade theory was built for the next thirty to forty years. As was noted in the fiftieth anniversary celebration of the paper, the significance of their result resided as much in the way they derived their result as in the result itself.[48] They worked with a formal general equilibrium model in which there were two of everything: two countries, two goods, and two factors of production. This made it possible both to write down and derive comparative statics results and to represent what was happening using diagrams. They represented the equilibrium quantities of goods produced using Leontief's diagram that combined indifference curves with Haberler's substitution curve.[k] To show what happened to factor prices and the allocation of capital and labor between the two industries, they used what is often called an Edgeworth or Edgeworth-Bowley box diagram, with which they would have been familiar from Wilson's course, for which Bowley's textbook had been essential reading. Such diagrams were, following their article, to become staples of international trade theory.

They had provided a formal general equilibrium model, going beyond the work of their predecessors and teachers—Taussig, Viner, Haberler, and Leontief—by describing explicitly the allocation of capital and labor between sectors. However, when it came to analyzing the effects of protection, they relied heavily on verbal arguments, for tariffs did not enter the model explicitly and neither did production conditions in the rest of the world. Even

k. See figures 9.2 and 9.1 this volume.

working out from their diagrams which good is the more capital intensive (a point critical to their arguments) required careful thought. It is therefore possible to sympathize with Homan, for there is a sense in which he and Ellis were entirely right to say that much of the article was not really about the problem that Stolper and Samuelson claimed it to be about. As the authors conceded, their results would not hold in the realistic case where there are more than two factors of production, and too much was happening "offstage."

Another feature of their article was coining the term "Heckscher-Ohlin model" to denote a model in which countries (usually two) were assumed to have the same technology (the same production function) but different endowments of capital and labor. Trade was then determined by the relative factor endowments of the two countries: the country with the highest ratio of labor to capital would export the labor-intensive good, and the other country would export the capital-intensive good. The significance of this model was that it provided a formal general equilibrium model that could be manipulated to work out what would happen to the equilibrium when one of the parameters changed. Although Stolper and Samuelson attributed the model to the Swedish economists Eli Heckscher and Bertil Ohlin, neither Heckscher nor Ohlin confined themselves to the assumptions of this model.[49] Instead, Stolper and Samuelson had simplified Ohlin's theory to the point where it could be translated into a simple set of either equations or diagrams—something neither Heckscher nor Ohlin had actually done.[1] In attributing the model to Heckscher and Ohlin, Stolper and Samuelson understated their own originality.

---

1. In the subsequent literature, the model was sometimes referred to as the Heckscher-Ohlin-Samuelson model (with possible injustice to Stolper), or even the Heckscher-Ohlin-Samuelson-Jones model, Jones being one of Samuelson's students who specialized in the field.

CHAPTER 12 | Alvin Harvey Hansen

The Conversion Myth

Samuelson had previously taken courses on business cycle theory and money and banking, but he developed a serious interest in these topics only while he was a junior fellow. His own explanation of this new direction in his thinking is simple: he and his friends discovered Keynes. In an article written to mark Keynes's death, he wrote, using the quotation from Wordsworth's *The Prelude* that he had used on several other occasions to describe his time in the Society of Fellows (see chapter 10 this volume):

> To have been born as an economist before 1936 was a boon—yes. But not to have been born too long before!
>
> > Bliss was it in that dawn to be alive,
> > But to be young was very heaven!
>
> The *General Theory* caught most economists under the age of 35 with the unexpected virulence of a disease first attacking and decimating an isolated tribe of South Sea islanders. Economists beyond 50 turned out to be quite immune to the ailment. With time, most economists in-between began to run the fever, often without knowing or admitting their condition.[1]

In this account, Samuelson became caught up in the excitement created by Keynes's revolutionary ideas. Though he thought that the joke had worn thin, he spoke of this revolution as if it were a religious movement: "[W]e find a Gospel, Scriptures, a Prophet, Disciples, Apostles, Epigoni, and even a Duality; and if there is no Apostolic Succession, there is at least an Apostolic Benediction."[2] He went on to spoil his opening generalization about economists under thirty-five having no immunity to Keynesian ideas by saying that, for two years, he had been immune, even though he was only twenty when the *General Theory* was published.[a]

> I must confess that my own first reaction to the *General Theory* was not at all like that of Keats on first looking into Chapman's Homer. No silent watcher, I, upon a peak in Darien. My rebellion against its pretensions would have been complete except for an uneasy realization that I did not at all understand what it was about. And I think I am giving away no secrets when I solemnly aver—upon the basis of vivid personal recollection—that no one else in Cambridge, Massachusetts, really knew what it was about for some 12 to 18 months after its publication.[3]

His initial resistance to Keynesian ideas was part of his claim, to which he attached great importance, of having been old enough to have understood the old theories.

The other element in this immensely powerful myth concerns the role of one of his teachers, Alvin Hansen, who arrived at Harvard from the University of Minnesota in September 1937. Samuelson presented him as having been converted to Keynes when he arrived at Harvard, the sole exception to the rule that economists over the age of fifty were immune to the Keynesian disease. "On the train from Minnesota, so to speak, Hansen must have seen the light."[4] In an article in *Newsweek*, he picked Hansen out as unique among his generation.

> As the great Max Planck, himself the originator of the quantum theory in physics, has said, science makes progress funeral by funeral: the old are never converted by the new doctrines, they are simply replaced by a new generation. He [Hansen] read Keynes, and disagreed. He read again, and agreed.[5]

"Singlehandedly," Samuelson wrote in the *New York Times*, "he converted a generation of Harvard (and American!) economists away from an ancient orthodoxy in macroeconomic policy."[6] Moreover, Hansen did not simply

---

a. The book appeared in February; his twenty-first birthday was in May.

convert a generation of academic economists; he also converted policymakers. In his second term, Samuelson claimed, it became clear that Roosevelt's "fireside chats," the National Recovery Administration (NRA), and planning rhetoric would not pull the United States out of depression: it was necessary to run deliberate budget deficits to restore prosperity.[b] "It was Hansen, and his Harvard-trained economists," he wrote, "who gradually converted the President and the Congress to an understanding of these facts of economic life."[7]

Several points in this story are problematic, but it nevertheless attests to Hansen's immense importance for Samuelson.[c] Prior to Hansen's arrival, though he revered Schumpeter and to a lesser extent Haberler, the main influence on Samuelson had been Wilson, whom he described as his intellectual father. He never traced an intellectual family tree back through Hansen, but there is no doubt that for around a decade Hansen became his most important mentor. Shortly after being awarded the Nobel Memorial Prize when he wrote a memoir of his graduate-student days, Samuelson mailed a photocopy to Hansen with the inscription, "To Alvin Hansen, who made it all possible."[8] Samuelson was liberal with praise, and this was a private communication in which one might expect to find flattery, but there are good reasons to believe this remark should be taken very seriously—and perhaps even literally. Once Hansen arrived in Harvard, their careers became entwined, and Samuelson's work developed in directions in which Wilson could never have led him.

Samuelson's account of Hansen echoes his account of his own intellectual development. Hansen acquired authority as a supporter of Keynes because he had been not only old enough to have known the old theory but also one of its most eminent exponents. Samuelson therefore pointed out that, though his business cycle theory may have been eclectic, Hansen had explicitly endorsed Say's Law—the notion that it is impossible for there to be a shortage of aggregate demand—the doctrine that had been the main target of Keynes's book.[9] Samuelson also stressed the critical tone of Hansen's review of the *General Theory*, remarking that it would have gone down well with the Harvard professors who appointed him.[10]

Given its centrality to Samuelson's whole career, this episode needs to be examined very carefully. Hansen's most perceptive interpreter, Perry

---

b. The NRA, established in 1933, sought to reduce the competitive price cutting that was seen to be undermining businesses by establishing industry codes of practice.

c. Not least among the problems with this story is its neglect of the role of Lauchlin Currie.

Mehrling, has written about the story of Hansen's conversion that Samuelson helped to establish as a myth.

> Among economists, Hansen is most commonly remembered as a popularizer of the ideas of the great British economist John Maynard Keynes. According to what has become the accepted view, Hansen's special genius was his intellectual flexibility, to wit his willingness to abandon the neo-classical orthodoxy of his first fifty years in favor of the fresh ideas blowing in from across the ocean. . . . It must be admitted that this makes a marvelous story: Hansen as convert, like Saul on the road to Damascus, overwhelmed by the Keynesian light on the train from Minnesota to Harvard.[11]

Unfortunately, as Merhling documents in detail, hardly any of this account is true. Hansen was never an orthodox neoclassical economist, and he was never a convert to Keynes in the sense implied by the conversion myth. The reason the myth took such deep root and was so powerful was that it was extraordinarily useful. Mehrling continued:

> The historical usefulness of the conversion myth must also be admitted. If Hansen at fifty could reject the barren orthodoxy he himself had promulgated for twenty years at the University of Minnesota, why should any mere graduate student delay? If Hansen was the Apostle Paul, then Keynes was the Messiah, and the young Keynesians were the early Christians, with a message destined to sweep the world.

There is no one to whom this conversion myth was more useful than Samuelson, who became, along with Hansen, one of the leading exponents of Keynesian economics in America. His own career became so closely tied to Hansen's and to the Keynesian revolution that his view of Hansen came to be entangled with his own self-understanding. When he wrote about how Hansen had developed Keynesian theory so that it could be used to analyze the effects of policy, Samuelson was talking about areas in which his own contributions were, despite Hansen's seniority, of a similar magnitude. Samuelson wrote about Hansen's modesty, the way he give his students space to shine, and the way he sought the views of his critics. These were clearly remarks Samuelson would like to have been said about himself. Demythologizing Hansen's conversion is thus central to any understanding of Samuelson's role in the Keynesian revolution and his relationship to Harvard. The key to this is placing the discussion in the context in which it was viewed at the time—business cycle theory.

Harvard Economists and the Depression

To understand the context in which Samuelson encountered Hansen, it is important to understand the widespread skepticism toward using government spending to cure depression. The prevailing view, consistent with what Samuelson had been taught at Chicago, was laid out in a book written by seven Harvard professors, *The Economics of the Recovery Program*.[12] Published in the second year of Franklin Roosevelt's New Deal, and the year before Samuelson arrived at Harvard, it analyzed the measures so far taken to promote recovery. It claimed to do this in a nonpartisan spirit, contending that because the authors held different political views, such agreement as there was reflected their scientific training.[13] They asserted that their views were a long way from nineteenth-century liberalism, with its focus on laissez-faire, but the essays were generally pessimistic about whether the measures Roosevelt had introduced would be effective. The reason was not that the measures were too limited, for more radical measures would be subject to the same criticisms.

Schumpeter started the book by reviewing past depressions, concluding that not only would recovery eventually come about by itself but that it was *best* it came about by itself. Measures to mitigate the worst effects of the Depression (presumably unemployment benefits) were needed, but it was important that such measures not injure the economic organism and that necessary readjustments be allowed to take place. While he struck an optimistic note in arguing that recession would eventually end, he was fatalistic in arguing that government could do nothing to speed up the process.

Measures to promote recovery by raising demand were covered by Edward Chamberlin, Seymour Harris, and Douglass Brown. Countering the popular view that purchasing power was too low and needed to be increased—"under-consumptionism," an idea in wide circulation in popular writing since the nineteenth century—Chamberlin argued that the notion of raising purchasing power was misconceived, whether the measures to achieve it took the form of raising consumption or raising wages. Consumption could be raised only at the expense of investment, so measures to raise consumption would benefit one sector of the economy at the expense of another. Raising wages would benefit employed workers, but only at the expense of the unemployed and of other classes. It might also be counterproductive in that high wages might induce companies to mechanize production and reduce employment. Many New Deal measures were aimed at raising prices, thereby raising incomes in the sectors affected.

Harris offered a wide-ranging discussion of such policies, and saw that it might be possible to stimulate recovery by devaluing the dollar, thereby raising prices and making the world's stock of gold (now worth more dollars) go further. He argued that moderate, controlled inflation was a possibility, and that it was wrong to argue, drawing on memories of wartime experience and what had happened in parts of Europe in the 1920s, that the country faced a choice between deflation and uncontrolled inflation. However, though less pessimistic than Chamberlin, Harris could hardly be described as optimistic about the prospects for promoting recovery.

Similarly, though Brown argued that public works could contribute to recovery, the thrust of his essay was to stress the difficulties involved. It was, for example, important that such spending be undertaken "when the maladjustments which preceded the depression have been sufficiently wiped out so that an increase in production and employment, once started, may continue," and that it was sufficiently large and well targeted—all difficult to achieve because of "lack of precise knowledge" and "administrative difficulties and impediments." None of the contributors was optimistic about finding a remedy for the Depression.

Other members of the department would have endorsed the generally pessimistic tone of *Economics of the Recovery Program*. For example, Haberler, while he recognized that public works spending could contribute to recovery, took the view that such schemes raised "numerous and complicated problems of a fiscal, administrative and political nature."[14] He also noted that "[i]t is by no means easy (though it is not impossible) to find methods of raising the necessary funds, apart from an alarming expansion of central-bank money, without giving rise at the same time or later to a decrease in the flow of money at some other point of the economic system." Similarly, in discussing wage cuts, Haberler presented it as depending on many factors, qualifying his conclusion that wage cuts would help end a contraction with the remark, "if we carry the argument to its logical conclusion."[15] He noted that wage cuts might work if accompanied by public works spending (the inflationary effects of such spending would counter the deflationary effects of cutting wages), but he hedged this otherwise optimistic conclusion with many qualifications.

Haberler's *Prosperity and Depression* appeared very soon after the *General Theory*, meaning that Haberler had had only a short time to digest Keynes's ideas. In the first edition, discussions of Keynesian concepts were isolated and often confined to footnotes. He took the view that Keynes's theory was not yet fully understood because Keynes used new concepts without making it clear how they related to well-established ones. He sat on the fence in that he was unsure how far Keynes's differences from conventionally held views were substantive and how far they were merely terminological.

Much clearer positions on the Keynes book were taken by other Harvard economists toward the end of 1936. In November 1936, the *Quarterly Journal of Economics*, edited by the Harvard faculty, carried four critical reviews, including one moderately critical one by the recently retired Frank Taussig, and a much more critical one by Wassily Leontief. Constructing an argument in terms of the theory of general competitive equilibrium, Leontief argued that Keynes's novelty was in denying the "homogeneity postulate": the idea that if all prices rise in the same proportion, demand will not change.[16] He concluded simply that, because Keynes had provided neither a theoretical argument for his position nor convincing empirical evidence, his case was unproven.

The following month, Schumpeter, though paying tribute to Keynes's brilliance, denounced the book as claiming to provide a general theory when it did nothing of the kind.[17] It was not even scientific, for it was offering policy advice that was valid only in very specific circumstances. Artificial definitions and highly specialized assumptions were used to produce seemingly paradoxical tautologies that were "invested with a treacherous generality."[18] By abstracting from the dynamics of capitalism, Keynes had lost contact with the modern industrial world.

The following February, Leontief mounted a more sustained methodological critique not just of Keynes but also of the entire Cambridge (UK) school: it was based on "implicit theorizing" that smuggled in unacceptable assumptions through the use of peculiar definitions.[19] The *General Theory* was a treacherous guidebook. One professor, Sumner Slichter, offered an eclectic and empirical view of the business cycle that led Samuelson to describe him as a closeted Keynesian, though he did not develop any formal theory. Burbank strongly disapproved of the way instructors of Ec. A, the introductory economics course for undergraduates, would insinuate Keynesian heresies into their teaching. One undergraduate who was later to become an eminent Keynesian economist, working closely with Samuelson, was introduced to the *General Theory* not by any professor but by his tutor, who urged him to read "this new book from England" on the grounds that "They say it may be important."[20]

Keynes was not popular among the senior members of Harvard's Economics department, but the nature of the opposition varied considerably. Schumpeter and Leontief thought it bad economic theory, resting on illegitimate arguments. A different line of criticism was taken by the majority of the department; they approached the book from the perspective of traditional American business cycle theory, in which many of them had been involved. They did not argue in terms of what came, in the 1940s, to be called a "model," but engaged in much looser verbal reasoning, constructing accounts in which the existence of many unquantifiable factors made it impossible to draw clear-cut conclusions. Although they did acknowledge that policy could affect total spending, and hence affect output, the absence of any way to judge the relative strength of different forces meant that, even when they reached "Keynesian" conclusions, as some of them did, they were often hedged almost beyond recognition. For example, Slichter's Keynesianism was never explicit.

The lack of formal, mathematical analysis explains why Samuelson had not been an enthusiast for business cycle theory before Hansen's arrival. Excited by the prospects for using mathematics in economic theory, he focused on those fields where his mathematical skills could be used to cut through the confusions found in the literature. His intellectual agenda was not at this point motivated by trying to solve the problem of unemployment—perhaps because he believed there was little government could do, or perhaps because he was caught up in his enthusiasm for mathematical economics. Business cycle theory as presented by his Harvard teachers did not present the theoretical challenge that was needed to get his attention.

Graduate Students and Keynes

Though their seniors were skeptical of the *General Theory*, many of the graduate students and instructors were enthusiastic. The key figure here was a Canadian, Robert Bryce, who graduated in engineering from the University of Toronto. In the summer of 1932, he went to Cambridge to learn about the causes of the depression that had prevented him from finding work as an engineer. Knowing no economics, he found himself attending Keynes's Monday evening Political Economy Club, listening to Keynes talking about the papers, and at the end of the evening, speaking on "anything and everything." After his first year, during which his tutor was the argumentative Joan Robinson, he came close to giving up what he considered a "messy" subject, but persuaded by his parents, he persisted. By the end of his second year, Bryce had become captivated by Keynes, entranced by his knowledge of markets and institutions, his incredible memory for the things that mattered, his prodigious versatility, and his intuition.[21,d]

---

d. He would have picked up the importance of intuition from Keynes himself, for this was

Though the arguments were not complete, these lectures contained a clear account of the theory to be published in the *General Theory*. With the new-found zeal of a convert, Bryce engaged in what he later described as "missionary endeavours," presenting Keynes's ideas to the unconverted at LSE, discussing them with students in Friedrich Hayek's seminar. Bryce remembers his experience in presenting Keynesian ideas at LSE as being what motivated him to go to Harvard, where he arrived in the same year as Samuelson. Though he wanted to learn from Leontief, Schumpeter, and other Harvard economists, he saw himself as propagating the gospel he had learned from the master in Cambridge.

Someone on whom Bryce had relied for support in Cambridge was a fellow Canadian student, Lorie Tarshis, who like Samuelson was to be attacked for writing a textbook based on Keynesian ideas. Unlike Bryce, Tarshis had studied economics at Toronto, and had even taken a course on money and banking based on Keynes's *Treatise on Money*, encouraged to take his studies more seriously by the dire economic situation. He attended the Political Economy Club and, unlike Bryce who just took another undergraduate degree, he stayed on for graduate work, focusing on the determinants of wages, in which he drew on Keynes's ideas. In September 1936, he took a teaching position at Tufts University, three miles from Harvard.

At Harvard, Bryce, together with Paul Sweezy, organized an informal seminar on Keynes's ideas that was attended by graduate students and young faculty members, including Tarshis and Sweezy's supervisor, Seymour Harris.[22] He remembers John Kenneth Galbraith, a specialist in agricultural economics working with John Black, as having attended occasionally, and Samuelson as having been involved in their discussions. Their discussions centered first on an account of Keynes's ideas that Bryce had prepared for use at LSE and then, in February 1936, on *The General Theory of Employment and Money* itself.[23] Because the New York publication date was several weeks after the book was available in Britain, Bryce arranged for copies to be shipped directly from Britain to Harvard. Bryce believed that for most of that academic year, he was the only person at Harvard who understood and appreciated the book: Leontief understood it but was skeptical; Schumpeter was interested in Bryce's paper, but did not absorb its message. It was the young economists, large numbers of whom remained at Harvard because jobs were

---

something Keynes stressed in the lectures in which he was trying to move forward from his *Treatise on Money*, which Bryce and his friends attended and recorded (Keynes 1971, Rymes 1989; see Backhouse 2010).

scarce,[24] who were attracted by Keynes, even if, at least at this stage, they did not fully understand his theory.[25]

Samuelson, who had taken Williams's course in money and banking along with Bryce in the previous term, was one of those who acquired early copies of the *General Theory*, together with the short summary of the book that Bryce had prepared. However, he resisted the idea of equilibrium unemployment, arguing with Bryce about it, his position reinforced by Leontief's derision of the book.[e] Samuelson later recalled that when, during his general examination, Seymour Harris asked him a question about "leakages" and the multiplier—two concepts central to the *General Theory*—he thought it was "off limits" and "felt uneasy about it."[26,f] If that memory is correct, not only was he not a Keynesian but also he did not even understand some of the central technical points about Keynesian theory.

In September 1937, as the United States began to fall back into recession, members of the Harvard-Tufts group had the idea of writing a book on the policies that needed to be pursued. They discussed drafts in the first half of 1938, and it was published as *An Economic Program for American Democracy*.[27] Samuelson recalled that he had the opportunity to be one of those involved in the book, but "wasn't much of a joiner" and so chose not to participate.[28] It is easy to see the influence of Keynes, for the book is a sustained argument for higher public spending to maintain a higher level of demand in order to achieve continuing full employment. This was needed not just for its own sake but in order to save America's "free democratic institutions." If no action were taken, there would be a danger that businessmen, "obsessed with a devil theory of government" would use economic power to institute a dictatorship. Presumably reflecting events in Germany, they opined that the economic activity revived by such a dictatorship would be "devoted increasingly to producing weapons of death and destruction which must sooner or later be used to plunge the country into a holocaust of slaughter and bloodshed."[29]

---

e. It is perhaps worth noting that Marion, in her UG thesis, which she discussed with Paul, used the phrase "implicit theorizing," which Leontief used to summarize his objections to the *General Theory*. See chapter 6 this volume.

f. Savings are considered a "leakage" from the circular flow of income, in that they constitute income not spent on goods and services and that do not generate further income. The contrast is to spending on goods and services, whether consumption or investment, which generates income for those people from whom goods and services are purchased. If saving is high, the multiplier—the total rise in income resulting from a one-unit stimulus to investment—will be lower.

The Harvard-Tufts economists used analysis that could easily be described as Keynesian, but they framed the problem in a way that was rooted in the type of analysis Hansen was offering. Samuelson remembered that on one occasion Hansen told him he did not think the book very original: "I thought it was just about what was in my lectures."[30] The household sector was a net saver; it did not spend all of its income. This meant that some other sector had to be a net borrower. Up until 1929, investment opportunities were sufficiently great that the private sector could fill this role. The expansion of the frontier and subsequent development of cities and the rise of industry created great investment opportunities. War and demand from the rest of the world had sustained expansion during the early twentieth century, but by 1929, investment opportunities had run out. This amounted to a structural change that, when combined with a severe downturn, produced the Great Depression.

The New Deal, they argued, had been a great success. It had increased government spending, filling the role that the private sector could no longer fill. However, by 1936, once the crisis had passed, the coalition supporting the New Deal began to fragment, spending was cut back, and the result was the 1937 downturn. What was needed, they contended, was to convert the emergency measures of the New Deal into a long-term program to sustain full employment. To that end, they formulated detailed proposals for expanding consumption (through increased welfare benefits and redistributive taxation) and investment (financed by borrowing).

Hansen as a Business Cycle Theorist

Alvin Harvey Hansen (1887–1975) arrived in September 1937 to join the Harvard Economics department, in which the younger and older generations were taking opposite positions on Keynes's *General Theory*. Like Samuelson, Hansen was the son of immigrants, though Hansen's parents came from Denmark rather than from Poland and they had settled in rural South Dakota, not in the Midwest.[31] He was the first member of his local community to attend Yankton College, a small liberal arts institution associated with the Congregational Church (his parents were strict Baptists). He majored in English, and after a spell teaching locally and a summer spent at the University of Chicago, Hansen decided to study economics and sociology at the University of Wisconsin. When Hansen enrolled in 1913, the university was an important center for American economics; it was the home of Richard Ely, the first president of the AEA, and John R. Commons, one of the major figures in the institutionalist movement that dominated the field up to the 1930s. Wesley Mitchell, another major figure in the institutionalist movement, was an important influence on Hansen, whose PhD dissertation, completed after he moved to Brown University, was very much in the mold of the quantitative empirical research that Mitchell was to encourage at the NBER after he became its first director in 1919.[g] Hansen then moved to the University of Minnesota, where he stayed for nearly two decades, before coming to Harvard.

Hansen came to Harvard as the Lucius N. Littauer Chair of Political Economy, joining the newly established Graduate School of Public Administration, which became known simply as the Littauer Center.[32] He was recruited by John Williams, the school's first Dean, though with the approval of the Economics Department in which he would spend part of his time.[33] Hansen's duties at the center included running its seminar on fiscal policy.[34] Their hopes for the center are reflected in Williams having approached Henry Morgenthau (U.S. Secretary of the Treasury), Marriner Eccles (chairman of the Federal Reserve), and Emanuel Alexander Goldenweiser (also at the Fed) about people they could attract as visitors. Hansen was enthusiastic about his new role, accepting it even after the University of Wisconsin's President Coffman invited him to name the salary and level of research assistance that would induce him to stay. One of the factors for his decision in favor of Harvard was the opportunity it afforded "to maintain close relations with Washington."[35]

There were very significant differences between Hansen and Samuelson— a Protestant upbringing in a farming community versus a secular Jewish family life in industrial Gary (although Samuelson had spent part of his very early years on a farm), as well as Hansen's education at a small-town college against Samuelson's at the metropolitan University of Chicago with its array of internationally known stars. But there were also significant similarities in their backgrounds. Coming from immigrant families, they were outsiders to the New England academic establishment, with its network of social connections, and lacked the extensive international connections of Leontief, Schumpeter, and Haberler. Both had a liberal arts education, and both had at one time focused on the humanities—in Hansen's case, it was literature and in Samuelson's, literature and history—before turning to economics. In Minnesota, Hansen and his family lived in modest circumstances in a working-class neighborhood, and this may well have had echoes in the decision made by Paul and Marion, when it became clear that

---

g. See also chapter 8 this volume.

Paul's textbook would significantly raise their wealth, to live on his university salary so that their lifestyle would not be out of line with that of their colleagues. Samuelson clearly admired Hansen's modesty, and he became a lifelong friend of Hansen and his family—to the extent that Hansen's daughters remembered "Sammy," as they called him, always being around at their home.

Hansen was, from the start of his academic career, a specialist in business cycles. His dissertation, *Cycles of Prosperity and Depression* (1921), focused on a single cycle: the dramatic crash of 1907. Using monthly data, he engaged in a type of statistical analysis that would have been appreciated by the economists, including Crum and Frickey, who were involved in the Harvard Economic Service. He decomposed data into seasonal, cyclical, and trend components, and used correlations to establish the place of different series in the cycle.[h] What were the relations between the groups of time series relating to investment, industry, and banking, and what were the relations between cycles in Britain, the United States, and Germany? Samuelson was right to say that this was a statistical survey in the spirit of Mitchell.[36] However, it involved more than "naive Baconian empiricism,"[37] for Hansen used his data on the relationships between movements in credit, prices, and outputs to evaluate alternative theories of the cycle.[38]

Starting from the presupposition characteristic of twentieth-century business cycle theory—that business should be seen "as a dynamic changing thing which must be studied as a process," rather than as a static condition of prosperity interrupted by crises—he reached the conclusion that cycles of prosperity and depression were driven by money and credit.[39] Significantly, in view of his later work, he sought to explain both cycles and long period trends, and he considered the under-consumptionist J. A. Hobson to have effectively rebutted the charge that over-production was impossible.[40] He used the accelerator, to which Haberler had attached such importance, to argue the fact that though fluctuations in investment were much greater than fluctuations in consumption, that did not prove the ultimate cause of a crisis lay with investment; a slowing down in the growth of consumption could be sufficient to explain a large fall in investment.

During the 1920s, as Hansen established his reputation as one of the country's leading business cycle theorists, his work remained, like his thesis, squarely in the institutionalist tradition. However, his views changed in

---

h. Persons (see chapter 6 this volume) was one of the economists with whose results he compared his own.

important ways.[41] Turning to the ideas of Albert Aftalion, Arthur Spiethoff, and other continental European writers, he began to see fluctuations in investment driven by population changes and waves of innovations as the root cause of the cycle. He still thought monetary factors played a role, but they merely served to magnify other forces, rather than being an independent factor.

One element in this was Aftalion's theory that the price level is determined by the level of money income in relation to the quantity of goods and services being produced. The important feature of this was that it focused on flows of income rather than on the stock of money. The other element was the idea, taken from Spiethoff, that there were certain investment opportunities available, and once these were taken up, investment would fall off, causing a downturn. The price system played a dynamic role, assisting the movement of resources into sectors with greater investment opportunities. A free enterprise system tended toward full employment because price flexibility encouraged a healthy level of investment and a high level of spending. However, though there was that tendency toward full employment, the business cycle was an inevitable feature of a dynamic, growing economy with rapid technological change. Only if the economy matured and accumulation slowed down would the cycle become a thing of the past.

It was in the course of expounding these ideas that, as Samuelson noted, Hansen expressed a different view on Say's Law, arguing that it was impossible to have unemployment caused by a shortage of purchasing power.[42] Perhaps part of the explanation lay in the fact that *Business Cycle Theory* (1927), the book in which Hansen expressed this idea, had originally been written for a competition to find the best critique of the work of two underconsumptionists, William Foster and Waddill Catchings.[43]

Just as Hansen's empirical methods and the theoretical resources on which he drew fitted well with the ideas of those who were to invite him to Harvard, so, too, did his policy conclusions. Because movements of resources from one sector to another were essential in a dynamic economy, and because the price mechanism served to bring about such changes, any policy that prevented price flexibility was liable to impede progress. He was thus suspicious of what John Maurice Clark, in a book that went through many editions in the 1930s, called *The Social Control of Business*.[44] Social control tended to produce rigidities that would hold back investment and slow down technical progress. He also questioned the need for government spending to get out of a depression, for there would eventually be a revival of investment that would bring the economy back to full employment.

These views conditioned Hansen's response to the Great Depression. It was a particularly deep depression, because it was the result of large monetary and technological shocks happening together.[45] Recovery required innovation and technological advance that would lower costs, raise profitability, and stimulate investment. If markets were left to themselves, recovery would eventually come. He thus opposed Roosevelt's National Recovery Administration, which, by allowing collusion, enabled certain sectors to isolate themselves from market pressures. However, the depth of the Depression meant that there was a problem, for complete price flexibility would push the burden of adjustment onto vulnerable sections of society. There was, therefore, a case for using monetary policy to prevent prices from falling, even if the end result was some inflation. Government investment posed a similar dilemma: it could lower unemployment, but the cost would be that it would take resources away from the private investments necessary for innovation and progress. A measure that could work, along with monetary policy, was unemployment insurance, for this would help stabilize purchasing power and prevent the Depression from worsening.

In the depths of the Depression, surveying business cycle theory in *Econometrica*, Hansen chose to focus on what he called "investment and savings" analysis, represented by Hayek and Keynes. He was critical of both Hayek's view that "neutral money" would be sufficient to tame the cycle and Keynes's excessive faith in "the occult powers of counter [cyclical] *monetary* adjustments."[46] Though it worked with a peculiar definition of income, he saw Keynes's theory as in essence the same as Aftalion's, and his main criticism was the way he used it: "as a kind of slot machine into which one may insert a question and draw out the correct answer."[47] Hansen clearly believed that increased government spending could improve the situation, but it needed to be undertaken very carefully, because if the government issued bonds to finance investment, it weakened confidence and thereby discouraged private investment. It was an error to argue that it did not matter whether investment was being undertaken by government or private investors, because they had very different effects on the psychology of the private sector. In an economy in which most production was being undertaken by the private sector, it was impossible to have any "sound revival of business until private enterprise enters the investment field."[48]

Though Hansen was still seeing the relationship between prices and costs as the crucial problem, he attached great importance to what he termed "the flow of purchasing power." He wrote of "three faucets" though which purchasing power could enter the economy: business spending (construction and investment); consumer spending of hoards of money; and government spending.[49] He even recognized that if new funds were sent through any of these faucets, the effect on total income was likely to be higher than the amount injected. Though still talking in terms of the velocity of the circulation of money, he was clearly thinking in terms of the multiplier, worked out by Keynes's colleague, Richard Kahn, a few years earlier. However, though Hansen thought interest rates were important in influencing investment, this mechanism was limited because interest payments were only one component of business costs, and it was reductions in costs that were necessary to restore business confidence. Increasing the investment (the business faucet) required both monetary measures and cost reductions.

The most significant feature of Hansen's thinking at this point is perhaps that, despite his emphasis on monetary policy and on cost reductions, he recognized that the flow of purchasing power was crucial, and that "business enterprises cannot be responsible for the maintenance of purchasing power."[50] The main responsibility for preventing a collapse in purchasing power lay with central banks, but there might be times when they needed help from government. To this end he proposed various measures to establish funds that could be used to increase the flow of funds through the consumers' and government faucets.

> It may be that we have reached a stage in the development of modern industry in which free enterprise and the price system cannot continue to function unless we develop new institutions, in coöperation with the central banks, to safeguard the maintenance of *purchasing power as a whole*. Without this, in a state of general collapse of producer confidence, each entrepreneur in self-defense contracts his operations—a policy which, if pursued by all, is suicidal to the general economy.[51]

The difficulty, as Hansen saw it, was to find a way to ensure that business as a whole did not experience losses without interfering with the risks facing individual businessmen.

Two years later, Hansen provided another appraisal of the multiplier, this time using the word and attributing it to Kahn and Keynes. He clearly accepted the idea, though he doubted that the proportion of income saved would be constant, calling into question their simple formula.[52,i] However, he believed that it was important not to lose track of the important technological forces contributing to economic progress, to which Schumpeter had

---

i. His point was that if the proportion of income saved were variable, calculating the multiplier as the sum of an infinite series was more difficult.

drawn attention. He also made it clear that part of his difference with Kahn and Keynes concerned his attitude toward mathematical models, and that he was becoming more receptive to such work.

> [T]here have been at least three developments with respect to the mathematical attack [on the problem of the business cycle], which should lead the "literary" business-cycle theorist to preserve an open mind as to its value. First, the devising and improvement of mathematical methodology have already progressed so that somewhat closer approaches to reality are now possible than was true earlier. Secondly, this new approach necessitates a rigorous statement of the postulates of the system and so leads to a reexamination of fundamental definitions and concepts which may have been inexactly stated or slurred over by the "literary" theorist. And, thirdly, the mathematical method, by its requirement of stating in definite form the assumed or agreed-on relationships among the variables, has pointed out a very specific lack of factual knowledge with respect to many fundamental relationships. With these results attained, we may await, at least without appreciable skepticism, the products which may flow from this newer mode of attack.[53]

Samuelson would have endorsed wholeheartedly the second and third of those propositions.

By the time he came to Harvard, Hansen had accepted some of the ideas usually associated with Keynes, but this was hardly a conversion, for he was gradually integrating Keynesian ideas into a theory of the business cycle that had been evolving since the beginning of the 1920s. He might at times sound Keynesian, as when he used the analogy of the faucets through which spending flowed into the economy, and the need to maintain aggregate purchasing power, but he was still talking about it in language taken from Aftalion; he insisted on seeing the cycle as an aspect of longer-run developments to which technological developments were central. These were to be important for Samuelson when he began to work on these problems.

The Fiscal Policy Seminar

Samuelson's contact with Hansen came through the Fiscal Policy Seminar that was run in the new Littauer Center by Hansen and John Williams, which was to be the main location for the development of Keynesian ideas at Harvard. This seminar was the result of careful planning by the Harvard Economics Department, as part of the new center and a venture to which they were devoting significant resources. In May 1937, Wilson had discussed its purpose with Burbank, when he had explained that he envisaged the seminar as concerning not traditional problems of taxation and the efficiency of government spending but the broader problem of the proportion of the national income being disbursed through government. "We are," he wrote, "dealing with even larger and more basic matters involving the division of income between government and other spending, being for these purposes regarded as a device for supplementing income in times of need and decreasing it (by debt paying) in good times."[54] The syllabus he proposed for the seminar, and the title he had proposed to Williams two days earlier,[55] was:

I. *Government and the National Income*

The economic, political, legal, social, and international effects of spending a considerable fraction of national incomes through governmental agencies and the rigidities or elasticities thereby introduced. The relation between public and private credit. The possibility of a compensatory mechanism for the business cycle. Deficit financing and debt retirement. Monetary aspects of expenditures and revenues. The possibility of creating or destroying vested interests.[56]

Though stressing national income, recently calculated by Simon Kuznets for the U.S. Commerce Department, this was framed in terms that reflected the American discussions of the cycle to which Hansen had contributed. However, it placed problems that were central to Keynesian economics squarely on the seminar's agenda.

When the seminar was eventually advertised, as one of a series of experimental seminars that would "bring together consultants drawn from the public service and a faculty group representing economics, politics, law, and business administration" to study "questions of broad governmental policy" in their "administrative, economic, political, social and legal aspects," it was given the title "Problems of Fiscal Policy," and was described in terms that were less precise than those suggested by Wilson:

This seminar is concerned with public finance in relation to economic, political, and social institutions and systems. It deals with the monetary aspects of expenditures and revenues, with public finance as a compensatory mechanism in the business cycle, and with the social and political implications of government spending.[57]

The importance of this agenda became even greater once war broke out in Europe, and it was clear that the major policy problem to be solved would be how to finance a massive rise in government spending on defense. But in 1937, that spending was still far in the future.

As the academic year began, news came in that the recovery, under way since early 1933, had begun to falter. Over the following four months, this turned into the most dramatic fall in output that the United States had experienced so far, with the possible exception of 1920–21. Yet unemployment was still well over 10 percent and manufacturing production was barely higher than it was in 1929.[58] This dramatic change challenged existing theories more profoundly than had the events of 1929, for it was not explicable in terms of existing theories of the cycle. These events and the policies appropriate to deal with them dominated the seminar, as well as Hansen's own thinking.

Samuelson's friends included two brothers, Walter and William (Bill) Salant. Bill had been in the same graduating class as Marion, and for a brief period Walter had been Samuelson's roommate.[59] Like Bryce and Tarshis, Walter Salant had attended Keynes's lectures in 1933–34, before spending four years at Harvard. He attended the Fiscal Policy Seminar in its first year and attested that the unexpected downturn in the economy established its character. Economic analysis was to be applied to current and anticipated policy problems. It was, however, a while before the attention turned to these events, because the program for the first term, involving many student papers, had been outlined early in the year, before the depth of the recession had become apparent. On Monday afternoons, from 4 to 6 P.M., in a crowded room with auditors often outnumbering enrolled students, there would be discussions either of student papers or of topics proposed by Hansen or Williams. On Fridays, there were informal talks by outside speakers, again late in the afternoon, but followed by dinner and further discussion, often till 9 or 10 in the evening. Given Hansen's and Williams's connections, these speakers naturally included government officials and figures from the private sector concerned with policy, as well as academics.

Walter Salant has written about the difference in temperament between Hansen and Williams. Hansen was continually advocating policy measures, but Williams was more skeptical and hence more cautious. They clearly disagreed, but did not confront each other openly, sometimes to the frustration of the students present. The advantage was that, at least in the first year, when the challenge of the 1937–38 recession was being confronted, and Keynesian ideas were being debated, neither of them dominated discussions: "they were more like mother hens encouraging the participants; the main intellectual pressure came from the graduate students."[60] Hansen and, less frequently, Williams, used the seminar to try out their own ideas. Thirty years later, Hansen wrote to Salant, "When I say that I learned so much [from the seminar in 1937–38] . . . I am simply telling the naked truth. And I think you will agree that I was never afraid to display my own ignorance. The great thing about that year was the fact that we were all students trying to find our way about."[61]

The reason why Samuelson took time to become committed to Hansen and the Fiscal Policy Seminar was probably that the year began with papers on technical aspects of taxation in which he would have had little interest, even though many of the Monday papers were given by his fellow graduate students, with some of whom he was later to work closely.[j] Apart from a talk on monetary and fiscal policy in Germany by Heinrich Brüning, former chancellor of Germany, on November 15, it was not until December that there was a paper relevant to the general economic situation.[62] Just before Christmas, Jacob Viner spoke on "The General Relations Between Fiscal Policy and the Cycle." The following term, there was a series of papers on monetary and fiscal policy, their interrelationships, and measures to achieve full employment, culminating with two sessions in which the Swedish economist Gunnar Myrdal, whose *Monetary Equilibrium* had just been published in English, discussed monetary and fiscal policy in Sweden.

Samuelson remembered dropping in on the seminar in its first year, and then attending it often in the second year.[63] A plausible reconstruction of what happened is that he attended Viner's talk, or Brüning's presentation, in the latter case attracted by the eminence of the speaker, and that he then got drawn into the seminar, falling under the spell of Hansen. By the following December, when the seminar hosted previews of three round tables scheduled for the forthcoming meeting of the American Economic Association, Samuelson's first paper on fiscal policy was among those under discussion.[64] After that, with speakers including Lauchlin Currie, then at the Federal Reserve, and Marriner Eccles, chairman of the Federal Reserve, there would have been much to interest him once he had started thinking seriously about fiscal policy and the business cycle. The seminar will have helped him to understand the arguments of the young economists involved

---

j. The list of graduate-student speakers included Richard Musgrave, Emile Despres, and Walter Salant.

in the Harvard-Tufts seminar, with some of whom he was to work during the war. However, though his career was to become increasingly entwined with Hansen's, this did not mean that he had become converted to Keynes: like his new mentor, he continued to distance himself from Keynes. The process of converting to Keynes involved the creation of a distinctive version of Keynesianism that owed as much to American sources as to Keynes.

| Hansen's Disciple

Hansen and Keynes

The downturn of 1937, when there was still massive unemployment and unused industrial capacity, challenged Hansen's perspective, for it made it clear that the Great Depression was no ordinary business cycle.[1] It had been particularly deep, but there were plenty of factors that could explain this whilst remaining within the framework of Hansen's existing theory of the business cycle: there had been an exceptionally dramatic expansion during the 1920s, an exceptionally deep financial crisis, and a terrible international situation. However, once recovery had started, Hansen's theory suggested that it should have continued until full capacity had been reached. Hansen needed to explain why this had not happened.

Hansen's answer was that recovery after 1933 had been led by consumption, which meant that as soon as consumption stopped growing so rapidly, there would be—through the accelerator—a fall in investment, and this could cause a downturn. Though it was easy to identify the immediate cause of why consumption had fallen in 1937—the decision to build up the Social Security fund—this raised the question of why the recovery had been so anemic. Hansen's explanation, taking up the theory that investment opportunities were crucial, was that the economy had entered a new era. Now that the American economy had matured, the pace of technological change was less and the population was growing more slowly. Both of these implied fewer opportunities for investment. Thus, unless action were taken, there would be long-term stagnation. There was need for what he called a "dual economy," in which the government created investment opportunities for the private sector, stimulating growth. This involved management of both the American and the international economies.

This was the context in which Hansen, very slowly, took up Keynesian ideas. He had always worked with other economists' ideas, "finding in each author some new insight to be integrated into his own thought," so it was not surprising that he should take up ideas from Keynes. He had already taken up Aftalion's income theory, which meant that, in principle, the step toward taking up Keynes's theory was a small one. However, for a long time he remained critical of Keynes, for at least two related reasons. Hansen was concerned with economic development and hence with dynamics, whereas Keynes's *General Theory* focused almost solely on unemployment, analyzing it in purely static terms. Hansen also held a different view of the role of government. A dynamic economy would be subject to frequent, unpredictable shocks, making scientific management of the economy an illusion. However, though discretionary management might be impossible, it was not difficult to identify unexploited productive investment opportunities and design policy to take advantage of them.

This perspective explains Hansen's response to the *General Theory*. In his first review (in June 1936), he offered a simple interpretation of Keynes's theory: that wealthy communities save more, but because outlets for new investment are limited, investment is low. Surplus savings do not get invested because the desire to hold money keeps interest rates low. Hansen concluded that Keynes's new theory would fare no better than his previous one because it assumed a rigid economy. In contrast, the United States was "a progressive and flexible community [that] is always busily at work raising the marginal productivity of capital and the rate of investment."[2] Thus, Hansen was not objecting to the logic of Keynes's argument: he merely believed that a state of technological stagnation had not yet been reached.

Hansen's second review (October 1936), written at much greater length for an audience of economists, engaged more seriously with the book and showed a much clearer understanding of Keynes's arguments. However, though he found the book exciting and in places brilliant, the review did not mark a conversion. This is clear even from his concluding paragraph.

> The book under review is not a landmark in the sense that it lays a foundation for a "new economics." It warns once again, in a provocative manner, of the danger of reasoning based on assumptions which no longer fit the facts of economic life. Out of discussion and research will come bit by bit an improved theoretical apparatus (Keynes's

interest theory contains promising suggestions) and a more accurate appreciation of social psychology (the brilliant chapter on long-term expectation) and of the precise character of the economic environment in which humans act as individuals and in groups. The book is more a symptom of economic trends than a foundation stone upon which a science can be built.[3]

These conclusions reflect Hansen's eclectic, open-minded approach to economic theory, which led him to appreciate certain chapters in the book. However, there were many reasons why Keynes's theory could not provide a foundation on which a new theory could be built. There were technical problems with Keynes's theory (for example, his definitions of saving and investment were not helpful for analyzing a dynamic economy). Hansen was more open to the idea that there were monopolistic rigidities in the economy, which would make Keynes's theory more relevant, but it was an open question whether these would be important in the long term. But, most important, Hansen attached great importance to the ability of technological advances to raise the productivity of capital:

> In brief, it is not improbable that the continued workability of the system of private enterprise will be made possible, not by changes in prevailing economic institutions (such as those advocated by Keynes), but rather by the work of the inventor and the engineer. Just as technological progress has been mainly responsible for the great advance in real wages and in standards of living during the last century, so also it may well turn out that in the future we shall have to look to new outlets for profitable investment—new discoveries in technique, new ways of utilizing nature's resources, new products, and new industries—if we expect the prevailing economic system to survive.[4]

He saw Keynes as reverting to a pre-capitalist mercantilism, endorsing leisure and luxury consumption that was a long way from his own emphasis on capitalism's ability to create new investment opportunities by developing "new resources, new products and new industries."[5]

The situation changed in April 1937, when Keynes published "Some Economic Consequences of a Declining Population" in the *Eugenics Review*, in which he argued that the rate of investment had fallen since 1913 because the growth rate of the population had fallen. This seems to have persuaded Hansen that Keynes had been converted to his own way of thinking, and prompted him to take Keynes more seriously than he had done in either of his two reviews.[6] After the 1937 downturn, Hansen developed the idea that long-term structural changes were depressing investment opportunities and contributing to stagnation into an explanation of why recovery from the Great Depression had stopped so abruptly in 1937: the factors making for technological dynamism in the nineteenth century were no longer present. This raised an important question about fiscal policy, for it implied that, instead of being "a cyclical compensatory device, designed to stimulate consumption, . . . public expenditures may come to be used increasingly as a means of directing the flow of savings into real investment. . . . This implies, moreover, a substantial shift in the rôle of taxation and of public debt in the functioning of the whole economy."[7]

Pump Priming

This was the way Hansen was thinking when Samuelson met him. Hansen recognized Keynes as a reformer with an eclectic attitude toward economic theory, but he remained critical. An idea of the view of Keynes that Samuelson might have learned from Hansen is given in a lecture he gave in John Williams's course on money and banking in May 1938, in which he discussed the *General Theory*. James Tobin, who was also attending the fiscal policy seminar, took careful notes.[8] According to these notes, Hansen began by saying that the book was not primarily about the business cycle, and that its explanation of the cycle in terms of fluctuations in investment driven by variations in the marginal efficiency of capital was not very original. Keynes's main concern was with unemployment, which might persist in the long run. Under such conditions, consumption and investment were not alternatives, for increases in consumption would lead to increases in investment.

The charge that Keynes's arguments lacked novelty was also applied to the notion that the level of employment depended on the rate of interest, along with prospective profits and the marginal propensity to consume. Incomes would fall if saving was not matched by sufficient investment. According to Tobin's notes,

> In rich community, marginal efficiency of capital low; propensity to consume low; but rate of interest can't keep falling because of liquidity-preference. Hence there is not adequate volume of new investment to maintain full employment.[9]

This echoed, very precisely, the interpretation of the *General Theory* offered in his first review. Hansen then went on to say that Keynes emphasized the rate of interest, whereas Spiethoff thought it was more important to consider factors affecting the prospective rate of profit: expanding markets, increasing population, inventions, and giant industries. These factors had led to expansion in the nineteenth century, but now they were leading to stagnation: the population was declining and there were no new markets being opened up. The lecture closed with Hansen's analysis of Keynes's proposed solutions. He doubted that low rates of interest would stimulate much investment; he thought that redistributing income to stimulate consumption would harm investment; and that public investment might be offset by private investment. The final remark in Tobin's notes, "Economic policies are choice among evils" is, unfortunately, not elaborated.[10]

This ambiguous attitude—interested and sympathetic, finding important insights that could be integrated into existing thinking, including Schumpeter's view of economic development—may have been what attracted Samuelson to Hansen. Though Samuelson had joined in debates about the *General Theory* with his fellow students, he resisted its message. Brought close to his teachers Schumpeter, Leontief, and Wilson by his mathematical skills, he sided with their criticisms of Keynes. He had successfully used mathematics to cut through the complex and imprecise verbal reasoning he encountered in consumer theory, and he was beginning to do the same with the theory of international trade, but the business cycle theory taught by Schumpeter and Haberler provided no such opportunities. Hansen provided a middle path, offering theories that took account of the arguments Schumpeter was making about the importance of technological progress while acknowledging the technical criticisms that Leontief was leveling against the *General Theory*. But at the same time, Hansen had accepted many of the points about effective demand and the multiplier that his fellow students were learning from Keynes's book. He was eclectic and open-minded. Just as important, though Hansen was a "literary" economist, he had come around to the view that, even though his own talents in this direction were limited, mathematical methods might have something important to contribute.

Clearly, Samuelson and Hansen got on very well, and perhaps their common background as children of immigrants contributed to that. In addition, it seems a near certainty that Wilson, who believed that Samuelson's prospects as a narrow mathematical economist were very limited, was encouraging him to enlarge his portfolio of skills to include more general economics. Working on the problem of the business cycle—the most important problem facing the United States, especially as recovery aborted in the summer of 1937—provided just such an opportunity. Though he continued to work on mathematical economics, discussing his papers with Wilson and Haberler, Samuelson began working with Hansen on the problem of the business cycle.

In December 1938, in Detroit, Hansen delivered his presidential address to the American Economic Association, titled "Economic Progress and Declining Population Growth."[11] Its central point was that population growth was declining and that this would lead to a large fall in investment unless there was a rise in technical progress. "We are," he argued, "rapidly entering a world in which we must fall back upon a more rapid advance of technology than in the past if we are to find private investment opportunities adequate to maintain full employment."[12] He also laid great stress on the accelerator, for what mattered was not the level of economic activity but its growth rate. It would be possible to compensate for a decline in private investment by increasing public investment "in human and natural resources and in consumers' capital goods of a collective character," but such compensation could be no more than partial. If government spending were taken too far, it might alter the cost structure so as to prevent the achievement of full employment.[13] There were thus difficult choices, with which economists would have to grapple for a long time.

One option was to refrain from expanding the level of demand so that "the recuperative forces to which we have long been accustomed will, in the absence of political interference, re-assert themselves."[14] The alternative was to use increases in government expenditure to achieve full employment. The danger was that doing this would cause inflation. Hansen argued for a compromise position: in 1929, U.S. national income had been $80 billion, and he believed that this was still a reasonable approximation to full-employment income. National income had fallen as low as $40 billion during the Depression, and Hansen proposed that government spending should be used to keep it above $60–65 billion, but once national income approached $70 billion, government spending should be tapered off. Recovery beyond that point should be left to the private sector because further government spending would simply set off a spiral of rising costs and prices. In short, fiscal stimulus should be applied only in the deepest part of the Depression.

Two days later, Samuelson presented his paper, "The Theory of Pump-Priming Reexamined," which formed part of a round-table discussion on "The Workability of Compensatory Devices."[15] This was not one of the sessions that Hansen had organized to complement his presidential address, though given the similarity of the topics, it could easily have been. Paul Ellsworth, from the University of Cincinnati, spoke on the use of monetary policy to counteract depressions. He recommended an easy money policy on the grounds that even if it did not work, it was unlikely to be harmful. The final speaker was Emile Despres. Like Samuelson, he came from the Midwest, born in Chicago and having graduated from Harvard in 1930. However, rather than stay on for graduate work, he went straight to the Federal Reserve Bank of New York, where he worked on short-term capital flows and U.S. monetary policy. Through the 1930s he had argued that expansionary policy would have helped mitigate the Depression; and in 1937, he had resumed his connection with Harvard as a consultant to the Littauer Center. Despres asked whether measures to tax hoards of money would be effective in stabilizing demand or in countering long-term stagnation. After reviewing many of the technical issues, he concluded that, while it was an interesting theoretical idea, it would probably not be very effective.

Samuelson's paper, sandwiched between the papers by Ellsworth and Despres, tackled the problem of fiscal policy. Some types of water pump work only when they are full of water, which means that they need to be primed—filled with water—before they can be used. "Pump priming" therefore refers to the idea that, in a depression, it is sufficient for the government to have a burst of spending to get the economy going and then, once recovery has begun, leave further expansion to private initiative. It is possible to discern Keynesian ideas in Samuelson's paper, as when he spoke about investment as being volatile and insensitive to changes in the rate of interest, and when he argued that the rate of interest could not equilibrate the demand for employment with the supply. However, at the point where he cited Keynes explicitly, Samuelson was critical: the instantaneous multiplier used in the *General Theory* "represent[ed] a backward step from the more general analysis of the lagged effects through time."[16] Though conceding the usefulness of the Keynesian multiplier, he emphasized complications that Keynes had not taken into account, including the accelerator. This critical use of selected Keynesian ideas was entirely consistent with what Hansen was doing.

Samuelson made it clear that he rejected the quantity theory of money, for he described as "completely fruitless" the attempt to analyze the effects of a rise in government spending through the velocity of circulation. The multiplier was more useful. However, this should not be read as a pro-Keynesian position, because opposition to the quantity theory was not an exclusively Keynesian stance. Hansen, like many other American business cycle theorists, had been just as dismissive as Keynes of the quantity theory. Samuelson's remark that "an insufficiency of [private net investment] would make long-term deficit spending mandatory" was Hansen's position. The published abstract does not make Samuelson's conclusions clear, and the conference proceedings contain no record of any discussion of his paper; perhaps the reason is that he was providing a technical review of the issues without offering any conclusions sufficiently controversial to provoke a response from the audience.

Business Cycle and Fiscal Policy

If the fact that Samuelson was working closely with Hansen was only hinted at in the summary of his talk to the American Economic Association, it was explicit in the article he published in May 1939, presumably written in late 1938 or very early in 1939, "Interactions Between the Multiplier Analysis and the Principle of Acceleration."[17] On the first page he acknowledged Hansen's help, saying that the paper had been written at his suggestion and that "Professor Hansen has developed a new model sequence which ingeniously combines the multiplier analysis with that of the *acceleration* principle or *relation*."[18]

Hansen produced a model in which the multiplier was ½ and the accelerator was 2, and to his surprise found that income went into decline. He thought that perhaps this could explain the 1937 recession and discussed it with Samuelson.[19] Samuelson recognized Hansen's system as a difference equation that would produce repeated oscillations Hansen would have discovered had he solved it for more periods. Samuelson formulated the model algebraically, allowing the values of the multiplier and accelerator to take any meaningful values, and he found a general solution, working out combinations of multiplier and accelerator, that would produce stability, instability, or periodic fluctuations.[a]

However, though Samuelson could readily understand such algebra, it was unfamiliar to most economists, which explains the way he chose to describe the theory. He started with an austere numerical example: initially government spending, investment, and consumption are zero. In the first period, government spending rises to 1 and stays at that level. Samuelson then worked out, period by period, the new levels of consumption and investment, assuming that the marginal propensity to consume was ½ and the accelerator was 1. These results were chosen so that the result was a cycle, with total income converging to its new equilibrium only after fourteen periods.[b] Then, to show that the problem was too complicated for such reasoning, he went through the same calculation for four more sets of values for the multiplier and accelerator, demonstrating that they generated completely different results.

---

a. The multiplier could be anywhere in the range zero to 1, and the accelerator had to be positive.

b. The new equilibrium is approached asymptotically; this calculation assumes very small discrepancies are ignored.

The only way to analyze the problem, Samuelson concluded, was to turn to algebra. Formulating the model as two difference equations, in which consumption depended on income in the previous period, and investment depended on the change in consumption from one period to the next, he was able to construct a diagram that showed how the system would behave for any combination of feasible values for the multiplier and accelerator. This led him to a methodological conclusion: "Contrary to the impression commonly held, mathematical methods properly employed, far from making economic theory more abstract, actually serve as a powerful liberating device enabling the entertainment and analysis of ever more realistic and complicated hypotheses."[20] The paper was used to argue the case for mathematical reasoning. Unlike some of his earlier papers, in this one he augmented his mathematics with verbal and diagrammatic explanations that made clear both the importance of the problem he was tackling and the usefulness of the mathematics. Perhaps this was because Hansen needed this type of explanation.

The paper is also interesting because of the way he framed the problem. His first sentence conceded that the new "multiplier" analysis had thrown light on the problem of government spending. He then went on to express the fear that "this extremely simplified mechanism" might be hardening into a dogma, "hindering progress and obscuring important subsidiary relations and processes."[21] This was precisely the situation with the multiplier that he had discussed in his presentation to the American Economic Association. What his analysis showed was that "the conventional multiplier sequences [were] special cases of the more general Hansen analysis."[22] A page later he reiterated this point by saying that "the Keynes-Kahn-Clark formula" was "subsumed under the more general Hansen analysis." In a footnote, he minimized the originality of his own work by claiming that his model was formally identical to the model sequences investigated by the Swedish economist Erik Lundberg and the Dutch econometrician Jan Tinbergen.

This makes clear that when he wrote this paper, Samuelson was following Hansen in fitting ideas that were coming to be associated with Keynes into the older framework of American business cycle theory, and that these ideas were widely held. This was made even clearer in his second article on the subject, published in the *Journal of Political Economy* in December.[23] Whereas his previous paper had used the accelerator to complicate the theory of the multiplier, this one used the multiplier to add a missing element to business cycle theories based on the accelerator. The idea behind the multiplier was not new—the idea that "actual movements of consumer demand depend on the movements of purchasing power; and these in turn are governed by the rate of production in general" was well established—but the mechanism and the mode of its interaction with the accelerator were not understood.[24]

Samuelson related his theory to debates that took place in 1931–32 concerning the role of consumer spending in the cycle and involving Charles Hardy, Ragnar Frisch, and John Maurice Clark. These writers, he claimed, realized that to explain fluctuations it was necessary to explain both investment and saving, but while they formulated the acceleration principle very clearly, they were less clear on what determined consumption. This is where Keynes came in, providing a clear statement of the multiplier that could be placed alongside the accelerator to make a fully specified theory.[25] The *General Theory* had been followed by work by Roy Harrod, Gottfried Haberler, and Hansen, who brought the two concepts together into a theory that could explain turning points, and hence the cycle. The problem with this literature was that there was no overall agreement on how to formulate the theory, and their work contained many flaws. There was, for example, confusion over the roles of net and gross investment, and about what caused the downturn at the top of the cycle.

After this brief review of the literature, Samuelson proceeded to cut though the confusion. His starting point was the consumption function. If consumption depended on current income, as shown in figure 13.1— and given the level of net investment—only one level of income was consistent with business not making losses, for only at this level of income would the amount business received from consumers equal the amount they paid out to factors of production. Significantly, the diagram was labeled "Determination of the Level of National Income." However, although the multiplier could be used to determine the level of income, the acceleration principle was needed to explain fluctuations in the level of income.[26]

This was one of the points at which the importance of mathematical analysis became clear. If the model was to generate cycles, it was necessary not only to introduce the acceleration principle but also to assume that consumption in any period depended on the *previous* period's income.[c] This was something that would have been difficult to establish without the mathematics. Having performed this analysis, though, Samuelson could then sort out issues that Harrod had been unable to settle. For the first time, he defended Keynes against the claims found in American business

---

c. Adding this lag turned what would otherwise have been a first-order difference equation into a second-order difference equation; a first-order difference equation cannot generate cycles, whereas a second-order one will do so for appropriate parameter values.

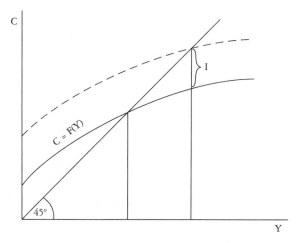

FIGURE 13.1 Income determination—consumption and investment.
Source: Samuelson 1939e, p. 790.

cycle theory: "From the long-run point of view Keynes was partially justified in ignoring the acceleration principle completely. The average level of
the system is independent of its operation, depending rather upon the level
of investment outlets."[27] However, though he was defending the Keynesian
apparatus as relevant for explaining the long-run level of national income,
his argument was grounded on a theory of investment that was very different from that found in the *General Theory*, where the analysis of investment
had focused on short-run fluctuations in the stock market. Samuelson's reference to "investment outlets" as the determinants of investment echoed
Hansen, not Keynes.

This diagram (figure 13.1), known also as "the 45-degree diagram,"
is important because it is the first use of what was to become, through
Samuelson's textbook, the standard method of explaining the central argument in Keynesian economics.[d] Not only was the determination of national
income central to Samuelson's exposition of economics, but it also adorned
the book's cover.[e] After that, it became synonymous, if not with Keynesian
economics then with "simple" Keynesianism, being used almost universally
in teaching introductory economics. However, though the diagram clearly

d. See chapter 27 this volume. Note that there are two versions of the diagram. Figure 13.1
   illustrates the condition that consumption plus investment equals income (C + I = Y);
   the other, shown in figure 18.1 later in this volume, illustrates the condition that
   saving equals investment (S = I), where saving is the difference between income and
   consumption.
e. See chapter 25 this volume.

drew on the *General Theory*, it arose naturally in the course of Samuelson's development and analysis of a theory that Hansen had developed.

The tone of Samuelson's conclusions was different in this paper. Instead of overtly praising the mathematics for opening up the analysis of more complex models, he pointed out that the assumptions were simplifications, and that "[o]bvious qualifications must be made before the results can be applied to the real world."[28] This reflects the different role played by diagrams in the two papers: in the first paper, a diagram was used to explain a complex situation; in the second paper, the diagram was used to illustrate a fundamental principle. However, despite this difference, Samuelson remained the mathematical theorist settling disputes. He did not praise the use of mathematics explicitly, but he criticized those who believe that economic problems can be solved by disputes over terminology. It is not definitions of saving and investment but, rather, "the numerical relations of the acceleration principle and the multiplier" that explain the cycle.[f] For Samuelson, quantifiable relationships were what mattered, and mathematics offered a useful way to analyze them.

Samuelson's continuing engagement with Keynesian ideas through 1939 is illustrated by his review of Gunnar Myrdal's *Monetary Equilibrium* (1939) for the *American Economic Review*.[29] The book had been translated from German by two of his friends, Bryce and Stolper. Samuelson showed that he had accepted some ideas from the *General Theory* when he criticized Myrdal for placing too much emphasis on price changes rather than changes in output and employment, and for not recognizing that monetary equilibrium might occur at high rates of unemployment. Having started from Hansen, Samuelson approved of Myrdal's more dynamic approach. In particular, he praised Myrdal's introduction of the terms *ex ante* and *ex post*, which were to become standard fare in macroeconomics teaching.[g] He described the Swedish school as "virile" and he recommended the chapter where Myrdal tackled saving and investment using the concepts *ex ante* and *ex post*, thereby clarifying points on which Keynes had been confused. Given that the book had been translated by his friends, that Myrdal had visited the Fiscal Policy Seminar, and that he had heard Samuelson present his paper at the American

---

f. He illustrated this point with reference to the dispute between Keynes and Dennis Robertson over whether saving and investment were equal.

g. Given the expectations and plans prevailing at the beginning of a period (*ex ante*), which would not necessarily be consistent with each other, the problem for the economist was to work out how differences between saving and investment were resolved by the end of the period (*ex post*).

Economic Association meeting, Samuelson would have engaged with Myrdal's ideas before reading the book for review. He might even have read the German version.

The way in which Samuelson's work was developing is shown in the manner he expanded the paper that he had presented to the American Economic Association to ready it for publication in the *American Economic Review*.[30] Though his title, "The Theory of Pump-Priming Reexamined," may have suggested a narrower topic, the paper was wide-ranging. He began by explaining the pre-suppositions underlying his arguments: the economic system was not frictionless, under-utilization of resources was possible, and there might be cumulative movements away from equilibrium. Given the desire to save, full employment required a high level of net investment, and there was no reason to believe that this would be achieved automatically, even with a perfect capital market. Indeed, this was very unlikely.

> The amount of net investment must be regarded as dependent on dynamic factors of economic progress such as the amount of as yet undeveloped innovations, trend of population, past net investment, as well as upon the shifting state of confidence and expectations. . . . This means that in any community there exists a possibility of insufficient net investment, and, perhaps in a wealthy community a likelihood of such an insufficiency.[31]

Despite citing confidence and expectations, two factors to which Keynes attached importance, this was a non-Keynesian analysis that could have been taken straight from Hansen. Samuelson made it clear that he did not consider Keynes to be his starting point when he included a footnote crediting Keynes with having made a similar point. That is, there was no need to adopt Keynes's theory of liquidity preference in order to explain why there might be insufficient net investment. His argument was that it was an advantage for there to be investment in capital that did not immediately increase production of consumer goods, applying a similar argument to government spending.

> [T]he present emphasis upon *self-liquidating* public investment may be misplaced. Aside from the fact that it is a poor social economy to saddle overhead charges upon the use of governmental services (as is done in the case of a toll bridge), it may be equally undesirable for government activity to ape the business practices of private enterprise. If the government employs the same calculations with respect to action

as a private business, it may soon find itself in the same dilemma as confronts a purely individualistic economy.[32]

In a footnote to this observation, Samuelson criticized the application of commercial practices such as amortizing deficits over fixed periods or a separate capital budget (an idea supported by Keynes).

The paper was less explicitly critical of Keynes than his earlier presentation, in that the comment on Keynes's theory being a "backward step" was removed, but he still presented the instantaneous multiplier used by Keynes as a special case of a more dynamic model. In writing that the doctrine of the multiplier was "nothing more than a recognition of the strategic importance of investment in determining the level of the national income,"[33] Samuelson placed himself squarely in the tradition of American business cycle theory as represented by Clark and Hansen. The need for a more dynamic model was not simply a theoretical nicety, for dynamic multipliers, such as used by Clark, were needed to work out the time for which changes in government spending would affect the time path of national income. This was central to the problem of pump-priming, and to the issue of whether government spending should be increased when the economy began to turn down or when the bottom of the depression had been reached. The argument for the latter was that the downturn produced changes in the structure of prices and costs that were important for the long-run health of the economy.[h] Samuelson questioned this, arguing that the downturn brought maladjustments of its own that might even be "far worse than those of the boom," and that he doubted there was much downward flexibility in modern economies.[34]

This paper is important because, in contrast to his more much more widely cited papers on multiplier–accelerator interaction, most of the claims he made in it were not derived from mathematical models. The multiplier was an inherently mathematical concept and was the basis for the claim that a rise in government spending must necessarily generate a larger government deficit because increased tax revenue would not be sufficient to cover the extra government spending. Mathematical reasoning also lay behind his argument that national income would be maximized if taxation were such as to equalize different households' marginal propensities to consume.[35] However, Samuelson's statement that the multiplier was useful "to examine various *mechanical* aspects of the impact of government expenditures" implied that there were other aspects that could not be analyzed that way.[36] He drew upon

---

h. This was a point associated with Friedrich Hayek, though at the time Sumner Slichter was making it.

the multiplier–accelerator model to take account of changes in investment that would occur in response to changes in other types of spending, but this was a minor point in his argument.

Most of his claims involved arguments that were not derived from mathematical models: he argued against waiting until the bottom of the depression before turning to expansionary fiscal policy on the grounds that it was perverse to let business become bad merely to improve it; and he challenged Hansen's interpretation of the 1935–37 recovery by arguing that Hansen's distinction between recoveries initiated by government spending and ones initiated by private investment did not make sense. Furthermore, when it came to determining the desirable long-term level of government spending, it was necessary to bring in political and ethical judgments. Using fiscal policy to reduce unemployment would raise the deficit, and this might have costs in the long term. His view was, while fiscal expansion to counter depression might have long-term costs, these costs, which were very uncertain, were less important than the benefits that could be obtained. "If the real national income can be increased by five or ten percent over a long period of years only at the cost of incurring a debt of some tens of billions of dollars," he wrote, "I for one should consider the price not exorbitant."[37]

Even by the summer of 1940, Samuelson had not been converted to Keynesianism. He used some Keynesian concepts and accepted ideas that came to be associated with Keynes, but he made it very clear that he considered Keynes to be one of many significant contributors to business cycle theory.[i] His writing gave no hint of the status to which he and others would later elevate Keynes, repeatedly being critical of Keynes for being insufficiently dynamic and for ignoring important factors. He was following Hansen, not Keynes. Samuelson's analysis of what had happened in the early 1930s—that new industries had grown to maturity, requiring no more than replacement investment, and "no new outlets appear on the horizon"—was pure Hansen.[38] Even where he challenged Hansen, he added the rider that Hansen's views on long-term stagnation were very interesting. His work with Marion on population growth supported Hansen's views on why the American economy was stagnating.[j]

Keynes's *General Theory* had caused excitement in Harvard, and many of the younger generation were converted, but Samuelson's response, like that of his mentor, was not to accept Keynes's claim to be offering a more general

---

i. This also applies to his work with Nixon, discussed in chapter 11 this volume.

j. See chapter 11 this volume.

theory but, instead, to integrate Keynesian ideas into the existing theory of the business cycle he had learned from Schumpeter, Haberler, and above all, Hansen himself. Consistent with this, the business cycle remained, in a way not true of Keynes, the context in which issues of fiscal policy were addressed. It is possible to discern hints of a changed focus toward income determination as the central problem, but they were no more than hints. Thus, when the thought arose that Samuelson should write a textbook, it is hardly surprising that its subject was to be business cycles.[39]

In August 1940, still expecting to remain at Harvard for at least another year, he signed a contract with Prentice-Hall to write a textbook for delivery on April 1, 1941.[40] It was to be co-authored with Erich Roll (1907–2005), who had arrived at Harvard as a visitor in 1939.[41] Born in the Austrian Empire, near Czernowitz, the city in modern-day Romania where Schumpeter had his first teaching position, Roll had come to Britain as a student in 1925, in the School of Oil Engineering and the Faculty of Commerce at the University of Birmingham. He was persuaded to stay on to do a PhD on the partnership between Boulton and Watt, two of the pioneers of steam power in eighteenth-century Britain. Roll obtained a teaching position at the University of Hull, and published two textbooks, one on money and the other on the history of economic thought.

Roll came to the United States in November 1939, on a Rockefeller scholarship. War had broken out in Europe, but he was encouraged to take up his fellowship because the authorities believed it would be useful to have young British scholars at American universities. Most of his time was spent at Harvard and Princeton, with many shorter visits to other universities. During his time at Harvard, Roll and his wife, Freda, were introduced by Svend and Nita Laursen (Svend was another Rockefeller Fellow who had arrived a few months earlier) to Samuelson and Marion, with whom they struck up a close friendship.[42] Freda later provided an account of time they spent together on a summer trip to Berkeley, California.

Together with the Samuelsons we sampled the pleasures of the neighbourhood. We sipped through straws exotic drinks in coconut shells at Trader Vic's in Oakland. We often drove over the Oakland Bay Bridge to San Francisco where we were greeted by the most delicious aroma of roasting coffee; we saw Alcatraz, a former penal settlement; we visited the Sally Rand nude ranch where scantily-clad girls lack-a-daisically lobbed ping-pong balls to each other; we ate excellent French meals at a little French restaurant for $1.95 including wine; we went to Chinatown; we gazed in wonder at the Golden Gate Bridge. We also visited Stanford University and lunched with the Haberlers, Machlups and other economists. We then said *au revoir* sadly to the Samuelsons as they set off for Harvard.[43]

Their friendship will have been a major factor leading Paul and Erich to decide to commit to writing a book together. Perhaps the opportunity to work together was one justification for their seemingly idyllic stay in California. However, there were good reasons for Samuelson's choice of co-author. Roll was eight years older, with a decade of teaching experience and two textbooks behind him, on the basis of which he could recommend Prentice-Hall as a publisher. He was also an applied economist: in his time at Princeton he worked on interwar balance-of-payments problems, and he had helped construct the first American index of industrial production.[44] At the same time, he was interested in economic theory and in using that to tackle empirical problems. Roll brought to the project skills that were complementary to Samuelson's.

The book was never completed. After the war, Samuelson wrote to Prentice-Hall to explain that it would never be finished.[45] In his letter he blamed their failure to complete the book on the war: they "never properly started" on the book because Roll moved to Washington and after that he moved to MIT; Samuelson had increasingly heavy teaching responsibilities and became involved in government service. Samuelson sought to save face by saying that they would have abandoned the book anyway because, almost immediately after issuing them a contract, Prentice-Hall had published another book, Estey's *Business Cycles* (1941), covering much the same ground at the same level of difficulty as their proposed book.[46]

Given Samuelson's later remarks, it is useful to see what the Estey book covered and to see the points Roll made when reviewing the book early in 1941. Almost a third of Estey's book was on data—distinguishing cycles from trends and seasonal fluctuations, the history of cycles including the Great Depression, and measurement problems. This was followed by a review of theories, including a chapter on Keynes's theories, and a lengthy section (almost 40 percent of the book) on stabilization, covering monetary policy, public works, stabilizing consumption, and policies directed toward wages and prices. Roll praised the book, contending that it was better than previous textbooks, all of which gave an old-fashioned picture of the field.[47] His main criticism, apart from the omission of a significant number of important theories, presumably to keep the book simple, was that the book paid insufficient attention to the change that had taken place in business cycle theory since the 1920s. "The most striking feature of recent cycle theory," he wrote, "is the way in which it has changed its character to become a study of the determinants of the level of economic activity through time."[48] The debates stimulated by Keynes had made it both more important and more possible to link business cycle theory with general economic theory, to the extent that business cycle theory "in the old sense" was rapidly disappearing. Even if Roll had not discussed these ideas with him, Samuelson would surely have read very closely a review by his erstwhile co-author of a book that he believed to be similar to one they were planning to write.

What Samuelson did not tell Prentice-Hall when he wrote about canceling his contract was that he had by then embarked on a textbook for another publisher—one that would take a very different approach to the problem of economic fluctuations. However, in 1940, that was a long way ahead, for he was still a student at Harvard who needed to secure his future. The first stage was writing a thesis, and the second was securing a more permanent and remunerative academic position. Moreover, though war had broken out in Europe, and though the U.S. government was preparing for war, it was not obvious what form American involvement would take and, a fortiori, it was not clear that this would have enormous implications for Samuelson himself.

CHAPTER 14 | The Observational Significance
of Economic Theory

Writing the Thesis

By the summer of 1940, Samuelson was establishing, through his publications, a research profile that would have been the envy of many young
professors. However, he remained a junior fellow—a privileged position but
nonetheless only a small step up from being a graduate student. He needed
to think about his future. Together with Marion he took the decision not to
apply for a renewal of his fellowship and to write a PhD thesis, something he
could not do if he were to remain a junior fellow. Perhaps he took seriously
Wilson's view that his long-term employability required him to demonstrate
his teaching ability, and this required that he return from the Society of
Fellows to the Economics Department.

He may also have thought that a PhD would improve his chances of finding a long-term academic position, and he may have been in a hurry to get a
position with a higher salary. It is also possible that he had the idea for a book
and decided that writing a thesis was the best route to publication. Whatever
his motivation, in the summer and fall of 1940 he composed and rearranged
material "at fever pace," dictating to Marion, who typed the entire first draft
of the thesis.[1] In the preface, he acknowledged her "all too many" suggestions and corrections, which had resulted in "a vast mathematical, economic,
and stylistic improvement" to which no perfunctory acknowledgment could
do justice.[2] Its title, *Foundations of Analytical Economics: The Observational*

Significance of Economic Theory, was in itself sufficient to make clear that he was setting himself a very ambitious task.

When, fifty years later, he came to look back on the published version of his thesis, Samuelson claimed that, though the thesis was written very quickly, his ideas had evolved gradually over the period from 1936 to 1941.[a] During this time, he had come to recognize that the existing corpus of economic theory involved "a limited number of qualitative relationships." Had he realized this at the outset, it would not have been necessary to ransack the mathematical libraries of Chicago and Harvard to find the answers to what he had initially assumed were completely different problems requiring different answers.[3] The thesis was, therefore, driven by "the internal logic of the economic puzzles" he was tackling.[4]

The thesis opened with an explicit methodological statement:

> *"The existence of analogies between central features of various theories implies the existence of a general theory which underlies the particular theories and unifies them with respect to those central features."* This fundamental principle of generalization by abstraction was enunciated by the eminent American mathematician E. H. Moore more than thirty years ago. It is the purpose of the pages that follow to work out its implications for theoretical and applied economics.[5]

The quotation in this passage was taken from *Introduction to a Form of General Analysis* (1910), by mathematician Eliakim Hastings Moore, a book he would have learned about from Wilson. It was based on lectures Moore had given at Yale in September 1906, where Wilson had just been appointed an assistant professor. The quotation is another way of expressing an idea that Samuelson stated explicitly as having learned from Wilson—namely, that problems can have a common mathematical structure even if they are different in other respects. This gave Samuelson the license to draw on ideas taken from thermodynamics, for the common structure of the problems in the two fields meant that it was possible to use the same mathematics even though the fields were otherwise very different.

In modern economics it is obvious to most economists that maximization and minimization problems arise in virtually all fields of economics; this is the reason why training in economics includes courses in quantitative

---

a. As will be explained in chapter 22 this volume, the book *Foundations of Economic Analysis* (1947a) contained a significant amount of material that was not in the thesis. However, most of the material in the thesis was changed little when included in the book, so comments he made about the book also apply to the thesis.

methods that expose students to optimization techniques. It is why micro-economic theory—the theory of how individual optimizing agents behave and interact—is considered the foundation for most applied fields. However, in the 1930s, the importance of optimization techniques was far from obvious to economists. The result was that, even when Wilson had planted the seed of the idea in Samuelson's mind, it took Samuelson a long time to see its significance. He wrote:

> Only after laborious work in each of these fields ["production economics, consumer's behavior, international trade public finance, business cycles, income analysis"] did the realization dawn upon me that essentially the same inequalities and theorems appeared again and again, and that I was simply proving the same theorems a wasteful number of times.[6]

The evidence from Samuelson's publications prior to the thesis supports the idea that it took time for him to realize there was a common structure to economic problems. His early papers focus not on the common structure lying beneath different economic problems but on the way mathematics could cut through the confusion in the existing economic literature. He was writing papers rapidly, but it took him considerable time to see the common theme running through them. His choices of mathematics to learn and of mathematics courses to attend may have been motivated by economics, but early publications, and his teachers' reactions to some of his papers, give the impression that his mathematics sometimes ran ahead of his understanding of economic problems. In later life he perhaps underestimated how early, and how thoroughly (by the standards of the time), he had trained himself in mathematics.

However, the thesis was not just about unifying economic theory. It had an even more important theme—namely, that economic theory should have implications for things that can be observed and measured. The importance he attached to this is indicated by his choice of subtitle for the thesis: "The Observational Significance of Economic Theory." He introduced this theme on the second page, arguing not only that there exist similar theorems in different fields but also that there exist "formally similar *meaningful* theorems in those fields." The word *formally* indicates that these theorems have the same mathematical structure and the word *meaningful* meant theorems that had implications for things that were observable. Claiming that "only the smallest fraction of economic writings" had tried to derive "*operationally meaningful* theorems," he defined meaningful theorems as "hypothes[e]s about empirical data which could conceivably be refuted, if only under ideal conditions."[7]

As was explained in chapter 10, this was an idea that had developed gradually over the years. In 1937, there had been little trace of operationalism in Samuelson's publications: the introduction of mathematics was motivated by its usefulness in clarifying thinking, and he had come close to accepting the Robbins position that the assumptions on which consumer theory were based could not be questioned.[8] His February 1938 article on consumer theory hinted at operationalism when it referred to his theory, founded on index number theory, as being "more directly based on those elements which must be taken as *data* by economic science" and "more meaningful" in its formulation.[9] But this was no more than a hint, for the article was framed by the concerns found in the existing literature and what he had learned from Haberler. His first clear commitment to operationalism, albeit one that sounds more like Popper than Bridgman, came in the paper he presented to the Econometric Society in December 1937, published in *Econometrica* in October 1938.[10] It is tempting, therefore, to think that the position he took in his thesis arose from discussions that occurred in his first few months in the Society of Fellows, after his article in *Economica* had gone to press and before he had finalized his paper for the Econometric Society meeting.

The term "operational" was clearly Bridgman's. However, the way Samuelson described operationally meaningful theorems was not Bridgman's. His emphasis on "data" and "observation" (a term that is given prominence by its use in the title of Samuelson's thesis) is closer to the ideas of the philosophers associated with the Vienna Circle. Though the idea that hypotheses are meaningful if they can be refuted is commonly associated with Karl Popper, whose major work had appeared in 1933, it is more likely that Samuelson learned them through Kaufmann and Sweezy, or through Rudolf Carnap, whom his friend Willard Quine had helped bring to the United States in 1936.[11] He might also have encountered such ideas through the senior fellow, Alfred North Whitehead.

The use of mathematics to cut through the confusions found in the existing literature and to unify economic theory solved the problem of where Samuelson would find meaningful economic theorems. Propositions about individuals could be derived from the hypothesis that "conditions of equilibrium are equivalent to the maximization (minimization) of some magnitude."[12] He no longer considered this an a priori truth but, rather, a hypothesis.[b] Samuelson then drew a clear distinction between propositions

---

b. However, given that Samuelson was building so much economic theory on this foundation, he must have believed that it would survive attempts to refute it.

about individuals and those about groups which could not be derived in this way, because nothing was being maximized.

> However, when we leave single economic units, the determination of unknowns is found to be unrelated to an extremum position. In even the simplest business cycle theories there is lacking symmetry in the conditions of equilibrium, without which there is no possibility of reducing the problem to that of a maximum or a minimum. Here the hypothesis is made that the system is in stable equilibrium or motion in terms of an assumed dynamical system.[13c]

The justification for this was nothing more than the observation that "positions of unstable equilibrium, if they exist, are transient, non-persistent states" that will be observed less often than stable ones.

Throughout this opening chapter, Samuelson was critical of existing economic theory, for very little of it had been focused on deriving meaningful or operational theorems. It is at this point, at the end of a short methodological chapter, that Samuelson expressed his much-cited difference with Marshall over the role of mathematics in economics.

> I have come to feel that Marshall's dictum that "it seems doubtful whether any one spends his time well in reading lengthy translations of economic doctrines into mathematics, that have not been made by himself" should be exactly reversed. The laborious working over of essentially simple mathematical concepts such as is characteristic of much of modern economic theory is not only unrewarding from the standpoint of advancing the science, but involves as well mental gymnastics of a particularly depraved type.[14]

What mattered in economic theory was the testable hypotheses and the need to derive them made mathematics central.

Equilibrium Systems and Maximization

The methodological claims made in the first chapter would be hollow if Samuelson could not justify them by showing how the goal of deriving operational theorems could be achieved. He did this in his second chapter,

---

c. Note that he was implicitly rejecting the representative agent model, which came to dominate macroeconomics in the 1970s, long before it had been enunciated.

"Equilibrium Systems and Comparative Statics." His starting point was the need to abstract from reality. Theories dealt not with the whole of reality but with carefully selected aspects of reality. The variables in which we are interested (prices, quantities, etc.) are the unknowns, and their values are assumed to be determined by equations or functional relationships that describe the situation under consideration. For example, the price and quantity of a good are assumed to be determined by supply and demand—two functional relationships between price and quantity.[d] We need enough equations to determine all the unknowns.

This was all well known. Where Samuelson went beyond this was in making the observation, considered trivial today but not so when he was writing, that we need something more. We need to introduce parameters (variables not determined by the system), changes in which will produce changes in the variables of interest. Suppose that we wish to ascertain the effect of a sales tax on the price and quantity of a good being sold. The functional relationships are the demand and supply curves for the product. If the sales tax is assumed to constitute a cost for producers (defining the market price as inclusive of the tax), then a change in the tax rate will shift the supply curve upward, changing the equilibrium price and quantity—the price and quantity at which supply equals demand. The task of the economic theorist, then, is to work out how changes in parameters such as the tax rate will change the values of the unknowns. If we can show, for example, that a rise in the sales tax cannot lower the tax-inclusive market price, we have a meaningful hypothesis, for if nothing else changes (the ideal conditions Samuelson referred to in his definition of meaningful theorems), it would be refuted by observing that raising the sales tax lowered the price. It is comparative statics because it involves comparing two static equilibria.

Samuelson made three important points about this use of equilibrium. The first was that equilibrium, as he was using the term, had no normative connotations: there was no reason to believe that equilibrium was desirable or undesirable. Equilibrium meant "the value of the variables determined by a set of conditions."[15] Any system can be represented as an equilibrium system. The second was that it abstracted from issues of time, an assumption that he

---

d. It is generally assumed that as the price rises, the amount demanded will fall and the amount supplied will rise, and that the two curves will intersect at some point. This point where supply and demand are equal is the equilibrium price. If either curve shifts—for example, a rise in income might cause consumers to demand more of a good—the point at which the two curves intersect will change, implying that the equilibrium price and quantity have changed.

proposed to tackle separately. The third was that there was no firm rule about which variables should be taken as data (parameters) and which should be explained by the theory. Traditionally, economists had taken as data those factors that they felt unable to explain—"tastes, technology, the governmental and institutional framework"[16]—but there was nothing fundamental about this. Systems could be as broad or as narrow as the theorist wanted. His illustration of this was that although government policy might be a parameter for many economic problems, understanding the business cycle might require a theory that explained government policy. In such a theory, government spending would be a variable to be explained, not a parameter. Such systems did not have to be stated mathematically, for any system could be stated in such terms, but it was useful to state it mathematically because, if it could not be, then "it must be regarded with suspicion as suffering from haziness."[17]

In the remainder of the chapter, Samuelson translated these arguments into mathematics—his subheading was simply "Symbolic Representation." His argument was presented in terms of variables, parameters, and functional relationships, without specifying any economic content. By keeping the analysis at a highly abstract level he made the point that he was presenting a method that could be applied to any economic problem, an important part of his argument being that it was "precisely *because* theoretical economics does not confine itself to specific narrow types of functions that it is able to achieve wide generality in its initial formulation."[18] However, the equations he wrote down were, he claimed, not completely without content, for he started with a set of equations describing equilibrium. He then manipulated these equations to derive equations that showed each variable as a function of the parameters.[e]

Given that his two sets of equations were equivalent, why not omit the first step? Why not omit talk of equilibrium and simply start with relationships between variables and parameters? For example, Cassel, whose general equilibrium system Director had introduced to him as an undergraduate, had argued that it was pointless starting with the assumption that consumers maximized utility (an equilibrium problem) and that instead the economist should start by postulating consumer demand

---

e. He started with n equations of the form $f^i(x_1, x_2, \ldots x_n; d_1, \ldots d_m) = 0$, where $i = 1, \ldots n$, the x's are the variables, and the d's are the parameters. This could be rewritten as $x^i = g^i(d_1, \ldots d_m)$, where $i = 1, \ldots n$. The former was a set of equilibrium conditions; the latter gave each variable as a function of the parameters of the system.

functions because that was all that could be observed. Samuelson's answer was that although two sets of equations might be equivalent, this might not be obvious, with the result that their identity might not be trivial "in a psychological sense."[19]

More important, the fact that relationships between variables and parameters were derived from an equilibrium system might imply something about them. To return to the example, the fact that consumer demand functions were derived from utility maximization might provide some testable restriction on their form, giving them meaning. Simply to state that demand for a commodity depended on prices of all goods had little content unless something could be said about functional forms, and the hypothesis of equilibrium might be able to do this. Samuelson then showed how testable predictions could be derived in this highly abstract framework, before working through two simple examples—a tax example where there was just a single variable of interest, and a market example where there were two.

This short chapter, covering highly abstract material, has been discussed in detail because it encapsulates the most important arguments in Samuelson's thesis:

(1) Many economic problems had the same structure, something that could be shown only by abstracting from the details of specific problems.

(2) When this was done, mathematical techniques (partial differential equations and matrix algebra) could be used to derive propositions that might not be obvious to those who confined themselves to verbal reasoning or simpler mathematics.

(3) Postulating that a set of equations was an equilibrium system might in itself be sufficient to provide information about relationships between variables and parameters.

(4) To derive testable relationships it was necessary not to describe equilibrium but to analyze how it changed in response to changes in parameters—to perform comparative static analysis.

Samuelson was providing an argument about how to do economics, arguing that the use of mathematical methods that were new to economists made it possible to turn long-held theories about economics operational. Given that he also described operational theories as meaningful, that was not just an argument that economists could use mathematical methods: it was an argument that they should do so.

Samuelson believed that, even if the behavior of individuals could be analyzed as the solution to a maximization problem, the behavior of *groups* of individuals could not be studied in the same way.[f] Given this, it was important to him that equilibrium systems might be of two types: equilibrium might be the result of maximizing behavior or they might be the point of rest in a dynamic system in which nothing was being maximized. Postponing the latter to the last two chapters of the thesis, he started by analyzing maximization, beginning with a long chapter on "The Theory of Maximizing Behavior." This was obviously relevant for situations where economic agents were consciously maximizing something, as when companies chose to produce the output at which their profit was maximized. The case of consumers was similar in that choosing their most preferred bundle of goods could be represented as maximizing an ordinal utility function. However, there might also be cases where no conscious optimization was involved, but which behavior could be represented as the solution to an optimization problem. He drew an analogy with physics:

> In some cases as we shall see later, it is possible to formulate our conditions of equilibrium as those of an extremum problem, even though it is admittedly not a case of any individual's behaving in a maximizing manner, just as it is possible in classical dynamics to express the path of a particle as one which maximizes (minimizes) some quantity despite the fact that the particle is obviously not acting consciously or purposively.[20]

He assumed that his readers would be familiar with the relevant physics, and did not provide any example.[g] He argued that even when economists defended their theories on other grounds—for example, as resting on plausible laws such as diminishing marginal productivity—they frequently rested on some implicit underlying optimization problem. He was therefore able to claim that, though some problems required the analysis of stability, the

---

f. This is related to what economists commonly call aggregation problems: the behavior of an aggregate need not be the same as the behavior of the individuals who make up the group. It can be proved rigorously that group behavior will be a scaled-up version of individual behavior only under conditions that are so special they can rarely be satisfied in any real-world context. For example, even if every individual's demand for a commodity falls when the price of the commodity rises, it is possible that, unless people are identical, market demand may not fall.

g. One of the simplest examples is the catenary—the shape of a cable suspended between two points—which can be calculated as the path that minimizes the potential energy of the cable. The example of the consumer did not fall into this category because, though consumers might not consciously maximize anything, their behavior was purposive.

theory of maximizing behavior could unify much, though not all, economic theory.

Samuelson's account of maximizing behavior, provided in chapter 3, emphasized three points. The first of these was Samuelson's discussion of what he called "the Generalized Le Chatelier Principle."[21] The principle is named after the French chemist Henri Le Chatelier, who in 1884 observed that, starting with a chemical system that is in equilibrium, if one of the variables is changed, the equilibrium will be changed so as to counteract the effect of the change.[h] Samuelson had learned from Wilson that this principle was not something specific to chemistry but was a general mathematical relation—a property of any maximum or minimum system—and that it might, therefore, be applicable to economics.[22] In Samuelson's hands, it became the theorem that if a system is at an maximum or minimum, the effect of relaxing a constraint is reduced by the presence of additional constraints. It was a "generalized" Le Chatelier Principle because it was shorn of any reference to chemical equilibrium.[i] To see its implications for economics, consider the example of a company employing labor. If the wage rate rises, the company may choose to employ less labor, possibly because it will choose to use mechanized production methods. However, if the company is prevented from employing the optimal amount of machinery, this will reduce the effect of the wage increase on the demand for labor. The implication that a company's demand for labor would be more elastic (more responsive to changes in the wage rate) in the long run, when the stock of machinery and other factors of production could be adjusted, than in the short run, when other factors could not be adjusted, was well known. Samuelson's point was that this had nothing to do specifically with economic arguments—it was simply the result of

---

h. For example, consider a mixture of nitrogen dioxide (NO_2), and nitrogen tetroxide (N_2O_4). If nothing is changed, there will be an equilibrium ratio of the two gases; if something changes, then the mixture will change until a new equilibrium is reached. For example, if energy is added to the system by heating it, the concentration of nitrogen dioxide increases because turning nitrogen tetroxide into nitrogen dioxide absorbs energy; if the temperature is reduced, the reaction goes the other way around.

i. He defined only his generalized version, writing, "Because of the almost metaphysical vagueness of its formulation, the latter's meaning [the meaning of the Le Chatelier Principle] is often in doubt, and it is used at one and the same time to cover diverse phenomena. The above formulation [Samuelson's generalized Le Chatelier Principle] explains why the change in volume with respect to a given change in pressure is greater when temperature is constant than when entropy is held constant and temperature is permitted to vary in accordance with the conditions of equilibrium" (Samuelson 1940a, p. 43, n12).

assuming that the company was in an equilibrium in which it was minimizing or maximizing some objective function.

The second point, one on which Wilson had insisted, was that Samuelson emphasized the importance of finite changes. It was very useful, and mathematically convenient, to use differential calculus and hence to analyze infinitesimal changes. However, real-world problems always concerned finite changes, and considering infinitesimal changes was useful only insofar as it provided information about finite changes. Finite changes were fundamental. This was connected to the point that the most general statements of equilibrium conditions typically involved inequalities, rather than equalities.

Finally, Samuelson argued that many economic problems, though they might not appear to involve maximization or minimization problems, could be restated as such problems. This was a variation of the well-known "integrability problem" in demand theory, which concerned whether, given a set of demand functions, it was possible to represent those as the outcome of maximizing some utility function. Once again, Samuelson was taking a specific problem and generalizing it, arguing that it was important to focus, not on the details of the specific economic example, but on the properties of the general mathematical problem.

Static Economic Theory

Only after these methodological and mathematical preliminaries, explaining how economics should be done, which filled almost half the thesis, did Samuelson turn to substantive economic problems. The first of these was "A Comprehensive Restatement of the Theory of Cost and Production." This was, presumably, a development of the paper on the theory of production that had failed to impress the audience at the American Economic Association when he presented it in December 1938.[23] Perhaps it was in reaction to that experience that he began by explaining the significance of what he was doing in relation to existing economic theory. "Economic theory as taught in the textbooks," Samuelson claimed, "has often become segmentalized into loosely integrated components, such as production, value, and distribution."[24] While this might be pedagogically useful, it obscured the fact that these were all aspects of the same problem. Given the technical conditions of production (the relationship between inputs and outputs), it was possible to analyze the activities of the profit-maximizing company as a single problem, covering the demand for factors of production (labor, land, capital goods) and sales of goods and services.

Brushing aside the issues over which economists had argued endlessly since Marshall's death, and which were of particular concern to his teacher Chamberlin, Samuelson noted that most of his results held irrespective of whether competition was "impure" or "pure." His method could cope with any number of factors of production, and he had attempted to derive "all possible operationally meaningful theorems" relating to the theory of the firm and production.

Though they may have been struck by the bravado in this claim, for most economists the main novelty in Samuelson's argument would have been the routine use of matrices and determinants, probably learned from Margarete Wolf in Madison in the summer of 1936. One of the most significant passages, echoing the point made in his chapter 2 about the importance of considering finite changes, was the following:

> It is curious to see the logical confusion into which many economists have fallen. The primary end of economic analysis is to explain a position of minimum (or maximum) where it does not pay to make a *finite* movement in any direction. Now in the case that all functions are continuous, it is possible as a means towards this end to state certain *equalities* on differential coefficients which will (together with appropriate secondary conditions) insure that certain *inequalities* will hold for finite movements. It is no exaggeration to say that infinitesimal analysis was developed with just such finite applications in view.[25]

Economic theory was replete with marginal conditions—so much so that they could be taken almost to define the content of the discipline—but economists had lost sight of their main goal. Propositions such as that the wage rate must equal the marginal product of labor, or that the company must produce to the point where price equals marginal cost, applied only in a world where functions were continuous. The general case involved inequalities, of which the equalities of traditional theory formed a special case. Aside from dismissing most previous theorizing as missing the big picture, Samuelson showed this formulation had the merit of encompassing not only traditional theory but also the input–output modeling of Wassily Leontief, from whom he had initially learned much of the economic theory he was analyzing.

In his three chapters on the theory of consumer behavior, which drew heavily on his published articles on the subject, Samuelson was even more critical of the existing literature, very little of which, he claimed, clarified the important issues. "Nowhere in the literature" was there "an adequate account of the theory" that made clear what content consumer theory had.[26]

There had been progress, in that consumer theory had moved progressively away from making ethical judgments, as in the utilitarian theories of Jeremy Bentham, Henry Sidgwick, and Francis Edgeworth; and along with this change there had been a move away from seeing consumer behavior as having a psychological or even physiological basis. Citing Alan Sweezy, as he had done in his earlier article, Samuelson argued that many economists had jumped to the conclusion that the whole theory was based on circular reasoning: behavior is explained by preferences, which are defined by behavior. This was wrong, because the theory did have implications: "modern utility theory with all its qualifications is not in a technical sense *meaningless*. It *is* an hypothesis which places definite restrictions upon demand functions and price-quantity data; these could be refuted or verified under ideal observational conditions." He continued with a strong criticism of previous writers,

> One should have thought that these empirical implications would have been the sole end of the theorists who concerned themselves with these matters. Strangely enough, means and ends have been so confused that only a small fraction of the literature has been concerned with this problem even indirectly; moreover, in this there are not half a dozen papers in which valid demand restrictions have been developed.[27]

Given that he presumably included some his own papers in this "not half a dozen," this amounted to a very strong criticism of his elders.[j]

When Samuelson turned to "Progression in Mathematical Thought," his story was one of increasing generality of the functional forms used for utility functions and to the recognition, by Pareto, that there was no need for cardinal utility functions. From here he went on to the device of indifference curves used by John Hicks and Roy Allen, arguing that there was no reason why these would be integrable into utility functions. Even the notion of an ordinal utility function was stronger than necessary. This led to the conclusion that it was sufficient to assume individuals select the most preferred combination of goods from those they can afford. All meaningful results could be derived from this. He pointed out that this did not imply anything about the way consumers thought or that they were rational in any other sense. Samuelson then proceeded to derive concrete results. As in his earlier papers, he emphasized that one equation contained *all* of the valid, meaningful results found in previous work on consumer theory.

---

j. He had by then published six papers on the theory of demand.

In two further chapters, drawing on his articles and the chapter written for the Schultz volume, he moved into a discussion of special topics, including cardinal utility functions and functions where the utility of each good depended only on consumption of that good; complementarity between goods; constancy of marginal utility of income; and consumer's surplus (a measure of the change in utility caused by a change in the constraints faced by a consumer). These chapters, relentlessly critical of previous economists, could be seen as exercises that demonstrated the value of the methods he was propounding by cutting through seemingly complex theoretical problems.[k]

Dynamics

The thesis ended with two chapters on dynamics. Samuelson introduced this discussion by, once again, criticizing previous generations of economists for failing to go beyond arguing that there were "laws" governing economics to investigating the character of those laws. If nothing is known other than that supply and demand determines prices, without knowing their shape, "the economist would be truly vulnerable to the gibe that he is only a parrot taught to say 'supply and demand.' "[28] He recapped points he had made earlier when he wrote that, though economists believed a rise in demand raised a good's price, they had no basis for making this claim. It was impossible to quantify such claims without numerical values for the parameters in supply and demand curves, but this was very time-consuming and expensive to do. (Samuelson would have remembered the statistical laboratory used by his Chicago teacher, Henry Schultz, to do just this.) This meant that the economist needed to derive qualitative results about whether variables would rise or fall in response to a change—to engage in comparative statics. The aim of his first chapter on dynamics was to show that deriving "fruitful theorems in comparative statics" was "intimately tied up with" the problem of stability of equilibrium.

This idea had been suggested to him by Wilson, in response to a paper Samuelson had written toward the end of 1938.[29] Wilson had complained that Samuelson's analysis was not "so general in some respects as Willard

---

k. The contrast with Marshall, who had emphasized the continuity between his work and that of his predecessors, was stark.

Gibbs would have desired." He told Samuelson that Gibbs used to lay great stress on the fact that it was important "to remain within the limits of stability." What Wilson appeared to be telling Samuelson was that he had not stated the conditions for optimization correctly and that these conditions were related to the conditions for stability. The significance of this for Samuelson's argument was that if one was solving an optimization problem, one could derive comparative statics results without paying attention to stability. However, when analyzing a system that did not involve optimization, it was necessary to assume stability to get comparable results.[1]

Wilson also reminded Samuelson of the need to consider the more general case where functions were not continuously differentiable—where functions might have kinks or discontinuities.[m] Wilson was describing the mathematics of convex sets (a form of analysis more general than differential calculus), a type of mathematics that became important in economics in the 1950s, when economists sought more general proofs of results in general equilibrium theory. His final advice was that Samuelson needed to explain himself better: "a little more text and not so many formulae in proportion to the text might make the whole decidedly easier reading."

Samuelson tackled the problem of deriving comparative statics results in three stages. Given that the existing literature contained little explicit discussion of the topic, Samuelson had to begin by defining dynamics and related notions such as equilibrium (which had a different meaning in this context). He defined a dynamic theory as one that determined how, starting from arbitrary initial conditions, all variables would change over time. This took the mathematical analysis to an even higher level, for it might be modeled using "differential, difference, mixed differential-difference, integral, integro-differential and still more general" sets of equations.[30] Even if some of the ideas would have been familiar to economists, Samuelson was using mathematical language in a way that only a tiny minority of mathematical

---

1. Wilson's concern was that Samuelson had not stated the second-order conditions correctly. Second-order conditions for a maximum imply stability.

m. Wilson wrote, "He [Gibbs] doesn't use derivatives but introduces a condition which is equivalent to saying that his function has to be on one side or in a tangent plane to it. He doesn't even assume that there is a definite tangent plane but merely that at each point of his surface it is possible to draw some plane such that at each point of his surface it is possible to draw some plane such that the surface lies except for that point and some other points entirely to one side of the plane." He went on to say, "Just how general a theorem one can get I don't know because I have never worked it out as carefully as I ought to have done."

economists would have previously encountered. Given a definition of equilibrium influenced by Ragnar Frisch, Samuelson defined two concepts of stability: a variable might get ever closer to its equilibrium value ("perfect stability of the first kind") or its motion might be bounded, meaning that it never remained on one side of the equilibrium for more than a finite time interval. These two types of stability could be analyzed for very small displacements from equilibrium, or for large ones. Again, these were distinctions that, while familiar to mathematicians who worked on such problems, would have been foreign to most economists. He was rapidly moving away from economics into mathematics.[n]

Though his discussion was to focus on stability of the first kind, Samuelson motivated stability of the second kind by noting that "no conservative dynamical system of the type met in theoretical physics possesses stability of the first kind." Given that he did not explain that "conservative" meant a system in which energy was conserved, few economist readers would have understood this. A footnote citing George Birkhoff explained that a system with friction (in which energy is dissipated as heat) might possess stability of the first kind. Though he did not develop it, Samuelson thus drew an analogy between stable economic systems and friction, implying that frictions were necessary to ensure stability of economic systems.

Comparative statics, the method he had advocated earlier in the thesis, was, Samuelson argued, a special case of a general dynamic analysis. While it might be possible to abstract from dynamic analysis, as Samuelson had done in his earlier chapters, it was important to take account of dynamics. He made this point by drawing out a series of examples from the literature, formulating each of them in the mathematical language of dynamic models. The first was supply and demand in a single market, where economists generally assumed that if supply exceeded demand, the price would fall, and if demand exceeded supply, it would rise. This was formulated as a differential equation that was then solved to obtain price as a function of time. Stability could be proved to depend on the relative slopes of the supply and demand curves.

Samuelson's second example was an alternative to the first. Instead of assuming that price changed in response to the difference between supply and demand, he made the "Marshallian" assumption that the quantity of goods traded rose or fell according to whether the demand price (the price

---

n. An example of stability of the second kind is considered later.

consumers were willing to pay) exceeded or fell short of the supply price (the price that producers required if they were to continue producing the product).[o]

A third dynamic model, also found in the previous literature although Samuelson cited no sources, involved postulating that demand and supply responded to prices with a lag: that they depended on the price prevailing one period earlier. The fourth model would also have been very familiar to economists, because it corresponded to the diagram Marshall had used to analyze international trade, and it involved countries adjusting the quantities they traded in response to the difference between what they were trading and what they wanted to trade. His final example, attributed to Francis Dresch, whose mathematical economics thesis had been submitted at Berkeley in 1937, differed radically from the other examples, in that it assumed that prices changed in response to accumulated stocks of goods: if producers failed to sell all their output, their inventories would increase and companies would respond by reducing prices.

Samuelson finished his chapter by applying dynamic analysis to the systems found in two very recent books. The first was the attempt by John Hicks, in *Value and Capital* (1939b), to generalize the stability conditions for a single market to multiple markets. Though Hicks had derived stability conditions, he had not derived them from explicit dynamic systems. Drawing on mathematical techniques he had used earlier in the thesis, as well as those relevant only to dynamic models, Samuelson analyzed stability more rigorously, showing why the absence of explicit dynamics was a problem for Hicks. The second was the Keynesian system, as formulated by interpreters such as Meade, Hicks, and Lange, comprising three equations: a consumption function, a marginal efficiency of capital, and a liquidity preference schedule.

Clearly this related to the system he and Hansen had previously analyzed, but it was different in that he did not incorporate the accelerator, thereby keeping closer to the issues then being debated concerning the coherence and meaning of the *General Theory*. Perhaps more important, though it was not the same type of supply and demand system, and though it originated in business cycles and not in "economic theory," Samuelson was treating the Keynesian system as something analogous to the other market systems he had been discussing in the thesis: he derived explicit comparative statics results (of precisely the sort that Hicks and others were trying to obtain).

---

o. Samuelson pointed out that although these two types of processes had become associated with Marshall and Walras, this involved a historical error.

This was the example in which he showed most clearly that dynamics—the assumption of a stable system—was closely related to the comparative statics results that were the goal of economic theory.

Samuelson achieved a number of things with these examples. The first was to show that dynamic processes were implicit in familiar economic examples, implying that economists could not argue that dynamics were unnecessary. They might not talk of explicit dynamic systems, but they were nonetheless using them implicitly. The second was to illustrate some of the different types of mathematics that could be used: differential, difference, and integral equations. One of his examples also illustrated stability of the second kind and the notion that systems might be subject to random shocks—that they might "take a random walk." In a random walk, a variable does not converge on any equilibrium; it simply moves up or down with given probabilities. For example, it was later argued that stock prices followed a random walk: in each day they might rise or fall, that day's price being the starting point for the next day's movement. Thus if, though chance, a stock price rose for several successive days, it could depart a long way from its initial value. Such a system can be seen as stable in that, although it will not converge on any value, there is a defined probability that it will not move more than a certain distance from the starting point.[31] His third major point was to show, through familiar examples, that stability analysis was not an esoteric matter that economists could ignore, but that it was important for deriving comparative statics results. As in his previous chapters, the tone was of showing economists how to do properly the things that they had previously been trying unsuccessfully to do.

Samuelson's second chapter on dynamics, chapter 9, "Foundations of Dynamical Theory," moved further from economics and into mathematics, citing mathematicians more frequently than economists. He distinguished between "causal" systems, in which the system was completely determined by the initial conditions, and "historical" systems, in which one also needed to know the historical date at which the system started. The latter were, he explained, incomplete causal systems.

The notion of a causal system led directly to the analysis of certain properties: whether the system could ever return to its initial point and whether any patterns might emerge in terms of relationships between variables. Though this argument was at a highly abstract level, it permitted discussion of problems with which economists were familiar, including the choice of variables to model and the fact that some variables changed more slowly than others. Dynamic analysis also made it possible for Samuelson to introduce randomness (also in one of his earlier examples) and to relate economic theory to econometrics (as the term eventually came to be understood). He provided a justification for representing economic equilibrium "as simply a statistically fitted trend," implying that the approach to estimating demand functions represented by Henry Ludwell Moore and Henry Schultz might have rigorous theoretical justification.[p]

Economists understood the notion of a stationary equilibrium, but Samuelson argued that there was a case for thinking in terms of moving equilibria—of equilibrium as something that changed over time. Citing Lotka's *Elements of Physical Biology* (1925), he noted that a dynamic equilibrium of supply and demand was "essentially identical with the moving equilibrium of a biological or chemical system undergoing slow change."[32] Though some economists, such as Frisch, would have had no problem with such ideas, it was far from the thinking of most economists. As has been explained already, he was moving away from economics into the realm of mathematics and physical systems in general, sketching directions in which economic analysis might develop.[q]

A Harvard Thesis

Though he had become an assistant professor at MIT by the time the thesis was submitted, it was, as Samuelson himself pointed out, essentially a Harvard thesis. This is trivially true, in that a work such as this could not have been changed fundamentally in the last few weeks before its submission.[33] However, there is a much deeper sense in which it was a Harvard thesis. As Samuelson repeatedly stated, his mentor was Wilson, who guided him continually. The earliest parts of the thesis, on consumer theory, involved tackling problems that Wilson had himself discussed. It was Wilson whose inspiration lay behind Samuelson's focus on analogies with physical science— notably thermodynamics and the Le Chatelier Principle—but also biology, where, though he might cite Lotka, Wilson's interest in these topics was never far away.

---

p. He cited Moore in this chapter (Samuelson 1940a, p. 233) and had cited Schultz, his former teacher, earlier in the thesis.

q. Most economics continued to be based on concepts of stationary equilibrium. It was not until the 1970s and 1980s, for example, that concepts of dynamic, stochastic equilibrium, such as Samuelson discussed in this chapter, became central to macroeconomic modeling.

However, Wilson was not the only influence for the thesis. In Schumpeter, Leontief, and Haberler, Harvard had a core of experts in the type of theory Samuelson was systematizing. Schumpeter might lack Leontief's mathematical skills, let alone those of Wilson, but he was an enthusiast for mathematical economics, and though his own work took him in a more historical direction, Samuelson's *Foundations of Analytical Economics* could be seen as providing the mathematical extension of Walrasian theory, so admired by Schumpeter, that he could not himself achieve. Though the thesis kept largely clear of business cycle theory, aside from some almost incidental references when Samuelson was discussing dynamics, his work with Hansen also found echoes in the later parts of the thesis. Discussions with his contemporaries are no less significant because they are harder to pinpoint.

The thesis was also a Harvard thesis in that it was a product of Harvard's "interstitial academy"—its profusion of academic spaces that arose outside established disciplines, the most important of which was the Society of Fellows, with which Bridgman, author of the term "operationalism," was connected. The interdisciplinary space of the Society of Fellows is reflected in the authorities Samuelson cited. Lawrence Henderson was not cited in the thesis, but as Samuelson later noted when revising the thesis for publication, his discussions of equilibrium echoed ideas about which Henderson would regularly have been talking during the three years Samuelson was a junior fellow. This is quite apart from Henderson's interest in Pareto, whose theory of economic equilibrium Samuelson had developed. In the published version of the thesis, Henderson's *The Order of Nature* was one of the first works cited.[34] Samuelson's friend, the chemist E. Bright Wilson (another junior fellow, not to be confused with Samuelson's mentor) would have discussed the physical analogies with him (the Le Chatelier Principle, to which Samuelson attached great importance, was derived in the context of chemical reactions).[35] Perhaps most important, the most heavily cited authority in the final chapter of the thesis, which offers the most general, and arguably most fundamental theory, is George Birkhoff, a senior fellow. Even if Samuelson did not attend his lectures on differential equations (though it seems very likely that he did), they were in close touch.

Of course, not all the ideas upon which Samuelson drew came from Harvard. Samuelson might be critical of Frisch in the context of consumer theory, yet when it came to discussions of equilibrium and dynamics, Frisch was the economist with whom he engaged more closely than anyone else, adopting some of his concepts. Samuelson had developed his ideas on consumer theory against the background of a literature in which the articles by Hicks and Allen were central. His articles show that Samuelson's ideas were already well formed before Hicks's *Value and Capital* was published in 1939, but he engaged with the book, particularly in discussing dynamics, where he treated Hicks in the same way as he treated other authorities: as an economist whose work needed placing on a more rigorous foundation.

Foundations of Analytical Economics was written in a few months, in a hurry, drawing on the journal articles he had written while a graduate student and as a junior fellow. It was, however, far more than a compilation of those articles. It proposed a new way of doing economics, to which certain types of mathematical analysis were central. When published as a book seven years later, it came to define the way much economic theory was done.[r] The derivation of comparative statics results, often using the mathematical methods he had pioneered, became standard practice. The same was true of his chapters on dynamics, though here the take-up of some of the methods he discussed (notably dynamic, stochastic equilibrium) was slower. Economists would turn to his book not just for its economic analysis but also as a primer on the mathematical methods they used. However, though he continued to work on this material, revising the manuscript for publication and writing new articles on dynamic theory, he was shortly to leave Harvard. Partly because of that move and partly because the United States became involved in the war then engulfing Europe, his career was to change dramatically. The specialist in mathematical economics was to become a leading figure in the development of Keynesian ideas, and he was to become the economist from whom an entire generation of students was introduced to economics. The next stage of his biography is to see how that change came about. It is probably little exaggeration to say that everything followed, in one way or another, from his move from Harvard to MIT.

---

r. The transition from thesis to book is described in chapter 22 this volume.

| Leaving Harvard

MIT's Offer

While at Harvard, Samuelson was still considered a specialist in mathematical economics who would find it difficult to get a permanent academic position, because positions in that field were scarce.[1] Wilson, who had been making efforts to find possible openings, expressed the problem in a letter to C. Griffith Evans, in the Department of Mathematics at the University of California at Berkeley. After praising Samuelson, saying, among other compliments, that Samuelson had given two "marvelously clear" lectures for him, and that he had married "a girl who is a grand economist," he wrote:

> Now the problem of placing Samuelson will not be wholly easy because not many people want mathematical economics. Moreover it seems to me that Samuelson thinks rather as a mathematician than as an economist. He tends to go into equations rather than into a literary form of expression without equations. While he has had a very fine training in mathematics and is entirely able to pick up what mathematics he needs he isn't as much a mathematician in the sense in which most departments of mathematics define the term just as he isn't as such an economist in the sense in which most departments define the term. Indeed I doubt whether he would be a great success teaching undergraduates economics from any of the standard texts now in use.[2]

Samuelson was a brilliant student who at that time simply did not fit into disciplinary categories. The reason Wilson thought he might interest

Evans was that Berkeley was building up its department to include a broad range of applied mathematics; Samuelson could do research in mathematical economics and would be able to do routine teaching in mathematics. Evans replied that they already taught mathematical economics and did not have the space for a second person in the field.[3] So, when at the beginning of December 1939 Samuelson received a letter from Harold Freeman, who had been a student with him in 1936–38, and was now an associate professor at MIT, inquiring about whether he would be interested in a position and on what terms, he jumped at the opportunity.[4] MIT was the one place where Wilson thought Samuelson would fit in because all students at the institute were required to study mathematics, and he would be able to take advantage of this in teaching even elementary economics.

Freeman told him that the professor who taught economic theory and business cycle theory was ill and might need to "rest up," which explains why Samuelson replied that he had recently become interested in business cycle theory and that he had been working with Hansen at the Littauer Center.[a] Samuelson explained that his appointment as a junior fellow ended at the end of the academic year and that he was interested in exploring all the alternatives open to him "at Harvard and elsewhere," and he suggested they arrange an interview. However, no offer from MIT materialized and on June 19, 1940, Harvard took the decision to offer Samuelson a one-year position as "Instructor in Economics and Tutor in the Department of Economics." On September 1, 1940, he began his teaching career at Harvard at a salary of $2,500 a year.

Events then moved rapidly, for by then several MIT faculty had been drafted for national defense purposes and its economics department needed to appoint someone very quickly. Harold Freeman persuaded Ralph Freeman, head of the Economics Department at MIT, that Samuelson would be a good appointment; not only was he a good scholar, but he would work with others.[b] When Ralph Freeman asked whether Samuelson was a cooperator, Harold Freeman allegedly replied, "Is Samuelson a cooperator? Why the man writes joint articles," the basis for this claim being the article Samuelson had written with Russ Nixon.[5]

This was the first, and far from the last, occasion on which Samuelson's career was significantly affected by the military situation. Anxious to behave

---

a. His expertise in economic theory would have been clear from his publications, so he presumably had no need to mention that.

b. Ralph Freeman was no relation of Harold Freeman.

properly, Ralph Freeman contacted Edward Chamberlin, who had by then replaced Burbank as head of the Harvard Economics Department, to ask permission to make an offer to Samuelson, no doubt explaining that MIT had been forced into doing so by the exigencies of preparing for war. Though this may have been a request that Chamberlin could not decently refuse, he placed the matter before his department's executive committee, which met on October 2.

The last item on the committee's lunchtime agenda read simply "Samuelson." They discussed Freeman's request along with a proposal to recommend Samuelson immediately for a five-year instructorship. Schumpeter apparently threatened to resign if Samuelson was not made an offer, but despite this drama, no offer was made and Chamberlin acceded to Freeman's request.[6] The outcome was that on October 10, MIT president Karl Compton officially offered Samuelson an assistant professorship, at a salary of $3,000 per year.[7] He decided to accept and moved immediately, a few weeks into the new academic year.

To understand the significance of this move, it is essential to note that Harvard had, along with Chicago, one of the leading economics departments in the country. It contained people, such as Chamberlin, Schumpeter, Hansen, Williams, and Haberler, who were acknowledged authorities in their field, as well as people such as Wilson and Leontief (still very young and only recently embarked on the project that was to bring him fame), who were engaged in mathematical economics at the level he was pursuing. Even those whom Samuelson did not respect, such as Crum and Frickey, were active in research. The list of Harvard's graduate students during the time Samuelson was there reads like an honor roll for postwar economics. In contrast, MIT had a Department of Economics and Social Science, in which the main research focus was in the field of industrial relations; its main function was providing service teaching for natural science and engineering students, half the department's teaching resources being devoted to a course in economics that was compulsory for virtually all students in the institute. MIT did not even have a graduate program in economics. If Samuelson moved to MIT, though he would be moving only two miles, he would be joining a department that was without the advantages Harvard, for all its faults, could offer.

In retrospect, Harvard's decision not to match MIT's offer seems like a monumental miscalculation. There is also a puzzle as to why, given the enormous disparity between the two departments, Samuelson chose to leave when he had the option of remaining at Harvard. The suggestion has been made that the answer to both questions was anti-Semitism, then rife at Harvard. It has also been suggested that some of his Harvard teachers were prejudiced against someone who was brighter than they were and, to boot, a Keynesian. Robert Solow, Samuelson's colleague for many years at MIT, who had been at Harvard in the 1940s, expressed the view that Harvard was prejudiced against Jews, Keynesians, and people who were very bright, so Samuelson had no chance.[8] It turns out, though there is considerable evidence to support this view, the story is more complicated.

Wilson and the Case for MIT

An important element in the story concerns Edwin Bidwell Wilson. On October 3, the day after the meeting of the Executive Committee, he wrote to Samuelson about the decision he was having to make. After saying that he did not want to make the decision for him, Wilson drew clear parallels between Samuelson's position and the situation he had been in early in his own career. Wilson had received an offer from MIT during his first year at Yale, and "although there were many people at Yale who couldn't understand why I should change from Yale to MIT under any circumstances and although I was very happy at Yale and perhaps better situated socially there than at MIT," he had never regretted his decision to move.[9] Wilson might now be at Harvard, but he knew what it was like to give up a much-prized position at an Ivy League university in order to go to MIT, and difficult as his decision had been, he was in no doubt that it had been correct. Wilson, who for three years had been co-president of MIT, then changed his tone to that of an MIT insider, saying that he had thought a lot about economics at "Tech." After the death of Francis A. Walker, first president of the American Economic Association and president of MIT from 1881 to 1897, economics had not been given the support it should have received. In particular, the mathematical and statistical side of economics had not been developed: the faculty at MIT had failed to take advantage of the fact that because it was an engineering school, their students were all required to have two years of mathematics, physics, and chemistry, with many of them having studied applied mechanics and thermodynamics (a subject that Wilson and Samuelson had discussed at length). If Samuelson went to MIT, he could take advantage of his situation there.

Realizing that Samuelson would be finding it difficult to break away from a department that included mathematical economists, Wilson wrote about the transformation that had taken place at MIT during his own time there; despite having thought he would be going into "utter mathematical darkness," MIT's mathematics department had developed into one of the best research departments in the country. This had been the result of appointing a group of able young people; though he could not be certain this would happen in economics if Samuelson went to MIT, he noted that "they are starting out well if they secure you."

Wilson then sought to weigh Samuelson's prospects at MIT and at Harvard. He thought that there was a very good chance that Samuelson would be offered a permanent position at MIT and that having the title of professor would also make it easier to get offers elsewhere. In contrast, there was great uncertainty about whether Samuelson would get tenure at Harvard; recent decisions had made it much harder for young people to get tenure, Harvard was well stocked with economic theorists (at least in relation to its teaching needs), and it had shortages of people in other fields that were becoming very important, such as agricultural economics. On the other hand, Samuelson would enjoy being at Harvard, and he would, Wilson thought, be very likely to be offered a five-year instructorship the following year. His knowledge of economic theory would make it possible for him to work up some other branch of economics, increasing his chances of advancement. There were arguments on both sides, but the decision was weighted heavily in favor of going to MIT. On October 9, Samuelson replied by saying that "in view of the age distribution and composition of the Department, and taking into consideration the rather attractive conditions at the Institute, it [accepting MIT's offer] seemed the best thing to do."[11]

On October 14, Wilson wrote again. Now that Samuelson had made up his mind, Wilson's tone changed and he explained much more explicitly than in his previous letter why he thought Samuelson's decision was the correct one. He laid out a vision of the advantages that could accrue to both MIT and Harvard from Samuelson's move, as well as the development of MIT. The letter needs to be quoted at length in order to show how deeply he was thinking about the question:

> Cambridge, Massachusetts is one of the best places in the world to study mathematics because there are two good departments, one at Harvard and one at Tech which taken together are perhaps better than can be found in any one place elsewhere. There would be a possibility of an exception in Princeton, New Jersey where Princeton University has a good department and where the Institute of Advanced Study concentrates a good deal of its effort into mathematical lines. In the same way Cambridge is a great center of research in physics since MIT built up a large research department in physics. Harvard has always

had a good department for many, many years. When I came to the Tech in 1907 Cambridge was a fine place to study geology because both Harvard and Tech had strong departments. I fear that the department at Tech has fallen down a good deal since then. Jagger went to Hawaii, Daly went to Harvard and I don't think the replacements have kept the department up.

In respect to all three departments there was enough difference in the environment and in the problems which came to the staff so that the combined departments undoubtedly covered the ground more widely than it would have been covered at either institution if the department there had been as large as the two departments combined and there had been no department at the other school.

Now I see no reason why there should not be some kind of fraternization between the Tech department of economics and the Harvard department whether in Cambridge or at the Business School as there was 30 years ago between the departments of geology (which may continue for ought I know) and as there is between the departments of physics in the two institutions. It seems to me clear that economics at Tech because it is at Tech will be kept closer to practical applied problems than in Cambridge though perhaps no more so than at the Harvard Business School. One reason there has not been very much influence of the Tech department on Harvard or of Harvard on Tech is because the department at Tech has been rather weak. For a long time the department of physics was weak and busied itself only with teaching and with rather low-grade practical research. For a long time there was no research done in mathematics worthy of the name. I think one of the good things about your going to Tech will be not only that the department is thereby greatly strengthened on the theoretical side but that you have a chance to broaden yourself out on certain types of application and that moreover this appointment may be but the beginning of a real interlocking in interest between the departments.[10]

Wilson was thus assuring Samuelson that he had made the right decision to go to MIT, not just for himself but also for Harvard. Going to MIT would pull Samuelson's research in new directions—it was still very much an engineering school—but due to the synergy that would result from having two strong but different departments, economics in Cambridge would be stronger than if Samuelson were to stay at Harvard and MIT were to remain weak.

Anti-Semitism at Harvard

The most widely canvassed explanation of departure from Harvard is anti-Semitism. The presence of anti-Semitism at Harvard is not in doubt.[12] A report on personnel problems written just before Samuelson's move to MIT took the issue seriously: after stating that "no graver reflection could be cast on the academic profession than that any of its members should be willing to compromise time-honored educational and scholarly standards by racial or religious discrimination," it noted that "comments volunteered in response to the Committee's questionnaire suggest that discrimination may exist in some departments."[13] Nine junior faculty had raised the issue, alleging discrimination in three departments, one teacher expressing the view that "racial prejudice is so thoroughly ingrained and taken for granted that no one takes much notice of it except in particularly flagrant cases."[14] It appears that, on investigating the issue, the committee was told that some faculty members objected to the appointment of Jewish teachers because they were thought unacceptable to undergraduates. This concern, the committee contended, was exaggerated and in any case should be challenged; the university should aim to liberate its students from such prejudice.

A major reason why anti-Jewish prejudice was so "ingrained" was that Harvard's mission in the early twentieth century was to train the Brahmins of New England society—the Protestant elite who would go on to positions of power and influence. Forty percent of Harvard's students came from Massachusetts and 47.3 percent came from families with incomes over $7,500, compared with a national average of 1.5 percent.[15] Alongside more serious students there was a significant intake of "frivolous, clubby students," in line for a "Gentleman's C," who despite their lack of academic prowess were important to Harvard.[16] However, Harvard sought students who were not just of the right social class but who also had "character," often represented by athletic ability; and here, competition with Yale and Princeton was strong, especially when President James Conant, appointed in 1933, tried to raise academic standards as part of his attempt to improve the university's academic standing. For this reason, Harvard introduced a quota to restrict the number of Jewish students. Traditionally, there had been no need to discriminate against Jews, for their numbers were small, but the influx of German and Eastern European Jews in the 1920s threatened the social mix. Harvard's problem was that if the number of Jews rose too high—at Columbia, the number of Jews had risen to 40 percent—well-heeled New Englanders might instead choose to go to Princeton or Yale, both of which had significantly fewer Jewish students than Harvard.

Conant sought to recruit academic stars, and his public pronouncements presaged modern university practices in which admission is based on merit rather than religion or ethnic origin. However, as Karabel has documented, he continued his predecessor's policy of favoring upper-class students by appointing as chair of the admissions committee someone who boasted of having handled the "Jew problem" at the private school from which he came.[17] Basing admission on factors such as "character" and "leadership" allowed discrimination to continue without inviting awkward external scrutiny.[18] Such criteria allowed them to admit those socially acceptable Jews whom, as potential donors, they did not wish to offend. As late as 1940, the head of Harvard's Eliot House could write to his colleagues asking what they were to do about the "Jew problem," opining that the number of Jews in his house was 40 percent and rising when they ought to have had no more than 20 percent.[19] There were Jews in the Economics Department, but the pressure was to keep this hidden. Frank Taussig, the long-time head of department who had retired just before Samuelson's arrival, had a Jewish parent, but his family had come from Germany, not Eastern Europe, and his appointment in 1892 was long before the issue of Jews gained prominence. Leontief's mother was Jewish, though this became known only much later.[20] Seymour Harris, born Ginsberg, was known to be Jewish, and though he eventually got tenure, it was not until 1948, twenty-six years after being appointed an instructor.

Typically for someone not wanting his decisions to be defined by his colleagues' prejudice, Samuelson played down this aspect of Harvard for most of his career, even denying its importance. He noted that, as would be the case for any non-Jew, the reason he went to MIT was simply that he got a better offer.[c] It was only after his retirement that he spoke more openly about anti-Semitism. In September 1989, responding to a conversation with his long-time tennis partner Henry Rosovsky, who played a major role at Harvard in challenging anti-Semitism, Samuelson expressed the opinion that Harvard economist Edward Mason, whose wartime recruitment of Jews into the Office of Strategic Services had marked a turning point, had been unfairly accused of being anti-Semitic. He went on to provide

---

c. Even years after the letter to Rosovsky, discussed later, in an article in which he made his contempt for Burbank very clear, Samuelson stated that he chose to go to MIT "without malice" (Samuelson 1998c, p. 1377). He does no more than hint, by referring to his "Protestant wife" (which could as easily imply that he was Roman Catholic as that he was Jewish), that this absence of malice referred to anything other than prejudice against economic theory.

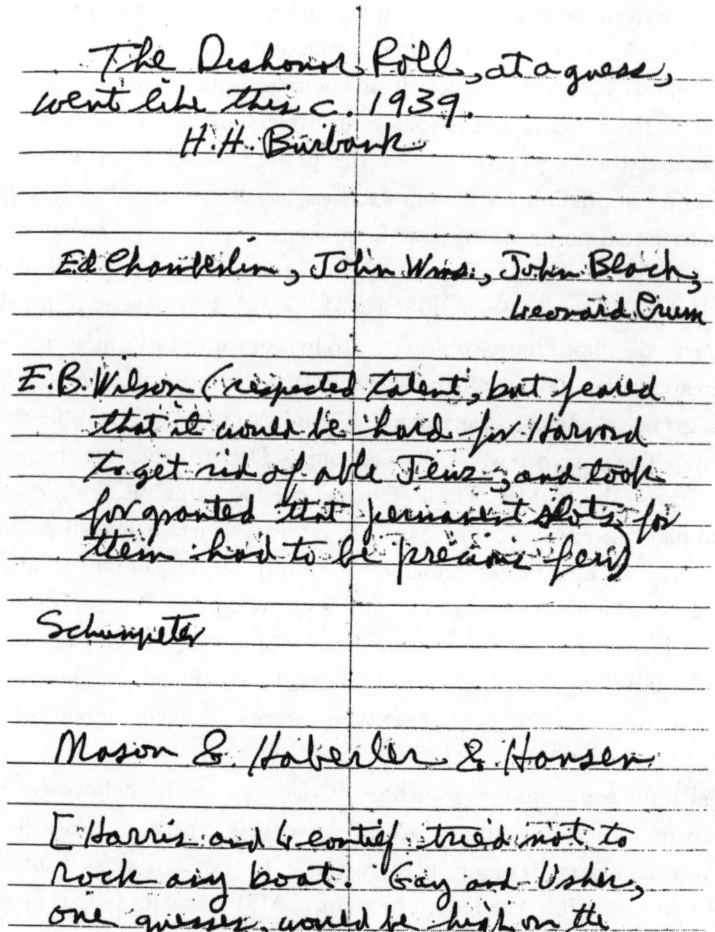
The Dishonor Roll, at a guess,
went like this c. 1939.
H. H. Burbank

Ed Chamberlin, John Wms., John Black,
Leonard Crum

E. B. Wilson (respected talent, but feared
that it would be hard for Harvard
to get rid of able Jews, and took
for granted that permanent slots for
them had to be precious few)

Schumpeter

Mason & Haberler & Hansen

[Harris and Leontief tried not to
rock any boat. Gay and Usher,
one guesses, would be high on the
page; Slichter perhaps in the
middle; Not Taylor perhaps low down.
Frickey was a cipher who voted with Crum.]
Econ was a better dept. Math, history, French ... ugh!

FIGURE 15.1 Samuelson's letter to Henry Rosovsky.
Note: The bottom line reads, "Econ was a better dept. Math, history, French . . . ugh!"
Source: P. A. Samuelson, September 26, 1989, Letter to Henry Rosovsky, PASP 63.

a "Dishonor Roll," reproduced as figure 15.1, in which members of the Harvard department were ranked in order of anti-Semitic prejudice. At the top was Harold Burbank, department chair from the late 1920s to 1938, followed by Edward Chamberlin, John Williams, John Black, and Leonard

Crum. At the bottom, innocent, were Mason, Gottfried Haberler, and Alvin Hansen. In between were Wilson and Schumpeter. Rosovsky's reply makes it clear that both of them realized that this letter would become part of their archives and eventually be read by historians, but that it would be a considerable time before this happened.[d]

Samuelson committed an account of anti-Semitism to print in the *Festschrift* for Mark Perlman. Perlman was eight years younger than Samuelson, but he was old enough to have experienced overt anti-Semitism, and his father, Selig Perlman, a distinguished labor economist and the economist who "discovered" Hansen, had experienced anti-Semitism at a time when there were even fewer Jews in the academy.[21] Mark Perlman was unusual in having published, in 1976, an article on Jewish contributions to economics, and given that Perlman was Samuelson's equal in vividly recalling and recounting stories about the past, they had presumably shared their experiences.[22] In this chapter, Samuelson focused on Harold Burbank, his department chair, of whom he wrote in uncompromising terms.[e]

> Burbank suffered fools gladly, but not Jews. On major departmental appointments, he could count on a near majority of cronies. Where patronage appointments in the lower ranks were concerned, he was absolute king. Being myself royally supported by Social Science Research Council and Harvard Society of Fellows stipends, like William Tell I felt no need to cozy up to him. That did not stop Burbank from advising me: "Samuelson, you are narrow. Keynes and Hawtrey are narrow. Don't take up economic theory until after you are fifty. This is what our great Allyn Young used to say." Alas, I had already lost my heart, and aspired to become even more narrow; and furthermore, Young had died young, just before his rendezvous with greatness. . . . I was always a young man in a hurry.
>
> Faced with a plethora of unsavory talent, H. H. B. [Burbank] solved his dilemma by confining the best of them to a ghetto of assistants in statistics and accounting under W. L. Crum and his satellite Edwin Frickey. Because Burbank had almost absolute pitch in his distaste for talent, such names as R. A. Gordon, Abram Bergson, Joe Bain and Lloyd Metzler made this a legion of honor. Metzler, a boy from Kansas

---

d. It is possibly significant that the letter was, unusually, filed both under "Rosovsky" and "M" (for Mason). If Samuelson, rather than his secretary, was responsible for this, it may have reflected his concern that the letter should not accidentally be lost.

e. It is worth noting that Samuelson's arrogance on his arrival at Harvard would not have endeared him to Burbank. See chapter 6 this volume.

with a German-sounding name, used to sing hymn duets with Marion Crawford—such as, "Jesus wants me for a sunbeam." But as has been said, an anti-[S]emite can smell out the last nine of the six Jews who have entered the room.[23,f]

Supporting evidence that Burbank was not anxious to assist Samuelson's career comes from correspondence with Wilson. In May 1939, Wilson wrote to Burbank explaining that Samuelson would be difficult to place in an academic position despite having a first-class mind. The problem was that he was not as good a statistician as a mathematical economist, and so, given the paucity of openings in mathematical economics, his only hope of getting a post was to be able to sell himself as a good teacher of general economics.

Wilson wrote at length, drawing on his own experience, to argue that Samuelson should be happy with a position in which he taught elementary economics, which would not make the same demands on his time as more advanced teaching, while getting on with his own research. Wilson pointed out that Burbank had lost a large number of teachers on Ec. A, the introductory course for undergraduates, and advised him to get hold of Samuelson and offer him a division of poor students, telling him that "you would have to place him as a teacher because of the scarcity of positions in mathematical economics and that to place him you needed to know that he had made himself a good teacher even for poor students."[24] Teaching a section of Ec. A would enable Samuelson to demonstrate that he could teach nonmathematical students, something he had up to that point not had the opportunity to do. If Burbank would do this, Wilson would square the teaching with the Society of Fellows.

However, despite Wilson's making a tightly argued case for a student who was now near the end of his fourth year at Harvard, and suggesting that he be made an offer that would be unattractive to many students, Burbank came up with excuses for postponing any action, even though he accepted the thrust of Wilson's argument:

Samuelson does present a problem. Sooner or later I suppose we will have to break him in. By all means the best place for him is in Economics A, but whether or not I can handle him next year I am doubtful, I will find it necessary to break in at least a dozen new men, and to add Samuelson with his particular problems to this difficult list

f. Note that this list contains Jews and non-Jews. Samuelson wanted to portray Burbank as a fool, as well as a bigot. The four economists all went on to distinguished careers.

is a bit more than I care to face, I agree with you that it is unlikely that he will be able to find a post in strictly mathematical economics. He must equip himself for general work.[25]

Burbank's refusal to accommodate Wilson's request is strongly suggestive of motives that were not stated explicitly. The result was that, before 1940, Samuelson's only teaching experience was statistics, considered by Harvard's anti-Semites to be a "Jewish" subject.[26]

As Samuelson's letter to Rosovsky made clear, his perception of anti-Semitism was not confined to Burbank, and even faculty members who were strongly supportive of Samuelson were to some extent complicit. Samuelson recalled a story told to him by Alfred Conrad, Schumpeter's assistant at the time of his death in 1950, on the way to Schumpeter's funeral:

ALF: Professor Schumpeter, what do you think of Nicky Kaldor?
JOE [SCHUMPETER]: Oh, these Asiatics. They are only early bloomers.
ALF: I am puzzled. Are you perhaps referring to Kaldor's Hungarian Magyar ancestry?
JOE: My dear Alfred. My figure of speech was to spare your sensibilities. It was my delicate way of referring to Kaldor's Mosaic ancestry.[27]

As Samuelson made clear, though Schumpeter shared with many other notable economists the belief that there were racially based character differences, he had probably done more than anyone else to place European Jewish émigré economists in academic posts.[28]

Schumpeter's complex attitude emerges even more clearly in an exchange with the Norwegian economist Ragnar Frisch. In 1932, Schumpeter had written to Frisch, raising doubts about the suitability of Jacob Marschak to be a fellow of the Econometric Society. Marschak was, Schumpeter claimed, "obviously working to create a majority of friends of a certain complexion on the German groups."[29] In response to Frisch's inference that Schumpeter must be objecting to Marschak's socialism, Schumpeter explained his position in detail writing on December 3:

You do me an injustice: I am not so narrow as to object to anyone because he is a socialist or anything else in fact. If I did take political opinion into consideration I should be much in favor of including socialists in our lists of fellows. In fact, I should consider it a good policy to do so. *Nor am I or have I ever been an anti-Semite. The trouble with Marschak is that he is both a Jew and a socialist of a type which is probably unknown to you*: his allegiance to people answering these two characteristics is so strong that he will work and vote for a whole tail of them and not feel satisfied until we have a majority of them, in which case he will disregard all other qualifications, this is the nature of a difficulty.[30]

However, despite believing that Marschak should not become a fellow of the Econometric Society because his commitment to advancing Jews and socialists would interfere with his scientific judgment, Schumpeter had no qualms about actively promoting Marschak's career, for he recognized that he had no future in Germany.

Though guilty of the racial stereotyping of his time, Schumpeter was a strong supporter of Samuelson. When Samuelson sent his friend Wolfgang Stolper a lecture he had written to commemorate their teacher,[31] Stolper reminded him that Schumpeter had threatened to resign over Harvard's failure to appoint him. Stolper recalled Schumpeter's having said, "I could understand it if it were anti-Semitism; but it is just that he [Samuelson] is better than they are."[32] Shigeto Tsuru, another fellow student and one of Samuelson's close friends, said that everyone had expected Samuelson to stay on as an assistant professor, and also believed Schumpeter held this view.[33] The idea that Samuelson was too good would be consistent with the fact that Schumpeter shared Samuelson's contempt for Burbank's scholarly standards, and given Samuelson's work, it could be seen as tantamount to prejudice against mathematical economics. However, it was common to use such language as a way of disguising anti-Semitic views.

Wilson is an even more significant case because Samuelson was so close to him. In Samuelson's "Dishonor Roll," Samuelson judged Wilson better than Chamberlin but worse than Schumpeter. His reason was a letter Wilson had written to Talcott Parsons in 1939,[34] which Samuelson had seen when Richard Swedberg, a biographer of Schumpeter, had found it in Harvard's archive. This letter stated that a Jew should not be appointed to a temporary position because it would be difficult to get him a permanent one. It argued that "in a social situation," the question of how to treat people fairly was a complicated one, even though the goals were simple: to recruit the best people to the permanent faculty and to ensure that all young people, including Jews, were appointed to positions appropriate to their talents. The problem was that because of anti-Semitism, at Harvard and elsewhere, Jews would take longer to find positions and therefore would need temporary positions for longer than non-Jews. The resulting large number of Jews in temporary positions, with poor prospects of permanent employment, was a reason why Parsons should not appoint another Jew from Chicago.

Though this made Wilson complicit in anti-Semitism, his arguments verging on casuistry, and though Samuelson was troubled when he saw the letter, he took a charitable view of his mentor.[g] When Samuelson came to write on anti-Semitism for Perlman's *Festschrift*, presumably after rereading the letter, he concluded that Wilson was not anti-Semitic but was trying to do the best he could in a bigoted society. His animosity was focused on Burbank, whom he saw not only as an anti-Semite but also as someone with very poor judgment about economics.

Decisions

News of the Harvard economists' disagreement over Samuelson reached MIT President Karl Compton, who on November 12 wrote to Wilson that he had heard that this had caused a disturbance: "I heard by the grapevine route . . . that there was subsequently a little disturbance over the matter in the minds of some members of the department."[35] Responding to Compton's anxiety about MIT having behaved properly, Wilson explained what had happened:

> Heads of departments at Harvard have very limited authority. They are really only chairmen and are according to the rules limited to a three year term although the rules are very often not followed in practice. Thus when your professor Freeman checked relative to Samuelson with Professor Chamberlin, Chamberlin could only represent his own attitude except as he called a special meeting of the department and took a vote on the matter. When some members of the department heard that Samuelson was likely to go to MIT they made a serious attempt to get the department to take some action which would keep

---

g. In the same letter, Wilson argued that because studying economics makes one conservative, it is appropriate to appoint liberals to junior positions. He also assumed that there might come a time when the appointment of Jews would be less of an emotional issue, and chances of success would be greater, concluding that it would have been better to focus on the appointment of women to the faculty (implying that this would have been less of an emotionally charged issue. Further evidence of Wilson's being complicit in anti-Semitism is contained in the letter, discussed in chapter 10 this volume, in which he had written, "My own personal contacts with him leads me to believe that he is not objectionably Semitic." This could be read either as implying that Wilson found some Jews objectionable or that though Samuelson might be a Jew, and even though he might be descended from Eastern European immigrants, he did not have those characteristics that caused other people to discriminate against Jews.

Samuelson at Harvard. . . . The discussion was entirely friendly to MIT and to Samuelson.[36,h]

Wilson then explained how this decision was consistent with Harvard's own teaching needs:

> Of course Professor Chamberlin would never have encouraged Professor Freeman to make an offer to Samuelson if it weren't for the fact that we are overloaded, so overloaded with high-grade people in economic theory that there really isn't much prospect that we can make a permanent position for a young fellow for a good many years especially as we are under-staffed in agricultural economies, in labor, and in social security and for that matter in economic history.

Wilson genuinely believed that Samuelson's profile did not fit Harvard's teaching needs, for several months later he wrote to Chamberlin saying that there was a need to bring on young people in applied fields: "there is no use of over-building theory and under-building agriculture, history and other items."[37]

The lack of fit with Harvard's teaching needs reinforced Wilson's conviction that MIT was the right place for Samuelson. In a letter that dealt mostly with other matters, Wilson added a paragraph that began by reassuring Compton that he had made the right decision in recruiting Samuelson: "I note with great satisfaction that you have taken on Samuelson in economics. He is one of the ablest young fellows I have ever met. I am sure he will have a distinguished career whether he stays with you or goes elsewhere."[38] Echoing what he had said to Samuelson three weeks earlier, he held out a vision of what could happen to economics at MIT if provided with adequate support from Compton:

> It seems to me that it is particularly appropriate for MIT to have in its department of economics persons who understand science and mathematics. Your students come to their economics with two years of mathematics, two years of physics, a year of chemistry and are simultaneously taking for the most part either physical chemistry or thermodynamics. It would seem to me that if the instruction in economics could be given in a way to use to the full the advantage of this long scientific training of your students it should be possible to give those

---

h. Despite the three-year rule, Burbank had been chair for many years, and was to become chair again after Chamberlin's term expired.

students in one year a broader and deeper course of economics than can be given to ordinary economic students in two years.

Significantly, Wilson then explained that this was not just his own view, for he had discussed this with at least one of his Harvard colleagues:

> In this opinion Leonard Crum agrees. Neither of us would mean that such a course should be in mathematical economics as such. My great trouble in teaching advanced economics at Harvard is to get the young economists to realize the importance of definitions, of consistency, and of logic. Even those who know considerable mathematics don't seem to know how to use it for scientific purposes.

Wilson was laying before Compton a vision of how MIT might develop its economics in a way calculated to make sense to MIT's physicist president.

In coming to the conclusion that Samuelson's profile was not a good fit with Harvard's teaching needs, it is important to realize the extent to which he was then regarded as a very narrow specialist. Hard as this is to imagine today, when academic economics is dominated by the use of mathematics, "mathematical economics" was then considered a specific field of economics—one specialization among many and, moreover, one the importance of which had not yet been established. In 1940, 70 percent of articles on economic theory in the *American Economic Review*, the journal of the American Economic Association, used no mathematics at all.[39] Immediately after Samuelson defended his thesis, Wilson, one of the examiners, wrote to him urging that he should revise the text so as to as to make it accessible to "good economic theorists who are not primarily mathematical economists," an end that required considerable rewriting and expansion of the text. Such rewriting would both make it clearer what they could learn from Samuelson's results and "help them to appreciate the value or rigorous mathematical economics of which not a few of them are rather skeptical."[40] The thesis might be accessible to himself, or to John Hicks and Roy Allen, but beyond such readers its audience was limited. Implying that Samuelson might not necessarily wish to remain at MIT, Wilson explained that if he became known as a "general theoretical economist," rather than a specialist in mathematical economics, he might find "first class positions" opening up all over the country.

At this time, as Schumpeter explained, many applied fields were defined in relation to policy problems: agriculture, labor, transportation, public utilities, control of industry, and public finance.[41] To teach such fields it was necessary, to an extent perhaps not true today when theory has spread much further, to venture into facts and institutions. This was an area in which Samuelson was still considered weak, even by Wilson, who supported him so strongly. The remark, quoted earlier, that Wilson made to Burbank that "Perhaps he doesn't know much concrete economics" might be seen as qualified (perhaps because he was trying to persuade Burbank that Samuelson should be allowed to teach economics), but he was more explicit when he wrote to Henderson, with whom he could presumably be more frank, recommending Metzler for the Society of Fellows.

> You may want me to compare him a little with Samuelson. As I see it he is nothing like the mathematician that Samuelson is though he has an adequate command of mathematics for an economist. As I see it he knows his economic phenomena and institutions a good deal better than Samuelson did when you took him on and is a better statistician.[42]

Though the comparison is with Samuelson as he had been in 1937, it remains an unfavorable judgment of his knowledge of concrete phenomena, reinforced by comments about the narrowness of Samuelson's work: "I doubt whether he [Metzler] has a so highly specialized technique or is working or would be willing to work in so narrow a field as that of mathematical economics." Wilson even expressed the view that Metzler might end up being more influential than Samuelson because "although he understands mathematical economics he can express himself, and prefers to express himself so far as possible in English."

Arguments about teaching needs could be used to cover not only anti-Semitism but also hostility to Keynes. Though Schumpeter and Wilson would not have considered Samuelson's support for Hansen's increasingly interventionist views a problem, even though they personally disagreed with them, others would have done so. Burbank, whose course on public finance Samuelson described as a course *against* public finance, would certainly have objected to the stance he and Hansen were taking on policy: in 1940–41, the academic year in which Samuelson had started teaching, it was, according to Robert Solow, common gossip that those teaching sections on Ec. A were not allowed to mention the *General Theory*.[43] Chamberlin, department chair for the critical meeting, was opposed to Keynes, as was Crum (and if Samuelson was right, Frickey would have supported Crum). It was not until after the Second World War that Harvard would choose to make tenured appointments to confessedly Keynesian economists.

A further problem arose from Harvard's reliance on a large number of instructors on fixed-term contracts, not all of whom could proceed to tenured contracts. This had come to a head in 1936–37, when the department recommended that two instructors, John Walsh and Alan Sweezy, have their contracts renewed for an additional three years, with prospect of renewal; but Conant's administration, in its bid to raise academic standards, would offer no more than a nonrenewable two-year extension.[44] Walsh and Sweezy were popular teachers, but Conant thought they had not published enough. Though Conant insisted that the reason was their poor publication records, he was accused of discrimination against economists who held radical political views.[45] On the advice of Walter Lippmann, then chair of the department's visiting committee, and in response to a petition from 131 faculty members, Conant set up a committee of senior professors, the "Committee of Eight" to look into the matter.[46]

The committee found that there had been no political bias, but that Walsh and Sweezy had not had a fair review and should be given a three-year extension as the department had recommended. However, by the time the committee ruled in their favor, the two had resigned. The following year, Conant tasked the committee to produce recommendations for tenure procedures, which it did. These rules had been implemented just before Samuelson's case came up, and an improved offer to Samuelson to match the one he had received from MIT would have involved making a special case almost immediately after instituting the new rule, and might have reignited controversy.

The undesirability of making an exception to the new rules was the reason why John Black opposed making an improved offer to Samuelson. He forgot to attend the executive committee meeting at which Samuelson's case was discussed, and the next day wrote apologetically to Chamberlin, saying:

> My vote is against this [giving Samuelson a five-year appointment].
> I think this is a fairly typical case of a young man whose services can be spared here for the next five years or so while he is getting experience and developing stature somewhere else. I always believed in this phase of the new program. My objection was to the precipitable way the change was introduced. Now that we are over the precipice, I see no reason for taking an action which is in variance with the policy.[47]

Wilson, too, thought Samuelson should be treated like anyone else and should wait his turn for promotion. He wrote to him:

> The question has been raised of course as to whether the department of economics would at this time recommend you for a 5 year

instructorship. I think you are pretty safe in counting on your getting a recommendation next spring for such an appointment if you don't get it now. For myself I agree in the main with Mr. Lowell's policy, as I understand it, which was the policy at Yale in the days when I was there, that able young people had to take their chances of getting what they wanted at the proper times and that a call to another institution shouldn't lead the university to make any future promises in advance of the regular time. I believe that as you advance in the academic world as you surely will you may yourself come to the conclusion that this is on the whole a sound policy no matter whether in your particular instance at the moment the university commits itself to a 5 year appointment for you or does not.[48]

It was not even clear that Samuelson was necessarily the strongest candidate for any permanent position that became vacant. He might be an exceptional candidate, but mathematical economics was widely considered a narrow specialization in which Harvard already had ample expertise. Harvard had to teach large numbers of undergraduates, most of whom lacked both the ability and the training to study mathematical economics.[49] Burbank's resistance to letting Samuelson teach introductory economics meant that he had been unable to demonstrate his ability to teach general economics, and even Wilson harbored doubts about whether Samuelson could communicate with economists outside the very small number who were trained in mathematics.

On Samuelson's side, there seems no reason to doubt his claim that he moved because he received a better offer. He was offered a higher salary, access to research grants, and better facilities than he could hope for at Harvard (including a telephone and a secretary). Not only that, but Wilson, who would have been well aware that MIT was being transformed from an essentially undergraduate engineering school into a full-fledged research university, had provided a clear vision of what could be achieved at MIT should Samuelson move there. However, in 1940, this was no more than a hope for the future. Samuelson faced a difficult decision and he agonized over it. While he was considering the offer, Rupert Maclaurin, who, as head of the Industrial Relations Section, was active in trying to build up MIT's economics department, phoned Samuelson daily, dangling before him the prospect of research funds.[50] Samuelson also claimed that Harold Freeman talked him into taking the job.

However, it is more likely the decisive push came not from Wilson, Maclaurin, or Harold Freeman but from Marion. Coming from a white, Anglo-Saxon, Protestant family and being an insider to Harvard—a Radcliffe graduate who spent two years as an assistant to Harris—she could see the institution's anti-Semitism and the barriers that would likely be in his way at Harvard more clearly than Paul could see them.[51] It was she who persuaded him to take the plunge and accept the MIT offer. While Wilson's vision of what Samuelson could achieve at MIT was to prove correct, his career was to develop in ways that neither he nor Wilson could foresee.

PART III | MIT, War,
Foundations,
and the Textbook,
1940–1948

CHAPTER 16

The Massachusetts Institute
of Technology

Economics in an Engineering School

At Harvard, which saw itself as America's preeminent university, home to
many academic stars in arts and sciences, Paul was at the center of the country's academic life. Its economics department was able to boast of being home
to some of the world's leading economists; as a junior fellow, Samuelson
mixed with eminent mathematicians, scientists, philosophers, historians,
and social scientists. The School of Public Policy provided a forum where
he could also engage with economic policymakers from Washington and
business. In complete contrast, MIT was an engineering school with a much
narrower focus.

Since its foundation in 1861, MIT had concentrated on training undergraduates in the practical skills required in engineering. This began to change
after the First World War, when two industrialists—Gerard Swope, of General
Electric; and Frank Jewett, of Bell Telephone Laboratories—decided that
industry needed engineers who had strong backgrounds in science and who
could contribute to the creation of science-based technologies.[1] Training in
practical engineering skills was no longer sufficient. Under their influence, the
Department of Electrical Engineering developed active research in physics. They
then turned to the institute as a whole, giving Karl Compton, a widely respected
experimental physicist who was recruited as president of MIT in 1930, the

task of "introducing a much more powerful element of fundamental science" into the engineering curricula.[2] During the 1930s, the curriculum was redesigned so that all students spent their first two years studying mathematics, physics, chemistry, English, and history, not specializing until their upperclass years.[3] Major laboratories were established, science departments were developed, and with the assistance of Vannevar Bush, who became vice president and dean of Engineering, Compton transformed MIT's other engineering departments. The result was that by the time Samuelson was recruited, MIT was still more specialized than Harvard but it had been transformed into an institution very different from the one it had been at the turn of the century.

According to historian Christophe Lécuyer, "From a polytechnic institution training practical engineers for positions of immediate usefulness in industry, it had become a full-fledged research university with leading research and graduate programs in physics, chemistry, electrical engineering, and chemical engineering." The institute had developed strong links with industry, and was also offering courses specifically for officers in the U.S. military: Navy officers could take courses in naval engineering, aeronautical engineering, meteorology, or torpedo engineering; Army officers could take specially designed courses in civil engineering or army ordinance, and there was a special course for chemical warfare officers.[4]

When Samuelson arrived, the Department of Economics and Social Science at MIT was very small, its composition reflecting MIT's history of offering the practical skills needed by engineers.[5] The head of the department, Ralph Freeman, was a former Rhodes Scholar and had served in the Canadian artillery during the First World War. When a separate Department of Economics and Statistics was established in 1930, Freeman, then at the University of Ontario, had been appointed as an associate professor, and in 1933–34, he became head of the department. The following year the department acquired the name it had in 1940, so as to reflect a broadening of its activities and the appointment of a sociologist to its staff.[6] Freeman had, according to Samuelson, absolute power in the new department, though out of courtesy he deferred to professorial votes on new appointments. Between them, the economists on the faculty had published very little: Armstrong and Tucker specialized in banking and finance, approached historically with a focus on institutions, while Thresher appears to have published nothing on economics.[a] Ralph Freeman published most

---

a. Google Scholar reveals only works related to student admissions.

frequently, but mostly book reviews. Three associate professors covered industrial relations and human relations, and there was an assistant professor covering each of social anthropology, psychology, statistics, and sociology, plus three instructors and four assistants.[7] There was no economics PhD program, though students could take graduate courses leading to an MSc in either economics and engineering or economics and natural science. They were primarily a service department, offering courses taken by engineers and natural scientists.

The 1940 edition of the MIT catalogue boasted that the institute "was the first technological institution to recognize and provide for the important place of economics in the training of the engineer."[8] Economics was a required part of the curriculum in all programs. Some courses were taught by specialists located in the engineering departments (for example, aeronautical engineering had a specialist in "air law and economics" and biology had an instructor in "marine economics," and there were courses in subjects such as "power system economics"), but the Department of Economics and Social Science provided most of the required economics teaching. Its main activity was an elementary course taken by virtually all students at the institute, which accounted for a high proportion of the department's teaching load and for which members of the department had collaborated on a textbook, *The Economic Process*.

First issued in 1934, this textbook was revised the following year, in which course offerings were increased to include American Government, Social and Economic Factors in City Planning, Methods of Social Investigation, Planning and Housing Legislation, and Economics of Transportation. The significant feature of these courses is that they were all introduced at the request of other departments. The department was not shaping its own activities. Five years later, Freeman was reporting a similar profile of activities: the economics textbook had been revised again, and a significant part of the department's efforts had gone into improving teaching in labor relations, sociology, and psychology.[9]

Ralph Freeman shared his surname with another member of the department, Harold Freeman (1909–1997), with whom Samuelson shared an office suite with telephones—a luxury that even Schumpeter and Haberler did not have at Harvard—and a secretary.[10] Samuelson described Harold Freeman as "the most unforgettable person I ever met," describing him as a cross between Peer Gynt and Baron Munchausen, whose versions of events rarely coincided with Samuelson's own.[11] Gregarious and full of gossip, he had studied at MIT in the late 1920s, in the days when it taught practical engineering skills, including handling ladles full of molten steel, a feat Samuelson found hard to believe given that Freeman was tall but weighed less than his IQ.[b] Graduating in 1931, he worked in a rubber plant, "pounding cheap heels into cheap shoes at 19 cents an hour" before becoming an instructor at MIT. He was a statistician, but from 1936 to 1938 he attended Harvard so that he could teach his share of economics properly. During this period he joined Samuelson at Schumpeter's and Wilson's lectures. At Harvard he wrote a thesis on *The Projective Differential Geometry of Plane and Space Curves*. He also undertook quality-control consulting work with industrial concerns, and published on statistical methods of quality control, before returning to MIT in 1939 as an associate professor to support the department's work in industrial statistics, in which there was extensive collaboration with the Mathematics Department.[12]

Samuelson's account of Harold Freeman, who became one of his closest friends, says as much about him as about its subject:

> [H]e told stories like Baron Munchausen. I never heard him describe an event as it happened. Usually his accounts were better than the real thing.... During the Korean War decade, Harold asked me how he could invest a small inheritance so as not to benefit from any war activity. It was a tough question in Leontief input–output networking. In the end I had to cheat him by not mentioning that Gillette and International Harvester did have some Pentagon contracts. During World War II he refused fees for consulting on quartermaster and ordnance matters. He did claim his travel expenses as tax deductions. The local IRS agent said: "Nix. You can be a good guy. But not at our expense."
>
> Every single day from September 10, 1927, to November 3, 1943, Harold ordered a chicken pie at the Walton Cafeteria outside MIT's main gate. By Laplace's Law of Succession, November 4, 1943 had an all but certain outcome. But never since has he eaten chicken.
>
> Once I asked him: "If the Devil promised you a theorem in return for your immortal soul, would you accept the bargain?" Without hesitation he replied, "No. But I would for an inequality."[13]

They shared a sense of humor, which is evident from their subsequent limited correspondence.[14]

---

b. Note that it is normal for an American to be weighed in pounds, whereas the UK uses kilos or stones.

Research and the PhD Program

The main responsibility for changing the research profile of the Economics Department was taken by W. Rupert Maclaurin (1907–1959), who had been one of those involved in recruiting Samuelson.[c] An associate professor when Samuelson arrived, he was promoted to full professor in 1942. Though born in New Zealand, Maclaurin was an MIT insider, being the son of the president of MIT who had been responsible for moving what was then Boston Tech across the Charles River to Cambridge, where it became the Massachusetts Institute of Technology.[15] Indicative of his position as an insider, the President's Report that announced his appointment in 1936 also contained details of the activities to establish a memorial to his father. Writing to the British economist Joan Robinson at the end of the decade, Samuelson described him as "an able chap with interests largely in the field of applied economics, particularly technological innovation. He is also what we in America would call a 'go-getter.' A type that you have perhaps not sufficiently encountered."[16] Samuelson claimed that MIT president Compton gave Maclaurin a "loose rein" on account of his having inherited "his father's green begging hand" (a reference to the funds Maclaurin's father had raised in order to move MIT to its new campus).[17]

In 1937, Compton, responding to suggestions from two businessmen, took the initiative in setting up an Industrial Relations Section, modeled on one established at Princeton. Assisted by Freeman and Maclaurin, he raised $125,000 to support the new unit in its first five years. Maclaurin was appointed its head.[18] It was responsible for research projects on topics such as hiring and layoff policies in a leading Massachusetts industrial company, industrial relations policies, and the supply and demand for labor in the paper industry.[19] Anticipating the establishment of a PhD program in economics, in 1939 Maclaurin approached Joseph Willits at the Rockefeller Foundation, asking for support.[20] Explaining that they believed their graduate program would be stronger with an organized research program, he proposed a three-year study of the labor market in a Massachusetts industrial community. Though Maclaurin was proposing research to be undertaken by economists, it remained closely tied to engineering.

In supporting the proposal, Compton drew attention to the fact that the Industrial Relations Section was the only organization of its type to be located in an engineering school, and he also pointed out the practical importance of the research for engineers. He claimed that many MIT graduates found

---

c. See chapter 15 this volume.

themselves having to determine or implement industrial relations policies, and this research would bring them into "intimate contact with the problems and personnel of the field."[21] The application was not successful and after some further unsuccessful attempts to apply for funds, Maclaurin changed his emphasis and approached the Rockefeller Foundation about a broader project that would be more suited to "appeal to the imagination and fitness of technical students."[22] He would devote less time to research in industrial relations and instead proposed to work out "an area particularly suited, such as the processes by which technical improvements spread through industry, or a study of the types of companies in different industries which are the initiators of technical change, whether the same types of companies initiated such changes."[23]

To support his case, Maclaurin pointed not only to the involvement of his own department with the Mathematics Department but also to the rising interest that many professors in engineering departments were showing in economics.[d] He argued that problems of mutual interest to economists and engineers could "best be developed if a special research fund were made available for graduate student and staff research devoted to the economics of industrial technology."[24] The topic he proposed to cover, "The Impact, Timing and Effect of Technological Change upon the American Economy," reflected his time at Harvard, where despite being in the business school, he had been one of Schumpeter's favorite students.[25] Under this Schumpeterian heading, Maclaurin proposed a broad program out of which he hoped that specific projects would emerge "after the ground had been thoroughly explored by means of graduate seminars carried on in co-operation with some of the technical specialists from the engineering departments."[26] Such a change would take the department's research away from industrial relations and toward a cross-disciplinary research venture involving economics and engineering.

Though it shows the direction in which Maclaurin was trying to shape the department's research, this was another grant proposal that came to nothing. However, in April 1941, Maclaurin submitted a successful application for $50,000, involving Samuelson, who had arrived a few months earlier, "to initiate a series of studies under the general topic of 'The Impact, Timing and Effect of Technological Change upon the American Economy.'" He wrote,

> We believe that this is an area in which an Economics Department
> with a young and growing Division of Industrial Relations located

---

d. This claim is borne out by the frequency with which economics was mentioned in the accounts of these departments' activities in the annual Reports of the President.

in an engineering school should be in a position to make a significant contribution. It would be our hope that over a period of years the specialists whom we might develop would help to interpret the processes of technological change and their economic and social implications to economists, government officials, labor leaders, and industrialists.[27]

It was an academic research project, but one that could have practical implications. It would cover three topics: factors in the individual firm influencing technological change involving substantial capital investment; case studies of union-management (or employee-management) relations and regulations concerning the introduction of technological change; and overall statistical studies of innovation. The description of the last of these topics adopted a Schumpeterian tone, in that it asked about the evidence for clustering of innovations and variation in the extent of innovation in different phases of the cycle. It also involved considering the character of new investment—how much was due to new industries and innovation, how much to growth in population and land, and how much to more intensive use of capital in old industries. The proposal reflected Hansen's thinking in proposing to establish whether a bias toward capital-saving innovations increased the likelihood of secular stagnation.

Maclaurin explained that MIT would contribute the spare time of himself, Samuelson, and Myers, and that $10,000 would be used to cover research assistance. If given support, he wrote,

> Our plan would be that while I would be in general charge, I would concentrate my own research efforts on company practices concerning technological change. Samuelson would work on overall statistical studies of innovation, and Myers on some case studies of union-management relations concerning the introduction of technical change.[28]

The Rockefeller Foundation decided to award $30,000 over three years.[29] This was less than Maclaurin had asked for, but it remained a substantial project, in which many MIT economists, especially instructors, were to be involved. The foundation's evaluation of the project focused on its interest to engineers and economists, as well as its potential practical value.

> The proposal represents an unusual attempt to define a field of interest to both engineers and economists. It is a field in which an Economics Department located in an engineering school should be in a position to make a significant contribution. The staff which will undertake the program rank well in their respective disciplines. It is the belief

of the officers that over a period of years the results of this program will aid in interpreting the processes of technological change and their economic and social implications to economists, government officials, labor leaders and industrialists.[30]

On receiving the grant, Maclaurin immediately obtained permission to use it to pay Samuelson's summer salary, so that he did not feel pressure to take on consultant work outside MIT.[31] Though wartime commitments soon forced him to withdraw from Maclaurin's project, Samuelson was being drawn into working on a predominantly statistical project that was intended to be thoroughly integrated into the main activities of an engineering school.

Maclaurin's research project began in July 1941, and the following fall saw the beginning of a PhD program in industrial economics. The title of the program was chosen to reflect the ethos of MIT: it reflected both Maclaurin's new interests and the department's expertise in industrial relations, most early theses being in the latter field. At the end of the year, the president reported that there had been a surprisingly large number of applicants, and that it was hoped to find, from those going through the program, "leaders for economic planning and coordination, especially after the war."[32] The entry requirements included not simply three full-year courses in social science, including economics, but also at least one full year of mathematics and a full year of science. As in other MIT programs, students were required to take a minor in a related field. In addition to specific program requirements, there was an MIT requirement that anyone entering its graduate school, in whatever field, was required to have taken several mathematics courses covering calculus and differential equations, at least one year of college chemistry, and at least two years of college physics, as well as the language requirements that were expected everywhere.[33] While industrial relations students, who were in the majority in the early years of the program, would no doubt have found business administration an attractive minor, those with interests relating to Samuelson's could opt for mathematics. In the second year of the program, several students were to take advantage of this option.

Samuelson's Activities

Samuelson moved straight from teaching undergraduates at Harvard to teaching at MIT, where in his first year he taught mathematical statistics and, probably, courses in economic theory and mathematical economics.[34] Samuelson remembers being assisted in his statistics teaching by his research

TABLE 16.1 Teaching Commitments Listed in MIT Course Catalogue (MIT 1941, p. 210; 1942b, p. 198; 1943, pp. 135–136)

	Ec. 17 Economic Theory	Ec. 18 Economic Theory	Ec. 19 Mathematical Economics	Ec. 26 Business Cycles	Ec. 37 Advanced Economic Statistics	Ec. 49 Public finance
1941–2	Y		Y			
1942–3	Y	Y	Y	Y	with HAF	
1943–4	Y	Y		Y	with HAF	Y

assistant, Leonid Hurwicz, and their introduction of a new and controversial grading system.[e]

> Even more melodramatic was the new Hurwicz-Samuelson grading system for my first regular statistics course. MIT engineers have always been notorious whiners. They are grade chasers beyond Philadelphia barracks lawyers anywhere. One of us—I will point no finger— said: "Let's add a hard extra credit exam question, with the proviso that it can only raise, but not lower, your grade." All hell broke loose when undergraduate commerce course nerds learned that their exam mark of 115 put them below the median of the class grades. It did not help when Leo explained that this was the famous Chicago grading system.[35]

Samuelson remembered the unpopularity of the Hurwicz-Samuelson grading system as potentially jeopardizing Hurwicz's future. However, Samuelson later wrote, "Leo had little to lose. It was my tenure and future life-time career that dangled on the razor's edge."[36]

The following academic year, as shown in table 16.1, his teaching load remained low, possibly because he was also teaching mathematics to Navy officers, a teaching commitment not evident from the course catalog, but which he remembered doing and which is consistent with the priority attached to military training during the war. This might have been where he began to think about the mathematics of ballistics and controlling gunfire that he was to work on later in the war.

By 1942–43, any concessions he had received as a new assistant professor were over, and his load rose to four and a half courses: he took on a second

---

e. Hurwicz's appointment is discussed in chapter 17 this volume.

course in economic theory, a course in business cycles, and he shared a course in statistics with Harold Freeman.[f] The year after that, he dropped the mathematical economics and took on public finance. Also, starting in the fall of 1942, Samuelson taught a course in international economic relations, running throughout the year, at the Fletcher School of Law and Diplomacy. The first graduate school in international affairs in the United States, the Fletcher School was based at Tufts University, in Medford, which was not far from MIT, with many of its teachers coming from Harvard. The course focused on the relationship between politics and trade: "the ways in which economic life is affected by the existence of political boundaries and of the ways in which political relations between nations are affected by economic factors."[37] Though the theory of international economics, covered in the first semester, related closely to Samuelson's published work, he would have had to engage in a different type of analysis in order to cover how political relations depended on economics. "The relation of economic activity to war" would also have gone beyond standard trade theory. Within two years of arriving at MIT, Samuelson was taking on teaching commitments that bore little relation to his published work.[g] In 1944–45, when MIT's teaching virtually stopped for the year and Samuelson moved full time to the Radiation Laboratory, he continued to teach at the Fletcher School.[h]

A major attraction of MIT was that Paul and Marion could continue to live on Ware Street, just two blocks from Harvard Yard, and he could maintain contacts with friends and colleagues still there. He grew increasingly close to Hansen, attending the Fiscal Policy Seminar and, from August 1941, joining him in a fortnightly commute to Washington, D.C. Though there were occasional activities at Harvard, the university had become increasingly empty. In a rare account of his life once war had broken out, he wrote to Bergson:

> I hope very much that I will be seeing you pretty soon. Both Marion and I have been wondering just what you all have been doing since we saw you last fall. I suppose that Judy must be running around in

---

f. Note that it is possible the catalogue, for which material would have been prepared several months in advance of publication, may not reflect who actually taught the courses. However, student notes confirm that much of this is correct.

g. It is tempting to link his interest in teaching potential diplomats to his own interest, as an undergraduate, in a diplomatic career, though it is as likely that he welcomed an additional source of income.

h. See chapter 21 this volume.

the Texas sun by now. It looks as if Harvard will be a morgue by next year—as somebody in Washington put it, "Pretty soon there will only be Paul Sweezy and enemy aliens left." The graduate enrollment is expected to shrink to nothing, and all the Ec. A staff are moving down to Washington in the hope that this will improve their draft status. At the same time they are working very hard in other directions with the result that a bumper crop of babies is already on the way. Let us hear from you soon.[38]

Close friends with whom he lost contact for a very different reason were Shigeto and Masako Tsuru. In June 1942, Shigeto wrote to him, "It is with the bitterest regret that we must leave without seeing you two. By June 12 we shall be on the Atlantic headed toward Japan."[39] As a result of conversations with Harry Dexter White, a high-ranking official in the Treasury whom he had known from his days at Lawrence College, Shigeto expected Japan to lose the war and wanted to be there so that he could take part in its postwar reconstruction.[40]

The opportunity came suddenly, on June 1, when he received a telegram saying that they could be part of an exchange between America and Japan. This offer came when Shigeto was in the middle of grading term papers for Seymour Harris, in which some of the students had reminded him of his status in the United States by writing "Remember Pearl Harbor!" on the first page of their answer books. He and Masako had five days to sort out their affairs, and though they had managed to see some of their friends, spending the previous evening with Paul Sweezy and Leontief, they were able to see neither Paul nor Marion, who were away visiting Marion's family in Wisconsin, before they caught the train at midnight from Boston's South Station. The Tsurus were among 1,500 Japanese who traveled on a Swedish ship, the *Gripsholm*, to Lourenço Marques in Portuguese East Africa (now Maputo in Mozambique), where they were exchanged for a group of Americans. They then sailed on a Japanese ship to Japan, arriving in August 1942.

Having too little time to sort out their possessions, Shigeto and Masako left Samuelson with several tasks, to which end Shigeto enclosed a letter, "To whom it may concern," authorizing Paul to act on his behalf "on all matters during my absence which is to extend at least for one year from to-day."[41] The implication that the war might last at least one year suggests that the advice he received from White might have been overly optimistic. Shigeto asked Paul to retrieve the camera, which as part of the restrictions placed on Japanese nationals, he had deposited at the Cambridge police station; and he asked Paul to look after money owed him by the Harvard Coop and various fees he was owed by Harvard University. He told Paul that he was giving him copies of books by Kalecki and Ohlin, and Pigou's *Economics of Welfare* (1932), that a mutual friend, Sven Laursen, would pass on to him. He also asked Paul to dispose of books that were stored in the basement of their apartment block. Books and papers from his room at Harvard had been moved into Leontief's office. Two days before the *Gripsholm* sailed, Paul sent a telegram, promising to look after their affairs and offering to wire him some money if he needed any.[42] Paul and Marion were to hear no more of the friend who had brought them together, until after the war.

One of the events that did take place at Harvard was a conference held on March 5, 1942, at the Littauer Center, on urbanism and the problem of towns and cities. The first session dealt with economic determinants of urban development, to which Samuelson presented a paper on "The Business Cycle and Urban Development."[43] He acknowledged that he was no expert on urban problems, but he believed that his work on the business cycle enabled him to challenge some beliefs about urban problems that had arisen during the Depression years. One of these was that the long-term trend toward urbanization had been reversed. Another was that unemployment was caused by problems that were specific to large cities: that "urbanism" was the problem.

There was, Samuelson argued, no evidence for a change in the long-term trend for people to move from the countryside to cities. There had been a movement the other way during the 1930s, but this was no evidence of a change in trend, for it was the result of people being unable to get work in the cities, moving back to the countryside to stay with families and help out on farms. Once back on the farm, they would be classified as "in work," even though they probably contributed nothing to farm output. It was thus an illusion to think that unemployment was an urban problem, for rural unemployment was disguised. As soon as prosperity was restored, as would happen after the war if a full-employment policy were followed, people would return to the cities. He argued, using census data, that unemployment was in fact no worse in large cities than in smaller ones.[i] He also drew on data that he was analyzing in his work in Washington on consumption patterns, arguing that with the return of prosperity, people would want to purchase a higher proportion of goods produced in cities, and less food, the dominant rural product.[j]

However, the expertise Samuelson brought to this topic was not just that of a statistician, for his conclusions also reflected his theoretical work

---

i. He used scatter diagrams to show that if cities were ranked in alphabetical order (i.e., randomly), one got as good a correlation with unemployment as if they were ranked by size.

j. Samuelson's activities in Washington are discussed in chapter 19 this volume.

on unemployment. The notion of disguised unemployment was theoretical, discussed in his article with Nixon, but more important was the idea that Hansen and others had developed: that unemployment was the result of economy-wide factors, notably the balance between saving and investment. This determined the overall level of unemployment, and the only question was how that was distributed, whether between open and disguised unemployment or between rural and urban locations. He argued that unemployment was not a problem pertaining to individuals.

> [A] single individual, if he studies Dale Carnegie, takes a correspondence course, works over-time, and does the thousand and one things which from time immemorial have been thought of as leading to success, can without doubt succeed in finding employment. But all cannot do so. If everybody became a go-getter, none would be much better off than before. One man can see the parade better by standing upon a chair, but what works for one will not work for all simultaneously, and the single individual who secures a job by self-improvement tends to do so by displacing another worker.[44]

It was because unemployment was not an individual problem that work and Social Security programs had been implemented. Cities were like individuals in that advertising by one chamber of commerce might improve the situation for an individual city, but such activities would not reduce national unemployment. He presented clearly the view that what is true for the individual is not necessarily true for the whole, of which the individual forms a part.

Later in March, Harvard was the place where Samuelson had his only encounter with John von Neumann, then working with Oskar Morgenstern on what was to become *The Theory of Games and Economic Behavior* (1944).[45] In January, Haberler had written to Samuelson describing the topic on which von Neumann, who had been invited to give a lecture on some aspect of mathematical economics, had proposed to talk:

> He suggested a talk on a system of equations or rather inequalities of production and distribution contained in an article he wrote a few years ago in Karl Menger's mathematical colloquium. He says that that would give him an opportunity to show that mathematical problems of a much different nature than in physics are apt to be raised by economic problems.[46]

Though Haberler doubted whether this was the best topic for the lecture, it is hard not to think that Samuelson would have been excited by it, for it directly challenged the approach that he, following Wilson, had adopted in his thesis and in the book he was writing, which involved making use of the common mathematical structure they believed underlay problems in physics and economics. He remembered Schumpeter being "pleasantly excited" by von Neumann's claim.[47] Samuelson recalled the incident in his Nobel lecture, likening the encounter to that of David and Goliath:

> This sets the state for my encounter with Goliath.... [V]on Neumann gave a lecture at Harvard on his model of general equilibrium. He asserted that it involved new kinds of mathematics which had no relation to the conventional mathematics of physics and maximization. I piped up from the back of the room that I thought it was not all that different from the concept we have in economics of the opportunity-cost frontier, in which for specified amounts of all inputs and all but one output society seeks the maximum of the remaining output. Von Neumann replied at that lightning speed which was characteristic of him: "Would you bet a cigar on that?" I am ashamed to report that for once little David retired from the field with his tail between his legs. And yet someday when I pass through Saint Peter's gages I do think that I have half a cigar still coming to me—only half because von Neumann also had a valid point."[48]

In a second account of the incident, Samuelson claimed he was, perhaps uncharacteristically, overawed by von Neumann's eminence.

> When he claimed it [his equilibrium model] meant economics had to find a completely new mathematics, I objected, saying it sounded to me like constrained-maximization theory à la Newton and Weierstrass (and, one would add today, à la Kuhn and Tucker). Von Neumann retorted belligerently, "Will you bet a cigar on that?" I was a brash young man but not so foolhardy as to grapple with the world's greatest mathematician. Still, on leaving the seminar room, I was heard to whisper Galileo-like, "Nevertheless, the world does move: *cherchez la* maximization." After these many decades I claim one cigar.[49]

He summarized his position, in 1989, by saying that though von Neumann's innovations had led to the development of "indispensable modern methods" (nonlinear programming, convex set theory, game theory, and optimal-control theory) the only real novelty he could see in von Neumann's work was "the philosophical complications introduced by games involving more than one person." Beyond that, he could see no novelty in this "so-called non-physics mathematics."

Economic Analysis

The course Samuelson taught in economic analysis provides the first evidence of how he approached the subject when he taught it to students who were neither economics graduate students nor specialists in mathematics. It was a course he had inherited, described in the MIT catalog as:

> **Ec. 17. ECONOMIC THEORY (A).** A brief historical review showing the interdependent growth of theory and fact, followed by the general theory of equilibrium under price competition and price monopoly from which will be determined, under the given conditions, wages, rents and interest. Findings will be revalued under conditions which more closely approach reality.[50]

After Samuelson took over, its catalog entry was modified so that, together with the course he took on in 1942, it was described as:

> **Ec. 17, Ec. 18. ECONOMIC ANALYSIS (A).** A review of the interdependent growth of theory and fact, followed by a study of the general theory of equilibrium under competition and monopoly. Findings will be revalued under conditions which more closely approach reality.

He had changed *theory* to *analysis*—the term he was to use in the published version of his doctoral thesis and in his introductory textbook.[k] A term that—suggestive of a less abstract approach and potentially engaging with the real world and that resonated with the operationalism of Samuelson's thesis—"economic analysis" was becoming increasingly frequently used in the 1930s and 1940s.[l]

Though it was a phrase Samuelson inherited from his predecessors, his description of the course as covering the "interdependent growth of theory and fact" reinforced the implication that the ideas under discussion were of practical relevance. Samuelson no longer offered "a historical review," but his reading list makes it clear that, like Schumpeter, he taught economic theory as a cumulative discipline in which students could learn from the classics, as well as from contemporary writings. For example, when covering the theory of costs and the company or firm, a topic under which he

---

k. See chapters 14 and 22 this volume.

l. A search of articles in the JSTOR online database shows that up to the mid-1930s, only 1 to 2 percent of economics articles used the phrase "economic analysis," after which the fraction increased until by 1950 it was around 10 percent. By the end of the century, it was around 12 percent.

included the distribution of income between profits and wages, he assigned readings from modern authorities—Joan Robinson, Edward Chamberlin (the only one of his Harvard teachers on the list), John Hicks, Roy Allen, Frank Knight, Paul Douglas, Jacob Viner (three of his Chicago teachers), and Frank Taussig, as well as from "classic" texts by Augustin Cournot (1838) and John Bates Clark (1899). There were a few pages from his fellow Harvard student Robert Triffin (1941), the only post-1939 reference. Samuelson attributed ideas to the economists who developed them; thus, he explained that Cournot, in 1838, had the idea of a stable demand curve and that Fleeming Jenkin, a relatively obscure figure writing before Marshall, was the first to use the idea in English. He explained that Cournot plotted the company's revenue as a function of price, whereas two more recent writers plotted it as a function of quantity. He explained that Marshall may have coined the term "elasticity," but he was not the first to have either the idea or the mathematics corresponding to it.[m]

Similarly, his coverage of consumer theory began with Adam Smith and the paradox that diamonds cost more than water, even though water is more important for life, failing to point out, as he had done with Marshall, that Smith's ideas on this topic were not original. The confusion he attributed to Smith was resolved with the idea of marginal utility, on which he cited the late-nineteenth-century economists Gossen, Walras, Jevons, Marshall, and the Austrians. The use of a logarithmic utility function was associated with the eighteenth-century writer Daniel Bernoulli; and the distinction between cardinal and ordinal utility, the concept of indifference curves, and the integrability problem were associated with Edgeworth and Pareto, both writing around 1900. He recommended material by his contemporaries Hicks and Allen—including Hicks's *Value and Capital* (1939b), augmented by Slutsky's recently rediscovered article from 1916, Leontief (on international trade), and Alan Sweezy and Georgescu-Roegen (on integrability). His own articles are conspicuous by their absence.

Marshall's *Principles of Economics* (1920) occupied a prominent place on the reading list, with the whole of Book 3 ("Wants and Their Satisfaction" being assigned, along with five chapters from Book 5 ("General Relations

m. Samuelson's course can be described in detail because one of his students in 1943, Elizabeth Ringo, preserved her detailed notes on his lectures. Ringo, a graduate of Swarthmore College, was studying for a master's and, supported by strong references from Samuelson, became an instructor at Wellesley College in 1944. Page references are not provided because I am working from a transcript, in the form of a word processor file, kindly provided by Irwin Collier.

of Demand, Supply and Value") and several notes from the mathematical appendix. The striking feature about Samuelson's recommendations from Book 5 are the chapters to which he did *not* direct his students. He omitted from his suggestions the chapters, considered by many commentators to outline the heart of Marshall's economics, on equilibrium of supply and demand over different time periods, in which Marshall sought to explain his ideas on "normal" values.[51] If they confined their reading to the assigned chapters, Samuelson's students would not learn about the difference between the short and long periods, something to which Marshall attached great importance. They would get a simplified treatment in which problems that could be discussed using algebra were more prominent.[n]

Despite the reference to "fact" in the catalog description, it was predominantly a course in economic theory, though it contained some empirical material. The reading list, used for more than one year,[52] contained references to *The Theory and Measurement of Demand* (1938) by Samuelson's former teacher Henry Schultz, which attempted to measure and test the theory of consumer behavior. Samuelson also recommended an article by the Oxford economists Robert Hall and Charles Hitch (1939), which used data on companies' behavior to challenge the notion that profit maximization could explain companies' pricing policies in the very short run (where it was not even clear what it would mean to maximize profits), and a paper by Horst Mendershausen (1939) on the relationship between family income and saving.[o]

Perhaps the most thoroughly empirical reading was a section from the proceedings of the Temporary National Economic Committee on the concentration of economic power. Though the heading on the mimeographed reading list was "U.S. Steel," the pages Samuelson assigned covered pricing policies in steel, lumber, turpentine, other building materials, and chemicals.[53] It is uncertain what lessons he wanted them to take away from this reading, but they would have learned that pricing policies were complex, reflecting different types of cost (in particular, production and transportation costs) and that the relationship between costs and price varied from industry to industry. There was no theory here, but an institutionally rich discussion of pricing that would have fit well with some of the chapters he had selected from Marshall, though there is no evidence that he discussed some

---

n. Marshall used algebra sparingly because many of the problems to which he attached great importance were too complex to be amenable to such analysis.

o. This was directly related to the research on consumer spending that Samuelson was undertaking in Washington, discussed in chapter 19 this volume.

concepts that one might have expected to occur, such as basing point pricing and transport costs. One conclusion he drew from such evidence was that marginal and average variable costs were horizontal up to full capacity, and then rose sharply—the "Reverse L-shaped Cost Curve. He told his students, "Empirically, this [constant costs up to full capacity] may be important, since you get MC from AVC which you do know."

The last remark suggests that Samuelson was emphasizing the need to construct "operational" theories—and that he was paying attention to the problem of measuring costs. His lecture on what happens when the demand curve shifts would have provided a natural occasion to discuss operationalism and testability, on which he had assigned readings that included Percy Bridgman's *The Logic of Modern Physics* (1927).[54] The normal way to present the material would have been to assume that companies maximized profits, and then to deduce that the demand curve rose. However, Samuelson did it the other way around. He started from the observable fact that the demand curve rose and then hypothesized that this could be explained as the behavior of profit-maximizing companies. He was applying to the theory of the firm the methods he had, as a student, applied to consumer theory.

Samuelson's lecturing style was informal: after discussing pure competition, he said he was going to cover other market structures, but he did not get around to them. And he was clearly not focused on making sure that students were able to get the details correct in their notes. The classes appear to have started with the case of pure competition, after which the discussion diverged into a discussion of operationalism, whereupon Samuelson listed three methodological texts where they could follow up on these ideas. Robbins was presumably cited as exemplifying the alternative view, with Bridgman and Hutchison (who argued for the testability of economic theories) representing his own position.[P]

Even though he provided extensive empirical readings and stressed operationalism, Samuelson's emphasis was overwhelmingly on economic theory. He presented the theory using algebra and diagrams. Though he referred to more advanced mathematics, the algebra necessary to follow the course was

---

p. Hutchison 1938. The garbled way Ringo noted the title of Hutchison's book, "Hutchinson. Postulational in or. Ec," makes it clear that Paul must have mentioned it quickly, with no concession to the students, such as writing it on the blackboard. He cited the first edition of Robbins (1932), even though a second edition, which might have appeared marginally less uncongenial to Samuelson's operationalism, had appeared in 1935.

confined to differential calculus, with the occasional appearance of integrals.[q] The course drew on Robinson's (1933a) diagrammatic exposition of the theory of the firm, and discussed a number of her ideas, such as her coverage of exploitation, as well as on Chamberlin's (1933) theory with its focus on factors such as product differentiation and advertising, not covered by Robinson.

The reading list for the second course on economic analysis included still more applied readings, including two articles on agriculture and one on basing point pricing (a technique used by companies to price products when faced with significant transport costs).[r] He included John Maurice Clark's "Toward a Theory of Workable Competition," perhaps citing the date incorrectly because he remembered hearing Clark deliver it at the meeting of the American Economic Association the year before it was published.[55] Significantly, the most applied articles, on the cement industry, railway rates, pricing policies, and a Temporary National Economic Committee monograph were listed only as "optional reading." Students were also advised to read Clark on the economics of overhead costs, articles on the location of industry, and something on the shoe industry. The added references to Henry Simons's *A Positive Program for Laissez-faire* (1934) and to Simons's review of Hansen's book on fiscal policy may indicate that Samuelson allowed himself to wander from the syllabus and discuss broader issues of topical interest.

Samuelson's discussion of dynamic problems illustrates his willingness to discuss problems that could not be analyzed using mathematical methods. Companies would know that demand fluctuated during the business cycle and uncertainty about future demand conditions might cause them to operate at less than maximum efficiency. For example, companies might choose not to build enough capacity to cover their peak level

---

q. There was mention of the fact that revenue functions could be approximated by Fourier series, and his discussion of monopoly pricing mentioned functionals.

r. It covered similar topics as the first course but went into some of them in more detail. Readings not covered in the other course included the article by Piero Sraffa (1926) that challenged Marshall's theorizing about returns to scale, initiating what came to be called the "cost controversy"; an article by Knight on costs and price; a chapter from Schumpeter on dynamic competition; and articles by Abba Lerner on monopoly power, Paul Sweezy on oligopoly, and Hicks and Roy Harrod on monopoly and imperfect competition. The course would have introduced students to a wide range of the contemporary literature on different market structures. Samuelson also mentioned references on welfare economics—articles by Kahn, Lange, Lerner, Hicks, and Bergson, all published in the 1930s—and a recent article by Lange (1942).

demand because doing so would mean that some of their capacity would stand idle most of the time. The result of this investment strategy would be shortages, fueling speculation, but it was nonetheless rational for companies to limit their activity in this way. Samuelson was arguing that there was a speculative element involved in monopoly, the operative factor being fear of underutilized capacity. When he turned to General Motors, he argued that average variable costs were considered constant and that a markup of 30 percent on the book value of the plant was added to cover overhead costs. This shows that Samuelson was incorporating in his lectures ideas about cost structures and company behavior that reflected empirical work being undertaken in the United States and, to a lesser extent, in Britain, even though they conflicted with conventional theories of the firm as expound by Robinson and Chamberlin. Companies did not operate in a world of the U-shaped average cost curves described in many textbooks.

Given the importance of the topic in economics after the Second World War, it is significant that Samuelson covered general competitive equilibrium. His reading list included Gustav Cassel's *Theory of Social Economy* (1923), the book that contained a simplified version of Walras's general equilibrium system, to which Aaron Director had introduced him when he was an undergraduate. He also recommended George Stigler's *Production and Distribution Theories* (1941), a book on late nineteenth-century economics, based on the dissertation he had been writing when Samuelson had been in Chicago. Perhaps more significant, he cited the German-speaking economists who had sought to provide rigorous proofs of the existence of general equilibrium in systems that were based on the one provided in Cassel's textbook, mentioning Abraham Wald, John von Neumann (with whom he had clashed at Harvard the year before), Heinrich Stackelberg, Karl Schlesinger, and Oskar Morgenstern. It is not clear how much students would have been expected to read of these, in that much of this literature had not been translated. Citing Oskar Morgenstern's (1941) review of *Value and Capital*, Samuelson made the point that taking account of this German literature might have saved Hicks from several errors, including the claim that having the right number of equations ensured that a system had a solution—a point on which he cited both Wald and von Neumann.

Samuelson exposed the students to a range of methodological views. He started with Jacob Viner, who was skeptical of the use of mathematics and who, echoing Marshall, saw economics as being like biology rather than mechanics. In expressing such views Viner would have been echoing Marshall. He gave three reasons why economists might hold Viner's view: people were fascinated by psychology, which caused them to become cranks; the social sciences deal with life and therefore need different methods; and different methods are needed because society is "organismic." In contrast, Samuelson's own view was that biologists used roughly the same methods as those in other disciplines, though they were perhaps less exact. In expressing this view he would perhaps have been thinking of the work of Lawrence Henderson and his recent correspondence with Alfred Lotka, who used mathematics to analyze population dynamics. One difference was that though biologists used the same methods, there was "more intuition, (cf. doctor-snap judgment) practical application, than theory." In other words, though biologists (and doctors) might of necessity rely more on intuition, this was essentially rushing to conclusions and did not involve any fundamentally different method.

Samuelson also covered capital theory, including Knight's critique of the Austrians, talking in detail about production and factor prices, sometimes too fast for even a bright student to understand.[56] Given its relation to Keynesian economics and the work he was doing on consumption, it is interesting to note that capital theory was the heading under which he discussed saving and consumption. Using a diagram (see figure 16.1), he illustrated optimal consumption for someone who had an uneven income stream, caused by an inheritance. The optimal strategy would be to borrow money that could be repaid on the aunt's death, making it possible to have a constant lifetime consumption (with the marginal utility of consumption the same in every year).

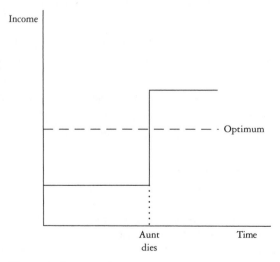

FIGURE 16.1 Consumption over time.

Samuelson went on to discuss what the consumer's budget constraint would look like if it were possible to borrow and lend at a constant rate of interest, if it were possible to lend but not borrow, and to borrow but not lend. This was tied into a discussion of time preference (the consumer's preference for present over future consumption) and whether the rate of interest could ever reach zero—topics that Knight and the Austrians had debated. In the 1950s, this view of consumption as smoothing an irregular income stream—associated primarily with Milton Friedman, Albert Ando, and Franco Modigliani—was to become an important element in macroeconomics, linked not to the theory of capital but to the Keynesian theory of income determination.

Samuelson rapidly settled into his new academic home. The department was small but free of the animosities that made life difficult at Harvard. Though its focus was teaching, its research program was being developed and Samuelson was integrated into it from the beginning. For the first two years he appears to have been given a light teaching load, and though in 1942 he had to take on new courses, by then the nation was at war. Suffering from hypertension, and anxious for his health after his father's death, he was convinced that if he were drafted he would be deemed medically unfit for military service. Concerned that he might not have long to live, and anxious to justify his draft status as someone in an occupation necessary for national defense, and not be classified as medically unfit for service, he threw himself into his work.[s]

Not only did Samuelson teach a course that revealed familiarity with a very broad range of literature—a task that would have been enough to keep most new assistant professors fully occupied—his research also continued unabated. As one might expect from someone who espoused operationalism so forcefully, he turned to statistics, developing his knowledge of theoretical statistics and getting involved in data analysis. Simultaneously with that he became involved in working out what came to be known as "the new economics" (the theory of income determination)—work that made use of

---

s. On June 9, 1941, his draft status was registered as 2B. His status changed back and forth between 2A (in necessary civilian occupation) and 2B (necessary to national defense), but it is hard to connect the dates to changes in his activities. Either there were changes in the way MIT employees were classified, or the changes to his classification reflected changes in his duties within MIT that have not been recorded, such as when he was or was not employed in training military recruits. His family have noted that he was desperate not to be classified 4F (physically, mentally or morally unfit for service).

contacts he made by entering government service as a part-time consultant to the National Resources Planning Board. He also embarked on revising his doctoral thesis for publication. Given the level of his commitments, it is not surprising that this proved a long, drawn-out process that was not completed until the war was virtually over.

CHAPTER 17 | Statistics

Statistical Analysis of the Business Cycle

Samuelson's thesis advocated the methodology of operationalism. He used this methodology to argue that economic theory should be about generating testable propositions. However, while at Harvard, with the exception of his paper on unemployment written with Russ Nixon, he neither engaged in empirical work nor wrote about how propositions might be tested. With his move to MIT, that changed. It is impossible to say how much this was a result of the ethos of MIT, dominated by engineering, or the result of the activities of his new colleagues, or a natural progression in his own ideas, but his approach to economics changed significantly. In the first few years at MIT, he read widely in mathematical statistics and he embarked on some empirical research projects.

Samuelson's first empirical project at MIT, on the business cycle, was supported by money donated by businessman Roger Babson. Babson, an MIT graduate from the 1890s, had become famous as the author of the "Babsonchart," a device used to predict the ups and downs of the stock market.[1] In 1929, at a time when most analysts were predicting a continued rise in stock prices, Babson forecast a decline; and after the Great Crash, he became a celebrity, his methods seemingly having been vindicated.[2] The principle behind the Babsonchart was Isaac Newton's third law: that every force produces an equal and opposite reaction. Believing that the future could be predicted on the basis of past trends, he interpreted Newton's law as justifying the line denoting normal business activity. The further business grew above this line, the greater the chance of a reaction that would take it below the line. Babson had learned about Newton while a student at MIT in the 1890s, and later made a donation to his alma mater for the study in economics of Newton's third law. Ralph Freeman proposed that part of this money be used to support a project led by Samuelson.

Samuelson's research proposal, which Freeman sent to the MIT treasurer on December 23, was clearly written with Babson's ideas in mind.[3] It began by praising "the triumph of Newtonian mechanics," arguing that its achievement was to formulate second-order differential equations that could fully determine the motion of a physical system. Though he criticized the approach as "primitive and rudimentary" in comparison with "the more advanced physical sciences," he pandered to Babson by saying that the notion of the depth of a depression being directly related to the height of the previous boom was an application of Newton's third law. His proposal was to make use of recent advances in statistics to go beyond such simple theories, implicitly claiming that he would build upon Babson's work.

> Recent advances in mathematics, statistics, and economic theory open up for the first time the possibility of empirical determination of *structural relations* in economic time series. These take the form of stochastic linear difference equations which yield as solutions damped or undamped harmonic series with coefficients varying according to some probability distribution.

Having constructed a theory in which cycles could be generated by a second-order difference equation, Samuelson was now proposing to estimate the coefficients in such a model, describing his project in terms developed by Ragnar Frisch during the 1930s. Though he had introduced his project in a way so as to impress Babson, Newtonian ideas were completely irrelevant to what he wanted to do. To undertake such an ambitious task—estimating such models was in their infancy—he needed a trained assistant, for which Freeman proposed to use $500 of the Babson funds.

Samuelson approached Oskar Lange, at Chicago, about whether he could recommend anyone, and in December 1940, Lange provided Samuelson with the names of four people who had a knowledge of mathematical statistics, including that of Leonid Hurwicz.[4] Two years younger than Samuelson, Hurwicz had been born in Russia, he had studied law in Warsaw, and after studying economics in London (with Dennis Robertson, a former collaborator with Keynes) and Geneva, he had come to the United States in 1940, where he was attending lectures in Chicago. After summarizing Hurwicz's background, Lange wrote,

He has an excellent mind, and is in my opinion, the best of the candidates on this list. He has quite a background in mathematical statistics, and has quite extensive knowledge of analysis. Before becoming an economist he was a theoretical physicist. He also did numerical work in experimental physics. He is really one of the very best I have had among students. In addition, he needs a job very badly, because he has no income at all.[5]

Samuelson later said he decided to take Hurwicz as he was the one in greatest financial need. Lacking any income other than support from the cousins with whom he was staying in Chicago, Hurwicz was willing to take the position even though it was for a single semester, from January to June 1941.

Later memories of the research the two of them undertook vary. Hurwicz remembered undertaking statistical work on how companies set prices.[6] He cited the example of a coffin manufacturer who started with the cost of a coffin, multiplied it by 3, and added $50. Such investigations were common at this time, both in the United States, where there was great interest in companies' pricing policies as a possible explanation for the Depression, and in Britain, where the Oxford Economics Research Group sought to explain the day-to-day setting of prices, a context in which it was believed that profit maximization made no sense. In contrast, Samuelson remembered Hurwicz as having worked explicitly on the business cycle: "We did early spectral analysis of Frickey's aggregate U.S. output for the time slot 1865–1935." Samuelson wrote,

> When I say "we" I do not refer to Leo and Paul only. Instead I can still see in my mind's eye Leo, whip in one hand, slide rule in the other, marshaling his crew of mostly young female National Youth Administration galley-slave computers. *Parallel* computer computation thus merits a marble marker at the northwest corner of Massachusetts Avenue and Memorial Drive. Leo began that there.[7]

In those days, a computer was a person, and a computer laboratory was a room in which rows of people sat doing calculations, which had to be broken down into components, each of which was worked out by a different person (the parallel computing) before the results were put together. This was Samuelson's first experience with directing a team of researchers.

Frickey, one of Samuelson's Harvard teachers, was concerned with developing indicators of the business cycle, writing a series of papers in the 1930s.[a]

---

a. See chapter 6 this volume.

Spectral analysis of his data—trying to identify the periodicity or frequency of cycles—would have been a natural extension of his work. It seems plausible that Samuelson, who had studied Fourier analysis and other techniques used for spectral analysis in the natural sciences, might have wanted to apply more advanced mathematical techniques to the problem, especially given that he had an assistant trained in physics. In modern econometrics, spectral analysis and structural estimation are generally seen as alternatives, but in 1940, estimation methods were much more fluid. Samuelson may well have been trying to use methods that would have been a more rigorous extension of the methods of his Harvard teachers, in order to estimate structural models.

This research project appears to have been unsuccessful, for it did not lead to any publications. Correspondence with the MIT treasurer makes it clear that it was understood the results of their work "would be presented in print at a later date" and that funds from the Babson grant had been reserved for this purpose, but no trace of such a printed report exists.[8] Furthermore, when Samuelson had to write a report on his use of the Babson money, he wrote to Hurwicz, who had by then returned to Chicago, asking whether he might list a paper Hurwicz had forthcoming in *Econometrica* as stemming from work done at MIT.[9] He asked him specifically whether he would be willing to insert in the paper a footnote thanking Babson.[10] Hurwicz's footnote described his work as having arisen from "interpreting the results of two business-cycle studies," one at MIT and one at Chicago.[11] While this was related to the subject of Samuelson's research project, it was based primarily on a paper that Hurwicz had written before he went to MIT, "The Phenomenon of Hysteresis in the Correlation of Time Series."[12] It went beyond Samuelson's model of the cycle, in that it analyzed stochastic models of fluctuations (Samuelson's earlier model had no stochastic terms), and it tackled problems relating to estimation, but it was entirely theoretical, containing no data analysis. There is no trace of the number crunching done by the "galley-slave computers" Samuelson remembered Hurwicz having supervised. If the project did fail, this was not surprising, for it was very ambitious, proposing to tackle an empirical problem for which standard techniques had still not been developed.

A few months after the Babson-funded project ended, Samuelson wrote a paper that did involve the analysis of statistical data: "A Statistical Analysis of the Consumption Function."[13] While there is no direct evidence that it was a spin-off from the business cycle research project, it would have been natural for them to have estimated a consumption function, for this was one of the two equations they would have to have estimated if the structural model was the multiplier–accelerator model that Samuelson had published the previous year.

Samuelson's paper began by surveying the literature on consumption and income, classified according to the methods used: from household budget data; from time series of national income; and "more or less plausible rough" estimates, such as those of Kahn, Keynes, and J. M. Clark.[14] Whereas Hansen had adopted the first method, Samuelson proposed to test the relationship using time series data on consumption and income. He started with data for the period 1921–35 produced by Simon Kuznets (omitting data for 1919–20 on grounds that they reflected anomalous wartime events) and added data that the National Resources Planning Board had produced for 1936–39. In order to find what he called "a reversible analytical relationship" rather than just a description of the historical data, he needed to adjust for price changes so as to relate real consumption expenditure to real income. Kuznets had used a complicated procedure to obtain his deflated series, but Samuelson discovered that using the wage earner's cost of living index produced by the Bureau of Labor Statistics provided similar results, so he used this simpler method to obtain the series he used for his analysis.

Samuelson fitted a least squares regression line to the data, relating consumption just to income. However, though this apparently fitted the data for the whole period, he noted that "the deviations from the line of best fit are not randomly distributed."[15] He deduced this not from a statistical test but from close observation of the data. If errors were not random, it implied that the least squares regression line was unsatisfactory from a statistical point of view, and so he then tested the hypothesis that a secular trend was operating by including time as an additional factor. He was thus testing the hypothesis that there was a consumption function relating consumption to income that shifted up or down at a constant rate. This worked for Kuznets's original data, but when the additional four years were added, the coefficient on the time variable was no longer significantly different from zero "in a sampling sense."[16] In other words, though including the extra variable inevitably made the equation fit the data better, the improvement was not sufficient to justify including it. Unlike his earlier observation that the errors were not random, based only on visual inspection of the data, this involved calculating test statistics.[b]

---

b. In the 1950s, it was Milton Friedman who developed the permanent-income theory of consumption, and Albert Ando and Franco Modigliani, authors of the life-cycle theory, who came to be associated with such ideas. These ideas were, however, already circulating in the early 1940s. See also figures 16.1 and 20.1, this volume, and the associated discussion.

Samuelson then explored whether the problem with the simple least squares consumption function could be explained by changes in business saving. The rationale for this was that this part of national income was not received by households, so it should not affect their consumption. To do this, he estimated consumption as a function, not of national income ("income produced") but of income received by households (national income minus business saving). This produced a marginal propensity to consume of 1.06, suggesting an unstable system. However, even with such a marginal propensity to consume, the system would not be unstable once account was taken of business saving. Moreover, he argued, retained corporate earnings should be reflected in equity prices, reducing the need for individuals to save out of income received. This meant that there was no reason to expect there would be a close connection between income received and consumption.

In this paper, Samuelson showed great familiarity with the data and the method by which they were calculated. He was also familiar with the idea that aggregate relationships could be tested statistically, and that such tests should be employed in working out the best specification for an empirical model. The tests he used were both informal (noting that the residuals from his regression equation did not appear to be random) and formal (noting that the coefficient on the time trend was not significantly different from zero). It has been claimed that his work "represented the first published diagnostic use of residual analysis in the econometrics of the consumption function."[17] The paper is important because it shows that, having written a thesis in which he argued that the task of economic theory was to derive testable predictions and to show the methods by which this could be achieved, he was now turning to the problem of testing theory. That is, he was ceasing to be just a mathematical economic theorist. Clearly, Hansen, in whose book the paper was published, was the major influence on this work, but the transition fits with his move into the more technical world of MIT. Not only did MIT provide the research grant that enabled him to recruit Hurwicz, but also he had moved to an environment where the emphasis was on solving difficult practical problems.

Statistical Theory

Though there is no evidence that Samuelson persisted with the Babson-funded project after Hurwicz departed, he remained focused on statistics, a subject he taught at one point with Harold Freeman. There was much interaction with the Mathematics Department, where courses in mathematical statistics were offered. In this environment, and thinking that there was a limit to the number of papers he could prudently submit to *Econometrica*, Samuelson began to publish his work in mathematical journals. In September 1941, the *Annals of Mathematical Statistics* had published an article in which he had derived the conditions under which the roots of a polynomial will be less than one.[c] This was, Samuelson explained, important in many fields—business cycle theory, probability theory, and in numerical calculations using iterative methods—for larger roots would typically lead to instability and systems would not converge on an equilibrium value.

Samuelson also took up a suggestion made in a recent issue of *Econometrica* that a regression equation should be calculated, not by minimizing the sum of squared deviations from the line (the usual method), but by minimizing the sum of absolute deviations. The advantage of this method, it had been claimed, was that it was not necessary to determine whether y depended on x or vice versa: one would get the same result whichever assumption was made.[18] This was, Samuelson pointed out, one of many ways in which a regression line could be calculated; and to choose between various methods, he listed six properties that might be thought desirable ones for a regression line to have and against which they could be evaluated. However, the most significant observation was that the dependence of one variable on another *should* matter.

> If the aim of the investigation is not simply a characterization of the properties of the multivariate distribution, but rather the search for a hypothetical "true" (in some sense) linear relationship, upon which has been superimposed a distribution of errors, then no definite method of determining the regression equation can be specified until some assumptions have been made concerning the nature of the disturbing causes. These assumptions must be in the nature of postulates; by no possible method can they be determined inductively from an examination of the data, even in an infinitely large sample.[19]

This article is not, in itself, of any great importance, but Samuelson's arguments show that he was engaging closely with the emerging literature on econometric methods. He cited Tjalling Koopmans's *Linear Regression Analysis of Economic Time Series* (1937), where attention had been paid to measurement errors in the variables. Samuelson was not clear on the nature of the errors involved (were they the result of measurement error or did errors arise because behavior was partly random?), but his arguments are consistent with

---

c. That is, the solutions to an equation of the form be less than one.

his having still been thinking along the same lines as Koopmans. His arguments are also consistent with the close attention Samuelson paid to residuals when estimating a consumption function the previous year. Though he does not use such language, the idea that statistical analysis required the specification of an underlying probability model, thereby making it possible to test hypotheses rather than simply to estimate relationships, was one of the crucial features of arguments that a Norwegian economist, Trygve Haavelmo, who was currently on a Rockefeller Fellowship to study in the United States, put forward in a working paper, *On the Theory and Measurement of Economic Relations* (1941).[20]

This paper, which was later published as a special issue of *Econometrica* (1944) and was very important in the history of econometrics, justified the use of statistical methods of hypothesis testing to aggregate data where no sampling was involved. Samuelson still had strong connections with Harvard, where Haavelmo had written the paper, and he was among those who received a copy when a limited number were produced in August.[21] Like Haavelmo, Samuelson believed that empirical work in economics involved integrating economic theory with statistical methods, for without economic theory it was impossible to specify the probability model to be tested.

In the 1942–43 session, two students who had arrived in the second cohort of the PhD program, Lawrence Klein and Joseph Ullmann, felt the need for additional knowledge of statistics, and they organized a seminar series involving speakers from inside and outside MIT.[22,d] Samuelson attended regularly. Samuelson and Harold Freeman gave papers, as did two of their students. There were several speakers from the MIT Mathematics Department, including Norbert Wiener, who expounded ergodic theory, to the bafflement of Economics Department chair, Ralph Freeman, who attended by accident and became trapped there. Wiener had begun his talk by reminding them that they were at war and that nothing heard in the room should be repeated outside, lest it give comfort to the enemy. To this, Freeman responded after Wiener had left, "Hell, Hitler and Himmler couldn't get a word out of me even if the speaker had been a coherent lecturer."[23]

Harold Hotelling came from Columbia to survey unsolved problems in statistics, covering the foundations of statistics, statistical decision making, and computational methods. Many of these problems were tackled in other seminars. Samuelson thought the best lecturer was Abraham Wald, the Romanian statistician who with Karl Schlesinger had proved the existence of

---

d. Klein is discussed further in chapter 24 this volume.

a competitive general equilibrium, and had been recruited to Columbia by Hotelling. He lectured on tolerance limits, a problem that was important to quality control in manufacturing. Harold Freeman applied Bayesian methods to the problem of industrial sampling—testing a batch of products to find out how many are defective, and E. B. Wilson came from Harvard to talk about contingency tables. William Feller came from Brown to talk about the theory of stochastic processes.

Perhaps the most significant paper was by Haavelmo, by then working for the Norwegian Shipping and Trade Mission, on March 30, 1943. When inviting him, Ullman explained that many of the participants in the seminar would have read *On the Theory and Measurement of Economic Relations* and were interested in the problem of applying Jerzy Neymann's theory of hypothesis testing to economics. The result was that Haavelmo chose to talk on the general problem of statistical inference in economics, giving the title of his talk as "Some Problems of Statistical Inference in Relation to Econometrics."[24] His starting point was that, while "econometrics should be an attempt, not only towards more precision in the formulation of economic theories, but perhaps still more an attempt to reach such formulations that the theories lend themselves to testing against actual observations," this was far from the case. To bridge the gap between theory and data, it was necessary to formulate models in probabilistic terms, for only then was a theory testable. Rather than talk in vague terms about "errors" and "unexplained residuals," economists should formulate theories in terms of probability distributions. This was prelude to a discussion of the problem of estimation in simultaneous equation systems along the lines he had recently outlined in a short paper in *Econometrica*.[25]

Klein, one of the seminar organizers and Samuelson's PhD student, quickly took note of Haavelmo's analysis and used it in a paper he published later that year.[26] Its effect on Samuelson is less clear, though he had been among the early readers of Haavelmo's 1941 manuscript and clearly understood the arguments involved. When he recalled the seminar many years later, he wrote of how it had changed econometrics. "His [Haavelmo's] MIT lecture," Samuelson wrote, was not "a routine review" but was "a first revelation of what was to be a major stimulus for the Chicago Cowles group."[27,e] He went on to say that, when explaining the problems involved in estimating simultaneous equations, Haavelmo had taken his (Samuelson's) version

---

e. The Cowles Commission, based at the University of Chicago from 1938 to 1955, was to play a major role in developing modern econometric methods along the lines laid down by Haavelmo in the early 1940s.

of the multiplier–accelerator model as his example and shown that what they "would have" done before his talk was, in general, wrong.[f]

Given that Samuelson and Hurwicz had tried to estimate a model of the business cycle, and that it would have been natural to have started with Samuelson's own model, it is tempting to conjecture that what "we would have" done before Haavelmo's talk was what Samuelson and Hurwicz had been trying to do two years earlier (though spectral analysis would have been something different). Though this is probably going too far, it is even conceivable that the appearance of Haavelmo's paper in August caused them to tear up results they had obtained from January to June. Samuelson's estimates of consumption later in 1941 might have taken account of errors, but they would not have met the criteria that Haavelmo was advocating.[g]

During the 1942–43 academic year, Samuelson published two further papers in the *Annals* and in the *Proceedings of the National Academy of Sciences*, edited by Wilson since 1915, on mathematical problems that, although they arose in statistics, might appear in any field where matrix algebra was used. In one, he developed a method suggested by his friend, the chemist E. Bright Wilson, for computing the roots of a characteristic equation of a matrix.[28] The other proposed a method for determining latent vectors of a matrix.[29] The *Annals of Mathematical Statistics* also published a paper, "Fitting Gram-Charlier Series," that was closely related to (if not the same as) the one he had presented to the statistics seminar that year.[30]

Following up on a suggestion made several years earlier by Wilson, this paper attempted to simplify and bring together two ways of representing a probability distribution. This attracted the attention of Lotka, who pointed out that the expansions of a probability distribution Samuelson had been using were similar to one he was using to represent birth and death rates in a population.[31] He noted that the field of possible applications of such functions was very broad. Of potentially even broader application was a fifth mathematical paper, also published in Wilson's *Proceedings of the National*

---

f. What they would have done was to calculate two ordinary least squares regression equations—of consumption on lagged income and of investment on the change in income (or capital stock on income).

g. Samuelson later wrote, "Econometrics was never the same after [Haavelmo's] famous *Supplement*," the 118-page article, published as a supplement to *Econometrica*, in which he provided the most complete statement of these ideas (Haavelmo 1944; Samuelson 1991b, p. 333) It is a view that Klein would have endorsed at the time, although Samuelson, who was still close to Wilson, might have been more doubtful.

Academy of Sciences, in which Samuelson proposed a new method of interpolation.[32] These papers all tackled problems arising in mathematical statistics that were also important in analyzing dynamic economic models.

The breadth of Samuelson's reading in statistics and the confidence with which he was prepared to criticize others' work at this time are illustrated by a review of *The Analysis of Economic Time Series* by Harold Davis (1941), a mathematician associated with the Cowles Commission since its foundation. Samuelson found material to praise in the book, including three of the chapters on statistical theory and the chapter dealing with the equation of exchange (the quantity theory of money). However, beyond that, though his review was at all times polite, he offered a critique of what was a long (620-page) technical volume. Samuelson criticized in detail the remaining four chapters on statistical theory: methods Davis was advocating were inferior to other methods found in the literature; Davis had failed to consider the efficiency of statistical tests he was using; and Davis had not taken account of important new work, notably "the modern theories of estimation and distribution associated with Fisher and Neymann."[33] As for the economic applications, Samuelson opined that Davis's comparative advantage lay in statistics, and clearly he was not impressed by his "economic time series" theory of history that forecast when revolutions were likely to occur. Samuelson's criticisms of the chapter on income distribution showed his familiarity with recent empirical literature. The review closed with the self-confident remark that he had focused on the book's shortcomings "because economic statisticians do not always have the necessary technical equipment to ferret out points of difficulty in a book that nonetheless contained 'many solid contributions.'"

This review was probably discussed when Samuelson encountered Davis at a conference the following year, for after such a substantial review, Davis might well have felt they had a lot to talk about. Their conversation prompted Samuelson to write a letter to Harold Freeman, in October 1944. Headed "Memorandum to H. A. Freeman," it read,

> Ours has been a beautiful friendship. But enough is enough. I hope you will not think that I have a prejudice against practical men—on the contrary, some of my best friends are practical men. And I'll go so far as to say that every department can afford to tolerate one such. But you introduce one practical man into the department and he will bring another, and another, and another. Moreover, his friends will be practical men, and one will be forced to utilize valuable time in talking to such practical men.

You will gather that I have been besieged for hours (or was it days?) by one Harold M. Davis—a good friend of yours—and that I hold you personally responsible for my anguish.

Therefore, I am taking this occasion to sever all relationships with you and yours; and I am instructing my wife and family to the most distant connection, to do the same. In the future if we should meet and there is no one, present, I shall, of course, not speak to you; and I shall expect you to return the courtesy. However, should it become necessary, in connection with my departmental duties, to have dealings with you, I shall submit with as good grace as I can muster; but that is my limit.[34]

There was, of course, no rupture, even if Samuelson had thought that Davis had taken too much of his time.

Population Dynamics

Alongside this work on statistics, Samuelson continued to work on the problem of population growth, on which he had begun to work with Marion while he was still at Harvard.[h] At the beginning of 1942, Alfred Lotka wrote to say that he had just read Samuelson's latest paper on stability, and that he presumed Samuelson realized that his system of equations was similar to one he had used in *Elements of Physical Biology* (1925).[35] Lotka also claimed that he had already discussed in print the relationship between the Le Chatelier Principle and stability.[36] He also noted not only that he had analyzed similar problems but also that Alfred North Whitehead, whom Samuelson knew in the Society of Fellows, had many years before asked him whether such systems might not be applicable to economics. In addition, he drew Samuelson's attention to a number of articles that had appeared since 1939, including one that was hidden away in the *Journal of the Burma Research Society*, of which he promised to send a copy.

Later that year, Samuelson became interested in the antecedents of his work on population dynamics. He had been reading the work of Robert Kuczynski, the author of a large number of works on demography in the 1930s, and had become convinced that one of Kuczynski's historical claims was wrong. This was the claim that the Russian statistician, Ladislaus Bortkiewicz, had derived a theorem showing that a population subject to

---

h. See chapter 11 this volume.

constant fertility and survival conditions would eventually approach a stable age distribution with an exponential rate of growth. Samuelson conjectured, in a letter to Lotka in July 1942, that what Bortkiewicz had actually done was to show that this was true of a specific numerical example.[37] Lotka was delighted that Samuelson had asked him about this, because his view was that Bortkiewicz had shown nothing of the sort: indeed, there was nothing new in his calculations, and he (Lotka) had been the first person to show that a population with given birth and mortality rates would converge on a fixed age distribution.[38] Familiar with developments in the 1920s, Kuczynski had, Lotka claimed, unconsciously read into Bortkiewicz things that were not there. Two days after writing this, he wrote to Samuelson again, making his point with two equations and arguing that there was a big jump from the system Bortkiewicz had been using, involving only the survival function (describing the proportion of people who survive to a given age) and systems that introduced the reproductive or fertility rate.[39]

This letter made Samuelson believe that he was finally becoming clear about the confusions in the literature, and that he had been "thrown off by the fact that Kuczynski had misinterpreted Bortkiewicz more than [he] had realized."[40] However, Samuelson argued that though Kuczynski had misunderstood Bortkiewicz, he had stumbled on a valid theorem that was independent of assumptions about fertility. To clarify this, Samuelson listed four theorems, all based on constant survival functions. The first two were straightforward: that a population in which births grow exponentially will achieve a stable age distribution in which population is also growing exponentially; and that if the age distribution is stable, the population must be growing exponentially. The third theorem was the important one that Lotka had derived in 1911—that any population with constant mortality and age-specific fertility would approach exponential growth. This left the fourth theorem, which Samuelson believed he was the first to have proved: that if population is growing exponentially, and mortality is constant, births must eventually grow exponentially. Samuelson then summarized the confusions in the literature in terms of these four theorems, asking Lotka whether he was correct.

Lotka replied with a list of his publications, explaining to Samuelson where he could find the first two theorems stated, repeating the point that neither Kuczynski nor Bortkiewicz had discovered anything new (he obviously agreed with Samuelson's statement about the third theorem). Then, rather than challenging Samuelson's claim about his own theorem, Lotka explained why he thought it was of limited practical value, "at least as applied to human communities."[41] It would be necessary to have just the right birth rate. His only concessions to Samuelson were that "in these days of controlled population policies it might have some bearing on problems of the future," and that it might be relevant to animal breeding or investment in industrial equipment. It appears that Samuelson then let the matter rest, publishing nothing on the subject until much later in life.[42]

This exchange with Lotka reveals Samuelson in pursuit of a problem that must have seemed to him to be an interesting piece of mathematics. Population growth had been one of Wilson's concerns, and it was also an important factor behind Hansen's explanation of stagnation. However, Samuelson's continued interest in the problem after the United States had joined the war shows how, even when busy with teaching at MIT, improving his knowledge of mathematical statistics, preparing a thesis for publication, working on the theory of fiscal policy, and organizing a major project in Washington (see chapter 19 this volume), he could not let this mathematical problem go.

Samuelson invested much time in statistics; he came to grips with the latest developments relating to the application of statistical methods to economic problems, and he used such methods to analyze macroeconomic data. These actions represented a major shift in the focus of his work, for at Harvard, despite his emphasis on generating testable hypotheses, he had mostly confined his attention to mathematical economic theory. However, now he chose not to venture further into formal statistical testing of economic theory. Instead, his research went in two directions. He continued to revise his thesis for publication, and he became involved in the very active debates over Keynesian economics and fiscal policy that were increasingly taking place in Washington, as economists were drawn into wartime government service. These economists were developing what rapidly came to be called the New Economics, or, as Samuelson was to call it in his textbook, the modern theory of income determination.[43] The theoretical foundations of this theory had been laid in the 1930s, but there was much that remained to be sorted out.

CHAPTER 18

Developing the New Economics, I
Theory, 1940–1943

The Theory of Income Determination

Samuelson's first Econometric Society meeting as a professor, rather than as a graduate student, was in December 1940, in New Orleans, where he took part in a session on Keynesian economics. Oskar Lange took up a theoretical question arising out of Keynes's *General Theory*: Could unemployment occur if wages were sufficiently flexible? If wages were flexible, so the "classical" argument went, the existence of unemployed workers who wanted jobs would push wages downward, increasing the demand for labor until full employment was achieved. Keynes controversially claimed that this mechanism would not work. Lange argued that so long as the money supply fell by less than prices fell, full employment would be restored, for the rise in the real value of the money supply would raise demand for securities (pushing down interest rates) and raise demand for goods.

Samuelson responded by discussing three meanings of Say's Law, the term used by Keynes for the idea that there can be no shortage of aggregate demand. The first, "most zealously held," was purely metaphysical and irrefutable: "supply is demand since goods exchange against goods."[1] This was empirically meaningless. The second was that purchasing power is indestructible: that what is not spent on consumption is automatically invested. This was empirically false, because effective purchasing power is constantly changing. The final meaning, which related directly to Lange's paper, was that involuntary unemployment was impossible if prices were sufficiently flexible.

Samuelson's most substantial argument against Lange was that while there might be a sufficiently *low* price level that would generate full employment, a *falling* price level might not eliminate unemployment. He was making a dynamic argument, present in the *General Theory*, but widely neglected in subsequent debates, because it was hard to make with a simple mathematical model such as Lange was using. Despite having advocated comparative static methods in his thesis, Samuelson could see their limitations.

The third speaker was Hansen, though it is not clear whether Hansen addressed this question, for *Econometrica* did not publish an abstract of his paper, merely a note that its substance would be included in his forthcoming book, *Fiscal Policy and Business Cycles* (1941a). This was a project in which Samuelson had become involved. The project had begun with Hansen writing a manuscript, "Fiscal Policy in Relation to the Business Cycle," which was discussed by leading economists at a conference organized by the Social Science Research Council in June 1939. During the following year, Hansen discussed the manuscript with many colleagues and students at Harvard, including Samuelson.[2] The published version opened with a statement of the relationship between depression and war, a situation then engulfing Europe and increasingly dominating American economic policymaking.

> The war now afflicting, directly and indirectly, the entire world, cannot be explained by overly simplified dogmas running in terms of competitive capitalism and imperialistic rivalries. But it has, nonetheless, an economic basis—the inability of the great industrial nations to provide full employment at rising standards of real income. The disastrous economic breakdown of the thirties let loose forces which have set the world in flames. The ultimate causes of the failure to achieve a world order in the political sphere must be sought against the facts of economic frustration.[3]

Economic policy could not be separated from international relations, an argument Samuelson would take up a year later, when he taught students at the Fletcher School about the relationship of economic activity to war.[a]

Perhaps the key point in Hansen's book was the emergence of a new aim for fiscal policy—ensuring full employment through high levels of government expenditure, financed either from progressive taxation or by a rise in the public debt. The crucial section of the book, "Fiscal Policy and the Full Use of Resources," began with a chapter on "The Cyclical Consumption–Income Pattern."[4] Arguing that consumption was largely determined by

---

a. See chapter 16 this volume.

income—that there was a consumption function—he made the case for high investment. He illustrated this with diagrams showing the relationship between consumption and income, including one similar to the diagram Samuelson had used in one of his articles on the business cycle.[5b] Unlike Samuelson's diagram, Hansen's consumption function was a straight line, but more significantly, there were numbers on the axes: a theoretical idea had been quantified.

Hansen had been able to do this using data collected by the National Resources Committee on the proportion of income spent on consumption by households with different income levels. There was, however, a problem that could not be solved using such data. Hansen calculated that raising national income from $50 billion to $80 billion would double the proportion saved, from 6.9 percent to 14.9 percent. However, data collected by Simon Kuznets showed that the proportion of income saved did not rise in the long term: the consumption function he had calculated held only when income changed within a short period of time. A different type of empirical analysis was needed. This was provided in an appendix, under Samuelson's name, titled "A Statistical Analysis of the Consumption Function." In this appendix, discussed from a different perspective in chapter 17 this volume, Samuelson used multiple regression analysis to estimate alternative forms of the consumption function from aggregate data.[c] It is remarkable that Hansen's chapter does not cite Samuelson's results, and Samuelson does not discuss the chapter to which his work was an appendix. However, the publication of two sets of estimates, derived using different methods, testifies to the importance Hansen attached to the consumption function, a concept that was central to both wartime and postwar planning.

A central element in Hansen's argument, as in virtually all analyses of income determination at this time, was the multiplier. The concept was discussed in detail in the *General Theory* and previous literature, but Samuelson believed that the theory was still not fully understood. So in the summer of 1941, he wrote a long paper, eventually published as "Fiscal Policy and Income Determination."[6] The paper's short second sentence sketched a view of progress in economics that he could well have picked up from Schumpeter, then working furiously on his history of economic analysis—that economic analysis advances discontinuously, taking large steps forward, and then needing time for gains to be consolidated.[7] Samuelson claimed that the theory

---

b. See figure 13.1 earlier in this volume.

c. These estimates are also discussed in chapter 17 this volume.

of the multiplier had immediate appeal because it "neatly expressed latent vague and intuitive notions of 'purchasing power,'" but because it was oversimplified, it received much criticism.[8] Though referring only to the multiplier, rather than to the Keynesian system as a whole, the sentence in which he made this remark encapsulated his view of what his graduate student Lawrence Klein was soon to label "the Keynesian revolution." The theory took off because it formalized ideas that were already in circulation, and it was opposed because it was oversimplified in ways that made it incorrect. The implication was that when the theory was elaborated—a task to which Samuelson's paper was to contribute—there could be a consensus. Samuelson thus set himself two tasks: to clear the ground by "isolating some current misapprehensions" and to take account of complications not discussed in oversimplified versions of the theory.

The first, short step was to isolate the multiplier from policy recommendations. Despite its use by Hansen and other advocates of fiscal stabilization policy, the multiplier was not the "rationalization of a free spending policy" that many economists thought it to be.[9] The doctrine had no implications with respect to public spending, for if a rise in government spending induced a fall in private investment, the multiplicand might be negative, meaning that there would be no case for raising government spending. However, the multiplier itself could not be negative, for if it were, the system would be unstable and it was impossible to derive meaningful results. Aside from this, statistical evidence confirmed that the marginal propensity to consume was less than 1, as was required for both stability and a positive multiplier. Some misconceptions about the multiplier, such as that the rate of interest adjusted to keep the velocity of circulation of money constant, were empirically false, but most misunderstandings were the result of incorrect analysis of dynamic processes. For example, confusion between one-shot rises in government spending (where spending rises for one period and then returns to its previous level) and changes where spending rises to a new level and stays there, had led to incorrect conclusions about the sensitivity of output to changes in government spending. The implicit message about the value of formal mathematical analysis will not have been lost on most readers of *Econometrica*, even though the article confined itself, for the most part, to verbal explanations.[10]

Samuelson's central message concerning the multiplier was that it was crucial to match the multiplicand—the expenditure being multiplied—by the appropriate multiplier. This was illustrated by the problem of government spending, where the multiplicand might be taken either as government spending on goods and services or as spending net of taxes (the deficit). If the former were used, then the multiplier had to be adjusted to allow for the additional taxes that would be paid as income rose.[d] The appropriate multiplier for government spending treated both saving and taxation as leakages, giving a much lower multiplier and a lower rise in taxation. It was impossible, Samuelson argued, for induced rises in taxation to cover the costs of the initial rise in government spending. As Samuelson put it, "Not even so powerful an agency as the Treasury can lift itself by its own bootstraps."[11]

The crucial point was that the marginal propensity to tax (the amount of tax raised by each dollar of extra income) was less than 1.

> This being the case, if a government spends, without at the same time making autonomous changes in tax *rates*, it cannot raise the national income *in a stable system* without at the same time raising deficits by *some* amount. The induced increase in taxes resulting throughout all time from given expenditure must fall short of that expenditure. Of course, the larger the propensity to tax, the less the Treasury will lose, but there must always be some finite loss.[12]

Samuelson immediately went on to point out that it might be possible to revise the tax system so as to reduce saving, making it feasible to maintain full employment even with a balanced budget.[e]

Having argued that raising government spending would increase the deficit if there were no rise in tax rates, Samuelson turned to the financial implications of deficits. His main aim was to explain how it had been possible to have a growing government debt at the same time as continuing low interest rates. There was simply no evidence that the Treasury or the central bank had "rigged" the market to achieve this; the purchases and sales of securities that would have been necessary to keep interest rates low had not taken place. The explanation he gave was that if the rate of increase in the debt was constant, as would be the case with a constant deficit, the interest rate would remain constant. It took an increase in the rate of growth of the deficit to push up interest rates. A higher deficit might raise interest rates, but those rates would not rise indefinitely. Once again, this was an argument about dynamics, but no doubt frustrating many mathematically competent readers of *Econometrica*, he gave no mathematical model to substantiate his claims, choosing instead to discuss U.S. policy on gold.

---

d. Suppose the marginal propensity to consume was ¾, so that the "basic" multiplier was $1/(1 - ¾) = 4$, and that the marginal rate of tax was 40 percent. It was fallacious to argue that a $2.5 billion rise in government spending would raise output by $10 billion, and that this would raise $4 billion in taxes, resulting in a reduced deficit.

e. He did not specify what changes in the tax system might achieve this.

Samuelson's next main point was to counter the argument, made by Hansen, that public works spending (on roads, hospitals, and other public projects) was more effective in raising income than was spending on relief and Social Security.[13] One argument was concerned with the immediate effect of any government spending. Samuelson pointed out that this could work either way. If the money allocated to public relief and Social Security would be spent more quickly than money allocated to public works, then relief expenditure would be more effective—the opposite of what Hansen was claiming. Another argument made by Hansen was that concentrating public spending on large projects would make it more effective. Samuelson's response was that being more visible did not mean that its effects would be greater, for numerous small projects could, taken together, have just as large an effect.

Samuelson also criticized what he chose to call the "velocity approach," more often called the quantity theory of money. The twentieth-century version of the quantity theory, expounded by Irving Fisher, centered on the equation $MV = PT$, where M is the stock of money, V the velocity of circulation, P the price level, and T the volume of transactions. If V and T are constant, then a change in M must cause P to change in the same proportion. "Income velocity," the term used by Samuelson, is the velocity obtained by defining T to include the transactions that enter national income, so that PT is national income.[f] He began with a mathematical point:

> It is unfortunate that ancient astronomers selected the period of revolution of the earth around the sun as the conventional unit of time reckoning, because with present financial habits this yields a figure for the income velocity of money of two or three, not dissimilar to the figure usually derived for the multiplier.[14]

However, though this gave Samuelson an opportunity to write with irony, this was irrelevant to his main point, which was that exponents of the velocity approach were making the same mistake as had many Keynesians. They were not distinguishing sufficiently enough between propositions that were true by definition and what were refutable hypotheses. The velocity approach, Samuelson argued, was based on the assumption that the velocity of circulation was stable. At full employment, this implied that changes in the money supply would induce proportionate changes in the price level—a theory

---

f. In the 1950s, Milton Friedman revived the quantity theory by arguing for a more flexible interpretation of this equation, in which V did not need to be constant.

Samuelson considered very important, even if requiring some modifications—but when there was unemployment, monetary changes would result, at least in part, in changes in output.[g] He argued that attempts to reconcile income velocity with the multiplier were unpersuasive, for they rested on manipulating identities and failed to explain anything. Even the argument that velocity played a role in the process of adjustment to a change in investment was not right, because normal velocity figures presumed stable payment habits—precisely what would not be found in a period when the economy was out of equilibrium. "At best," he wrote, "the normal speed of turnover of money is one minor limiting factor; at worst, it is irrelevant and misleading."[15]

Samuelson wrote with great confidence, boldly criticizing a theory with a long history; even his characterization of the quantity theory as the velocity approach served to trivialize it. He stressed that he had "avoided glossing over fundamental differences of opinion and logic," and he implied that he had understated the objections to the velocity approach when he wrote that he had made no effort "to indicate the substantial unanimity now achieved by informed writers on many issues."[16] Yet behind this clearly implied claim to authority, the issues about which he was writing were still not sorted out.

The theory of the multiplier and income determination had still not stabilized, with the result that his paper was disjointed, driven by the positions he was criticizing: it reads as a series of loosely connected points. There is a great contrast here with his papers on consumer theory and international economics, for both of which there was an established set of assumptions that defined a theory that he could systematize by applying more rigorous mathematical analysis than was being employed by his contemporaries. When it came to the multiplier, he wrote as though he were doing the same thing: using formal mathematical analysis to cut through the confusion found in previous work. However, his position was different because, despite the existence of mathematical models that encompassed Keynesian and classical systems, he had not found a single model from which he could derive the results he wanted to derive. This meant that although his thinking about dynamics was informed by his thinking as a mathematician, he did not present a dynamic model from which his conclusions could follow.

g. Using the notation defined here, if there is full employment, T, which measures real activity, cannot change, and so a rise in MV must cause P to rise; in contrast, if there is unemployment, monetary changes may cause T to rise or fall, implying that P need not change. The claim that V and T are constant, and that changes in P are therefore proportional to M, is a testable hypothesis; the claim that MV = PT, with nothing said about V and T, is true by definition.

The editors of the *American Economic Review* gave Samuelson an opportunity to link such ideas to the dispute over Keynes and classical economics, to which he had contributed in his AEA debate with Lange, when they invited him to review *Employment and Equilibrium,* the latest book by the Cambridge economist A. C. Pigou (1941). Samuelson contended that, in debating what classical economics was, Keynes's interpreters were "very much in the position of the man who, having lost his donkey, had no recourse but to ask himself what he would do if he were a jackass, and then do the same thing."[17] As the economist whom Keynes had chosen to exemplify classical theory, Pigou could tell Keynesians how a jackass thought.[18,h] Samuelson praised the book highly as "one of the most important books of recent years."[19] He thought the book's methodology was "almost ideal," and it revealed common ground between classical and Keynesian economics. The concluding words of the review were that Pigou's book "reveals with remarkable force the extent to which the Keynesians all along have been speaking classical prose, at the same time that 'classicists' have thought in Keynesian poetry." The review shows, more clearly than does his previous work with Hansen on the cycle, or his discussion of fiscal policy, how Samuelson was thinking about the Keynesian system in 1941.

The concepts of saving and investment were being widely discussed and were causing great confusion. Samuelson conceded that Pigou was correct in accepting the Keynesian definitions, according to which saving and investment were defined as being equal.[20] However, there might still be disequilibrium, in that the amount that households wished to save out of their income might not be the same as that which entrepreneurs wished to invest at the same level of income. Because it was necessary to deal with magnitudes that were not necessarily observed, he suggested that, rather than using the terminology advocated by the Swedish economists—of saying that *ex ante* saving and investment might differ even though *ex post* they had to be equal—the terminology of *virtual* and *observable* would seem more suitable.

The reason Samuelson thought the book almost ideal from a methodological point of view was that it derived comparative statics results, and it focused attention on dynamic processes—methods that had been central to his dissertation, defended earlier in the year. Disequilibrium, or the "inappropriateness" of the desired saving and investment, was what brought about change, something that was recognized in the "fruitful detailed

---

h. He used the jackass analogy when discussing his own education at Chicago (see chapter 5 this volume). An analogy he first used to establish Pigou's authority was later used to establish his own.

time-sequence analysis" of "Robertson, Kahn, J. M. Clark, Lundberg," and, critically, "Keynes *at an earlier stage.*"[21] Samuelson argued that there was no inconsistency in analyzing a short-run equilibrium, even though it was changing in the long run. To support this he alluded to the paradoxes of the ancient Greek philosopher Zeno that he had used previously in criticizing Keynes: just as an arrow moves even though at any time it is at a particular place in the air, so saving and investment could be equal and yet changing.[22]

In early 1942, Samuelson followed up this review by writing a note in which he claimed that he and another reviewer, Nicholas Kaldor, had been right to argue that investment would depend on the level of employment.[23] He adopted the strategy he commonly used in such cases of starting with a simple model and generalizing it. The simplest model adopted an aggregate production function in which output was a function of labor and capital.[i] The rate of interest was assumed to equal the marginal product of capital, which depended on employment and the capital stock. Investment (the growth rate of the capital stock) could be anything—the investment function was horizontal. He then followed Pigou in postulating different production functions for the production of consumption and investment goods. Pigou might be right to argue that as production of investment goods rose, the marginal productivity of capital in producing investment goods would fall, giving a negative relationship between investment and the rate of interest. The problem with the argument was that it failed to take account of relationships between the two sectors.

Samuelson's first conclusion was that Pigou's assumptions defined a system that was much more complicated than Pigou realized, and that these additional complications added nothing substantial to his argument. However, there was a more interesting message. Pigou was presenting a classical system in which full employment could be achieved. Samuelson argued that high investment would lead to high employment and a high marginal product of capital. What he called "perfectionist diddling of the market interest rate" might ensure that precisely the right level of investment was undertaken to achieve full employment. However, even if monetary policy could achieve this perfect result, it was achieved by flouting "the tyranny of the strict acceleration principle." Samuelson was implicitly using a non-Keynesian concept, taken from traditional American business cycle theory, to criticize Pigou's classical theory.

---

i. He attributed this way of posing the problem to the Cambridge economist Frank Ramsey (1927, though it seems likely that this was an error and he meant 1928).

As in his earlier writings, Samuelson was critical of Keynes. Not only had Keynes abandoned the dynamic analysis of his earlier work, which was important for deriving operational theorems, but he had also accepted too uncritically the law of diminishing marginal productivity—the idea that when employment increased, the wage employers would be prepared to pay would go down. However, he also found fault with Pigou. Perhaps the most important problem was that he was skeptical of Pigou's assumption that the central bank could determine the level of money income: cheap money might fail to raise demand, either because it might be impossible to lower interest rates or because investment did not respond to changes in the rate of interest. The message of his later note was that American business cycle theory, represented by Hansen, had focused on important relationships that neither Keynes nor Pigou understood.

Consumption and Investment and the Multiplier

The unsettled status of the theory of income determination is illustrated by correspondence Samuelson had with his friend Abram Bergson early in 1942. Bergson was writing a paper in which he analyzed the role of price changes in income determination.[24] His method was to argue that, whether companies operated in competitive markets or had monopoly power, it was possible to argue in terms of a function in which price depended on both output and the marginal cost of labor.[j] Different authors, including Keynes, Hicks, and Pigou, reached different results, Bergson claimed, because they made different assumptions about the responsiveness of price to these two variables. This required rethinking the theory of saving and investment to take account of price changes that went along with changes in output.

While working on this paper, Bergson contacted Samuelson to ask whether stability required that the marginal propensity to save in terms of money had to be greater than the marginal propensity to invest in terms of money (Samuelson's analysis had all been in real terms). This led Samuelson to explain the position he had taken. He justified leaving out price changes "as a first approximation in conditions of deep depression." The wage rate was given "for institutional reasons," and it was assumed that prices were proportional to wage rates because of constant returns to scale. These were admittedly "drastic assumptions," but they were "necessary for the validity

---

j. This is a simplification, for Bergson allowed for other inputs that might need to be used alongside labor, but it does not affect the argument.

of the more rudimentary multiplier models involving wage units, etc."[25] He then went on to explain that the only way to understand how stability conditions would change when a more realistic model was assumed would be to specify a dynamic model. For example, one might assume that the change in output equaled the difference between saving and investment, both of which depended on real income and other variables. In the published version of the paper, Bergson followed this approach, producing an equation similar to one Samuelson had used in an earlier article, but modified to incorporate the prices of consumption and investment goods.[26] A month later he acted as a referee on Bergson's paper, recommending that Dickson Leavens accept it for *Econometrica*, saying that it was a contribution on a very difficult subject, and suggesting that Bergson be asked to insert the full set of equations from which it was derived, so as to clarify the assumptions on which it was based.[27]

Samuelson made further progress toward providing a systematic treatment of the theory of income determination when, at the end of 1941 or early in 1942, he wrote a long paper, initially titled "Consumption, Investment, and Income" but changed at some point to "The Modern Theory of Income."[28] Its main purpose was expository: to present a simplified version of the modern theory of income determination and to draw conclusions about the relative importance of consumption and investment in stimulating output. However, when the argument moved into dynamics, the exposition became much less simple. The paper shows the direction in which Samuelson was taking Keynesian theory, and it shows him writing about fellow economists in what was to become a characteristic style. He resorted to irony in discussing the work of his contemporaries.

> While *wise* economists have undoubtedly always been in perfect agreement as to what constitutes the correct theory of output as a whole, just what that theory is, until recently, no wise economist would ever tell. But in the last half-dozen years [since 1936, when Keynes's *General Theory* was published] the secret has slipped out, although its full implications are only gradually becoming familiar.[29]

Though the effects of the secrets having slipped out had generally been salutary, an unfortunate effect of recent developments had, Samuelson claimed, been "the glorification of the expansionary stimulus of real investment as compared to consumption." His aim, therefore, was to correct the misunderstandings that lay behind this view. Irony was even more evident in a footnote discussing economists at the University of Cambridge (UK), with which Keynes was associated. He saw the lack of continuity between Keynes's two major books as "worthy of a doctor's dissertation" and that clues to when ideas in Cambridge (UK) changed were to be found in articles by Joan Robinson, "who holds among other offices that of public relations expert between the 'Cambridge school' and the rest of the world."[30]

Samuelson wrote explicitly in terms of different schools of thought—classical, neoclassical (and even neo-neoclassical), and Keynesian. Though he clearly approved of Keynes's main arguments, he did not identify with any single school, implying he stood above them all. His tone was that of someone who understood the mathematics and was able to point out error by virtue of getting the mathematics right, something other economists had not managed to do. Thus at one point he remarked, "I should like to make it clear that I am not accusing any one school of thought, such as the anti-Keynesians, of being more confused than their opponents. The Keynesians too have sinned, including the Master." In a footnote to this passage, he pointed out errors in four "mathematical versions of the Keynesian system some of which have received the apostolic benediction."[31] He patronizingly accused Robinson of being confused and having "corrupted" the Polish economist Michal Kalecki.[k]

An illustration of the importance of understanding the mathematics occurred in the opening section in which he explained that one reason economists believed investment to be the driving force was that the output of investment goods industries, such as pig iron, was known to fluctuate much more than the output in consumption goods industries. Because fluctuations in investment seemed to come before changes in consumption, it had been assumed that causation must run from investment to consumption. Against this, Samuelson, drawing on his mathematical experience, could easily see that if investment was compared with *changes* in consumption (as implied by the accelerator), the timing was reversed, immediately undermining any presumption about causality.

The paper is also significant for being the first place where Samuelson used the diagram that was later to adorn not only the pages of his best-selling introductory textbook but also its cover; it showed the level of income as being determined by the intersection of an upward sloping saving function with a horizontal investment function. This diagram, figure 18.1, was a variation on the diagram he and Hansen had

---

k. Kalecki, who had left Poland for Cambridge, had developed a theory that had much in common with that of Keynes, but with Marxist elements. Robinson was, in 1942, discovering Marx.

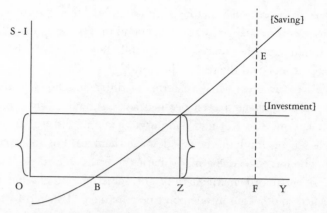

FIGURE 18.1 Income determination—saving and investment.

previously used (figure 13.1), but instead of plotting consumption against income, he plotted the difference between them (saving) against income.[1] Equilibrium output is Z, at which *ex ante* (planned) saving and investment are equal (he was using what was coming to be the accepted terminology, despite his own preference for the term "virtual saving").[32] If Z is less than full-employment output, F, then F cannot be an equilibrium. Samuelson claimed that, though this account of income determination was oversimplified, it was based on "firm empirical patterns which every theory must take into account"—notably the stability and broad shape of the consumption function that he had estimated in his previous work— and it was sufficient to correct misunderstandings.[33] He compared his diagram with the Marshallian "cross," the well-known supply and demand diagram, using Marshall's analogy of the two blades of a pair of scissors to explain that it was neither saving nor investment but the relationship between them that determined income. The diagram therefore came to be known as "the Keynesian cross."

However, while such diagrams could do much to explicate the relation between saving and investment, they needed to be used in conjunction with other arguments, for a crucial role was played by the rate of interest, which brought in the money supply and central bank policy. More complicated was the role of time. One of the additions made to the earliest draft was an eight-page section on the dynamics behind these static diagrams. This required

---

1. If saving is defined as the difference between income and consumption, the gap between expenditure (consumption plus investment) and income must be identical to the gap between investment and saving.

that Samuelson make assumptions about the lags involved. One possibility was to assume that current consumption depends on income in the previous period. Another was to assume that it takes time for production to respond to changes in sales, with any difference between the two being met from inventories. The relationship between saving and investment out of equilibrium would be different in each case. It was here that he made the remark, cited earlier, that both Keynesians and anti-Keynesians had made mistakes in equal measure.

Samuelson argued that it was optimal to have a propensity to consume that was sufficiently high to produce full employment, for if there were unemployment, consumption and investment could both increase. However, once full employment was reached, consumption and investment became competitive, which meant that "optimal behavior then involves deliberate social decision and cannot be decided upon mechanical behavioristic grounds."[34] Probably, he argued, "societies desire neither the largest possible rate of capital accumulation per unit time nor the smallest." The paper ended with a review of what Samuelson called the "under-consumptionist school," going back to Malthus, which had argued that unemployment could result from the level of consumption being too low.[m] They had consistently been dismissed, even by writers such as Hansen, and yet modern thought was, Samuelson noted, moving in their direction. How was this possible?

His answer was that the analysis of effective demand was "one of the most difficult problems of economic analysis," to which advances in value theory (the theory of how individual prices are determined) could contribute little.[35] Whereas the theory of value was well developed and could be reduced to a few basic principles (as he had shown in his thesis), he contended that "It would be too much to expect . . . that any one writer should have developed a beautiful, logical, and complete theory [of effective demand]." Quoting Keynes's *General Theory*, he observed that "the underconsumptionists 'saw truth obscurely,' and they often combined with it naive, cranky, and refutable points of analysis."[36] He was no doubt

---

m. It was widely held, at least since the time of Adam Smith, that saving (refraining from consumption) was beneficial. High saving would lower interest rates, raise investment, and stimulate economic growth. Malthus argued that there was an optimal propensity to consume (conceptually equivalent to assuming an optimal propensity to save) because, after a certain point, saving was harmful because spending would be insufficient to buy all the goods that could be produced. The result would be unemployment. This idea, the basis for under-consumptionism, was considered heretical, for it challenged the idea that saving was always a virtue.

addressing his teachers when he claimed that such errors were not a reason for rejecting the theory.[n]

The concluding message of the paper was that, though differences over economic policy were real, there was great agreement on economic analysis. His remark that "[i]t is particularly important to emphasize the great consensus of analysis which has been reached by almost all present day economists" implicitly gave authority to his own arguments, in a paper in which he had found fault with the writings of his many of his most eminent contemporaries.[37]

One of Samuelson's main targets in this paper—certainly if judged by the number of pages devoted to it—was an article in which Oskar Lange (1938) had taken up the idea, made in the early nineteenth century by Malthus, that there was an "optimum" propensity to consume. This idea was important because it challenged an orthodoxy that was deeply entrenched in economic thinking. Using a model similar to Samuelson's, but also having an equation in which supply and demand for money determined the rate of interest, and in which the rate of interest affected investment, Lange had shown that there would be some propensity to consume at which investment was maximized. If consumption were lower than this, the rate of interest would be lowered and investment would rise; if consumption were higher, the rate of interest would rise, thereby lowering investment. This vindicated, so Lange claimed, the under-consumptionists, who claimed that an economy could be held back by a lack of consumption, thereby contradicting the orthodoxy according to which saving was always beneficial. However, Samuelson believed his argument to be mistaken on several counts, and that Lange's claim that there might be an optimal propensity to consume that resulted in less than full employment was completely wrong.

Samuelson had corresponded with Lange about his earlier work on consumer and welfare economics, and naturally sent Lange a copy of this paper. Lange replied that he had read it with great interest.[38] He offered many suggestions for improving the paper, as he had done on a previous occasion when Samuelson had criticized him and he had conceded that Samuelson was right to find fault with his algebra, but he claimed that Samuelson's own algebra was not right either, and that if the mistakes were corrected, his own conclusions were justified. Lange said he was "inclined to be more charitable

---

n. He criticized Slichter, whose textbook he had used as an undergraduate (see chapter 3 this volume), and Williams, who had taught him money and banking at Harvard, and ran the Fiscal Policy Seminar with Hansen (see chapter 12 this volume) for objecting to under-consumption on grounds that were merely verbal.

to the neo-classical theory than I was before or than you appear to be." His reason was that neoclassical writers assumed all prices were completely flexible, which meant that if the propensity to consume fell, prices as well as output would fall, reducing the demand for money. Moreover, if people did find themselves with excess cash balances, this would have a direct effect on both demand for durable consumption goods and investment.° The theory presumed that the supply of money did not fall as fast as demand, which would certainly be true if, as did most neoclassical economists, the money supply were assumed constant. Lange concluded by saying that in a month's time he hoped to have the draft of a booklet, "Price Flexibility, Employment and Economic Stability," that would explain the neoclassical theory. Aside from a footnote, the notion of the "optimum" propensity to consume did not appear. Lange said that he might send it to Samuelson if he was not too busy.

Not surprisingly, Samuelson found this letter helpful. He wrote Lange that he was particularly grateful for spotting his mathematical error, for "it would have been embarrassing for this to have occurred in print," implying that Lange should be embarrassed about his own mistake.[39] He went on to say that, on rereading, he had come to realize that his wording had not made sufficiently clear the complete generality of Lange's case. He had implicitly taken Lange to be talking about a world in which there was unemployment. In such a world, wages may be taken as constant. It was only as full employment was approached that wages would rise. In contrast, he presumed that Lange had intended to encompass the full-employment case in his equations.

Samuelson then explained why he was not convinced by Lange's argument about real cash balances. This effect presumed imperfect capital markets, for in a perfect capital market, in which companies could borrow and lend unlimited amounts at the market rate of interest, cash balances should not matter. However, though he accepted that capital markets were imperfect, he thought that the effects Lange discussed would be "completely overshadowed" by the effects of a falling price level on the marginal efficiency of capital.

> Under realistic conditions, therefore, I think that the neo-classical position is utterly fallacious, despite the fact that it is possible to construct models in which the curves do not have the flatnesses and steepnesses of the real world and in which wage reductions would temporarily increase employment.[40]

---

o. The investment function would take the form $I = F(i, C, M)$, where i is the rate of interest, C is consumption, and M is cash balances.

He then made his objections to the neoclassical theory clear, explaining why he hoped that the manuscript Lange had promised him would not compromise on the crucial questions.

> In contrast to this for our world, the armament period included, a real thorough-going application of their [the neo-classical economists'] plans would lead to the introduction of hyper-deflation with disastrous consequences to our economic and political system. I shall be very sorry, therefore, if in your monograph you give way on these points. The optimum propensity to consume should occupy much more than a footnote.[41]

In a postscript to his letter, Samuelson explained that though he was not anxious to publish his paper quickly, Hansen wanted him to get it out as soon as possible, suggesting that this would be easier if it were divided into two parts. To avoid this, he wondered whether Lange thought that the *Journal of Political Economy* might be willing to take it at its current length. However, the paper was submitted, unfinished, to the *American Economic Review*, asking for advice on what was needed to make it publishable. The editor wrote that he would be happy to accept it when Samuelson was satisfied it was ready for publication, though without waiving his "editorial prerogative to suggest improvements."[42] However, he confirmed Samuelson's view that he should take plenty of time to revise the paper thoroughly.

> If I were you, I should not be in too great a hurry with it. In other words, the manuscript will bear careful reworking. In particular, I suggest you try to put your positive analysis into a more orderly relation to your commentary on Hansen and Lange. The two strands get a little in each other's way. Could some of the critical comment be reduced to footnotes? In the last section you devote too much space to commenting on Slichter and not enough to bringing your paper to a good end.[43]

The letter ended with an invitation to lunch when Samuelson was next in Washington. However, despite everyone Samuelson consulted thinking the paper was sufficiently important to publish, it was never published, and the ideas were to come out in other ways. The explanation is no doubt that Samuelson was becoming increasingly busy with teaching in MIT and with fortnightly visits to Washington.[p]

---

p. See chapter 19 this volume.

The Keynesian System

In October 1942, Samuelson received a letter from a former MIT student, Arthur Ashbrook, who described himself as "a hireling in OPA's iron and steel branch" in Washington, but who thought that he would be in the armed forces before the end of the year.[q] Ashbrook told Samuelson that, being unable to suppress "some of my more pernicious vices acquired at MIT," he had been reading the *General Theory*.[44] "Horrible doubt" had crept into his mind, for it seemed to him that Keynes's argument about why there would not be full employment was confused. It was important to distinguish between full employment in the classical sense and in the statistical sense.

> Involuntary unemployment should be linked with frictional and voluntary unemployment as qualifications of the classical concept of full employment. When we talk of "millions of unemployed," we are speaking principally not about a lack of full employment in the strict sense, but of a low MPC and a low MEC, coupled with an I [interest rate] that because of institutional factors will not fall below a rate substantially above o. In other words, we always have full employment to a first approximation; what our real goal is statistical full employment.[r]

He asked Samuelson whether he "would be willing to restore my faith in the bible" by pointing to some articles that explained why unemployment could remain high even when supply and demand for labor were high. After all, it was "all right to doubt that Joshua stopped the sun in its course, but when one begins to doubt that man was born sinful. . . ."

Samuelson replied that he was uncertain about whether he could restore Ashbrook's faith. "You must remember," he wrote, "that not all the books of the Bible are to be given the same weight" and he had "always thought that Keynes['s] discussion of involuntary unemployment was the weakest part of the book."[45] He conceded that if all markets were frictionless and competitive, it was hard to see why wages would not fall. If that were the case, Keynes's attempt to explain this using money illusion was not likely to be very important. However, though he agreed with Ashbrook up to this

---

q. The OPA was the Office of Price Administration. Ashbrook was to complete his PhD, under Samuelson's supervision, in 1947.

r. Full employment as measured by unemployment statistics.

point, he questioned the usefulness of Ashbrook's definition of the term "full employment":

> It conceals more problems than it illuminates. In particular it does not explain the huge swings in effective demand which determine how far from what you call "statistical" full employment the system's actual full employment will be.

Unemployment was not explained just by the structure of wages. The labor market was highly imperfect, in that people were often unable to sell their labor whatever the wage they were willing to accept. This was the reality irrespective of any theoretical justification for it.

> If you don't believe this, just wait until the next depression. Try chaining yourself to the desk of the personnel officer of a huge company brandishing evidence of your high IQ and the fact that your family is starving. For a thousand and one reasons the employer cannot take advantage of your offer to work for less, even if he should want to . . . and if he were a man of good will he would not want to since he himself believes in a fair minimum wage, regardless as to whether or not this belief is well founded.

Samuelson went on to explain that belief in a fair wage, and that cutting wages would not help, were important.

> In explaining the unwillingness of workers to cut wage rates when their families are almost starving, we must appeal to the same vague beliefs in a fair wage, to this intuitive notion that this will not help, to their group and class sympathies.
>
> All in all it is only too easy to explain why wage rates are sticking. Keynes should have let it go at that, pointing out that frictions explain the rigidity of wage rates but not unemployment. For if frictions were removed and wage rates were made flexible, the result under some conditions might be only to initiate a vicious downward spiral of prices and wages.

Drawing on points that Keynes had made, Samuelson challenged Ashbrook's assumption that a man could get work if his wage were less than the marginal product of labor; even if true for an individual, it was not true for large groups. Ashbrook was only partly convinced, replying to Samuelson in a long letter in which he defended his position that it would make more sense to work simultaneously with more than one concept of full employment.[46,s] Unfortunately, we do not have Samuelson's reply.[t]

Samuelson's opinion that Keynes's discussion of involuntary unemployment was the weakest part of the *General Theory* is significant, given that this was to prove the Achilles' heel of Keynesian economics.[47] When Ashbrook, drawing on standard supply and demand theory, confronted Samuelson with what he believed were theoretical inconsistencies in Keynes's treatment of involuntary unemployment, Samuelson did not respond by defending Keynes's reasoning; he appealed to the reality of involuntary unemployment, saying that though such explanations were not part of the theory, it was easy to explain why wages would not bring labor markets into equilibrium. This meant that even in the absence of a formal theoretical justification, it made good sense to talk about there being involuntary unemployment, rather than fit the analysis into categories that kept it closer to traditional price theory. Samuelson's response also makes clear the importance of dynamics. As Keynes had realized and, as Samuelson had pointed out in an earlier paper, he took seriously Keynes's belief that cuts in wages might be destabilizing.

Ashbrook was not the only economist to contact Samuelson seeking explanations of the new theory. Hans Neisser, also working at the OPA, had written in July to point out that if there were no lag between the receipt of income and spending on consumption, the multiplier–accelerator model would not produce a cycle, merely exponential growth.[48] He wrote again in November, having read Samuelson's "Fiscal Policy and Income Determination."[49] After a point about investment that Samuelson was able to dismiss as a misunderstanding, Neisser questioned whether a rise in the propensity to consume would necessarily conduce to full employment. There was the definitional point that unemployment statistics might not measure unemployment

---

s. The letter is fascinating because of the picture he gives of life inside the OPA. He writes of a "price-fixers' school" in which staff members had the opportunity to listen to big shots "sounding off about prices and the state of the union." Galbraith had explained that, though most economists thought price control naive, the OPA had taken actions that either emptied the shelves in stores or led to rationing. The only "dynamite" in the meetings was criticism of other agencies. Seymour Harris, as chairman, had been peculiarly gauche, and though he was apparently a hard worker, "could best use his time for some concentrated thought on various subjects, not excluding economics." Gilbert had made a good impression and Clark (Ashbrook wrote J. B. but must have meant J. M.) came across as very modest.

t. Ashbrook was called up, and his next appearance in Samuelson's papers is after the war, when he returned to MIT to complete his PhD.

DEVELOPING THE NEW ECONOMICS, I: THEORY, 1940–1943 | 373

correctly, as well as the point that full employment might require a reduced standard of living. This elicited from Samuelson a clear statement about the assumptions he was making about the supply side.

> Your second point, which I did not get into, was whether or not an increase in effective demand can result in extra employment only by reducing the real wage. I do not think that Keynes would agree with this—I know that I should not. It would depend upon the exact nature of the loss of returns, external and internal, and upon the degree of monopoly.[50]

The effect of a rise in the propensity to consume would depend on the degree of monopoly power and cost conditions facing companies, about which he and Neisser were making different assumptions.

> I should say that we differ in our emphasis upon the importance of limited capital as a bottleneck causing an increase in effective demand to dissipate itself in an incipient inflation, short of full employment. After 1929 I think the American economy was singularly lucky in having excess capacity in physical equipment so that during the great depression this was not an important consideration, However, after a long period of stagnation, when capital equipment had finally gotten adjusted to maximum levels of income far below full employment, this might become an extremely important factor.

In response to this, Neisser replied that costs could be constant "only over a limited range" and that there was no reason to believe that the point at which costs began to rise would be full employment.[51] In other words, he was suggesting that there might not be sufficient productive capacity to employ the entire labor force without a fall in real wages. This elicited a further clarification from Samuelson.

> I agree that the full employment point need not coincide with the bottleneck point at which capacity gives out—nor, for that matter, with the point at which workers will begin to push up money wages. After a period of long stagnation the bottleneck point is certain to be considerably below the full employment point so that there is a [serious] problem of an upward price spiral even though people are still unemployed. On the other hand, after a boom period the reverse could conceivably be true and I am not sure that after 1929 this was not the case. Of course certain assumptions with respect to monopoly, expectations etc. would be involved in any explanation of this fact.[52]

This shows that Samuelson was well aware of capacity issues and the need to consider the supply side. His argument that capacity would fall during a long period of stagnation no doubt reflects the experience of 1937, when recovery stopped well short of full employment. It is also worth noting his repeated emphasis on monopoly and expectations.

A point Samuelson found more difficult to answer, and more interesting, was an argument Neisser made about whether there was a point at which a rising propensity to consume would lower investment, a point Lange had also made. Samuelson explained that Neisser needed to distinguish between what people intended to save and what they actually saved. If people tried to consume all their income, or if savings were taxed away, and there was investment going on, there must be forced saving: people would fail to consume all their income. Part of the problem, Samuelson confessed, was that he had caused confusion by not defining sufficiently precisely what he meant by the "propensity to consume." But the real problem was that Neisser had not appreciated that increased consumption would be causing income to rise. "My point," Samuelson wrote, "may be summarized in the assertion that the producers goods industries are benefited, not hurt, by an autonomous increase in consumption up to the point where output ceases to be expansible," a point that might or might not correspond to full employment.[53]

The end result of their correspondence was to reduce their disagreements considerably. Neisser explained that he had viewed Samuelson as one of the "mature economy" theorists who "deny the necessity of net savings in the present stage of capitalist development," but that he had been wrong to do so. He excused his misunderstanding because he though Samuelson had talked about "taxing away saving" in a misleading way. "You should explain," he wrote, "how a tax system would look which reduces savings and raises consumption as long as utilization and income does not exceed, say, the level of 1939 but does not reduce to the same extent the marginal propensity to save for higher incomes. Our present system of graduated income taxes seems to have the opposite effect."[54]

Samuelson shared Hansen's view that there might be a shortage of investment opportunities, but was distancing himself from more radical positions. Neisser drew a clear distinction between Samuelson's view and that of Keynes, suggesting that this might reflect differences between the European and American situations.

As to the problem of the mature economy, I should like to point out that the impossibility of sufficient investment is not proved at all for the European economies, and is in particular disproved for Germany by the experience up till 1929 and for England by the experience after 1933. It is this experience which presumably led Keynes to take a different view from the mature economy theorists, viz., that it is not the absence of investment opportunities (the inelasticity of the marginal efficiency function), but the inelasticity of the money supply which was mainly responsible for the English unemployment situation before 1930.

Neisser agreed that there was no shortage of investment opportunities in Europe—how could there be, given the contrast with the situation in America during the 1920s—though he did not accept that Britain's problem had been an inelastic money supply. On the other hand, though there was more evidence to support the mature economy thesis in relation to America, he opined that "no conclusive proof ever has been tried. And the great obstacles our tax system and other institutions put in the way of investment make such a proof rather difficult."

In this correspondence with Neisser, not only do we see Samuelson discussing the new economics in relation to what had been experienced over the previous decade, debating its relevance as much as its logical consistency, but we also see him explaining results about which he was confident because he had proved them mathematically. Neisser could follow his mathematics—he had read and appears to have understood at least one of Samuelson's very technical articles on the stability of equilibrium—and he was sympathetic to the ideas Samuelson was proposing.[55] His problems arose in relating results from simple mathematical models to the world they saw around them. The exchange also shows the way in which Keynesian ideas were being used by two economists who did not completely accept them.

The merits of Keynesian ways of thinking about employment were also raised by an exchange that Samuelson had with Abba Lerner in the same month. Lerner tried to persuade him that it was possible to conduct the analysis in terms of the supply and demand for saving, thereby relating the Keynesian theory to older theories that ran in terms of supply and demand for loanable funds.[56] While Samuelson contended that Lerner's argument was wrong, suggesting an alternative way of deriving such curves, he disputed that this had anything to do with the old theories.[57] Lerner was trying to find a way to reduce the problem to a two-dimensional diagram involving familiar ideas such as supply and demand. Samuelson's letter showed him finding fault with Keynesians, as well as with the anti-Keynesians.

[T]he Keynesians have sinned grievously in not understanding their own system. I believe this to be true of Harrod, Joan Robinson,

Kalecki, and that at one time even Lange was confused as to whether the marginal propensity to save and to invest had to be equal. Keynes himself is a split personality on these subjects. In fact it can be shown that in the Treatise and in his earlier writings he made similar blunders by not recognizing the senses in which things are equal at the intersections of schedules, but "virtually" away from the intersections.... In the Keynesian system for the first time the non-mathematical economist has had to work with many dimensional relationships. It is not surprising but it is nevertheless deplorable that the confusions of a century ago with respect to the equality of supply and demand should rise once again to plague and confuse us.[58]

Using appropriate mathematical analysis was vital, because the Keynesian system was multidimensional. Yet despite this, Samuelson persisted with trying to help Lerner understand it by arguing in terms of two-dimensional diagrams. If he had constructed an algebraic model that could capture all dimensions of the problem, Samuelson did not reveal it.

Samuelson also pointed out the benefits of using mathematical reasoning to analyze the multiplier in print. When reviewing a book by Fritz Machlup in early 1943, he found a long list of points where he believed Machlup had made mistakes, and claimed that Machlup's 200-page book could have been compressed into a single mathematical article.[59] His belief that the use of mathematics simplified arguments was made even explicit when he argued that Machlup's more technical chapters were the easiest to understand. In these, Machlup had used mathematics to analyze the working out of the multiplier in systems of international trade: analyzing the effects of a shift in demand from domestic to foreign products, and the effect on one country of an increase in investment in another country. The multiplier was being used increasingly widely.

However, despite all the attention paid to the multiplier, there remained unanswered questions. Samuelson discovered one of these while working on some numerical examples where he suspected a computational error.[60] Samuelson noticed that, though the multiplier was used in two different ways, no one, including himself, had proved they were the same. One was the case in which there is a one-time increase in spending, and the other was one in which spending rises to a new level, at which it remains constant. In the first case, the multiplier gives the cumulative rise in income; in the second, it gives the higher level of income in every period. He sought to show that these two multipliers were the same, over whatever period the multiplier was calculated.[61] He extended his analysis to multi-country multipliers and applied to it techniques learned from studying problems related to engineering.[62]

Samuelson's notion of a "truncated" multiplier—a multiplier calculated over a finite number of periods—was taken up by Oskar Lange, who generalized his result, allowing for changes in spending in every period.[63] Lange stepped up the mathematical analysis, drawing on a number of techniques Samuelson did not understand, and in April 1944, Samuelson wrote to him asking for some references and questioning some of his results.[64] He suggested that one of the problems might be the way one represented a one-time expenditure increase in continuous-time models—a single impulse of spending would have to be represented as "a momentary impulse of infinite magnitude—i.e., like an improper Dirac function."[65] The multiplier might appear to be a simple concept, but it raised difficult mathematical problems that few economists were able to handle properly.

The Rate of Interest and the Stationary State

The *Review of Economics and Statistics* devoted its February 1943 issue to thirteen articles marking what Schumpeter called "a lamentable event"— his sixtieth birthday.[66] This was obviously something to which Samuelson would contribute, and he chose to discuss Schumpeter's theory that the rate of interest would be zero in a stationary equilibrium.[u] Samuelson began by analyzing the terms "static" and "dynamic," central to Schumpeter's theory of economic evolution, a literature that he contended was unsatisfactory.[67] Understanding the relationship between statics and dynamics in theoretical physics was fruitful, but few possessed the necessary technical knowledge to handle this correctly, a criticism that he illustrated with his Chicago teacher, Frank Knight.[68] Attempts to approach dynamics though biology had also been disappointing: "one looks in vain for any new weapon, secret or otherwise, for discovering scientific truths." After seeking to clarify the discussion by proposing a consistent set of terms, he turned to Schumpeter's notion that the rate of interest would be zero in a stationary state.

---

u. One reason why he may have been interested in this problem at this time is that Everett Hagen, with whom he was working closely in the National Resources Planning Board (see chapter 19 this volume), turned to Frank Knight's theory of capital in order to analyze the implications of net investment for the distribution of income, which was central to their work on consumption (Hagen 1942).

Samuelson reviewed the theories of Schumpeter, Lionel Robbins, and Frank Knight (together with his "disciple," George Stigler), claiming that Schumpeter's critics, Robbins and Knight, had failed to understand basic ideas such as the difference between a static situation and a stationary equilibrium that was the end result of a dynamic process, or the difference between reaching zero and approaching zero asymptotically. Citing the literature on stochastic processes associated with Yule, Slutsky, and Frisch, and drawing heavily on an article by the Cambridge mathematician Frank Ramsey, his message was that economists ignored mathematics at their peril.[69] Even Schumpeter did not escape criticism, for it made no difference to his theory of the business cycle whether, in the absence of innovation, the rate of interest converged on zero or on some positive rate of interest. Samuelson saw Schumpeter's arguments as having "dramatic value," even though Samuelson's preference was not to "reify" Schumpeter's stationary state but, rather, "to concentrate on the dynamic path" toward such an equilibrium. The question of whether or not opportunities for productive investment were limited was an important one, but it was a "factual question," not the theoretical one that Schumpeter, Robbins, and Knight had made it out to be.

However, while there were reasons for him to be thinking about such problems in 1942 when viewed against the background of his other work, this article, clearly written because he wanted to honor a teacher whom he held in high regard, appears to be a throwback to the work he was doing as a junior fellow in the late 1930s. Rather than developing theoretical ideas in discussion with his contemporaries, he was using mathematical argument to show that the debates of his elders, who did not understand the mathematics, were confused and misleading. Perhaps more telling than the criticism of his elders' mathematical failures was his dismissal of their concerns as "esoteric." This was very much the attitude he had taken to the literature on consumer theory that preceded his own. The mathematical models he cited might lead to seemingly unrealistic results, but this was the fault of the assumptions made, not of the mathematics. For example, if the rate of interest approached zero, the mathematics of discounting implied that a permanent asset should have infinite value. Echoing a theme from an earlier paper, he wrote,

> If the infinite value of permanent assets in a zero interest rate economy seems anomalous, the paradox springs from the unreal character of the assumption that men maximize utility in terms of an infinite horizon. It is questionable whether the whole process of saving is illuminated by the attempts to explain it in terms of adjusting consumption streams over time.[70]

This statement makes it clear that, though he was familiar with mathematical theories in which saving was the result of households' optimizing over time, he rejected such an approach as unrealistic. He was thereby rejecting the framework that would, in the 1950s, become the standard approach to modeling consumption and saving. As his remark about the importance of limited opportunities for investment makes clear, he was viewing Schumpeter's theory of the rate of interest through the lens of Hansen's theory. Moreover, though he attached great importance to the theory of optimizing behavior, he did not view saving as determined by intertemporal optimization.

Schumpeter told Samuelson that he found the paper very stimulating and that he hoped to have an opportunity to discuss it with him, continuing,

> If you get reprints do not forget to send me one. I like to have a complete collection of Samuelsonia. Most of all of course I value the sign of goodwill on the part of one of the ablest economists of our time.[71]

This episode shows that, despite the criticisms contained in his article, Samuelson still held Schumpeter in high regard, and that this respect was reciprocated. It also serves as a reminder that, though Samuelson's work was moving on, he was still willing to point out the confusions into which his elders had fallen. Taking a problem that was important to Knight as well as Schumpeter, he was arguing that, because they did not understand the mathematics, his elders had made serious mistakes. As in his thesis, he was using mathematics to clarify ideas, rendering old debates redundant, and thereby breaking with the past. In contrast, in his other work during this period, he was involved in developing the theories that would become the foundation on which most postwar macroeconomics would be based and that would be disseminated through his textbook. Some of these made it into print, but because of the pace of his activity, he failed to get some important papers to the point where they could be published.

The ideas being discussed in this chapter—the "New Economics"—centered on the multiplier, now appear very simple and naive to most economists: they are considered suitable for introductory economics courses and can be passed over very quickly by more advanced students, who may not even take them seriously as a starting point. In the 1970s, these Keynesian models were displaced by other models based on the systematic application of the intertemporal optimization framework that Samuelson rejected as unrealistic and they were widely seen as being misconceived. However, for many years, economists did take these models seriously, developing and complicating them, using them as the basis for forecasting and policy analysis. What the sometimes convoluted debates discussed in this chapter and chapter 20 this volume show is that in the early 1940s, these ideas were far from simple. The mathematics might be trivial to a modern graduate student in economics but the conceptual basis for the theory was far from trivial especially when the ideas had to be related to the national accounts. Ideas that Samuelson was to present in a simple form in his introductory textbook a few years later were simple only because they had been extensively discussed and the conceptual problems clarified during this period. Just as important, they were central to the main policy issues faced by the United States in wartime. This meant that the primary place where the New Economics was being discussed was among the network of economists working in government agencies in Washington. Samuelson joined this network in 1941, when, though he continued to live in Cambridge and though teaching remained his main occupation, he began to commute to Washington to work as a consultant to the National Resources Planning Board.

CHAPTER 19

Hansen and the National
Resources Planning Board,
1941–1943

Hansen and the Keynesian Network

Alvin Hansen, with whom Samuelson had begun to work very closely shortly
before his move to MIT, and whose work had been the basis for Samuelson's
theory of the business cycle, had worked as a consultant to branches of the
federal government throughout the 1930s, but after his move to Harvard, he
became much more prominent as a public figure. In 1938, he began to work
together with Lauchlin Currie, an economist who had been an instructor at
Harvard until 1934, where he and others had advocated expansionary policies to
combat the Depression.[1] In 1934, after a brief spell at the U.S. Treasury, Currie
made similar arguments at the Federal Reserve in his role as assistant to its new
governor, Marriner Eccles. He became the major figure in a group of Keynesian
economists in Washington. Currie and Hansen came into the public eye in May
1939, when they testified before the Temporary National Economic Committee
(TNEC), a committee set up by the U.S. Congress to investigate the concentration of economic power. Their testimony was instrumental in shifting the focus
of attention from market power as the cause of depression to the failure of the
financial system to equilibrate saving and investment, the problem Keynes had
identified in the *General Theory*. Currie recalled the occasion vividly.

> In any case, sometime in 1938 I believe it was, we welcomed Alvin
> Hansen with open arms as our most important recruit. I recall very

well arranging for him to be our star witness in the TNEC hearings, rehearsing together our testimony and going over a long list of "good" and "bad" words prepared for the use of the government witnesses by Stuart Chase. Unfortunately, somebody slipped the list to the press, which had great fun with it.[2]

Keynes was not mentioned in this testimony, even though it would have been perfectly natural to do so—perhaps his name was one of the "bad" words that was not to be mentioned—but in correspondence with Dennis Robertson, a friend and colleague of Keynes, Hansen was less discreet. After reading his presidential address to the AEA, Robertson had written to him with criticism of his use of the accelerator.[3] In reply, Hansen asked what he thought of the observation, made in his TNEC testimony, that through its social security and tax systems, England had made the transition to a high-consumption economy. "Perhaps," he wrote, "I am getting too Keynesian."[4]

In July 1939, Currie moved to the White House as an assistant to Franklin Roosevelt. More than anyone else, Currie was responsible for the recruitment of Keynesians to Washington during the war. His later memory of this describes the extensive network that was being created.[a] In 1940, Hansen became part of this network when he took up position as an advisor to the Federal Reserve, where he remained throughout the war, and the National Resources Planning Board.[5] He combined his work in Washington with his teaching duties at Harvard by spending Thursdays and Fridays in Washington and taking the overnight train there and back, spending the rest of the week in Cambridge, a commute on which Samuelson was soon to join him.

---

a. "By 1939 I had become the first economist in the White House and we were becoming a formidable group. I had recruited Dick Gilbert and his group—V. L. Bassie, Rod Riley, and the rest—for Harry Hopkins at Commerce, which gave support to Bob Nathan, long a lone outpost in hostile territory. I had turned my post at the Federal Reserve over to Emile Despres. I was, I am happy to say, responsible for bringing Ken Galbraith to Washington and for getting Gerhard Colm placed in the Bureau of the Budget, now moved to the Executive Office of the President. Walter and Bill Salant, Griff Johnson, Alan Sweezy, Arthur Gayer, Malcolm Bryan, George Eddy, Albert Hart and Martin Krost were my former students or associates and were occupying key posts. Our position in the Treasury was getting stronger as Harry White gained influence, and we had close working relationships with Gardner Means and Tom Blaisdell in the NRPB and the members of the Board, and with Ezekiel and Louis Bean in Agriculture, with Isador Lubin in Labor and, of course, with Leon Henderson and Jerome Frank in the SEC. Hansen was winning converts outside" (Keyserling et al. 1972, p. 141). This list includes many people with whom Samuelson was to interact during the war.

In Washington, though the immediate problem was meeting the needs of war, Hansen was concerned from the outset with the problem of postwar prosperity.[6] The scale and nature of his activities are shown in a long memorandum he sent to Goldenweiser, a colleague at the Federal Reserve, detailing topics being investigated and interdepartmental conferences that had been held. Staff from the numerous government agencies had discussed various aspects of the defense program and its impact on the economy.[7]

A preliminary report, dated September 25, 1940, included in Hansen's memorandum, made clear both the scale of the problem and the extent of the uncertainty involved. On current plans, defense expenditure was predicted to rise from $4.5 billion in 1941 to $10 billion in 1942 and $9 billion in 1943. In the event of a negotiated peace in which "England emerged as undisputed sea power," these plans would be adequate, as the United States would feel safe even if Germany dominated the European continent. If Germany conquered England, defense spending would need to be higher, possibly $15 billion in 1942 and $25 billion in 1943. However, if the United States entered the war, expenditures might rise rapidly to $40 billion. To put this into perspective, national income in 1940 was estimated to be $74 billion.[8] Hansen concluded that, given these uncertainties, it was hardly worthwhile to try to estimate the effect of the defense program beyond 1942.

Also included in his memorandum was a list of problems for which the Federal Reserve needed to reach conclusions. These included the obvious wartime issues of bottlenecks in specific industries, taxation, federal borrowing, and control of inflation through monetary and other means. At the end, Hansen included a section, "Long Range Planning with Respect to a Post-Defense Slump."[9] Taking the likelihood of a post-defense slump for granted, this section was very sketchy (half a page), focusing on financial issues, and comprising no more than a list of four policies that might be considered. All four policies aimed to increase the flow of purchasing power into the economy once defense spending was reduced.

In May 1941, more than six months after he had flagged the issue in his memorandum at the Federal Reserve, Hansen wrote a paper in which he made the case for what he called "post-defense full employment."[10] It began with a bold statement about why military victory alone was insufficient; there was a need to plan for peace.

> The immediate war aim is to defeat Hitler and to preserve and safe-
> guard political freedom. But a military victory for the democracies is
> not enough. If the victorious democracies muddle through another

decade of economic frustration and mass unemployment, we may expect social disintegration and another international conflagration.

A positive program of postwar economic expansion and full employment, boldly conceived and set forth in a vigorous manifesto, is the only thing that can touch off any spark of mass enthusiasm at all comparable to Wilson's "Fourteen Points." Such a manifesto would awaken a tremendous popular response in this country, in England, and in the conquered countries.[11]

National income could be raised to $100 billion during the war, but because very different goods needed to be produced in peace and war, and because it would take time to retrain people and fit them into new types of productive work, planning was needed to make sure that national income did not fall when the war ended.

Hansen analyzed the problem using national income. In 1940, national income of $75 billion had been divided: $66 billion for consumption, $8 billion for investment (including inventories and foreign investment), and $3 billion for defense. He estimated that, given population and productivity growth, potential output would be at least $100 billion in 1943–44. If consumption per head remained at its 1940 level, consumption would take $65 billion of this. Investment could be reduced to $5 billion, leaving $30 billion for defense. If full employment were to be maintained after the war, when defense spending fell sharply, other sources of spending would have to rise. He sketched a scenario in which defense spending fell to $10 billion (including $3 to $4 billion for international reconstruction), investment rose to $10 billion to cover restocking and investment in housing, leaving $80 billion for consumption. He then analyzed the sources of the extra $15 billion for consumer spending and its implications for the federal budget deficit, making assumptions about taxes on consumer goods and corporate profits. By 1947, after the transition from war to peace, defense spending (including international contributions) should be down to $3 billion; and if potential national income had by then risen to $110 billion, and investment rose to $12 billion, then consumption needed to rise to $95 billion.

These were hardly forecasts, for they did no more than indicate the scale of the problem. However, they indicated a clear program for post-defense policy, all geared to maintaining consumption at the required levels. This created a need for a considerable program of public spending, requiring that the federal government keep a shelf of public investment projects ready to be implemented when the need arose.[12] The political implications of such analysis, based on simple calculations of national income, are obvious. It shows, moreover, that Hansen perceived the central problem in relation to post-defense planning to be maintaining consumption at a high level.

Though Samuelson had been involved in Hansen's work, he had remained in Cambridge for 1940 and much of 1941, outside the Washington circles in which ideas on maintaining full employment through regulation of saving and investment were being worked out. His entry into Washington circles came through the NRPB.[13] The NRPB originated in the National Planning Board (NPB), set up by Harold Ickes in 1933 as part of the Public Works Administration. Chaired by Frederic Delano, Roosevelt's uncle and an experienced planner, its other members were Wesley Mitchell, economist and founder of the National Bureau of Economic Research, and Charles Merriam, a political scientist from Chicago, its objective was to bring scientific thinking to bear on social and political problems. In 1934, this became a presidential board, comprising the secretaries of key government agencies, but with an advisory committee comprising Delano, Mitchell, and Merriam in active charge of the work. In 1939, Congress then reestablished the NPB as the NRPB, and as part of the Executive Office of the President. The main functions of the board were to advise the president and improve communication between different government agencies. To this end, the NRPB produced numerous reports, prepared by its own staff and outside consultants. Some were printed (and published) and some mimeographed, but all were based on extensive statistical data. Most of these covered the staples of planning, from transportation to urban and regional development, and from natural resource management to conservation.

The NRPB also produced reports on how to avoid unemployment. In April 1937, Ickes, Merriam, and Beardsley Ruml had persuaded Roosevelt to agree to a survey of consumption spending, in order to be able to achieve "a more balanced economy," which resulted, after interviews with 300,000 households, in the construction of new, highly detailed statistics, published in three reports, in 1938, 1939, and 1941.[14] These reports revealed not only patterns of consumption spending but also the distribution of income, including the conclusions that most Americans were relatively poor and that most income was in the hands of a relatively small minority.[15] One of the most marked findings concerned savings: households with incomes below $1,250 a year had negative saving, whereas at the other extreme, households with over $20,000 saved 40 percent of their income.[b] In November 1940, the

_____

b. Recognizing that the survey covered a period (1935–36) when incomes were abnormally low, the reports focused on normal income as influencing expenditure. It should, therefore, not be surprising that Samuelson's analysis of consumption in this period (see

NRPB published a further report, prepared by John Kenneth Galbraith, on the effects of public works spending.

Thus when, in September 1939, with the outbreak of war in Europe, the NRPB turned to what it called "post-defense planning," it had a body of data on which it could draw.[c] At first, planning for the postwar world was controversial, for even Roosevelt thought this was looking too far ahead. However, in November 1940, Roosevelt authorized the NRPB to work on how to avoid a "post-emergency slump." This was the project for which Samuelson was to be recruited.

The Full-Employment Stabilization Unit

On July 10, 1941, Alvin Hansen wrote Samuelson from the Federal Reserve. Reminding him that he had not yet replied to a previous proposal for research in connection with the NRPB, Hansen wanted to make another suggestion, "perhaps more interesting and more feasible."[16] Drawing on its earlier studies of the distribution of income, the NRPB was trying to work out what the distribution of income would be if full employment were achieved and if family allowances were in place to improve the position of the poorest families. Twisting the income distribution in this way, through raising the incomes of the poor, should reduce the gap between consumption and income. This would build directly on the data for household expenditures collected in the 1930s. Hansen wanted to know whether Samuelson was interested in being a nonresident consultant, advising them on this work. He would have staff working for him in Cambridge, who would criticize the work being done by the NRPB and suggest ways in which it could be improved. He and Thomas Blaisdell at the NRPB were both anxious for Samuelson to be involved.

Samuelson agreed and on July 23, Blaisdell wrote to Samuelson saying that the NRPB was very interested in recruiting him, but it would be a couple of weeks before he could provide details. Samuelson filled in his formal application on August 5, and on August 11 he received a letter confirming his appointment, for not more than fifteen days per month, at a salary of

---

chapters 17 and 20 this volume) contained echoes of what later came to be called the permanent income and lifecycle theories of consumption. Clawson notes that Milton Friedman, the author of the former theory, was on the staff that prepared one study and he assisted with another.

c. The terms "post-defense" and "post-emergency" were in use even though the United States had not yet entered the war and would not do so for another two years.

$12.77 per day's work.[17] His plan was to follow Hansen's example in commuting fortnightly to and from Washington on the overnight train, spending at most one night away from home.[18] When in Washington, he would stay with friends—Erich and Freda Roll (Erich was with the British Supply Mission), John D. Wilson (then with the Office of Strategic Services), and David Lusher (at the Office of Price Administration).[19]

Two weeks later, Samuelson wrote memoranda outlining his project and the resources he would need.[20] He reckoned that he would require one or two senior people with the rank of "economist" or "associate economist" and a further two "assistant economists."[21] These would be based in Washington, and at least one of the senior people would have responsibility for liaison with other units when Samuelson was not present. He also asked to have at least one assistant economist based with him in Cambridge. His conception of the project is shown by his claim that, because it would involve the "use and interpretation of varied statistical data," the most important quality required of these recruits was "imagination sufficient to formulate the right questions and enough ingenuity to dig out the answers."[22] "Specialized high powered theoretical and statistical tools" were less important.

Though Samuelson was proposing to employ people to do further work, he must already have done a significant amount of work on the problem, perhaps as a result of earlier discussions with Hansen. His memorandum, "Consumer Demand at Full Production," could hardly have been written from scratch in a single month.[23] It was based on the assumption that policy should have two aims: to maintain full employment and to substantially reduce poverty. These were connected, for changing the distribution of income in favor of the poor would increase spending, thereby raising the level of demand, and it would also affect the composition of demand. So Samuelson's memorandum addressed the technical question of the types of commodities that people would choose to purchase if there were full employment, by taking consumption patterns of 1935–36, the date of the NRPB's surveys, and projecting them forward to the "objective year" of around 1950 (chosen on the assumption that hostilities would end in 1944). The key assumption was that by 1950, national income would be $125 billion, the result of population growth and technical progress (in 1929, it had been $80 billion), of which $120 billion would accrue to households. Breaking consumers down by income category and location (urban, rural farm, and rural nonfarm), consumer demands were calculated on the assumption that the distribution of income in the objective year would be the same as in 1935–36, modified in one crucial respect: measures would be taken to ensure that no household would have an income below $1,200 a year, this being the level that was considered necessary to cover basic needs. The result of this was that inequality would be significantly reduced; according to their way of measuring inequality, it would be halved.[d]

The rationale for making such estimates was planning. Samuelson drew an explicit analogy between wartime and peacetime planning.

> It is the responsibility of those who direct our armed forces to say what is needed under modern conditions in guns, tanks, airplanes, warships and munitions. Essential to the production of those implements are the necessary raw materials, productive plant, labor force, energy resources, and transportation facilities. Our organizing and productive genius must then turn its attention to the things that must be done in order to provide us with the required instruments of defense.[24]

Samuelson then continued by claiming that "[t]he same technique could be utilized in providing for consumer satisfactions—the fundamental purpose of our peace time economy." It was not necessary to "provide all Americans with an American standard of living," so "a production goal might be set by a more or less arbitrary determination of what Americans need and ought to have." If it was to be democratic (unlike planning being undertaken elsewhere), it would "preserve as large a measure of consumer choice as possible."

Samuelson's memorandum suggested a method of planning that was consistent with consumer choice, and in an appendix he provided a checklist of what needed to be done:[25]

I. Set up the bill of goods, the men, the machines.
II. Define the transitional requirements.
III. Design the programs for moving toward the objectives.
IV. Explore the usefulness of directives already available to government.

This was a very wide-ranging program, involving detailed planning of the entire economy and a spectrum of government policies, from vocational training and the maintenance of purchasing power, to housing, education, and recreation programs. One of its remarkable features is the centrality of income distribution to the analysis. It was sufficiently important for Samuelson to include an appendix that explained how to calculate a curve showing the cumulative distribution of income across consumer units, and another that provided thirty pages of tables of the distribution of various types of spending across consumer units. His project was closely connected to Hansen's

---

d. The Lorenz curve would be shifted almost halfway toward the line of perfect equality.

work, and he described Hansen's memorandum on "Post-Defense Full Employment" as "a masterly statement of the problem."[26] Points Samuelson covered included the need to take account of the distribution of income in working out how government spending would affect demand, and the problems with creating enough opportunities for private investment.

The economist with whom Samuelson was to work most closely at the NRPB was Oscar Altman, head of the Full Employment Stabilization Unit, to which Samuelson was attached. Six years older than Samuelson, he had overlapped with Samuelson in Chicago where he had been a graduate student, obtaining his PhD in 1936.[27] His thesis had been related to taxation and the law, two chapters being published in a law review, though by the end of the war he had acquired training in statistics, publishing an actuarial analysis of the life of B-29 aircraft engines.[28] As an NRPB staff member he had been responsible, in May 1939, for writing up the deliberations of the TNEC concerning saving and investment. In *Saving, Investment and National Income*,[29] published as Monograph 37 in the TNEC series on the distribution of economic power, Altman baldly asserted that saving and investment were the two main determinants of national income, and that *all* witnesses agreed that "savings had to be returned to the income stream—spent for investment goods or in other ways offset" if national income were to be maintained. As an example, he cited Hansen's testimony in support.

> It is highly essential that all that part of the current flow of income which is not expended on consumption goods, namely that part which is saved, shall be expended either directly by the saver himself or indirectly through a borrower on new plant and equipment of some sort. If the amount which is saved is large, as it is likely to be at a high income level, it is necessary that equally large outlets be available for these savings in equipment and plant expansion, and in residential and public construction.[30]

As befits a report for a committee on the distribution of economic power, Altman's statistics sought to analyze who was doing the most saving, with statistics on business saving, government saving, and saving by households with different incomes. Concentration of national income was one of the main factors determining saving. Concentration was also a factor he analyzed when considering how savings were transmitted to investors—notably concentration in financial institutions associated with the institutionalization of saving through pensions and life insurance companies—and in discussing the direction of investment. Investment was, he concluded, more concentrated than it had been twenty years before, a conclusion backed up with many tables that showed the distribution of saving and investment between businesses of different sizes. This increased concentration made savings institutions more liquid and implied an uneven flow of saving into different sectors. In his conclusions, Altman made the case that investment was needed as an offset to saving, irrespective of whether it could be made to yield an income.

Samuelson and Altman were responsible for a small part of the NRPB's planning activities. When listing the planning tasks being performed, NRPB director Charles Elliott categorized them as concerned solely with "consumer market, etc." under the general heading of "Private Activity," which itself was listed as one of eight "substantive programs."[31] Separate sections dealt with programs such as demobilization of manpower and machines, industry, and the public sector. "Finance and fiscal problems" were allocated to Hansen. It was therefore crucial to ensure that there was coordination between the activities of different units within the NRPB. It was also essential to liaise with other agencies, both to get information and to coordinate their activities. The NRPB had no authority to "assign" work to any other agency, though some agencies were required to report their activities to it.

One route through which Samuelson became involved with other agencies was that of regular conferences, such as one apparently chaired by Hansen at the NRPB on October 30, a few weeks after he had begun his fortnightly visits to Washington. It involved representatives from the Bureau of Agricultural Economics, the Bureau of Labor Statistics, and the Bureau of Foreign and Domestic Commerce, as well as Hansen, listed as representing the Federal Reserve Board, and Samuelson for the NRPB.[32] The purpose of the meeting was to exchange information about research that would shed light on postwar readjustment. Lest anyone thought that their concern was solely with the volume of investment, Hansen made it clear that they were concerned with "capital improvement of all kinds." In order that there should be continuing contact, they agreed to meet every other Thursday at 11:30, and to continue over lunch afterward. There was then a review of research being undertaken in the different departments represented.

The Commerce Department was preparing a breakdown of gross national product into sixty-three categories, and was planning work on the expansion of investment by private industry. The Bureau of Foreign and Domestic Commerce was planning a study of foreign trade patterns at full employment. The National Economic Unit was planning to investigate how much investment would be undertaken at different levels of income. The Bureau of Labor Statistics was studying the composition of employment and the employment effects of the defense program, and was planning studies of the cost of living (subject to available funding). The minutes of the meeting described Samuelson's project in more detail:

> Mr. Samuelson is directing a project that will begin by making vary-
> ing assumptions about income distribution under a stalemate econ-
> omy, high consumption economy, a redistributed income economy,
> and a full employment economy. Income distribution is a first step in
> projecting consumer purchasing under each of these conditions. Then
> it is expected to approach the needed levels of private capital forma-
> tion from this angle.[33]

It is not clear how much coordination of research work took place as a result of the meeting, but it will have provided Samuelson with a much clearer picture of what Washington economists were doing than he could have gotten by working in any single department.

The first task facing Altman and Samuelson was to recruit staff, and so in August and September Samuelson approached possible candidates and departments who might have recent doctoral students whom they could suggest.[34] One list of thirty possible names shows that he was considering people currently working in other agencies, as well as people still in universities, and that many of these were unavailable. In several cases this was because they might be called for military service.[35] It was not the best time of year, as many potential recruits were already committed. The secretary at Chicago's Economics Department reported that one of the two people Samuelson asked about had an academic post, and the other had gone to the Bureau of the Budget.[36] Howard Ellis, at the University of California, Berkeley, wrote, "So many of my students have recently gone into government service, or into academic positions left vacant by the migration to Washington that I have only one suggestion."[37] Walt Rostow and Rutledge Vining both expressed interest, but explained why they could not be involved.[38] Word that Samuelson was looking for people got around, and he had people approach him,[39] but in October he would tell George Jaszi and the Federal Reserve that he was "still desperately hunting for competent economists who can qualify for a Civil Service rating."[40] On December 11, Altman was able to report that within a few days they would be in a position to recommend at least half the necessary appointments.[41]

If the work were to be completed on time, it would be necessary to hire the others within a few weeks. By December 30, Altman had found eight people to work on the project, an increase in the numbers Samuelson had proposed in the summer, most of whom were transferred from other government agencies or from other activities within the NRPB.[42] His attempts to recruit outsiders from universities seem to have come to nothing, and it was probably Altman, with more extensive contacts in Washington, who found people, though Samuelson was involved in interviewing and selecting them. The job description of one of the senior recruits was:

> To prepare and direct, under general supervision, studies in the patterns of consumption and public and private investment at various levels of national income; to investigate past and prospective trends in these patterns; to conduct studies in the distribution of individual and corporate income at various levels of national income, and to advise junior members of staff with respect to statistical source materials and methods of analysis and presentation.[43]

Junior recruits had similar duties except that their responsibility was to assist rather than direct such work.[44]

Preparing a Report

In the first months of the project, Samuelson and Altman consulted widely. In addition to those at the October 30 meeting, they were in touch with economists at the Bureau of the Budget, the Department of Labor, the Office of Price Administration (OPA), the Securities and Exchange Commission, and the Board of Economic Warfare.[e] These consultations, Altman claimed, confirmed the importance of their work, for studies of consumer demand were considered basic both to maintaining full employment and to understanding the problems of transition.[45] Their own work up to March 1942 entailed the analysis of basic statistics. Their basic data on consumer income and expenditure came from previous reports, so they had reviewed the criticisms of these published in academic journals. This had revealed, among other problems, that the Bureau of the Budget's estimates of incomes in the higher income brackets (always a problem because samples were inevitably small) were clearly wrong and that these errors affected the whole of the income distribution.[46] So they had recalculated household income data on the basis of more recent evidence; they had examined corporate saving, studied forecasts made by the Department of Agriculture, and examined work on rural–urban migration. All of these

---

e. Gerhard Colm, Leontief, Hildegaard Kneeland, Raymond Goldsmith, and Louis Bean, respectively.

would form the basis for their estimates of the distribution of income in the "objective year."[47]

As part of his response to a request from the NRPB director for a progress report, Altman provided a detailed rationale for their work.[48] Clearly, their results would assist more specialized planning. He emphasized that their work would inform not just government but the American people as a whole, for it would give them an understanding of the roles of government, business, and individuals in maintaining full employment. People would thus be able to make better choices about how best to achieve full employment. Such objectives no doubt meshed with the work by Charles Merriam, in another part of the NRPB, on democratic planning. To achieve this objective, there would be a need for research on matters beyond consumer spending. Altman argued that there was a need for studies of corporate saving, the issue of bonds and equities by companies, and the behavior of financial institutions (the last two being important in the channel through which saving flowed into investment), the demand for investment goods, and the production side of the economy (to translate demand for goods into production and employment in different sectors). If their unit was to achieve this, he and Samuelson would be taking on tasks that went beyond their initial remit of analyzing consumer spending.

An illustration of the way that their work was expanding beyond determining consumer spending is provided in a memorandum Samuelson sent to Blaisdell on March 24, 1942, titled "Expansion in Non-Essential Civilian Capacity."[49] This was concerned only indirectly with full-employment consumption, for it addressed the problem of what would happen during the war, as the economy approached full capacity. Up to now, Samuelson argued, the various sectors of the economy had been able to expand together. Thus, despite the massive increase in defense spending, one in six tons of steel had gone into automobile production in 1941. Production of consumer durables was higher than ever before. He might well have had Leontief's input–output analysis in mind when he wrote, "In a thousand ways the system is geared to move forward together, each component waiting on the slowest." However, now that full employment was being approached, this would no longer be possible, and some activities would have to be restricted. It was vital to ensure that non-essential activities did not use resources that were useful for war production. For example, most consumer durables competed for resources with war production. He proposed a number of specific measures that could be taken, including control of inventories and discriminatory qualitative credit controls.

A few days after writing this memorandum, Samuelson agreed to write something that could form part of a memorandum on the control of investment, a piece titled "Investment in 1941 and the Business Inflationary Gap in 1942." The terminology of the inflationary gap, worked out by Keynes for the analysis of British inflation, was widely used at this time to denote the gap between the total demand for resources and what was available, the assumption being that such a gap would lead to price rises.[f] His primary concern, however, was not with the problem of inflation per se but with how much investment would be choked off by shortages of construction materials and other goods.[50] He hoped that Mordecai Ezekiel in the Department of Agriculture, and two of those in his unit, would be able to shed light on what would normally be invested. A note records one of his staff, Goodman, having contacted the Commerce Department for an explanation of their statistics on inventories. That this was being done at a fairly disaggregated level is shown by a memorandum in which one of their team calculated that 2.4 percent of the output of pig iron went directly toward consumer goods.[51]

The project faced a potential crisis in April 1942, when Altman thought he might have to leave the NRPB to join the air force. Clearly, an experienced economist would be needed to replace him, and he approached Albert Hart, whom he and Samuelson had known in Chicago, about whether he would be interested.[52] Hart responded favorably to the idea of taking on the work, but was not enthusiastic about moving to Washington. It was important, he argued, that teams of economists outside Washington be kept up to strength, and were free to criticize what was going on there. For this reason, he thought it would be wrong to abandon his department at Iowa State University. However, might it make sense, he asked, to transfer the whole project to Ames, Iowa? It would fit with the policy of decentralization, staff might like to move out of Washington, and Ames made sense in that the university was the chief center for "consumption economics," so the project would have a lot of support.[53] Hart made an even stronger case when he visited Washington on April 23—including that he might be able to attract Martin Bronfenbrenner, then in Chicago, to Ames—and Altman put the proposal to Blaisdell the next day. Nothing came of the idea, presumably because Altman's draft position changed and he was able to remain at the NRPB. Though Altman recommended that Blaisdell consider it very seriously, it is hard to see how it could have worked, for commuting to Ames would have been harder than commuting to Washington, and even more

---

f. The pervasiveness of inflation gap analysis is shown by the fact that Milton Friedman (1942), though he doubted the concept would be useful in peacetime, considered it a useful tool for wartime planning.

important, Altman and members of his unit relied on being in frequent contact with other agencies.

In May, they managed to get the services of the first of the academic economists whom Samuelson had hoped to recruit the previous year. Abram Bergson was hired for three months, starting June 1, to work on a specific part of the consumption study. In addition to assisting with the general tasks of the unit relating to consumption at different levels of national income, he had the task of undertaking much more disaggregated analysis: he was required to supervise or carry out studies of: "(1) the distribution of income in various fields of business enterprises and industrial activity, (2) the distribution of income by geographical area, and (3) the distribution of income by individuals and families."[54]

The way the project was developing is shown by a contents list for the material that Samuelson hoped they could "whip into shape" for the annual report, summarizing their work.[55] It comprised four sections: whether there would be a boom or depression after the war; the financial situation of businesses and families during and after the war; the distribution of income, saving, and spending after the war; and policy implications. A draft of the first section had already been completed on May 28.[56] In it they questioned the claim, sometimes made, that demobilization after the First World War showed that planning was unnecessary.

Over the summer, Bergson began to make an input into the program. On July 7, he sent members of the unit a critique of a consumption function that Ezekiel had published in a recent issue of the *American Economic Review*, arguing that it was flawed: it did not use appropriate, or even consistent, definitions of saving and investment, he worked in current dollars, and he had not justified the use of a time trend.[57] All pointed to things the unit needed to do better. A progress report submitted at the end of the month showed him playing a major role in the supervision of research in the unit. In addition to supervising the work of junior colleagues, he had written a memorandum on John Dunlop's work on cyclical variations in the structure of wages and on Joseph Pechman's thesis on how changes in income were linked to distribution, and he was investigating the relationship between marginal and average propensities to save at different income levels. He outlined a list of eight projects that someone, not necessarily himself, should undertake.

That month, Goodman reported a conversation with a member of the Progressive Urban Planning Section of the NRPB, out of which arose a number of suggestions that would have broadened the activities of the Full Employment Stabilization Unit in the direction of giving a broader picture of the likely economic situation after the war.[58] Goodman also reported on activities being undertaken elsewhere in the NRPB that they might find useful.[59]

A draft of the report covering this work, *Studies in Wartime Planning for Continuing Full Employment*, was completed in August.[60] It was a report by the staff of the Full Employment Stabilization Unit, ten of whom were listed, Altman (head of the unit) and Samuelson (consultant) appearing at the top of the list. However, in his bibliography, Samuelson listed it as jointly written by himself and Everett Hagen, one of the three senior economists under Altman and Samuelson. It is not clear whether this means they drafted most of it together or whether, given that Samuelson had apparently drafted the first section, the drafting of the rest of it was by Hagen. However, there seems no reason to doubt that it was a report to which the entire unit had contributed.

The report followed the table of contents Samuelson had proposed to Eliot back in June, and it started by examining the experience of demobilization after 1918. There had been a small boom immediately after the war, but that was because, in economic terms, the war had not ended in 1918, even though fighting stopped then. Many government contracts had to be completed—ship construction, for example, carried on after hostilities had ended—and the government was committed to payments for veterans. The result was that "government deficit expenditure of a magnitude approaching that of the last year of the war prevented economic distress during the demobilization period, and that too early discontinuance of that support resulted in depression."[61] It went on to argue that there were significant differences between the wars: the current war was total war, whereas the previous one had been only partial, with only a quarter of national income going to the war effort and without the need, until the last two months, to curtail consumption. Because mobilization had been greater in the present war, demobilization would be more difficult, creating many structural problems. There was also the problem that, unlike the situation in 1917, because there had been prolonged depression before the war, there was no expectation of continued growth after the war.

Unemployment after the Second World War would depend on the level of demand, and so they devoted much of their report to estimates of consumption spending, adopting a disaggregated approach as in the previous work on which they drew, and exploring the effects of different ways of making the distribution of income more equal. The report argued that investment would not rise sufficiently to maintain full employment, because there had been a massive increase in plant and equipment during the war. The conclusion reached was that, in the absence of government intervention, there might be unemployment after the war. Because industry would not have had time to adapt to producing the consumer goods that would be in immediate demand after the war, scarcity of consumer goods might lead to price rises. Their forecast was of "large-scale unemployment accompanied by price inflation" unless price controls continued.[62] In a section provocatively entitled "Raising our Sights," the report expressed the view that

> The war has taught us what levels of national income, consumption, and investment are within our grasp if we pay attention to economic essentials instead of to economic shibboleths. If public policy after the war is devoted to maintaining employment and economic opportunity, ... the American people will be able to have within this decade national incomes one third larger than in 1941 and twice as large as in the middle thirties.[63]

It argued for spending on things such as veterans bonuses to maintain incomes, but was cautious about lowering taxes: corporation and excess profits taxes should come down from their wartime rates, but these should be kept at levels that were "high compared to pre-war standards."[64] The reason was the need not only to maintain incomes but also to reduce inequality. The report also argued that defense spending should be tapered off gradually and that the Public Works Reserve should be recreated.[g]

Wartime Planning for Continuing Full Employment was mimeographed, with a smaller circulation than had it been published. Producing the report in this way was consistent with the NRPB's task as making available "confidential 'ever current recommendations' for activities to stabilize employment and maintain a high national income, to be continuously filled out and improved month by month, as long as the war lasts."[65]

The interim report was sent out for review, and no fewer than nineteen people offered criticisms and suggestions.[66] Many readers approved of the report, though most of them found points of disagreement or places where the exposition needed improvement. One of the most critical was George Stigler, whose views were summarized in an internal memorandum:

> The report in its present form is not suited to governmental publication according to George Stigler who also "differs strongly from the author's implicit political and social views." He also states "that there

---

g. The Public Works Reserve was a scheme for maintaining a reserve of public works projects that could be implemented during a depression so as to alleviate high unemployment.

are too many cases where statements are made which are with your facilities capable either of proof or disproof."[67]

The memorandum did not elaborate on what these social and political views were or what statements should be tested. The first section, on previous experience, was best received by the reviewers, though even this was criticized. Harold Moulton of the Brookings Institution, who had previously written a critical review of Keynes's *General Theory*, considered it fallacious to argue that the fluctuations in government spending controlled the level of activity, for this argument failed to take account of the fact that aggregate purchasing power was the result of both private and government spending; he did not accept that they had moved together after the First World War.[68] Jacob Marschak, of the New School for Social Research, made a similar comment in that he thought the section suggested excessive reliance on "net government spending," though he thought that this defect had been corrected in later sections of the report. He found the section on the transition to peace after the First World War, and the comparisons with the current war, "particularly illuminating" and thought it would "obviously have very great practical use."[69]

Criticism of other parts of the report can be seen as paying tribute to the ambitious nature of the task that had been undertaken, given the unsettled state of economic theory at the time. For example, Marschak questioned the assumptions about how demand would respond to price changes. An interesting comment was made by Samuelson's Harvard friend Paul Sweezy, a Marxist, who criticized the perspective underlying the policy analysis in the final section.

> When it comes to prescribing solutions to economic problems, the authors seem to assume that all that is required is a proper analysis and the indicated cure will naturally be adopted. In other words economic problems are treated as essentially technical problems; that they are also social and political problems which arise from and are inextricably bound up with a given social structure of class power and class aims does not enter the picture. [These] seem to me to be definite limits on the scope of the report.[70]

The overall verdict would seem to be that the interim report needed considerably more work before it became the final report. It could be that it was because he had heard some of these criticisms that Hansen made the somewhat defensive suggestion that Goldenweiser tell Delano "that Mr. Hansen has had a number of conferences with Messrs. Blaisdell and Samuelson on the report and that he has offered extensive comments and criticisms."[71] Samuelson might be the academic consultant responsible for the report, but Hansen was following it closely.

The Public Face of the NRPB

If the NRPB had merely produced confidential reports for use within government, it would have been less likely to provoke strong political opposition. However, the reports that entered the public domain when transmitted to Congress, and the pamphlets it published, gave it a high and controversial public profile. The most controversial reports were those on unemployment policy, to which the work of the Full Employment Stabilization Unit was related, even where they were not directly involved in writing them. During the time Samuelson was a consultant, the NRPB published *Security, Work and Relief Policies*, prepared under the direction of Eveline Burns and presented to President Roosevelt on December 4, 1941, but not transmitted to Congress until February 10, 1943.[72] Its message was reinforced by the *National Resources Development: Report for 1943*.[73] The first of these was politically controversial, for it made the case for a wide-ranging system of social welfare provision. The introduction makes clear that it was a political as much as a technical document.

> This report is concerned particularly with making adequate provision for those who have no means of livelihood or only inadequate means. Some of the causes of suffering are personal in character.... But the suffering which comes from economic maladjustment is just as real as that which comes from personal.... It is sometimes alleged that a complete system of social security would ultimately have the effect of discouraging self-reliance and even fostering unemployment by destroying the incentives to industry, by removing the rough but salutary influence of discipline. There are doubtless some marginal persons who would deliberately choose to avoid work even if guaranteed a minimum subsistence. But these must be balanced against the millions of cases where deep anxiety, haunting fear of want, acute suffering and distress blight and sear the lives of men and women, and children too. Most of the drifting souls are those on whom the door of hope has been closed either by nature's equipment or by the unfortunate circumstances of unkind social experience.[74]

The report argued forcefully for measures to ensure a minimum level of income.

> Discipline that is enforced by deprivation of the elementary necessaries of life, the discipline of cold, hunger, illness, should not be permitted to operate below the level of a minimum standard of security, certainly not in a land of plenty where there is enough to go around. Above that level, it is not fear but hope that moves men to greater expenditures of effort, to ingenuity and emulation, to sharp struggle for the values they seek in life—hope set in a framework of justice, liberty, fair play, and a fair share of the gains of civilization.[75]

To achieve this, it recommended both measures to ensure full employment, public assistance for those whose incomes are interrupted, and public provision of health, education, and welfare for those who need it. This would require coordinated activity, involving fiscal and monetary policy, by the federal government. The two volumes of the *Report for 1943* tied this vision into the practicalities of postwar planning, a task which, they argued, could not wait. The political nature of this program was made explicit when the report explained about how planning had to be undertaken in a democracy: "There is at the heart of tyranny and autocracy in our day ... an internal conflict which cannot be resolved and which leads inevitably to weakness and disintegration.... Trying to use reason as a tool for injustice, violence, inequality, slavery, leads in the end to revolution."[76]

There seems little question that *Security, Work and Relief Policies* was tied up with the fate of the NRPB. It is possible that Roosevelt thought the report would be politically useful in reassuring the American people that the United States was releasing a report comparable with William Beverage's *Social Insurance and Allied Services*[77]—the report that laid the foundations for the British postwar welfare state. However, whereas the Beveridge report proved so popular that British governments were under great pressure to implement its recommendations, the reaction to its American counterpart was very different, and its publication may have weakened the position of the NRPB. One historian of the NRPB has contended that the delay in publishing the report until after Beveridge's report made it easier for Congress to reject it as involving a "socialistic," "cradle-to-grave" program of planning.[78] As Samuelson became more closely associated with Hansen and the NRPB, he inevitably became associated with such ideas.

In order to reach an audience that would not read reports transmitted to Congress, the NRPB published pamphlets. In January 1942, they had published a pamphlet by Alvin Hansen, *After the War—Full Employment* (1942a), in which he argued the case for using the federal budget to stabilize the level of demand; public debt, he contended, was not something to fear, but an instrument of government policy. In the words of one historian,

> This pamphlet, almost as much as any other NRPB publication, aroused fierce and emotional criticism, in the Congress, in the business world, and in at least part of the press. Senator Robert Taft, then the leading Republican intellectual and a powerful figure in the Senate, was particularly incensed by it.[79]

In September of the same year, they published another pamphlet, *Post-War Planning—Full Employment, Security, Building America,* which, following up on Roosevelt's call for "four freedoms" on January 6, 1941, argued for a new Bill of Rights, which would be the basis for the postwar planning strategy.[80] As one historian has put it, "just as the Four Freedoms speech represented FDR's response to fascist ideology and aggression overseas, so the planners' document represented their view of domestic American liberal democracy at home."[81] Those rights included economic rights: to work; to fair pay; to adequate food; to clothing, housing and medical care; to freedom from fear of old age, want, dependency, sickness, unemployment and accident; and to education. The right to live in a system of free enterprise was framed so as to restrain private business as well as government, for it carried the rider, "free from compulsory labor, irresponsible private power, arbitrary public authority, and unregulated monopolies."[82] The aim was not just to summarize existing rights but to extend them "through planning and cooperative action." Two months later, this statement was further publicized by being summarized graphically on a single, folded sheet of paper. The proposed Bill of Rights was also printed at the beginning of the *Report for 1943,* emphasizing its connection with the planning process.[83]

On August 21, 1942, after their report had been drafted, three members of Samuelson's unit (Bergson, Goodman, and Hagen) proposed to Blaisdell that they capitalize on the studies their unit had done by writing a series of pamphlets that would follow on from Hansen's by covering postwar economic problems.[84] They justified this by arguing that their results could be made generally accessible, and that in addition to providing much-needed teaching materials on a topical issue, would help inform the public—an important task in a democracy. They proposed ten titles, ranging from "The National Income at Full Employment" to "A Conversion Crisis after the War?"[85] At this time, the funding of the NRPB was in question, but Blaisdell took the line that they should proceed on the assumption that funds would be forthcoming.[86] Bergson soon moved to the Office of Strategic Services (OSS), working on Russia, but in his final fortnight at the NRPB he tried hard to get the first pamphlet under way.[87] Bergson may have achieved this, for on September 15, the date when Bergson moved to the OSS, Hagen circulated an outline pamphlet on national income in 1950 to his colleagues for criticism.[88]

Samuelson was not named in any of these publications, but he was known to be a consultant for the NRPB, and materials expressing radical ideas were coming out of the unit with which he was associated. The result was that by the end of 1942, some outsiders were already associating Samuelson with advocacy of high public spending after the war. One of Samuelson's former students, in a junior position at the OPA, wrote,

> A professor friend of mine working down here in Washington read something put out recently by NRPB, dealing with the post-war economic organization of the U.S. Your hand was in it. He said the authors had gone "hog-wild" for government spending after the war. I haven't read the report, but I thought you'd be interested in his reactions.[89]

Any doubts about Samuelson's association with these ideas would have been dispelled the following June, when the NRPB published a pamphlet based on the first section of the interim report—*After the War: 1918–1920*, written by Samuelson and Hagen.[90] Perhaps they chose this section to publish because it was the part of the report that had the best reception from the critics to whom it had been sent. Though clearly drawing on the first section of their report and containing the same message—namely, that the experience of 1918–20 demonstrated the need for planning the transition, not the success of unplanned markets—it was very different in character, suggesting they had learned from their critics.

After explaining the importance of learning from past experience, the pamphlet began with a history of America's involvement in the First World War, in which it is possible to discern traces of both *Economic Consequences of the Peace*, the book in which Keynes made his reputation by attacking the Treaty of Versailles after the First World War, and the ideas about secular stagnation that Hansen was proposing.[91]

> The days before 1914 were far enough away to seem Utopian in retrospect, so that one could speak glibly of a return to "normalcy." Those with more accurate memories might have known that in 1914 there were signs that the world was about to enter upon a depression period and that, but for the World War, the Wilson administration might

have had to face the same type of problems which were to become acute only two decades later.[92]

The war had saved the United States from depression. As Keynes had argued two decades earlier, Samuelson and Hagen argued that the return to "normalcy" for which people longed was impossible. Hansen's ideas were reflected in their analysis of how the recovery from postwar depression took place: Recovery required something to drive investment. They then took up Hansen's idea (discussed in chapter 12 this volume) that, with the closing of the frontier, slower population growth, and without new industries to drive investment, depressions would become more common and would last longer. The pamphlet documented the extreme haste with which demobilization had taken place after the First World War. Everyone was anxious to get the troops home, and military contracts were cancelled as soon as possible. The result was a hard winter in 1918–19, with much open and disguised unemployment. Production rose in 1919–20, but this was accompanied by inflation, with prices rising 25 percent above their wartime peak, before both collapsed in 1920–21. Possibly aware of the way their interim report had been criticized, they illustrated this with charts showing the course of production, employment, and prices.

They could then turn to the heart of the report: the analysis of causes. There had been depression after the war, but though it was bad (it would have seemed worse had there been statistics to measure the rise in unemployment), it had been short-lived. The depression of 1920–21 had also been very short-lived, apparently vindicating those who thought government need do nothing to ease readjustment. Responding to critics of their interim report, they paid much attention to factors other than the government deficit. They sought to undermine the argument that after the war there was "deferred demand" that could sustain expansion by pointing out that, in 1919, households saved more despite a fall in income. The brief prosperity of 1919–20 was not driven by consumer expenditure.

Government spending was part of the answer. A chart vividly illustrated the government deficit, which remained until well into 1919. Even when the deficit had been eliminated, government spending remained high. Samuelson and Hagen concluded that though this was not intentional, government spending and the deficit had "prevented demobilization from causing national income to spiral viciously downward and had caused the upturn in early 1919," when other factors came into play.[93] Exports rose more than imports, and there was a burst of speculative activity, including a massive rise in inventories. There were bottlenecks in production and transportation, and shortages as well as financial and real estate speculation. Much of this was linked to rising prices and easy credit conditions (in which the Federal Reserve resorted to ineffective warnings to member banks not to fund speculative activity). It was thus not surprising when the recovery in 1919–20 collapsed. A graph was used to show the dramatic decline in world trade, worst in Europe, which contributed to depression in the United States.

The pamphlet closed with a comparison of the First World War and what was currently happening, arguing that the problems of readjustment were going to be worse. The scale of the war effort was much larger; the government deficit was much higher; many industries were more fully mobilized for wartime production, and some civilian industries had been shut down completely. If government action had been essential in avoiding catastrophe after the First World War, it was even more important at this time. Perhaps recognizing the political sensitivity of the issue, they focused very much on the *immediate* problem of reconversion.

> *Whatever one's belief as to long-run issues*, it will be agreed that at the end of this war there is a great danger of a critical short-run period in which employment and incomes must fall. Clearly industry and Government should do everything possible to maintain minimum income standards by means of dismissal wages, unemployment compensation, demobilization bonuses payable in installments, and direct and work relief. *Even though the desirability of long-run public works may be debatable*, none can deny the pressing urgency of providing a shelf of short-run useful public and private projects of the "filler" variety, devised to provide employment in the demobilization and reconversion crises.[94]

Their prognosis was for simultaneous inflation and unemployment.

> *We shall have a boom and a slump simultaneously.* There is every indication that the end of the war will let us in for a "spotty" period, with all of the superficial aspects of a boom—inflationary pressure on prices, shortages, attempted inventory accumulation—at the same time that we shall have all the disadvantages of a depression involving dislocations of manpower and plant, losses, unemployment, and less than potentially obtainable real income.[95]

Given their Hansenian perspective, they clearly believed that government would have to play a role in the longer term, as when they noted that there was "a need for new conceptions and responsibilities on the part of both private and public enterprises," but they played this down in the interests of focusing on the immediate postwar problem.[96]

In his work for the NRPB, Samuelson had immersed himself in the problems of data analysis and had organized a substantial team to tackle a far more elaborate and complicated problem than he had previously tackled. The extent of the criticisms made of the interim report must have been a setback, indicating the need for further work that, given the uncertainties over the future of the NPRB, might never be undertaken. The pamphlet he wrote with Hagen drew on this work, but avoided the technicalities, and soft-pedaling the more radical ideas found in the writings of Hansen and the NRPB, it represented a highly polished analysis of First World War experience and its implications for the present. It relied on neither formal statistical analysis, such as he had used a few years earlier in his analysis of the consumption function, nor complex forecasting models, such as those used to make projections of consumer demand after the war. It relied on simpler data analysis and a historical narrative.

The following year Samuelson claimed, in correspondence with Walter Salant at the OPA, that the pamphlet's main purpose had been to debunk "the generally held views concerning the postwar boomlet."[97] He thought it had achieved this purpose, but he knew it had shortcomings, due as much to lack of data as to interpretation of the facts that they did have. His letter to Salant also explained that he did not think there was a direct relationship between aggregate demand and price changes.

> For some time I have been distrustful of analyses which try to relate too closely the rate and direction of price changes to demand factors alone. Too little or too much demand operates as a permissive factor and it creates the environment which shapes price-setting and wage-fixing. But it is often changes in wages and prices (other people's costs) which [are] the direct or proximate cause of price increase. From this point of view it would probably not be difficult to specify a number of physical (shortages, transportation) and psychological (industrial unrest, postwar fatigue, etc.) factors making for price increases at this time.[98]

The result was that price rises would be uneven.

The pamphlet helped to link Samuelson more firmly with Hansen, the NRPB, and the radical policies with which they were associated. He and Hagen may have expressed their views cautiously, but the pamphlet was an NRPB publication advocating planning, which was sufficient to damn it in the eyes of some businessmen and politicians. Moreover, using the same title, "After the War," served to link it to Hansen's highly controversial pamphlet.

This may not have brought him fully into the political arena, but it was a big step nearer. He was becoming more than just a mathematical economist, known only to other economists.

Samuelson reached a different lay audience when he found time to review two books for the trade journal *Mechanical Engineering*. This project originated at MIT, as one of a series of reviews of economic literature affecting engineering by members of the Department of Economics and Social Science, requested by the American Society of Mechanical Engineers. The two books, on the current economic situation and the outlook for the future, were by Stuart Chase, an MIT-trained engineer turned freelance writer who had admired central planning and had been the only highly enthusiastic reader of the report Samuelson's unit at the NRPB had produced a year earlier. Chase said much with which Samuelson would have agreed. Chase argued that when resources were needed for military purposes, people did not ask where the money was coming from, but just spent it, as Germany had done. It was shortages of physical resources that would stop Germany, not financial bankruptcy. "Adam Smith may heave in his grave," Chase claimed, "but no nation in this dangerous world of 1942 is meekly going bankrupt because some textbooks say it ought to."[99] Faced with such arguments by someone known to be a supporter of Soviet planning, and addressing an audience of engineers, Samuelson adopted a very cautious tone, ostensibly taking the position of a conservative. "Because Chase represents a growing school of thought, intelligent conservatives with a sense of history will be interested in his viewpoint."

Like a prize fighter riding with the punch, "the thoughtful moderate can hope to avert cataclysmic, revolutionary change," embracing gradual reform and conserving what was good. Samuelson illustrated Chase's argument with lengthy quotations, carefully selecting one in which Chase offered a summary of Hansen's theory of the Great Depression as caused by a saturation of investment outlets—an assessment with which he agreed. When it came to evaluating Chase's attempt to outline a "budget" of essential resources—food, clothing, shelter, health, and education—Samuelson concluded that there was need for "a tremendous *joint* effort on the part of government and business." Though conservatives might be suspicious of what it implied, it was noncommittal and it was not even clear whether Samuelson was expressing his own view or merely summarizing the views in the book he was reviewing. His closing sentence claimed that even readers who did not agree with the book would gain insights into what lay ahead.

Samuelson was being positive about the book without laying himself open to the charge of agreeing with someone known as having once been an enthusiast for Stalin's central planning. Samuelson was learning how to write very diplomatically when covering politically sensitive issues, a skill that was to prove invaluable when he wrote his textbook.

The End of the NRPB

Like many of President Roosevelt's New Deal institutions, the NRPB was highly controversial, strongly criticized by conservatives. For example, a Republican senator criticized the NRPB for accepting Hansen's fiscal spending policies and for "fronting 'a gigantic move to plan the new social order' in 'this communistic program' aimed at invading 'the domain of the sex life of our young people,' while ultimately aiming at 'the complete destruction of all free enterprise.'"[100] In addition, there were widespread doubts about its role, for its work seemed to overlap considerably with that of other agencies. There was a widespread lack of awareness of the coordinating role it played.

The NRPB also became entangled in disputes between the Executive Branch and Congress, for it reported directly to the president, not to Congress. Quite apart from partisan opposition, which became stronger when the Republicans made gains in the 1942 elections, many in Congress took the view that they, not the president, should be making plans for after the war. It was also felt that Roosevelt had started postwar planning much too early, and that he should have waited at least until the outcome of the war had become clearer. In 1943, this criticism came to a head, and in June 1943, the decision was made to disband the NRPB, effective at the end of August.[101]

Beneath such disputes lay an ongoing hostility to the New Deal and to the idea that government should play a role in stimulating the economy. Merriam, Chase, and others associated with the NRPB had been arguing, in widely read media such as *The Nation* and *Harper's* magazine, that government controls on economic activity should continue after the war, and critics took this as indicating a desire to change the nature of the American economy.[102] Senator Robert Taft argued that "a mixed economy really meant a fifty percent socialist economy," an idea picked up by much of the press, who saw government as trying to control business. The strength of this criticism was such that a few months later, Harold Ickes, one of those behind the NRPB, felt the need to protest, with a three-page article in *The New Republic*, "Bureaucrats v. Business men."[103] Businessmen might be critical of bureaucrats, but it was businessmen, brought into government by Roosevelt, who were running the war.

The attacks on the NRPB, according to one historian, peaked after the publication of the *Security, Work and Relief Policies* and the *Report for 1943*, which were read as implying that the NRPB supported the idea of a constantly increasing national debt.[104] Taft claimed, in Congress, that "constant debt increase would lead to the ruin of our entire system and the destruction of all the values that constitute the past savings of the people of the United States." An article in the *New York Sun* criticized the theory on which the NRPB policies were based:

> the theories upon which they [the NRPB] base their fundamental calculations constitute such a radical departure from the established and accepted laws of economics as to suggest, subtly, the need for revising many of the basic axioms on which scientific progress has rested for centuries. It is just possible, for example, that Newton's head really fell up and hit the apple.[105]

Taft's position was supported, in even stronger language, by Yale professor Fred Fairchild, who warned the Chamber of Commerce about the dangers of planning, in an address that was reported in the *New York Times*. He attacked not only planning but the idea that the United States could afford to play a major role in the world.

> We must abandon illusory expedients for the control of business cycles, curtail military expenditures, balance the budget, avoid repudiation of the public debt and start reducing it. And we must abandon grandiose notions of America policing, feeding, reconstructing the world. We must give up the Atlantic Charter and all the things it proposes to have America do for the world, and do for nothing. They are out of the picture. America cannot afford to do those things.[106]

Control of business, Fairchild argued, was a fantastic or impossible illusion.[107] The vice president of the American Federation of Labor adopted a similar stance, claiming that corporation tax policy was being used "for the destruction or conversion of our society into some idealistic state."[108]

Fairchild's isolationist remarks pointed to the two very different views of America's role in the world that dominated public debate at this time and that stood in stark contrast with Samuelson's view, outlined two years earlier:

> American humanitarian zeal will desire the feeding of the war-devastated populations of the world once the present conflict is ended, and the nation may want to assist in the rebuilding of destroyed productive plant upon which depends the provision of better standards of living

for other peoples. In part the goods and services America provides to other areas of the world may be paid for with raw materials and services rendered us. On the other hand, it may be necessary to give away certain goods and services without the expectation of reimbursement.[109]

There is no evidence that Fairchild had these remarks in mind, or even that he had read them—they were in an internal memorandum. Insofar as he drew any distinctions between NRPB personnel, Fairchild's target was Hansen, by then the leading public advocate of Keynesian policies and author of the controversial NRPB Pamphlet, *After the War—Full Employment*. However, Samuelson was aligned firmly with Hansen's policies, was a contributor to Hansen's major academic publication on the subject, and was the author of a pamphlet that, for all of its caution, was advocating essentially the same policies as Hansen had under virtually the same title.

The NRPB staff had carried on functioning through this period when the organization for which they worked was under attack. In March, Hagen wrote to Samuelson saying that he had an offer from the War Labor Board and that he was discussing a similar position with the Office of Strategic Services.[110] He admitted that the situation facing the NRPB seemed to be improving and that Blaisdell was optimistic, but he was not convinced about the unit's future, so he was likely to accept one of these two positions. The pamphlet he and Samuelson wrote had been completed in March, but revision of the interim report was ongoing.[111] A memorandum from Samuelson to Blaisdell shows his awareness of the situation. He had been asked to comment on a manuscript by his friend David McCord Wright, on the problem of the national debt. He found the manuscript lucid and well balanced, with just a few technical queries that needed attention. However, he had doubts about the strategy of publishing it.

> From a tactical point of view, it sometimes seems to me desirable simply not to discuss the debt at all. In bringing it to explicit attention and analysis, unless we do succeed in convincing doubters, we may simply be turning the knife in the wound or waving a red flag before the bull. After all, the fear of the debt is largely irrational and logic is not always the best weapon in such a case.[112]

Thus, although he thought it would do a lot of good if published in the *Atlantic* or *Readers Digest*, he thought it might "come with bad grace from the Board which is already looked upon with suspicion in these matters."

Members of Samuelson's unit kept working until the very end. Toward the end of May, Samuelson received a memorandum on "liquid saving," providing figures on how much of their savings businesses were holding as cash.[113] On June 10, Hagen sent a manuscript on "National Output at Full Employment in the United States in 1950" for transmission to Blaisdell. Recognizing that the NRPB would probably not be able to publish it, he asked permission to publish it elsewhere.[h] On July 1, another member of the unit sent Samuelson a memorandum on British saving during the First World War that he had drafted the day before, with the remark, "It took a lot of discipline and courage to finish this memo, things being as they are. Mary was a real soldier, working while everyone else relaxed."[114]

No sooner had the NRPB been disbanded than Samuelson began to receive inquiries about his availability to do similar work elsewhere. On August 6, 1943, Walter Salant wrote, saying that those at the Office of Price Administration thought it was time that they got into such work, and asked whether he would be interested an arrangement with them similar to the one he had with the NRPB.[115] Even though the closing of the NRPB should have freed up his schedule, Samuelson replied that he was so busy that there was no possibility of taking up any consultancy work for at least the next few months. However, while Samuelson, secure in his position at MIT, could turn down such invitations, his staff were busy looking for work in other government agencies.[116] Hagen took a position with the Office of Strategic Services. Samuelson's contract terminated on August 31, bringing to an end his commuting to Washington.[117]

Though Samuelson had spent only two days a week in Washington, for just two years, the experience was crucial to his development as an economist. He had been in charge of a large empirical project involving extensive data analysis; through working with Altman, an economist with more experience in government work, he had gained experience in directing a project, recruiting staff, and trying to turn the results into a report that would stand up to criticism by people predisposed to challenge its conclusions.[118] Through Hansen, he had been introduced to the work of other government departments and developed an extensive range of contacts that would have been difficult had he remained in Cambridge. He was also becoming more and more closely identified with Hansen and a set of internationalist and interventionist positions on economic policy.

The failure of the NRPB prompted some soul-searching in an apparently unfinished and unpublished draft, "Post-war Planning as Seen by a Retired

---

h. It subsequently appeared in the *American Economic Review*, jointly written by Hagen, by then at the Federal Reserve, and Nora Kirkpatrick at the Office of Strategic Services.

Post-war Planner."[119] Samuelson confessed to having begun postwar planning "six months before there even was a war" and of having spent two years commuting to Washington.[i]

> Often in the wee-hours of the night, the theory of opportunity cost would rear its ugly head to remind him of the important cargo which his occupation of scarce space had displaced—to which his conscience had only the reply which is the last refuge of scoundrels, "If I don't use the Pullman space, some other post-war planner will."[120]

The pangs of guilt he felt also concerned the additional burdens his absence was placing on his colleagues back at MIT. He wrote of "sacrifices and harrowing experiences," such as the difficulty of finding hotel rooms and making train reservations, leaving implicit the comparison with those whose sacrifices and harrowing experiences were much less trivial. However, Washington did have its advantages: for a college professor "from the sticks," it could seem "like a glorified post-graduate school, teeming with the gossip and camaraderie typical of such institutions," and it provided opportunities for "the economist's wife to carve out a career for herself."[121,j] Samuelson must have felt doubly privileged spending part of his time in this atmosphere and the rest of it in Cambridge, where he had the luxury of being involved with MIT's graduate program and attending seminars at Harvard.

It is also possible to see feelings of guilt about the comfortable position of noncombatant economists in Samuelson's attempt to justify the high salaries that young economists could command. He argued that the agencies employing them received a very high return per dollar spent.

> The cream is skimmed so to speak from the knowledge of the consultant, so that even if he were to devote his remaining time to the Agency this would be subject to rapidly diminishing returns. More important the consultant neither sells nor does the Agency buy *working time*, but rather a *responsibility* for a certain task or field of research. This responsibility is indivisible. It cannot be turned on and off. It weighs as heavily if one is working 5¼ days a month as under full time.[122]

---

i. He appears oblivious to the fact that there was then a war, even though the United States was not yet a combatant.

j. Against this assumption about economists' gender, it should be mentioned that Samuelson was shortly to supervise two PhDs by women who went on to assume positions as professional economists.

Samuelson claimed to be speaking without prejudice, on grounds that he had never been more than a part-time consultant. He then addressed what must have been the crucial issue, for him and others in his position.

> It would be a grave misapprehension, almost a reversal of the actual facts of the case, to think that one anxious to avoid military service would do well to go to Washington. On the contrary, a check-up of the experience of recent economics majors would show that the Federal Agencies have leaned over backwards in their attitude toward selective service. In no sense has the government service provided an escape from the draft.[123]

The dubious logic of some of Samuelson's arguments, and the attempt to leaven parts of the argument with humor, suggests that his conscience was struggling with his having had such a privileged position during the war. If it were written in 1943, it might help explain why, despite his fascination with economic problems, he became involved with technical military problems relating to fire control. It was certainly important to him later on to be able to tell his correspondents that he was engaged in classified war work.

| Developing the New
Economics, II
Policy, 1942–1943

The Balanced-Budget Multiplier

At some point between March and June 1942, Samuelson wrote a chapter, "Full Employment After the War," for a volume that Seymour Harris was editing on *Postwar Economic Problems.*[1] Whereas elsewhere Samuelson's concern was the need to take action, in this chapter he focused on economic theory. Sensitive to the political implications, Samuelson emphasized repeatedly that he was talking about a technique of analysis that was "neutral on policy questions," and that, though the framework being used to analyze the problem of unemployment was usually named after Keynes, it had roots in earlier thinking.[2] As he had done consistently since his first encounters with the problem of fiscal policy, he distanced himself from Keynes.

The existence of a stable relationship between consumption and income was central to the theory of employment. Samuelson explained this stability by talking about the stability of the proportions of household budgets spent on different commodities, something he was becoming very familiar with through his work at the NRPB. Over short periods of time, Samuelson argued, the fraction of income saved rose with income. There was a level of income at which people saved nothing, but as income rose, so did the proportion of income saved. This was shown by the consumption function, AA, in figure 20.1. Over time, the consumption function shifted upward, indicated

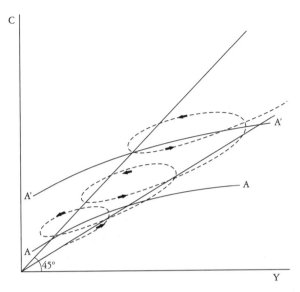

FIGURE 20.1 Consumption and income.
Source: Samuelson 1943d, p. 35.

by the move from curve AA to A′A′. Because income fluctuated over the business cycle, the time path followed by consumption and income was like that indicated by the dotted line in figure 20.1.[a]

The reason why Samuelson emphasized the relationship between consumption and income was that he believed it to be central to all business cycle analysis: interest rates and stocks of wealth were less important than income as determinants of how incomes were divided between consumption and saving. The relationship between consumption and income had historically been very stable, but it could be altered by *"deliberate social action."*[3] The reason why this was mattered was that savings had to be "offset" by spending, either business investment or government spending. If there were to be full employment, there must be sufficient spending to offset the amount that people wished to save. If not, there would be a downward spiral of income and employment until saving was reduced accordingly.

He countered the argument that flexible wages would be sufficient to maintain full employment by causing prices to fall, hence lowering interest

---

a. The diagram is reproduced here to make it clear that this chapter contained a view on the behavior of consumption function that is commonly, but incorrectly, thought to have surfaced only later. The diagram is very similar to ones that were later used to justify the permanent income and lifecycle theories of consumption.

rates and stimulating investment. The problems with this argument were that low interest rates—cheap money—did not work: the argument relied on continuously falling prices, but this would have "adverse psychological effects." It was thus possible that ever-falling prices would make unemployment worse, not better. There was, likewise, no reason to believe that the economic system would automatically generate full employment. By the same token, there was no reason to believe that there would necessarily be unemployment. It was an empirical question. Samuelson did not point out that the same argument was to be found in Keynes's *General Theory*.

This chapter is also the first publication in which Samuelson referred to the saving and investment diagram he had used in "The Modern Theory of Income" (see figure 18.1), as "analogous to the 'Marshallian cross' of supply and demand."[4] This diagram and its equivalent showing consumption, investment, and a 45-degree line (figure 13.1) came to be associated so closely with Keynesian economics and Samuelson's textbook that it is important to note he remained skeptical of it. The reason was that it oversimplified the factors behind investment:

> However valid this [the S and I diagram] may be formally, it is necessary to insist that investment in anything but the shortest run cannot be related to income in the way that savings can. Even in the shortest run it is not the statical level of income, but its time pattern of change taken in conjunction with the existing stock of capital equipment, which determines investment. In the present writer's opinion, this cannot be emphasized too much.[5]

Once again, he was stressing the importance of dynamics. Perhaps this was the reason he was in no hurry to publish his earlier paper, despite Hansen's urging him to do so.

Reviewing the "offsets" to saving that might contribute to full employment, Samuelson covered various possibilities, including business investment, government spending to redistribute income, foreign investment, the development of new wants to stimulate consumption, deficit-financed government spending, and "government spending matched by equivalent taxes."[6] The last of these was a recent discovery.

> Only recently have I become convinced that item 6 [the last factor in this list] does provide a genuine offset to saving—that a balanced budget at a high level, with "nonprogressive" taxes and expenditure, is nevertheless employment- and income-creating. A proof cannot be attempted here. However, if valid, this form may provide an important

method by which our economy can hope to maintain the level of effective demand.[7]

This was what came to be known as the "balanced-budget multiplier:" the idea that an increase in government spending *matched by an equivalent rise in taxation* is expansionary. The political significance of this is hard to exaggerate, given the extent to which opposition to Keynesian ideas focused on the danger of perpetual government deficits.

Shortly after discovering the balanced-budget multiplier, Samuelson had a conversation with Bill Salant, one of two brothers whom Samuelson had known as a student in Harvard, discovering that the two of them had worked out essentially the same result.[8] Samuelson was confident that the result had not been published, at least in the English-language literature, and suggested they write it up together. In July 1942, Salant, who was then a member of Lauchlin Currie's staff in the White House, wrote up the idea as "Taxes, the Multiplier and the Inflationary Gap."[9]

Salant's starting point was the claim that the government deficit had an effect on national income that was the same as an equivalent increase in investment. This led economists to deduce that, provided the deficit remained unchanged, alterations in government spending would have no effect. He then proceeded to explain why this was incorrect. The key was in considering changes in government spending separately: government spending would raise national income directly, and it would also do so through inducing rises in consumption. If taxes rose to fund the rise in government spending, they would reduce consumption and exactly offset the rise in consumption induced by the rise in government spending, leaving just the rise in government spending.[b] The balanced budget multiplier would be precisely one.

---

b. A rise in government spending of 1 would immediately raise income by 1; that rise in income would generate a rise in consumption and a further rise in income of c, where c is the marginal propensity to consume. This in turn would induce a further increase in consumption of c^2, and so on. The total increase in income would be given as $1 + c^2 + c^3 + \ldots = \dfrac{1}{1-c}$. This was well known. However, suppose that taxes rise by 1, too. By reducing consumers' disposable income, this reduces consumption by c, lowering national income, which reduces consumption by a further c^2, and so on. The total reduction in national income is $c + c^2 + c^3 + \ldots = \dfrac{c}{1-c}$. The net effect is $\dfrac{1}{1-c} - \dfrac{c}{1-c} = 1$. That is, a \$1 rise in government spending financed by a \$1 rise in the taxation raised national income by \$1.

Another way to think about this is that the balanced-budget multiplier arises because the only difference between government spending and taxation is that the former is a component of national income, whereas taxation is not (taxes are treated as a transfer payment, like Social Security payments or gifts from one person to another that are not associated with the production of any commodity or service). The balanced-budget multiplier thus depended on the way the national accounts were constructed, which provided one reason the idea had not been discovered sooner.[c] The earliest national accounts defined national income so as to include only the part of government spending that was financed by taxes, a procedure that, even if it made sense during the Depression, certainly made no sense during the war, when the deficit increased to an unprecedented fraction of national income. Similarly, when Currie had used multiplier analysis to work out the cause of the 1937 recession, he had used the deficit—the net contribution of the government to income generation.[d] Samuelson added another explanation of the failure to see the balanced-budget multiplier that applied specifically to him and Salant—they were both concerned with foreign trade multipliers, where it makes sense to see the stimulus as being the trade balance, or exports minus imports.

Samuelson was right to be surprised that the result had not been discovered earlier. Looking at the algebra alone, it is hard to understand why Samuelson did not see the idea when he was analyzing the difference between public works and relief expenditure in the paper he wrote the previous summer.[10,e] Had he asked how much income would have been generated by transferring money from the public works budget to the Social Security budget, he would have gotten the same answer. Those who were concerned with

c. In modern national accounts, "national income" is defined as consumption plus investment plus government expenditure on goods and services plus net exports (exports minus imports). The rationale for not subtracting taxes is that they are a transfer payment, not a payment for goods and services. (Samuelson 1975b, pp. 44–45).

d. The previous year, when Currie was analyzing the spending program for an unpublished memorandum, he had written, "when the Government spends money that is collected in taxes and would have otherwise been spent by the taxpayer, there is a transfer of buying power rather than a net increase. Although the *net* activity-stimulating expenditures of the Government cannot be exactly measured an attempt was made to approximate it by deducting from total expenditures . . . all taxes except estate taxes which are assumed to decrease in some measure the expenditures of the public" (Currie 2004, p. 302; emphasis in original).

e. There, he compared series $(1, \frac{1}{2}, \frac{1}{4}, \frac{1}{8}, \dots)$ and $(\frac{1}{2}, \frac{1}{4}, \frac{1}{8}, \dots)$. Given that Social Security payments are treated, as are taxes, as transfers in modern national income accounting, it would be natural to associate the former with public works and the war finance, such as Salant at the White House and his brother Walter at the Office of Price Administration, were using the concept of the inflationary gap, and it was in this context that Keynes had implicitly employed the idea of the balanced-budget multiplier when writing a statement for the 1940 budget in the United Kingdom.[11] However, perhaps the most telling interpretation is that their failure to see the idea illustrates the way in which theorizing about the multiplier was driven by policy issues rather than theoretical questions internal to the discipline. Neither of Samuelson's two papers on the multiplier had the theoretical precision and focus that he achieved in papers in which the goals were purely theoretical.

Samuelson and Salant continued to correspond about publication. In October, Samuelson wrote with suggestions for how that paper could begin, saying that material Salant had already written could follow this. Samuelson also suggested adding an alternative explanation of the result.

> Originally the community is in equilibrium at that level of income where savings and investment[,] in the schedule sense, are just equal. After the proposed change the national income produced for the civilian population can only be in equilibrium at the same level on the assumption that private investment is unchanging and that savings depend only upon disposable income. Any other result would lead to a contradiction. Hence the total of government employment is superimposed upon the old level of employment so that there is a dollar increase in employment for each spent dollar increase in taxes.[12]

This makes it clear that, although the mathematics behind the result was very simple, they were still struggling with the conceptual issues, deriving the theorem in different ways. The reference to national income produced for the civilian population shows that their work was rooted in wartime discussions, a point reinforced by reference not to an abstract concept of national income but to specific income series developed in government agencies. Even the correct concept of national income to be used was unsettled. Samuelson closed by insisting that their names appear in alphabetical order, and that he hoped they could meet a week later when he was in Washington. However, the paper was not finished, because Salant moved to London, working for the Office of Strategic Services, to analyze bombing targets.[13]

---

latter with Social Security payments. In fact, Samuelson had them the other way round, arguing that public works were less likely to be spent fully. He was focusing on whether incomes would be spent, ignoring the critical question of which payments contributed to national income and which did not.

Walter Salant and Forecasting Employment

In November, Samuelson began a correspondence with Bill Salant's brother, Walter, who was working with Hans Neisser at the Office of Price Administration (OPA), concerning a paper by Richard Gilbert and Victor Perlo, also of the OPA, that had been presented to the Econometric Society in December 1941 and that had recently been published in *Econometrica*.[14] That paper argued that the traditional method of forecasting, which involved combining separate forecasts for each industrial sector, had not proved successful. The problem was not lack of knowledge about the industries, for forecasts were typically produced by people who were very well informed about the industries concerned. Instead, they proposed to approach the problem the other way round, starting with "general economic factors" and only then constructing forecasts for individual industries. The theoretical framework Gilbert and Perlo used was an extended version of the multiplier.[f] Using least squares regression analysis, they had estimated ten relationships they believed were stable. This formed a set of simultaneous equations that could be used to generate forecasts that, they claimed, were much more successful than traditional methods.[g]

Samuelson, who was by this time involved in post-defense forecasting at the NRPB, argued that their multipliers were much too large, for he

---

f. The crucial difference between their model and Samuelson's multiplier–accelerator model was that, instead of finding a relationship between the level of investment and the change in income, they found relationships between changes in investment and changes in income. This difference completely changed the dynamic properties of the system.

g. The time path of income was explained by three sets of equations:

> (1) The multiplier: the increase in gross national product (GNP) was three times the increase in "weighted offsets to saving" (variables such as investment and net government spending).
>
> (2) Equations for each of three types of investment: the increase in private investment in equipment was 0.1 times the increase in GNP; the increase in private investment in plant was 0.06 times the increase in GNP; and the increase in housing investment was 0.05 times the increase in GNP.
>
> (3) Equations to determine federal receipts (a nonlinear relationship) and state and local government net receipts.
>
> (4) The rise in imports was 0.03 times the rise in GNP.

> Once they had calculated the change in GNP, they could use two further equations to calculate changes in industrial production and nonagricultural employment. Though these equations had been calculated using regression analysis, they did not report the results of any statistical tests, as would be routine in modern econometric work (Gilbert and Perlo 1942, p. 312).

was skeptical of the propensities to invest that were central to their calculations. "My own inclination," he wrote, "is to distrust mechanical relationships between income and investment; at best I would use propensities to invest only in the very short run."[15] He suggested that their methods had worked during the previous two years simply because private investment had risen during "the defense period," irrespective of whether or not there was a "reversible, repeatable relationship like that between consumption and income." This makes very clear Samuelson's strong belief that, despite the formal similarity between saving and investment functions in Keynesian models, their behavior was fundamentally different. He then went on to explain his view of the business cycle.

> My own view is that the business cycle represents contagious swings of investment, set off by autonomous factors and changes in the level of income. How far these quasi-induced bursts will go depends upon the accumulation of investment opportunities due to technological change, changes in capital stock, outlook for extensive growth, etc.

He clearly thought that investment was a dynamic problem and, like Hansen, emphasized long-term structural factors. However, despite his skepticism of the OPA forecasts, Samuelson felt that Perlo and Gilbert had avoided many of the pitfalls in the forecasting being undertaken in other government agencies, such as Agriculture and Commerce.

Samuelson's criticisms of the Gilbert-Perlo study were discussed within the OPA, and in December 1942, Salant sent Samuelson a memorandum from a colleague, Murray Geisler, explaining that a crucial equation had been left out of the *Econometrica* article.[16] This stated that "weighted offsets" (the spending to which the multiplier was applied) was in fact a weighted average comprising 0.6 times current "offsets" and 0.4 times the previous year's figure. This introduced a lag into the system that greatly reduced the multiplier—to a more normal level of 2¼. If no account were taken of the lag, the unreasonably high figures Samuelson had found would be correct. The problem Samuelson had found was due to a typing error.

However, Samuelson was not satisfied and looked at the problem again. What bothered him was that, if correct, this explanation undermined a basic idea—that lags could not affect the final value of the multiplier after all induced spending had taken place. This was an idea he had held since his early work on the business cycle, when he viewed the multiplier as determining the level of income and the accelerator, in which a lag is essential, determined fluctuations. He rejected the idea that Geisler had not allowed the multiplier process to work through, and he found another mistake: they had forgotten to include the lagged term, 0.4 times last year's offsets, in their calculations.[17] Perlo wrote a memorandum to Salant, passed on to Samuelson, in which he said that Samuelson's view that lags could not affect the final equilibrium was correct, but "the point is that under the conditions which have prevailed in recent years, the system has never settled down."[18] In a corrigendum, Gilbert and Perlo explained that an equation had been left out of their paper, noting that, "[t]he total effect [of a change in public spending] over a whole business cycle is just as great as if there were no lag, but the timing is considerably modified."

They continued to argue about technical details of the calculations, Samuelson not convinced by Perlo's explanation. Their discussion led to more substantial points concerning the methodology of forecasting and the statistical issues being confronted by forecasters at this time. Perlo noted Samuelson's claim that, were it not for federal taxes, the system would be explosive: it was dangerous to assume that the system would remain the same whether federal expenditures were high or low. Wartime had led to such a large increase in government spending that applying the same system to pre- and postwar spending was hazardous. Samuelson responded that his main criticism still stood.[19] They obtained high multipliers by assuming a mechanical relationship between saving and investment. The correlation between investment and income proved nothing, for it said nothing about causation and because the same data were being used to deduce saving and investment schedules. This would produce marginal propensities to save and invest that were essentially the same and "almost infinite" multipliers. The same problem applied to results obtained by other forecasters, Mordecai Ezekiel, Richard Bissell, and James Tobin.

Here, Samuelson made two methodological points. If the OPA's methods produced good results for the period in which they were interested, they were justifiable. However, correct forecasts did not imply that the theory was correct: to prove that, it would be necessary to prove that the investment function was invariant, reversible, and that shifts over time were either negligible or predictable. This went against the trend of modern business cycle theory, which was "in the direction of placing the greatest emphasis upon the capricious, volatile, and shifting character of the net investment schedule." In saying that, he was concurring with Keynes.

Perlo's comments, Samuelson concluded, bore on the basis upon which postwar forecasting was being undertaken, for if people believed that it was possible to find a *reversible* relationship holding in the twenties and thirties, one could not blame them for extrapolating it to the postwar world.[h] This was very important because "plenty of people are using what I consider to be a false part of the theory in their policy thinking concerning the post-war outlook and it will not do to tell them that the post-war world will assuredly be different from the pre-war world." Much more was needed.

The following summer, Samuelson sent Walter Salant a copy of his chapter in the Harris volume, eliciting the following remark.

> Your comment that a budget balanced at a higher level with non-progressive taxes is employment-creating was certainly put in a tantalizing way. Can you let me know briefly what you have in mind? It sounds something like a point that my brother was making about a year ago, but I can't remember exactly the line of reasoning.[20]

Samuelson replied that it was the same point, and that he and Bill Salant had arrived at it independently. He added that it was a conclusion he had "been resisting subconsciously for some years."[21] He told Walter about his discussions with Bill, discussed earlier in this chapter, and that he was feeling guilty about being too busy to work on their joint paper. He said it would have been much better had he not interfered and left Bill's manuscript in its original form, and so he suggested that, if Bill agreed, Walter should now see Bill's original paper through to publication.

He also pointed to another way of presenting the result. The budget deficit measures the stimulus to private sector national income, so if there is a balanced-budget increase in public spending, private employment will not change; but there is nothing to cancel out the rise in public sector employment, resulting in an increase in total employment. Samuelson also explained why he thought the result important. Its wartime significance was that it showed the inflationary gap to be larger than the budget deficit. In peacetime, it could be important for discussions of the burden of taxation, potentially changing the "whole analysis of the incidence of taxes."

> Possibly in the postwar world it may become necessary to levy non-progressive, dead-weight taxes. When we come to ask who shares the burden of these, it may turn out that nobody does; the government gets resources which would otherwise be idle, and their work is the only burden of the tax.[22]

---

h. Samuelson used the term "reversible," underlining it for emphasis. He appears to mean a stable structural relationship rather than a correlation that would disappear as soon as circumstances changed.

The reference to the possible need to impose dead-weight (lump-sum) taxes shows the way that, even a year later, they were not thinking of this as a general proposition but, rather, as something relating to a specific tax regime.

The idea of the balanced-budget multiplier also occurred to Hansen, who after discussing it with Walter Salant and Abba Lerner, wrote to Samuelson about it in September 1943.[23] By then, Samuelson had stopped commuting to Washington and they had not met for a while, and Hansen expressed the hope that they could meet on one of the days when he was at Harvard. Hesitant about the mathematics, Hansen wanted reassurance that the idea was right, and when Walter Salant had said that his brother had come up with the idea, he remembered that Samuelson had mentioned it to him several months previously, as well as stating it in the Harris volume. Samuelson and Bill Salant may not have finished their paper, but the main idea in the paper was circulating in Washington.[i]

Teaching the New Economics

At MIT, Samuelson taught the ideas he was working on in two courses, Business Cycles and Public Finance. When he took over the first of these courses, he changed its description to reflect the new approach to economics, offering "A statistical, historical, and theoretical examination of the determinants of income, production, and employment. Modern methods are brought to bear on the problems of analysis, forecasting, and control."[24] Notes taken by a student show how Samuelson's ideas on macroeconomic problems had evolved by early 1943. He began with a lecture on the problem of the business cycle and then turned to the analysis of saving, investment, the multiplier, fiscal policy, and aggregate demand.[25] Concluding with an overview of the Keynesian system ("Putting Keynes Together") and the inflationary gap, he offered thorough coverage of what would later be called Keynesian macroeconomics, engaging with contemporary debates over Keynesian theory

---

i. Correspondence with Hansen in the period when Samuelson was at the NRPB is sparse, probably because they were meeting, as members of a committee and over lunch, every fortnight, as well as in Cambridge at the Fiscal Policy Seminar; it therefore fails to document the extent of Samuelson's interactions with Hansen. For example, a letter from December 1942 shows that they had been discussing the marginal propensity to consume of rich and poor families and the role of Social Security spending, a problem central to Samuelson's work at the NRPB (P. A. Samuelson, December 16, 1942, Letter to Alvin Hansen, PASP 36 [Hansen]). Hansen was following Samuelson's work closely.

and wartime policy concerns. The value of Keynes's system, Samuelson contended, was not that he got everything right, but that he provided a system that could accommodate the idea that aggregate demand might be too low.[j]

However, although Samuelson praised Keynes for providing a logical system, he struggled to explain the interdependence of its various parts. Samuelson tried a complicated "four quadrant" diagram but it contained some very awkward constructions and was cumbersome to use. One of the criticisms that he made repeatedly was that both the Keynesian and the classical theories neglected forms of wealth other than money. The demand for money in the Keynesian system should depend on these other assets. At one point he suggested that total wealth could be estimated by calculating the present value of income, excluding wages and salaries (the sum of money that would, if invested at the market rate of interest, yield that part of national income not accounted for by wages and salaries).[k] Such criticisms appear remarkably prescient, given the role that wealth effects were to play in macroeconomics in the late 1940s and 1950s.

Theory dominated Samuelson's course, though data were never far away—hardly surprising, given that he was simultaneously commuting to Washington to discuss issues that he was also discussing in class.[l] For example, citing data that he was using at the NRPB on saving by households in different income brackets, Samuelson paid close attention to the distribution of income, explaining Pareto's law of distribution and using the Lorenz curve and the Gini coefficient to measure inequality.[m] The distribution of

---

j. Ringo, the student whose notes are the source here, noted "PAS. real contribution of General Theory is that it is a logical, interdependent system and takes account of the problems of ineffective demand."

k. He wrote "$W = \dfrac{mY}{i}$ = present value of [income], excluding wages and salaries

(m = roughly 33%)." ("Wealth" has been replaced with "income," presumably being a note-taking error by Ringo.) The demand function for money should therefore be

$$M = M\left(i, Y, \frac{mY}{i}\right).$$

l. Students were required to write term papers on the aftermath of a single war, perhaps the Civil War or the Napoleonic War, a topic that directly paralleled the work he was doing on the First World War.

m. The Lorenz curve is constructed by ranking income recipients from poorest to richest, and then plotting the proportion of income earned against the proportion of the population. If there is perfect equality, the bottom 10 percent of the population will have 10 percent of income, the bottom 50 percent will have 50 percent, and so on. The result will be a straight line at 45 degrees to the horizontal axis. If there is inequality, it will trace out a

income, which changed over the cycle, mattered because of its effects on saving. However, because the marginal propensity to consume did not vary very much across households, the effects of redistribution on consumption would be small: it had to be justified on social grounds, not purely because of its effects on saving. He used a figure similar to the one used in his chapter in the Harris volume (see figure 20.1) to illustrate the relationship between the consumption function in the short run and the long run, though the two short-run consumption functions were labeled "1776" and "Today."

In the course of explaining how saving and investment determined income, he made a number of significant remarks. Samuelson noted that full employment was not a definite point, and he used the term "hysteresis effect" to denote movements that changed a schedule in an irreversible way. Whereas in print he might have to use generally accepted terminology, in his course he explained his own preferences more forcefully. The student noted: "Samuelson doesn't like 'ex ante' and 'ex post'" and "Doesn't like 'planned' vs. 'Unplanned'.... Confusion of schedules, expectations, identity." The crucial point Samuelson was making was that what mattered was whether investment was maintainable. *Ex post*, saving and investment would be equal, but investment would not be maintainable except in equilibrium. To avoid having to "drag in a little angel in order to make the process instantaneous," it was better to talk in terms of "observable" versus "virtual" magnitudes. If this account is not completely clear, it may reflect the fact that, though Samuelson understood the arguments, he had not settled on a particular way to express it.

Even national accounting concepts were unsettled, for economists working in government agencies were then developing different frameworks for the national accounts.[n] This no doubt explains why, certainly to modern readers, his discussion appears to lack clarity. What is perhaps most noticeable is the absence of the notion of value added (he simply treated the private sector as a single unit) and the absence of any reference to Leontief's input–output analysis that was later used to clarify the way the national accounts were organized.

When Samuelson turned to government spending, he introduced the balanced-budget multiplier that he and Bill Salant had recently worked out

---

curve below that line. The distance of the curve from the 45-degree line (measured by the Gini coefficient) can be taken as a measure of inequality.

n. Samuelson mentioned Kuznets and Milton Gilbert, but he could also have mentioned Robert Nathan or, in Britain, James Meade and Richard Stone.

but not yet published. Again, his discussion reflected the extent to which such issues were discussed but had not yet stabilized. There was still no agreement on whether the multiplier should be applied to government expenditure or to the government deficit, and exactly what should be included in the multiplier. He illustrated this by citing the claim by Federal Reserve Chairman Marriner Eccles that the "way to balance budget was to spend freely, raise income, and then collect taxes out of the higher income." Eccles had, Samuelson explained, forgotten to include the marginal propensity to tax in the multiplier: his conclusion might be right, but his logic was wrong.

The multiplier was also topical owing to the problem of America's wartime relationship with its allies and debates about the need to support European countries after the war; it provided evidence to counter the conservative claim that the United States could not afford to support other countries, for additional spending might lead to additional output. Samuelson used multiplier reasoning to establish whether foreign lending would reduce domestic investment by raising interest rates, and whether it would raise exports. The latter might happen through two mechanisms: the "classical mechanism," whereby the foreign loan altered prices in the two countries; and the "modern mechanism," which changed spending by changing incomes.

Samuelson also extended the Keynesian model to allow for changes in the capital stock. Here, too, he was grappling with problems for which there was no accepted mode of analysis. Clearly the problem of capital accumulation mattered, but the reason why he discussed it was probably that he wanted to address the argument made by Oskar Lange about the existence of an optimum propensity to consume.[o] Discussing this required him to talk about capital accumulation, for Lange's arguments raised the question of whether it was appropriate to maximize national income, the capital stock, or the rate of investment.

Samuelson had touched on fiscal policy in his course on business cycles in the first quarter, but went into it in much more detail in the course he taught on public finance during the summer. Public Finance was a new course. It focused on public works spending, deficits, and their effects on aggregate demand and employment. Even though Samuelson covered a lot of theory in the lectures, the reading exposed the students to up-to-date institutional and empirical material, including several NRPB and NBER reports.[26] If there was a textbook for the course, it was *Deficit Spending and the National Income* by

---

o. See chapter 18 this volume.

Henry Villard (1941).[p] It probably approached the topic much as Samuelson would have done. Its coverage—90 pages on the business cycle, no fewer than 160 pages on the multiplier, and 150 pages analyzing "recent public net income-increasing expenditure"—shows clearly the state of discussion: the concept of the multiplier was still one that had not stabilized and needed detailed explanation. One reason for this was that the multiplier was tied up with definitional issues necessary to use it in practice.

Samuelson started the course by noting that government activities had to be appraised on the basis of their direct usefulness and their influence on effective demand. The latter was important because public works were the "only *respectable* weapon government has which operates in anti-cyclical manner" (he seems not to have said what the non-respectable weapons were). After reviewing discussions of public works in the thirties, Samuelson jumped ahead to the postwar situation and the consequences of demobilizing 10 million men and women. He made the same point as was obsessing him in Washington— namely, that there had been insufficient planning to implement the public spending needed to prevent unemployment. He presented the theory about public works spending in terms of three schools of thought. The first school, associated with Herbert Hoover, was that policy was all about adjusting the timing of public works that would be undertaken regardless. It rested on the idea that there was a normal level of activity and that policy was merely about stabilization around this level, and not about raising it. The second was the "pump-priming" school, which held that because the Depression had been caused by speculation, it would be sufficient to have a small amount of public works spending to restore confidence. Within this school were those, such as Sumner Slichter, who held that stored-up purchasing power would create a long period of prosperity after the war. The third school, associated with Hansen and Abba Lerner, held that more than pump-priming would be needed and that the government might have to run a continuous deficit.

Samuelson defended Hansen's policies against two accusations that conservatives often made: that they were socialist and that they would lead to an unsustainable burden of government debt. He contended that, with the exception of public utilities such as the Tennessee Valley Authority and the Boulder Dam—both enormous projects—public works spending had not led to socialism. Though there was a sense in which public works competed with private activities, the effect was tiny. Also, as federal spending rose, state and local government spending, especially relief, fell. Samuelson defended Social

---

p. Ringo noted that it should be "read 'copiously.'"

Security spending, arguing that Roosevelt's policies did not involve any break with previous policies and that they would not undermine the private enterprise economy. Indeed, there were good reasons why the Social Security Act, passed in 1935, was the most popular New Deal measure. Samuelson countered a range of arguments about why government debt was a problem, ranging from fear that the government would one day default to the idea that high values of debt were inflationary: it was government spending, not government debt, that was inflationary, and it was interest payments, not the debt itself, that was a burden. Britain had been able to bear a high debt burden for hundreds of years, and in any case, much American debt was internal, involving just transfers within the United States. He dismissed the argument, made by Gayer, that government debt had been the cause of the 1937 depression. Though he clearly sided with Hansen on much, he dismissed as "nonsense" Hansen's idea that a consumption boom would stop as soon as the stimulus was withdrawn, whereas an investment boom would be self-sustaining.

Despite Samuelson's convictions that mathematics was important, he used it sparingly.[q] Samuelson obviously believed that the important issues that students needed to think about were not ones to which answers could be found simply by solving sets of equations.

American Keynesianism

Accounts of the development of Keynesian economics after the *General Theory* typically focus on the IS-LM model, sometimes called the Hicks-Hansen IS-LM model.[27] This model provided a graphic representation of the interaction between the goods and money markets, which could be used to analyze the consequences of monetary and fiscal policy. Central to the model is the relationship between national income or output and the rate of interest.[r] However, most of the time, Samuelson and the network of economists with whom he was working argued not in terms of the IS-LM model (which shows the interaction of the markets for goods and money), but in terms of a simple multiplier model that ignored the money market and took no account of the effect of rising output on the rate of interest. Though economists eventually

---

q. He spoke of the problem of maximizing employment while keeping the debt low as an isoperimetric problem, formulating this using integrals over time.

r. For example, if a rise in government spending causes output to rise, this will raise the demand for money, and hence the rate of interest; the rise in the rate of interest

confined their use of this model to introductory textbooks, as something to be covered before students moved on to the more sophisticated IS-LM model, the discussions covered in chapters 18 to 20 show is that in the early 1940s the ideas expressed in this mathematically very simple model were far from straightforward. Economists had to grapple with conceptual issues about how the model in which income was determined by the interaction of saving and investment fitted in with the national accounts, the structure of which was still under discussion. Though the model was simple, the results often seemed paradoxical when viewed against an understanding derived from traditional theory.

Part of the reason for this emphasis on fiscal policy was the war. The need for a dramatic increase in military production made inevitable a massive expansion in federal government expenditure—an enormous fiscal stimulus. Though it was important to prevent inflation, there was no question of allowing monetary policy, through interest rate increases, to interfere with this, for the nation's top priority was winning the war. Rising government spending could lead to rising output, rather than rising prices, because the United States, even when it entered the war, had still not recovered from the Great Depression and had large reserves of productive resources that could be brought into use. Fiscal policy and public finance became the big topical issues on which economists, privileged by not having to fight on the front line, felt obliged to work. This motivation meant that economists' discussions of Keynesian economics were dominated by practical concerns related to measurement and the implementation of policy. Though using theory, Samuelson and those with whom he was working were first and foremost applied economists for whom meticulous data analysis was more important than theoretical sophistication.

Not only did government spending rise dramatically, so too did the deficit—the gap between federal spending and taxation.[s] This was generally accepted in wartime, even by conservatives, but there was fear about deficits carrying on into peacetime. Samuelson, like many of his colleagues, believed that the danger facing the United States after the war was a return to the conditions of the Great Depression, and in planning for peace, they began to articulate a view of fiscal policy as a tool that could be used to maintain

---

will partially choke off the rise in output, causing the multiplier effect of government spending to be lower than had the interest rate not risen.

s. In 1943, federal spending was $817 billion, or 42.5 percent of GDP. Revenues were a mere $250 billion, resulting in a deficit of $568 billion, or 29.6 percent of GDP (http://federal-budget.insidegov.com/l/45/1943, accessed March 3, 2016). The budget had almost been balanced in 1938.

prosperity. This approach to policy can legitimately be called "American Keynesianism," even though many of its proponents, including Samuelson, were cautious in their endorsement of Keynes, preferring to credit him with having made theoretical innovations that needed to be combined with other ideas. Where Keynes had focused on the need to raise investment, there was a stress on raising consumption, and where Keynes had sought to avoid advocating unbalanced budgets, it was argued that continuing budget deficits were not a problem. This incurred the wrath of conservatives, for whom balancing the peacetime budget was the hallmark of sound finance.

Working increasingly closely with Hansen, Samuelson was moving toward a position on economic policy that was politically controversial. Within the network of Washington economists, his positions were standard and he could debate technical details, but in the wider world he was enunciating views that were strongly attacked. In 1943, he had not yet ventured into the public arena, where Hansen was the main target of conservative attacks, but he was becoming known as a significant figure within the NRPB, a source of radical ideas on socioeconomic reform such as the proposal for a Bill of Economic Rights, and through his pamphlet he was identifying himself with Hansen. Two years later, Samuelson was to take the step from the world of academic and government economists into journalism, but before that he was to become closely involved with a different world—that of physicists working in MIT's Radiation Laboratory. And on top of all of these activities, Samuelson was preparing his thesis for publication.

CHAPTER 21

Scientists and Science Policy,
1944–1945

Technical War Work, March–December 1944

Following the closure of the NRPB, Samuelson's visits to Washington ceased and his activities at MIT increased. In March 1944, he wrote to his friend Walter Salant, "Except for a visit of 2 hours, I have not been to Washington since last June. I have been extremely busy here and may perhaps in the next week or two make one or two fateful personal decisions."[1] One of those decisions concerned what to do in the coming year. To focus resources on what was needed for the war effort, MIT was winding down most of its economics teaching and none of his courses would be taught in the academic year 1944–45. He needed to do something else.

On Saturday, March 18, Compton discussed with Samuelson the possibility of his working for the Office of Field Services (OFS). This was a division within the Office of Scientific Research and Development (OSRD), headed by Vannevar Bush, and from 1943 to 1945, Compton was its director.[a] The following Tuesday, Samuelson wrote to Compton, saying that he had reached the conclusion that he should instead move to MIT's Radiation Laboratory, the reason being that his "past activities in testing anti-aircraft" made him think his comparative advantage lay in carrying on with this work.[2] It is not clear where or when he had done such work. One possibility is that mathematical

---

a. There is no indication of the work he was offered.

problems related to fire control were covered in the teaching of navy officers that he had been doing for the mathematics department. Another is that his contact with Norbert Wiener had caused him to think about the problem of fire control. Wiener ran, with physiologist Arturo Rosenblueth, an interdisciplinary seminar in which the theory of cybernetics was developed, and at some date between 1937 and 1942, Samuelson began attending.[3b] These seminars covered physiology—a topic to which Samuelson had been introduced by Lawrence Henderson—and machines, and involved problems of information feedback and control. From 1940 to 1942, Wiener worked on the problem of anti-aircraft fire control, trying to solve the problem of how a gunner could anticipate the movement of an aircraft controlled by a human pilot who was trying to take evasive action. This was modeled as a stochastic process involving random changes in the direction in which the aircraft was flying.[4] In 1942, when his grant was terminated, he applied the ideas to other problems. Samuelson briefly cited Wiener's work in *Foundations,* and beginning in the 1950s, he began to use similar methods in his work on finance.

On the same day as Samuelson spoke with Compton, he also wrote his local draft board, saying that he had been released from his instructional duties so as to take on duties of a full-time staff member in the Radiation Laboratory to do work described as "[r]esearch and development of highly secret military devices in the field of high frequency electronics."[5] He started work the next day, on March 22, 1944, in the Theory Group, Mathematics and Statistics, working on "[d]esign and research in fire control problems."[6] He told Abram Bergson that he found it "quite exciting," though it was "very strenuous and working from 8:30 to 6 leaves me little time for the economic reading which I should like to do. In fact, it is only with the greatest effort that I am able to make progress on the remaining chapters of my own manuscript."[7,c] Given that he had been working there for just two weeks, it suggests he had underestimated how time-consuming his work there would be.

In the Radiation Laboratory, Samuelson was a member of Ivan Getting's Fire Control Division. Getting, almost three years older than Samuelson, had graduated from MIT in 1933, before taking a doctorate in astrophysics

---

b. Karl Deutsch, a historian and political scientist who arrived at MIT in 1942, wrote, "In Wiener's informal 'seminar' in the backroom of a nearby restaurant these young scientists, as well as Paul Samuelson, Jerome Wiesner, Frank Piore, Julius Stratton and other research leaders[,] would take part in these discussions which were a great experience for me" (Deutsch 1980, p. 326). Stratton was later to become president of MIT.

c. This refers to the revision of his thesis, discussed in chapter 22 this volume.

at Oxford. He then became a junior fellow at Harvard, overlapping with Samuelson for three years. In 1940, he had joined the Radiation Laboratory, co-directing the project that developed the SCR584 radar which, brought into service late in 1943, greatly improved the army's ability to track and shoot down enemy aircraft. Following this success, in 1943 he turned to developing the Mark 56 gunfire control system for the U.S. Navy. The goal of this project was to make it possible for a ship's guns to be fired "blind," able to hit targets at night or when fog or atmospheric conditions made seeing them impossible. Aiming for a completely automatic system was conceptually and bureaucratically very ambitious, for Getting believed that to achieve this goal, it was necessary to control both the design and the production of the system. The system was first tested in the spring of 1944, with the first automatic firing of live ammunition taking place the following December.[8]

Samuelson was part of a theoretical section that included the logician and cognitive scientist Walter Pitts, who had recently proposed a mathematical model of a neural network and who had come to Cambridge to work with Norbert Wiener.[9] Their focus was on entire systems, this being one of the reasons why Getting had went to considerable lengths to get control of all aspects of the project—something in which he was not completely successful.[10] It was necessary to integrate analysis of ballistics with understanding of the mechanical system and the human operator.

The details of Samuelson's activity within this group in which he worked long hours are unclear, no doubt because the classified nature of the work precluded his leaving a paper record of what he was doing. When writing to colleagues, declining their invitations to take on work, he obviously took pride in being able to explain that he was engaged in classified, technical war work. Given his concerns that his work as an economist at the NRPB had not contributed sufficiently to the war effort, it was important to him that he was doing something that justified his not being called up. He was not confined to the Radiation Laboratory premises at MIT, however, for in October he told Arthur Smithies, then at the State Department, that he had spent most of his last trip to Washington at the Naval Research Lab in Anacostia, "a million miles away from the economics profession."[11]

One surviving draft shows Samuelson taking a broad view of the fire control system: "A Suggestion for a Generalized Fire Control Correction Box."[12] This looked at the general problem of attacking a moving target. It was a mathematical problem involving predictions in which the relevant variables were determined simultaneously. That is, if a shell were being fired at a moving target (and for long-range guns, the movement of the earth may also need to be taken into account), the position of the target when the shell arrived (assuming it is to be hit successfully) depended on the time it took for the shell to travel to its destination; but this time depended on where the target would be, so the solution involved solving a pair of simultaneous differential equations. This was inherent in the problem and had to be solved with some sort of dynamical feedback mechanism. Samuelson assumed that the target was moving in a straight line, so that its position could be calculated from its initial position, as well as its velocity and the time the shell took to reach the target. This time was determined by ballistic considerations including the type of shell, its initial velocity, air density, and the direction in which the gun was aimed. In solving these two equations, a formula could be found that related the direction in which the gun was aimed to various positions and velocities. Samuelson did not actually solve such a system, but he described the equations using abstract functions, deriving its properties.

This was the simplest version of the problem, for in practice it would be necessary to take into account the movement of the ship on which the gun and the gun director (the radar) were placed, wind, and parallax effects arising from the gun director's not being in exactly the same place as the gun (there was expected to be one radar set controlling guns placed in different places on the ship). The box he was proposing was concerned with dynamic corrections—ones that depended on the motion of the target. He explained the importance of such dynamic corrections with an example.

> To return to the example of horizontal parallax, imagine a torpedo bomber which is crossing the bow of a ship some 2000 yards ahead at the rate of 150 yards per second. If the gun is further from the target than the director, it will not suffice to change the fuse setting in the hope of preventing the shell from going off between the ship and the target. By lengthening fuse setting we can make it go off in the previous predicted position. But still this will be too late, the plane will have gone past already. Actually the proper dynamic correction will result in a new fuse setting and in a new lead angle.[13]

This meant that the ideal was to recompute the problem taking into account the corrected data.

The problem was that this was not always possible. The Mark 56 director, as it stood, did not allow for certain factors such as variable air densities. More important, the effects of disturbances might be different for different guns served by the same director. Corrections would be different for 5-inch and 400-millimeter shells, and would be different if the objective was to aim two guns at two different aircraft in a formation. Samuelson then developed the theory of the correction box, which involved differentiating the equations describing the motion of the system and solving for the changes to the shell's flight time (which might be needed to set a fuse) and the direction in which the gun needed to be fired. The problem became a nontrivial one only when dynamic corrections were introduced. The paper ended with a numerical example—using a gun director designed for a 90-millimeter shell to control a 40-millimeter gun—to show that dynamic corrections were very important. If no correction were made, the 40-millimeter shell would burst 200 yards short of the target. Applying a static correction and using a proximity fuse could reduce the error to 21 yards, while applying a dynamic correction led to a negligible error.

The paper, intended for circulation only to specialists familiar with the project, gave no indication of the relationship of Samuelson's work to that of his colleagues. It is possible that the idea of a correction box was Samuelson's idea for solving a problem that members of the unit had identified, or even that it was Samuelson who had identified reasons why the existing director would fail to work as required, though given Getting's experience of such problems, this seems unlikely. It is more likely that others, perhaps Getting, had identified the problem and that Samuelson had been tasked with working out the theory of such a correction box. Whichever of these is correct, the paper makes it clear that Samuelson was thinking about the system as a whole, and was not just working on mechanical calculations.

Two other papers show Samuelson tackling narrower problems. "Differential Corrections in Anti-Aircraft Trajectories" was concerned with finding a simpler method for solving differential equations so as to reduce the number of calculations that needed to be done, a critical problem given the absence of powerful computers and the need for calculations to be done at great speed.[14] The other paper was completely different in character—a statistical analysis of tracking data, circulated as a Radiation Laboratory report. By this time, a prototype of the Mark 56 director existed and before testing with live ammunition, the accuracy of the mechanical apparatus was being tested using a motion picture camera mounted on the radar dish to record "the actual elevation and traverse position errors." The paper's abstract read as follows:

Breadboard model of the gun director Mk 56, mod. o, angular position errors and gyro torque motor rate currents have been subjected to statistical analysis and examined for consistency. Autocorrelation, rectangular smoothed rates, double exponential smoothed rates, mean square errors, and other statistics have been calculated.

On all four of the courses analyzed the root mean square error in traverse rates smoothed for 1.5 seconds was 0.7 mil/sec or less. On the one course subjected to intensive comparisons it would appear that the rates derived from the gyro current are fairly consistent representations of rates as derived from position data.[15]

This was a nontrivial statistical problem because data were measured subject to error, with the result that they had to be smoothed using a variety of methods. Once again, the need to economize on calculations was a major constraint. Samuelson noted that it was possible to take a short-cut, noting that there was a relationship between the error they were trying to measure and the auto-correlation function, a statistic that was comparatively easy to calculate, thereby avoiding a more complicated set of calculations. Five pages of text were followed by twenty-three pages of graphs. Unlike the other papers, this was clearly one in which he had a team of assistants to complete the computations. His conclusion was that "this is good tracking."

Samuelson was impressed by his colleagues and their mathematical abilities. His later remark that working at the Radiation Laboratory was the first time he experienced a situation in which he was not the brightest person in the room may even indicate that this was a shock to his self-confidence.[16] However, although it was a project controlled by physicists and engineers who had skills with which he could compete, it was also one to which bright outsiders, such as Samuelson and Pitts, could contribute. His mathematical knowledge—of statistics, differential equations, and the theory of equations—was important, but he was not working simply as a mathematician. Had that been the case, he would not have had to visit the Naval Research Laboratory. To be able to analyze the system and work out the theory of a correction box, the ability to make the link between the mathematical analysis and the physical problem was just as important.

Though working long days as a mathematician, he was never cut off from his economist friends and colleagues. In June 1944, he described what was going on in Cambridge to a former student, Bob Roosa.

> Things in Cambridge go on very much the same. I am now on full-time leave from the Department working on hush-hush matters at the Radiation Laboratory. There is not very much instruction in economics on the graduate level these days, I guess, but the undergraduate teaching load seems to be holding up. Bob Bishop, Art Bright, and Vandermeulen are still around and most of the members of the permanent staff are also here, in between their many important consultations with various and sundry important groups.

Except for the fact that all the students are Chinese and South American, Harvard proceeds along its usual way. Hansen is on the same old schedule, Haberler, who was at the Federal Reserve, is returning, Harris is full-time in Cambridge and is writing no less than four (4) books. Schumpeter is in residence except during the summer months, however, we haven't seen very much of him. Burbie is again chairman of the department.

This spring there has been a series of evening lectures at Littauer during which numerous visiting experts discussed problems of reconstruction. On the whole they were not too good. As usual, Williams, in his comments upon the speakers, started out brilliantly but unfortunately he had to begin repeating himself before the series was well underway and so the result was something of an anticlimax. Believe it or not, he talks now of the necessity for getting consumption up, but he doesn't say how it's to be done; and he seems really to believe that with the vast technological productivity of American industry, unemployment is inevitable.[17]

Samuelson's time in the Radiation Laboratory was very important to him. This was not just because it involved making a contribution to the war effort that justified his not being in the army. He had always been concerned with science, and here he worked closely with physicists and mathematicians on a major project. It was salutary for him to mix with such people who made him aware of his own limitations. He always stressed the long hours and the hard work involved, well aware that many of his contemporaries in the armed forces were facing much worse. He remembered being bored by the work, perhaps because he knew it was an environment in which he could not excel, claiming that "by 4 pm my slide rule seemed heavy and I would play hookey in MIT's math library."[18] His workload was not so heavy that it prevented him from continuing to work as an economist. He attended lectures and seminars at Harvard, and although his teaching at MIT was suspended, he continued to teach at the Fletcher School; he also continued to revise his thesis for publication, worked informally as a consultant to the War Production Board, and took his first steps into journalism.[d] The work also meant that his position at MIT became much more than that of a member of a comparatively marginal department: he was doing work that was central to MIT's activities, work that could be understood by the scientists who were in control of the institution. He also became interested in the problem

---

d. See chapters 22 and 23 this volume.

of government policy toward science, probably because he discussed what was going on in the Radiation Laboratory with its official historian, Henry Guerlac, a historian of science who had overlapped with him in the Society of Fellows. This became more than a passing interest, and grew to take up a significant portion of his time.

Planning Postwar Science

In the summer of 1944, while he was working in the Radiation Laboratory, Samuelson and Rupert Maclaurin turned their attention to the problem of science policy after the war. This was controversial owing in part to the efforts of Harvey Kilgore, the populist U.S. senator for West Virginia, who had introduced a series of bills into Congress proposing measures to provide federal support for science funding after the war. Kilgore's proposals raised objections not only from conservatives, who were suspicious of any expansion of government activity especially after their experience of the New Deal, but also from scientists themselves, who feared that government control of science funding would mean political interference.[19] Maclaurin was interested in the problem as part of his ongoing research project on the economics of innovation. Begun in 1941, this project had produced some results on innovation in the paper and glass container industries, but the major studies that were to result from it had yet to materialize—notably Maclaurin's study of the radio industry—and it was still ongoing.

Samuelson had worked on Maclaurin's project in the summer of 1941, but been forced to withdraw very early on because of his commitments to the NRPB. His interest in the science funding would appear to have grown out of his work in the Radiation Laboratory, where he had first-hand experience of what federal support for science could achieve, as well as discussions with his extensive network of contacts in Washington and his conversations with Guerlac. The immediate stimulus to write about the subject came from the appointment of a committee chaired by Charles Wilson, president of General Electric, which had been formed to advise on the best way to carry out the fundamental research needed by the military after the war, following on from the wartime success of the Office of Scientific Research and Development (OSRD).[20]

Samuelson was especially worried about the possibility that government-supported research would be scaled down substantially once the war ended, and he expressed his concern about the plans of the Wilson Committee even before they were published. In August 1944, he wrote to John Coil of the National Planning Association, warning that the committee was formulating plans that "some navy men consider ... to be an utterly inadequate program." As he wrote about the committee, "At least three of the civilian members seem to be interested in soft peddling the whole business, or at least in reducing its scope and effectiveness." He added, "Jewett of Bell Tel[ephone] Lab, Hunsaker of M.I.T., and the [N.]A.C.A. [National Advisory Committee on Aeronautics, of which Hunsaker was president], and President Compton of M.I.T. are looking with some favor upon a modest program, *which will not have to come before Congress for funds*, and which can be handled by private negotiation between the armed services and the *National Academy of Arts and Sciences*."[21]

Coil shared Samuelson's letter about the Wilson Committee with Bruce Bliven, the editor of *The New Republic*, who asked him to find someone who might write an article on the subject. When Bliven, with whom Samuelson had been in correspondence earlier in the summer about two articles on the problem of postwar unemployment, contacted Samuelson directly, Samuelson suggested Guerlac, though he feared that because of his role as Radiation Laboratory's official historian, Guerlac might feel he was party to too much confidential information to be able to write on the subject.[22,e] When Samuelson suggested to Bliven that he might write an editorial himself, he got an enthusiastic response.[23,f]

Samuelson eventually produced a draft editorial for Bliven, but by this time their original concern had been overtaken by events. The Wilson report had been published, and on November 17, 1944, Roosevelt invited Vannevar Bush, the MIT engineer who was head of the OSRD, to prepare a report on the problem. Samuelson explained to Bliven that the situation was not as bad as it had been in August, for it looked as though the policy of rapidly winding up government research activity had been reversed.[24] "However," he continued, "there are still no indications of an adequate postwar program. This is an understatement. I am hoping that the favorable elections and probable discussion will improve prospects but I am not optimistic." The situation had improved but there was still great cause for concern.

Samuelson then listed a number of points that he had not been able to make in his draft, which Bliven had asked to be less than a thousand words.

---

e. Samuelson's other articles in *The New Republic* are discussed in chapter 23 this volume.

f. While Samuelson was having these discussions with Bliven, Maclaurin drafted a proposal to study, through a survey, the relation between fundamental research at universities and industrial development. This proposal was Maclaurin's, but it contained ideas that so clearly echoed Samuelson's thinking that it is virtually certain that they had discussed it.

Though defense might be the initial motivation, "Military research should be simply the opening wedge in a forward program of encouraging technical progress" that would be of benefit to industry. Government research might lead to a reduction in the "relative prestige" of large companies, currently responsible for much research, but they would not suffer in any absolute sense. Smaller companies that did not have research capabilities would, of course, benefit and the result would be healthier competition. Samuelson also drew on his own experience in the Radiation Laboratory to claim that "centralized research in OSRD laboratories" was much more effective than research funded by federal grants-in aid.

Given both the appearance of the Wilson report and the publication of Roosevelt's letter, it was inevitable that Bliven would ask for alterations: the material was more topical than ever, but it did not reflect what had happened. He told Samuelson that he had been impressed with a recent article in *Science*, written by Rear Admiral J. A. Furer, a navy representative on the Wilson Committee.[25] Furer made a case for the committee's proposals, citing the example of the National Advisory Committee for Aeronautics as a precedent for a coordinating body made up of "civilians of distinction in science, engineering and industry" plus military officers. A point he made that appealed to Bliven was that the board should not operate its own laboratories, but should contract research to existing organizations, though where no suitable facilities existed, it might establish laboratories for specific purposes and then hand them over to another agency for operation.[26]

Samuelson, in his reply to Bliven, agreed that the Wilson report was "somewhat impressive, especially in view of what might have been expected from it," but he was not convinced.[27] He responded to Furer's argument about the NSRB's not having its own laboratories by pointing out that the Radiation Laboratory's being at MIT was "a mere formality." In fact, he pointed out, it "has little to do with M.I.T. and it *is* the OSRD" (emphasis in original). Making his point with non-MIT examples, he continued,

> Ask any producing scientist whether grantsinaid to the Applied Mathematics Panel or to, say, the Radio Research Laboratory at Harvard[,] are more productive. He is sure to select the latter and this is always the case.

The most productive research had been organized in precisely the way Furer was arguing against. He suggested Bliven talk to Merle Tuve, a geophysicist at Johns Hopkins, who had "the best grasp of the problem of anyone on the committee." Though he made it clear that he was not in any way questioning his integrity, he argued that Jewett's position reflected a way of thinking that stemmed from his position as president of the National Academy of Sciences. The implied message was that Bliven should continue to work for better policies; it was only "because of continuous pressure" that the Wilson Committee had made reasonable recommendations.

Bliven proposed that they add a new introduction, because Samuelson jumped into the middle of the problem without explaining that science had contributed much to the war effort and that science would continue to play an important role. Bliven also translated Samuelson's comments on the attitudes of those involved into more diplomatic, though still hard-hitting language:[28]

> A good many well known scientists, however, take their coloration from the conservative business men who are their associates, and seem terribly alarmed lest government aid to scientific research should interfere with the sacred fetish of "private enterprise." There is a real danger that they may cripple scientific research by turning it over to the same auspices which helped bring us to such a perilous condition in 1941.[29]

Samuelson thought this revised introduction "first rate," though it perhaps underestimated the extent to which the scientists themselves held conservative views.[30] Bliven's introduction led straight into an account of the Wilson Committee, pointing out that it was concerned narrowly with "technical military scientific research," and describing it as "an able but cautious report which shows the marks of compromise." In arguing that the president should appoint the board, he suggested that giving this responsibility to the National Academy of Sciences would be like suggesting "that the carpenters' union should elect members of a board which is to plan public works."[31] Given conservative attitudes toward unions, this was a strong claim. Science was, he contended, too important to be left to scientists.

Explaining that the full extent of scientific advance was still a military secret (the first atomic bomb had not yet been dropped on Hiroshima), Samuelson picked out a few achievements that relied on scientific advances (interception of enemy aircraft, victory over submarines, continuous blind-bombing of Germany), and emphasized that this had involved "a great deal of luck," because before 1939, "only pitiful driblets were available for fundamental research in the same fields which now engage hundreds of physicists and electrical engineers." The need for luck should be reduced by establishing an organization that would provide grants-in-aid to universities and laboratories, and undertake sustained fundamental research and development." Samuelson argued that the country could no longer afford *not* to do this: imaginative plans were also needed in nonmilitary fields. If scientists did not come up with an adequate program, there was the danger that others might do so, and the result would be something that was less effective.

The Bowman Committee

When Roosevelt asked him to prepare a report on postwar science policy, Bush immediately set up four committees to advise him, writing answers to each of the four questions that Roosevelt had posed. The key question was the third: What could the government do to aid research by public and private organizations? Bush selected Isaiah Bowman, professor of geography and president of Johns Hopkins University, who had much experience with government committees, to chair the committee that was to answer it. Its members included distinguished scientists and science administrators from universities and commercial research laboratories, including John Tate, a Minnesota physicist; Oliver Buckley from Bell Laboratories; Warren Weaver from the Rockefeller Foundation; and Caryl Haskins, a biophysicist who ran a private research laboratory. Its most distinguished member was Isidor I. Rabi, a physicist and associate director of the Radiation Laboratory, who was also heavily involved in the atomic bomb project and was the latest (1944) recipient of the Nobel Prize for physics. Maclaurin, who was working on innovation and was well known to Bush, was an obvious choice as secretary of the committee, and Samuelson joined him as assistant secretary. Samuelson, Bush claimed, was "exceptionally qualified" for the task in view of his work at the National Resources Planning Board and his work on "the economic effects of technological change and various national planning studies."[32] Given that he was now employed by the Radiation Laboratory, this involved his being "loaned" back to MIT from January 1, 1945.[33] The expectation was that he would be returning after three or four months. His role was to take minutes of the meetings of the main committee and its steering committee. The committee was provided with a substantial secretariat, directed by Henry Guerlac, to assist in finding materials and drafting reports. Samuelson's main collaborator on this task was Guerlac.[34]

Samuelson drafted the memorandum that formed the basis for discussion at the first meeting of the Steering Committee on January 3, 1945.[35] It began by establishing the breadth of Roosevelt's directive, beginning with "pure (or fundamental) and applied research," carried out in universities, private and government laboratories, and industry. It listed the reasons why research was desirable for the nation, as well as reasons why funding for research had declined: the distribution of income was becoming more equal, so that the wealthy could provide fewer funds; bond yields were low; too little research had been undertaken during the Depression and wartime; the purchasing power of the postwar research dollar had been halved; and universities were under pressure (high teaching loads and low salaries).

This memorandum, presumably prepared in collaboration with Maclaurin, flagged important issues to be discussed. Should economies of scale be sacrificed by decentralizing research across large and small universities? Should research be used to aid backward industries (textiles, housing, agriculture), and should it be used as a weapon against monopoly? Could government support research without controlling it? How were pure and applied research to be defined? What conditions were to be applied to the distribution of research funding? It concluded with a note on "possible instrumentalities"—branches of the Office of Education or the Department of the Interior, or an independent Executive Office combining military and civilian research agencies. It provided a comprehensive outline of the tasks to be undertaken.

One of the issues occupying the committee was how to define different types of science: Should they use the terminology of pure and applied science, or prefer terms such as "basic" or "fundamental" science? This was crucial because it was widely assumed that applied research, which resulted in ideas that could be protected by patents and exploited commercially, would be undertaken by industry, without any government support. The problem was research that was essential in the long term, which might not be funded if government support were not available.[g]

The dominant voices on the Bowman Committee were clearly those of the natural scientists and engineers. These came with deeply held views about science that they had been developing for many years. The key players—Bush, Conant, Compton, and Jewett—were all suspicious of government control, concerned with preventing federal support for science being provided in such a way as to reduce scientists' freedom. Though they had different visions of the institutional setting in which scientists would prosper—laboratories in which scientists engaged in long-term collaborative projects, or common rooms in which individuals conversed—Conant and Compton were agreed on enhancing the role of pure scientific research driven by the curiosity of the scientist. But although it was the scientists on the committee whose views

g. Samuelson recommended that Guerlac would be a good person to deal with the problem of defining pure science, but the committee did not take up this suggestion.

dominated, the members of the secretariat were not mere scribes. They had strong views of their own, and their role gave them the power to influence the committee's discussions.

Samuelson, with his recent experience at the Radiation Laboratory, and Guerlac, whose views went back to his PhD thesis on military research in eighteenth-century France, were convinced that wartime experience of planned research could carry over into peacetime.[36] They had a powerful ally in Rabi, who could also see the importance of planned science. However, theirs was a minority view, for most committee members were fearful that planned science would undermine the freedom of the individual scientist, and that government funding would likely lead to undesirable government control. It was necessary to find a balance that would ensure adequate funding while minimizing the control and interference by nonscientists feared by committee members.

The term "scientific high command" was the heading on an undated note, presumably written early in the Bowman Committee's deliberations, and clearly not intended for wider distribution on account of its sharp criticism of prominent scientists, especially of Jewett.[37] Its tone and conclusions reflect the position taken in Samuelson's editorial in *The New Republic*, suggesting he might have been its author.[38] It assessed the current situation, described the sentiments of leading scientific decision makers in scientific matters, and provided an inventory of possible solutions. The last ran from the most conservative to the most radical: letting the army and navy do everything, using existing institutions such as the National Academy of Sciences, or creating a permanent government bureau.

There had been, so this document argued, a "gradual realization" even among the more conservative voices that "some planning" was necessary to ensure "adequate use of science by the State." Cooperation between civilian scientists and the armed forces had been successful in wartime, and a way should be found to continue this. Moreover, the reality of the situation was that there was a "small number of scientists" who would remain in "key positions" regardless of what would happen.[h] This is what the document described as a "close inner gang" of "Eastern seaboard and MIT" Republicans, who were anti-bureaucratic and, though conservative, were patriotic rather than reactionary. This group had done an "extraordinary job" in bringing civilian scientists to the study of war-related problems, and they determined to go "all out" in keeping this active after the war. The document then

---

h. Such as Bush, Jewett, Conant, Hunsaker, Tuve, and Compton.

discussed alternative organizational forms, but subsequent discussions in the Bowman Committee exposed the sensitivity of any such proposal.

A draft report, partly written by committee members and partly by the secretariat, was discussed at the end of March, in a meeting held at Johns Hopkins University in Baltimore.[39] The minutes, written by Samuelson and another member of the secretariat, show that even at this point there was deep disagreement over the need for federal funding. On one side were those who argued in favor of government support for science. Four arguments were presented against them: (1) federal funding would lead to federal control; (2) the unpredictability of pure science meant that it was dangerous to let it be planned by any single group; (3) government funding would discourage other funding, leaving pure science completely dependent on it; (4) civil service regulations were unfavorable to fostering pure science. For example, Weaver, who as a representative of the Rockefeller Foundation had a commitment to private funding of research, challenged the claim that the wartime success of federal funding could be carried over to peacetime; wartime methods, focusing on immediate needs, had harmed pure science, and in peacetime, scientists would not tolerate the same conditions as they had accepted in wartime. Rabi countered these arguments by suggesting that Weaver had been too much influenced by mathematicians, claiming that three out of four scientists in the Radiation Laboratory would like to work in a similar environment after the war; universities had fought for freedom in the past and could learn to fight "against government dictation."

The dispute was resolved by prefacing the report with what Bowman called a "statement of social philosophy."[40] Starting with the familiar trope of the closing of the frontier, it argued that even if the geographical frontier had closed, "there always remains one inexhaustible national resource—creative scientific research."[41] It expressed pride in existing institutions and spelled out arguments against federal control made by committee members, before explaining that federal funding was a conclusion to which the committee had been "forced." It then argued that the committee's proposals for federal funding were rooted in American traditions.

Basically this problem is but one example of a continuing series of similar problems raised by the American experiment. All our important political decisions involve the necessity of balancing irreducible national functions with the free play of individual initiative.... In the opinion of the Committee an increased measure of federal support will raise new problems. We have therefore carefully considered the possibility of increased federal aid for scientific research without at the same time introducing undesirable paternalism. In order to be fruitful, scientific research must be free—free from political influence, free from pressure for immediate practical results, free from planning of means or ends by those who are not scientists, free from dictation by any central board.[42]

Setting up a new institution was presented as a necessity to which the committee had agreed only reluctantly, and it must be done in such a way as to avoid centrally planning science.

The organization or instrument finally set up should be such as to eliminate political influence and to escape undesirable pressures. It should not itself attempt to play the role of an all-seeing, all-wise planning board attempting to guide in detail the normal growth-processes of science.[43]

The report was agreed upon and transmitted to Bush, who used it as the basis for his own report, published in July 1945 as *Science: Endless Frontier*, to which it was published as an appendix.[44,i]

In a letter to Bush, Bowman pointed out the importance of what he called the statement of social philosophy.

This statement was very carefully drafted. It contains the best judgment of the committee. It is a deliberate judgment following wide differences of opinion at the beginning. It is a unanimous judgment. Without these few pages on social philosophy about half of the committee would be unwilling to sign our report. I would be among that half. We must express our fears regarding Federal control and we must state explicitly how we would avoid such control. Having done so, we are ready to present our recommendations regarding the scale of support and the method of distribution.[45]

Samuelson's involvement with the Bowman Committee might seem far removed from his other concerns, for none of his own publications had dealt with the topic, but it was not. Working with Hansen, he had become convinced that government had an important role to play in sustaining a mixed capitalist economy. The same political philosophy, emphasizing individual freedom and initiative, but with government action to undertake tasks that private business would neglect, can be seen in his work on the management

---

i. This explains why Samuelson could include the Bush report in his bibliography, with a note saying that he had written much of it.

of science and economic management.[j] And, at least since his undergraduate years, science had been a particular concern; mixing with scientists in the Society of Fellows, at MIT, in the Radiation Laboratory, and in the Bowman Committee was undoubtedly very important to him. Being able to bring his expertise as an economist to help create an environment in which science could flourish would have been something to which he attached great importance. The Bowman Committee also exposed him to the arguments that were used to attack not just government-funded science but government involvement in the economy more generally. These arguments were wielded by people whose scientific credentials he respected and that merited being taken seriously. The experience of producing a document that was acceptable to the entire committee would have been a lesson to Samuelson in how to present state intervention in a manner that was acceptable to those who equated being American with opposing government control of individual activities.

After the Radiation Laboratory

By March 22, when he was busy drafting the report, Samuelson had completed a year at the Radiation Laboratory, and on April 4, its director, Wheeler Loomis, wrote to ask him about extending his leave of absence from MIT.[46] Samuelson explained that he would prefer not to agree to this, on two grounds. The first was that, though he had so far been able to fend off such pressure, the Economics Department was unwilling to extend his leave beyond July 1, 1945. The second was that, after canvassing opinions on the manpower situation in his division of the Radiation Laboratory, and knowing the need for economists to work on problems of reconversion, he believed that "such talents as I have would best be used" by returning to work as an economist.[47]

Shortly after the Bowman report had been transmitted to Bush, Samuelson had a conversation with Getting, and he decided he needed to clarify his situation to Loomis.[48] He made it clear that, if his duty lay in continuing at the Radiation Laboratory, he would do so:

> My previous letter to you reflected my belief that the day is approaching when it will no longer be in the national interest to convert a good economist into a mediocre mathematician. However, it is not up to

---

j. On the latter, see chapter 23 this volume.

me to define when that day has arrived. It is my intention, therefore, in this letter to rescind my statement in the last letter. I am willing to continue on at the laboratory for as long as I am needed.

He then expressed a preference for any continuation to be on a three-month basis rather than for a longer period. There were two other considerations. The Economics Department had "a necessary project" that he alone could do—writing new materials for the introductory economics course.[49] However, in relation to the national emergency, this was not decisive. A potentially more important consideration was that Rabi had approached him to write the history of the Manhattan Project to build an atomic bomb at Los Alamos.[50] This was a paradoxical offer because, officially, he was not allowed to know that there was such a project, and yet he was being asked whether would like to write its history. He was not trained as a historian, but he was a mathematically trained social scientist, and though his mathematical knowledge would have been important for the task, he later noted that "wild horses could not have drawn me to that, or any, history job"—though when replying to Loomis, he was more diplomatic:

> My off-hand reaction [to Rabi's request] was that after four years of heavy load with no customary academic vacation the thought of taking on an entirely new job requiring creative energy was not an attractive one; that I should prefer to make my contribution to the war effort in the Radiation Laboratory where I am already familiar with the work.[51]

In addition, the war was nearing its end and he had no desire to embark on a project that would probably take a long time to complete.[k]

Samuelson continued within the Radiation Laboratory until July 14, 1945, when he returned to his duties at MIT.[52] In the first part of May, he was no doubt involved in the further revisions that needed to be made before the final version of the Bowman Committee report was sent to Bush.[53] By the middle of May, as the war was ending in Europe, this was completed, for on May 19, Bush's secretary congratulated Maclaurin on the "splendid job" they had done.[54,l]

---

k. Even had he been interested, he would have known from Guerlac, the official historian of the Radiation Laboratory, about the difficulties involved in writing such a history. He may have been aware of the conflict Guerlac faced between the type of history he wanted to write, paying full attention to the social and political context of scientific developments, and the type of history his employers wanted him to write.

l. Beyond this work for the Bowman Committee, it is not clear what work, if any, Samuelson was doing for the Radiation Laboratory for the last two months.

Samuelson was presented with a further opportunity to become involved with scientists (and philosophers) when Leontief conveyed to him an invitation to join the Inter-Scientific Discussion Group.[55] This group was an part of the Unity of Science movement, which had come to be associated with Harvard, beginning with the Fifth International Congress for the Unity of Science, held there in 1939, and the move to Harvard of the exiled Austrian physicist-philosopher Philip Frank. The Inter-Scientific Discussion Group was a successor to the Science of Science Discussion Group that had met in the fall of 1940, organized by psychologist Stanley Smith Stevens. A common theme among those behind the discussion group was an affinity with Bridgman's operationalism, which Stevens had advocated in psychology, and the logical positivism of Rudolf Carnap, brought to Harvard by Willard Quine, and the Vienna Circle. Given Samuelson's emphasis on operationalism in his thesis and the book he was currently writing, it would be natural to deduce that it was these links that induced him to accept Leontief's invitation by return post.

The first meeting he attended was on March 21, when George Wald, a biochemist who specialized in studying vision, spoke on "Biology and Social Behavior."[56] It would have been a gathering of familiar faces, for not only were his teachers—Schumpeter, Leontief, and Haberler—present, but so too were John Edsall, working alongside him in the Bowman secretariat; Percy Bridgman, whose lectures on thermodynamics he had probably audited and whom he knew from his days as a junior fellow; and Norbert Wiener, in whose cybernetics seminar he had participated. Because of illness, he missed the meeting on April 18, at which a philosopher, Curt Ducasse, spoke on "What Is Science?"[57] He resumed his attendance on June 18, when Edsall was talking about "Stability and Flux in the Living Organism," after which he attended no further meetings until February 1946, when the topic of discussion was von Neumann and Morgenstern's *The Theory of Games and Economic Behavior* (1945), which brought out a large contingent of Harvard economists: Haberler, Leontief, Hans Staehle, and Richard Goodwin. Though he was busy teaching in the 1945–46 academic year, it would seem that he had little interest in the group, returning simply to hear Oscar Morgenstern talking about what was clearly a very important book. A year after that, he returned for a session on "Automatic Calculating Machinery," but that appears to have been the sum total of his involvement.

Samuelson was busy, but given his capacity for fitting commitments into his schedule, it is hard not to conclude that, despite his emphasis on operationalism in his thesis and in *Foundations*—the latter then in the hands of Harvard University Press—he had no deep interest in the philosophy of science.[m] He attended the first meeting after his invitation, and after that appears to have attended only sessions on topics closely related to his own work. This strongly suggests that, although he chose to use the term *operationalism*—rather than alternatives such as *testability, refutability,* or *falsificationism*—there is no evidence that he engaged seriously with the related philosophical issues. As with Henderson's Pareto seminar almost a decade earlier, he sampled it and moved on.

The period covered in this chapter was very brief, and despite the demands made by the Radiation Laboratory, Samuelson's commitment to natural science was never full time, as he kept working as an economist throughout. But even though it was only a small part of his life, it was very important to him. It was important to him that he worked on radar—something that was, without question, important for the war effort. This would have been consolation for any concerns he may have had that his unfinished work at the NRPB had not been successful. He had, of course, been teaching students for much of the war, including helping out in the Mathematics Department, but although teaching was important, its contribution to the war effort or the essential task of planning for peace was only indirect. As suggested earlier, he may have been inspired by E. B. Wilson's successful move into aeronautics in the previous war. If so, the experience of working alongside some of the world's leading scientists may have helped him confirm that he wanted to be an economist. However, even if he wanted to be an economist, and could be an outstanding one, it was undoubtedly very important to him to have rubbed shoulders with top scientists.

m. On *Foundations*, see chapter 22 this volume.

CHAPTER 22 | *Foundations of Economic Analysis,*
1940–1947

From Thesis to Book

While he was working at the Radiation Laboratory, Samuelson sent the final draft of *Foundations of Economic Analysis* to Harvard University Press. When it was published in 1947, this was to cement his reputation as the leading economist of his generation. The book had had a long gestation period, being a revised version of the PhD thesis (discussed in chapter 14 this volume) he had submitted in 1940.

Fifty years after the book's publication, Samuelson provided his own account of the problems encountered in turning the thesis into a book and why it took so long.

> Alas, World War II came to U.S. shores via Pearl Harbor. Nights and Sundays, while working on radar and mathematical fire control at the Radiation Laboratory, I toiled over revisions and expansions. By 1944 I handed in the finished draft.[1]

He claimed that the manuscript then sat in the Economics Department, which had to give approval because it was appearing in a series sponsored by the department, gathering dust, owing to the long-time department chair's lack of enthusiasm for those who engaged in economic theory before the age of fifty.[a]

---

a. Elsewhere, Samuelson attributed Department Chair Burbank's aversion to him as anti-Semitism; see chapter 15 this volume.

Burbank, Samuelson claimed, also tried to sabotage the book by ordering too few copies and destroying the type:

> Less lucky was the department chairman's decision to have a first printing of only 500 copies. I objected. We compromised on 750 copies. But he had the last word. His orders were to destroy all that beautiful mathematical type after the first run.[2]

However, Samuelson's memory of these events, colored by his attitude to Burbank, was not completely accurate.[b]

Samuelson had defended his thesis soon after his move to MIT. The examination took place on December 4, 1940, the examiners being Wilson, Chamberlin, and Taylor, with Schumpeter as the chair. Wilson was concerned not with Samuelson's competence in mathematical economics—he had no doubt that he was "a consummate mathematical economist" whose command of the subject was comparable to his own and better than that of any other member of the department—but with Samuelson's ability in economic theory more generally. He had heard that Samuelson was "a little short in his knowledge of economic theory . . . that cannot yet be put into mathematical form."[3] As he did not consider himself qualified to assess this, Wilson therefore impressed on Chamberlin, shortly before the examination, that those present should ask questions to probe Samuelson's knowledge of such work. The outcome of the examination was, in Wilson's view, not a foregone conclusion. In any event, the panel concluded that Samuelson's performance was excellent in general economic theory, as well as in mathematical economics.[4] In the new year, Wilson wrote to him to say he had done a fine job in his examination, expressing the view that Schumpeter had been too busy to read the thesis properly beforehand, for he had asked questions to which answers could be found in the thesis.[5]

Samuelson's thesis was a natural candidate for the Wells Prize, awarded each year to the best PhD thesis in economics, and which carried with it the promise of publication by Harvard University Press. However, the Harvard Corporation ruled that, having been examined so late in the year, Samuelson's thesis could not be considered for publication by the Prize Committee in 1941,

---

b. The first clue is that, no doubt because of the importance he attached to the episode, he leaves the reader free to infer that he worked in the Radiation Laboratory throughout the war; as was explained in chapter 21 this volume, his employment in the Radiation Laboratory did not begin until March 22, 1944, and that from January 1, 1945, he was seconded to the Bowman committee. If he worked there informally outside these dates, such work is not documented.

but had to wait until 1942. On learning this,[6] Wilson advised Samuelson to take advantage of the delay by rewriting it: though he or other mathematical economists might not benefit from such rewriting—they could understand it in its current form—it would make the book far more valuable to economists who were less mathematically inclined. He explained that there were "too many formulas which would scare them off" and that expanding the text would "help them to appreciate the value of rigorous mathematical economics of which not a few of them are rather skeptical."[7] Alluding to the precept of Alfred Marshall that Samuelson had criticized so strongly in the opening pages of his thesis, Wilson explained that he thought Samuelson should give more illustrative examples and turn as much of the mathematics as possible into English.

Writing to Harris, chair of the Wells Prize committee, expressing relief that the thesis could not be considered for another year, Wilson named some of the economists whom he thought that Samuelson could reach by writing in a different style.

> The important thing, however, is to get this book out in such a form that it won't be too difficult reading for men like Taylor and Chamberlin and Frank Knight or J. M. Clark or other of our first-class economic theorists who are not particularly trained in mathematics. [Such economists] ought to know what [Samuelson's] results are in order to avoid certain confusions which might otherwise arise.[8]

He pointed out that Samuelson implied as much in certain passages of the thesis. Wilson's view of Samuelson's thesis followed from his belief that the potential audience for works in mathematical economics was very limited. Given that Chamberlin and Taylor had been among the examiners, Wilson's remark that they would not understand it was probably well founded.

Writing to Chamberlin, Wilson opined that the 284 pages of the thesis should be expanded with around 100 pages of additional text. And in addition to providing illustrations of "actual economic problems," he recommended that there should be "many more references to the standard treatises on economics like Marshall's [*Principles of Economics*]" and that where he did refer to such works, detailed page references were needed.[9] He made it even clearer to Chamberlin than he had to Samuelson that he disagreed with Samuelson's treatment of Marshall:

> Samuelson quotes Marshall's remark that you ought to be able to translate your mathematical economics into English composition and

he quotes it with disapproval, I would quote it with approval. I realize fully that a complete translation may not be possible but I further realize that in our day and generation theoretical economists will not be highly trained in mathematics and that it is of the greatest importance to do all the translating one can and make the translation just as readable and effective as one can.

Such remarks, when taken together with his earlier doubts about Samuelson's employability in most economics departments, show that Wilson failed to anticipate the extent to which the audience for mathematical economics would grow.

The Wells Prize for that year was awarded to Samuelson's friend David McCord Wright for his thesis on "The Creation of Purchasing Power" and Samuelson's thesis was considered at the beginning of 1942. A committee comprising Harris, Haberler, Hansen, and Leontief decided to award him the prize, a decision that was endorsed by the department on February 10, 1942.[10] Burbank wrote to him of his good fortune on March 16, saying that one of the factors behind the award was "the condition of the essay relative to publication" and that he hoped a manuscript could be sent to Harvard University Press as soon as possible. As well as covering the costs of publication, the prize included a payment of $500, but this could be paid only when the final manuscript was sent to the publisher, which did not happen until February 1945.[11]

On May 29, 1942, David Pottinger, of Harvard University Press, requested a summary of the book and various biographical details so he could prepare some advance publicity.[12] In reply, Samuelson explained that he was undertaking "fairly extensive revisions" and that, because of his work as a consultant for the National Resources Planning Board, it was being delayed. He did not expect the manuscript to be finished in 1942. He explained that the book was very important: "the problems which it analyzes are not at all of an esoteric or narrow type, but rather are the fundamental ones underlying all economic writings, literary or symbolical, theoretical or applied." However, he warned Pottinger that the book would be mathematical. He hoped that nonmathematical economists would be able to learn from it, but he was not very optimistic about this.[13] He then went on to summarize the book's contents:

It is an attempt to elucidate the basic hypotheses common to value and price theory and modern business cycle theory. These prove to be of two distinct but related types. The first hypothesis holds that the equilibrium conditions determining the values of certain economic variables arise from the maximizing behavior of a given firm or household. In particular, interest is centered on the non-circular, refutable, meaningfully observable implications of the hypotheses in counterdistinction to any alleged *a priori* validity.

The second principal hypothesis involves the assumption that the interactions of the schedules summarizing the behavior of different economic units are subject to certain "stability" conditions. This latter term presupposes a rudimentary implicit or explicit theory of dynamics. The second part of the book is concerned with developing a theory of dynamics and its relationship to the derivation of useful information about the statical properties of the system. These are illustrated by application to some of the more fundamental problems of economic theory and business cycles.[14]

This suggests that very early on, in 1941 or 1942, Samuelson had decided that the book should be expanded by being extended into business cycle theory, for though the thesis had mentioned this (there had been an analysis of the stability of the Keynesian system, and references to business cycle theory), such material was very limited. There is no indication that, at this point, he had the idea of writing a chapter on welfare economics.

As Samuelson anticipated, progress was slow. On July 8, 1943, Samuelson wrote to Abbott Usher, who was dealing with the press on behalf of the department, about his progress with the book.

This is just a line to let you know that I finally found the leisure necessary to prepare my dissertation for publication. The manuscript will be ready for the printer by the first of September. However, this is not a definite prediction as I may hit snags in the latter portions.[15]

Usher was encouraging Samuelson to finish the book quickly. Making it clear that Samuelson was free to revise as he wished, he expressed concern that trying to bring the manuscript up to date might cause Samuelson to get bogged down. He suggested Samuelson consider adding notes rather than starting "so large a revision that it remained incomplete."[16] The following month, after describing all the activities that were taking up his time that summer, Samuelson wrote to Walter Salant, "To cap all this, I am trying desperately to make minor revisions in my dissertation so that it can finally be sent to the press. I have put this off for so long, and now that I am on the home stretch, I hope that I can finish it once and for all."[17]

In April 1944, a fortnight after he started at the Radiation Laboratory, he told his friend Wolfgang Stolper that it was only with great difficulty that he could make any progress on "the remaining chapters of my own manuscript."[18] Unfortunately, he did not say which chapters he had already finished. Given his comment to Salant, a year earlier, that he was making only minor revisions and that he was "on the home stretch," it is clear that at some point in 1943–44 he had decided to include new material.[c] It is not known when he submitted the manuscript to the department. As he was still struggling to find time to finish it in April, it would seem unlikely to have been earlier than the summer of 1944, and it could well have been later in the year. The book was forwarded to Harvard University Press in February 1945, which means that the time it sat on Burbank's desk—presumably because he had to find time to read it, possibly also consulting colleagues, and give his approval—was probably at most six months, though if Samuelson and Marion had worked on it for a significant part of the time he was employed at the Radiation Laboratory, it might have been much less. Having submitted it, he was probably impatient to know that it had been sent to the press, and he may well have remembered the delay as being longer than it was.

On February 27, 1945, Samuelson wrote to E. B. Wilson saying, "My Wells Prize dissertation has finally been handed to the University Press. That is a great relief."[19] When they received the manuscript, Harvard University Press immediately raised the question of how soon it should be published. There was a paper shortage, and given that the Economics Department had sent them another book to be published that year, they thought it unlikely that they could also proceed with Samuelson's.[20] Usher, who was dealing with the press, explained that although he did not expect the print run to be more than 750 copies, he would also like a quotation for printing 1,200 copies, so as not to prejudge the size of the edition.[21] However, the first problem the publisher encountered was that the Harvard University Printing Office said that because of the mathematics involved, they were unable to give an estimate of the cost, because much of the typesetting would have to be done by hand.[22] Rather than proceed on a cost-plus basis, Usher asked the press to get estimates from printers who specialized in such work.[23] Faced with this, the Harvard Printing Office came up with a price that the press thought excessive.[24] Instead, the decision was made to use a Pennsylvania printer, Lancaster Press, on grounds that they had greater experience and were known to be reliable.[25]

---

c. He did not mention what the new material was. A possible candidate, discussed later, is the chapter on welfare economics.

However, work did not begin, and in December 1945, Harvard University Press asked the printer to return the manuscript, as it would shortly be going into production, noting that in addition, Samuelson wanted to do some more work on it.[26,d]

In April 1946, the press reported to Usher that Lancaster Press was so busy they would not be able to start work for another few months.[27] Later that month, Samuelson settled on what would be the book's final title, *Foundations of Economic Analysis.* The reasons he gave for this was that it was more accurate, given the new material he had added and that he thought it would be more popular—a change that Usher strongly approved.[e] It was not until December, though, that Lancaster Press sent Harvard University Press the galley proofs of the first two chapters for approval.[28] That month they also learned that their supplier would begin producing suitable paper in January 1947.[29] Though Samuelson had to insist on the printer reproducing certain symbols precisely, and the printer had to have new type cast,[30] the book was ready for printing in June. A print run of 1,200 copies was agreed—significantly more than the figure Samuelson remembered. Samuelson also negotiated an order for 100 offprints of the mathematical appendices.[31]

Once the plates were made, there was pressure to kill the type, coming entirely from the printer. In April 1947, Lancaster Press wrote to Alfred Jules, production manager at Harvard University Press, to say that they were getting close to being able to print the book and they did not want to hold the metal plates any longer than necessary.

> The composing machine metal shortage is still acute and what metal is available is priced at almost double its normal cost. For these reasons we hesitate to tie up too many pages after a printing of a book is completed, and we have been wondering whether you would want to consider having us electrotype this book before this first printing and in that way have printing plates available for any subsequent issues that may be needed.[32]

This letter went back and forth between Jules and the press's business manager. Jules asked, "OK to kill after presswork is complete?" and was told, "We'll have to get dept. OK." Jules then wrote to Lancaster Press, explaining

---

d. The letter refers to "the authors." It is not known what changes Samuelson wanted to make at this stage.

e. The thesis title had been *Foundations of Analytical Economics: The Observational Significance of Economic Theory.*

that "we cannot plate this book for obvious reasons, but I can well appreciate your metal situation and will do all I can to hasten the decision of the department."[33] However, nearly two months later, a decision still had not been received. Lancaster Press asked Jules again whether the type could be killed, in a letter that was passed on to Smith, who then contacted Usher.[34] Jules wrote to Lancaster Press:

> I have taken up with our business manager the matter of killing the type and hope to get a decision one way or the other today. It takes some time to get an approval from the department involved, as in most cases, they prefer to have the type held for a length of time. As they have no understanding of the type metal shortage, we are more or less helpless.[35]

In July, Usher confirmed that the type could be killed.[36]

Lancaster Press eventually shipped 887 copies of the book on October 1, 1947, and copies were distributed on October 10.[37] It appears that the shortage of paper was still a factor, for a letter from the press to Usher explained that it was expected that the War Production Board would soon revoke controls on the use of paper, when it would be easy to scale up production quickly.[38] Because costs had risen so much since the contract had been signed almost two years earlier, Lancaster Press was allowed to raise their price by 10 percent, though owing to the subsidy from the Wells Prize fund, the book could still be sold for $5, a price similar to that at which McGraw-Hill were to sell Samuelson's introductory textbook.[39] As Samuelson had noted the previous year, the extended time from submission of the manuscript to publication had been caused primarily by the shortage of paper.[40]

Statics—Production and Consumption

Samuelson was entirely correct to say that he expanded his thesis as well as revised it, for about half the material was new and yet it is striking how little the text of the thesis was changed.[41,f] However, one change was very significant. In the introduction to the thesis, Samuelson had explained the link between comparative static and dynamic theory by writing, "Here the hypothesis is made that the system is in stable equilibrium or motion in

---

f. He added four new chapters and an appendix, which amounted to 181 of the book's 439 pages. A further 47 pages of new material were added elsewhere to the book.

terms of an assumed dynamical system. This implies no ideological or normative significance."[42] In the book, that became:

> Instead, the dynamical properties of the system are specified, and the hypothesis is made that the system is in "stable" equilibrium or motion. By means of what I have called the Correspondence Principle between comparative statics and dynamics, definite operationally meaningful theorems can be derived from so simple a hypothesis. One interested only in fruitful statics must study dynamics.
>
> The empirical validity or fruitfulness of the theorems, of course, cannot surpass that of the original hypothesis. Moreover, the stability hypothesis has no teleological or normative significance.[43]

Similarly, in the chapter "Stability and Comparative Statics," after explaining that dynamics and comparative statics were connected, he added the sentence, "This duality constitutes what I have called the *correspondence principle*."[44] The content of his argument had not changed, but Samuelson introduced a name for the idea and elevated it to the status of a "principle."[45] Naming the idea gave it a prominence that it would otherwise not have had; it drew attention to Samuelson's claim that it was important to specify a dynamic system, for without this the derivation of comparative statics results might be impossible. Given that most previous work failed to specify explicit dynamic systems, this was a bold claim, marking Samuelson's work apart from what had gone before.[g]

He gave an example to illustrate this point in the first substantial addition to the text of his thesis—a section titled "The Calculus of Qualitative Relations." Samuelson argued that even if we know the signs of all the parameters in a system (and typically economic theory says nothing about the size of coefficients, merely whether they are positive or negative), it can be impossible to work out comparative statics results. For example, in the Keynesian system, with only three equations determining three variables, even if we knew the signs of all the parameters, it would still be complicated, if not impossible, to work out comparative static results. What he was doing, thus, was explaining to the reader why it was necessary to use mathematical methods such as he was about to present. "Intuition and a general feeling for the direction of things does not carry one far in the analysis of a complex many-variable system."[46]

---

g. Even Hicks, in *Value and Capital*, had analyzed dynamics, but without specifying equations governing the behavior of a system out of equilibrium.

Having sought to shape his work in this way, most of the thesis's discussion of maximization, cost and production, and the consumer remained unchanged. Samuelson added two pages on "indeterminacy in purest competition?" but this was essentially an aside.[h] He clarified a few passages and expanded his discussion of the analysis of the consumer in Hicks's *Value and Capital,* a book he had by now had time to read more carefully. He significantly shortened his discussion of the constancy of the marginal utility of money on the grounds that, though it had once been central to debates about the consumer, it was of no more than historical interest. He had to cover it because Hicks and others were trying to reestablish the concept of consumer's surplus as providing a way of doing welfare economics.[i] However, Samuelson argued that the concept of consumer's surplus, though it raised some interesting mathematical problems, was unnecessary for welfare economics and was a vestige of an age when economists used literary methods and failed to see the underlying mathematical structures.

The direction in which Samuelson thought consumer theory should move was indicated by a completely new chapter, "Transformations, Composite Commodities and Rationing." He was even more critical than he had been in his thesis of Marshall's concept of elasticity; it served to conceal problems and was of little use "except possibly as mental exercises for beginning students."[47] Index numbers were more important because they were central to national accounting, where they were needed for measuring concepts such as industrial production or the price level that involved aggregation over many commodities. The "cost of living," for example, referred to a basket of goods, for which there was no natural unit of measurement, as did most of the "commodities" in which economists were interested. Even an apparently simple commodity such as wheat did not have a single "natural" price, for it is a composite of many different types and grades of wheat. Index numbers took him into the problem of aggregation, to which he had been exposed as a graduate student, and on which Leontief and Hicks had both worked. Samuelson praised Hicks's *Value and Capital,* claiming that one of the reasons for the book's success was an aggregation theorem that enabled Hicks to treat groups of commodities as if they were a single commodity.[48]

---

h. His point was that if companies face constant costs and a single price at which they can sell their product, there was nothing to determine the output of individual companies because changes in output change neither price nor average cost. However, this was not a problem, because the output of all companies taken together was determinate: it did not matter how output was distributed among companies.

i. On the concept of consumer's surplus, see chapter 10 this volume.

A major problem with index numbers was whether they could be used to ascertain whether an individual consumer would be better or worse off after a change had taken place. Using arguments about revealed preference that went back to his first articles, he argued that there was an *inevitable* area of ignorance, in the sense that no simple index number could be a perfect measure of well-being. With any index number, there would either be some circumstances where, for example, a measure of real income would rise even though someone were worse off, or fall even though someone were better off. This indeterminacy, which many economists tackling the problem in the 1920s and 1930s had tried to eliminate, was inescapable. He stressed this point:

> I should like to state as strongly as possible that this final indeterminacy is intrinsic and inherent. No amount of ingenuity can remove it, grounded as it is in the fundamental convexity properties of the indifference field, or more accurately in the consistency behavior of the individual.[49]

He also noted that the problem arises only when finite changes are involved, echoing the point Wilson had stressed, following Gibbs, about the importance of considering finite changes. Though the theory might be abstract, it led to the practical conclusion that, in the absence of a perfect index number, it was necessary either to work with more than one index number or to choose the one that was the best approximation for the purpose at hand.

The same mathematics could be used to analyze the problem of rationing, which was topical during wartime. Rationing might involve either a limit on how much of a good could be bought, or it might involve "points rationing," where goods required payment of cash plus points. In both cases, the equations describing equilibrium needed to be modified, and when this was done, the Le Chatelier Principle, discussed in his thesis, enabled Samuelson to deduce that when rationing is introduced, the consumer would be less responsive to price changes than in the absence of rationing. He also investigated whether allowing people to trade their ration points for cash would increase or decrease their well-being.

Statics—Welfare Economics

In his thesis, Samuelson had not tackled the problem of welfare economics, though he had worked closely with his fellow student, Abram Bergson, who had published a paper on the subject.[j] Samuelson shared Bergson's views on

---

j. See chapter 11 this volume.

how the subject should be tackled, but in his publications before *Foundations* his remarks were confined to noting, albeit emphatically, that the problem of welfare bore no relation to the concept of utility as that was understood in consumer theory. He had made welfare judgments in his work on international trade, but in this work he was simply using welfare criteria, not analyzing them.

Since Bergson's article, there had emerged a rapidly growing literature on the analysis of welfare, described by Hicks as "the new welfare economics."[50] It was widely held that judgments of welfare were subjective—dependent on the values of the individuals making the judgments—and that nothing scientific could be said about them. "One's welfare economics will inevitably be different according as one is," Hicks argued, "a liberal or a socialist, a nationalist or an internationalist, a Christian or a pagan," something he found "rather a dreadful thing to have to accept." The problem of welfare economics was to find a way out of this impasse—to find a way to analyze welfare scientifically. The standard method was represented by Marshall and Pigou, who had sought to ground welfare economics in utility theory. The problem was that this was conceptually flawed, the main problem being that it involved adding up the utilities of different individuals—something for which there was no basis.[k] Fortunately, Hicks went on, recent work had pointed to ways of discussing the efficiency of the economic system without resorting to arbitrary subjective judgments about how one person's welfare should be valued against another's.

The first stage in Hicks's argument was to define an "optimum" as one in which everyone is as well off as he or she can be without making someone else worse off (what later came to be called a "Pareto optimum"). In such an optimum, any change will make at least one person worse off. There might be many such optima. The second stage was to reduce the number of potential optima, considering as improvements those changes where those who gain can compensate the losers and still remain better off. Such a compensation test establishes, so Hicks and others argued, that an allocation is efficient. If compensation is not actually paid, it may not be possible to demonstrate that social welfare is higher—comparing the benefits to some people with losses experienced by others would require value judgments—but it

---

k. Marshall and Pigou were actually more skeptical about utility measurement than this statement implies, but it is a sufficiently good summary for the point made here. They might have wished to avoid interpersonal comparisons of utility (or satisfactions), but their methods presumed this. On consumer's surplus, see p. 210, note w.

establishes that the new allocation has the *potential* to make everyone better off. Compensation tests, therefore, so it was claimed, opened up the possibility of a scientific welfare economics that did not rest on subjective value judgments; it rested solely on individuals' own judgments about their own welfare.

It seems likely that what prompted Samuelson to write his new chapter on welfare economics was the publication in the *American Economic Review* of a critique of the new welfare economics by his friend from his Chicago student days, George Stigler. We know that shortly after the exchange with Stigler, he decided to add significant new material to *Foundations,* and the chapter on welfare economics, which is very different in style from the rest of the book, could well be what he added. It is plausible that it was Stigler's failure to understand the new welfare economics that made him realize there was a need to improve on Bergson's exposition of the theory. In his article, Stigler claimed that the "new welfare economists" (in which he included Samuelson's article on international trade) claimed that "many policies can be shown ... to be good or bad without entering a dangerous quagmire of value judgments."[51] Claiming that the new theory, though usually presented using formidable mathematics, was simple enough to be summarized in half a page, he offered what he believed was a strong critique: if the precepts of the new welfare economics were followed, thieves would be rewarded for their crimes and wars should be fought with checkbooks, a remark that had added significance, given that it was published in 1943.[52] The problem with these arguments, Stigler contended, was that societies were concerned with more than maximizing national income. Policy changes would lead to changes in individuals' preferences, making it impossible to use these as the basis for welfare analysis. What societies required, Stigler contended, was consensus on the ends that society is to seek. Without such consensus, and a belief that the system is fair, the social system would disintegrate.

Samuelson responded to Stigler by saying that he agreed with much of what Stigler was saying—economic welfare was not necessarily the main goal in society, and tastes would change—but Stigler had gotten the new welfare economics completely wrong.[1] The new welfare economics was not intended to displace the old, but to derive *necessary* conditions for social welfare, basing them on the very mild assumptions that it is better to have more than to have

---

1. These points on which he agreed with Stigler were ones to which Knight, who taught them both, had attached great importance.

less, and that "individual tastes are to 'count' in the sense that it is 'better' if all individuals are 'better off.'"[53] In saying that the new welfare economics is no substitute for the old, he implied that stronger ethical judgments could and should be made, though this was not a point he chose to stress. The new chapter on welfare economics—a substantial chapter spanning fifty pages and with much less mathematics than other chapters—clarified the new welfare economics that Stigler had so badly misunderstood.

Samuelson approached the problem historically. Economics had, Samuelson claimed, always been associated with the notion that "in some sense perfect competition represented an optimal situation," exemplified by the case for free trade.[54] The idea that competition was socially optimal had often been used to defend the status quo against arguments for government intervention, but Samuelson argued that it could also be a radical idea, used to challenge the status quo, as when it was used to justify anti-monopoly legislation. It had in the past been bound up with teleology—with arguments about natural rights, natural selection, or the Malthusian doctrine that competition was necessary to bring out the best in people—but there were also arguments that did not depend on teleology. The argument that some trade was better than no trade could easily (albeit, illegitimately) become an argument for free trade. This was reinforced by the argument that in an equilibrium, every agent is doing the best he or she can for himself or herself. Though some economists had gone further, by the end of the nineteenth century economists had generally concluded that, subject to some caveats, perfect competition was optimal provided the distribution of income was appropriate. However, all of them made mistakes, with the result that none of them provided a proof of this claim. The economist who got closest was Pareto, who had argued that competition produced "a *maximum d'utilité collective* regardless of the distribution of income, and indeed even if the utilities of different individuals were not considered to be comparable."[55] He obtained this result by defining his maximum position in terms of a *"requirement that there should not exist any possible variation or movement which would make everybody better off."*[56] This was a valid argument, but Pareto failed to make it clear that the optimum he had defined was not unique.

In the 1920s, economists had developed Pareto's ideas and Samuelson claimed that this literature had culminated in the work of Bergson:

> He is the first who understands the contributions of all previous contributors, and who is able to form a synthesis of them. In addition, he is the first to develop explicitly the notion of an ordinal social welfare function in terms of which all the various schools of thought can

be interpreted, and in terms of which they for the first time assume significance.[57]

Bergson's paper introduced the idea of the social welfare function, which Samuelson was adopting as his own approach to the problem.

Samuelson's defense of the notion of a social welfare function began with the charge made by Lionel Robbins that value judgments had no place in scientific analysis.[58] However, while such a view was useful in culling bad reasoning, it went too far.

> It is a legitimate exercise of economic analysis to examine the consequences of various value judgments, whether or not they are shared by the theorist, just as the study of comparative ethics is itself a science like any other branch of anthropology.[59]

Contrary to Robbins and many proponents of the new welfare economics, Samuelson contended that even propositions that rely on interpersonal utility comparisons have "real content and interest for the scientific analyst," though the economist may not wish to deduce or verify the ethical judgments on which they rest, "except on the anthropological level." He summed this up when he explained his use of a social welfare function.

> Without inquiring into its origins, we take as a starting point for our discussion a function of all the economic magnitudes of a system which is supposed to characterize some ethical belief—that of a benevolent despot, or a complete egoist, or "all men of good will," a misanthrope, the state, race, or group mind, God, etc. Any possible opinion is admissible, including my own, although it is best in the first instance, in view of human frailty where one's own beliefs are involved, to omit the latter.[60]

This made it clear that all the economist could do was examine the consequences of ethical beliefs: choose a different set of beliefs and a different evaluation of social welfare would follow. All he assumed about such ethical beliefs was that they provided a consistent ordering of possible states of the world: that if A is considered better than B, and B better than C, then A must be better than C.[m]

Though Samuelson followed Bergson in using what they both called a social welfare function, he cut his analysis free from the tangled debates of the 1930s in a way that Bergson had not. This is precisely what he had done with

---

m. This is the assumption of transitivity.

the theory of the consumer: building on previous work, but presenting the theory in such a way that when one had read his account, it no longer seemed necessary to go back to the previous literature. Cutting himself free from the earlier literature involved outlining—far more clearly than Bergson had done—ethical judgments that might be used to give structure to the social welfare function and make it possible to derive substantial results.

Samuelson did this by starting with a function that was even more general than Bergson's, and with less content, for it simply stated that social welfare was a function of all variables that are thought relevant to social welfare.[n] Indeed, it had no content at all. To give it content required making ethical judgments that restricted the form of the function. Its use lay in providing a framework both to analyze the implications of specific value judgments and to assess what value judgments were implicit in welfare criteria, such as Pareto optimality.

After observing that the variables in the social welfare function were not normally taken to include prices (itself a value judgment), he explained that many of the variables would be specific to individual households. The consumption of different households—who consumed what—did matter, and the services (including labor) provided by different households were not interchangeable. The crucial assumption, however, was that individuals' preferences "count." This assumption was far from ideologically neutral, for the essence of Nazi and communist "totalitarianism" was held to be that individuals' preferences did not count; but it was one that most American economists, who took for granted the importance of the individual, could be assumed to find acceptable. Samuelson implicitly noted the ideological dimension of this assumption when he referred to the attitude of the "soap box speaker," who said, "When the revolution comes, you will eat strawberries and cream, and like it!"[61] More serious were problems such as conspicuous consumption—enjoying something because others did not have it—and envy, but these could be minimized by assuming individuals' preferences were to depend only on their own consumption and not that of others.

Thus far, the ethical judgments made were, Samuelson contended—ones that most economists would accept. He then explored more controversial ones: that the social welfare function be nearly symmetric with respect to the consumption of all individuals (that everyone counts for approximately the

---

n. $W = W(z_1, z_2, \ldots)$, where the z's are any variables that are thought relevant to social welfare.

same); and that welfare was the sum of individuals' cardinally measurable utilities. These involved judgments about the distribution of resources. It is important to note that Samuelson was not arguing that such judgments were illegitimate; it was merely that they *do* involve value judgments, even though they might appear to be mere technical assumptions.

Samuelson then turned to the mathematical analysis of welfare, using this list of value judgments to reach two conclusions. The first was that the variables in the social welfare function should include quantities of commodities consumed and quantities of productive services provided, such as labor. The second was to argue that these would affect social welfare only if they affected the utilities of individuals.[o] Even with these restrictions, the social welfare function was still vague, but it was sufficient for Samuelson to derive conditions for a social optimum comparable with those derived by Hicks and others—the conditions that later came to be called the conditions for a Pareto optimum. He summed up what could be achieved by arguing that the optimum conditions he had derived defined what he called a "utility possibility function," which stated that the maximum utility an individual could achieve given the utilities achieved by everyone else in the society. It made it clear that there was an infinite number of social optima and that choosing between them involved evaluating what some people gained against what others lost.

He then turned to the claim that any "individualistic" ethical optimum (that is, one of the optima defined by the conditions discussed in the previous paragraph) could be a achieved by lump-sum taxes. The attraction of this theorem was that it made possible separating questions of resource allocation from questions of distribution between individuals. However, Samuelson contended that not only was it not a fundamental theorem in welfare economics, it was not even universally true.[p] Among the reasons he cited were that people might have preferences that rendered the equilibrium unstable, that it would not hold if the optimum conditions were achieved through price discrimination (through different individuals being charged different prices), and that it was in practice very difficult to devise truly lump-sum taxes (taxes that did not depend in any way on an individual's actions).

---

o. $W = W(U_1(.), U_2(.),...)$, where the U's are the utility functions of the individuals in the society being evaluated.

p. It later came to be known as the second of two fundamental theorems of welfare economics: that any competitive equilibrium is Pareto efficient; and that any Pareto efficient allocation can be achieved as a competitive equilibrium by suitable redistribution of resources.

Perhaps echoing issues that he had been discussing in the National Resources Planning Board, which wanted to reduce income inequality, he noted that separating out the problem of income distribution simplified "the problem of formulating political slogans and beliefs which will command wide approbation."[62] However he claimed, without providing any explanation, that even if this was politically desirable, "it must never be forgotten that from a consistent ethical point of view decisions should be made concerning the welfare function itself. Beliefs concerning the distribution of income are derivative rather than fundamental." In a footnote, he implied that understanding the mathematics of the problem could shed light on the clash between equity and efficiency in capitalist economies; oversimplified analyses based on separating resource allocation from considerations of efficiency were misguided.

Whereas other economists were searching for a way of doing welfare economics that could stand independently of any ethical judgments, Samuelson denied that this was possible. The attempt to eliminate ethics from welfare economics was completely misconceived because welfare judgments were inherently ethical. The starting point for any welfare analysis had to be a set of ethical principles or value judgments. It also meant that if different people or different groups adhered to different ethical principles, the result would be different judgments about welfare. A social welfare function, therefore, had to reflect a particular set of ethical views; it could not be completely objective and independent of who was making the evaluation.

In taking this position, Samuelson was assuming the view of Frank Knight, under whose spell he had fallen while an undergraduate in Chicago.[q] Though Samuelson was generally taking a very critical stance toward the mentor with whom he had once been besotted, there are clear parallels between Knight's views on the relationship between ethics and economics and Samuelson's welfare economics. The chapter on welfare economics refers to Knight four times, and in every case Samuelson is praising Knight.[63] Possibly his exchange with Stigler had prompted him not only to clarify his views on welfare economics but also to reread the work of the teacher in whose circle they had once both moved.

This analysis of welfare economics, Samuelson argued, completed his static analysis of maximization. In previous chapters, he had analyzed maximization by companies and consumers, and in the chapter on welfare, he tackled the problem of maximizing social welfare. Because it was less clear

---

q. See chapter 5 this volume.

what should be maximized, the nature of the discussion had to be very different, focusing on more philosophical, conceptual problems, resulting in a chapter that had a balance of words and equations that would have pleased Wilson. Mathematics was, as in his other work, used to clarify his arguments, but in comparison with the mathematics used elsewhere in the book, it was comparatively simple. Samuelson's chapter took up Robbins's challenge that value judgments should not be part of economic science. Scientific economic analysis might not be able to arbitrate between competing value judgments, but it could analyze the implications of different sets of values; Samuelson did not accept the view that economists, in their role as economists, could say nothing about interpersonal comparisons, and hence that welfare economics could not go beyond what became known as Pareto optimality.[r]

Bergson and Samuelson took their analysis in a direction that was very different from that of the new welfare economics as defined by Hicks, in that instead of trying to do welfare economics without making any subjective value judgments, they placed ethical judgments at the center of the field. However, their work came to be seen as part of the New Welfare Economics. They were all agreed that utility could not be measured in the same way that, for example, temperature can be measured. In addition, they were prepared to make similar judgments—notably, that individual preferences counted. As economists came to accept that compensation tests were conceptually flawed, and as other approaches to welfare economics were developed, Samuelson's approach appeared to have even more in common with that of Hicks.

Dynamics and the Business Cycle

Though Samuelson started *Foundations* with static analysis, dynamics were just as important. The obvious reason was that some economic problems, such as the business cycle, were inherently dynamic. The less obvious reason was what he called the Correspondence Principle—a label for the idea that it was possible to use the assumption of stability to derive comparative statics results. This led to a two-way connection between comparative statics and stability: not only could the assumption of stability be used to derive fruitful comparative statics results, but "known properties of a (comparative)

---

r. It should be noted that Robbins held views that were less austere in relation to welfare judgments than the position with which he came to be associated in the light of his book.

statical system [could] be utilized to derive information concerning the dynamic properties of a system."[64] This was what justified elevating an idea to which he had not attached a name when writing his thesis to the status of a "principle."[s] Most of the material on dynamics was first presented in a series of articles in *Econometrica* and the *Review of Economics and Statistics*, only the first of which had been a chapter in his thesis.[65] It was in the second of these articles that he introduced the Correspondence Principle, making the claim that, with it, a radical change was taking place in economics.

> An understanding of this principle [the Correspondence Principle] is all the more important at a time when pure economic theory has undergone a revolution of thought—from statical to dynamical modes. While many earlier foreshadowings can be found in the literature, we may date this upheaval from the publication of Ragnar Frisch's Cassel Volume essay of only a decade ago. *The resulting change in outlook can be compared to that of the transition from classical to quantum mechanics.* And just as in the field of physics it was well that the relationship between the old and the new theories could be in part clarified, so in our field a similar investigation seems in order.[66]

Samuelson would have had in mind Keynes's comparison of the revolution to be wrought by his *General Theory* with that brought about by Einstein in physics. Samuelson was not claiming to have initiated this revolution, potentially even more fundamental than the Keynesian, but he staked a claim to be playing a vital role in it.[t]

The third of Samuelson's three articles on dynamics, "Dynamics, Statics and the Stationary State," did not become a chapter of *Foundations*, but it was the source for a substantial section titled "Statics and Dynamics." In this section, Samuelson provided less technical definitions and explanations of basic terminology, arguing that given recent progress in the field, it had become possible to provide a rigorous differentiation between "statics and stationariness, between dynamics and history."[67] However, the details of these distinctions were perhaps less important than his criticism of economists who

---

s. This was a point he had learned from Wilson in 1938. See chapter 14 this volume.

t. It is surprising that he cited "an unpublished manuscript" dealing with the distinction between "complete causal systems" and "historical or incomplete causal ones" (Samuelson 1942f, p. 2), but did not cite his thesis. The unpublished manuscript could have been either the thesis or the article published the following year. In *Foundations,* the latter was reproduced unchanged, aside from a three-sentence summary of his results and an indication of his future work.

treated the word *dynamic* as nothing more than a synonym for *good, complex,* or *realistic*. The problem was that though economists might make analogies with theoretical physics, they were generally hampered by their lack of technical knowledge, causing them to get "bogged down in the search for economic concepts corresponding to mass, energy, inertia, momentum, force and space." Here, he was conveying something he had learned from Wilson: the reason why methods taken from physics could be useful was that the economic and physical problems could exhibit common mathematical structures, and it was a mistake to look for detailed parallels between economics and physics. He accused his Chicago teacher Frank Knight of making just such a mistake, the implicit message, here and at many other places in his writings, being that it was important to understand the mathematics.

Similarly, just as it was wrong to look for exact analogies with physical systems, it was also wrong to look for exact analogies in biology. Here, his main target was Marshall, whose use of biological analogies he found very vague. There were no differences in principle between physical and biological sciences:

> if one examines the more exact biological sciences, one looks in vain for any new weapon, secret or otherwise, for discovering scientific truths. If the bloodstream is capable of a simple, abstract, rigorous description in terms of the usual laws of physical thermodynamics, so much the better; if not, one must be content with more complicated unwieldy explanations.[68]

Indeed, Lawrence Henderson had pointed out that the idea of a stable equilibrium, central to physics, had first been formulated in relation to the body's resistance to disease. This undermined Marshall's contention that mechanical analogies needed to be replaced with biological, for there was no difference in principle.

Samuelson proposed a fourfold classification of economic systems, using this to criticize Hicks for being too vague in saying that dynamic analysis was where variables must be dated.[u] He was offering something more rigorous. In the article, he went on to use this terminology to tackle the concept, discussed by many economists, of a stationary state and the problem, important to both Knight and Schumpeter, of whether the rate of interest would be

---

u. Samuelson argued that systems could be grouped under four headings: (1) static and stationary; (2) static and historical; (3) dynamic and causal (nonhistorical); (4) dynamic and causal.

zero in a stationary state. However, in *Foundations*, he omitted all discussion of stationary states and the rate of interest, and simply included his nontechnical classification of different types of system, using it as the prelude to the more technical account of the same concepts, using mathematics, drawn from his thesis. Stationary states were discussed, after a section on causal systems, but as a particular solution to a set of functional equations. He also extended his classification of types of system by including adding stochastic systems.[v]

Samuelson completed this chapter with a discussion of business cycle theories. After explaining that part of his purpose had been to show that the problem of dynamics was not synonymous with that of the cycle, he explained that he was not going to provide a survey based on economic characteristics but, rather, was going to focus on the "analytical differences involved."[69] In other words, the "nature" of the business cycle was defined by the mathematics used to model it. The result was a section that was less a survey of business cycle theories than a survey of different mathematical methods that could be used to model the cycle. The basic distinction was between endogenous models (which explained the cycle as self-generating, determined by factors within the system being analyzed) and exogenous theories (which explained fluctuations in terms of factors outside the model).

The problem of endogenous theories was that they required that there be no damping—that the parameters of the economic system were such as to generate a system where fluctuations neither faded away nor exploded. In physics there were constants that might generate such systems, but there was no reason to assume such constants in economics. Thus, he was critical of the Polish economist Michal Kalecki for imposing the condition that cycles not be damped.[70] This was a milder version of an even more critical appraisal of Kalecki that he had made privately in a letter to Hurwicz:

> By the way, have you read Kalecki's most recent "Studies in Economic Dynamics?" He has a chapter on "pure" business cycles which, in my humble opinion, hits the low as far as method is concerned. In order to obtain his favorite mixed difference-differential equations he approximates differences by derivatives, but not all the way thru—then he

---

v. Given that random shocks had been used in business cycle theory for many years (for example, by Frisch), it is not clear why he did not introduce these ideas in his 1943 paper. Possibly he had not thought about the problem, or perhaps he had not thought it necessary for his discussion of stationary states. Dynamic stochastic systems became the dominant approach to macroeconomic modeling during the 1970s and 1980s, but few economists linked such work to the very brief coverage in *Foundations*.

would have had a simple differential equation. Also, he makes it non-linear to maintain stability regardless of coefficients, but he does not integrate the system explicitly, nor even write out the non-linear term.[71]

Kalecki, Samuelson believed, did not understand the mathematics he was using.

Samuelson then went on to say that the problem with linear endogenous models was that they could not explain the amplitude of the cycle: as with a pendulum, the amplitude could be of any magnitude, depending on where the system started. One way out was to drop the assumption of a purely endogenous cycle and to assume that external factors kept the system going (though he did not cite it at this point, this was Ragnar Frisch's "rocking horse" model of the cycle, according to which a rocking horse hit periodically by outside shocks would exhibit a continuing cycle). The other was to go for a nonlinear model, exemplified by "billiard table" theories in which output bounced up and down between a full-employment ceiling and a floor.[72] A problem here was that, as Hansen had shown, there was "no (relevant) natural bottom to the economic system." Not surprisingly, he favored mixed endogenous-exogenous systems, this being the section in which he cited his own work. His multiplier–accelerator model was an endogenous model in that it could generate cycles, but it could be augmented with external shocks.

Finally, he turned to "Mixed Systems of a Linear Stochastic Type"—linear models subject to random shocks. Such models had been analyzed by the Russian economist Eugen Slutsky and by Ragnar Frisch, the latter whose paper he described as brilliant, but Samuelson linked the method to his MIT colleague Norbert Wiener, the key figure in the development of cybernetics and whose informal seminar he had been attending.[w] He also linked Frisch's approach to the cycle with the problem of estimation, citing Trygve Haavelmo's "The Probability Approach in Econometrics."[x] Though such models were much more difficult to handle, he also outlined the problem of modeling the cycle as a nonlinear stochastic system.

Leaving aside the Correspondence Principle, the chapters on dynamics were perhaps the most original and also the most unfinished; and for many economists, the most difficult parts of the book. In the chapters on statics, Samuelson was refining a body of ideas that had been around for decades—treating it rigorously, correcting errors, and codifying it. He could do this

---

w. See chapters 9 and 21 this volume.
x. See chapter 17 this volume.

only to a very limited extent with dynamic theory, and as a result he drew on a much more disparate mathematical literature. To a much greater extent than in the chapters on optimization, the chapters on dynamic analysis were about the mathematics, explaining its relevance for economics. The reason for this was that there was much less dynamic economic theory to codify, and much of what did exist was based on different conceptual foundations. For example, Keynesian models were conceptually distinct from dynamic Walrasian general equilibrium theory, and the many business cycle models in circulation were conceptually heterogeneous. Under these circumstances, it was inevitable that Samuelson would focus on the mathematics and that his discussion of dynamics and the business cycle would have a more unfinished appearance. It was probably also inevitable that this section of the book would contain much material that many economists would not understand.

Samuelson also discussed the demand for money, an important component of many business cycle theories, at the end of his chapter on the theory of consumer behavior.[73] This is notable for his decision to start not with recent literature, such as Keynes, but with Walras, who had analyzed the demand for cash balances in the context of his theory of general equilibrium. In part, this discussion has the feel of an exercise designed to show that his theory of demand could be applied to money, as well as to ordinary goods and services.

He did not engage with the literature on money. Given his growing knowledge of probability theory and statistics, it is perhaps remarkable that this section contains no suggestion that mathematical analysis is needed to resolve the issues at stake, such as whether liquidity preference (the term used by Keynes to refer to the holding of money because of uncertainty about what might happen to interest rates and bond prices) was necessary to ensure a positive rate of interest.

The Book's Reception

Reviewers were generally enthusiastic about *Foundations*, seeing it as a very important contribution to economic theory. This may be because most of them were young—few of the older generation would have been able to follow the book's arguments in detail.[y] The mathematical appendices were welcomed as providing much-needed teaching materials, and the book

---

y. Reviewers (and their ages) included Roy Allen (41), Gerhard Tintner (40), Kenneth Boulding (37), George Stigler (36), Wolfgang Stolper (35), Lloyd Metzler (34), Kenneth May (32), Leonard Savage (30), Charles Carter (28), Melvin Reder (28), William Baumol

stimulated discussion of the role of mathematics in economics, which in 1947 was still a controversial issue.[74] Not surprisingly, some reviewers took up the comparison with Marshall, whose view of the role of mathematics in economics Samuelson had challenged. For example, Melvin Reder character-ized Marshall as having sought to clarify concepts, using mathematics when it served that purpose, whereas Samuelson "begins with systems of equations and attempts to deduce their empirical or operational implications."[75] He concluded that if one followed Samuelson, mathematics was far more likely to be useful. In a similar vein, Roy Allen compared Marshall's use of math-ematics to the use of steel to provide scaffolding, whereas Samuelson used it as part of the structure.[76] The book was almost inevitably compared with Hicks's *Value and Capital*, Reder and Allen providing extensive comparisons.

Celebrating the fiftieth anniversary of *Foundations*, Samuelson described Hicks's book as "an expository tour de force of great originality, which built up a readership for the problems *Foundations* grappled with and for the explosion of mathematical economics that soon came."[77] However, few reviewers saw the relationship in this way. Allen, who had collaborated with Hicks on consumer theory in the early 1930s, argued that whereas Hicks had tried to work out a complete economic theory, Samuelson had done no more than show the common mathematical basis underlying different fields of economics.[78]

Even more critically, William Baumol noted that the book lacked a theo-retical unity, some chapters amounting to "collections of his miscellaneous thoughts and brilliant analytical sorties lumped together on the basis of some tenuously established common characteristic."[79] That was a well-justi-fied criticism of the chapters on dynamics and the business cycle with which many reviewers were disappointed.[80,z] Three major problems were identified. Discussions of dynamics rested on very special assumptions, meaning that there could be no confidence in the results; they focused on the mathematics, with very little economic content; and no attention was paid to expectations. The point was also made that Samuelson's methods were incomplete, in that he did not discuss methods for quantifying the theory.

Unlike *Value and Capital*, *Foundations* could be interpreted in many ways. For example, *Foundations* came to be associated with a neoclassical orthodoxy

---

(25). Samuelson's fellow students in this list were Stigler (at Chicago), and Metzler and Stolper (both at Harvard).

z. In contrast, Lloyd Metzler (1948b, p. 906), who had used similar methods, considered the treatment of dynamics as the most important part of the book.

based on optimization and calculus-based methods, but there was another side to the book. Following Wilson's advice, Samuelson had paid much attention to the analysis of finite changes, and he denied that aggregates could be analyzed in terms of maximization—points picked up by some reviewers.[81] His friend Metzler, with whom he had had extensive discussions of dynamics before the book's publication, stressed Samuelson's departure from traditional theory, going so far as to claim that Samuelson believed that "*most* of the important economic problems" could *not* "be reduced to simple problems of maximization."[82] A mathematician assessed the book as containing "an implicit basic critique of economic theory" in that "much economic theory turns out to be banal or meaningless when stripped of its vague literary formulation."[83]

Though Samuelson attached importance to the Le Chatelier Principle, this was not something that impressed his reviewers, whether economists or mathematicians. The only reviewer to mention it did so in a footnote, pointing out that Samuelson had gotten a minus sign wrong.[84] The reason was presumably that, though the Le Chatelier Principle had been an important step for Samuelson, it was not a necessary step; it was sufficient to begin with results on optimality conditions and the Correspondence Principle. Perhaps this was his own fault, in that though he had stated that the Le Chatelier Principle played a role in natural science, his reference to the "metaphysical vagueness" with which it was stated will not have encouraged economists to follow up on this unfamiliar idea.

It is arguable that the rival to *Foundations of Economic Analysis* was von Neumann and Morgenstern's *The Theory of Games and Economic Behavior*. Where Samuelson, following Wilson, sought to base economic theory on traditional mathematics, finding the same mathematical structures in physics and economics, making it possible to use the same mathematical techniques, von Neumann and Morgenstern believed that it was necessary to turn to more modern mathematics, different from that used in physics. As was explained in chapter 16, this volume, Samuelson saw optimization as lying beneath much of their work. Unfortunately, given his early interest in interactions between small numbers of individuals, evidence for which is found in one of the essays he wrote for Chamberlin (see chapter 6, this volume) *The Theory of Games and Economic Behavior* appeared too late to be taken into account in *Foundations*. Haberler wrote to Morgenstern suggesting that von Neumann might wish to review *Foundations*. However, when he received the request, von Neumann, though admitting he was tempted, declined. He found the book "very interesting and very detailed," but to review it conscientiously would require more work than he was able to undertake.

[T]he whole subject off the use of mathematical methods in economics is one which I wouldn't like to deal with in print except after a very careful study of the corpora delicti and of my corresponding formulations. The methodological questions which are involved are very delicate and it is very easy with respect to them to sin by overstatement as well as understatement.[85]

Foundations cemented Samuelson's reputation as one of the world's leading mathematical economists, and its publication played a major role in changing the way economics was undertaken. The use of mathematical models to derive comparative statics results became a standard technique that, by the 1960s, all graduate students had to master. The book was very much the product of Samuelson's Harvard years in that, though he had made substantial additions, including innovative material on welfare and dynamics, the fundamental ideas behind the book had been developed under Wilson's tutelage in the late 1930s. The new interests he had developed between moving to MIT in 1940 and submitting the manuscript to Harvard University Press in 1944 had not caused him to change the book in any substantial way. The result was that there developed a certain distance between his mathematical economics, for which Wilson was his mentor, and his work on macroeconomic problems, with Hansen as mentor. With continuing involvement in debates over economic policy, the gap between the two sides of his work was to increase even further.

| Postwar Economic Policy,

1944–1947

The War Production Board

In October 1943, Samuelson received a letter from Raymond Goldsmith, a German-Jewish economist who had immigrated to the United States in 1934, after which he had engaged in statistical work for a series of government agencies. He was to go on to become one of the leading specialists in the measurement of income and wealth, and was shortly to help draft a plan for German currency reform. He asked Samuelson whether the disbanding of the National Resources Planning Board left him free to do some work for the War Production Board (WPB), which was about to turn its attention to the problem of demobilization and the transition to a peacetime economy.[1] Samuelson's response was that he was resisting such invitations because he was being kept very busy in Cambridge, with an increased teaching load and "engaged in certain technical wartime research."[2] Though he does not give details, it is possible that this involved research related to fire control, on which he was later to work full time.[3] However, he was sufficiently interested in Goldsmith's invitation to say that his technical work might terminate at the end of the year, and that if it did, he would be free to take it up the invitation. He described his interests.

> I am quite interested in the technical problems of reconversion— disposition of government owned property, final renegotiation, termi- nation of war contracts, etc.—rather than in speculation concerning

the overall magnitude of demand, prospects for boom, etc. I realize that the latter are important subjects but I feel that I have put in enough time on them already.[4]

Despite his workload, he could not let go of the opportunity provided by Goldsmith's invitation. After further discussion, Samuelson suggested that his comparative advantage probably lay in "the use of critical rather than creative faculties."[5] Being offered the equivalent of $8,500 a year, a rate much higher than his MIT salary, would have added to the attraction of Goldsmith's offer.

Despite this interest, Samuelson wrote to Goldsmith in January 1944, saying that he could not work for the WPB, a decision that Goldsmith regretted. Explaining that Samuelson's letter had not arrived in time to stop the bureaucratic machinery, and that his appointment as an economic consultant had been approved by the Civil Service Commission, Goldsmith was clearly not going to accept no for an answer. He suggested that Samuelson could take the oath of office, but need do no work until his schedule allowed it. Samuelson protested that this missed the point, which was that he needed to be protected against himself: "because of my essential interest in the problems at hand, it is the more important that I protect myself against myself, and *not* make it easy to take on responsibilities."[6] As proof of his interest, he enclosed a memorandum he had already written on whether the costs of converting industry back to peacetime production should be included in estimates of the cost of the war. His memorandum gave reasons why they should not be, though since writing it he had changed his mind. The cost of fighting a fire, he pointed out, should include the cost of getting the engine back to the depot afterwards.

On whatever terms—presumably what Samuelson jokingly called "a lend-lease basis"—Samuelson engaged in at least intermittent discussions with Goldsmith.[7] He made proposals for alleviating the financial problems faced by businesses converting from military to civilian production, discussing proposals ranging from expediting the termination of war contracts (which would make companies' financial problems worse) to providing tax reliefs and "V loans" to war contractors and "government boon-doggling via private business"—subsidizing private companies to continue to provide jobs.[8] He took it as a premise that there could be a recession if this were not handled correctly.

There was a dilemma in the government's recouping as much as possible of the cost of the war from selling assets (factories and equipment) it no longer needed but ensuring that these assets got into the hands of those who could use them most productively. The memorandum making these proposals involved no economic theory, but was a long and inconclusive survey of the practical difficulties involved in conversion. Mobilization had massively distorted the structure of the economy, expanding some industries and reducing others, but there was no simple way to work out which industries could continue at wartime levels and which needed to return to pre-war levels; neither was there any simple way to reconcile the competing pressures on financial policy during the transition. Detailed statistical data on the private sector's financial position were required, but this was to be part II of the paper, which Samuelson did not write.

Samuelson's discussions with Goldsmith did not stop after he started working at the Radiation Laboratory.[a] In June 1944, Goldsmith sent Samuelson some "additional data sheets" explaining how war outlays were calculated, and in July, Samuelson visited Washington and established that the WPB estimates agreed with his own.[9] An economist at the WPB followed up this visit with a letter to Samuelson in which he endorsed Samuelson's view that $23 billion was the "rock bottom" estimate of the expected fall in national income—it being based on a multiplier of only 1.5, when actual multipliers were in the range 1.6 to 1.8.[10] The paper in which Samuelson developed this estimate began by contrasting the rosy optimism of the economists who were forecasting a national income of $200 billion, with the view of businessmen who could not see how their production could be higher than it had been before the war.[11] What the optimist forgets, Samuelson explained, was that high wartime levels of income were sustained by "the most colossal levels of deficit spending which any economy has ever experienced."[12] He sounded like a traditional business cycle theorist (such as Schumpeter) when he argued that by most standards this was an artificial boom—justified by the national emergency, but a boom nonetheless. He even likened the optimists to the royal court in Hans Christian Anderson's story "The Emperor's New Clothes." However, even if the wartime boom was artificial, it was important to make sure that the national income did not fall back to its pre-war levels ($90 to $100 billion), for this would be a disaster.

Samuelson offered a nontechnical explanation of how the problem should be analyzed. Spending could be divided into "relatively stable magnitudes whose behavior has been and can be expected to be passively and predictably related to other magnitudes" and "relatively autonomous elements" that need to be explained in terms of "the unique circumstances expected to prevail in

---

a. See chapter 21 this volume.

the period ahead."[13] Consumer expenditure on nondurable goods, Samuelson believed, fell into that category, each dollar of disposable income producing a 60¢ rise in spending. Given taxes, $1 extra income would result in a rise of 70¢ or 80¢ in disposable income. In contrast, spending on consumer durable goods would be limited only by supply, because people had not been able to maintain their stocks of automobiles and other goods during the war. Federal spending and private investment were also relatively autonomous. These could not be forecast on the basis of past behavior or with variables like business saving, which was liable to enormous fluctuations. The skill of the forecaster lay in working out how these autonomous factors would change. Only after explaining this did he write down a mathematical model of the multiplier. Using these figures, he estimated that a $15 billion cut in federal spending would reduce national income by $25 billion, and cause unemployment of 4 million people.

By October 1944, the pressure on Samuelson's time was less, presumably because his work in the Radiation Laboratory had eased. Anticipating that it would reduce even further, he told Goldsmith that he would now like to do some consulting work.[14] One of the reasons he gave was that he had realized it was "hopeless to work in isolation" when analyzing contemporary economic events, a situation that doing consultancy work would remedy. He remembered with pleasure his work for Blaisdell at the NRPB. However, despite his appointment having been approved in January, the bureaucratic formalities were slow to be completed. It turned out that the Civil Service Commission required evidence that he would not be paid for the same work by two organizations, a problem Samuelson overcame by getting permission to take up to four days a month off without pay from MIT. Goldsmith welcomed this, and hoped that the Civil Service Commission would not raise "the same silly objections as last year."

This was not to be, and the bureaucratic formalities, including getting approval from Samuelson's draft board, were not completed until March 1945. Formal notification of the appointment came on May 7, and he was sworn in the next day—the day when war officially ended in Europe—by which time the Bowman report on science policy had been sent to Bush.[15] His salary, the daily equivalent of $6,500 a year (raised to $7,175 two months later), was significantly less than Samuelson had told Goldsmith other agencies had offered him, but was still much higher than his MIT salary and what he had been receiving for the NRPB work.[16] It seems likely that one of the bureaucratic hurdles that Goldsmith was trying clear was to get Samuelson assigned a higher grade than the Civil Service Commission believed appropriate for someone of his age and experience.

Goldsmith wanted Samuelson not as a mathematical specialist but as a general economist.[17] Goldsmith had to prepare a report on reconverting industry to peacetime activities, and he proposed to do this by reviewing what had happened to industry in the six years since 1939, covering the utilization of plants, the distribution of industrial production between industries, and changes in the distribution of industry across regions.[18] This was the basis for assessing the size and structure of the economy after reconversion. The transition would be considered in two stages—from V-E Day (May 8, 1945) to V-J Day (still unknown), and from V-J Day to "postwar normality."[19,b] The report would also assess the arguments for continued government control over industry during this transition. Projections of military spending, on the basis of different assumptions about the date of V-J Day (June 30 and December 30, 1946), were already available in a memorandum by Everett Hagen, with whom Samuelson had worked at the NRPB.[20]

The way Samuelson proposed to tackle the problem involved estimating the effects on industry of different levels of income (on which he had worked at the NRPB), but it was also necessary to take into account how this income was being generated. Estimating full employment income at $170 billion in 1943 dollars, he explained that this level of income could be achieved through high private investment, high consumption, or government support: each of these would produce different patterns of industrial output. Samuelson also attached importance to regional imbalances, in that wartime industrial expansion had caused certain cities to reach sizes that might be unsustainable in the long term. Interestingly, he also argued that supply-side factors—bottlenecks affecting resources needed for recovery—could have adverse effects on aggregate demand and that there were financial problems that needed attention. His was a world in which aggregate demand might fail to generate the requisite level of output and one in which money and finance mattered.

A week after his appointment, Samuelson spent two days in Washington. A week later, Goldsmith sent him forecasts of GDP and its components through 1947, asking for a reaction by telephone, so urgent was it to get his input quickly.[21] The method Goldsmith and his colleagues had used was consistent with the views Samuelson had expressed in his earlier memorandum. Nondurable consumption was modeled using estimates of income and assumptions about tax rates and the propensity to consume. Nondurable spending was assumed to be constrained by productive capacity, in the belief

---

b. V-E and V-J refers to the Allied Forces' victory in Europe and later in Japan.

that accumulated savings would generate sufficient demand. These assumptions meant that their forecasts, of a fall from $206 billion in 1946 to around $156 to $160 billion in 1947, changed little across the different scenarios for reductions in military spending that they were considering.

Samuelson's response to these figures is not on record, but a few days later he wrote a memorandum to Goldsmith on how to estimate industrial production.[22] The 1941 ratio of industrial production to national income would probably provide an upper limit; plotting the ratio over recent years and extrapolating would probably give a low figure. Alternatively, Samuelson argued that it might be possible to make use of studies undertaken by the Bureau of Labor Statistics (BLS) and Wassily Leontief's input–output tables for 1939. Input–output tables made it possible to work out how much industrial production would be generated by a given level of consumption, and BLS data could be used to work out the relationship of consumption of different types to national income. If productivity increased and working hours could be forecast, this would give estimates for employment. At the very end of his memorandum, Samuelson noted that he was assuming there would be sufficient outlets for investment, and that a way of checking would be to compare the estimates of productive capacity in different sectors, derived by using Leontief's input–output table with those produced by the WPB.

These communications show that Goldsmith was relying on Samuelson not only as an authority on the multiplier and the theory of income determination but also as a source of technical advice on empirical methods. For example, he asked for his views on of some estimates of the capital stock— "industrial facilities," or capital plant and equipment for manufacturing and processing—produced by the Twentieth Century Fund. The problem was that regression analysis did not produce equations that fit the historical data very well (the correlation between capital stock and GNP was not high).[23] There was also uncertainty about how much of the capital investment made during the war would be useful in peacetime, and the effects of direct controls on industry were hard to estimate. Samuelson's view was that in an economy with full employment, such problems made it difficult to be sure about the value of the multiplier.[24] There was no reason to believe that the multiplier would be the same when military spending was reduced as it had been during the expansion of 1943–44. Such analysis, taking account of problems on the supply side, was a long way from the simplistic focus on aggregate demand of which Keynesians such as Samuelson were later accused.

Over the summer, Goldsmith, having problems getting the report done in time, turned to Samuelson for something else:

> Meanwhile, there is one thing which I should like you to do. I want to include in the report a fairly short description, running to something like five pages, of the basic mechanism through which, under present conditions, inflation or deflation (or more generally changes in aggregate demand) operates and of the main forces involves [*sic*].
>
> I would regard such a section mostly as a venture in the economic education of the top administrators. Therefore, it would have to be written in non-technical style. However, this piece should go well beyond the over-simplifying and elementary statements that are generally given to the lay public. Some simple algebra might well be used. What is more important, the limitations to which the broad statements usually made are subject and the time lags involved in the process should be brought out. Similarly, some indication should be given which processes are cumulative and which are not. In other words, what I am after is a statement on the one hand understandable to administrators who have a reasonable knowledge of economic facts though not of theory, but on the other hand fully consistent with the results of up to date economic analysts. This may be an order almost impossible to fill but I think you are as likely to handle it successfully as anybody.[25]

Whereas he had previously called upon Samuelson to advise them on how to handle data, he was now asking him to draw on his pedagogic skills.

Goldsmith continued to turn to Samuelson for technical advice, asking for comments on forecasts of GDP up to 1950 and estimates of GDP for 1945–47 based on two very different assumptions about the end of the war in the Pacific—September 30, 1945, and December 31, 1946; the possibility that the war might end in 1945 was now being taken seriously.[26] Samuelson suggested that rather than "substantially full employment" during the transition, it would be better to assume the most optimistic figures for the minimum level of unemployment (probably 4 percent of the labor force) and to allow for some shrinkage of the labor force as "extraordinary war workers" stop being available for paid work. He also paid great attention to how workers would respond to unemployment. High unemployment would induce some people to enter the labor force and would discourage others, and it was hard to tell which effect would dominate. Many women would be pushed out of the labor market and would not seek employment, unless their husbands and fathers were unemployed. There were also problems relating to hours worked that the forecasts had not taken into account. Samuelson also expressed views on the estimates of agricultural output and productivity in the service sector.[27] He was expressing views on all aspects of the modeling process.

In the meantime, Goldsmith had raised a further point concerning the expository pages he wanted Samuelson to write.[28] It had become fashionable to argue that inflation and deflation could occur at the same time, making it easier to reconcile the views of different government officials.[c] He thought this sufficiently important that he wanted Samuelson to say something about it—whatever conclusion he came to—that could be included in his own introductory chapter.[29] The pages that Samuelson sent, headed "Determinants of National Income and Inflation," explained that while economists were not agreed on their forecasts, there was widespread agreement for the need to focus on saving and investment. This was not a new method of analysis, and it could explain why there was a boom during the First World War, why there was a boom of limited duration in the 1920s, and why the Great Depression gave way to wartime prosperity. He then tackled the objections that were raised to this method of analysis. It was right to argue that production was what mattered, but as most business people realized, "the factors which determine over-all production are to a large extent financial."[30] He then explained why government had to be involved. Business people had no authority to use their shareholders' money to stem the tides of prosperity and depression, and in any case they did not have the "bottomless purse" that was needed. Samuelson hammered away at the idea that both conservatives and liberals agreed the free enterprise system would not automatically generate the right level of effective demand—too much demand and there would be inflation, too little demand and there would be depression. After a digression on "the mysterious multiplier," which he suggested could be omitted on a first reading, he explained why saving had to be matched by some form of spending. If this did not happen, income would not flow back to businesses, which would then have to cut back on production. The "offsets to saving," as he called the required spending, could include private investment, but also foreign lending (exports minus imports), autonomous increases in consumption, or government spending. Because private investment was irregular, government fiscal policy had to act as "a stabilizing fly-wheel."[31]

The inflationary gap was based on the argument that "[i]f 'full employment' were as sharply marked a condition as the edge of a billiard table,"

---

c. As Samuelson was to point out, this remark raises questions about how inflation and deflation are defined.

rises in demand would have no effect on prices until full employment was reached. If demand rose past the point of full employment, output would not be able to rise any further and there would be a gap between demand and output that could only be reduced by rising prices. However, the story would not end here, for rising prices would raise corporate profits, and eventually wages would rise, resulting in an inflationary spiral. This would have no end, because it involved competition for a limited quantity of goods.

> This can be put in an even simpler way. At full employment, there is 100 percent of output to be distributed. But if total effective demand is very high, consumers may want 90 percent of national product, government 20 percent, and capital producers, 40 percent. This adds up to a total of 150 percent, which is an impossible situation. Each group cannot get all that it wishes. But it can bid prices up in the attempt. The only thing that keeps prices from rising infinitely fast, is the fact that there is necessarily some delay between the receipt of income and its expenditure. By the time people go to spend their money, they will find it will buy a good deal less than 90 percent of the national income.[32]

To reinforce the point, he explained that "the attempt of each group to better itself during an inflation by raising prices has been compared to the comic spectacle of a fat man, who in bending down to pick up his derby hat, only succeeds in giving it another kick in front of him."[d]

Responding to Goldsmith's request to write about the problem, he explained that it would be possible to see simultaneous inflation and deflation, for prices did not have to move in the same direction. Equally important, whereas *inflation* always meant rising prices, *deflation* was used to refer both to falling prices and to depression; that is, prices could rise even when there was considerable unemployment, as had happened in 1937.

On August 6 and 9, 1945, atomic bombs were dropped on Hiroshima and Nagasaki, respectively, bringing the war to an abrupt end. Goldsmith wrote to Samuelson on the day of the Nagasaki bombing, saying that finishing the report had become even more urgent and asking him come to Washington to discuss it.[33] The WPB was wound down and Samuelson's appointment was terminated at the end of September, but Goldsmith continued to approach him for advice. Goldsmith had written a nontechnical

---

d. Given the widespread accusation that Keynesian economics, up to the 1960s, ignored the effects of expected inflation, and feedback from inflation onto wage increases, it is important to note that Samuelson was thinking in this way at this time.

account of the topic that was based purely on Samuelson's memorandum (he explained he had been too busy to read anything else), but he feared it made demands on the reader that were as great as those made by Samuelson's paper.[34]

An interesting feature of the draft for which Goldsmith sought Samuelson's advice was that he avoided talking in terms of saving and investment, which he thought potentially misleading, and adopted his own fourfold classification of transactions.[e] Goldsmith's alternative classification reflects the thinking of someone who had worked extensively on the national accounts, wanting an exhaustive scheme for classifying expenditures, and seeking a clear rationale for putting particular items in one category rather than another. He took many ideas from Samuelson, and in places used his wording, though he made extensive modifications of his own, such as paying much more attention to the distinction between plans and what ended up being recorded in the national accounts. He was not just recycling Samuelson's material; rather, he was trying to develop it in theoretically innovative ways, which was why he wanted Samuelson's reassurance that it was "unobjectionable from the point of view of the present status of professional discussion."[35] This shows that, although the Keynesian terminology of saving and investment was becoming widely used, it was still not taken for granted. Unfortunately, Goldsmith needed a quick response and Samuelson's response, presumably over the telephone, is not recorded.[36]

Samuelson's work for the WPB shows a set of interests that contrasts strongly with the conventional image of a mathematical economist and Keynesian theorist. The concept of the multiplier and the analysis of aggregate demand were central to the WPB's forecasts, but Samuelson's interests lay as much in the technical, statistical problems and the institutional details as in theoretical factors. Moreover, his command of these issues was such that his advice was respected even by someone who had spent his whole career on problems related to national income accounting. Goldsmith was also pushing him to write in a style accessible to a lay audience, a skill that he was beginning to develop through forays into journalism.

---

e. E-transactions were ones made out of current income and flowed back into the income stream. S-transactions (so named because saving was the prime example) were made out of current income and did not flow back into the flow of income. I-transactions (named after investment) were not made out of current income but entered the income flow, while N-transactions were completely neutral.

Unemployment Ahead

Samuelson had taken his first step into national journalism when, on July 20, 1944—the day when the plot by German officers to assassinate Hitler failed—he submitted an article to *The New Republic*. Still working at the Radiation Laboratory, he introduced himself as someone who had worked at the NRPB for two years prior to its demise, and who had been concerned about the unwarranted air of optimism that was building. Economists in Washington, he claimed, were anticipating "a postwar period in which private industry would be able by itself to create a high level of prosperity." "I consoled myself," he wrote, "with the thought that as the postwar became more imminent, this illusion would be dispelled. Unfortunately a recent trip to the Capitol suggests that this is not yet the case."[37] During August, he discussed this paper with Bruce Bliven, the editor of *The New Republic*, who suggested that he had been too hard on Washington economists, whom he had not named.[f] In response, Samuelson presented himself as someone who had once been a Washington insider but was no longer. "A little over a year ago," he wrote, "I attended my last dinner meeting in Washington."[38] At this meeting, attended by presidential assistants and heads of spending and planning agencies, he had discovered that no one was concerned about the absence of a "shelf of public works projects" that could be implemented should there be a postwar depression. He conceded that complacency might be fading as the war's end approached, but stood his ground:

> I can testify from personal experience that among many persons, themselves engaged upon estimating transitional unemployment, there has been a rather remarkable optimism.... I myself checked with people at the Federal Reserve Board, the Department of Commerce and the Bureau of the Budget. In the last few weeks I have been doing informal consulting for a unit in WPB [War Production Board] charged with making estimates on these matters, and it was only with the greatest difficulty that I was able to make anyone believe that national income might fall by as much as 23 billion. To me, some of the recent public utterances of so good a New Dealer as Ezekiel are quite incomprehensible.[39]

---

f. Samuelson claimed not to have given names because his observations were based on confidential material that he wished to respect.

He might now be an outsider, but he still had contacts that enabled him to report insiders' views with confidence.

Samuelson responded by accepting many of Bliven's suggestions, deleting some passages and simplifying others, and making the piece more topical by mentioning the conflicts between the WPB and the military, including references to WPB staff who had resigned in protest against military interference with their work.[40] He also added a chart to illustrate the problem, taking it from a recent article in the *Federal Reserve Bulletin*.[41] It turned out that the article had to be split into two parts, and Bliven asked whether he could provide some pictograms to illustrate it. Samuelson was unable to provide pictograms, though he provided two charts, of which one was eventually used in the second part. "In normal times," he wrote, "I would make more strenuous efforts to take care of such matters, but working from eight-thirty to six on military matters makes this quite impossible."[42]

The first installment of Samuelson's article was published on September 11, under the title, "Unemployment Ahead: A Warning to the Washington Expert."[43] It began with a description of how a recent trip to Washington had brought home to him how soon the war was likely to end.

> Happily, we are entering upon a time when the end of the war in Europe is in sight. Each day's newspaper makes this more and more clear, but its real imminence was only brought home to me by a recent trip to Washington, the first in a year. Everywhere I went I could smell cuts in war production; in the corridors of the Social Security Building, where WPB [War Production Board] dollar-a-year men are still a dime a dozen; in the sweltering "temporaries," where OPA [Office of Price Administration] dignitaries hide; and the scent had even penetrated the marbled tabernacle of the Federal Reserve Board.[44]

With this paragraph, Samuelson established himself as an outsider, albeit one familiar with the corridors of power. Munitions production was being cut, stockpiles were high. General Brehon Somerville was pushing for production of heavy trucks, airborne radar, and heavy bombers, disagreeing with Donald Nelson, head of the WPB, on the need to start planning for reconversion; but if the war went well, Samuelson explained, even Somerville would have to come around. Private businesses were becoming less enthusiastic about bidding for military contracts, anxious not to get left behind in the race to peacetime production. Ship construction might hold up, owing to the continuing naval war in the Pacific, but Samuelson thought that there would soon be "about a 40-percent slash" in military production, reducing production by $25 billion a year. This was roughly the amount by which consumption fell from the peak of the 1920s boom to the depression of the 1930s—a massive fall.

The effects would be even bigger than this because of the multiplier, "that bit of glorified common sense which economists of all schools now largely recognize."[45] Suggesting he was doing no more than articulating a common-sense view that his readers would readily accept, he turned to a criticism of the economic experts in Washington.

> Once acquainted with the above facts, any reasonably well informed layman . . . will instantly recognize that a serious storm is on the horizon. If we can expect this from the amateur, what can we presume to be the view of the professional Washington economist, the full-time expert with all of the statistical resources of the government at his disposal, the experienced executive whose official responsibility it is to foresee and forestall by appropriate policy measures all threats to our prosperity? Surely he has an elaborate set of plans, ready to go into effect the moment the emergency arises. Or at least he must be working frantically to make good the deficiency before the zero hour is upon us. Unfortunately, this is not the case.[46]

The diagram Samuelson had taken from the *Federal Reserve Bulletin*, projecting alternative scenarios for production and unemployment after the war, was then reproduced. Although it was not converted to a pictogram, the magazine's staff had added pictures of a factory and an unemployed worker, head bowed as he contemplated the possibility of hard times ahead. Unfortunately, Samuelson continued, the Washington economist could not see what ordinary people could see and was not devising measures to combat unemployment: "His digestion is good, and at night he experiences no nightmares."[47] Economists did foresee some problems, but only temporary ones. He saw this as paradoxical because only a few years earlier, as academic economists, they had been preaching the dangers of secular stagnation.[g]

Samuelson made it clear that he was not critical of economists in general. The public needed to know that economists had performed an extraordinary task during the war.

> It has been said that the last war was the chemist's war and that this one is the physicist's. It might equally be said that this is an economist's war. . . . [T]he Washington economist has done an excellent job,

---

g. The doctrine of secular stagnation was in this period strongly associated with Hansen and his younger colleagues. See Backhouse and Boianovsky 2016.

either in comparison with reasonable expectations or in comparison with the business executives who have been called to the government service. At a time when bureaucracy is anathema, it is well to emphasize that no administration in history has commanded the services of men of equal zeal, honesty or competence.[48]

After discussing whether economists had much influence on policy (concluding that some policies stemmed directly from economists' recommendations), Samuelson explained why economists in Washington had got so out of touch.

Nevertheless, perhaps because of his successful wartime preoccupation with scarcity of supplies, shortages of manpower and resources, excesses of purchasing power and inflationary gaps, the Washington economist has for the moment lost his perspective concerning the immediate postwar problem. . . . The Washington economist lives in a world frequented by his own kind. I know, for I have lived in that happy world. When he hears that someone else has arrived at the same optimistic estimate as his own, he takes this to be independent corroboration of the truth of his view instead of realizing that it is simply a reflection of his own last week's expression of opinion. This process of mutual infection and amplification of opinion is cumulative and self-aggravating, so no wonder his conviction grows without bound.[49]

The article ended with another homely touch, the story of an investment counselor who made a careful estimate of the effects of the end of the European war and took his conclusion, that incomes might fall from $150 billion to $110 billion, to Washington, only to be laughed at. "Why, you talk like Leon Henderson [the unpopular head of the OPA who, after the 1942 election, retreated to a career in business], who thinks that there will be eight million unemployed." It was, Samuelson concluded, Henderson's strength and salvation that he was not considered "an economist's economist."

Immediately after the article appeared, a friend from Samuelson's Chicago days, Jacob Mosak, wrote from the OPA to congratulate him. "I think most Washington economists have needed the warning for a long time," he wrote. "I have argued along the same lines for about a year."[50] He added that people at the OPA had been very pessimistic about the postwar outlook, both in the transition and in the long term, enclosing a clipping from the *Washington Post* that quoted an estimate of the likely multiplier in the coming years. Samuelson replied that it was reassuring to discover that they were in agreement, and he explained to Mosak the multiplier he had calculated for the WPB.[51]

The problem was that the consumption function could not be estimated from past data: personal and corporate tax schedules had changed, and some elements of consumption would be independent of income in the reconversion period. Taking separate account of personal and business saving, and the different tax rates on individuals and businesses, Samuelson calculated a multiplier of 1⅔, from which he concluded that it was "fairly safe" to assume it must be somewhere between 1½ and 2. He then added, "Keynes says that a man working by himself can dress up the most God-awful moonshine. I would be interested to know if I am completely wide of the mark."

The New Republic published the second installment of Samuelson's article, bearing the subtitle "The Coming Economic Crisis," a week after the first.[52] Reminding readers of the complacency of the Washington expert he had discussed the previous week, he listed various grounds for optimism. The First World War demobilization was unplanned, yet it did not produce complete disaster; there was a backlog of deferred demand, owing to very high wartime savings waiting to be spent; memories of unemployment were fading; and there were the wonders of new technology—"television, [F]livver planes, synthetics, air-conditioning, plastic autos."[53] There was merit in all these arguments, but Samuelson explained that they missed the point that wartime prosperity was fueled by $100 billion of government spending—the equivalent of two Tennessee Valley Authorities every day. Using language common to interwar business cycle theory, he argued that this was "artificial" prosperity. It was based on increased production of automobiles, aircraft, ships, and electronics that could not possibly be sustained after the war. It might sound terrible to say so, but the fact was that war *did* generate prosperity.

> To the civilian population the war period is scarcely more real [than the depression years].... Even more precious than the augmented family weekly takehome is the enhanced sensation of personal security which a high level of effective demand has created. In the last war, many observers were shocked to hear the frank assertion, "Say what you will, this war has made many a happy home." It is a sad commentary upon our peacetime management that the same feelings should be entertained today by more people than would care to admit it.[54]

However, even to those experiencing it, this prosperity seemed transient and insecure. The feeling would soon be exploited by those wanting to deny that war really had produced such a massive increase in production.

> I predict that the campaign to debunk wartime increases in production, which is just beginning, will swell into a mighty chorus. We

shall be told that war prosperity was an illusion; that we did not produce what we did produce; that even if we did, such output is incommensurable with civilian goods and proves nothing about peacetime real incomes, etc., etc.

There were even some people who feared the return of full employment.[h] There was an urgent need to demonstrate that high peacetime income was possible.

Returning to the theme with which he had begun his first article, he argued that so long as policymakers were aware of the grave situation ahead, common sense would guide them.

> Let them [the policymakers] proceed in a common-sense way from their own diagnosis of the origins of wartime prosperity. Let them disregard the shibboleths, inconsistencies and confusions of so-called orthodox finance. Let them do these things, and they will not need the advice of high-powered theory or statistics to determine in which direction correct policy lies.[55]

His most specific advice, entirely consistent with common sense, was that adjustment should come slowly: cuts in government spending should not run ahead of civilian expansion by more than $10 billion. "Economically, the war did not begin with Pearl Harbor. Nor will it end with the defeat of Japan. Our economic system is living on a rich diet of government spending. It will be found cheaper in the long run, and infinitely preferable in human terms, to wean it gradually." It would be possible to achieve slow adjustment by stockpiling obsolete munitions, but much better to embark on a substantial program of social security and worthwhile public construction projects.

Despite Samuelson's targeting of Washington economists, Morris Livingston of the Bureau of Commerce wrote to compliment him on his articles, to which Samuelson replied that he greatly valued the contributions coming from Livingston's office.[56] He received a follow-up letter from Mosak, who said that they had calculated the multiplier in essentially the same way as Samuelson.[57] He enclosed a copy of a paper on "Forecasting Postwar Demand," which he had presented a month earlier at a session of

---

h. Samuelson did not explain why it was feared. It is possible that it was believed that full employment would lead to inflation, or simply that it would be associated with an unwanted degree of planning.

the Econometric Society and the American Statistical Association meeting, to which Livingston and two other economists had also contributed.[58] Mosak estimated that by 1950 (a date chosen to allow time for reconversion), potential national income would be $200 billion; and to ensure that there was sufficient demand for this to be realized, there would be a need for policies to raise the propensity to consume well above pre-war levels, as well as government spending to meet the gap that private investment would be unable to cover. The point was that the government should guarantee full employment—something that private sector bodies could not do.[59]

Samuelson's response to Mosak's article was that he was "a little startled" by the amount of government spending required to maintain full employment.[60,i] He had one suggestion to make—that Mosak should consider the possibility that by 1950, the consumption function might have shifted upward, something that would be likely if reasonably full employment had been maintained for a few years (if people became more confident about high incomes they would have less need to save).[j] Having said that, he immediately qualified it by saying that there was no "mysterious hand guaranteeing a miraculous increase in consumption habits precisely sufficient to meet our needs" and the war might even have increased thriftiness. The significance of this is not so much the precise arguments as the uncertainty about what would happen; for all Samuelson's emphasis on there being a stable consumption function, he recognized that major changes to the system, such as wartime and the transition to peace, could significantly alter consumption behavior.[k]

---

i. Mosak did not specify the level of government spending required; it depended on what was assumed about private investment.

j. Another statement reminiscent of what Friedman was later to label the permanent income hypothesis.

k. Though Samuelson will presumably not have seen this until the proceedings were published in January 1945, the same conclusions could be drawn from the discussion at the session on September 14, where Mosak had presented his paper (Roos et al. 1945). Charles Roos had argued that the uncertainties were sufficiently great that the type of national income studies produced by Mosak should be regarded less as forecasts than as guidance similar to that provided to a company by its operating accounts. A set of accounts was invaluable in diagnosing the health of a company, but it was not a forecast. Leonid Hurwicz raised the possibility of structural changes in spending patterns and Everett Hagen noted that there might be no reliable way to forecast consumption.

The Case for Low Interest Rates

During the war, the Federal Reserve pegged interest rates to suit the U.S. Treasury. In the summer of 1944, Samuelson took up the argument that the interest rate should have been much lower. High interest rates, he argued, benefited banks, a claim that was challenged by bankers. The argument to which he took exceptions was that, because rises in interest rates lowered the value of their security holdings, rises in interest rates were harmful for banks.[1] He argued his case to both his fellow economists and to readers of an engineering trade journal, *Modern Industry*.

In the summer of 1944, Samuelson wrote a paper that was eventually published in the *American Economic Review*.[61] It was certainly correct that the present value of bank assets—the value they could be sold for in the market—would be reduced by a rise in interest rates, but this did not mean that they were made worse off. To the contrary, banks were made better off by such changes. His purpose was not to say that interest rates should be raised. To the contrary, he believed that interest rates should have been lower—the war was a 2 percent war, but it should have been a 1 percent war, for this would have reduced its cost, and in a world of direct controls and inflationary gaps, interest rates had no effect on consumption or investment.

The central part of his argument was that the mistake lay in looking only at the value of bonds held, and not at the streams of revenue accruing to banks. He began by considering a university that had invested endowment funds in government securities, an example that would be familiar to his predominantly academic audience. If interest rates fell, the value of the bonds held would fall, but so long as the securities were held to maturity, the university would be no worse off, its income being unchanged. Of course, it would have been better to have delayed purchasing the bonds until their values had fallen, but that was a completely different argument. He then turned to an insurance company, where the problem was slightly different, owing to the nature of its liabilities, but the conclusion was the same. Samuelson then argued that the same arguments applied to banks, providing an example in which all interest rates rose by one percentage point. This was, he claimed,

---

1. There is an inverse relationship between the rate of interest and the market price of fixed-coupon securities. For perpetuities, the yield on such a security, i, is AP/V where V is the value of the security and AP is the annual interest payment. This yields the relationship $V = AP/i$. For fixed-term securities, the equivalent formula is more complicated, but V still falls when i rises.

equivalent to an annual subsidy to the banks of $600 million. The obvious problem caused by the loss in capital values was that if there were a sudden withdrawal of deposits, the bank would need to liquidate assets. However, Samuelson argued that, given the situation banks then faced, this was simply not going to happen.

Though Samuelson presented these conclusions as obvious—he described himself as "giving away the secret which all wise men know but which no wise man will tell," defending them required his going into technical details.[62] He produced data showing that banks held very little of the long-term debt that would be most affected by interest rate changes; he calculated the relationships between interest rates, security prices, and revenue streams; and he spoke with apparent authority on how the U.S. Treasury and the Federal Reserve would behave after the war. However, though demonstrating, for the first time, his credentials in the field of finance, the underlying lesson involved an elementary point: high interest rates benefited creditors and harmed debtors.

In the middle of November, Samuelson was invited to take part in a "Debate in print" in *Modern Industry* over the question of whether the federal government should abandon its easy money policy.[63] His opponent was to be Christian Sonne, a merchant banker (president of Amsinck, Sonne & Co.), who had written a book about eliminating corporate taxes and was chairman of the Executive Committee of the National Planning Association. He was told that the debate should discuss issues that mattered to the fifty thousand managers in manufacturing who subscribed to the journal. After arranging to discuss the issues with Sonne when he visited Boston so that they did not talk past each other, Samuelson quickly drafted a short paper, and in December he sent a copy to Hansen, who thought it "excellent" and saw nothing in it to criticize.[64]

When the article was published on January 15, 1945, alongside advertisements for industrial gloves, roller bearings, and silent hoist equipment, a box (see table 23.1) on the first page summarized the opposing arguments.[65] Samuelson's was a simple point: that low interest rates stimulated business investment through making it more profitable. However, he needed to allay fears about what was happening to the federal debt, which he did by arguing that easy money was different from deficit spending, for it involved increasing the supply of capital, not keeping rates low by using government to push money into the economy. In any case, although the federal debt exceeded $200 billion, "the Government's credit was never so good" and there was nothing to worry about. The government could lower interest rates and could

TABLE 23.1 A Debate About Easy Money

Samuelson	Sonne
1. "Easy money" makes investment funds more available to business.	1. "Easy money" cannot lower interest rates, which are determined by national production, confidence, and savings.
2. Low interest rates encourage private borrowing demand; high interest rates, caused by reducing supply, do not increase savings.	2. Low interest rates prevent businesses building up a reserve of funds high enough to justify lending to small businesses.
	3. Interest rates need to be high enough to attract capital from abroad.

Note: This table summarizes the contents of the boxed feature in the Modern Industry article, in which their photographs and short biographies were also presented.

have made them even lower, had the U.S. Treasury so desired. High interest rates might control inflation in a postwar boom, but they would not stimulate investment and could cause depression. Against Sonne's argument that the United States needed to attract funds from abroad, Samuelson reminded readers that the United States was the world's greatest creditor, and that it should follow Britain's example of keeping rates low, as the rest of the world wanted.

Samuelson had closed his article in the *American Economic Review* by asking to hear from "the wise men" about whether the government's policy of keeping interest rates at 2 percent had been "uninspired."[66] This challenge was taken up by Seymour Harris, at Harvard, and George Coleman, an economist with the Mississippi Valley Trust Company. Harris, who claimed to be supplementing rather than criticizing Samuelson's "brilliant" article, defended government policy, arguing that the government had done a good job of preventing banks from profiting excessively from war financing, and that banks were less profitable than other enterprises.[67] Coleman, on the other hand, was more critical. He began by turning Samuelson's rhetoric about this being a secret shared by all "wise men" against him:

> This plea [to hear from "wise men"] leaves anyone who might wish to comment on this article in the temerarious position of being accused of thinking himself to be a "wise man." This difficult position becomes somewhat more tenable, however, when realizes that his evaluation of

a "wise man" is subject to a substantial discount since he believes that barbers know more about banking practices than bankers do.[68]

Samuelson, Coleman claimed, had made an error in his calculations—perhaps too small to worry an academic economist, but significant enough to make the difference between profit and loss in a bond transaction. Samuelson had also used the wrong basis for valuing assets and correcting this changed the capital loss from raising interest rates from Samuelson's 3 percent to 25 percent. More important, "even the lowliest bank clerk" could have told Samuelson, even if his barber could not, that banks were taking short positions precisely because they feared the interest rises that Samuelson was saying did not matter.[69] "Mr. Samuelson and his barber" should have devised a better argument for lower interest rates.[70]

In responding to Harris and Coleman, Samuelson abandoned the patronizing tone of his earlier articles, and rather than enter "a titanic battle between Mr. Coleman's bank clerk and my economic sophomore," he chose to talk about changes that had taken place in the government bond market since his article had been written. The most he conceded was that there was "some interest" in Coleman's suggestions about how securities should be valued.[71] Though the language was less arrogant, he did not soften his criticisms of bankers. Since 1942, the U.S. Treasury had, in effect, guaranteed a particular pattern of interest rates; the fact that banks did not shift to higher yielding bonds showed that they either did not believe this or that they did not understand it. Samuelson turned this account of how the Treasury had achieved such a firm grip on interest rates into a reiteration of his call for "another turn of the 'cheap money' screw."[72] He presented himself as someone intimately familiar with the institutional details of government financing and its implications for banking and the economy.

These arguments about interest rates were one of his first forays into finance, a field in which he was to become a major contributor in the 1950s. The episode, like the reference to the emperor's new clothes cited earlier, marks the emergence of a highly confident and ironic style that was to become a feature of Samuelson's writing.

Hansen's New World

As the war drew to a close, plans for the postwar world had to be implemented and debates in the political arena became more active. On January 3, 1945, President Roosevelt presented his Annual Budget Message to Congress.[73] He made it clear that government spending would be dictated by the military situation, and though he estimated that $73 billion would be needed for war purposes in 1946, this would depend on the course of the war. However, he also spoke of the need for reconversion and the necessity of strengthening the Social Security program, as well as the need to secure "world-wide economic co-operation." While large-scale demobilization would not begin during the period covered by the budget—planners were expecting the war with Japan to continue much longer—it was necessary to prepare for peace. As a framework for thinking about the problem of employing 60 million men and women, he presented figures for national income, showing how it had grown during the war. Federal spending had risen tenfold, to $95 billion, and its deficit was $47 billion. This was not at the expense of the private sector, for consumer income had doubled from 1939 to 1944, and saving had risen more than sixfold, from $5.6 billion to $36 billion, while business saving had risen from minus $2.6 billion to $9.7 billion. Gross national product had more than doubled, from $89 billion to $196 billion.

Roosevelt linked domestic prosperity with foreign policy. The United States had learned that it could not stand "the malignant effects of economic isolationism" and that "full employment after the war is not only a matter of immediate self-interest, but also part of our stake in world stability and prosperity." He concluded with a statement about what needed to be done.

We must develop the human standards and material resources of the Nation, which in turn will tend to increase our productivity and most effectively support business expansion and employment. Our program should include provision for extending social security, including medical care; for better education, public health, and nutrition; for the improvement of our homes, cities, and farms; and for the development of transportation facilities and river valleys. We must plan now so that these programs can become effective when manpower and material are available. . . . Our productive achievements during the war have demonstrated once and for all the progress which this Nation can support, the progress which will be required if all our resources are to be put to adequate peacetime use. The war, however, will also leave us deep distortions in our economic life which must be overcome. We owe it to those who give everything that we set our sights as high for peace as we set them for war.

Though it stopped short of saying how much spending would be needed, this was a clear statement of the policy Samuelson had long been arguing for. In an unsigned editorial Samuelson had written for *The New Republic*, published on

January 29, immediately preceding an article by Henry Wallace on "Jobs for All," he welcomed the president's message as "a landmark of progress toward a rational fiscal policy."[74] Roosevelt's figures showed that "even amid the crescendo of total war," federal spending accounted for less than half of national income.[m] However, Samuelson claimed that this did not go far enough. The budget should be defined in terms of "full-employment income." If this were calculated, it would define national goals and the president could plan federal spending so as to avoid unemployment or inflation. The national accounts would cease to be a mere record of past history and would become a method of control.

On March 26, as the Bowman Committee deliberations were drawing to a close, Samuelson took up another theme from Roosevelt's message—the need for the United States to support international institutions—this time in a signed article in *The New Republic*. Billed on the cover as the main article, under the heading "Hansen's New World,"[75] this was a response to Hansen's recently published book *America's Role in the World Economy*.[76] The book began with the war that was on everybody's mind. The power of the United States and Russia, supported by China and a still strong British Empire, opened up the possibility of an international security organization that might ensure a stable international political order. However, this would be possible only if prosperity were maintained in the United States and the rest of the world: peace could not be maintained by countries that did not have the material resources. The implication was that it was important for international security that the United States introduce measures to ensure full employment, for one of the main uncertainties hanging over the world was the future of the American economy, which had been "a major disturbing element" before the war.[77]

Economic problems were, Hansen argued "infinitely complex and difficult" and though we had "only reached the Kindergarten stage in learning how to manage complex economic problems," a start had been made.

> We have freed ourselves in large measure from the restraints that formerly tied us hand and foot and made it impossible to act. We are increasingly developing the tools and mechanisms needed for the task. But we have yet to work out a comprehensive, far-reaching program both on the domestic front and the international, adequate to give us confidence and faith that our economic future is secure.[78]

---

m. He could have pointed out that the rise in national income from 1939 to 1944 more than covered the rise in government spending.

The international institutions being put in place were needed to make sure that the world did not experience another Great Depression.[79] This was a call for both an end to isolationism and for policies to ensure full employment. Hansen endorsed the measures being taken in Britain to establish the welfare state and establish full employment, along with Australian calls for governments to enter into an international agreement to maintain full employment in their own countries.

Samuelson pointed out that this was Hansen's first book aimed at the general public and the most important of the many books to appear on international problems. Central to the book, he explained, was the argument that the best contribution the United States could make to the world economy was to put its own house in order and to maintain a high level of income and employment. Samuelson left the reader in no doubt that, like Hansen, he supported the new institutions being created; the nearest he came to criticizing his mentor was when he accused him of being "much too gentle" in his criticisms of the "Key Kurrency" objection to the International Monetary Fund (IMF), an objection that Samuelson claimed neither he nor even *Time* magazine could understand. It was a very clear public identification with Hansen's internationalism.[80,n]

Hansen's book had avoided technical discussions of economic theory, but in his concluding paragraphs, Samuelson used an analysis of Hansen's career to tell readers about the Keynesian revolution, about which his student Klein had recently written his dissertation.[o]

> Hansen himself illustrates beautifully the painful process by which the economist divested himself of old misconceptions and inched laboriously toward a better comprehension of economic reality. Trained just before the First World War, he began to stand out among American business-cycle theorists in the decade of the twenties. Toward the end of that "new era" there grew up the belief that the business cycle was gone forever and even Hansen thought that the business cycle represented simply the growing pains of the capitalistic system and might be expected to disappear in the years ahead; as may be seen in his Business Cycle Theory (1927).[81]

Describing the 1927 Hansen as "Neanderthal," Samuelson continued,

> Possessing that quality, rare among academic persons beyond the age of thirty, of being able to change his mind, Hansen became one of

---

n. The spelling and capitalization are as in the original. This refers to the central role of the U.S. dollar as an international reserve currency.

o. See chapter 24 this volume.

the most important contributors to the revolutionary innovations in thought associated with the name of Keynes. The revolution is in economic theory; the new doctrines themselves are profoundly capitalistic in nature. After reading this book, every intelligent reader will know which are the true friends of the enterprise system: Keynes or Hayek, Ruml or Queeny, Stuart Chase or Carl Snyder, Alvin Hansen or Henry Simons.

The friends of enterprise were those who supported measures to maintain full employment, not those who branded government intervention as socialist.[p] The internationalism and full employment policies that he and Hansen supported were linked explicitly to the Keynesian revolution in economic theory. Equally significant, Samuelson was arguing forcefully that it was Keynesians, not critics of the state, who were the real defenders of the free enterprise system. The bankers who opposed such ideas did not know what they were talking about.

> The notion that a banker understands money or finance is a quaint one which will not stand up under empirical observation. A barber can discuss as cogently whether or not banks create money, while from time immemorial economic sophomores have had a field day at the expense of bankers' writings. It is for this reason that bankers always employ hack economists to server as their trigger-men and ghost-writers.

He does not seem to have worried about making enemies.

Arrangements for a postwar economic order had been thrashed out at an international conference in Bretton Woods, New Hampshire, in July 1944, but the proposals still needed to be ratified by Congress. In April, Samuelson contributed to the debate with another article in *The New Republic*, "Bretton Woods, Pro and Con." He took five of the accusations made by critics of the plans and attempted to rebut each one. Before doing so, he made it clear how important were the issues at stake. "It is no exaggeration to say that the peace of the world and the future of international political and economic cooperation hang in the balance. Failure of Congress to accept these proposals would have repercussions far transcending even the terribly important immediate issues."[82]

Two objections were quickly disposed of. Despite claims to the contrary, no economist, banker, or international trade expert had been able to find any

---

p. The first name in each of these pairings was a liberal; the second, a conservative.

fundamental technical flaws, and the plans were far from hastily devised. The objection that the plans involved a radical departure from the gold standard was also misconceived. Because the plan of Harry Dexter White, the U.S. negotiator, was adopted instead of the Keynes plan, gold would be at the center of the Bretton Woods system. To see what the plans might mean, Samuelson speculated on how the economic history of the interwar period might have been different had Bretton Woods been in operation after the First World War. Several bad mistakes in exchange rate policy would have been avoided. Those who argued against Bretton Woods (notably the bankers he had lambasted in his previous article) had opposed Roosevelt's abandonment of the gold standard in 1933, as well as his establishment of the Securities Exchange Commission and the Federal Deposit Insurance Corporation, measures that were widely accepted to have been beneficial.

The most frequently heard argument, according to Samuelson, was that the agreement would make "Uncle Sam a Santa Claus." This was clearly wrong, because there were strict limits on what other countries could borrow from the IMF, and U.S. liabilities were limited to $3 billion. Critics were inconsistent in arguing both that overseas dollar holdings were much too large and that the IMF would run out of dollars within a couple of years. The argument that the agreement needed to be amended was no more than an attempt by its opponents, in the face of strong public support for it, to pretend to compromise. Amending the agreement would be to destroy it, because everything would need to be renegotiated. The *only* real issue before Congress, Samuelson argued, was "isolationism." If the proposals were defeated, he added, "let those responsible for the resulting international anarchy be clearly recognized."[83] His support for Bretton Woods was uncompromising.[q]

Alongside his efforts to create a new international order Hansen was arguing for domestic reforms, and to this end he had helped draft the Full

---

q. Though not teaching at MIT during 1944–45, Samuelson had continued to teach budding diplomats at the Fletcher School, where his courses on The United States in the World Economy and Commercial Policies of the United States covered the same issues as he had discussed in *The New Republic*. He provided his audience of specialists in international relations with arguments for the liberal, internationalist world order for which Hansen was arguing. It is tempting to conclude that what he was doing here echoed arguments he heard as an undergraduate in Chicago, when he was himself taking a broad social science course with the thought of becoming a diplomat. The following year (1945–46), he reverted to teaching the course in International Economic Relations in place of U.S. Commercial Policy, and the year after that he dropped the latter course. In 1948–49, after his textbook was published, he stopped teaching at Tufts.

Employment Bill that had been brought before the Senate in January 1945. The bill sought to establish a right to work and to ensure that the federal government had an obligation to make sure jobs were available to those who wanted them.[84] Rather than simply requiring that the president be asked to report on the state of the economy and make recommendations on how to achieve full employment, Hansen proposed a carefully planned program to stabilize investment.

> My proposal is more specific with respect to recommendations by the President on an integrated program of public construction and development projects, Federal, State and local, with a view to placing construction public and private on a high and stable level.[85]

The president's recommendations at the beginning of each session of Congress should include "a long-range program of Federal public works and developmental projects together with an integrated plan for Federal aid to State and local public works and capital projects" covering at least six years.[86] Hansen wanted to make it clear that the goal of policy was stability of public and private construction and the avoidance of both inflation and deflation.

Discussion of the bill was delayed by more pressing matters—such as approval of the Bretton Woods agreement—but with the sudden end of the war in Japan on August 15, 1945, anxiety about the need to avoid unemployment during the process of reconversion became acute. There were to be public hearings on the bill until September 1, after which closed sessions began. Samuelson had been busy during the summer, both writing his textbook and advising Goldsmith, and there had been a lull in his journalism, but on September 2, the *Washington Post* carried a piece he had written to influence congressional deliberations.[87]

In this article, Samuelson did not try to explain any of the technical economic arguments, but focused entirely on the political case. It was, he argued, "well wishers of the capitalist system who have by far the greatest stake in the maintenance of a high level of jobs and of effective demand." The fact that liberals and unionists supported the bill was no reason for business to oppose it. "If the CIO were to come out against sin," he wrote, "it would not be in the true interests of the Chamber of Commerce to come out in its favor." Well-functioning markets needed high employment, without which individual initiative could not be rewarded. Responding to the publicity surrounding Friedrich Hayek's *Road to Serfdom* (1944b), which had emphasized the dangers in government intervention, Samuelson contended that it was wrong to draw a sharp distinction between "serfdom" and "laissez-faire"; the United States had a mixed economy in which government was needed to act as a "balance wheel" against booms and slumps. In a mixed economy, business and government had different but "mutually helpful" responsibilities. In an italicized paragraph he wrote,

> *Business enterprise cannot be expected to create its own market and generate demand in just the right amount, avoiding on the one hand excessive purchasing power and inflation and on the other hand deflation and widespread unemployment.*

Without government action, economic progress would be bumpy, for businesses had no incentive to adjust their actions so as to regulate economic activity. Objectors to the bill were, Samuelson contended, really offering arguments about the desirability of full employment itself, which was a mistake. He argued strongly that to deny either the desirability of achieving full employment, or that government had a role to play in achieving it, was "to play into the hands of the avowed enemies of free private enterprise."

Though the bill passed the Senate, when it was considered by the House of Representatives in November, conservative opposition was much stronger, and after tortuous negotiations, a substitute "Employment Act" became law in February 1946. In place of a right to work, guaranteed by the use of compensatory spending, the president was simply urged to aim for a high level of employment. The president would be advised by a three-person Council of Economic Advisers, and there would be an annual report on economic conditions. It seems safe to conjecture that Samuelson would have endorsed Hansen's view that the most important feature of the original bill was its spending provisions, and these had been removed.[88]

Forecasting Failure

Samuelson was one of the economists who was convinced that, in the absence of strong government action, the end of the war would be followed by a depression. However, even though the war ended abruptly before the measures he thought necessary were in place, the predicted slump never materialized. The result was a controversy over the methods by which these forecasts had been made, in which the focus of attention was as much on the Keynesian theory upon which it was based as the statistical techniques employed.[89] Samuelson's involvement in the production of the most recent forecasts had been behind the scenes, privately advising Goldsmith, but he had clearly associated himself with them though his articles in *The New*

Republic. Moreover, he was even more strongly committed to the methods through which they were derived. He took the opportunity to publish a response, "Unemployment Forecasts: A Failure," in the pilot issue of *The American Economist*, an academic journal established in 1946 with the aim of publishing widely accessible articles.[90] Articles in the journal were unsigned, so he remained anonymous.

Samuelson wrote that he would not have been surprised if the reason for failure was that they had failed to forecast investment correctly, because the difficulties in forecasting investment were well known. However, the failure arose because forecasters failed to get right the relationship between disposable income and nondurable consumption, the latter being $10 billion (roughly 5 percent of 1945 national income) higher than predicted. As Samuelson put it, this error "brings into question the stability of what in economic terminology is called the 'consumption function.'"[91] It had been assumed that, because the reconversion of industry would take time and consumer durables would be in short supply, consumers would respond by postponing their consumption until more durable goods were being produced. Instead, they had massively increased spending on nondurables.

This, however, was a narrow, technical point. The failure of forecasting also raised questions about the whole basis on which forecasting was done. The complexity of the issues is shown by exchanges Samuelson had with his one-time co-author, Everett Hagen, who after leaving the NRPB had worked at the Federal Reserve before moving in February 1945 to the Office of War Mobilization and Reconstruction.[92] Drawing on work he had done with Samuelson at the NRPB, Hagen wrote two articles on forecasting, about which they entered into correspondence at the end of 1944.[93]

This correspondence seems to have begun with some handwritten comments on a draft of one of Hagen's articles.[94] After discussing technicalities relating to the estimation of business and household saving, Hagen turned to Samuelson's criticisms of "Washington economists" in *The New Republic*. "I don't think you got around town enough before you wrote your articles for the *New Republic*," he wrote. "You certainly didn't reflect the OPA correctly."[95] Samuelson's failure, he claimed, lay in not having distinguished between two distinct concepts: the single estimate of the most probable course of events, and "the contingencies against which policy measures should be adopted." Hagen said that he, like several other Washington economists, had been concerned only with the former and, had time permitted, he might have drafted a reply to Samuelson's criticisms.

Samuelson interpreted this as implying that his *New Republic* articles might have done harm, and explained that he had written them to counter what he saw as excessive optimism about the postwar situation, though he realized that they were out of date even before they were published.[96]

> I am sorry if my *New Republic* articles did any harm. As you know, the OPA has certainly been as pessimistic as I; but both Walter Salant and Jack Mosak were kind enough to write that in their opinions the articles did some good. And I know for a fact, because of informal consulting which I was doing for them, that the WPB, the agency concerned with cut-backs, was living in a fool's paradise as far as their effects were concerned.[97]

He went on to discuss Hagen's point about different types of forecast.

> Certainly there are and have been important differences in your subjective probability distribution as to the future level of national income and mine. Your single most likely expectation differs from mine and so does your spread. I suspect the same could be said about the views of Colm, Smithies, Ezekiel and myself. When I asked Smithies whether I was wrong in my belief that there were not at hand anywhere in the federal government substantial plans for alleviating unemployment, his reply was ingenious: "do we ever in this country plan for anything?"[98]

Hagen reassured Samuelson that he had misunderstood what was "an offhand reaction" to the comment about Washington economists (of which Hagen was one), and that the *New Republic* articles had indeed done some good.[99]

Hagen's reflections were signed and appeared, much more prominently than Samuelson's confessions, in the *American Economic Review*.[100] Hagen admitted that forecasters should have done better. They had been overconfident owing to their great success in predicting consumption both during the years before Pearl Harbor and during the war itself, when their models had forecast better than they could have expected. More important, during the war they had correctly forecast that conversion to war production could take place much more quickly than business people believed was possible, and this experience should have taught them that reconversion might also take place very rapidly, as did in fact happen. In contrast, Samuelson argued that forecasters had failed to predict things that were unpredictable, such as the expenditures of returning veterans, or how people would react when the durable goods that they would have been expected to purchase were not available.

Hagen raised a more general question about what methods should be used, claiming that there was a need for "far more, and far more systematic econometric work—of the sort that is being done at the Cowles Commission."[101]

> It would be a disastrous error to conclude from the experience of the reconversion forecasts that the use of "nation's budget" models should be discontinued. It would be folly to assume that the use of economic barometers, or of the "qualitative-historical" method, or dependence on "informed judgement," can *take the place* of quantitative estimates of the relationship between aggregate demand and its components, and aggregate supply.

Samuelson supported the use of such formal forecasting methods, but his support was much more guarded.

> It would be as foolish to lose all faith in the worth of such careful forecasts as to make the opposite error of blindly swallowing as Gospel-truth any pseudo-scientific estimates that come wrapped up in the impressive trappings of advanced statistical, mathematical, and economic techniques. The experience of the last year has shown that economists cannot entirely rely upon routine extrapolations of past statistical curves and regressions. So much the better. One good lesson will have been snatched from the postwar forecasting debacle if it is again made clear that forecasting involves more than an assistant's turning the crank of a calculating machine and grinding out the answer.[102]

The Cowles Commission methods that Hagen was advocating, and about which Samuelson was more skeptical, were those about which Trygve Haavelmo had spoken when he visited the MIT statistics seminar, and which by the 1960s were to become the dominant approach to empirical work in economics.[r] They involved specifying formal mathematical models and then using formal statistical inference both to attach numbers to coefficients in the models and to test whether they could explain the data.

Samuelson did not respond publicly to Hagen's call for economists to adopt the Cowles Commission's methods, but not long afterward he expressed his views privately to Seymour Harris, editor of the *Review of Economics and Statistics*, when he acted as a referee for an article Rutledge Vining, at the National Bureau of Economic Research (NBER), had written in reply to an article by Tjalling Koopmans, from the Cowles Commission.[103] Titled

---

r. See chapter 17 this volume. It was the approach to empirical work that Lawrence Klein, who moved to the Cowles Commission after finishing his PhD with Samuelson, was to make his own, his macroeconomic models inspiring many others.

"Measurement without Theory," Koopmans's article was a response to the latest NBER study of the business cycle by Wesley Mitchell and Arthur Burns (later chair of the Council of Economic Advisers).[104] This was a massive volume full of data, whose authors sought to provide a detailed statistical description of the business cycle. "Measurement without Theory" was a defense of the Cowles Commission's methods that Hagen wanted to see used more widely. In his reply, defending Burns and Mitchell, Vining criticized those methods from the point of view of the NBER. His main argument was that the Cowles Commission took it for granted that the correct theory to use was Walrasian general equilibrium theory, but their methods were not of much use if one did not accept this and needed to discover the correct theory. If one had to discover what was the correct theory, the NBER's methods were more useful. Samuelson's verdict on Vining's paper was, "Many of us will say 3 cheers with Vining when he defends empiricists against the perfectionistic-formalism of the Cowles Commission."[105] Where he parted company with Vining was that he did not agree that the alternative was to revert to thirty-year-old NBER methodological procedures that had "grown decadent."

The exchange confirms Samuelson's ambiguous attitude toward the methods that came almost to define what later generations would call "econometrics." A few years earlier, he had written a favorable report on an econometric paper by Gerhard Tintner, revealing his familiarity with such work and his support for it.[106] He thus favored the use of Cowles Commission methods, but believed that they should be used pragmatically, and he saw a significant role for less formal work. This attitude, of showing great interest in such work but being skeptical of the necessity of pursuing empirical work this way, was consistent with the view expressed by Wilson in a review of Haavelmo's *Probability Approach to Econometrics*, published the year before Koopmans's review of Burns and Mitchell, attacking the NBER's methods. Wilson's main argument was that, although it was desirable "from an ideal point of view" to specify and take into account the behavior of error terms (the essence of Haavelmo's method), it was a puzzle that scientists in other disciplines—astronomy, physics, engineering, biology, psychology, and medicine—had not found any need to do this.[107] Why, he asked, does "the backward science of econometrics" need to be "more critical with respect to its probabilistic hypotheses than other sciences need be?" Though he was open to persuasion, he found no answer in Haavelmo's work.[s] It would appear that Samuelson

---

s. Wilson also made the same criticism of Haavelmo that he had made of Samuelson's doctoral thesis: that he had things to say that were important for economists at large and writing in a less technical style would increase the accessibility of his work.

shared Wilson's ambivalent view of Cowles Commission methods, and that despite sharp differences in expression, his disagreement with Hagen was one of emphasis as much as substance.

The Guaranteed Wage Study

Toward the end of 1944, the War Labor Board (WLB) was involved in a dispute between the Carnegie-Illinois Steel Corporation and the United Steelworkers of America.[108] The union was demanding that, during the life of the contract, the company offer a guaranteed wage to each employee. The WLB did not agree to that, fearing that it would subject the industry to intolerable financial risk. However, as part of its ruling, it recommended that the president set up an independent body to undertake a comprehensive, national study of the issue of guaranteed wages, of which fifty to sixty schemes were believed to be in operation. The outcome was a comprehensive report by Murray Latimer, chairman of the Railroad Retirement Board, under the title *Guaranteed Wages*. The report's analysis of the economics of guaranteed wages was taken from a document prepared by Hansen and Samuelson, printed as an appendix to the Advisory Board's report, and it summarized one of its chapters.[109] Hansen and Samuelson had first discussed writing this in February 1946, signing a contract three months later.[110,t] Their report was finished by December and published along with comments from John Maurice Clark, Edward Mason, and Sumner Slichter, as well as their response to the comments.

Given that they met regularly (apart from the week when Paul and Marion's daughter, Jane, was born and his duties at home were "somewhat distracting," though not arduous), there is little written record of their collaboration. An exception is a letter in which Samuelson, in addition to mentioning two articles and book on the subject, drew attention to a number of passages in J. M. Clark's *Economics of Overhead Costs* (1923),[111] and sent him a copy of twenty short quotations that he had marked in his copy of the book.[112] These show that Samuelson was thinking in terms of the behavior of costs over the business cycle. Of particular importance was the fact that there

---

t. It appears that Hansen was approached, he discussed it in person with Samuelson, and in this letter Samuelson is saying that he had decided it would be feasible. They received a single fee ($7,800, representing eleven months' full-time work—six months for Samuelson and five months for Hansen) that they could divide between themselves as they saw fit.

were overhead costs attached to labor; this included both the cost of training and the minimum level of consumption necessary to maintain the worker's health. These costs had to be borne by someone irrespective of whether the worker was employed, with the result that paying workers only for hours worked created a divergence between the cost of labor to the employer and the cost of labor to society. Moreover, cutting employment in a recession might not actually benefit business if the result was lower sales.

Their final report paid much attention to the business cycle. Guaranteed wages could, they argued, smooth out consumption spending, especially on durable goods, and hence ameliorate fluctuations in aggregate demand. An important advantage of such schemes was that, unlike other counter-cyclical measures, they were instant in their operation: as soon as demand faltered, guaranteed wage schemes would boost household incomes. However, they were not a substitute for other measures; their most useful role was smoothing out seasonal and other irregularities in employment, not as a cure for unemployment. They would do little about the main factor behind the cycle—fluctuations in business fixed investment. Moreover, even if they covered the entire labor force, they would not be sufficient to smooth out consumption. Guaranteed wage schemes had, therefore, to be used in conjunction with other policies.

Although they focused on the business cycle, Hansen and Samuelson did not neglect the effects on individual firms and workers. Clearly, guaranteed wage schemes were beneficial for workers, but only if they were not accompanied by significantly lower wage rates. Guaranteed wages could also benefit companies, for greater job security could increase worker productivity; it was also possible that, if a guaranteed wage scheme were in operation, employers might respond to downturns by looking for way to improve productivity instead of by laying off workers. It was here that they had to get into technicalities about the way schemes were funded, because different types of scheme could have different effects on companies' incentives to invest and to innovate.

Hansen and Samuelson concluded that guaranteed wage schemes should not be legislated, but should be achieved through collective bargaining between companies and unions. Agreements should contain limitations on employers' liability, so that in the event of a sharp decline in production, their financial viability would not be threatened. What government was encouraged to do was to revise tax provisions to encourage companies to adopt guaranteed income provisions, such as by favorable treatment of reserves they held and integrating guaranteed income schemes with Social Security. These recommendations were modest, no doubt reflecting both the conflicting arguments they had discussed in their report and their sense of what was politically feasible.

Clark agreed with the caution and realism of their conclusions. However, he criticized them for "here and there, by tone and implication," conveying an impression that guaranteed wages might yield greater results "than are wholly consistent with the cautious character of the actual recommendations."[113] Throughout his comment, he questioned whether the report had paid sufficient attention to the way guaranteed wages and commitments to full employment would undermine the operation of the price mechanism. All three commentators were more cautious than were Hansen and Samuelson, concerned with the effects on investment and possible adverse effects on employment, and proposing ways in which employer liability could be reduced. In short, they were less convinced that guaranteed wage measures would be effective.

Latimer's report broadly endorsed the recommendations made by Hansen and Samuelson. It concluded that guaranteed wage schemes could be economically beneficial, provided they were properly designed. For this to happen, they had to be integrated with unemployment insurance, so that the cost to employers would be limited to the difference between someone's wage and his or her unemployment benefits, and funds to cover guaranteed wages needed to be regarded as an expense for tax purposes. Guaranteed wage schemes would also improve industrial relations by making workers more secure. Latimer's board accepted Hansen and Samuelson's judgment that such schemes could help smooth out seasonal and other small fluctuations in economic activity, and also their view that other stabilization policies would be needed. The report's summary concluded on a positive but cautious note.

> The guarantee of wages is not a panacea but a tool, and a tool which becomes sharper, not duller, with wide and more intensive use. . . . And to suppose that any single tool—be it the guaranteed wage, or public works, or any other device—can become a multipurpose instrument by which all the ills of the economy can be remedied can lead only to confusion and failure. The guaranteed wage, used with care, with full recognition of its limitations, and with eyes open to dangers in exceeding those limitations, can become an integral part of a rounded program for greater security, for harmonious industrial relations, and for a more lasting prosperity.[114]

Though Hansen and Samuelson had done no more than write the document on which one chapter was based, they had clearly influenced the tone of the report, and the importance of their role was made clear in the transmittal letter to President Truman. They generated further publicity for their work with an article, "Making the Annual Wage Work," in the *New York Times Magazine*.[115] This presented the guaranteed wage as an idea introduced by enlightened business people, who believed that it would reduce labor turnover and increase labor productivity: it was a legitimate goal for labor, for households were not concerned about hourly wage rates, but about "take-home pay over the long pull" and guaranteed wages represented a better form of labor contract. The current system did not make sense because, although a company could cut its costs by firing people, it was "an optical illusion to believe that society could slough off the wastes and losses resulting from unnecessary unemployment."[116] This was the prelude to a statement of the case for stabilization policy.

> The stabilization of employment at high and productive levels represents a challenge that we must face up to in the post-war period. But the guaranteed wage can function effectively only as a part of a broad program including fiscal and monetary measures to maintain full employment and adequate social security.

Samuelson's consultancy work, both at the WPB and in the report on guaranteed wages, involved a continuation of his role at the NRPB in the early years of the war. In contrast, his forays into journalism marked a new departure and were to become an activity to which he devoted an increasing fraction of his time. Though he never ceased to be a mathematical economist, he clearly loved the very different challenges posed by policy analysis and the need to be familiar with economic institutions and economic statistics. Why else would he have begun to assist Goldsmith when his nine-and-a-half-hour days at the Radiation Laboratory and the pressure to finish *Foundations* would have provided ample reason for declining to take on an additional burden? He must have had a similar motivation to continue lecturing at the Fletcher School. As Goldsmith had perceived, Samuelson had become a general economist, as qualified to discuss the technicalities of the national accounts as to explain the mathematics of economic theory. He was no longer the narrow specialist in mathematical economics whom his teachers thought might find it difficult to get an academic position. Perhaps even more important, Samuelson had acquired a clear political position that he was to hold for much of his life.

In that he confessed to having supported Roosevelt, his claims to have been a conservative while at Chicago must be questioned, but there seems little reason to doubt his claim to have moved toward a much more liberal position. Anyone who read NRPB reports in 1942–43 would have picked up his links to Hansen, but as the war came to an end, his identification with Hansen had become public, epitomized by the support for Hansen's vision of the postwar era in *The New Republic* and his collaboration with Hansen on the guaranteed-wage report.

Up to this point, Samuelson had generally distanced himself from Keynes. However, in *The New Republic* articles he could hardly avoid taking a stance on the economist with whom liberal, interventionist policies were widely associated, and he defended him as a true friend of the free enterprise system. This changing position with regard to Keynes clearly owed much to Hansen, but it cannot be understood apart from his supervision of Lawrence Klein, his first PhD student.

| Keynes and Keynesian Economics

The Keynesian Revolution

The first student to complete an economics PhD at MIT was Lawrence Klein. As an undergraduate at the University of California, Berkeley, where he graduated in 1942, he had spent most of his time in mathematics and economics classes.[1] He was fascinated with university mathematics and was convinced that it could play a role in economics. For his summer work as a research assistant he estimated the demand for Californian lemons. While still an undergraduate he published a note in the *Quarterly Journal of Economics*, in which he pointed out critical flaws in a recently published article that used correlation analysis.[2] He recalled that he encountered Samuelson's name when browsing the early issues of *Econometrica* in the Berkeley library, and Samuelson was the reason he chose to go to MIT for graduate work. Klein was assigned to Samuelson as his research assistant, and spent at much time with him as he could.[3] He found Samuelson exciting to work with because he generated ideas so fast, and being his assistant simply involved picking up a problem of interest.[4]

One of the problems that concerned Samuelson was that of trying to identify separate saving and investment functions from a single set of data, for he was not convinced by the ways in which people were trying to do it. When Trygve Haavelmo circulated a paper that analyzed the identification problem—the problem of how to decide whether data on prices and quantities traced out a demand curve or a supply curve—Samuelson was very interested, and he set Klein the task of investigating the equivalence between the saving–investment problem and that of identifying demand and supply functions.[a]

Samuelson believed that the two problems were formally identical, implying that the methods used in one problem could be applied to the other.[5] Klein used that idea to criticize a major study by Mordecai Ezekiel of the relationships between saving, investment, and income.[6] Ezekiel had tried to identify an investment function separately from a saving function by dividing investment into four categories, estimating separately the relationship between each of them and national income. The idea behind this was that though total investment was equal to saving, the components of investment were not. Klein challenged this, arguing that the conditions needed to identify separate saving and investment equations were not met, for Ezekiel's data did not contain enough information. Though he did not make use of these methods, Klein argued that Haavelmo's procedure of specifying a joint probability distribution for all the variables was preferable. One of the problems related to investment in housing, where Klein argued there was as much evidence that housing was changing in response to income as that it was causing changes in income. When Ezekiel replied that Klein had mistaken the evidence for his treatment of housing, Klein responded by denying that this was his main point, which was that estimating an investment function was very difficult and that the techniques available had not so far made it possible to do so successfully.[7]

The problem of estimating saving and investment functions fell squarely within the range of problems that Samuelson was tackling at this time in both his academic papers and at the NRPB. Samuelson had himself criticized Ezekiel's estimates of the consumption function in July 1942, just before Klein's arrival. Another paper Klein wrote while at MIT also related directly to Samuelson's work at the NRPB—"The Cost of a 'Beveridge Plan' in the United States."[8] He took the eight categories of social spending, from retirement and unemployment benefits to marriage and funeral grants, and estimated what they would cost to implement in the United States—a task that involved deciding on levels of benefit and working out how many people would be entitled to those benefits. He emphasized that his aim was simply to evaluate the cost of the scheme, not to comment on whether such benefits were appropriate, but he concluded that the cost was "not excessive in terms of expected level of postwar national income," representing not more than 10 to 13 percent of a high level of income.[9]

---

a. See chapter 17 this volume on discussions of Haavelmo in the MIT statistics seminar.

The connection between Samuelson's work and Klein's could hardly have been closer.

The most important topic to which Samuelson directed Klein was analyzing the Keynesian system, on which Klein wrote his thesis. In the preface to the thesis Klein wrote that "Oftentimes I feel that I have in many cases done nothing more than paraphrase what I have learned in classes and innumerable discussions with Professor Samuelson."[10] Despite Klein's penchant for using mathematics, and his econometric skills, the thesis comprised a historical analysis of Keynesian economics, tracing the ideas of Keynes, then still alive and frequently visiting the United States on wartime missions, from his early work to the *General Theory*. Klein painted a picture of Keynes as having started out adhering closely to "orthodox doctrines" and exhibiting marks of "extreme classicism," but as having broken with that tradition.[11] There were continuities in Keynes's thinking—the need to avoid deflation and unemployment and a critical attitude toward the rentier, as well as a belief that fluctuations in investment were the prime mover of a capitalist economy. Intuition came first and led to the development of a formal theory. Theoretical revolution came when Keynes realized that the saving–investment process determined the level of effective demand, the new theory being conceived in the middle of 1933.

There seems no reason to doubt that Samuelson was the source of many of the ideas in Klein's dissertation. His key historical point, that the Keynesian revolution involved seeing that the interaction of saving and investment could determine national income, and its dating to the middle of 1933, can be viewed as a direct response to a challenge Samuelson had posed in "The Modern Theory of Income"—to explain what had happened in Cambridge between articles Joan Robinson published in 1932 and in 1933.[b] He wrote:

> Professor Samuelson has pointed out to me a very interesting development in the economic literature of 1933. We can never be quite sure what goes on behind the political scenes in Cantabrigian economics, but we do know that there is a good deal of exchange of information among individuals within certain groups. If we take Joan Robinson as a reliable sounding board of opinion within the Keynesian group, we find a great change in ideas during 1933.... [In Robinson 1933b] Mrs. Robinson was over-generous to the master and was actually writing one of the first expositions, in which she is so lucid, of the really essential parts of the *General Theory of Employment, Interest, and Money*.[12]

---

b. See chapter 18 this volume.

On the next page he reiterated this view, writing, "The differences in theoretical structure between these two articles of Mrs. Robinson are quite amazing and should lead us to suspect the occurrence of the Revolution in Cambridge during 1933."[13]

Klein's dissertation echoed many of the themes that Samuelson had been developing in his writings on the multiplier over the previous two years. These include the importance of arguing in terms of schedules, or virtual movements, and relationships between observables that are true by definition and the claim that unemployment arises because of the shapes of certain schedules (investment and savings being unresponsive in relation to rates of interest), not because of rigidities.

> In a system of real economics with no frictions, it is necessary only to assume that certain schedules have different shapes from those assumed classically. If the savings and investment schedules are both interest-inelastic, as we now believe, then it is easy to see why there is no perfect equilibrium of perfect competition possible.[14]

Like Samuelson, Klein attached less importance to Keynes's theory of money and the rate of interest than to his theory of income determination, and he used the distinction between full employment and the level of output at which bottlenecks developed. He emphasized that the theory of the inflationary gap he had presented was entirely operational. It is even tempting to see Samuelson's influence in the remark that Schumpeter, despite his claim to be completely non-Keynesian, had to admit great similarities between his own theory of the cycle and Keynes's, for both stressed the primacy of investment, and that many of the critical reviews of the *General Theory* were constructive.[15]

The state of thinking about Keynesian economics when Klein was writing his thesis is nicely shown by a letter he wrote to Hansen in March 1944. In a conversation the previous day, Klein had failed to explain to Hansen what he had meant when he said "that the level of income is determined in the Keynesian system by savings and investment."[16] In his letter he explained the difference between an equation that would be satisfied for only one value of a variable and an identity true for all values of the variable. He then turned to the "statical Keynesian system used by Hicks, Lange, Samuelson and many others," which comprised two equations: supply equals demand for money, and savings equal investment, where everything except the money supply (constant) depends on both income and the rate of interest.[c] The first

---

c. The equations are $M = M(i, Y)$ and $S(i, Y) = I(i, Y)$.

equation could be solved for the rate of interest as a function of income and the money supply. This could then be substituted into the saving equals investment equation to obtain a function in which income was the only variable.[d] If investment were assumed not to depend on output, the result was a diagram such as figure 18.1, earlier. Klein's conclusion was that shifts in investment determined fluctuations in income, a result that was central to the Keynesian system. If the interaction of saving and investment did not determine income, the Keynesian system would be indeterminate. These ideas are now the staple of introductory macroeconomics courses, but were then less well understood.

Klein had come to MIT as an enthusiast for using mathematics in economics, possessing considerable statistical and econometric skills that he augmented while studying with Samuelson, attending courses in the mathematics department. It seems safe to assume that if Samuelson had pushed him toward writing a more mathematical thesis, Klein would willingly have gone along with this. The implication has to be that Samuelson, despite his enthusiasm for using mathematics in economics, encouraged Klein to take a different route, just as he was doing in his own work on the business cycle. Klein made the important methodological point that mathematical models were essential:

> Keynes was quite unkind to the mathematical economists in the *General Theory*, but it is hoped that this book along with basic works of Lange, Smithies, Hicks, Samuelson, Kaldor will show that only by laying bare the mathematical skeleton models of the theory can all its implications be traced.[17]

However, the mathematical skeleton was not enough on its own, hence the need to go back into history to understand the systems they were being used to analyze. Thus, he wrote,

> Mathematical models of the skeleton system of the *General Theory* are very useful in bringing out certain important structural aspects of Keynesian economics, in disproving certain false conceptions about the new theory, and in contrasting the Keynesian and classical systems. The models show the building blocks on which the complete, interrelated system rests.[18]

There is a clear distinction here between "model" and "system."

---

d. $S(i(M_0, Y), Y) = I(i(M_0, Y), Y)$.

Klein provided a cogent discussion of the relationship of a model to the world, and to policymaking, using the analogy of a physical machine.

That is to say, the Keynesian economic system is essentially a machine which grinds out results according to where the several dials controlling the system are set. The dials are the functional relations and the setting of the dials is taken care of by the banking system, the government, the psychology of consumers, the attitudes of investors, the achievements of the technologists, etc. Is it correct to blame the machine if the dials are consistently set at pessimistic levels? If the machine is a true model of the way the system of the real world behaves, then we are not justified in criticizing the machine because other factors set the dials at particular levels. It is just as easy to explain one phase of the business cycle as any other with the Keynesian analysis provided we take into account the correct structure of the relationships involved during each phase. Our experience in the past has been that the relationships have been sufficiently alike over a period of years so that we can take the stationary system for an equilibrium solution. If the conditions of our time are such that this stationary solution is not one of full employment, then we must realize this fact and do something about it. On the other hand, the future may be such that we get a continuously changing structure for the economic model. Without serious modification, this can be incorporated into the theory. There is nothing to make us work with constant, unchanging functional relations. Shifting equilibria and dynamically changing relations can also be ground out of the machine. The principles of the Keynesian Revolution need not be discarded; rather they must receive elaboration and be extended to handle more complex situations.[19]

Samuelson did not express himself this way—in his publications up to this point he had not talked in terms of "models," though in his unpublished paper "The Modern Theory of Income," he had referred to his own simplified equation systems and those of others as models. In contrast, Klein's dissertation is littered with the term, which appears on at least 43 of its 195 pages.[20] It contains some themes that can be found in Samuelson's work, such as the importance of invariant, structural relationships, but it can be read as expressing an optimistic strategy for empirical modeling that goes beyond what can be found in Samuelson's writings. It is a view that arose out of Klein's ongoing relationship with Samuelson and with which Samuelson must have engaged even if he did not himself go down this route.

Klein's views on the nature of the Keynesian revolution are very different from the views Samuelson had expressed in his publications up to this point, which had been colored by his having approached Keynes from the perspective not of classical economics but from American business cycle theory as represented by Hansen. Samuelson's earliest work on business cycle theory followed Hansen closely, seeing Keynes as having added the concept of the multiplier to a body of literature that adopted a more dynamic perspective on business cycle theory than was to be found in the *General Theory*. There was no suggestion that he thought in terms of a dichotomy between Keynesian and classical theory. Even in "The Modern Theory of Income," he wrote of the Keynesians from the perspective of an outsider: adopting a modern theory of income determination was not the same as being a Keynesian.[e] For example, he criticized "the Keynesians" for having two different theories of the equality of saving and investment, between which they continually switched back and forth. This is very different from the picture painted by Klein of Keynes as the economist who had put everything together to create a new system. Moreover, when Klein compared Keynes's theory with the ideas of other economists, his list included no Americans, unless Schumpeter is counted as American.[f] This raises the question of whether, despite Klein's claim that in many of his discussions he did no more than paraphrase what he had learned from Samuelson, Klein had helped shift Samuelson to a different stance on Keynes.

Samuelson's lectures in early 1943, when Klein was working on his thesis, focused on "the Keynesian system," a significant change compared with earlier work in which he wrote in terms of incorporating Keynesian ideas into the more general Hansen theory.[g] Whether or not it was Klein who persuaded Samuelson to change his emphasis, it was while working with Klein that Samuelson began to talk of Keynes rather than Hansen as the key figure in the New Economics. Klein was also politically much more committed than Samuelson. He believed in socialism, and shortly after leaving MIT, he even became a member of the Communist Party.[21] In contrast, Samuelson was never a socialist, but as he came closer to Hansen, the roots of whose political ideas lay in the New Deal, he grew to adopt a more interventionist position that was branded socialist by its conservative critics. The two had much in common, and it seems certain that their relationship was less unequal than Klein suggested.

---

e. This judgment is based on the way he uses the terms "Keynesian" (to refer to ideas of Keynes) and "Keynesians" (to refer to an identifiable group of economists).

f. His list comprised Hayek, Schumpeter, Myrdal, Pigou, Hawtrey, and Hobson.

g. See chapter 20 this volume.

Debating Keynesian Economics

During the war, Samuelson was repeatedly in contact with Oskar Lange, engaging with him both as a mathematical economist and as a business cycle theorist. The terms of their engagement are illustrated by a letter Samuelson wrote to Lange in April 1944. He began by raising some problems with Lange's "The theory of the multiplier" article published the previous summer.[22] These were highly technical mathematical points, involving whether equations could have the properties Lange assumed. In claiming that "the key to the paradox lies in the fact that in the continuous case of a single impulse of expenditure must be thought of as a momentary impulse of infinite magnitude—i.e., like an improper Dirac function," he was talking as one mathematician to another.[23] Few economists, even readers of *Econometrica,* would have followed the point. Yet on the next page he adopted a completely different approach when discussing a recent paper by Franco Modigliani, an Italian economist who had fled to the United States in 1939, where he studied for a PhD under Jacob Marschak at the New School.[h]

Modigliani's dissertation, which formed the basis for "Liquidity Preference and the Theory of Interest and Money" published in *Econometrica,* sought to reconcile the Keynesian theory of interest with the classical theory, thereby assessing the interpretations of Keynes offered by John Hicks and Abba Lerner.[24] This article is notable for its explicit presentation of his aggregative model, involving physical output, investment, and the price level, as a simplification of a Walrasian general equilibrium system in which every good is considered separately. Like Hicks, Modigliani analyzed this simplified system in terms of two equations relating the rate of interest and national income—labeled an IS curve (on which investment equaled saving) and an L curve (on which demand for money, alias *Liquidity* preference, equals the money supply).[i] The diagram illustrated the stationary solution to an explicitly stated dynamic model.

Modigliani's conclusion challenged the Hansen-Samuelson-Klein view that there was a causal relationship between investment and national income. They did indeed move together, but this was because low investment and low employment were "the effect of the same cause, namely a

---

h. In the 1960s, Samuelson, Modigliani, and Robert Solow were to be colleagues at MIT, with reputations as three of America's leading Keynesian economists.

i. Hicks 1937. In his diagram, two alternative curves were labeled $L(M = M_0)$ and $L'(M = M_1)$. This notation was close to the one that was to become standard a decade later, when textbooks talked about the IS–LM model (its other component was I = S).

basic maladjustment between the quantity of money and the wage rate. It is the fact that money wages are too high relative to the quantity of money that explains why it is unprofitable to expand employment to the 'full employment' level."[25] In his letter to Lange, Samuelson said that he had read this letter with great interest. However, he thought Modigliani, in common with many economists discussing the Keynesian system, had not handled money and prices correctly.[j] In Modigliani's system, a rise in the money supply and a fall in the wage rate both led to a fall in the rate of interest and a rise in the rate of investment. The exception was "the Keynesian case," where there was a minimum below which the rate of interest could not be pushed because, at this rate, people would be willing to hold unlimited amounts of money. In contrast, Samuelson argued that in the classical system, there was full employment whatever the quantity of money, and that wage cuts (which would increase employment) were not equivalent to an increase in the money supply (which would not increase employment). Here, Samuelson was not challenging Modigliani's mathematics, but the economic assumptions on which his theory was based. He hoped Lange's forthcoming monograph would resolve the difficulties he was having, closing by saying, "I hope that this letter is not too incoherent. It is written on the run in between other activities."

Though Samuelson still taught Keynesian economics under the heading of the business cycle and had not changed his view that dynamics were important, the business cycle no longer framed his work on the economy as a whole in the way it had done in 1940. The demands of war production, which it clearly made sense to analyze as an exogenous shock to the system and not as part of some cyclical process, would have played a role. Equally important was the need to understand the multiplier. The concept of the multiplier had been known since the early 1930s, but even in the early 1940s it was still not properly understood. There was no agreement on the terms in which the relationship between saving and investment should be discussed, and theoretical problems were connected to practical problems relating to the measurement of national income. Through his academic research, his consultancy, and his teaching, Samuelson was engaged with all of these. The result was that the determination of national income through the interaction of saving and investment schedules came to be central to his thinking. Keynes came to be increasingly prominent as the

---

j. He claimed that Modigliani had not handled correctly the point, standard in the general equilibrium literature, that demand functions were homogeneous of degree zero in prices.

creator of a new system; seeing him this way was more compatible than were Samuelson's earlier views with Klein's claim that there had been a Keynesian revolution.

Though Samuelson came to be identified with the Keynesian revolution in America, his own identification with Keynes and the idea of a Keynesian revolution was slow. It is tempting to see his reluctance to identify himself as a Keynesian as political, for Hansen's ideas on policy were already being attacked by conservatives who objected to any suggestion that governments should run deficits in peacetime.[k] However, there were intellectual reasons for his distancing himself from Keynes. His reaction to the *General Theory* had been strongly influenced by Hansen, and though interwar American business cycle theory, represented by Hansen and Clark, became less prominent in his work, it flavored his interpretation of Keynes. Whereas Modigliani, under Jacob Marschak's influence, followed the mathematical logic of his general equilibrium system to conclude that frictions—wage rigidity—must underlie Keynesian results (except in special cases), Samuelson never went down that route. Cheap money had not stopped the Depression, and so it did not make sense to rely on any mechanism that involved investment responding to changes in the interest rate. He took for granted the belief, widespread in the 1930s, that markets were not competitive. The notion that there might be an insufficient level of investment to sustain full employment was a conclusion learned from Hansen that he never abandoned and which continued to color his interpretation of Keynesian economics. He was developing a Keynesianism that was distinct from the one that came to dominate postwar macroeconomic theory.

Keynes and Keynesianism, May 1946

On April 21, 1946, John Maynard Keynes died, almost exactly ten years after the publication of the *General Theory,* and Samuelson was invited, on Marschak's recommendation, to write a commemorative article for the July issue of *Econometrica.*[26,l] Frisch hoped that Samuelson's article would run alongside an article by William Beveridge, offering personal reflections on Keynes, but Beveridge's article failed to materialize and Samuelson's article

---

k. Such attacks had led to the closure of the NRPB. See chapter 19 this volume.

l. Samuelson was then in Marschak's mind, because Marschak was trying to persuade the University of Chicago to hire him. See chapter 28 this volume.

was published on its own.[27] Though Samuelson had engaged with Keynesian theory, a semi-historical article like this represented a new departure. He generously acknowledged his debt to Klein, and it is probably his knowledge of Klein's thesis that explains his close familiarity with the evolution of Keynes's ideas and his background. On the grounds that Beveridge and others would cover them extensively, he chose not to discuss the personal details of Keynes's life but, rather, to confine his attention to the effects of his work on modern economic analysis.

Samuelson's article began with his remark, quoted in chapter 12 earlier, about economists under thirty-five having had no resistance to the *General Theory*. However, rather than praise Keynes, he went on to find fault with the book in language that was as critical as that used by his Harvard teachers, Leontief and Schumpeter, a decade earlier.

> It is a badly written book, poorly organized; any layman who, beguiled
> by the author's previous reputation, bought the book was cheated of
> his 5 shillings. It is not well suited for classroom use. It is arrogant,
> bad-tempered, polemical, and not overly-generous in its acknowledg-
> ments. It abounds in mares nests and confusions: involuntary unem-
> ployment, wage units, the equality of savings and investment, the
> timing of the multiplier, interactions of marginal efficiency upon the
> rate of interest, forced savings, own rates of interest, and many oth-
> ers.... [It] resembles the random notes over a period of years of a
> gifted man who in his youth gained the whip hand over his publishers
> by virtue of the acclaim and fortune resulting from the success of his
> *Economic Consequences of the Peace*.[28]

The result was that Keynes had set up "an indoor guessing game": "Wherein lies the essential contribution of the *General Theory* and its distinguishing characteristic from the classical writings?" The *General Theory* was "an obscure book," the obscurity and polemical character of which would, Samuelson conjectured, serve to maximize its long influence. And yet it was, Samuelson claimed, a work of genius, its analysis both obvious and new.

But what was the book's novelty? He dismissed Keynes's theory of liquidity preference on grounds that the rate of interest was of minor importance, and he argued that though Keynes had brilliantly called attention to the importance of expectations, he had hardly provided any theory. The novelty of the *General Theory* lay not in its theory of liquidity preference or its conception of expectations but in its analysis of effective demand.

I myself believe the broad significance of the *General Theory* to be in the fact that it provides a relatively realistic, complete system for analyzing the level of effective demand and its fluctuations. More narrowly, I conceive the heart of its contribution to be in that subset of its equations which relate to the propensity to consume and to saving in relation to offsets-to-saving.

There was no mechanism to ensure that investment was equal to saving at full employment. The *General Theory* might have been an obscure book, needing a companion volume that could provide a guide to its contents, but it provided a new system, and that was what was needed to defeat the classical theory.[m]

Samuelson wrote favorably of Keynes's wartime analysis of inflation using the concept of the "inflationary gap" as the modern theory of inflation. This theory might have been the reason why the inflation rate was much better during the Second World War than in previous major wars. This established that the theory was not simply about the economics of depression, but applied in times of prosperity, too. However, even here, Samuelson was critical of Keynes, for he believed that inflation was not determined entirely by aggregate demand. Writing at a time when price controls were still in operation, Samuelson expressed the view that their removal might lead to "a considerable, self-sustaining rise in prices," even if there were insufficient effective demand.[29]

The book had been influential because economists in Britain rapidly realized that effective demand was not to prove a passing fad, but was part of the "wave of the future," and American economists soon followed.

Obviously, exactly the same words cannot be used to describe the analysis of income determination of, say, Lange, Hart, Harris, Ellis, Hansen, Bissell, Haberler, Slichter, J. M. Clark, or myself. And yet the Keynesian taint is unmistakably there upon every one of us. (I hasten to add—as who does not?—that I am not myself a Keynesian, although some of my best friends are.)[30]

Having established that Keynes provided a system, and that his economics did amount to a general theory, applicable in times of prosperity as well as depression, Samuelson sought to establish that his philosophy was "profoundly capitalistic" in nature, aimed at saving the existing system. Keynes

---

m. A few years later, Hansen (1953) was to write such a guide.

himself was an "urbane and cosmopolitan provincial English liberal" who found nothing in "the turbid rubbish of the Red bookshops."[31,n]

Samuelson then turned to the development of Keynes's ideas, arguing that the *General Theory* could not have been anticipated, given his previous work. Though he criticized orthodoxy, such as Irving Fisher's quantity theory of money, Keynes was not an original economic theorist, his work being notable only for its "political novelty and persuasiveness." He had even made a number of serious mistakes, such his views on population and his arguments with Bertil Ohlin on reparations payments. "He has been at once soundboard, amplifier, and initiator of contemporary viewpoints, whose strength and weakness lay in his intuition, audaciousness, and changeability."[32] Keynes never had any interest in economic theory. The only time Keynes showed any interest in economic theory was in his appreciation of Frank Ramsey's theory of saving, about which Samuelson wrote, "his reasoning is all the more brilliant—and I say this seriously!—because it is mathematically unrigorous, if not wrong."[33] The exaggerated importance Keynes attached to the article could be explained only in terms of his personal affection for Ramsey.[34,o]

So why did Keynes have so little interest in economic theory, and why was he so bad at formal theorizing? Samuelson's answer was,

> Perhaps because he was exposed to economics too young, or perhaps because he arrived at maturity in the stultifying backwash of Marshall's influence upon economic theory—for whatever reason, Keynes seems never to have had any genuine interest in pure economic theory. It is remarkable that so active a brain would have failed to make any contribution to value theory; and yet except for his discussion of index numbers in Volume I of the *Treatise* and for a few remarks concerning "user cost," which are novel at best only in terminology and emphasis, he seems to have left no mark on pure value theory.[35]

Reading between the lines of this article is a complex task. Given that Samuelson was well aware of his own precocity, it is remarkable that he criticized Keynes for coming to economics too early. His likening of Keynesianism to a disease suggests that either one caught it or one did not; yet in distancing himself from Keynes he implied that, while he might not have been

---

n. Other than that he wanted to recognize Keynes's qualities without conceding too much, it is not clear precisely what he meant by describing him as cosmopolitan and provincial. Perhaps his love of the language got the better of him.

o. Samuelson was later to hold a more positive view of Ramsey's theory of saving, which in the 1980s came to be seen as one of the main foundations of macroeconomic theory.

immune, he never succumbed completely. The vehemence of his attack on Marshall, which goes beyond anything in *Foundations*, makes it impossible to avoid conjecturing that this was an article on which he sought Schumpeter's advice. In describing Keynes as someone who "stumbled upon and formulated a new system of analysis," with no interest in economic theory and as reasoning incorrectly, Samuelson presented him as having brilliant intuitions but leaving a gap that Samuelson was to fill with the "Keynesian savings-investment-income cross."[36]

A large part of the explanation of Samuelson's attitude toward Keynes is that he came to "Keynesian" problems through Alvin Hansen. Hansen had come to terms with Keynes's ideas by incorporating them into his own theory. This explains the paradox that, as Samuelson put it, "The Keynesian notions are old and new at the same time."[37] Samuelson sometimes disagreed with his mentor, as when he had tried to explain that consumption spending could have the same impact on demand as investment, or when he had to argue dogmatically that it made no difference whether one argued in terms of saving and investment or in terms of income (saving plus consumption) and expenditure (investment plus consumption), a point Hansen could not understand as late as 1947. However, Samuelson and Hansen remained extremely close, personally and intellectually.[38] This explains why, in 1946, though admiring Keynes, Samuelson could still distance himself from him, putting forward an interpretation of the *General Theory* that stressed precisely those elements that fit into Hansen's way of thinking. The myth of Hansen's conversion to Keynes that Samuelson was to propagate later was not yet part of his thinking.[39]

There had, however, been a change in Samuelson's position in relation to Keynes. Possibly by realizing the powerful role that the analysis of aggregate demand could play in policymaking, or perhaps by working with Klein on his thesis, he had changed from seeing Keynes as having simply provided concepts that could be worked into a preexisting, dynamic theory, to seeing Keynes as having put forward a system, albeit one that was so badly formulated that it needed others (Hansen and himself) to sort it out. This brought him closer to the view of J. M. Clark, who had written to Keynes shortly after the *General Theory* appeared:

> It has seemed to me that what I call the "income flow analysis," of which yours is the most noted presentation, has done something which has not been done in comparable degree since Ricardo and Marx; namely constructed a coherent logical theoretical system or formula having the quality of a mechanism, growing directly out of current conditions

and problems which are of paramount importance and furnishing a key for working out definite answers in terms of policy.[40]

Though he would not have seen this letter, this was Samuelson's position: that the Keynesian theory of income determination, if made properly dynamic, could formalize the income flow analysis of Clark, Hansen, and others. Though he was no mathematician, Clark conceived of economics as dynamic and concerned with the relation of fluctuating demand to a relatively inelastic supply. In *Studies in the Economics of Overhead Costs*, he had written that his book was "a study of the discrepancies between an ever fluctuating demand and a relatively inelastic fund of productive capacity, resulting in wastes of partial idleness and many other economic disturbances."[41] He might talk of "unused capacity" rather than unemployment, and he might stress the role of imperfect competition, but the subject was the same. In 1946, Samuelson had occasion to reread *Studies in the Economics of Overhead Costs*, and he wrote Clark, praising it.[p]

> I cannot refrain from writing to tell you what a seminal work it is.
>
> A dozen or more years ago, as an undergraduate at the University of Chicago, I first read it. I have been astonished to discover how many ideas in my mind trace back to that first reading—and incidentally how much of the current discussion of unemployment reflects its influence. I was also amused to note that as an undergraduate, steeped in the orthodox Chicago tradition, I jotted down critical marginal notes which today I would no longer hold against you.[42]

By the time he wrote these words, Samuelson's views had changed dramatically in a way that enabled him to appreciate Clark's work; but though Keynes's ideas had been crucial to that transformation, he had not simply converted to Keynes, any more than his mentor had. When Lewis Haney, at New York University, who was to become the harshest academic critic of his textbook, classified him as a Keynesian in his textbook on the history of economic thought, Samuelson replied that after being hostile to the *General Theory*, he "finally came round to the view that his work is characterized by numerous logical flaws and omissions but that his tools represent an important addition to our economic knowledge" and that he held "no

---

p. Overhead costs are costs that have to be incurred whatever the level of production. As output rises, such costs will be spread over a larger quantity of output, with the result that cost per unit of output will fall. Facing such cost conditions, companies could not be in competitive equilibrium and there must be an element of monopoly.

particular brief for the particular policies advocated by Keynes or for his general weltanschaung."[43]

Though they might prove useful for other reasons, given a postwar political climate that was increasingly hostile to Keynesianism, there is no reason to think that such statements about where he stood in relation to Keynes were anything other than an accurate reflection of a position he had reached over several years during which he had been engaged in the urgent practical problems related to the war and its aftermath.[q] This version of Keynesian economics, rooted as much in the ideas of Clark and Hansen as in the *General Theory*, was shortly to be popularized in what became a bestselling textbook.

q. He could also joke about his views. When Paul Douglas, as president of the American Economic Association, asked Samuelson to participate in a session on Keynesian economics in 1947, for which he wanted to include a true defender of Keynes, a strong opponent, and two others with intermediate positions, Samuelson replied that he was not sure "as to which of the backfield posts—'true defender,' 'strong opponent,' or 'intermediate position'"—he was slated for. P. H. Douglas, April 28, 1947, Letter to Paul A. Samuelson, PASP 24 (D [1942-64]); P. A. Samuelson, May 20, 1947, Letter to Paul H. Douglas, PASP 24 (D [1942-64]).

CHAPTER 25 | Drafting the Textbook, 1945

A Textbook Centered on National Income

In the summer of 1945, Samuelson began work on the book that was to make him a household name among the college students who were to study economics in increasingly large numbers. His articles in academic journals and his *Foundations of Economic Analysis* were read by most economists who entered graduate school, but the book that introduced him to the much larger audience of undergraduates who took an elementary economics course was *Economics: An Introductory Analysis*.[1] Published in 1948, this was to go through eleven editions before, in 1985, a co-author took over responsibility for further revisions.[a] The book dominated the rapidly growing market for introductory textbooks to the extent that, at one point, it was claimed that all such books were clones of Samuelson. The book made him a fortune, selling worldwide and being translated into many languages.

Samuelson remembered the book as being the result of a conversation with his MIT department chair, Ralph Freeman, shortly after he had returned from working full time in the Radiation Laboratory.[2] "Entering my office and closing the door," Freeman made a proposal:

Eight hundred MIT juniors must take a full year of compulsory economics. They hate it. We've tried everything. They still hate it. We even

---

a. When William Nordhaus took over, the character of the book changed significantly. By then the textbook market had changed, being much larger and with more competition than when the first edition was published.

did a departmental joint product. It was the worst editorial experience of my life. After our senior colleague turned in his chapter, I had to say, "Floyd, this is not a chapter on public finance. It's a chapter against public finance." Paul, will you go on half time for a semester or two? Write a text the students will like. If they like it, yours will be good economics. Leave out whatever you like. Be as short as you wish. Whatever you come up with, that will be a vast improvement on where we are.[3,b]

There was, however, another reason for wanting the course rewritten. Writing to Compton, Freeman stressed that the reason was not the inadequacy of current teaching materials, but the need to revise the course to fit into the new humanities course that MIT was introducing.[4] This involved studying English in the first year, modern history in the second, and social sciences, including economics, in the third year. Included within the social sciences was Economic Principles, the course for which Samuelson was being asked to rewrite the course materials. Far from making use of the training that scientists and engineers were receiving in mathematics, those courses were all intended to emphasize written and oral expression.[5] This feature of the program was stressed in the MIT President's Report, which stated that the emphasis on "good writing and expression" would "continue to be emphasized in other subjects throughout the remainder of the four-year program."[6] Through the book that would interest MIT's science and engineering students, all of whom learned mathematics, Samuelson was tasked with producing a text that was well written and *not* one that focused on mathematics. Freeman cited the need to have Samuelson write new teaching materials when he asked Compton to inquire whether it would be possible to release Samuelson from his duties in the Radiation Laboratory without taking him away from important war work.

Though Samuelson credits Freeman with inviting him to write the book to meet the needs of the MIT department, he soon had the idea of writing something for a wider audience; in July 1945, a few days before he officially left the Radiation Laboratory, McGraw-Hill had sent him a draft contract for a book to be titled *Elementary Economics Handbook*.[7,c] During the 1945–46

---

b. The phrase "against public finance" hints at the possibility that there may have been a political element involved. However, caution is required in attributing the phrase to Freeman, because Samuelson used exactly the same phrase to describe Harold Burbank's course in public finance at Harvard.

c. Samuelson's last few months at the Radiation Laboratory were spent working on the Bush report, so he may have remembered the conversation with Freeman as having taken place after he left the Radiation Laboratory, even though he was still on its payroll.

academic year, he worked on the book, and as soon as chapters were finished, they were duplicated and distributed to students.[8] Though these materials were put together under the title *Modern Economics: An Introductory Analysis*,[9] it was clearly unfinished and he was unwilling for it to be used outside MIT. However, in early 1946, he had a much more polished draft, in which the word *modern* had been dropped from the title, on sale in the MIT bookstore to anyone who chose to purchase it. After further revisions, the book was eventually published in 1948 by McGraw-Hill.

The reasons Samuelson gave for taking on the task were his susceptibility to flattery, the fact that he already had so many journal articles to his credit that it could hardly damage his reputation, and the mistaken idea that it would take him no more than three months. *Foundations* was already on its way to the publisher, and he recognized that there was a window of opportunity, in that the existing textbooks were out of date. A further factor was that he was offered a reduction in his workload to write the book, though it is hard to find evidence of this in the MIT course catalogs.[d] A textbook by a friend from his Harvard days, Lorie Tarshis, had been half-written before the war and would appear a year before Samuelson's, but in 1945 Samuelson knew nothing of this.[10] In the end, writing the book would take three years and was to involve him in unanticipated controversy.

As Freeman told Samuelson in 1945, the department had been trying to reform the introductory curriculum at MIT for some years. In 1942, two instructors, Richard Clemence and Francis Doody, neither of whom had yet taken their PhD, published an article in the *American Economic Review* on what should be taught in an introductory course, making arguments with which Samuelson would have been familiar. They were in his department, and a friendship developed with Clemence that continued while Samuelson was writing his book. Clemence's wife, Ellie, was among those Samuelson thanked for providing editorial and secretarial assistance.[11] When Clemence submitted his doctoral dissertation to Harvard, in the same year that Samuelson's

---

d. In 1945–46, when teaching resumed after being virtually suspended for a year, Samuelson was listed as teaching the same courses as before 1944, and the following year he was listed as teaching two additional courses. These were more elementary courses—Economic Principles (Ec. 11) and Prices and Production (Ec. 13)—and were presumably the ones where his book was tried out on students. If the catalogue is correct, and it may be that his teaching was different from what was anticipated when the catalogue went to press, the "reward" for writing the textbook must have involved postponing by a year the date when he would take over these courses himself. However, there is the possibility that the catalogue, which would have gone to press months before teaching began, may not indicate correctly who ended up teaching each course.

textbook was published, he sent him a copy, and Samuelson offered him advice on publication: if Clemence could persuade publishers that he might one day offer them a textbook, they would be more likely to take a chance on a more specialized book that would sell less well.[12]

Writing just as the United States was entering the war, Clemence and Doody argued that teachers had a duty to explain to their students the great changes that were taking place in the world.[13] However, it was widely agreed that most general courses were not successful in doing this. The theory taught was too static, and teachers were unsuccessful in showing students how it could be applied to solve real-world problems. Students needed to be taught about the business cycle, even if there was not unanimity among economists on how to analyze it. Clemence and Doody argued that Keynesian theory provided a way of supplementing static theory with a model that was closer to reality. Teachers should avoid requiring students to learn a mass of facts that they could not themselves remember from one year to the next, and economic history should be taught in such a way as to explain how theory and facts fit together.

Clemence and Doody suggested that economics should be seen as the study of economic systems, where an economic system was "defined as any set of arrangements by means of which a group of people attempt to satisfy their wants for scarce goods and services."[14] If this definition were adopted, there remained the problem of integrating the material, and here they suggested using the concept of national income.

> The entire course may be regarded as an attempt at the solution of a single economic problem. That problem is to explain the forces which determine the size and composition of the national income, its fluctuations over time, and its distribution in both space and time.[15,e]

Business cycles would be a part of this, but they would not be the only topic of discussion: the study of national income was much broader. The course should begin with a discussion of statistics on U.S. national income "since the early period," which students could discuss even before they were taught any theory. They should then be taught the idea of equilibrium, "beginning with a brief discussion of the principal institutions forming the structure of a capitalist system, with emphasis on the free market."[16] This would cover business organization, the corporation, trade unionism, collective bargaining, public

---

e. It should be noted that this approach was not entirely new, in that it is reminiscent of the approach of Pigou's before the First World War.

finance, and international trade. The key point was that institutions were presented as relevant to the principal problem of explaining national income.

The preface to *Economics*, dated April 1948, promised a book that would meet the criteria set out by Clemence and Doody six years earlier.

It aims at an understanding of the economic institutions and problems of American civilization in the middle of the twentieth century. *National income provides the central unifying theme of the book.*[17]

Traditional topics were omitted in favor of what Samuelson described as "a rich array of quantitative material." The book was up to date in that much of this material had been available only in the previous half-dozen years. The subjects were those that were needed to understand the postwar world and those that people found interesting. Just as nonspecialists studying physics deserved to learn about atomic energy and nuclear structure, so economics students deserved to learn about the big questions of economic policy. The book should enable students to understand public statements from bodies such as the Committee for Economic Development, a middle-of-the-road business group led by businessmen, newspaper publishers, and a Republican senator, or the President's Economic Report to Congress. The book might present modern theories associated with Keynes, but Samuelson was claiming that it was emphatically not radical in its politics: teaching national income was consistent with adopting a middle-of-the-road position.[18]

Samuelson's conception of the book had been reached very early on. In March 1946, he summarized his approach in a letter to Emile Despres.

I proceed on the conviction that the elementary course is primarily designed for people who will never be professional economists or even concentrators in economics. (I also believe, but I am not so sure of my ground, that the introductory course for concentrators should not deviate much from that for anyone else.) The elementary course, therefore, should concern itself with the important economic problems that confront any intelligent adult. It follows automatically that all "important" questions will be of interest to the student. In fact, interesting the student would be the primary aim of the course. This may sound cynical, but I do not believe it is[,] since the intuition of the ordinary layman as to what is interesting is usually a pretty good one.[19]

A very similar statement found its way into the book's preface, where he wrote that the topics people found interesting overlapped "almost perfectly" with the topics that were important for understanding the postwar world, and that "the instinct of the nonspecialist is nearly infallible."[20] The earlier letter makes it clear that this near-infallibility referred to the identification of important problems: he was not implying that the layperson's understanding of these issues was infallible. Samuelson then told Despres what this meant in practice.

> Certainly, this means pretty much soft-pedaling all so-called value and distribution theory. A little bit of supply and demand, cost, production and profit analysis of the firm will do no harm; and probably the same thing can be said for a fairly rigorous treatment of comparative cost. Aside from this, I would place emphasis upon national income, money, unemployment, the business cycle, fiscal policy, public debt, social security, etc., along with preliminary exposition of the elementary facts of life about corporations, trade unions, stock market, etc.

His "preliminary exposition of the elementary facts of economic life" was so important that it covered almost 250 of the book's 600 pages.

The First Draft, 1945

Samuelson's starting point was the book produced by various members of the MIT department, put together by Ralph Freeman, known as *The Economic Process*, a revised edition of a book originally written in 1934.[21] Like Taussig's textbook used at Harvard, it comprised two substantial volumes of nearly 500 pages each. Chapters had been drafted by nine members of the department, but so Freeman wrote, "[t]here has been ... so much interchange of ideas, and the editor has so freely used his power of amendment, that it would be difficult to trace to particular individuals the various errors and imperfections which may appear."[22] It was this book, used by all instructors, that was the starting point for the debates over the curriculum that led Clemence and Doody to write their article.

Though the organizing principle of the book may have been that proposed by his former colleagues, and though he started from the text Freeman had edited, the opening gambit in Samuelson's book appears to be entirely his own. He began by citing an unnamed professor at the Harvard Law School who used to address the entering class, "Take a good look at the man on your right, and the man at your left; because next year one of you won't be here."[23] Samuelson used this story, which any student in that first class would understand, not to make a point about the need for hard work but to argue that unemployment could strike anyone; it was not something that people brought on themselves but something that affected companies and even whole industries. According to Samuelson, the rise of the dictators, and hence the Second World War, stemmed from the failure to maintain high employment. Economics could hardly be more important. It explained the existence of poverty within a society in which goods were plentiful.

From here Samuelson tried to persuade his student readers that economics was an intellectually challenging activity—that it was not simply a matter of expressing personal opinions about what should happen—and that economic analysis involved more than mere description. Using analogies from science, he explained why economists had to distinguish between understanding the world as it is and what they wanted to happen.

> At every point of our analysis we shall be seeking to shed light on these policy problems [controlling the business cycle, furthering economic progress, and achieving an equitable distribution of income]. But to succeed in this, the student of economics must first cultivate an objective and detached ability to see things as they *are*, regardless of his likes or dislikes. The fact must be faced that economic subjects are close to everybody emotionally. Blood pressures rise and voices become shrill whenever deep-seated beliefs and prejudices are involved. A doctor passionately interested in stamping out disease must train himself to observe things as they are. His bacteriology is not a different one from that of a mad scientist out to destroy the human race by plague. *Wishful* thinking is *bad* thinking and leads to little wish-fulfillment.[24]

There was, Samuelson claimed, not one economics for Democrats and another for Republicans. People might have different ethical positions, yet agree on economic analysis. Economics might not be obviously difficult, like mathematics, and it deals with things that everyone knows about, but this simplicity could be deceptive. Words could be treacherous because they elicited emotional reactions. Like any science, economics involves simplification, idealization, and abstraction. What is most noticeable about this passage is how Samuelson refrained from using terms such as "positive" and "normative" economics, even though these had been well established in the literature since the nineteenth century. He was avoiding jargon, however simple it might appear to economists. Philosophical jargon was not completely absent, but it was confined to terms he could be sure his students would already understand, as when he wrote about theory.

> Properly understood, therefore, theory and observation, deduction and induction cannot be in conflict. Like eggs, there are only two kinds

of theories: good ones and bad ones. And the test of a theory's good-
ness is its usefulness in illuminating observational reality. Its logical
elegance and fine-spun beauty are irrelevant. Consequently, when a
student says, "That's all right in theory but not in practice," he really
means, "That's *not* all right in theory" or else he is talking nonsense.[25]

Here, as earlier on, he was trying to persuade students that economics was
saying something substantial—that it was not simply a matter of opinion.

Samuelson's introductory chapter closed with a section "The Whole
and the Part," driving home the point that what was true for an individual was not necessarily true for society as a whole. He was thus clear-
ing the ground for analysis that would go counter to the conclusions
students would draw from their own experiences. Individual behavior
might be unpredictable, but it might be possible to predict how large
groups would behave. After all, he explained, the planets did not understand that they were following elliptical paths. Behavior that benefited
one person (such as standing on tip-toe to see a parade) might not be of
any value if everyone did the same. This led Samuelson to explain that
when there was unemployment, "we move into a topsy-turvy wonder-
land where right seems left and left is right; up seems down, and black
white."[26] Picking up the analogy used by Keynes almost a decade earlier,
he continued in terms his students, all of whom were trained in mathematics and physics, would understand:

> Mathematicians tell us that in addition to Euclidian geometry there
> exist non-Euclidian geometries. In these non-Euclidian worlds, two
> parallel lines may meet—thus on the spherical surface of the earth two
> "parallel" lines perpendicular to the equator meet at the pole. What
> is true of one kind of world may be false of another. Similarly, for the
> modern world of unemployment, the conclusions of the old classical or
> Euclidian economics may not be at all applicable.

He pointed out that the benefits derived from moving gold from mines
into Fort Knox, of exporting more goods, and of saving more all depend on
whether there is unemployment or full employment. This was why it was
important to start with the analysis of national income and unemployment.
However, again following Keynes, he argued that if unemployment could be
banished, then traditional economics would come into its own.

Samuelson then gave his view of what economics was about. He argued
that any society had to solve three economic problems: (1) What is produced?
(2) How is it produced? (3) For whom is it produced? These questions helped

define the subject matter of economics, but they did not do so completely. What was produced would depend on individual tastes—the province of the psychologist, the anthropologist, or even the biologist. Explaining institutions was for the sociologist or anthropologist, and technology was the realm of the physicist and engineer. Economists, he argued, should take the results reached by other scientists as a starting point: "The institutional framework of society, the tastes of individuals, the ends for which the strive—all these must be taken as being given. These and more. For the character and quantity of resources and the technological facts about their combinations and productive transformations must also be taken as given."[27]

This somewhat abstract definition of the subject matter of economics was then made more concrete with a simple example, of a society facing a trade-off between guns and butter. A numerical example was presented not just using a table and a graph but also with a pictogram of stylized artillery pieces and packets of butter—a pictogram such as Bliven had wanted for his article in *The New Republic*—shown as figure 25.1.[f] Technical concepts such as the "production-possibility curve" and "substitution" could explain the different wartime experiences of the United States, Germany, and Russia. In the United States, "the arsenal of democracy," eliminating unemployment made it possible to have more guns and more butter, and living standards rose. In Germany, the slack created by unemployment all went into military production, while Russia, already on its production possibility frontier, increased its military production only at the expense of hardship for the civilian population. This could hardly have been more relevant to students coming to the subject in 1945.[g]

As his discussion of the wartime experiences makes clear, Samuelson saw the problem of unemployment as central to economics. However, a further influence was that of his Chicago teacher, Frank Knight. In the second edition of the textbook, he added a footnote to his exposition of the three questions faced by society, saying that "This viewpoint, with minor adaptations,

f. Though this choice is believed to date back to press reporting of the National Defense Act of 1916, the most notorious use of it was by Joseph Goebbels in 1936, when he argued that guns would make Germans powerful whereas butter would make them fat. The use of illustrations such as this was a novelty of his textbook.

g. This can be seen as a compromise between traditional definitions of economics that sought to identify the subject matter of economics (for example, as the study of the business system) and the analytical definition made famous by Lionel Robbins (1932), which defined economics as analyzing the implications of the fact of scarcity, an aspect of all behavior. Samuelson accepted the fact of scarcity, even writing about "the law of scarcity," but his definition defined a specific subject matter. See Backhouse and Medema 2009.

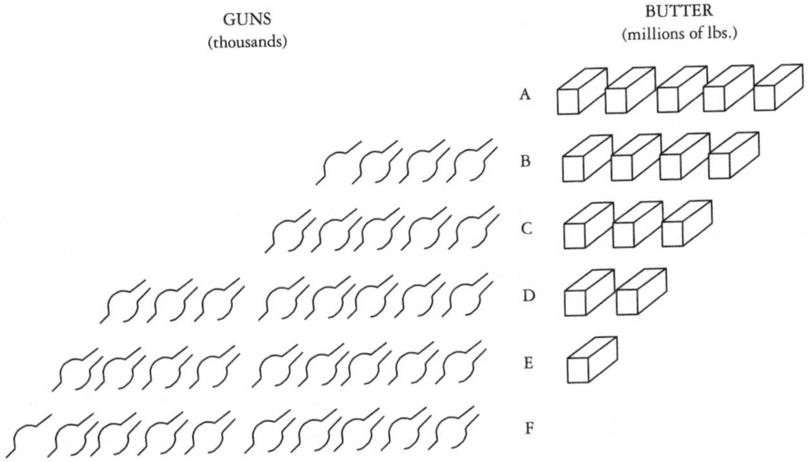

| GUNS (thousands) | | BUTTER (millions of lbs.) |

FIGURE 25.1 Guns or butter?
Source: P. A. Samuelson, 1945, Modern Economics: An Introductory Analysis of National Income and Policy, PASP 91, p. II-6.

corresponds to that worked out by Frank Knight . . . [in his] *Social Economic Organization*," which he had used as an undergraduate.[28,h] Like Knight, Samuelson objected to very broad definitions of economics that made it synonymous with rational behavior, and he wrote in terms of the different functions of an economic system. However, Samuelson conceded too much to Knight when he described the modifications to Knight's perspective as only minor. Knight's five functions were reduced to three, and they did not correspond exactly to Samuelson's. Knight wrote of "fixing standards" and "efficiency"—terms that Samuelson did not use, presumably because he wanted to keep clear of ethical issues—and Knight's functions of "economic maintenance and progress" and "adjusting consumption to production within very short periods" have no counterpart in Samuelson's list. Samuelson's functions for an economic system were both simpler—easier for beginning students to remember—and less nuanced, shorn of many of the philosophical points that Knight wove into his discussion.

However, although Samuelson acknowledged a debt to Knight, it is not difficult to see a similarity between Samuelson's three opening chapters and

---

h. It is not clear why this acknowledgment was added in the second edition. Around the time that the second edition was being prepared, Knight had had a somewhat acrimonious exchange with Samuelson, and perhaps Samuelson was trying to make amends. Possibly he had written the first edition without thinking fully about the source of his ideas (he had started by revising the department's textbook) and the parallel with Knight's text was drawn to his attention later.

the equivalent chapter in the department's textbook from which he had started. That talked not of economic organization but of the economic process, making the point that production involved more than engineering. Economic problems arose from scarcity, which implied the need for choice and economizing.

Samuelson's most obvious innovation was his writing style, beginning with his opening sentence. Whereas the text of Freeman and his colleagues had been dry and analytical, Samuelson's opening chapter abounded in paradoxes—poverty amid plenty, differences between the whole and the part—and imagery involving money and spending. In place of an abstract discussion of choice, Samuelson posed three much more concrete problems that societies had to solve. Samuelson described a concrete choice between guns and butter, using a diagram to help students visualize it, as previously mentioned. Where the earlier book had written in abstract terms about social institutions—practices, laws, methods, and customs—that molded individual behavior, Samuelson dispensed with such general discussion to cover in detail those institutions about which students needed to know: families, businesses, and government.

National Income and Its Uses

The first draft of the textbook was circulated to students in 1945 with the title *Modern Economics: An Introductory Analysis of National Income and Policy*. As Clemence and Doody had recommended, national income provided the unifying theme. Not only did the subtitle come close to equating modern economics with the study of national income, but the first section, comprising eight chapters, culminated in an explanation of national income. The idea of income was introduced in two chapters on "Individual and Family Incomes," grounding the idea of income in a context that would be familiar to students.

These chapters centered on statistics compiled by the National Resources Committee, which had been the data on which his wartime work on forecasting consumer spending for the National Resources Planning Board was based. He included tables displaying the number of families receiving different levels of income, and showed how the degree of inequality could be represented on a diagram.[i] There was an extensive discussion of income

---

i. He used a Lorenz curve, defined in chapter 20 this volume.

distribution, including differences between male and female earnings and between earnings of black and white households. He discussed poverty and the industrial revolution, and Marx's views about class struggle, noting that the Soviet Union appeared to have similar levels of inequality to the United States. His second chapter on individual incomes focused on occupational differences, both within and between occupations. These two chapters, exploring issues of social mobility and the question "Is college worthwhile?" clearly covered issues to which the students could relate. A diagram showing starting salaries for chemical engineering graduates could hardly have been more directly aimed at MIT student concerns. They will have seen very clearly that engineering graduates prospered during the war, this being due, Samuelson explained, to "our rather short-sighted national policy of drafting scientific, medical and engineering students into the armed forces."[29,j] It was a simple and very clear lesson in supply and demand before Samuelson turned to a more formal discussion later on.

He then went on to "Business Organization and Income," a chapter that was very different in tone, comprising sections taken directly from the text Freeman had written previously.[k] It was far more taxonomic in its coverage, focusing on institutional forms—individuals, partnerships, corporations—and methods whereby businesses raised funds. The last topic took him into a discussion of financial assets, the stock market, and speculation. He explained how to read balance sheets and analyze corporate income streams. In the course of this, he included a diagram, out of Freeman's book, showing how funds flowed in and out of businesses (figure 25.2). Supporting this emphasis on the interpretation of company accounts. Samuelson included the 1941 earnings report of the International Harvester Company, replete with balance sheets, different sets of income and expenditure accounts, and overseas transactions, from which were derived a series of questions for students to answer.

Corporate financial accounting led straight into the national accounts; the table of contents specified a chapter on government, but this was not present in the first draft. There was a clear link between the discussion of individual and household incomes and the breakdown of national income by type of income. The difference between real and nominal incomes led into a discussion of national product (the sum of the different types of goods and services produced) and the relationship between saving and capital accumulation. The

---

j. Even if subconsciously, perhaps this was a justification for his own activities during the war.

k. Footnotes sourced the material as "Adapted from 'The Economic Process.'"

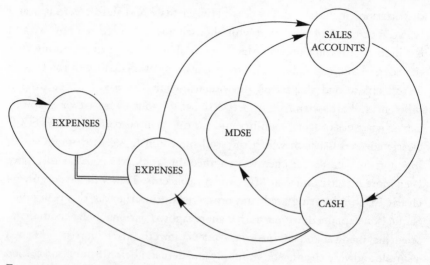

FIGURE 25.2 Financial statements.
Source: P. A. Samuelson, 1945, Modern Economics: An Introductory Analysis of National Income and Policy, PASP 91, p. V-15.

chapter on national income culminated in two graphs. The first depicted the course of national income during the Great Depression, showing the waste arising from actual national income being below its full employment level. The second showed that, despite inflation, real national income had risen enormously during wartime. The challenge Samuelson posed to his readers was understanding how the economic situation could have been so different in the early 1930s and the early 1940s.

Focusing on income was one of the ways in which Samuelson made economic ideas seem more concrete, for household income was something to which students could relate, especially when it was laced with up-to-date statistics on the distribution of income across households. The chapter that stood out as not following this pattern was the one on business income, with its more comprehensive, almost taxonomic approach. The reason for this difference is clearly that Samuelson had not had time to rewrite this the way he wanted, and although he had shortened and rearranged the material, the chapter was a series of sections from Freeman's book. The concrete but fictitious example of the "Santa Claus Manufacturing Company" used to present company accounts was taken directly from Freeman's text. However, Samuelson's addition of a genuine company report, presumably in facsimile, served to persuade students to take this fictitious example seriously. Closing part I of the text with a chapter on national income not only integrated the previous chapters but rendered the discussion of the economic system as a whole more concrete in the same way as he had done in the chapter on individuals and families. The changes Clemence and Doody had advocated were useful, not just for making the material more dynamic and for linking it to history, but also for making it less abstract.

In part II of the first draft, to which he gave no title, the tone was completely different. Using simple numerical examples, Samuelson explained supply and demand curves in a way that did not presume prior understanding of graphic representations of data. His tables and the graphs derived from them involved artificial examples illustrating assumptions that were based on pure theory—diminishing rates of substitution, linear demand curves, U-shaped average cost curves. He explained not just the economics but also how one should read a graph, the meaning of optimum conditions, and how to justify using continuous functions when some products (e.g., eggs) were indivisible.

Equilibrium under perfect competition was illustrated using a supply and demand diagram, but when Samuelson turned to monopolistic competition, he used no diagrams or numbers and instead invited his readers to place themselves in the position of a company president having to take advice from his accountants and sales managers (all of whom could be presumed to be male in 1947) before deciding what prices to set. " 'Boys,' you will say, 'what will our volume of output approximately be if we stay on our toes and keep our share of the market?' "[30] The manager's decision was then to decide what markup to apply to the costs these accountants came up with. This might not conform with the theory of profit maximization, but Samuelson believed it was realistic.

> Many investigators of actual business pricing policies have testified that corporations often do follow the above described practice of quoting prices on a "cost and mark-up" basis, hoping thereby not only to recover their full costs, but also to make a return on their investments. This theory is therefore realistic.[31]

Though realistic, this statement was not very informative because it did not explain the markup. To take the analysis further, Samuelson turned not to theory but to empirical work, arguing, "There seems to be nothing to do about this unsatisfactory situation but to try to specify a number of different competitive and monopolistic patterns characteristic of various important industrial situations." These included chronically overcrowded sick industries, few sellers of identical products (oligopoly), monopolies maintained by research and advertising, and publicly regulated monopolies. He was adopting Chamberlin's strategy of classifying market structures, but the examples he used were more reminiscent of the institutionalist studies of pricing found in the reports of the Temporary National Economic Committee.

Theory, again illustrated with numerical examples, and with graphs in an appendix, returned when Samuelson moved on to the problem of "Production Equilibrium and the Problem of Distribution." The point that he emphasized was that the marginal productivity theory explained how much of each factor a company would hire given the prices it faced: it did not explain factor prices. He was very critical of the economists who had developed what he repeatedly called the "so-called marginal productivity theory of distribution."[32] The search for a marginal productivity theory of distribution, in which each factor was paid according to the amount produced by the last unit employed, was a "will-o-the-wisp" and "ill-conceived."[33] The theory could say little about the problems that were of concern to society.

> Unfortunately, there is little that can be said about this general supply and demand problem which is very useful in understanding the distribution of income between rich and poor, between labor and property owner, between one kind of property owner and another. This is unfortunate, and admittedly a deficiency in our economic knowledge. But in any case, the problem of "distributing social product" is a false one, and the difficulties which [a]rise in its solution are irrelevant ones.[34]

There were also technical problems with marginal productivity theory, of which the main one was joint production. If capital and labor had to be used together, withdrawing one factor would mean losing the whole output. Marginal productivity theory could do no more than establish the limits within which factor prices must lie (and in extreme cases, it might say no more than that a factor get between 0 and 100 percent of total product). Given this, there was scope for bargaining to influence factor payments, which led Samuelson to ask whether trade unions could raise wages. His answer was that they could change wages, though only within certain limits. These limits might be very hard to define, but they were real. However, Samuelson was not wholly on the side of unions, for wage rises could have harmful effects, and there was the danger that worker demands would be insatiable.

In its coverage, part II was the most traditional part of the book. Here, he did not seek concreteness by discussing real-world data but, rather, through simplifying the theory, explaining concepts by reducing them to essentials that could be explained using the easiest possible mathematics. This was much more what one might expect from the author of *Foundations*. Where Freeman, like Taussig and others before him, had enunciated a set of economic principles, whether on consumer behavior, the distribution of income, or the process of saving and investment, Samuelson was much more clearly providing students with a set of analytical techniques they could use to solve economic problems. His chapters on supply and demand, consumers, and firms were exercises in economic theory, clearly separated from discussions of real-world markets.

From the theory of production, Samuelson moved to international trade, using similar diagrammatic techniques to illustrate the theory of comparative advantage. His main expository tool was a numerical example, in which the United States and Europe traded food and clothing. The lesson was on the importance of specialization and hence of international trade. One diagram showed "a very advantageous triangular trade" in which America exported autos to England, England exported clothing to the East Indies, and the East Indies exported rubber to America. The system of multilateral trade in 1938 was illustrated with a more complex diagram, showing trade flows between the United States, the tropics, regions of recent settlement, continental Europe, and non-continental Europe. The point of this diagram was to show how tragic bilateralism (trade deals negotiated between countries two at a time)—a policy he associated with continental fascist countries—would be. He reminded his readers about the United Nations' having set up the International Bank for Reconstruction and Development (now the World Bank) and the International Monetary Fund to create conditions in which multilateral trade could flourish, and that Franklin Roosevelt's policy of pressing for tariff reductions remained U.S. national policy. This discussion, which exposed his student readers to the internationalist position he had taken in *The New Republic*, provides a clear illustration of how his wartime experiences were informing his writing.

This internationalist position was supported by a chapter, devoid of technical theory (though theoretical ideas lay beneath many of his arguments), on tariff protection and free trade. His starting point was the fact that "*unhampered free trade promotes mutually profitable international division of labor, greatly enhances the potential real national product of all countries, and makes possible higher standards of living all over the globe.*"[35] This was presented as "a fact," not an abstract theoretical conclusion. He then discussed various arguments for protection, but even here he challenged common arguments. Non-economic goals, such as national defense, might be important, as in the case of fostering domestic rubber production. However, in this instance, subsidizing industry would be better than imposing a tariff. Other arguments for tariffs, such as keeping money in the country, raising money wages, or serving special interests, were completely fallacious. Even tariffs to raise revenue or to protect home markets or domestic labor were misconceived. "Infant industry" and "young economy" arguments had more validity, but they applied more to "backward nations" than to the twentieth-century United States. Samuelson's commitment to free trade was clear.

Explaining National Income

The final chapters of the 1945 draft, covering saving and investment, prices and money, and the banking system, are clearly less polished than the earlier ones.[1] The chapter on saving and investment begins by telling the reader that the most important fact about saving and investment was that, in a modern industrial society, they were undertaken by different people and were undertaken for different reasons. Investment was "extremely variable." Samuelson's explanation echoed Hansen's arguments about investment opportunities.

> This capricious, volatile behavior is understandable when we realize that investment opportunities depend on new discoveries, new products, new territories and frontiers, new resources, new population, higher production and income. Note the emphasis on new and higher. Investment depends on the dynamic and unpredictable elements of growth in the system, on elements outside the economic system itself: technology, politics, optimistic and pessimistic expectations; governmental tax, expenditure and legislative policies, etc.[36]

"As far as total investment is concerned," Samuelson wrote, "the system is in the lap of the Gods."[37] Like Keynes, he concluded that there was no assurance there would be sufficient investment, though he got there using arguments drawn from Hansen.

---

1. Though bound together with the earlier chapters, the first of these three chapters, none of which is listed in the table of contents, is unnumbered, the second is numbered 18, and the third is numbered 19. The numbering of the diagrams in the first of these chapters begins with "Figure 5." This initial draft of the textbook was clearly put together using some materials he had prepared for other courses, which have not been found. He might have been using some material produced by his colleagues, though that seems less likely, given his acknowledgment that an earlier chapter did draw on such material.

In contrast, the main determinant of saving was income, there being observable patterns in consumption. He illustrated these in a diagram that showed how spending on food, shelter, clothing, recreation, education, and saving would rise with income. Total consumption was thus explained as the sum of a number of components, each of which was related to income, which he supported by citing the statistical work done by the National Resources Committee on consumer expenditures that had been the basis for his work at the NRPB.[38] The diagram was then simplified by omitting all curves other than total spending, and its importance was stressed by also providing a graph which showed saving and investment against income and placing it on the cover of the book.[m]

In this last diagram, saving was determined by the multiplicity of factors listed earlier, and income was adjusted so that saving equaled investment. A change in investment would change income, which led Samuelson to explain the multiplier, the paradox of thrift (whereby a rise in savings reduced income), and the concepts of deflationary and inflationary gaps. After discussing the role of private investment and foreign trade, Samuelson ended the chapter with a section in which he explained how government monetary and fiscal policy should be used to stabilize income. As the main objection raised against this was the effect on public debt, he pointed out that even the conservative President Hoover had sought to schedule public works so as to smooth out the cycle. Samuelson acknowledged that public debt was an important problem, but he contended that it was not the most serious problem the country faced.

This chapter on saving and investment was arguably the most innovative in the book.[n] Freeman and his co-authors also had a chapter with the title "Saving and Investment," but its content bore no relation to that of Samuelson's. Freeman's text had been rich in definitions, but though it made a clear distinction between saving and investment, and although it offered a long discussion of what caused saving and explained alternative ways in which savings could be invested, there was no analysis of how they were related. Saving and investment were as much classificatory devices as analytical concepts. What the student encountered was a series of principles. Some were beliefs about businessmen's attitudes, such as "Safety of the principal is of primary importance: investors look chiefly

---

m. As in figure 18.1 given earlier, this volume.

n. Tarshis, one of the participants in the Harvard seminar discussed in chapter 12 this volume, introduced Keynesian ideas into a textbook published the following year, but at this point Samuelson knew nothing about it. See chapter 26 this volume.

at the certainty of the future income."[39] Others appeared to be empirical generalizations, such as "The amount of intentional saving is controlled by the size of the national income and its distribution,"[40] or simply classificatory schemes (that saving might result in the creation of unproductive goods, durable consumers goods, business assets, or idle funds).[41] Others were theoretical propositions, though not presented as such, as with the proposition that "Credit expansion by commercial banks may compel real saving."[42] Unlike Samuelson, his predecessors had not made clear distinctions between economic theory and propositions about how real-world markets operated.

In contrast, using the diagram with which the book was to become associated, Samuelson showed why the market would not necessarily generate the right level of investment to ensure full employment, the argument to which his conservative critics took exception. Other conservative doctrines that Samuelson sought to undermine were the view that inflation was necessarily harmful, and the "mystical belief" that the money was valuable because it was backed by gold. He explained how inflation redistributed wealth from creditors to debtors, and hence between economic classes. Mild inflation kept "the wheels of industry ... well lubricated," making it possible for everyone to benefit: creditors were compensated by receiving higher interest rates than if prices were constant. However, rapid rises in inflation would dislocate production, though he explained that there were few cases of hyperinflation except during wartime or in the aftermath of war.

As for money, though dollar bills might say "silver certificates" or "redeemable in lawful money," this meant nothing other than that you could change a $10 bill for a "crisp new bill" or for a mixture of $5 and $1 bills.° Money had a high value because it was kept scarce. If a government issued more than was demanded, then its value would fall—there would be hyperinflation—but as long as it did not, it would retain its value. Samuelson argued that, like individual prices, the overall price level was determined by supply and demand—by the level of national income in relation to full employment. Money was relevant because it was one of the factors affecting spending and saving. Writing in 1945, Samuelson was well aware of the importance of household assets for consumption, for during the war American families and businesses had accumulated cash and liquid assets to the tune of $200 billion, which might lead to higher spending after the war. Even though it involved a detour into the past, the text would hardly have been complete

---

o. This was incorrect, in that silver certificates could be redeemed for silver dollars or quarters.

without an account of the quantity theory of money—the theory that the price level was proportional to the money supply, which was the doctrine that Milton Friedman was to resuscitate in the 1950s. The problem with this theory, Samuelson claimed, was that prices were not proportional to total spending, and total spending was not proportional to the money supply. The famous "equation of exchange" (money supply times the velocity of circulation equals the price level times the quantity of output) was a truism—it was true simply because the velocity of circulation was defined as the ratio of money income (PQ) to the money supply.

Criticism and Feedback

MIT was not the only university having problems with its teaching materials. In one letter, Samuelson went so far as to joke that "it is the great academic indoor sport to deplore the current status of elementary textbooks and teaching."[43] In February 1946, Alan Sweezy, a friend from Samuelson's Harvard days, wrote to say that he had heard that Samuelson was working on a textbook.[44] "As usual," Sweezy wrote, "we are worrying about the elementary course" and they wanted to find a better textbook. He asked when Samuelson's book might be available and whether the publishers would object to him and his colleagues at Williams College trying out some of his material on their students. Samuelson replied that although he thought the book had been a success, engaging students, and that he would be pleased to show Sweezy chapters for comment, he thought it would be premature to use them for teaching outside MIT because there remained gaps and "rough places in need of revisions."[45] He promised to send copies on March 1, by which time he would have more copies for the new term.

Samuelson had already sent copies to Wolfgang Stolper and Erich Roll. Stolper told several publishers' representatives about it, in the hope that Samuelson would land a "good fat contract,"[46] and when, a month later, the McGraw-Hill representative told him that Samuelson had already signed, he replied that he could count on orders of 500 copies a year from Swarthmore. Roll praised the manuscript to Emile Despres, who asked Samuelson for a copy. Returning from government service to a position at Williams, he wrote Samuelson that he was baffled as he contemplated "the problem of teaching in general, and teaching the introductory course in particular."[47] He got the same response as Sweezy and Stolper: he was welcome to comment on material, but it was too incomplete to be used outside MIT.[48]

By this point, Samuelson had a clear idea of what he was doing; as he explained to Despres, his target was students who were not concentrating in economics, and it followed "automatically" that the course should confront questions that they thought were important.[p] To David McCord Wright, he wrote that "the needs of the student are those of an intelligent citizen."[49] This might have accounted for why the course had been well received, though as he had conceded to Sweezy, the returning veterans who filled the classrooms were more interested in broad questions of economic policy than pre-war students ever were.[50] The result was that he "ruthlessly soft-pedaled" value and distribution theory, aside from a bit of supply and demand, cost and profit analysis, and a fairly rigorous analysis of comparative cost. Instead, he focused on national income problems of policy, along with what he called "preliminary exposition of the elementary facts of life about corporations, trade unions, stock market, etc."[51,q]

A point he repeated to several of his friends was that he had enjoyed the work— something about which he expressed embarrassment. To Sweezy, he wrote, "I started the job with a certain amount of shame, but I must confess that I have been enjoying the task."[52] Given the consistency with which he made such remarks around this time (March–April 1946), and that that these remarks were expressed to close friends with whom he had no need to cultivate an image, there seems no reason why they should not be taken at face value.[53] One element in his feeling of shame could be that he was having to simplify and compromise in the interests of making the book accessible. However, against this we have to set his view that he was tackling real, if difficult, problems that his readers needed to understand. Another possible source of his embarrassment was that *Foundations,* then making its way through Harvard University Press's production process, developed in detail precisely the theory that he was "soft-pedaling" for his introductory students.

The friends to whom he had sent the manuscript offered feedback. Stolper criticized the manuscript for being too long and detailed, with too many examples, for it left the instructor with nothing to add to the book.[54]

---

p. The correspondence with Despres is discussed earlier in this chapter.

q. He had also worked out, very clearly, what he thought was wrong with other textbooks. Hicks had written a book that was "too brief, rather arid, and too little concerned with the economic 'physiology'—rather than 'anatomy' for the non-economic concentrator." Boulding's book was too analytical. Bowman and Bach was good, but "voluminous, theoretical and rather difficult for elementary courses." He confessed to a "secret liking" for a book by Bruce Knight, often dismissed as "a work for freshmen and girls at junior colleges," but he was not enthusiastic about that, either.

This contrasted with the experience of Samuelson's colleagues at MIT, who liked it because the material had provoked the students so much they never had time to discuss "incidental matters suggested by the readings." Alan Sweezy strongly criticized the chapter on money and prices.[55] He argued that Samuelson had got things the wrong way around, in that he discussed the relationship of the money supply to the price level before explaining what money was. The process of money creation needed to come first. He also argued, in a Keynesian vein, that Samuelson should introduce spending as the factor influencing prices right from the start. He was far more critical of the quantity theory than was Samuelson.

> It's [referring to the velocity of circulation] a pretty useless concept: worse than useless, in fact, since it implies a mysterious process of causation which simply doesn't exist. Just because we were brought up on it and had to fight our way through to clarity later on is no reason to make the present day student repeat that painful experience. Spending is what actually makes money "circulate" and I think it's very important to emphasize that simple truth from the beginning and keep it constantly before the student's eyes.[56]

It would seem that Samuelson took seriously Sweezy's criticism that it was wrong to adopt a historical approach to teaching theory, for a few days later he responded to being sent a copy of the new edition of Stigler's *The Theory of Price* (1946) by saying that it was "the *only* book" he could recommend on intermediate or advanced price theory courses because "Up to now we have all been perpetrating the pedagogical crime of making the student repeat the historical meanderings of the developing body of economic thought."[57]

Samuelson's friends pushed him in different directions. Where Stolper had found the book too comprehensive, Sweezy found it too brief. After saying he liked the book on account of its having more "punch and flavor than any elementary textbook he knew" and that touches such as "Fat men fish, lean men hunt, and smart men make medicine" were superb, he said that much of it was too concise. Points were made once, very clearly, but for elementary students it was necessary to elaborate on apparently simple points: "You have to play with them [seemingly obvious points], turn them over and over, introduce illustrations, repeat what you've said with slight variations over and over again." Samuelson was getting a lesson from someone whose Harvard career had given him much experience in teaching elementary economics. He also urged Samuelson to cut things out so as to spend more time on the big, important ideas.

At this point, at the end of February 1946, Samuelson was hoping to finish his revisions by June, so that the textbook would be available for the fall.[58] In early April, he had doubts about this schedule, questioning whether he would finish before the end of the summer, saying that the book was consuming most of his leisure time.[59] By the end of April he had changed his mind again, saying that the "final version" was almost finished.[60] In May, when Fritz Machlup wrote saying he had heard about the book, and perhaps Samuelson would like to consider Blakiston as a publisher, he replied that it was almost finished and that McGraw-Hill would be bringing it out in the fall or the winter.[61] Shortly afterward he signed a contract for another book, *A Primer of Economics*, aimed at intermediate students.[62] However, this proved much too optimistic and the process of revising the text dragged on for much longer.

In the midst of this process of redrafting, Samuelson produced a "Second Preliminary Edition," this time titled *Economics: An Introductory Analysis*, to be used by students beginning their studies in October 1946.[63] This edition was an expanded version of the first draft. With the exception of a single chapter, discussed below, his changes were confined to the reordering of chapters and writing new ones. The most substantial of the changes, shown in figure 25.3, was to bring the three chapters on saving and investment, money and prices, and the banking system forward, to become part II of the revised draft, following on directly from the chapter on national income, which came at the end of part I. Most significantly, he proposed to begin part II with a chapter on "The Business Cycle," which shows that he was still thinking in a traditional way, according to which the theory of saving, investment, and income determination is seen as part of the theory of the business cycle.[r]

The result of the rearrangement was that the traditional material, beginning with supply and demand, became part III, coming after the analysis of the business cycle, now titled "The Economics of Full Employment." Given that part II began with a discussion of the cycle, he appears not to have accepted the message of Keynes's *General Theory* that the business cycle could be an addendum to a theory of employment rather than its setting, but he

---

r. Two points about the 1945 draft are not clear. The first is the reason why the chapters on saving and investment, money, and banking were placed at the end. Was this because Samuelson had not yet worked out where he wanted to fit them in, or was it because they were simply not ready in time to be included earlier in the text? The second is whether some chapters were omitted because they were still unwritten or because they were not needed for the students who were being taught that year.

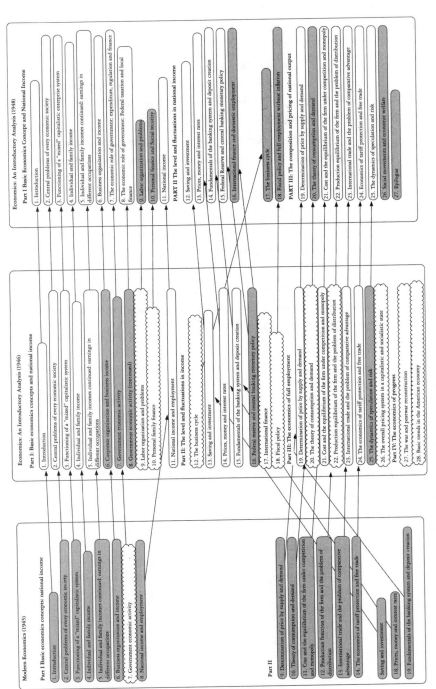

FIGURE 25.3 Successive drafts of the textbook, 1945–48.

Note: "Clouds" indicate chapters listed but not present in the draft. Chapters that are newly written, or substantially revised, are shaded. Several instances where material has been moved from one chapter to another are not shown.

had accepted the claim made by Keynes in the final chapter of the *General Theory* that traditional theory applied at full employment.

Though still marked as being "For private circulation only," an arrangement was reached with Addison-Wesley to print hardbound copies that were placed on sale at the MIT bookstore for $3. When people asked about obtaining copies, Samuelson directed them to the bookstore, sometimes going to the trouble of checking inventory levels himself.[64] However, despite being made available in this way, the book was still not finished and revisions continued. In August, he wrote one friend that the chapter on central banking was only just completed, and solicited comments.[65] In September, he wrote to an MIT colleague that he hoped to finish revisions in the fall.[66] In October, he told a former student, Dan Vandermeulen, that he had just revised the national income chapter, and that he was about to revise the one on saving and investment. The process of revising the book dragged on into 1947.[67]

However, by then a controversy had erupted over the book that was to involve not only Samuelson and Freeman but also the president of MIT, Karl Compton. This controversy related to the second preliminary edition; this was the one his critics were reading and that he was sending out to colleagues in other universities as late as January 1948.[68]

CHAPTER 26

Controversy over the Textbook,
1947–1948

Controversy Within MIT

On March 3, 1947, a Visiting Committee appointed by the MIT Corporation held a meeting at which they discussed activities in Samuelson's department.[1] It was chaired by Walter J. Beadle, an MIT graduate who had moved on to DuPont, a company that was also represented on the MIT Corporation by two family members. The significance of the DuPont connection was that it was three DuPont brothers, Pierre, Irénée, and Lammot, who in 1934 had decided that Franklin Roosevelt was going to do much more than repeal Prohibition (one brother had supported Roosevelt because of this) and that he was going to implement policies they considered hostile to business. They became the center of what one historian has described as "the businessmen's crusade against the New Deal."[2] Beadle was, therefore, not the only person in DuPont who was interested in Samuelson. Later in March, Edmond Lincoln wrote to Harvard's Harold Burbank from DuPont's Delaware offices, asking for an opinion on Samuelson, reassuring him that he should feel perfectly free to speak his mind on the matter.[3] In reply, Burbank began by praising Samuelson highly.

> In all respects, Samuelson's career since he came here has been one of the most outstanding we have ever had. I think it is safe to say that he is already about as well known as most of the older economists in this country. He is regarded by many as the most promising young

economist in this country. Among those on our own staff who would support him unqualifiedly and in preference to any other men are Harris, Hansen, Schumpeter and perhaps Leontief and Mason.[4]

However, Burbank went on to raise doubts by saying that opinion was divided over "a young man who has risen so rapidly and gone so far especially in contentious subjects."

Some considered Samuelson the most outstanding economist of his generation, others believed that he had not learned how to use his undoubted ability effectively, while a third group considered him extraordinarily proficient in the narrow field of mathematical economics but lacking the knowledge and capacity to work effectively outside that field. Burbank mentioned no names for the last two groups, though the last category describes accurately the attitude Wilson had picked up from his colleagues in 1940, before Samuelson's final examination.

Describing himself to Ralph Freeman as "a businessman who had spent thirty years in the field of applied economics," Beadle had a particular interest in economics teaching.[5] The previous year he had written to express the hope that MIT would avoid the problem of providing an "unbalanced" coverage of economics to students who took the subject for just one or two years.[6] When he expressed a particular interest in the introductory course, Ralph Freeman explained that the course was centered on the problem of maintaining full employment, a radical departure from the traditional syllabus, though one that was thought more meaningful and interesting for the students.[7] The fact that Freeman had already explained that the department did not try to indoctrinate students, but to place them in a position where they could "adopt that philosophy and theory which they believe to be best," suggests that even before the meeting questions had been raised about what the department was teaching.[8] After the meeting, the committee attended the MIT Corporation luncheon, at which Samuelson's text was discussed, and several members of the corporation expressed an interest in reviewing it.

Samuelson spoke with Beadle on MIT's graduation day, June 13 1947, and, presumably having been told of the corporation's interest in his textbook, appears to have said that he was happy for him to give the text a critical review. Before reading the book himself, Beadle wrote to Ralph Freeman, recommending that he invite economists such as Wilford King (New York University) and Fred Fairchild (Yale) to review it.[a] At the end of the month,

---

a. Fairchild was on record as opposing Hansen's internationalist policies. See chapter 19 this volume.

he read the text carefully and in July, he wrote to Freeman about it. He explained that the text was very important because of its connections with MIT. Not only was the book used for teaching elementary economics at MIT but also any text by an MIT professor would be read "widely and critically."[9] Because of MIT's reputation, and because of the new four-year course in economics and social science, it was important to make sure that any text was "thoroughly objective and mature."

Beadle was positive about some aspects of the book, writing "I want to compliment Professor Samuelson on having presented a wealth of interesting material in a lucid style which, I would expect, intrigues the interest of the students far more than the prosaic Taussig text used when I was an undergraduate."[10] However, he expressed the opinion that at times the attempt to enliven the presentation had resulted in flippancy, as when Samuelson wrote of railroad presidents having "a rather humdrum job." Though Samuelson was trying to be objective, Beadle thought that he sometimes slipped up, as when he said that the federal government had an unlimited source of funds, and when he wrote that mistakes made by private investors could be avoided by "advanced centralized planning." Beadle claimed the latter remark implied that federal employees were more infallible than ones on private payrolls. He was also disturbed by statements such as that the text could not treat "the problem of radically changing the economic system" as thoroughly as it deserved to be treated.

Saying that he was pleased that Samuelson had asked Freeman to edit his text, Beadle suggested that he had "a major editorial job" on his hands. If Samuelson were to approach his task "as objectively as a professor in an engineering school should approach a problem of this kind," he was optimistic that the book would bring credit to both MIT and the author. Beadle clearly thought that anyone in an engineering school had a particular responsibility to be objective.[b]

Another member of the Visiting Committee asked Nicholas Peterson, an economist at the First National Bank of Boston, to review the text. Though noting that several important chapters were still missing, Petersen claimed that the author presented it as "established fact" that some sort of "managed capitalism" was necessary, and he failed to present alternative points of view. He argued that a student would be able to understand the subject only if given more historical background, on how the economy had evolved through history and "the fundamental principles of the American Enterprise

---

b. Was this a perhaps implicit criticism of Harvard, with its greater emphasis on the humanities?

System," as well as information on "advantages and disadvantages apparent in the American economy."[11] Samuelson wrote in a "flip and cocky" style, and he gave the impression of "being somewhat immature in his thought as well as lacking in scholarly background on economic and political history." Peterson attached a list of passages where the author's views came through even though he claimed to be offering factual analysis.[c]

Beadle sent a copy of his letter to Freeman to MIT President Karl Compton and to three other members of the MIT Corporation. He drew upon what Burbank had written to Nelson, his colleague at DuPont, to provide an assessment of Samuelson:

> I have never met Professor Samuelson but it is my understanding that he has a brilliant record and is proficient to an extraordinary degree in the area of mathematical economics. While he is regarded by many as the most promising young economist in this country, others feel that he has not yet learned to apply effectively his undoubted ability, and some even believe that he lacks the knowledge and capacity to make himself effective outside the narrow area of mathematical economics. The fact that he is only thirty-two years old and took his Ph.D. only six years ago suggests to me that under adequate administrative supervision the Institute may be able to bring him to maturity to the mutual advantage of the Institute and himself.[12]

One member of the Corporation and MIT alumnus, Ellis Brewster of the Plymouth Cordage Company, shared Beadle's view that Samuelson was not always objective and that he had a tendency to expect too much from government.[13] Samuelson had taken a rather short-term view and paid too much attention to recent economic events, a fact that was easily explained by his being only thirty-two years old.

However, another recipient, Frank Chesterman, of the Bell Telephone Company and another alumnus member of the corporation, took a much harder line, implying that Samuelson was close to being a communist and possibly even a member of the Communist Party or some similar organization. He was, he wrote, "astonished to find that a teacher at MIT shall enunciate some of the absurd thinking which is quoted in Walter's letter to you."[14] He continued,

> It is perfectly obvious that the young man is socially-minded if not strictly communistic. It would be a terrible reflection on MIT if the

---

c. This list appears not to have been preserved in the archives.

book in its present condition were published. . . . I question whether Samuelson is a member of some of the subversive societies we hear so much about because his line of reasoning and method of expressing his thought are those of that group.

Chesterman was less optimistic than Beadle and Brewster that Samuelson's "false ideas" could be corrected, and he suggested that action should be taken so as "not to involve the Institute in the consequences of Samuelson's publication." His tone was completely different from Beadle's—it was threatening. Chesterman, who had not been a member of the Visiting Committee, and so was perhaps less familiar with the department, expressed his extreme unhappiness at the thought that "Professor Freeman and Samuelson are apparently allowing the teaching of our young men to proceed in accordance with the data included in Samuelson's book."

Samuelson treated Beadle's letter as providing constructive suggestions, and he replied, on July 31, in a conciliatory tone, thanking him for his very helpful comments.[15] He explained that the manuscript had now gone to the publisher, but that it had been changed significantly and was "quite different" from the version Beadle had seen. He had taken care to indicate where opinions differed and where his material was controversial. The book was not intended primarily for use at MIT, and elsewhere it would not get an "inside track" and thus would face competition. To reassure Beadle, he explained that he had sought advice from precisely the places to which Beadle would have wished him to turn: "A number of Federal Reserve economists have read the banking sections; a number of Carnegie Tech, Williams and Yale faculty members . . . have been kind enough to go over the manuscript, and I have also had some of the business economists at Standard Oil of New Jersey read the text."[16] He might not have consulted Fairchild, but he had consulted his successor in teaching public finance at Yale. Of course, he did not point out that these economists were mostly his friends from Harvard and a few of his former students.

Samuelson also noted that he had modified the wording in almost all of the ten passages identified by Beadle as being suspect. Beadle replied on August 6 that he was sorry to hear that the manuscript had gone to press, because he doubted the rewriting had gone far enough to bring credit to Samuelson and MIT. The instances he quoted were no more than illustrative of problems that pervaded the text, and simply correcting these would make little difference. The fact that Samuelson had made such remarks at all suggested that the "general immature tone" was probably still there.[17] He concluded by saying that if Samuelson's aim was to foster independent thinking, should the student not have a better grounding in the economic lessons of history? As might be expected from someone who learned economics at MIT many years previously, he advocated a more historical approach to economics. However, while he replied personally to Beadle, Samuelson appears, quite understandably, to have left it to his superiors to reply to Chesterman.[18]

In replying to Beadle, on August 6, Vice President James Killian defended the entire department, arguing that all its members supported free enterprise.

> There is no question but that every member of our Economics Department is a wholehearted advocate of the free enterprize system. No one of them is a Socialist or Communist. I believe, however, that many of them may sincerely believe that policy founded on no economic controls or balancing by (or sponsoring by) the Government is one of the surest ways to wreck the free enterprize system.[19]

Recognizing that Beadle might question this last point, Killian explained that the same views had been held by most members of the Business Advisory Council, a large group that included conservatives as well as liberals, and that was "certainly not predominantly New Deal." He also defended Ralph Freeman as someone who had been nominated for the position of department chair by Davis Dewey (who had held the position when Beadle had been a student), on account of his having the properties of "ability, sound and objective judgment, conservative but with a liberally open mind and a background including both industrial and academic."[20]

Given that Beadle's letter had taken the line that Samuelson's book would bring discredit on MIT, Killian chose to focus not on his ideas but on his loyalty to MIT:

> there is no question but that he is our most brilliant scholar in the field. He is also a young man of extraordinary fine personal qualities. At considerable professional sacrifice during the war he took some classes in the Department of Mathematics to help in an emergency. He similarly did a most helpful job in analyzing the performance and requirements for certain radar equipment. He is modest and cooperative to a high degree, and his loyalty to MIT is the only reason we have held him on our staff.[21]

Killian, who will have discussed the matter with Compton, supported Samuelson unreservedly.

Killian also challenged Beadle's view of Samuelson's text, implying that Beadle found it objectionable only because he was predisposed to do so. The statements Beadle had quoted were, in his view, "sound statements of policy" provided they were "carried out in a spirit of supporting the free enterprise system and not as a means for wrecking or weakening it." Whether one was disturbed by Samuelson's remarks depended on whether or not the reader "happened to be particularly 'sensitized' to and suspicious of a subversive motive in respect to the free enterprise system."

Moreover, even though Beadle's criticisms were unjustified, Samuelson had been willing to amend the text, and he had discussed it with many economists, incorporating their criticisms. This did not indicate dogmatism. Killian then returned to defending the department, explaining that students needed exposure to different schools of thought. The only requirements in a teacher were competence and loyalty to "our American ideals." He reiterated that there was no subversive intent, and that there was full support for the free enterprise system; he closed by thanking Beadle for his constructive advice.

Despite Killian's attempt to set the record straight, the dispute escalated. Killian's letter to Beadle crossed in the mail with one from Beadle to Compton. He had learned from Samuelson that the text had already gone to press, and because he doubted that his revisions would be satisfactory, Beadle decided that stronger measures were needed. "Would it not be possible," he asked, "for you personally to get hold of the rewritten text and give it a thorough reading before it is published?"[22] It was necessary to establish whether, as he had presumed in his earlier letter, the problems with the text stemmed from Samuelson's "lack of maturity" or whether from "an ingrained socialistic philosophy." If it was the latter, then it would seem that "more drastic correctives would be required with respect to the teaching of economics at the Institute." Beadle had shifted his ground, and while not accusing Samuelson of being a communist, he had come much closer to Chesterman's position. He also broadened his attack from criticism of Samuelson to criticism of the whole department.

> In any case, I believe that the Department administration is subject to severe censure for having permitted the text, in the form in which the Committee reviewed it, to be passed out to the students of Ec. 11 and used as a basis for classroom instruction. It raises a question in my mind as to the competence of that administration.

In view of this he suggested a further meeting with Compton, but without any representatives of the department being present.

Samuelson also wrote to Compton, on August 7, sending a copy of a letter he had sent to Beadle.[23] His main defense was that his book represented the methods of analysis used by "90% of the active academic economists under the age of 50 over the last decade."[24] The older generation of economists might disagree, but the field had changed, and Samuelson was doing no more than reflecting a consensus among the younger generation. Contrary to what Beadle was now suggesting, he and Beadle did not disagree at all on "general questions of socialism, communism and capitalism," but only on specific policies. He gave Compton a clear and explicit statement of his beliefs in regard to both politics and academic freedom.

> It may be added that the book is in no sense a "left-wing" work; and I have never, myself, been associated with left-wing organizations of any kind, or with organizations working with such groups, or—for that matter—with any labor organizations whatsoever. This does not mean that I do not recognize the rights of other teachers to entertain their own convictions; and speaking for myself, I would not hesitate to recommend for appointment in our department any person loyal to the American government who was by temperament and training a desirable teacher and researcher—even if he held views on, say, socialism or pacifism which I do not share.[25]

Here, he was defending himself not just against Beadle but also against Chesterman's accusation that he must be at least a communist sympathizer, if not a member of an affiliated organization. He had no problem denying any such involvement, for he had no history of political activity beyond writing articles in *The New Republic* and national newspapers in support of Hansen's policies. However, his friends included many socialists—Russ Nixon was then developing a career in the United Electrical, Radio and Machine Workers Union (which had many communist members), albeit one interrupted by a distinguished military career; Paul Sweezy and Shigeto Tsuru were avowed Marxists; and Lawrence Klein was then involved with the Communist Party—and he was defending their right to their own convictions.[d]

The charges being made were escalating rapidly, and Compton probably did not need any prompting from Samuelson to see that he had to take a much stronger line if it were not to get out of control. As Samuelson's critics were members of the MIT Corporation, claiming to defend MIT, he chose to explain the role of the MIT Corporation in relation to academic freedom.

---

d. Perhaps his reference to pacifism reflected his sensitivity to questions about his contribution to the war effort.

The entire university tradition from the beginning, and the conditions under which creative scholarship and effective education have flourished, rest basically upon what is sometimes called, and sometimes abused, "academic freedom." An educational institution is not a "line organization" in which directives flow from the controlling body and the administration down to those who are directly performing the functions of the institution. Universities are more like cooperative aggregations of scholars and teachers. To support this valuable work boards of trustees voluntarily have associated themselves to provide business leadership and facilities. Their influence on the views of the faculty or what is taught by the faculty or how it is taught can be by advice, suggestion and criticism, but not by directive or control. The only legitimate control of such matters by a board of trustees is through the appointments of the administrative and teaching staff.[26]

The clear implication of this position was that it would be wrong for either Beadle's committee or the MIT president to go "beyond suggestion, advice and criticism." Compton wrote that, while he had presumed that Beadle did not intend to go beyond this, the tone of his recent letter obliged him to clarify his position. While action could be taken in cases of "moral turpitude, disloyal or subversive activity, or demonstrated incompetence," Compton made it clear that he would not issue any orders or directives infringing on academic freedom, "nor will any such be issued by the Corporation so long as I am President." Beadle's criticisms of Samuelson had reached the point where Compton was not prepared to compromise. He asked to know the names of everyone to whom Beadle's letter had been sent so that he could make sure that they also received his reply.

Faced with this ruling by Compton, Beadle hastily retreated, saying that his remarks were intended to be constructively helpful and not intended as dictation or control.[27] Samuelson's letter of July 31, he wrote, reflected the "fine personal qualities" to which Compton had referred, and he opined that Samuelson has simply not understood the scope of the comments he and his colleagues on the corporation had made. Compton responded positively to Beadle's suggestion about a meeting to discuss the matter further, but as he was not available at the end of August, he suggested that Killian represent the administration. Brewster and Charles Spencer (unlike the other critics, a permanent member of the MIT Corporation) agreed that there were still procedural matters that should be resolved, and supported the idea of a meeting.[28] Now that it was too late to influence the content of Samuelson's book, they took the line that academic freedom required that students be exposed to all points of view, and they wanted to ensure that procedures were in place to make sure this happened.

During August, Beadle tried to gather support for his criticisms of Samuelson's book. Beardsley Ruml, an economist with experience at the Rockefeller Foundation and the Social Science Research Council, expressed the view that as a matter of principle, members of the Visiting Committee should not comment on the text used in a particular course in the department. The furthest he would go was to express the view that some parts of Samuelson's book were not as good as others, and that he would be happy to discuss this with him.[29] Samuel Stratton of Middlebury College initially formed a negative view of Samuelson's book: it gave the reader the impression that there was a lot wrong with the free enterprise system, not because of what Samuelson actually said but because of the way he expressed himself.[30] However, when he had time to read the book properly, he changed his mind. He conceded that Samuelson had oversimplified the problem of achieving full employment, and some of his conclusions were too dogmatic, but he found the book was very stimulating and he would enjoy teaching from it, because it would provoke lively classroom discussions. He concluded that Samuelson was obviously familiar with orthodox theory, and parts of the book (on price determination and central bank policy) were very well done.[31]

Killian met with Beadle, Spencer, and Brewster on August 27, all sides hoping to draw a line under the affair. Summarizing the meeting to Compton, Killian said that he had explained that the remit of the Visiting Committee was confined to offering advice on the teaching of economics in the department, and that Samuelson was free to publish any book he liked. However, while Spencer and Brewster agreed with this, Beadle did not. Killian summed up the meeting:

> Beadle repeatedly returned however to an attack on Samuelson, and was most vehement and bitter in his criticism of the book. There is an evangelical fervor about his judgments that make it futile, it seems to me, to discuss dispassionately the points of view held by Samuelson.
>
> I came away from the meeting greatly discouraged with Beadle's point of view, and troubled by what could only be construed as threats. He said for example that he could not conscientiously give his approval to the Institute's fund-raising program if it continued to teach economics as it now does, and he reported that he had finally decided to take the whole matter up with Lammot duPont and that Lammot had said that he dreaded to think of what Samuelson was pouring into the

minds of Institute students. There were other remarks by him which were belligerent and authoritarian.[32]

Killian concluded that the matter should be taken up by MIT's Executive Committee, as it was clear that Beadle intended to pursue the matter and that he could do much harm.

The day after the meeting, Killian framed a statement of policy on teaching economics that amounted to a very broad declaration of principles.[33] As he explained when he sent it to Beadle, it supplemented the descriptions of different courses contained in the course catalogue.[34] He also tried to defuse the situation by saying that he could make available to the committee the results of questionnaires issued to students taking Ec. 11. However, he pointed out that MIT administrators and faculty had no right to question students on their beliefs or opinions.[35] Beadle, however, implicitly questioned this on the grounds that, if students were not questioned about their beliefs, it might be impossible to demonstrate that instruction was not as biased as he thought it was.[36] In addition, given that he was arguing that Samuelson's treatment of the subject failed to meet the criteria of presenting "a scholarly treatment of the subject" and "all relevant facts and points of view" listed in Killian's statement, he asked for information about how Freeman intended to apply the statement of policy in future.

It was the dean, Robert Caldwell, who saw a way to placate Beadle. Students were assigned not just a textbook but also a set of recommended readings, and these could be used to ensure that different points of view were represented in the teaching. This possibility enabled him to claim that Beadle's letter of September 10 contained a suggestion "of real educational value."[37] Whether or not he was reading more into Beadle's letter than was there, this was a possible way forward.

MIT and Keynesianism in America, Fall 1947

One of the defenses made of Samuelson's book was that he was teaching up-to-date material that was widely taught in American universities. Within MIT, this was a strategy that made good sense. However, at the same time as Samuelson was defending his book within MIT, Keynesian teaching was under attack elsewhere. In August 1947, an organization called the National Economic Council published a review of another textbook, *Elements of Economics,* by Lorie Tarshis, a professor at Stanford.[38] This review, by Rose Wilder Lane, sought explicitly to undermine the trust Americans placed in the textbooks used to teach their children.[39] She urged her readers to look at textbooks, so as to see the lies and propaganda they contained. She had chosen the book by Tarshis not because it was unusual but precisely because, she claimed, it was typical of what was then taught in universities:

> It teaches in every day words the Keynesian theory that has dominated economic teaching for years, and is now orthodox in universities and powerful in Washington.
>
> This textbook contains many lies; I mean contradictions of fact, which a competent economist knows are lies, such as (p. 53) "a hundred years ago ... great depressions, like those of recent years, were simply not known." ... It contains also many lies of omission and distortion, such as emphasizing business profits without mentioning a loss, though every economist knows that 50% of American corporations normally show losses and nearly a third of them are in the red at the top of the biggest booms. But I have not the space to discuss the text's lies and you may read them for yourself. The importance of *The Elements of Economics* is its effective propaganda for the Keynesian theory.
>
> Not to go into the theory's ancient, pre-Christian theological origins, in modern economics it represents Karl Marx's theory of "the inherent contradictions of capitalism."[40]

Though Lane acknowledged that Keynesians were "emphatically not communists," but lay in the center seeking to save capitalism, they shared "the Marxian-Keynesian explanation of depressions" and denied "the *fact* that government's economic action caused every depression in this country's history." The real problem with Tarshis's book was the "emotional effects" it produced through its slant, and innumerable repetitions.[41] "I cannot," Lane wrote, "do justice to this textbook's charm for the immature. I cannot convey the impact of its grave passages upon their deepest and best emotions." The book was not even an economics text.

> *The Elements of Economics* plays upon fear, shame, pity, greed, idealism, hope, to urge young Americans to act upon this theory, as *citizens*. This is not an economics text at all; it is a pagan-religious and political tract. It inspires an irrational faith and spurs it to political action. From cover to cover there is not a suggestion of any action that is not political—and Federal.[42]

It has been argued that Lane was motivated as much by Tarshis's conception of democratic politics and the role of the economist within society as with the details of his economic arguments, for she was also very critical of an anti-Keynesian, Ludwig von Mises.[43] The review named fifteen colleges that used the book, and the publisher sent letters to the universities' trustees.[44,e]

Among those sent a copy of the review were members of the MIT Corporation. On receipt of it, Lammot DuPont wrote to Beadle, saying that he assumed that it constituted "an aggravated example of what the M.I.T. Professor has done in a milder way."[45] He was relieved to see that MIT was not listed as one of the colleges that had adopted the book. He then bemoaned the hold that "leftists" had in some universities, citing "a professor at a well-known university in the east," who had been advised to look for an appointment elsewhere. His friend's problem was that the department comprised eleven professors, of whom seven were leftist and only four were "sound"; the democratic process meant that retiring sound people would be replaced with leftists. Beadle was sent a copy of the review by a colleague in the corporation and sent it, along with DuPont's letter, to Compton, explaining that it pointed out the problems with economics teaching in the United States.[46]

Compton had seen the review while on a summer camp with his family, and thought it "an exceedingly effective statement"—a comment that might have worried Samuelson had he heard it. He also made a connection with a comment made in *Fortune* about Klein's *The Keynesian Revolution*.[47,f] This review identified Samuelson as "one of the most brilliant contemporary economists" and focused on Keynes's conservatism: because Keynes provided a cure for unemployment, "conservatives should have been more grateful to Keynes (whom he correctly classes with them) than they were." The anonymous reviewer did find Klein guilty of "an excess of enthusiasm" and criticized his poor sense of the social and political consequences of Keynesian ideas, but considered his account of the technicalities "sufficiently masterful"

---

e. When controversy over his book erupted a second time, in 1950, Samuelson provided Killian with a detailed account of its circulation: "About three years ago the so-called National Economic Council launched an attack, under the name of Rose Wilder Lane, on *The Elements of Economics* by Prof. Lorie Tarshis of Stanford University. In bitter viciousness it makes the present piece look like a love pat. This was the first anyone had heard of that organization or of Miss Rose Wilder Lane as an economist. Copies of this attack were sent to 15,000 banks (with a request that each contribute $500 to the task of purifying the college textbooks.) And copies were sent to *every* trustee of *every* college using Tarshis' book. The Tarshis book by the way, was a respectable job, favorably reviewed by the academic journals, and any criticisms that have ever been made of it had nothing in common with those of Miss Lane" (P. A. Samuelson, August 22, 1950, Letter to James R. Killian, PASP 87 [MIT Archives]).

f. See chapter 24 this volume.

to make up for this.[g] Perhaps Compton hoped that the opinion of a business magazine would carry weight with Beadle.

In the fall, the administration continued to liaise with the Visiting Committee about the teaching of economics in the department. Beadle suggested that Killian might look at a statement by Harvard's President Conant on education for business responsibility at the Harvard Business School. He drew his attention to the paragraph in which Conant argued that equality of opportunity could "have meaning only in a competitive society in which private ownership and the profit motive were accepted as basic principles."[48] There was a clear suggestion that MIT should consider enshrining such a commitment to free enterprise in its statement about economics teaching. Killian replied by reassuring him that different perspectives were discussed in the classroom and sent him one of Conant's speeches on academic freedom.[49,h] There were discussions about the supplementary readings assigned for Ec. 11 and, on Beadle's request, the companion course on industrial economics, Ec. 12.[50]

Beadle discussed the situation with Yale's Fred Fairchild, known to be hostile to Hansen's internationalism, and at his suggestion tried to interest Compton in the procedures followed at the University of Pittsburgh by Vincent Lanfear, dean of Pittsburgh's business school.[i] In words Beadle quoted in a letter to Compton, Fairchild endorsed Lanfear as "about the only administrative officer who I know has taken a firm stand on the kind of teaching that is delivered by members of the Economics faculty, particularly with reference to false and reckless statements about business and propaganda about Communism, collectivism etc."[51] Beadle sought to arrange a meeting between Lanfear and the MIT administration, but Killian held back from inviting an outsider to make judgments about MIT's Economics Department. It would be much better for Beadle to review the matter with him.[52] Dean Caldwell, too, reacted negatively to the idea of consulting Lanfear, on grounds that the University of Pittsburgh had been widely criticized for its policies.[53] While they wanted to be as accommodating as they

---

g. The review is too brief to specify what Klein's failings were; he might have been alluding to his belief that the Soviet Union had solved the problem of ensuring full employment.

h. Another life member of the MIT Corporation, Redfield Proctor, of the Vermont Marble Company, thought Samuelson gave the impression, reinforced by some wages statistics about which he was skeptical, that everyone ought to be paid the same, and deduced that he could not be "a really sound teacher" (R. Proctor, October 21, 1947, Letter to Karl T. Compton, PASP 87 [MIT Archives]).

i. On Fairchild, see chapter 19 this volume.

could to members of the MIT Corporation, they did not want to become embroiled in discussions with other universities.[j]

The Visiting Committee's Report, February–April 1948

Having been told by Compton about Klein's *The Keynesian Revolution*, Beadle had a new reason to be concerned about Samuelson. In January 1948, he wrote to Freeman asking whether its final chapter, "Keynes and Social Reform," had also been in Klein's thesis. In this chapter Klein outlined a program of economic policy, claiming it had the support of Hansen, Samuelson, and others. If the chapter had been in the thesis, Samuelson must have approved of it, which would indicate that his teaching was not as harmless as was being claimed.[54,k] Klein's book was also used as evidence against Samuelson by Donald Carpenter of the Remington Arms Company, a member of the corporation whom Killian had asked for advice on other matters.[55] Carpenter had been talking to Beadle, and on his suggestion had read the final chapter

---

j. While these discussions were going on within MIT, Tarshis was receiving strong support within the AEA. In October, Harvard's Seymour Harris wrote to Paul Douglas, president of the AEA, drawing his attention to the threat posed to academic freedom by an organization run by someone widely reported to be "a well known Fascist" and noting that Carl Shoup, of Columbia, had drafted a reply to Tarshis's critics (S. E. Harris, October 27, 1947, Letter to Paul H. Douglas, PASP 37 [Harris]). Because he believed that it was important that instructors not be subject to outside pressure in their choice of textbooks, Harris recommended that the AEA set up a committee to strengthen the hand of those disposed to fight for academic freedom. Forecasting that the problem would become increasingly important, he suggested that the AEA also investigate "what the National Economic Council is and where it receives its funds." The outcome was that on December 30, 1947, the AEA approved a statement saying that "university and college teachers must have the free and untrammeled right to select for use in their teaching and research such textbooks and related materials as they, and no others, believe will promote the purposes which their courses are intended by their teachers to serve" (American Economic Association 1948, p. 533). A committee of three past presidents was formed, which would review cases, express their own judgment on their merits, and where necessary refer them to the American Association of University Professors. However, it proved difficult to circulate the document and advertise the committee, owing to lack of a mailing list, and it was a year before further action was taken (see American Economic Association 1949).

k. Klein's thesis did not contain this chapter, closing with one that countered the charge that Keynesian theory was simply "depression economics."

of the book.[56] His reaction was that "if this represents the type of economics Samuelson is teaching ... I, too, am somewhat concerned.... [I]t is pretty difficult for me to subscribe to some of the statements made, and I would seriously question the advisability of teaching this kind of economics at M.I.T. I hope, sincerely, that the book does not correctly reflect the doctrine which is being taught."[57]

Though conceding that it was unfair to take sentences out of context, he quoted a few from Klein's final chapter in case Killian wished to take the matter further. These quotations included statements about the need to redistribute income from rich to poor so as to reduce saving and the need to have a program of social reform even after the program of unemployment was solved. One sentence praised the work of the highly controversial Office of Price Administration, as having "served us beyond all best hopes and wishes during the War and it did not infringe upon any fundamental liberties, only upon the liberty of greedy profiteering."[58] In a postscript, Carpenter mentioned he had discussed it with a friend, whose reaction was: "this is not the type of economics that I would like to have my son taught."[59] Carpenter made one concession:

He [Carpenter's friend] went on further to state (in which I agree) that if the professor pointed out that this is one type of economic thinking, and here (giving the conservative type) is another type of thinking, stating both impartially, tho I would prefer it that he stated a preference for the conservative type, then that type of teaching could not be seriously criticized.

Two days later, Beadle wrote to Killian, enclosing a copy of Klein's book and saying that if he and Compton had not read it, they might wish to do so.[60]

Before replying, Killian checked with Dean Caldwell, who commented that the last paragraphs of Carpenter's letter did contain a constructive suggestion, and that his own discussions with the department confirmed the view that a wide range of viewpoints was presented. Samuelson and Professor Tucker, also involved in teaching, held very different views, and he had been surprised by the number and variety of materials to which students were "constantly" referred.[61] As for bringing in Klein, Caldwell discounted this on the ground that students' views did not always reflect those of their teachers, and that Samuelson would have expressed his views more cautiously and in a less extreme form than someone younger and less experienced. Caldwell's response was relayed to Carpenter in great detail. The point about his being more cautious than his student was the basis for saying that Samuelson should be judged on his own statements, and that they should wait for the textbook to be published before commenting on it. Killian also stressed, as he had done earlier to Beadle, that Samuelson was a pioneer in economic thought and a creative scholar, who was committed to seek the truth, and whose work was "governed by the highest ideals of scholarly work."[62] Samuelson might have different ideas about what makes the free enterprise system successful, but he believed in it.[1]

Killian tried to persuade Carpenter to look beyond a single course:

> Perhaps of more importance is what might be called the general intellectual climate in which the students at the Institute operate. The whole atmosphere is one of objectivity, and even if a single course were to become—despite our policy—biased in its material, I think the chance of it having an undesirable effect upon our students is extremely small. I have too high a respect for the critical sense of our student body to feel that they could be seriously misled by propaganda, even if it existed.[63]

However, Beadle did not relent in his attempt to persuade the MIT authorities that Samuelson's views were dangerous. In April, he wrote to Killian, drawing attention to a very critical review of Klein's book in the latest issue of the *American Economic Review*. Its author, David McCord Wright, a Harvard friend of Samuelson's, had criticized the book on technical grounds as well as pointing out, in a passage to which Beadle drew Killian's attention, Klein's apparent sympathies with Marxism.

> Nor does Klein ever seem to consider that at least a partial incentive for activity is not merely to enjoy income but also to accumulate and transmit wealth. The explanation for his oversight and others is, I believe, ideological. From the text, Dr. Klein seems to have strong sympathies with socialism if not Marxism.[64]

This was, of course, true. As evidence that Samuelson did not object to the way Klein attributed certain ideas to him, Beadle quoted his contribution to a recent volume edited by Seymour Harris, in which he stated that his chapter owed much to discussions with Klein, whose "rewarding study" was shortly to be published.[65] To link Samuelson to Klein's views was to show that he was guilty of the charges being made against him. Beadle also drew attention to McCord Wright's closing remark.

---

1. On this occasion, he was able to support this claim by quoting in full the citation Douglas had read out when presenting the Clark medal. See chapter 28 this volume.

> If economists are ever to be anything more than bickering apologists
> for the factions of the hour, they must learn to remember alternative
> assumptions, policies, and philosophies; and to be less jaunty before
> the vastness and variety of that life process which our finite minds are
> striving so desperately to describe.[66]

Beadle clearly thought Samuelson a "bickering apologist for the hour" who
needed to be pushed into considering alternative views.

Under these circumstances, Samuelson must have been reassured by the
series of letters he received from instructors who had either seen his 1946
draft or had heard about it, and asked whether the published version would
be available in time for use in their courses. In the first half of 1948, he was
actively involved in preparing both an instructor's manual to accompany the
book and a collection of readings to supplement the book, the latter being no
doubt influenced by the events surrounding the visiting committee.[67]

Given that the department felt under attack from Beadle, and that Beadle
felt frustrated in his "altruistic desire to make a contribution to the department's progress," it was crucial to air the matter at an open meeting of the
Visiting Committee. In preparation for this meeting, Beadle consulted
Beardsley Ruml, with his experience at the Rockefeller Foundation. Ruml
explained that he personally favored an economics course on the relationship
between the state and individual enterprises, whether in controlled, planned,
or free enterprise systems. However, his main interest was in the structure
of the entire program, which he thought should be focused on political and
economic power rather than economics.[68] Beadle read the book Ruml recommended, arguing that Ruml's chapter "Profits and Compensation" should be
made compulsory reading in the course, as the most powerful statement he
had read on the "incentive aspects of our economy."[69] He also recommended
a criticism of planning.[70]

This meeting of the Visiting Committee eventually took place on May
3, 1948, its agenda taking the form of a series of questions to Freeman. The
committee was satisfied with the statement of policy contained in the booklet
"Humanities and Social Sciences," but it sought an assurance that the policy
was being carried out and that bias would not be introduced because students happened to get an instructor with a particular point of view or failed
to read optional materials. Ruml's chapter on the importance of incentives
had been included on the reading list, and it was suggested that an article
in which Keynes stated that "the classical teaching embodied some permanent truths of great significance" should also be added.[71] The committee
also asked whether students' attention might be drawn to five propositions

critical of planning: that government planners were as fallible as those in private industry; that political pressure on government administrators might lead to "grave economic error"; that government errors were likely to have more serious consequences than private ones; that the absence of profit or loss accountability might make government errors more prolonged; and that government activity and controls might deter private initiative and investment.[72] This list showed that though they claimed to have accepted that a variety of positions be represented, the committee clearly sought to make sure that students were exposed to its own critical view of government activity.

The final report expressed appreciation for the department's cooperation and support for its policies, but noted that its teaching, like that at other universities, had been "greatly influenced by the writings of the late Lord Keynes."[73] Noting that such views were associated with central government planning, they suggested that when a student was studying a theory concerning possible benefits of planning, attention should also be drawn to a number of reasons why planning might be harmful. Admitting that the committee was concerned particularly with the presentation of "conservative or classical standpoints," they accepted a policy statement by Freeman to the effect that readings would present points of view different from those in the textbook. They also recommended that faculty appointments reflect the desirability of representing different points of view. Though couched in diplomatic language, stressing diversity of views and the need for objectivity, and avoiding anything that might be embarrassing to MIT, this was an attempt to move the department's teaching in a more conservative direction. What might have been a crisis over Samuelson's influence on the students had been averted, if only temporarily.[m]

---

m. Controversy was to erupt again, after the book was published, and continued throughout the 1950s.

CHAPTER 27 | *Economics*, the First Edition, 1948

Modern Economics

Economics: An Introductory Analysis was published in May 1948. The initial print run was unusually large, at 20,000 copies, but within two months this had sold out, and McGraw-Hill arranged for a further 25,000 copies to be printed. By August it had been adopted at Yale, Harvard, Princeton, Duke, Columbia, Purdue, and many other universities.[1]

Samuelson's book could dominate economics teaching because it provided an account of modern economics. The word *modern* may have been removed from the book's title, but the opening pages made it clear that modern economics was about explaining "the dizzying ups and downs of business activity."[2] The Great Depression, the aborted recovery of 1937, and the unprecedented expansion of activity during wartime were recent memories, and the theory needed to explain them had been developed only in the previous decade. Economics teaching had to be brought up to date, especially for a generation of students that included returning veterans who would be older, more confident, and less tolerant of irrelevance than most students. Meeting this demand, Samuelson's book was innovative both in content and in style. Lorie Tarshis's *Elements of Economics*, which had appeared the year before, was similar in content, but more traditional in style; once Samuelson's book appeared, its sales rapidly fell.[a]

---

a. Samuelson attributed the fate of the Tarshis book to the attacks on him as a "Keynesian-Marxist," discussed in chapter 26 this volume, attributing the ability of his own book

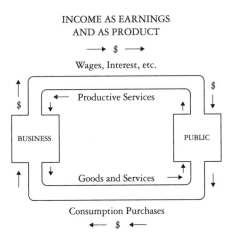

INCOME AS EARNINGS
AND AS PRODUCT

→ $ →

Wages, Interest, etc.

Productive Services

BUSINESS   PUBLIC

Goods and Services →

Consumption Purchases

← $ ←

FIGURE 27.1 Two definitions of income.
Credit line: Samuelson, Economics: An Introductory Analysis, *1948, p. 226, McGraw-Hill.*
Reproduced with permission of McGraw-Hill Education.

As in the early drafts, and as Clemence and Doody had proposed several years before, national income—a concept that had become central to policymaking during the war—was central to the book. However, in the published version, Samuelson took his break with the past a step further. The traditional approach was to see fluctuations in economic activity as part of a broader theory of the business cycle. In contrast, Samuelson placed the theory of income determination at the beginning, and though he did include a chapter on the business cycle, it came later. The static theory of income determination became independent of more complicated and arguably less well established ideas about dynamics, as it had in Keynes's *General Theory*.

He explained the theory using a diagram not used in the earlier drafts, depicting the circular flow of income that would become a standard feature of such books. He used two versions of the diagram. The first, reproduced as figure 27.1, was used to explain how national income could be measured in two ways: either as income or as output.

In the following chapter, the interpretation of the diagram was transformed into figure 27.2 with the addition of pipes and a water pump representing the flow of investment into the circular flow, and an exit at the bottom representing

to withstand such attacks to its more scientific style. The attacks were indeed vicious, but there appears to be no hard evidence that they caused any institution to drop the book, and there is some evidence that they were ineffective. It is possible that its sales fell simply because most instructors preferred Samuelson's textbook.

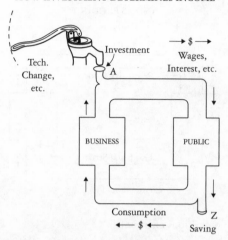

FIGURE 27.2 Investment and the flow of income.
Credit line: Samuelson, Economics: An Introductory Analysis, *1948, p. 264, McGraw-Hill.*
Reproduced with permission of McGraw-Hill Education.

leakage of savings from the system. It was now clearly a hydraulic system, and even if it is not clear how it could physically be constructed (the pump suggests it is driven by gravity, which does not fit with the circular motion), this made it easy to visualize the central feature of the theory he was expounding.

The image's antecedents can be traced to the "Wheel of Wealth" used by Samuelson's Chicago teacher Frank Knight, making it remarkable that the idea of using this diagram did not come to Samuelson until 1947.[b] However, Knight's schematic diagram was changed into a depiction of something physical. There were precedents for this, notably in the hydraulic models used by Irving Fisher in the early twentieth century and in diagrams used by others in the 1930s, but Samuelson modernized the idea and gave it a centrality to economics teaching that it had not had before. It led directly into his analysis of saving and investment, handled through the saving and investment diagram that adorned the book's cover and that provided a static representation of equilibrium, analogous to the supply and demand diagram that had been a staple of economics teaching for half a century. This simplification of the theory was possible because, despite the Hansenian roots of his analysis, Samuelson had cut himself free from the idea that a dynamic theory of the business cycle had to be the starting

---

b. See figure 3.1 given earlier in this volume.

point for the analysis of problems relating to the level of national income and unemployment.

Samuelson also broke with the past in the style of his writing. Hansen was himself the author of a successful textbook that, although written before the transformation of his thinking in the late 1930s, provides a good illustration of the older generation of textbooks with which Samuelson's needed to compete.[3] Defining economics as "a study of the price and value aspects of human activities and institutions," it would have struck Samuelson's engineering students as much drier, less directly related to their immediate concerns or contemporary events. Hansen and his co-author clearly saw the Great Depression as an important event of great interest, but it was placed in the context of over a century of economic controversy. The book's claim that there were "economic laws," though quite consistent with everything Samuelson wrote, would have been more likely to evoke skepticism from MIT's engineers, though Samuelson did talk about the law of scarcity.

Samuelson may have taken some ideas from Hansen's book—given their closeness it would have been surprising if he had not—but the tone was very different. To see this, consider the treatment of national income in the older book. The Hansen book started with national income, but having provided the statistics, it went on to discuss its distribution across households, the distinction between consumption and investment, and ultimately, the production of different types of goods.[4] From there it went into a discussion of alternative methods of economic organization.[c] In contrast, Samuelson, after explaining the problems that an economic system solved and describing how "a 'mixed' capitalistic enterprise system" worked, continued with matters to which his student readers could immediately relate: families, businesses, and government. Equally important, he wrote in a completely different style. Nowhere is this more evident than in two of the chapters not in the previous draft.[d]

---

c. A further difference is that, in contrast with Samuelson, national income played no analytical role. There was a discussion of how to control the flow of purchasing power, but this did not come until much later in the book, not linked to the opening discussion of national income. Where Hansen's book progressed from a discussion of how money was created, moving through the price fluctuations and the business cycle to "the control of purchasing power," Samuelson reversed the order. He began with saving and investment; it was only after he had explained why the money supply mattered that he turned to explaining how it was created.

d. It is also evident in Samuelson's decision to play down the emphasis on traditional price theory, with its heavy reliance on analytical diagrams. The result was a book in which such diagrams were less prominent than in modern rivals, such as Boulding's *Economic Analysis* (1941, 1948a) or Tarshis's *Elements of Economics* (1947). Samuelson's remark to Despres that Boulding's book was weighted too far toward the analytical side makes it

In his discussion of family income, Samuelson emphasized the differences between households and the unequal distribution of income within the United States. The chapter on labor problems developed this point. He began with a history of the American labor movement, the growth of unions, and the differences between craft unions (the American Federation of Labor, or AFL) and industrial unions (the Congress of Industrial Organizations, or CIO). Then, drawing on skills he had no doubt acquired in his high school years when he was focusing on literature and journalism, he did something none of his predecessors would have done: he used a series of fictional stories to explain labor problems and implicitly to show the class structure of American society. He began with the life story of John Kennedy, a carpenter who was a member of the United Brotherhood of Carpenters and Joiners, affiliated with the AFL. He described his terms of employment and his experiences during the housing boom that followed the First World War and the remainder of the 1920s. John Kennedy had been a supporter of La Follette's Progressive Party, but he had no time for communists and had never met one. In contrast, Shelby White, the auto worker in the United Automobile, Aircraft, and Implement Workers of America (CIO), recognized that the communist minority in his union fought for things he also wanted, but it was necessary to make sure that they did not outsmart him at union meetings.

After giving different perspectives through stories about a labor lawyer, a "philanthropic capitalist," and a congressman, Samuelson then provided a broader view through the life of a professor of labor economics, Gordon Bruce, age forty-five, at a "Middle Western State University," several of whose students worked for the Department of Labor and the National Labor Relations Board.[5] This professor was very well informed on the labor market, but was nonetheless "a troubled and perplexed man" for he realized that there were no simple solutions.[6]

> If he ever began to list his doubts and fears, Bruce could go on almost indefinitely. For example, he is concerned over the problem of keeping unions democratic, and he is beginning to wonder whether the trend of collective bargaining toward a wider and wider industrial and national scale will intensify the danger from strikes and inevitably call forth strong, almost totalitarian government action which will infringe on individual freedom. But that is his job, to worry over all

---

clear that this was a conscious decision (P. A. Samuelson, March 2, 1946, Letter to Emile Despres, PASP 28 [Sub-committee on the problem of economic instability]).

matters connected with labor. When called upon to summarize his attitude toward the labor problem, he is still reasonably optimistic.[7]

This last case study is significant because Bruce is clearly the subject with whom Samuelson most closely identified. The economist does not have an easy life mediating between competing claims of labor and capital, needing to balance factors ranging from curbing industrial power to maintaining individual freedom. Samuelson ended the chapter with the remark, "It goes without saying that this viewpoint [in the previous quotation] is condemned alike by the typical conservative farmer and the small-town editor, and by the left-wing agitator. That too he has come to expect as part of his job."[8] Though this would not have been evident to his student readers, Samuelson was alluding to problems he had faced in writing the book.

The chapter "Personal Finance and Social Security" illustrates the way in which Samuelson linked the core ideas about national income to problems that students could relate to. "Not everyone," he wrote, "will come into first-hand contact with the workings of the gold standard or of Federal Reserve banking policy; but everyone will encounter, each day of his life, the problem of acquiring income, spending it upon consumption goods, and investing his savings so as to afford maximum protection against the vicissitudes of life."[9] He presented evidence on how spending patterns varied with household income, and from there it was a short step to more abstract concepts such as the marginal propensity to save, central to the theory he was shortly to present. Students' interest was maintained by relating the discussion to wartime experience, pointing out how many consumers had benefited from the war and the connection between liquid assets and saving. Explanations of government bonds, the cost of owning a house (funded by a loan), and life insurance led into a short but strongly argued defense of social security, presented as a form of insurance.

> Leaving all humanitarianism aside, a social security program is simply a cheap and sensible way of providing the individual care that would have to be provided or financed some other way. Private insurance is not a subtraction from national output and income; neither is social insurance. The statement is sometimes encountered that "a poor country like England cannot afford a Beveridge Plan calling for cradle to grave security against the chief vicissitudes of life—against the expenses of unemployment, old age, sickness, pregnancy, and large families." Such a statement is not good economics. These contingencies have to be met in any case, and the question is whether they should be budgeted

in a systematic, efficient, and sensible way, or be left to fall upon the individual or upon haphazard charity.

Ideas that would, in a traditional textbook, have been dry and remote were related to students' own experiences and to current policy problems. He had changed not just the content of an introductory textbook, he had also adopted a new style, as even most persistent critics recognized. His style might be criticized as being taken to the point of flippancy, but it changed the way textbooks were written.[e]

Free Enterprise and Socialism

Samuelson was still working out his ideas in the three years he was developing the book. This is shown by the way he rearranged the chapters and by new material he brought in. Some changes were the result of criticism by colleagues, such as changing "The Economics of Full Employment" to "The Composition and Pricing of National Output." However, it is remarkable how many of the chapters he wrote in the summer of 1945 remained essentially unchanged by the printed version. Given the controversy that had erupted in 1946 and his admission, on the book's fiftieth anniversary, that he wrote *Economics* as if a lawyer were looking over his shoulder, it is important to consider how he presented the choice between capitalism and socialism.

In the 1946 draft, Samuelson had explained that, though the choice between different economic systems was an important problem, it was not something about which economic science could say anything. He had written:

> It is not our task, especially at this stage, to evaluate the advantages and disadvantages of different economic systems. No board of scientists could weigh this subject and come out with a scientific answer—because it is not simply a scientific question. But the study

---

e. Beadle wrote, "In some instances, however, this effort to enliven the presentation has been pushed to the point of being rather flippant; for example, 'Presidents of railroads, who usually come up from the ranks *and have a rather humdrum job.*' (V-6. Underscoring supplied)" (W. J. Beadle, July 15, 1947, Letter to Ralph E. Freeman, PASP 87 [MIT Archives]). Some academic reviewers of the book made similar remarks. Looking back at the book, four editions later, Samuelson confessed to having written in a deliberately colloquial style, and that although some teachers were offended, it had probably been commercially advantageous (P. A. Samuelson, May 16, 1961, Letter to Ralph P. Agnew, PASP 87 [Economics (1945–2008, Folder 2]).

of economics can provide part of the material necessary in answering the question.[10]

In the book, he removed the reference to choosing between economic systems and wrote simply that the study of economics could provide part of the material necessary to answer the questions of "What?," "How?," and "For whom?" that faced any society. Lower down the page, he deleted a reference to competing systems.

> When we come to the third question of the desirable distribution of wealth and income between individuals, we leave the field of science altogether. *De gustibus non est disputandum*: there is no disputing (scientifically!) tastes; and the same goes for ethics. We must leave the definition of social ends to the philosopher, the theologian, the statesman, and to public opinion, *confining ourselves to the more prosaic task of improving the workings of a given system with respect to continuously accepted goals rather than changing the system itself. Because of time limitations, we cannot treat the problem of changing the economic system with the thoroughness it deserves, and must be contented to point out a few considerations bearing on this important question.*[11,f]

Though Samuelson would appear to have made a significant modification of the text, this is mitigated by the fact that both paragraphs are about what economic science is *not* about. The effect of the changes is to focus attention on what economics *can* do, a change that could be justified on pedagogic grounds, quite apart from avoiding an issue on which he had been attacked.

The question of alternative economic systems was postponed to the final chapter, "Social Movements and Economic Welfare," where Samuelson was able to provide a much more nuanced discussion. His starting point was the crisis that had afflicted capitalism in the 1930s and the variety of responses to it—"[a] bouquet of isms"—fascism, communism, socialism. After a brief but thoughtful historical sketch of socialist movements in the United States and Europe, he spent three pages on the history of fascism and Marxian communism in Russia. His accounts may have been brief, but they were serious explanations of what these movements were and how they had evolved. He distinguished sharply between communism and socialism, noting that the socialist governments of Sweden and Britain represented "a middle way." He explained that in Britain, owners of nationalized industries had been compensated and that "[a]nyone who opposes the Labor party's government—and

---

f. Italicised text at the end of the quotation was in the 1946 draft but not in the book.

most English newspapers do—is free to express his opinion and organize politically. Even communists are granted full civil rights and liberties as of 1948."[12] He made it clear that the advocacy of "peaceful and democratic evolution" was "often more than a tactical move; rather a deep philosophical tenet of faith." This was clearly a sympathetic account of British socialism that stood in sharp contrast with Soviet communism, under which phases such as "industrial democracy" were used to denote positions very different from those how they were in the West.

A point that his conservative critics would not have liked was his equally sharp distinction between political freedom and economic control. After commenting on fascist and communist suppression of civil liberties, he continued,

On the other hand, socialist Britain (1948) has more civil liberties than did the United States in the 1920 era of rugged individualism, when Attorney General Palmer imprisoned and released hundreds of people alleged to be "reds."

It is one thing to tell a corporation what it may charge for electric power and quite another thing to tell a man what he can say, what he can believe, how he must worship. It will not do to confuse the two.[13]

Samuelson made it clear that regulation of industry was consistent with a free society.

Beadle had criticized Samuelson for implying that people on the federal payroll were "more infallible" than ones employed privately.[14] Samuelson modified the offending text as follows (words appearing in italics were struck out and replaced with those in square brackets):

But *sometimes* [some of] the mistakes which a flock of independent competitors make—for example in all overbuilding as in 1929, or in continually entering the already overcrowded grocery store business— *could have been avoided by advanced centralized planning* [would be lessened in an economy characterized by planning. (Of course fallible bureaucrats might perpetrate a series of planning errors of their own, and new problems of individual liberty would be introduced)].[15]

Samuelson softened the claims for what central planning could achieve but only slightly, and he made it clear that he *did* intend the paragraph to bear the interpretation Beadle placed on it—that planners could sometimes do better than business people. He conceded Beadle's point about the imperfections of planning, but made it clear that he thought this obvious. However, though he was more nuanced in his claims for what planning could achieve, the message of the section in which it occurred was not changed. It remained a forthright critique of business people and their ambiguous attitude toward competition, approving of it when it was in their own interests and characterizing it as "chiseling," "unfair," or "ruinous" when it was to their disadvantage. Competition was used to eliminate rivals and create monopoly, and workers complained about competition when it threatened to depress wages.[g]

This discussion of the limitations of free enterprise set the scene for an explanation of the role of government as doing things that private business could not do. This section was not weakened at all. Indeed, it was strengthened, for in addition to the provision of collective services and setting the framework within which private enterprise functioned, he added a third function: using monetary and fiscal policy "to enable private enterprise to maintain a steady level of high employment and rising productivity."[16] This might be coercive, but it was necessary because, as Samuelson made clear in what was effectively the book's conclusion (chapter 26), a laissez-faire system did not produce a social optimum. It did not generate an optimal distribution of income and there was great waste owing to unemployment and the business cycle. In addition, drawing on the theory of monopolistic competition that students would have learned in the intervening chapters, Samuelson wrote of the "evils" of monopoly: restricting output for fear of spoiling the market, wasteful advertising, needless product differentiation, and an inefficient division of production among too many companies. The word *evil* was used three times in a short paragraph.[17]

The Business Cycle and Economic Policy

Though Samuelson modernized both the content and the presentation of economics, a striking feature of Samuelson's book is its roots in interwar

---

g. There are other places in the book where he strengthened his criticism of business people. For example, he replaced the example, congenial to his critics, of "a union leader [who] has quarterbacked a successful strike" and feels "an expert on the economics of wages," with other examples: "Because a union leader has successfully negotiated several labor contracts, he may feel that he is an expert on the economics of wages. A businessman who has 'met a payroll' may feel that his views on price control are final. A banker who can balance his books may conclude that he knows all there is to know about money. And an economist who has studied the business cycle may be under the illusion that he can outguess the stock market" (Samuelson 1948, p. 6. The previous example is from P. A. Samuelson, 1946, *Economics: An Introductory Analysis*, PASP 91, p. I-3).

"institutionalist" economics, a fact that must have been in his mind when he described it to friends as being very "institutional."[18] Part I—in which, after describing the economic problems facing any society and sketching how a capitalist system worked, he discussed families, business organization, and government—was always a crucial part of the book. Judging by the 1945 manuscript, it was the part of the book he wrote first, and although it was expanded with the addition of chapters on government, labor markets, and personal finance and family income, its basic structure and focus never changed.

An important feature of this coverage of the facts of economic life was the provision of voluminous statistical information, much of which originated in New Deal institutions. This was, as he explained to Alan Sweezy, an important part of the book: "I have tried to draw upon the plentiful up-to-date statistical materials concerning National Income, corporations, etc.—material only recently available in the *Survey of Current Business* and other sources."[19] However, the data he used came from a much wider variety of sources than just the *Survey of Current Business*. The coverage of family incomes relied on the statistics on income distribution and inequality produced by the National Resources Committee in 1935–36 (data with which he had become familiar during his work with the NRPB). The data were also the basis for the discussion of spending patterns that led into his analysis of saving. He used data on the distribution of income across different occupations dating from the late 1930s and 1940s. The account of national income drew on Department of Commerce figures, available only since the mid-1930s. He turned to Arthur Burns at the National Bureau, whose *Measuring Business Cycles* had just appeared, for business cycle data,[20] and he referred to publications of the Temporary National Economic Committee for data on market structure. His denunciations of the evils of monopoly owed as much, if not more, to the Temporary National Economic Committee than to Chamberlin's analysis of market structures.

Samuelson and Hansen were very close while he was writing the book. Samuelson's coverage of the business cycle and economic policy were entirely consistent with Hansen's empirical-institutional approach. He began his account of the cycle with a statistical description such as would have been familiar to economists in the 1920s, complete with a "barometer" of business activity. Attempts to forecast had proved little more reliable than those of fortune-tellers, and aside from allowing for seasonal variations and long run trends, it was possible to do little more than describe the phases of the cycle. Though his description of the four phases of the cycle was taken from

Mitchell, he turned to Hansen for a summary of the business cycle in the United States, in which construction activity was a key factor.[21] He paid his respects to Schumpeter by discussing long waves in economic activity, but concluded that it was too soon to tell whether these were any more than historical accidents.

Hansen's linking the business cycle to activity in the building industry provided the first clue to understanding the cycle. The greatest fluctuations take place in industries producing durable goods—something supported by the graphs he had presented. He reviewed alternative theories, concluding that what was needed was a synthesis. Of the mechanisms internal to the economic system that had been proposed, the one on which he chose to focus was the acceleration principle. Using a numerical example, he showed that this principle led to instability, amplifying fluctuations in demand.[h] The chapter confirmed the conclusions reached in several other chapters that "the economic system is more or less without a steering wheel"; even if business people and workers act selflessly and efficiently, the system may experience inflation or deflation "depending upon the chance circumstances of the complex interaction between investment and saving."[22]

The solution to this problem was clearly fiscal policy. The least controversial version of this was "compensatory" or "anti-cyclical" policy, keeping the budget balanced over the cycle, but increasing spending in recessions and reducing it in booms. Samuelson described this as a "rather conservative" doctrine—too conservative for some of "the present generation of economists."[23] Even though he viewed this as a conservative doctrine, associated with previous generations of economists, he discussed it in detail, covering public works, welfare payments, and adjustments to taxes. He also pointed out its limitations, though the main objection Samuelson raised was that spending that started out being counter-cyclical might end up being long term. He illustrated this with the 1930s, pointing out that the period 1933 to 1938 involved a complete cycle and that, according to the theory, there should have been a surplus in its best years, 1935 to 1937. "However, at the time, with almost 10 million unemployed, putting on the fiscal brakes hardly seemed rational or 'political.'"[24] Given the implication that it would

---

h. The acceleration principle states that investment is proportional to the change in output. Thus, if output grows more slowly, investment will fall, which may, via the multiplier, cause a fall in output. Samuelson's use of the accelerator is discussed in chapter 13 this volume.

have been unreasonable to put on the brakes at such high unemployment levels, the effect of this was to undermine the objection he had raised to compensatory fiscal policy.

This took him straight into an account of Hansen's views on secular stagnation and the argument for long-term government deficits.[25,i] Though it would see rapid technological innovation, Hansen argued that a mature economy such as the United States had would be susceptible to stagnant investment: the frontier, which stimulated an enormous amount of investment in the nineteenth century, had closed, so to sustain investment there was a need for innovations on the scale of electricity and motor vehicles. In the absence of sufficient innovation, and given the tendency of saving to rise, the result would be that aggregate demand would not rise sufficiently fast to maintain a high level of employment. Samuelson portrayed Hansen as being flanked on one side by less cautious supporters and on the other side by conservatives who agreed with him on the facts but believed the causes lay in government interference with business. Hansen was also opposed by economists who challenged the thesis that secular stagnation was likely. Here, Samuelson cited a recent book by George Terborgh (1945), who adduced many reasons why investment would remain high enough to maintain demand. Terborgh saw saving and investment analysis as neutral, a point to which Samuelson clearly attached great importance.

Samuelson may have expunged the statement to which Beadle took exception about the government's being able "to take the social point of view whatever the financial cost,"[26] but it is hard to see any compromise in his conclusion:

> In short, there is no technical reason why a nation fanatically addicted to deficit spending should not pursue such a policy for the rest of our lives or even beyond. The real question is whether such a policy will impinge on an economy that is inflationary or deflationary. So long as private and government spending are only enough to offset saving, that is one thing. If a nation or Congress is misguided enough to continue heavy spending and light taxing after total consumption and private investment have become too large, then inflation will be the outcome.

---

i. This is an idea recently revived by Lawrence Summers. See Backhouse and Boianovsky 2016.

His key point was that the appropriate level of government spending depended on the balance of saving and investment in the economy as a whole, not simply on what was happening to the government debt.

If inflation became a problem only at full employment, then the concepts of deflationary and inflationary gaps, explained in the chapter on saving and investment, would be sufficient to calculate the optimal fiscal stance. But this was not the case, for prices usually started to rise before full employment was reached. This meant that maintenance of full employment required more than just fiscal policy. The problem was a psychological one, for it arose from businesses and trade unions reacting "perversely" to increases in demand. The solution of having a reserve army of the unemployed to keep prices down was not acceptable; neither was the solution of direct price and wage controls, with its implication of a high degree of centralized control, consistent with what Samuelson believed were the "philosophical beliefs of the great majority of the American people."[27] Some people believed a little inflation had to be tolerated, but the problem of finding "a wage and price policy for full employment" was "America's greatest problem and challenge."[28] It was a problem that involved thinking not just about the balance of saving and investment, but also about the allocation of resources within the economy.

A new chapter, "International Finance and Capital Movements," supported the internationalism associated with Hansen that Samuelson had defended in the pages of *The New Republic* a few years before. He sought to undermine fallacies such as that it was always good to have a surplus in the balance of payments. Countries, he argued, went through stages of development in which foreign investment, which raised production, subsequently produced flows of income in the other direction. In general, people understood this, but "[w]hen nationalism rears its ugly (or beautiful) head, matters change."[29] People who would never grumble about interest payments made from one part of a country to another would object to absentee ownership by foreigners. Trade and politics were intertwined, but in a way that Samuelson argued was too complicated to discuss. Some people sought a world without wars or nationalism, with the freedom to invest and trade freely wherever they liked; others saw military glory as more important than comfortable living, believing that one "super-race" should be able to strip others of their goods so that they could "have [their] cake and cannons too."[30] The world of the last two centuries lay somewhere in between these extremes.

Relegating the more technical discussion of topics, such as fixed and flexible exchange rates, the gold standard, and the international trade multiplier to an appendix, Samuelson turned to contemporary problems. His target was isolationism. After reminding readers that exporting goods could create prosperity, as had happened when European countries suddenly demanded American goods during the First World War, and when many loans had been made to the rest of the world in the 1920s, Samuelson listed a series of policies that might raise employment. These "[b]eggar-my-neighbor" policies included tariffs, import quotas, exchange controls, and depreciating the dollar. If other countries did nothing, these policies might work, but if, as was certain to happen, they retaliated in kind, the result would be a downward spiral in international trade and the United States would end up worse off. These policies were foolish even for "hard-boiled" or "selfish" nations. The lesson was that the United States should turn to domestic policies to conquer unemployment, and rely on trade "only to increase our present and future standards of consumption, or to serve our political aspirations and responsibilities."[31] "Economic isolation will not work," he continued. "On this, if on no other proposition, 99$^{44}/_{100}$ per cent of all economists are agreed." With this he turned to the policies that *should* be pursued.

The first of these policies was the maintenance of full employment through domestically created purchasing power, making it possible to remove tariff barriers and subsidies for inefficient industries. The Marshall Plan was also important, for establishing Western European prosperity was crucial to the containment of communism.[j] Canceling wartime debts was a smart move, not something that would hurt Americans. It was also necessary to support Britain with loans, for otherwise it would be impossible for Britain to free its trade and return to convertibility—two policies to which the United States attached great importance. Perhaps most important of all was international collaboration through the newly established International Bank for Reconstruction and Development (later the World Bank) and the International Monetary Fund (IMF). Samuelson explained how these institutions worked, pointing out that the United States was not acquiring unlimited liabilities. The World Bank was a commercial operation that should be able to cover its costs, but in the event that debts did turn bad, the tab would be picked up by all member nations, not just by the United States. The IMF would create greater exchange rate stability and the whole package of reforms would make it possible to move toward freer international trade. It was an unashamedly internationalist policy, supported by domestic demand-management policies.

---

j. The text was written before the Marshall Plan had been approved; President Truman's approval came a month before the book was published.

When defending his position against Beadle, Samuelson had argued that he was trying to keep to a "middle-of-the-road" position, a phrase that implied balance and hence that the textbook was one that could safely be used for teaching.[32] This introduces the question of where that balance rested, given that this was the age of the cold war, when certain positions were considered to lie outside the range of acceptable beliefs. Samuelson provided no analysis of this problem, but his friend Arthur Schlesinger Jr. did, in a book published very shortly after Samuelson's textbook. *The Vital Center* sought, as its title implied, to stake out a center ground.[33] Shaped by the cold war with the Soviet Union, it was uncompromising in its anti-communism, unrelenting in its denunciation of those who, in their allegiance to the Communist Party of the United States, were blind to the perils of Soviet totalitarianism. Yet he was also critical of capitalism, for modern industrialism had contributed to the anxiety that lay beneath contemporary politics. Civilization had become "the victim rather than the master of industrialism," which had shattered the personal ties that held preindustrial societies together.[34] Schlesinger's attack on the right was an attack on business people; they had, he claimed, been effective in raising productivity, but they had become less effective the further they got from the counting house. "Men accustomed to the exclusive pursuit of their own interests find it hard to assume the rôle of the politician, who must balance and reconcile the conflicting interests of many groups."[35]

Schlesinger even likened communist societies to company towns like Pittsburgh: "Soviet Russia is a Pennsylvania or West Virginia from which there is no escape and in which the steel companies and the government are united in indissoluble bonds."[36] He made the case for a class analysis of American society, contrasting plutocracy unfavorably with aristocracy and its sense of *noblesse oblige*. The business community was not capable of defending a free society, and government was the means through which the nonbusiness classes could protect themselves. Thus, the New Dealers were advancing cautiously out of "the jungle of private enterprise" and "the tyranny of the irresponsible plutocracy."[37,k]

Samuelson had known Schlesinger since they had been students at Harvard, and in the 1950s and 1960s they were both active in advising Democratic Party politicians. We do not know how much contact they had during the time when Samuelson was writing his textbook, but Schlesinger presented a political philosophy that is entirely consistent with the view Samuelson,

---

k. His understanding of the phrase "middle-of-the-road" is illustrated by his use of it to describe the German social democrat Karl Kautsky (Schlesinger 1949, p. 132).

following Hansen, represented in his textbook.[38] Samuelson may not have been quite so critical of business and business people as was Schlesinger, but they held the same view on the necessity for government action to regulate, and hence to maintain, a free society. Samuelson's arguing that a middle-of-the-road position called for significant government intervention, in a book that effectively concluded by talking of redistribution, of the evils of monopoly, and of the wastes that are found under laissez-faire, could be seen as helping to place the center just where Schlesinger believed it had to be.[39]

The Book's Reception

Economics was an MIT book, unlike *Foundations,* which though published seven years after his move to MIT, was essentially the product of his Harvard years. Samuelson's most persistent critic, Beadle, clearly viewed the book not as the product of an isolated professor but as one produced by MIT for which collective responsibility should be taken. This attitude explains why, when Freeman said that Samuelson had asked him to go through his draft, Beadle understood him to be saying that he would be editing the book, in the same way that he had edited the volumes the department had previously produced.[40] However, though Beadle had misunderstood the level of editorial input that Freeman would be providing, he was right in seeing Samuelson's book as an MIT product designed to meet the MIT's needs. MIT did not require a technical book, because economics was part of a humanities and social science sequence aimed at teaching students how to write. And though he drew on resources from his own student days—in particular, the textbook written by his one-time idol Frank Knight—Samuelson's starting point was the textbook written by his departmental colleagues a decade earlier; in revising it, he took up ideas that emerged from discussions among MIT's instructors about how such a textbook should be written.

Economics was also Samuelson's own book, and it shows how much he had changed since completing his thesis at Harvard. It was a book that someone who was no more than a specialist in mathematical economics could never have written, and it reveals debts to the education he had received in wartime, working as a consultant for government agencies and engaging with other young economists in the same situation. This work had given him a familiarity with data—not just where to find statistics but also understanding how they were constructed and how they could be used—and it had affected his conception of the economic system. The claim that the Second World War was an economist's war as well as a physicist's war reflected a deeply held belief that a mixed economy, in which businesses interacting through the marketplace were guided by intelligent planners, could work. The United States experienced unprecedented prosperity, as well as having won the war. The next task was to win the peace. Samuelson's commitment to the internationalism represented by Hansen was no accident; rather, it was the fruit of his experience. He had ceased to be an "ivory tower" economist.

Samuelson's attitude toward his book changed as he wrote it. In July 1945, soon after he had started writing, he wrote to Klein: "To my shame, I am putting in some time writing an elementary one semester text book along the lines we discussed. Don't breathe it to a soul."[41] However, as he got further into the task, and once his text was being used by students, his attitude began to change. A year later, he confessed to Despres that the compromises he was having to make left him "wide open as far as my professional colleagues are concerned," but that there was consolation in the fact that he had "(rather shamefully) enjoyed writing the manuscript."[42] However, the following month, when he wrote to McCord Wright, he stated simply that "I must confess I have rather enjoyed doing this, although the result is full of compromises and does not satisfy me completely."[43] By the start of the next academic year, when his second, more complete manuscript was being made available to students via the MIT bookstore, his attitude had turned full circle. In a letter to Max Millikan, he wrote about the difficulty of the task involved: "it is a monumental task to cover the richness of modern economic reality in one volume and at the same time give some analytical insight."[44]

A significant change is that, instead of deprecating the book for being about institutions, Samuelson focused on the need to capture the richness of economic reality, a task that he seems to have conceived as being different from analysis. It was necessary to engage in anatomy before one could turn to physiology, and there was no shame attached to doing this.[45] He no longer referred to it as a *very* elementary book. His work for government agencies and his engagement with not just Hansen but also economists such as Oscar Altman and Raymond Goldsmith—both committed to rigorous empirical work—appears to have changed his view about how economic inquiries should be conducted.

The first recorded response to the published book came from Samuelson's Chicago friend Martin Bronfenbrenner, who wrote to the publisher that there was no chapter from which he had not learned something.[46] Where conservatives criticized Samuelson for expressing his own views, Bronfenbrenner praised this feature of the book: "Economics textbooks have maintained for entirely too long the tradition of artificial impartiality and it is a great relief to see Samuelson coming out clearly with his own views." The organization of the book, he remarked, offered a solution to the problem of how to teach economics to the current generation of students. Seymour Harris, a friend and Keynesian from Harvard, described the book as a landmark, saying he was surprised that such a distinguished economist could write so effectively for students.[47]

On August 31, before the new academic year had properly begun, Samuelson was able to report the book's commercial success to Compton. He also told Compton about a glowing review in *Fortune* and a briefer one in the *Economist*, and that Columbia's Albert Hart had written an enthusiastic review for the *American Economic Review*. The book had been widely adopted, he wrote, and "it has been a profitable venture beyond my fondest expectations."[48,l] He told Compton this, so he claimed, not to pat himself on the back but so that Compton should know his confidence in him was not completely misplaced. In conclusion, alluding to conservative criticisms about his lack of objectivity, he reflected on the changes taking place in economics:

> I should add, however, that though the national income approach to elementary economics is now the rage, it may not be approved of by all of the authorities in the field of economics. This I suppose is inevitable in a field of the social sciences which touches upon controversy and emotions. I think, however, there is gradually coming to be greater consensus on the more neutral and objective tools of analysis as distinct from policy prescriptions.[49]

Samuelson tried to counter the claims of his critics by arguing that neutrality and objectivity resided in the tools of analysis, a position that echoed the view of his former Harvard teacher and friend, Joseph Schumpeter.[m] Objectivity did not rest, as his critics claimed, in simply presenting conflicting points of view.

When reviews were published, they were mostly enthusiastic about the book. The first academic review to be published, in the October 1948 issue of the *Southern Economic Journal*, argued explicitly that, though the language was Keynesian, it was not a Keynesian textbook, for "with admirable self-restraint" Samuelson had "leaned over backwards to avoid expounding pet policy prescriptions."[50] The reviewer for the *Journal of Farm Economics* found part III, on the composition and pricing of national output, the weakest section of the text, in contrast to part II, on aggregative

---

l. The royalties on these two print runs roughly equaled his annual MIT salary.

m. It is questionable whether tools are as neutral as Samuelson and Schumpeter claimed.

analysis, which was "the *piece de resistance* ... replete with relevance," the stimulating effect of which could be neutralized only by an unimaginative instructor.[51]

Hart's review, on which Samuelson had reported to Compton in August, appeared in December. The book had weaknesses, many of which Hart discussed in detail, but these were more than offset by the book's many merits. As if to counter Samuelson's conservative critics, Hart emphasized its middle-of-the-road position.[52]

> The supreme merit of the book, to my taste, is a systematic effort to find points of contact between different points of view which students and their neighbors in society may hold. Samuelson's own policy position is middle-of-the-road, favoring private employment for the great bulk of the labor force, and allocation of inputs and outputs primarily through private decisions of households and firms. On the other hand, Samuelson stresses the responsibilities for economic stabilization which fall upon government because of the inherent instability of the private economy, and the fact that government cannot evade responsibility for the distribution of income and wealth.[53]

It was, of course, the points made in the last sentence, accepted by Hart, that Samuelson's conservative critics could not accept.[n] Hart, in contrast, saw Samuelson as discussing the "real merits" of socialism largely in order to understand Western Europe (Britain then had a government committed to an explicitly socialist program): "he does not mince words about the evils of fascism and communism."

The main exception to this enthusiastic reception was Lewis Haney at New York University. Writing in the *Annals of the American Academy of Political and Social Science,* Haney was scathing about the tone in which the book was written.

> Samuelson's "Economics" has a snappy style which may be appreciated by some. It drops to wisecracks at times. The language or use of words is too often shaky and inaccurate. And not unrelated to these characteristics is its glorification of ignorance—repeated statements such as "The instinct of the non-specialist is nearly infallible," "Every one of college age knows a good deal about money, perhaps even more than he realizes" (!), and "An expert is entitled to only one vote along with

---

n. Note that Hart had, like Samuelson, been trained at Chicago under Knight and Simons.

everyone else." This sort of talk may make the inferior student (and teacher) feel good, but is it true?[54]

The book had good points, but these were opposed by the main slant of the book:

> On the whole, Samuelson suggests that individual and social interests clash, that the average of prices is adequate, that the quantity theory is good enough for most purposes, and that the main "task" of "economics" is to find "proper" economic policies designed to establish what, as he sees it, is "useful," "wise," "suitable," and "equitable." The references to other than his so-called "modern economics" are on the whole derogatory.

Samuelson's economics was, Haney claimed, the economics of Keynes and involved collective action to control national income. Haney even objected to national income's being defined as the sum of consumption, investment, the trade balance, and government spending. Samuelson got "tangled up" in discussing banking and the creation of money (a chapter that Samuel Stratton, initially a critic of an early draft, had picked out as being well done),[55] and he had focused on the quantity rather than the quality of money: "What about the quality of being valuable? In this economics of assumption, echo answers."[56] Haney was to play a role in the attacks on Samuelson's book that intensified when the young William F. Buckley selected it as a major target in *God and Man at Yale*, the latter being one of the foundational texts for the modern conservative movement.[57] He and his associates might condemn the book as Keynesian, but this remained a minority view that failed to stop Samuelson's book from being a runaway success.

Returning to Normal

When *Economics* was published, MIT's group of economists was still very small. If the two specialists in personnel management are excluded, economists in the Department of Economics and Social Science were outnumbered by the psychologists. However, it had the strong support of the president, Karl Compton, and was poised for expansion.[a] Above all, it was a harmonious department, MIT being free of the anti-Semitism that Samuelson had encountered at Harvard.[1] Equally important, it was by now clear that he was considered the star whom they needed to keep, and he will have known full well that this attitude extended to the new president, James Killian. The controversy over the textbook, though it had taken much of Compton's and Killian's time, had not hurt him at all; to the contrary, it had made the institute's two presidents much more aware of his stature within the economics profession. A few years later, when Killian wrote his memoirs, he said of the "one man, recognized by all, who came to personify the quality of the Department":

> So brilliant had Samuelson's record been at Harvard and so immediately productive was he at M.I.T. that he soon became a magnet

---

a. Over the next two years, it would recruit Charles Kindleberger, Morris Edelman, Max Millikan, George Schultz, and Robert Solow.

drawing still other able economists to the Institute, who together were to help build a department famous the world over.[2]

He was, moreover, in what had during the war become one of the world's preeminent centers for natural science and engineering—an environment in which, after his wartime work, he was a perfect fit. Chicago and Harvard might have their attractions, but MIT was now his home.

Samuelson had also become established within the economics profession. Marks of this recognition had been his appointment, in 1942, to the editorial board of *Econometrica*, and two years later, at the age of twenty-eight, as one of the editors of the *American Economic Review*. This latter appointment was for a three-year term, 1944 to 1946, and involved working as one of a group of six, under the management of a managing editor who farmed out the manuscripts and to whom recommendations about publication or rejection had to be sent. He had agreed to take this on the month before starting in the Radiation Laboratory.[3]

Possibly the reason why he considered this work compatible with other activities was that Paul Homan, the managing editor, reassured him that, as long as the war continued, the flow of manuscripts would remain low and the task would not be onerous.[b] However, the problems that could arise in such a role were immediately made clear, for Samuelson had to advise Homan on a dispute in which a senior economist at the Brookings Institution, Harold Moulton, had complained that a recent article by McCord Wright, one of Samuelson's friends at Harvard, had questioned his integrity in a way that reflected badly on the editorial process. After rereading both Wright's article and the book by Moulton he had criticized, Samuelson explained to Homan in detail why he did not believe Moulton's charges were justified. But after a demanding start, with three requests to read papers in as many months, Homan's forecast of a low workload proved correct.[4] However, Samuelson's few reports amply justify Homan's remark that, at the end of his term, he had never known anyone who performed his duties "so usefully and without stint."[5] Not surprisingly, Samuelson continued to be used by Homan as a referee after his term as editor had ended.

Samuelson's practice as a reviewer is nicely illustrated by his response to a manuscript by the Dutch pioneer of econometric modeling, Jan Tinbergen.[6] Though he recommended rejection, he explained in detail why it was important for a journal such as the *American Economic Review* to

---

b. For the second of his three years, Homan was replaced by an acting managing editor, Fritz Machlup.

be willing to publish technical papers, even though only a minority of its readers would understand them. Readers could benefit from articles even if they did not fully understand them, and his view, based on systematically reading back issues, was that the articles most widely cited ten or twenty years later were frequently "theoretical and difficult papers which at the time may have seemed formidable and abstract to many readers."[7] He expressed the opinion that the *American Economic Review* had been so bad because its previous editor had presumed a division of labor, in which the *Quarterly Journal of Economics* would publish the technical articles. In contrast, the *Economic Journal* under Edgeworth and Keynes had been so good because it was willing to publish technical papers. Samuelson was, of course, making the case for why the *American Economic Review* should publish papers such as he often wrote. His reason for recommending rejection of Tinbergen's paper was that he believed Tinbergen was unaware, presumably owing to living in a German-occupied country, that others had derived similar results and that the results were wrong in ways that he explained in detail in his review. He recommended passing the article on to *Econometrica*, even though he doubted it was acceptable for publication there.

No sooner had Samuelson's term with the *American Economic Review* ended than he was invited to serve as one of the editors of the *Review of Economic Studies*, a journal founded in the 1930s by a group of young British economists. This was a more significant role, for he was responsible for being the conduit through which American economists would submit papers. On taking over, he wrote to one of the British editors, Nicholas Kaldor, about the "unbelievable" flood of graduate students in American universities who would soon be trying to publish their work.[8] This gave him confidence that he would be able to increase the flow of submissions. However, his role involved much more than soliciting manuscripts. Unlike his work at the *American Economic Review*, where his role had been to advise Homan and Machlup, he was asked to accept or reject papers by American economists, while Kaldor and Ursula Hicks would decide the European submissions.[9,c] In practice, the decision making was collective, for Samuelson would consult Hicks about whether an article would be of interest to Europeans, and she would consult him about papers submitted by Europeans. The difficulties involved in duplicating the papers and sending them back and forth may

c. The idea behind this was that this would speed up the decision making because transatlantic mail was much slower then than it is today, even without taking account of email.

seem strange by today's standards, as they frequently discussed papers that only one party had been able to read.

Samuelson's involvement with the *Review of Economic Studies* was part of an increasing engagement with European economists that became possible with the end of the war. Samuelson was having a stream of European visitors to MIT, and American economists were visiting Europe. For example, John and Ursula Hicks visited the United States at the end of 1946; it was no doubt Samuelson's presence that caused MIT to be part of their "grand tour"; before the war, a European economist visiting Cambridge, Massachusetts, would simply have gone to Harvard. Samuelson told the Cambridge (UK) economist Joan Robinson, who in the 1950s and 1960s would become one of his most regular correspondents as they argued over capital theory, that "we exploited them shamefully—making them perform day and night."[10] He told Ursula that their visit was the high point of the academic year.[11]

A friendship developed with Ursula Hicks, with whom Samuelson exchanged frequent and often long letters in which they shared news about developments in their two countries. Samuelson passed on news about American economists and who was moving where, as well as about the birth of his second daughter, Margaret.[12] He shared with her his relief at getting the textbook off to McGraw-Hill, after spending "an unbeliev-able number of man-hours personally verifying the old age assistance pensions in the state of Mississippi and the dates when reserve requirements were changed for central reserve city banks, etc., etc."[13] Hicks reported having entertained Aaron Director and Milton Friedman on their way home from a "wonderful Liberal conference" (where "Liberal" was used in the European sense of those committed to individual liberty) organized by Hayek in Switzerland (the meeting at which the Mont Pelerin Society was formed). "As they were all in 100% agreement to take all controls off immediately," she wrote, "I don't know quite what there was to discuss." Samuelson reciprocated with news of Leontief and a colleague going to Salzburg for "a 6-week chautauqua designed to bring American culture to the Central Europeans," alerting her to the possibility of making contact when they returned through Britain.[14] The visit to Europe that Samuelson's leave of absence was to make possible in the fall of 1948 was part of this recreation of a transatlantic community of economists that was to become even closer as the European recovery got under way and as the speed and cost of transatlantic travel plummeted.

As with most American economists, it was Europe that was the most important international connection. However, Samuelson's connections with Japan were also to be very important for him, the crucial link being his close friend from his Harvard days, Shigeto Tsuru. They had completely lost contact, but he needed to get in touch because he had been looking after Tsuru's affairs since his abrupt departure from Harvard in 1942.[d] News came in early 1946 when he attended a talk by John Kenneth Galbraith, who had recently been in Japan. Galbraith told Samuelson that Tsuru "had ceased being a pure Marxian and has entered upon a 'New Dealer' phase."[15] However, it was not until September that Samuelson learned Tsuru's address from Leontief and wrote to him, explaining that he had tried to be in touch earlier but this had been difficult because people who visited Japan as part of the occupation administration did not stay in one place very long. He had sent a package of books, but it had been returned after spending several months in the western Pacific. Samuelson told the Tsurus of the birth of their daughter, Jane, noting that, "Needless to say we are fond and doting parents."[16] He reported on those of their friends who had children, on one divorce, and on developments in Harvard.

> Life in Cambridge goes on pretty much the same as always. Harvard now has 300 graduate students and all the courses are very crowded. Haberler, Burbank, Taylor, Chamberlin and all the other professors continue as usual. E. B. Wilson has been retired and Schumpeter, Usher and Black are only a couple of years away from the retirement age.[17]

Samuelson also explained how the war had affected research in economics.

> During the war there was a considerable diminution in economic research except as it referred to war finance and current problems. Consequently most progress was made in the field of Keynesian economics and fiscal policy. Pretty much everybody who was in active service feels the need to reconvert and catch up. However salaries in the government are so much better than at universities and the cost of living is up so much that many economists have decided not to return to academic life. (Robert Triffin by the way has gone to work for the Internation[al] Monetary Fund in Washington. He is really a Latin American expert these days. They now have two little boys.)[18]

Samuelson explained that in 1942, they had tried to collect the money owed to Tsuru, but had been unable to do so. He would try again, for he knew that Tsuru was still owed the money by Harvard and the Coop, and most important, was due a tax refund. Samuelson also told him that he would find "the old janitor on Martin St" to see whether the books were still there. He

---

d. See chapter 16 this volume.

promised to send Tsuru his copies of Kalecki, Ohlin, and Pigou along with books their friends had recently written and a few reprints of his own articles. He had recovered Tsuru's camera from the U.S. Marshall's office in Boston, and was intending to take some pictures of Jane with it. Fearing that it was too delicate to post, he asked for advice on how he might send it. He closed by saying that he and Marion often wondered how Shigeto and Masako were getting on, having heard indirectly that Shigeto was writing a book on the United States, and offering to send food: "we shall be making inquiries to see whether we are permitted to send coffee or anything else without a written request."

However, this letter did not reach Tsuru and was returned to Samuelson. Contact was made only six months later, when Paul and Marion received a letter from Shigeto written in March 1947. Tsuru reported that he had heard much about Samuelson from economists who came to Japan. He picked out Jerome Cornfield, who had described Samuelson's article on Keynes in *Econometrica* as "a masterpiece," motivating him to write to ask for a copy. He described the shortage of economic literature in Japan.

> Generally we still suffer from the literary isolation (excepting, of course, the ubiquitous presence of the *Time* and the *Reader's Digest*), especially of the kind I am keenly interested in, namely the academic economic literature. Anything along this line you could get hold of will be infinitely appreciated if you could send them to me. Lange sent me his recent book on Price Flexibility and Mosak his. And I am wondering whatever happened to your own book which I thought you were on the verge of bringing out some years ago. I also would like to obtain a copy of Metzler's book if it has come out.[19]

He went on to summarize his own situation:

> In my own case, as you may easily imagine, academic pursuits have been shamefully neglected for the past five years. But somehow I am attracted again to that darkest of dark sciences.

This letter reached Samuelson quickly and he immediately replied, on March 11, sending a copy of the letter he had sent a few months before and reiterating his offer to send "coffee, food, books, or whatever else you might enjoy most."[20] A few weeks later he took the precaution of sending another letter and saying that if Tsuru could send an official power of attorney, he would try to reclaim the money owed him.[21] In June he reported that Tsuru's notes had been found in Leontief's office, and that they had been mailed to him and that the Leontiefs had sent a parcel of food, but that he had had little success in recovering other books. Haberler had given most of Tsuru's books to the Widener Library.[22] Paul gave the news that Marion was expecting a second child within a few weeks and he sent a photograph of Jane.

Tsuru wrote in September to thank Samuelson for the parcels of books and reprints he had received. The main reason for the delay was his entry into government service as executive chairman of the Program Committee of the Economic Stabilization Board. "This job," he wrote, "has kept me busy as never before; often I had to sit up three nights in a row with conferences and the translation of documents. Although the goal of stabilization is far from being achieved, routine works of day to day have become somewhat less intense; and I am beginning to find time to catch up on personal affairs."[23] Stabilization of the Japanese economy meant finding a way to reduce inflation, which in 1946–47 was running at over 100 percent per annum.[24]

Reconnecting with Tsuru was to prove important for Samuelson. He and Marion were, personally, very close to Shigeto and Masako, keeping in regular contact and visiting Japan frequently. Tsuru was eventually to translate Samuelson's textbook into Japanese and, crucially, provide a link with Japanese economics that was to be important for both his academic publications and his journalism.

The Lure of Chicago

At the beginning of 1946, when Samuelson was working on his textbook, the University of Chicago made moves to recruit him.[25] One of Samuelson's supporters at Chicago was Jacob Marschak, at the Cowles Commission, who had encouraged the university's chancellor, Robert Hutchins, to recruit both him and Milton Friedman. If Chicago could get them both, it would have a formidable team, leaving Harvard, Oxford, and Stockholm far behind.[26] They would complement each other, with regard to both their academic temperament and their politics. However, if a choice had to be made between them, Marschak favored Samuelson, whom he considered a genius, an opinion shared by Alvin Hansen. Samuelson had published a lot, in contrast to Friedman, who had published "little of note, presumably because of the deadening atmosphere of crass empiricism at the National Bureau in which he has spent his last 10 years; and because he indulges in destruction more than construction."[27] While Friedman's contributions to statistics and quality control were interesting, as regards economics, he had become "a collector of economic tit-bits." In contrast, Samuelson was a "system builder."

Samuelson has shown that all assumptions of rational economics—in whatever fields—can be reduced to that of stability. He applies powerful tools to test stability empirically. He thus revolutionized both "micro-economics" (theory of the firm and the household and of relative prices) and "macroeconomics" (theory of the economy as a whole), far transcending Hicks as offering a key to questions in all fields of economics.

He then explained to Hutchins why he was having difficulty in getting the department to support Samuelson. "Since macroeconomics—which is, after all, the foundation of all economic policy other than that of doing-nothing[—]is considered a Keynesian heresy," he wrote, "I have a difficult stand in the department in defending this candidature." Samuelson was seen by some colleagues as duplicating Lange, but this was no objection. After explaining why it was not a problem to have two people who used similar methods, he wrote,

> If, on the other hand, the opponents of Samuelson mean that he and Lange have similar creeds and that we must work on a well-equilibrated two-party (or two-sect) system, and if such non-scholarly, politician-like view should be at all granted—which I hope it won't—then it is only fair to say that at present the equilibrium is very harshly distorted in the other direction. As long as this distortion was due to the presence of men of the reputation of Knight and Viner, and as long as the economic depression and the war experience did not show the short-comings of the old tradition, this "under-representation" of the new currents was all right. It is not all right any more.[28]

If Marschak's favored option of appointing Samuelson and Friedman were pursued, this would not alter the political balance of the department, though he protested that the problem was the reluctance of most colleagues to take "detached, non-partisan, non-personal action."

Marschak wrote to Samuelson requesting the materials he would need to convince his colleagues, though Samuelson had to explain that as he had only one copy of *Foundations*, he could not send that.[29] On March 20, the department chair, Theodore Schultz, invited Samuelson to visit the department and to talk with Chancellor Hutchins and President Colwell.[30] In the same post was a letter from Marschak, telling Samuelson how he was perceived by certain people at Chicago and what he needed to do on his visit.

> The main difficulty to overcome is to convince people here that 1) you are not a passion-blinded partisan, 2) you are not self-centered,

haughty or rude. I believe that at least some of the people here, both in the department and in the administration are fully aware of your importance as one of the very few living system-builders in economics. While this can be easily proved by showing your published work, there remains the difficulty which I just mentioned. It will be up to you to dispel any prejudices of a personal kind. These seem to go back to your days as a young student. Everyone would get more "mellow" after such passage of time; but few people here met you since those childhood days.[31]

In reply, Samuelson explained his attitude to his student days by quoting Wordsworth's "Blessed was it in that dawn to be alive, / But to be young was very heaven!" and observing that in those days "Giants walked the earth."[32] However, though Stigler, Friedman, and Allen Wallis had been his idols in those days, he now found himself trying to convert his idols. This was prelude to a statement of his political philosophy.

> As far as ends are concerned … I haven't changed much during the years. … I have still a bias in the direction of "individual freedom." But more or less unwillingly, I have had to revise my notions concerning the interest-elasticity of motivated private investment, concerning the finality of James Mill's views on effective demand, and on a number of other technical matters.
>
> On the strategic policy level, I have therefore had to change my judgments somewhat. And so here I stand today, possessed of a few fiscal notions which the Chamber of Commerce might consider suspicious and which the C.I.O. would consider reactionary.[33]

In the possibly misguided hope that these statements of political philosophy would reassure him that Samuelson was no "passion-blinded partisan," Marschak forwarded Samuelson's letter to Hutchins to inform him about his personality and attitude.[34] Arrangements were made for Samuelson to visit Chicago during April 18–20.[35]

Immediately after returning to Cambridge, Samuelson wrote to Schultz thanking him for a pleasant visit and implicitly signaling his interest in receiving an offer.[36] He thanked Marschak for making the visit possible, saying that his only regret was the lack of opportunity for scientific discussions, aside from an exciting conversation with Tjalling Koopmans, who had told him about some things the Cowles Commission was doing. Conscious, to a degree that he had not been before the visit, of the extent to which the invitation had been the result of Marschak's activity, he explained that it would be hard to pull himself away from Cambridge.

> Naturally, even the contingent prospects of working with such a large and strong department of Economics is an exciting one. The only hesitation which I have arises from a natural reluctance to tear my roots from the Cambridge community, where opportunities with respect to research stimulus and teaching load, and total financial income have been so attractive. Indeed, the only circumstances under which I could, with conscience, consider leaving my present post—assuming that I would be honored by a call from Chicago—would be if I were convinced that the Chicago department, would in the years to come become preëminent as a world center for Economic study, and that I could make a harmonious and important contribution to that development.[37]

The reference to harmony within the department, and to not wanting to put Marschak in an "uncomfortable position" by agitating for his appointment, makes it clear that he understood the tensions within the department.

However, no offer was forthcoming and there was not even any acknowledgment of his claim for travel expenses, until he wrote Schultz on June 6 to inquire whether his earlier letter had gone astray. Schultz apologized for the delay, explaining that he had wanted to wait until he could report a definite decision.[38] Given that the department dispersed during the summer, there was unlikely to be anything decided before the fall. In the midst of this process, Henry Simons, one of Samuelson's teachers and the most prominent monetary economist in the Chicago department, died unexpectedly at the age of forty-six. On hearing the news, Samuelson wrote to Schultz to express his sympathy and his admiration for Simons. He suggested that Simons be commemorated by publishing several of his articles as a book.[39] By then, however, Schultz was in India and would not be back until the end of July.[40]

When the Chicago department reassembled after the summer, there were further discussions of Samuelson, and on November 11, 1946, the decision was made to offer Samuelson a position as associate professor, starting October 1, 1947, at a salary of $7,500.[41] Faced with the need to make a decision in his role as president, Colwell wrote to Hutchins asking about the opinion he had formed at the interview he had had with Samuelson.[42] Hutchins had clearly formed a bad impression of Samuelson, for he sent a telegram to Colwell saying, "Samuelson is a vicious character with a high intelligence quotient. They say he will be the Viner of the future but I don't like Viner."[43] (Viner was not only considered an outstanding economic theorist; he was also thought vicious.)

In mid-November, Schultz made a trip to the East Coast, in the course of which he met Samuelson and explained Chicago's "long term interest in having you come to the University of Chicago as a colleague."[44] He laid before Samuelson the opportunities that would be created for him at Chicago, and discussed possible other recruits, including Samuelson's Harvard friend Lloyd Metzler, whom Schultz had just invited for a second visit to Chicago. Koopmans, in consultation with Marschak, tried to persuade Samuelson by explaining why Chicago needed him and what it had to offer.

> Chicago needs you because its present teaching does not pay sufficient attention to the problems of full employment, and more generally to the problems of relationships involving economic aggregates, which are especially your field of interest, and to which you have contributed so much.[45]

However, the main reason for needing Samuelson was that his work would fit with what was going on at the Cowles Commission.

> Chicago also needs you because the sharper mathematical formulation of economic theory which in your research interest has a complement in the sharper formulation of statistical procedures, and their adaptation to the economic application, in which particularly the Cowles Commission is engaged. I believe that the 2-hour conversation we had when you were here demonstrated a unity of purpose as well as a complementarity of efforts which makes me hope strongly that you will come to Chicago.[e]

Koopmans gave samples of the work he was referring to and then explained in more detail why Samuelson was needed. They had made progress in their work on statistics, and this was causing them to make increased demands on economic theory.

> Both in the research activity of the C.C., and in the teaching in the Department, there is at present a risk of hypertrophy of statistics. Because, of all economic theorists, you will be most sympathetic to our re-adaptation of statistical methods to meet[46] economic problems,

---

e. This was the discussion Samuelson had described as "exciting" in his earlier letter to Marschak.

and to our urging the theorists to develop their results in such a way as to give a real foothold for econometric measurement of relationships.

Samuelson was the economic theorist most likely to engage with the statistical work they were doing, thereby rebalancing the activities of Chicago economists toward economic theory.

Against the enthusiasm of Marschak and Koopmans for Samuelson, there was strong opposition that now included Friedman, who had joined the department on September 1. On November 27, he wrote to George Stigler, blaming Paul Douglas for the decision to make Samuelson an offer.

> The Samuelson matter was again forced to a head—by Douglas—& thanks mainly to his efforts we lost badly. The dept has voted to make Samuelson an offer. We don't know the end of the story. But whatever it is, I am very much afraid that it means we're lost. The Keynesians have the votes & the means to use them. Knight is bitter & says he will withdraw from active participation in the dept. [Lloyd] Mints, Gregg [Lewis], & I are very low about it.[47]

This letter makes it very clear that it was Samuelson's alleged Keynesianism that upset those who were opposed to his appointment, and also that had Samuelson accepted the offer, he would have joined a very divided department in which feelings were running high between factions. Friedman may also have thought that Samuelson's appointment would reduce Stigler's chance of an offer, for Stigler was doing the rounds of top universities, hoping to find a position.[48,f]

By January, Schultz had heard nothing so he wrote to Samuelson, asking him to set aside time to talk at the AEA meeting in Atlantic City later that month.[49] This elicited a letter from Samuelson, explaining in detail why he had decided not to accept the invitation. He accepted that Chicago had a much better economics department and that the intellectual stimulation he would receive from Knight and Marschak would be second to none. However, MIT was an ideal environment. It was sufficiently close to Harvard for his relationships there to be "symbiotic without, I trust, becoming parasitic."[50] Time, money and facilities for research were "virtually unlimited," and because the graduate program was so small, he was able to enjoy teaching a wide variety of courses. The final aspect of MIT, which would no doubt be in stark contrast to what he would find in Chicago, was that "there is an

---

f. Later that year, Stigler moved to Columbia.

atmosphere here of serenity and congeniality which is very enjoyable and very conducive to scholarly productiveness and balance." He might have mentioned the strong support he was getting from President Compton when members of the MIT Corporation were attacking his textbook as being insufficiently supportive of free markets.

Samuelson's final reason was that being on the East Coast enabled him to engage in a greater variety of activities than if he were in Chicago, where his professional activities would be confined to the university.

> I also have the feeling—perhaps I am wrong in this—that being upon the Eastern seaboard and not being limited by the University of Chicago form of professional contract, I shall find myself actively participating in more worthwhile outside consulting activities; activities, which have, to a potentially "narrow" theoretical economist, a value far beyond their pecuniary return; but which might gradually die out were it not for the pecuniary element to the transaction.[51]

He then partially retracted this, saying that it was a minor point and that the terms of the offer meant that he needed to pay little attention to the financial aspect of the decision.[g] However, he added that he and Marion had settled in Cambridge and were reluctant to leave.

Despite this comprehensive case for not accepting Chicago's offer, Schultz kept up the pressure on Samuelson, talking with him at the AEA and then writing to him with details of the housing situation in Chicago, including details of five houses and apartments, with analyses of what they would cost to purchase and to run. It appears that in his discussions with Schultz he had stressed the personal ties that kept him in Cambridge, for almost immediately after the meeting Paul Douglas wrote Samuelson, trying to reassure him that he would get a very warm welcome in Chicago. He described the stimulation he had received from having Samuelson, Jacob Mosak, and Gregg Lewis in his classes, but said that he was not just regarded as a former student of whom they were proud: he would come as an "honored colleague with whom it would be a pleasure and honor to be associated." Though discussion in the department was sometimes "sharp and intense," and occasionally on a personal level, Douglas wrote that he had "never known any real department politics to be played."[52] Roy Blough, whom Samuelson knew through consultancy at the U.S.

---

g. Chicago offered a contract that involved the university's receiving a professor's outside earnings. Given this, his remark indicates either that he had no idea of the royalties that his textbook would generate or he was being disingenuous.

Treasury just before he moved to Chicago, wrote to say he was distressed at Samuelson's decision, asking him to reconsider.[53,h] He reassured Samuelson about the neighborhood, saying that though he had anxieties about coming to Chicago, he and his wife had settled down well, liking the "informal society" better than other places they had lived. He praised what Schultz was doing for the department, reassuring him that there was complete independence about what everyone did.

Recognizing Samuelson's reluctance to move, Schultz switched to offering him a one-year visiting professorship, discussing it with Samuelson on the telephone on February 27. Samuelson then talked to Ralph Freeman, their dean, and Marion before writing to Schultz, the next day, to decline this offer, too. A year's leave would come at the worst possible time for MIT, given the influx of returning veterans, and he and Marion had decided that, with two babies, one only a few weeks old, it was the wrong time to be considering a temporary move.[54] On the same day he also wrote Douglas, expressing his appreciation for what he had written, and saying how much he had enjoyed his classes.[55] His main reason for staying, he explained, was that he found his current environment "extremely pleasant and stimulating," and given that few people are really content in their jobs, it seemed silly to tempt fate by moving.

Samuelson made it very clear to Douglas that ideological differences with other Chicago economists had not played any role in his decision.

> Neither on the conscious (nor, I believe, subconscious) level did the factor of my possible differences in policy viewpoints from, say Professor Knight, on such problems as the validity of the Savings-Investment analysis of unemployment, play a role in my decision. As you know, I have never been a shrinking violet. Moreover, it is only on the level of means rather than ends that I have to some degree altered my opinion in the last 10 years. And even on this level, our differences are not to be exaggerated. A little cross-breeding between Keynes and James Mill may produce something more viable than either.[56]

Three days later, Samuelson received a letter from Killian saying that he had been promoted to full professor, with a salary of $7,500, with effect from July 1.[i]

---

h. This activity has not been discussed, because it had only just begun in the period covered by this book. It was an activity with which he would continue in the 1950s.

i. There is no indication that this was a response to the Chicago offer; it could well have been set in motion some time before.

Schultz, however, was still not deterred and continued to put pressure on Samuelson. On March 4, he told him about three new positions they were going to fill, asking for advice on whom they might appoint, thereby making Chicago more attractive.[57] This caused Samuelson to change his mind, and he telephoned Schultz to accept the offer of a permanent position. On March 7 (Friday), Douglas wrote to say how delighted he was at this decision.[58] Samuelson's explanation for this change of heart was that after refusing Chicago's offer, he had regretted doing so.[59] However, it was evident to Marion and to his colleagues that he was uneasy with his decision, so they urged him to get away for a quiet weekend during which he could think it through.

The outcome was that on Tuesday, March 11, he wrote to Schultz saying that he had decided to remain at MIT, for the same "intangible non-professional" reasons he had given when he turned down the job before. He apologized profusely for the trouble and confusion he had caused, saying that he had "cut rather a sorry figure in this whole affair." He was clearly acutely embarrassed. Shortly afterward, he and Marion purchased a new house in suburban Belmont, suitable for their growing family; it was a sign that they had decided to stay in Cambridge for good.

Though Samuelson's reluctance to move was clearly the main reason for staying put, it cannot have hurt that on Monday Killian had written saying that, as evidence of MIT's desire to support his work, they had approved an increase in his salary to $8,500, and that they would offer him a term's leave of absence with full salary so that he could make that trip to Europe that he had been wanting. A month later, Killian wrote again to say that his salary from July 1 would be raised to $9,000.

Chicago was not the only other university interested in Samuelson. Early the following year, when Rupert Maclaurin heard rumors that Harvard had three vacancies and that they would be interested in recruiting Samuelson and another colleague, Richard Bissell, he felt sufficiently confident to write to Compton, "as far as I can observe from quite intimate association both Professors Samuelson and Bissell are happy here now and that only a major effort would persuade either of them to leave. I also believe that this is known at Harvard."[60]

And Schultz did not give up, continuing to harbor the hope that Samuelson might change his mind again. In November 1947, he wrote to Samuelson asking whether they might meet when he was in Washington or New York to "discuss afresh our genuine desire to have you become a colleague and a member of our faculty."[61] Samuelson was unable to meet Schultz in New York or Washington, but by then he had changed his mind on going to the AEA. He explained to Schultz that his whole family would be spending the Christmas holidays in Wisconsin, and they might get together if he were able to get to the AEA for a couple of days.[62] Not knowing that Samuelson had turned down Chicago and that he could have moved to Harvard had he wished, chairmen of other departments sounded him out, incorrectly assuming that any economist at MIT would wish to move if the opportunity were to arise. In every case, his response was that he had no intention of leaving. Samuelson was now in a position where he could have moved to almost any economics department that had a vacancy, but he was firmly committed to MIT.[j]

The Clark Medal, November–December 1947

A week later, Samuelson received a very different letter from Douglas. Writing in his capacity as president of the American Economic Association, the letter was to tell Samuelson that he had been awarded the inaugural John Bates Clark Medal, as "the younger economist who has made the most distinguished contribution to the main body of economic thought and knowledge."[63] Douglas impressed on Samuelson the need for him to attend the presentation at the AEA dinner at the Knickerbocker Hotel in Chicago that December. Samuelson immediately responded, saying "Atomic bombs could not keep me from attending the dinner on the 28th" and that he would keep silent about it until then.[64]

Given that it was the first time the medal had been awarded, and that any economist under the age of forty was eligible, it was remarkable that it was awarded to a thirty-two-year-old, for there were many strong candidates and Samuelson would have remained eligible for several years to come. His nomination was based purely on his articles; by the time voting took place, the committee knew that *Foundations* would soon be published, though they had not seen it or known the how economists would react to it.[k]

---

j. Machlup had tried to recruit him to Johns Hopkins, even though he knew he had turned down Chicago. Though he surmised that Samuelson would get a call from Harvard, he thought he might be impatient, and assured him that Johns Hopkins could be built up into a first-rate department, thereby implying that MIT could not (F. Machlup, December 2, 1947, Letter to Paul A. Samuelson, PASP 51 [Machlup]).

k. The other candidates were Kenneth Boulding and George Stigler (on the final ballot), with Albert Hart and John Dunlop having been in the final five. Unlike more recent medals, no specific reason for the award was cited, voting being on the basis of a list of publications and positions held.

Ralph Freeman was not able to attend the dinner, but several MIT faculty members did. One of them, Erwin Schell, from the Department of Business Administration, wrote to him about the occasion, copying his letter to all members of the two departments, quoting Douglas's remarks in full.

It is now my happy privilege to confer the John Bates Clark Medal upon a brilliant young economist, who, master at an early age of both mathematics and economic theory, has made extraordinarily penetrating contributions to the theory of employment, production, distribution, and value, and whose recent book [*Foundations*] stamps him as one of the masters of our craft. With an amazing production record behind him, he faces the future with the promise of even greater achievements before him. In the name, therefore, of the American Economic Association, I now confer the John Bates Clark Medal upon Mr. Paul A. Samuelson of the Massachusetts Institute of Technology, the university which Francis A. Walker [MIT economist and first President of the AEA] loved and which he did so much to promote.

I feel that from somewhere in Valhalla, the mighty figure of Francis A. Walker is beaming with happiness.[65]

Given such remarks, it is not surprising that Samuelson afterward wrote to Douglas to thank him for the "warm and gracious way in which he personally awarded the Clark medal," saying that it was "an occasion that I shall long remember and cherish."[66]

Though Samuelson promised to keep silent, a copy of the letter telling him about the award had reached Killian. So on December 15, two weeks before the public awarding of the medal, when sending Beadle the list of supplementary readings for Ec. 12, Killian forwarded a copy of the letter to him, quoting to him the criteria according to which the award was made. Noting that the AEA's other major award was named after a former president of MIT, he was leaving Beadle in no doubt that Samuelson's activities were in no way undermining the reputation of MIT. To the contrary, he wanted Beadle to know that the growing reputation of MIT's economics department was closely connected with that of Samuelson, who had now made the decision to stay for good.

CHAPTER 29 | The Young Samuelson

Samuelson and the Modern Economics

This book has told the story of how a student who specialized in mathematical economics to an extent that some of his teachers thought him unemployable achieved, in less than a decade, a position from which he could dominate the discipline. During that period, marked by the Second World War, Samuelson transformed himself from a narrow specialist to a general economist, as proficient in analyzing data as he was in manipulating equations. However, it was not just Samuelson that had changed; he could become such a dominant figure only because economics had become very different from what it had been a decade earlier.

An age in which American economics was dominated by figures such as Frank Knight, Jacob Viner, Warren Persons, Wesley Mitchell, Edward Chamberlin, Joseph Schumpeter, and Alvin Hansen gave way to one of which younger, more technical, mathematically proficient economists such as Tjalling Koopmans, Jacob Marshak, Milton Friedman, Kenneth Arrow, Trygve Haavelmo, Lawrence Klein, James Tobin, Robert Solow, and, above all, Samuelson himself were representative figures. Samuelson's career could prosper because the profession became more open to mathematical economics, his own work making a significant contribution to that transformation. That process was not completed by 1948—far from it, for nonmathematical economists, including Viner, Chamberlin, and Hansen, remained important right up to the 1960s—but by then the trend was firmly established; mathematical economics was no longer a marginal field.

Samuelson achieved this as an outsider who, with a large element of good fortune, passed through the two leading economics departments of his day. As the son of Jewish parents whose family had left Poland for the Midwest, whose money came from ventures including a drugstore and a restaurant, Samuelson was not part of any establishment that could give him assistance. His talent was recognized and opportunities opened up—notably, the scholarships that took him first to Chicago, then to Harvard, and then into the Society of Fellows. In the course of that journey he encountered many of the leading economists of the period, absorbing the ideas of one teacher after another. Sometimes the ideas of one teacher displaced those of another, as when his involvement with Hansen changed his views on economic stabilization. Sometimes, as with Haberler and Wilson, he was able to make connections between what he had learned from different teachers, producing something different from what either had taught him.

One of the main claims of this book is that this experience makes Samuelson a transitional figure. There is no doubt that he became a thoroughly modern economist, whose work could look fresh even to students coming to it in the 1970s, and who continued to produce innovative work for many years after 1948 (such as the theory of public goods, the consumption-loan model, efficient markets theory, growth theory, and the theory of capital). However, his work retained traces of the way economics was done by his teachers. Skepticism about applicability of the mathematical theories he was developing pervaded the articles he wrote as a student, and some of this skepticism survived in his bestselling textbook. Modern, more technical economics did not come from nowhere to displace the older way of doing economics: it evolved out of it. This is obviously true of mathematical theories of the consumer and the firm, where Samuelson refined ideas that had been in circulation for the entire twentieth century. But it was also true of "Keynesian" economics, where Samuelson's response to Keynes was rooted in the work of Hansen and interwar American business cycle theory. The story of how Samuelson drew on the work of his teachers to write two books—one that was modern in the prominence it gave to mathematics, the other modern in its style and its presentation of the new theories of income determination—can be seen as the story of how modern economics emerged from the older approaches to the subject.[a]

---

a. Though I have chosen not to use this terminology, the transition can be characterized as involving a move from pluralism to neoclassical economics (see Morgan and Rutherford 1998). Using this terminology, the argument is that Samuelson, though very much a

Chicago to MIT

Samuelson could reflect fondly on his childhood. He recalled the drugstore in which his father taught him how to do arithmetic, an experience that was clearly important to him. His mother was a more distant figure, perhaps because given the conventions of the day, according to which she would have been the prime caregiver, he blamed her for being sent off to the farm for long spells. This was something he never understood; was she pursuing a career before it became normal for woman to do so? Or, were there other reasons such as family illness that forced her into this? He stressed repeatedly that he was well looked after and loved by his quasi-foster caregivers, and when writing his putative autobiography he could adopt the conventional attitude of saying that this was something about which be bore no resentment.[1] But family and friends testified otherwise—that this was not only something he resented, increasingly, as he grew older but also something that nagged him because he did not understand why it had happened. His two brothers, Harold and Robert, on the farm at different ages, were much less affected.

When Paul grew close to Marion, her hometown of Berlin, Wisconsin, became another home, at least during the vacations. He still visited his parents in Chicago, but this was out of duty. At some point after his father's death in August 1939, his mother moved to San Francisco, and in 1950 she remarried; a year later, he had still not met her new husband, despite having made trips westward. Harold and Robert lived close by and looked after their mother.

Despite being a commuter, Samuelson became immersed in the University of Chicago when he arrived in January 1932, describing his arrival there as a second birth. It is hard to resist reading this as implying a commitment to a new home that went beyond the purely intellectual stimulation of the Malthusian theory of population growth he encountered in the first lecture he attended. He became close to his teachers, including ones whose courses he did not take for credit. Though he grossly understated the theoretical sophistication of Chicago monetary theory to the point of distortion, there seems little reason to doubt that his politics became conservative—not surprising in a young student (only sixteen on his arrival) who fell under the spell of Frank Knight, and whose closest friends included Aaron Director and George Stigler. He described himself as having been "besotted" with Knight

---

neoclassical economist, retained traces of the more pluralist intellectual environment in which he had been trained.

and wrote of Knight as having been his "idol." He was taken by their icono-clasm. Their political views were also shared by Harry Gideonse, another of Samuelson's teachers who was important to him.[b] He was personally close to the more liberal Paul Douglas, but if Douglas's political views tempted him, Samuelson had the example of Director, who moved rapidly away from Douglas into Knight's circle.

Despite talking of a second birth when he arrived in Chicago, his com-mitment to economics did not happen for an additional two years. Hutchins's Chicago required that all students take a broad program covering the natural and social sciences and the humanities. Samuelson had no regrets about this program, even though it meant that specialization was delayed. The first prize he won was not for economics but for an essay on civil government—something that would have been very significant for him, given his interest in a diplomatic career. When he did specialize, it was in the social sciences, and in his junior year his courses included anthropology, sociology, and polit-ical science. His commitment to economics came in the middle of his junior year, seemingly as a result of Director's course on labor problems, an essay written for Director being not just one that he preserved but also one he later included in his publications list.

Many of those who entered economics during the Great Depression (such as James Tobin) were motivated by a desire to do something about the prob-lem of unemployment. However, although Samuelson entered Chicago when the Great Depression was at its worst, and although he did cite this reason at one point, he usually provided a much more self-centered motive—his suit-ability for economics. He claimed he had been born to be an economist. This attitude is entirely consistent with his having being besotted with Knight, ever the skeptic and iconoclast, and with his claim to have absorbed the conservative economics advocated by many of his teachers. However, in his last two years at Chicago, his belief that mathematics was key to economic theory represented a significant departure from Knight's position. He took the important graduate theory course not with Knight, but with Jacob Viner. His ability to notice and correct Viner's mistakes gained him a reputation in a cohort of graduate students that included many who were to become central to American economics in the 1940s.

Though he may not, at that stage, have thought of himself as a "math-ematical economist," this was the path on which he had embarked, and there

---

b. Gideonse, Knight, Director, and Stigler all attended the initial meeting of the Mont Pelerin Society in 1947.

seems little reason to doubt his claim that he took more mathematics courses than any previous economics major had done. When, at Harvard, he began to espouse operationalism and the idea that meaningful theorems were testable, he was moving away from Knight's position. However, his economics remained detached from any significant political involvement, which came only after he started working with Hansen. When, during the Second World War, Samuelson became identified publicly with a clear political stance, the gulf between his views and Knight's became even greater.

Had he been able to do so, Samuelson would have remained at Chicago, but the terms of the SSRC scholarship that Viner was instrumental in obtaining for him forced him to leave his newfound home. He chose Harvard, though initially without any expectation that he would settle there. At Harvard, he encountered Joseph Schumpeter, perhaps the most eminent economist then working in the United States, with whom he formed a lifelong friendship, and other European émigrés: Gottfried Haberler and Wassily Leontief. From them he obtained a training in economic theory that was more rigorous than he had obtained from Knight or Viner, and which complemented the training in mathematical economics and statistics he got from E. B. Wilson.

The clearest sign of his acceptance into Harvard, temporarily at least, was becoming the first economist to be appointed a junior fellow. He had joined an elite whose reach extended beyond the confines of economics and whose paths would repeatedly cross his own. His contemporaries included historian Arthur Schlesinger Jr., mathematician Stanislaw Ulam, chemists E. Bright Wilson and Bob Woodward, physicist Ivan Getting, and though he had recently ceased to be a junior fellow, philosopher Willard Quine. The freedom and resources given by the Society of Fellows lie behind the stream of articles on which his later reputation was to rest.

Unlike the decision to leave Chicago, leaving Harvard for MIT in October 1940 was a choice Samuelson was not forced to make. He took up an instructorship at Harvard and was assured that it would likely be renewed, but MIT offered him a position with higher status and better salary and conditions. The MIT department, devoted to service teaching for scientists and engineers, was no match for Harvard's, but it was only two miles away and he could remain in touch with his friends and colleagues. He continued to live a stone's throw from Harvard Yard. There was also the question of whether his Jewish ancestry might prove a barrier in the undoubtedly anti-Semitic environment of Harvard. Given the strong support he received from Schumpeter and the esteem in which many other faculty members held him, Samuelson had been able to turn a blind eye to this. He had been accepted into the Society of Fellows and though some, such as Department Chair Harold

Burbank, might be less supportive, Samuelson could attribute their apparent antipathy to political differences, or to doubts about someone cleverer than they were, rather than anti-Semitism. Marion, on the other hand, could see more clearly than Samuelson that Harvard's anti-Semitism would be a problem and that moving to MIT would liberate him from this. She persuaded him to accept the MIT position, and within a month of joining the Harvard faculty he moved down the road.

His colleagues at MIT welcomed him: to have recruited him was, for them, a significant coup, and though he might be no more than an assistant professor, he was well supported. They might be doing service teaching, but it was a close-knit department with a common purpose that strengthened as the war developed. He got on well with Ralph Freeman and Rupert Maclaurin, and was very close to Harold Freeman. Shortly after his arrival, MIT instituted a PhD program in economics, and during the 1940s further appointments were made, including many scholars of Jewish background whom Harvard did not want, that expanded the department. He was rapidly promoted, and when the chance came to return to Chicago, much closer to Wisconsin and his own family, the attractions of MIT had grown too strong.

As with his move to MIT, it was Marion who could see most clearly that he would be happier remaining where he was, with their growing family and a house in the suburbs. Economics at MIT might still be tiny in relation to places such as Chicago or Harvard, and they remained economists in an engineering school, but with the wartime development of enormous research laboratories, of which the Radiation Laboratory was one, postwar MIT had acquired great prestige as one of the preeminent locations of American "big" science. It might take time for economists in other universities to appreciate this—the inquiries he continued to receive about his interest in a position elsewhere clearly reflected the perception that an economist at MIT must be hoping for an opening elsewhere—but for someone committed to the idea that economics was a science, it was a natural place to be.

MIT was near Harvard, which conferred advantages in terms of course availability and research collaboration. But there was also intense competitiveness, with the result that when MIT acquired someone who was clearly better than his counterparts at Harvard (in this period most academics were male), such as Norbert Wiener or Noam Chomsky, that person would be celebrated as a star. By 1948, after the enthusiastic reception of *Foundations of Economic Analysis* and the runaway success of *Economics: An Introductory Analysis*, Samuelson was in such a position. Compton's successor as MIT president, James Killian, came to view him as *the* reason for the success of

MIT's economics department: he was the magnet who pulled other good economists toward MIT. It was a role he was very comfortable with.

Mathematical Economist

Samuelson had made the decision to study a lot of mathematics while in Chicago, and his teachers in mathematical economics at Harvard included Schumpeter, who encouraged the use of mathematics even though he was no mathematician himself, and Leontief. But the person who shaped his conception of mathematical economics was the professor of Vital Statistics and part-time member of the economics department, Edwin Bidwell Wilson. "Operationalism" had been in the air in Chicago, the term being used by Henry Schultz and Paul Douglas, and it was obviously familiar at Harvard, home of its creator, physicist Percy Bridgman. But it was Wilson who guided Samuelson to the mathematical apparatus by which he was to operationalize economic theory. He introduced Samuelson to the work of Willard Gibbs, seeking to instill in him the rigor that Gibbs would have expected. Wilson stood apart from many developments in mathematics during the twentieth century, including some that were to become fashionable in economics, but he nonetheless provided Samuelson with as rigorous a training in mathematical economics as he could have obtained anywhere else.

The central idea Samuelson acquired from Wilson was that seemingly different problems might have a common mathematical structure. The fact that a system involved equilibrium, whether physical, chemical, biological, or economic, might be sufficient for it to exhibit certain properties that could be derived without knowing anything about the field in question. Samuelson extended this insight—his Correspondence Principle—to the idea that one might need to assume the equilibrium was stable. This led Samuelson, guided by Wilson, to focus on linear algebra as the means by which comparative statics results could be derived in systems that might contain many variables, and to work on the theory of difference and differential equations, needed to study dynamics. This focus on linear algebra and on difference/ differential equations set Samuelson's work apart from other important work on mathematical economics in the 1940s, such as *The Theory of Games and Economic Behavior* by John von Neumann and Oskar Morgenstern. Samuelson understood their work, but he remained a skeptic of the usefulness of game theory, and guided by Wilson, chose not to follow their approach to the use of mathematics in economics.

There is an obvious parallel between Samuelson's wartime work on ballistics and Wilson's First World War move into aeronautics. It is not clear when Samuelson started this work, for he claimed to have worked on the problem of fire control before he entered the Radiation Laboratory full time. He taught in the mathematics department, and it is entirely plausible that, in teaching in the mathematics department in wartime, his focus was the mathematics of projectiles, to which calculus and differential equations are directly applicable. He might also have discussed the problem in the seminar run by Norbert Wiener, in which cybernetics was worked out. However, whereas Wilson went on to write a textbook in aeronautics, Samuelson ended his time in the Radiation Laboratory, impatient to return to working full time as an economist.

When he described himself, to Wheeler Loomis, the Radiation Laboratory director, as "a second-rate mathematician," he was no doubt comparing himself with colleagues such as I. I. Rabi, Ivan Getting, and Stanislaw Ulam, realizing that in their company he would never be the star that he could be in economics. He was clearly respected by the scientists and mathematicians with whom he was working, for otherwise Rabi would never have invited him to become the official historian of the Manhattan Project to develop the atomic bomb. His response to Goldsmith's attempts to recruit him as a consultant to the War Production Board show that, instead of choosing to immerse himself completely in science and engineering, he remained fascinated by economic problems. He wanted to be somewhere he could excel.

Given Samuelson's commitment to operationalizing economic theory, it is no surprise that in 1940 he embarked, with Leonid Hurwicz, on an empirical project on the business cycle, focused on data analysis. This highly ambitious project clearly failed to produce the anticipated results, and Samuelson did not follow it up with other, similar projects. He was acquiring a thorough knowledge of mathematical statistics, working alongside Harold Freeman and the new cohort of economics graduate students at MIT, and could have continued a project using the methods being developed by Haavelmo and others at the Cowles Commission, but he did not. He chose not to become an econometrician in the modern sense of the term.

One reason why he remained skeptical of econometric results was E. B. Wilson, whose course had introduced him to mathematical statistics. Wilson had the mathematical expertise to engage in formal statistical or econometric modeling, and yet he is on record as admiring the work of Wesley Clair Mitchell, seeing the need for taxonomic work analogous to that involved in identifying species in biology. Theory had to be combined with close awareness of economic data. This explains why Wilson could work closely with his Harvard colleagues, Crum and Frickey, whose work Samuelson disparaged. Attaching importance to a good understanding of data (how it was constructed and what it meant) was consistent with his view that theory should not be applied unless there were evidence that doing so increased knowledge, and corresponded with his sympathy towards Stephen Leacock's skepticism of complicated mathematical theories.

Samuelson's most systematic engagement with statistics came during wartime. His work at the National Resources Planning Board (NRPB) did not involve complex formal modeling, let alone the estimation of a probability model, as advocated by Haavelmo, but did call for meticulous analysis of consumption patterns and the consequences of changes in the distribution of income. Inference was not involved, just careful data analysis. Data were also at the forefront when Samuelson discussed the multiplier with economists in wartime Washington. He was obviously concerned with theoretical problems—such as what came to be known as the balanced budget multiplier—but data were never far away because to be usable for policy, a number needed to be attached to the multiplier. Samuelson clearly paid as much attention to the appropriate data as to getting theory right.

Coming from this perspective, it should be no surprise that, faced with the exchange between Koopmans and Vining over "measurement without theory," Samuelson would give at least partial support to Vining's defense of empiricism "against the perfectionistic-formalism of the Cowles Commission."[2] Samuelson did not share Wilson's enthusiasm for Mitchell's economics—he regarded the approach taken at the National Bureau of Economic Research as having grown decadent in the thirty years from Mitchell's first book on the business cycle to his last (with Arthur Burns). Samuelson could never have written, as Wilson had done in 1938, that he endorsed everything Mitchell had done. However, Samuelson's pragmatic use of different methods of data analysis, maintaining a distance between theorizing and data analysis, but undertaking theory while being immersed in facts, closely reflected Wilson's position.

The New Economics

Samuelson was, through and through, a mathematical economist, forever turning his mind to developing new theorems; and throughout the 1940s, he published in addition to his two books a stream of articles on mathematical economics and applied mathematics. For reasons given in the previous section, this work was largely shaped by ideas he learned from Wilson. But beginning in 1937, he began to fall under the spell of Alvin Hansen, the new Littauer Professor of Public Policy, who pulled him in other directions. Hansen was no mathematician, which meant that Samuelson could demonstrate his value to him by working out a model of the business cycle that Hansen could formulate but not analyze. The multiplier–accelerator model, developed by Samuelson as a theoretical exercise, was Hansen's model. However, Samuelson's relationship with Hansen was to involve much more than being the mathematician who solved the technical problems Hansen could not solve. He was drawn into the Fiscal Policy Seminar and at the 1938 American Economic Association meeting, he provided a verbal analysis of alternative forms of fiscal stimulus, very much in the vein of Hansen.

Hansen was instrumental in bringing Samuelson to Washington during the war, where at the NRPB he became involved in tackling the problem of what would happen when the war ended. Through Hansen, and regular meetings at the Fed, he developed a wide circle of contacts, augmenting those he already had through Harvard and Chicago. He threw himself into not only his empirical work at the NRPB but also debates over the multiplier and public finance—the main issues facing economists in wartime—with friends and contacts at other agencies. He developed expertise as an applied economist, his contacts being as likely to approach him with a problem relating to the meaning of data as to solve a theoretical problem they could not solve.

Samuelson claimed that for a while he resisted the lure of Keynes's *General Theory*. Starting in 1939, he began to take up the concept of the multiplier and the idea that the level of aggregate demand determined the level of employment. However, like Hansen, for most of the 1940s he continued to distance himself from Keynes. The two of them accepted the multiplier as a useful, if not invaluable, theoretical tool, but they used it within the intellectual framework, rooted in earlier continental European and American business cycle theory, developed by Hansen. Samuelson's version of "the new economics" or "the modern theory of income determination" became a distinctively American form of Keynesianism, emphasizing the role of innovation and technological change in determining the level of investment.

While working with Hansen, Samuelson was revising his doctoral thesis for publication. In *Foundations of Economic Analysis*, his analysis of income determination remained separate from his new theory of the consumer because, contrary to the common view in economics today, he did not believe that economy-wide relationships could be grounded in optimizing behavior. Instead, his analysis of the economy as a whole was based on relationships that were determined empirically—the consumption function and the acceleration principle. He provided an account of dynamic modeling that drew on theorems about the stability of systems of differential and difference equations, and was never integrated with his theories of how consumers and companies behaved.

Though the unit to which Samuelson was a consultant had a narrower remit, the NRPB at this time was the source of radical proposals that would have transformed American society. This fed into his unit's forecasts of postwar consumption, based on the assumption that poverty would be eliminated and the distribution of income would be made more equal. But it also implied a strong political stance, for these proposals were anathema to conservatives already incensed about Roosevelt's New Deal. Samuelson sided strongly with Hansen, the first time a clear political position was evident in his professional work; it is as if Hansen not only persuaded him to work on applied macroeconomic problems but also brought him round to taking a political position. His association with Hansen would have been clear from the pamphlets he was writing at the NRPB, but it became even more explicit when he started producing articles supportive of Hansen's internationalist political positions in *The New Republic*. In these, unlike in his previous work, he developed a strong political voice—and a taste for journalism that never left him.

Samuelson also took a strong political stance in relation to the problem of postwar science policy, an issue in which he had become interested while working in the Radiation Laboratory. When he feared that the Wilson Committee was not going to be sufficiently bold in its recommendations, he tried to persuade both a contact in the National Planning Association and the editor of *The New Republic* to take action. In early 1945, he had the opportunity to try to shape the views of the Bowman Committee, helping write one of the reports on which Vannevar Bush's *Science: Endless Frontier* was to be based. Even with the support of that year's Nobel Prize winner, I. I. Rabi, he could not win out over conservatives opposed to planning; but right to the final report, he and his friend Henry Guerlac were trying to get as good an outcome as they could. Samuelson had become a supporter of planned science, such as took place in MIT's large research laboratories, to one of which he and Guerlac were then attached.

Samuelson's support for Hansen hardly took him out of the political mainstream, but going even this far implied a break with the anti-interventionist and anti-Keynesian stance of his Chicago teachers, Director and Knight, and drew him closer to Paul Douglas, whose views on policy he must have rejected while at Chicago, however much he appreciated his introduction to economic theory. Traces of their teaching can still be found in his work, however. In his textbook, Samuelson framed his conception of the economic process in terms taken from Knight, and he drew upon what Knight had called the "Wheel of Wealth" for one of the key visual aids in his textbook.

It is impossible not to see a connection between Samuelson's lifelong interest in the theory of capital and the debates in which Knight and Schumpeter had engaged. Most strikingly, the stance Samuelson took toward ethics—that welfare economics must of necessity embrace ethics, for without ethical judgments there is no basis for reaching any conclusions about welfare—was one of Knight's main themes and the subject of numerous articles. Samuelson came to reject much of what Knight wrote—in 1950, Knight even complained to a mutual friend that Samuelson never missed a chance to get slurs against him into print.[3] Samuelson later denounced Chicago monetary economics as living in pre-Keynesian darkness, far darker than the most cursory glance at what Chicago economists were saying would indicate. However, for all his vociferous and highly public denunciation of his former teachers, in important respects—Samuelson's focus on capital theory and his approach to welfare economics were to become very important—his outspoken criticism conceals the fact that he had learned things from Knight that he never abandoned.

The Two Books

There is a seeming paradox in Samuelson's having produced two very different books within a short space of time: *Foundations of Economic Analysis*, the technical work on economic theory, and *Economics: An Introductory Analysis*, a textbook so elementary that at times he wrote of being embarrassed by it. Despite their close publication dates, these books reflected ideas and skills that he had learned at two different times. *Foundations* bore the mark of Wilson's rigorous approach to economic theory and the types of mathematics to which he directed Samuelson, notably the theory of linear equations and of difference and differential equations. In complete contrast, *Economics* bore the imprint of economic theory and quantitative and pedagogic skills learned through working with Hansen and through his engagement with wartime government agencies. The senior administrators for whom Raymond Goldsmith wanted Samuelson to write a simple account of the theory of the multiplier might, on average, be more intelligent and more informed than a typical undergraduate student taking economics for the first time, but they would be equally intolerant of writing that was not clear. Wartime had given him the expertise he needed to write the textbook he would probably have been unable to write in 1940.

Yet, he did not reject Wilson in favor of Hansen, even if he did end up espousing policy positions that Wilson, who favored "sound" finance, could not support (perhaps Samuelson's distancing himself from Keynes for over a decade was in part influenced by Wilson). The heart of *Foundations* may have been written by 1940, but turning it into a book took place while he was working on wartime problems. As is the case with Adam Smith's two great books, *The Theory of Moral Sentiments* and *An Inquiry into the Nature and Causes of the Wealth of Nations,* we have to presume that he considered *Foundations* and *Economics* complementary.[4,c] The reconciliation involves not just the gap between micro and macro that Samuelson postulated in *Foundations,* but a skepticism toward direct application of abstract theory that he had learned from Wilson and that Hansen exemplified: Hansen was the nontechnical economist who needed to be taught the implications of his own theory, but who nonetheless reached judgments on economic policy that Samuelson respected and took very seriously.

Samuelson was clearly not an "institutionalist" economist in the sense in which that term was used in the 1920s and 1930s—he was too much infected with mathematical economics and with Keynesian ideas for that—but some of his work, aided and abetted by both Wilson and Hansen, had institutionalist features. In reviewing *Foundations,* Samuelson's friend Lloyd Metzler commented that Samuelson was cynical about the modern theory of the consumer that he had helped to rewrite.[5] It is hardly surprising, therefore, that when he wrote about real-world companies and markets in his textbook, he offered a perspective that was informed by the empirical work undertaken during the New Deal, on which his wartime work at the NRPB had drawn so heavily. Samuelson represents a strand in American Keynesianism that was different from the "monetary Walrasianism" that sought to integrate the theory of income determination with optimizing models of consumers and businesses.

In the period covered by this volume, it is appropriate to speak of Samuelson being close to one or two in a series of mentors, the most important among whom were Knight, Wilson, and Hansen. However, though he followed their ideas closely—perhaps more closely than one might immediately realize—he was learning rapidly to take positions independent of

---

c. The significance of this comparison is that there has long been debate about the relationship between these two books, which appear, superficially, to be based on contradictory assumptions about human nature.

theirs. As he never tired of saying, he was full of self-confidence, so when an idea came to him, he would follow it up, engaging in discussions with people other than his mentors. Interested in population dynamics, one of Wilson's concerns, he entered into extended discussions with Lotka, branching out in new directions. Though it was Wilson who taught him mathematical statistics, he engaged with many statisticians and econometricians whom his graduate students, with his support, brought to MIT in the early 1940s. Hansen provided him with the entrance into wartime Washington, an opportunity Samuelson pursued vigorously, discussing fiscal policy with the main economists responsible for applying Keynesian ideas in government.

As an undergraduate at Chicago, Samuelson had made friends with several of the graduate students, and when these were added to his friends from Harvard, Samuelson's address book contained a high proportion of the best economists of his generation. With the opportunities provided by war, when economists were in great demand in government, and then by the postwar boom in universities resulting from the GI Bill and its commitment to subsidizing the education of returning veterans, this generation could progress rapidly; Samuelson was at its center, knowing virtually everyone and respected by many. Samuelson never tired of celebrating the achievements of his friends, notably the cohort of graduate students who, he claimed, did as much as their teachers to create Harvard's golden age. He was generous to a fault in crediting his friends with ideas, minimizing his own role. His friends valued his talents, illustrated by the lectures in mathematical economics he gave for them, and they could see the importance of the methods he was using more clearly than could some of their teachers. His friends may have helped Samuelson see that *Foundations* could be successful without the need to add the hundred pages of additional verbal explanation that Wilson had wanted him to provide so that nonmathematical economists could understand it.

His closest friend chose not to participate in all of this, except through him. Marion was unambitious for herself, but guided her husband through an important decade, persuading him to move to MIT and later to remain there and to decline an offer from Chicago. She had also been closely involved in his academic work, in the theory of protection, population dynamics, and, crucially, the writing of *Foundations*. Above all, she gave him the home he needed. Samuelson's lifelong friend and colleague, Robert Solow, has remarked that, when he hears people respond to the difference between the two books by suggesting that if Samuelson wrote *Foundations,* Marion must have been the one who wrote *Economics*, he responds, "You've got that the wrong way round: it was Paul who wrote *Economics*, and Marion wrote *Foundations.*" Though made in jest, there is a serious element in that remark, for her role in *Foundations* was substantial. In contrast, *Economics* was in part the product of the MIT economics department and in part the product of his wartime experiences. By that time, Marion was less involved in his academic work, increasingly occupied with their growing family.

Economics after the War

In the period from the end of the Second World War to the 1960s, economics was transformed. It became more technical, with greater use of formal theory. It became normal for articles in academic journals to make a clear distinction between theoretical and empirical work; the first part might present a theoretical model and the second part an empirical application, perhaps estimating the coefficients using statistical data. Samuelson's *Foundations*, with its focus on operational theorems and comparative statics results, provided economists with the toolbox they could use to construct theories with the newly expected standards of rigor. It not only showed economists how to solve an economic model but also provided a compendium of the necessary mathematical techniques. It was used by graduate students and it became an important work of reference. At the same time, Samuelson's *Economics* transformed the introductory economics curriculum. It covered the new theories of income determination and made the case for a modern mixed economy in which government, even under Eisenhower's Republican administration, played a role far greater than had been the case a generation earlier. Economics did not change overnight, many economists carrying on as they had done before the war, but especially within the younger generation, new approaches were rapidly being adopted.

Samuelson was not the only creator of the new ways of doing economics. The Cowles Commission was mathematizing economics on the basis of Walrasian general equilibrium theory in ways that looked very different from anything in Samuelson's book. With the support of the U.S. Air Force, methods of "activity analysis" were rapidly being developed, bearing a family resemblance to the input–output modeling of Samuelson's teacher, Wassily Leontief. John von Neumann and Oskar Morgenstern had proposed a radically new conception of economic equilibrium in *The Theory of Games and Economic Behavior*, using advanced mathematical techniques such as fixed-point theorems, that Samuelson did not use, but that were taken up at Cowles and elsewhere. Econometrics, increasingly understood as the use of statistical inference to estimate the coefficients of theoretical models—was being developed at the Cowles Commission along lines laid out by Haavelmo, while at the National Bureau of Economic Research, the tradition of quantitative research established by Wesley Mitchell was still going strong. Milton Friedman, just a little older than Samuelson, had worked there with Simon Kuznets, and at Chicago he initiated a research program in monetary analysis that was in the Mitchell-Kuznets mold.

Although none of these approaches to modernizing economics was Samuelson's, he was close to most of them. He might be skeptical about the econometric estimation of complex models, the techniques for which were being developed at the Cowles Commission; but beginning in 1948, he began to work closely with one of its leading figures, Tjalling Koopmans. And his first PhD student, Lawrence Klein, after a period at the Cowles Commission, became the leading figure in large-scale macroeconometric modeling in the 1950s. Samuelson became heavily involved in linear modeling; together with his MIT colleague Robert Solow and Harvard's Robert Dorfman, he wrote an advanced textbook, *Linear Programing and Economic Analysis*, for RAND, a think tank established in 1948 that was to play an important role in both economics and policymaking.[6]

Samuelson was never a national income accountant, but during the war he had developed a close working relationship with Raymond Goldsmith, who was. He could also cooperate with and support those, such as Rutledge Vining, who continued to work in the National Bureau institutionalist tradition at the same time as being very close to those who were much more rigorously "neoclassical" in their approach, such as Solow and James Tobin, a Harvard graduate who soon was the dominant figure at Yale. Alongside Solow, Tobin, and Franco Modigliani (eventually hired at MIT), Samuelson became one of America's leading Keynesian economists.

Samuelson was at the center of American, and arguably world, economics from the publication of his two books until his retirement. The reason he could do this from a position at MIT was that, building on the position it had achieved in the natural sciences and engineering during wartime, the economics department at MIT became central to American economics. By the 1960s, its graduate program was producing the economists who would go on to become leading figures in the field. With the rise to prominence of Milton Friedman and his successors, Chicago might eventually displace MIT in the league of Nobel Prize winners, but MIT economists remained in prominent positions and ideas emanating from MIT were important in most branches of economics. Samuelson was not personally involved in all of these, although he was active in many major developments, including finance, public economics, modeling intergenerational transfers of resources, the theory of capital, and economic growth. He was a major presence in the department, making MIT the place where others wanted to work.

In this respect, he had much in common with the British economist Alfred Marshall, whose attitudes he disparaged so prominently in *Foundations*. They both had a mission that involved establishing a new, scientific economics by building up a center of economic research and teaching. Of course, MIT in 1948 was not the University of Cambridge in 1885, and Samuelson was an enthusiast for mathematical economics in a way Marshall never was. However, though both of them contributed to the theory of profit-maximizing businesses and utility-maximizing consumers, neither was a simple neoclassical economist; both were cautious in applying such theories to real-world problems and had the ability to appeal to widely differing groups of economists— even to economists who did not accept the value of their more formal theoretical work. Just as there is a strong historicist strand in Marshall's work, it is possible to discern institutionalist traces in Samuelson's.[7]

This book is the story of how a student with a humanities background came to economics through an interdisciplinary education in the social sciences, recognizing as an undergraduate that mathematics could be key to unlocking the secrets of the subject. Discovering an aptitude for such work, he developed under the guidance of Wilson and then Hansen into the economist who could dominate the field in the 1950s. In 1948, still only thirty-three years old, settled at MIT as a full professor, his eminence was recognized by the American Economic Association, and he soon had two important books to his name. From that point, the story of Samuelson changes. It ceases to be that of a young person finding his way and becomes that of an established figure in the field. That story is for a different book.

LIST OF REFERENCE ABBREVIATIONS AND SOURCES

AHP   Alvin Hansen Papers, Harvard University Archives,
           HUGFP 3.xx
Direct   Supplied by author of document, recipient of letter, or by
           family member of the author
EBWP   Edwin Bidwell Wilson Papers, Harvard University Archives
GHP   Gottfried Haberler Papers, Harvard University
           Archives, 12516
HUA-E   Harvard University Archives, Economics Department,
           UAV349.10
HUESR   Harvard University, Economics Student Records
HUPF   Harvard University Press Archive, Foundations Folder
JHWP   John H. Williams Papers, Harvard University Archives
JTP   James Tobin Papers, Yale University
LAMP   Lloyd A. Metzler Papers, David M. Rubenstein Rare Book
           and Manuscript Library, Duke University
MIT-AC04   Massachusetts Institute of Technology, Office of the President,
           records of Karl Taylor Compton and James Rhyne Killian,
           AC0004, Massachusetts Institute of Technology, Institute
           Archives and Special Collections, Cambridge, Massachusetts
MIT-AC20   Massachusetts Institute of Techology, School of Humanities
           and Social Science, Office of the Dean, records of John
           E. Burchard, AC0020, Massachusetts Institute of Technology,
           Institute Archives and Special Collections, Cambridge,
           Massachusetts

MIT-AC394   Massachusetts Institute of Technology, Department of Economics Records, AC0394, Massachusetts Institute of Technology, Institute Archives and Special Collections, Cambridge, Massachusetts

OSRD   Records of the OSRD, National Archives and Records Administration, College Park

NARA   National Archives and Records Administration, St. Louis

PASP   Paul A. Samuelson Papers, David M. Rubenstein Rare Book and Manuscript Library, Duke University. Citations take the form PASP n (folder), where "n" is the box number. The folder name is omitted if it is the same as either the document or, for correspondence, Samuelson's correspondent

RMSP   Robert M. Solow Papers, David M. Rubenstein Rare Book and Manuscript Library, Duke University

RFP   Rockefeller Foundation records (FA386), Record Group 1.1: Projects, Series 224.S: Massachusetts—Social Sciences, Box 6, folders 60–64, "MIT—Industrial Relations"; dates indicate the appropriate folders

STP   Shigeto Tsuru Papers, held in Library of the Institute of Economic Research, Hitotsubashi University

UCOP   University of Chicago, Office of the President, Hutchins Administration Records, 1892–1951

WSP   Wolfgang Stolper Papers, David M. Rubenstein Rare Book and Manuscript Library, Duke University

ENDNOTES

Introduction

1. E. H. Schell, December 31, 1947, Letter to Ralph E. Freeman, PASP 87 (MIT).
2. This terminology comes from Morgan and Rutherford 1998.

Chapter 1: Childhood

1. The archival record of Paul's early years is thin. There is a brief exchange of letters with his teacher and neighbors dating from the 1970s, but otherwise the sources appear to be confined to his own reminiscences in autobiographical essays and interviews. Fortunately, these are numerous, because of his habit of lacing publications with autobiographical remarks. Unfortunately, these are typically brief and often lack details with which to pin down the events recounted. The most substantial pieces relating to his early life and his family background are: a long unpublished and untitled "Autobiographical fragment" (undated, PASP 149 [Autobiographical]); an unpublished, handwritten, and incomplete "Brief history of the Samuelsons" (undated, PASP 149 [Autobiographical]); a piece he wrote in March 1989, "Portrait of the scholar as a young pup" (PASP 149 [Autobiographical]); and a short piece, with a significant part of its two handwritten pages crossed through, "Roots," written in 1987 (PASP 149 [Autobiographical]). It is possible that the striking through may have been done by a typist, indicating passages that had been copied. Had he intended to delete all the material struck through, it is not clear why the document would not have been thrown away. There were also numerous remarks made in various interviews. He had clearly thought about his past, having some clear memories of his childhood, but never brought the material together into a single narrative.

2. P. A. Samuelson, Undated, Autobiographical fragment, PASP 149 (Autobiographical). Ch. 1, p. 9.

3. The exact relationship of "Uncle Jimmy" to Samuelson is not clear.

4. Given his father's change of name, it is not clear whether these are merely the names by which Samuelson knew his aunts and uncles or the names given by their parents. Samuelson lists five names, saying that he believed there may have been another sister. Sarah's name and all the birth dates are taken from the 1910 U.S. Census.

5. Samuelson writes Hankanson, but that would appear to be a misspelling.

6. This is the arrival date given in the 1910 Census. Samuelson's account simply refers to the Edwardian decade.

7. P. A. Samuelson, Undated, Autobiographical fragment, PASP 149 (Autobiographical), Ch. 1, p. 11.

8. The 1920 Census gives Frank's immigration date as 1908, though note that transcription errors are not uncommon in such records.

9. Samuelson's account suggests she may have been closer to fifteen, though he made it clear he did not know her age.

10. Samuelson, Autobiographical fragment.

11. A later copy of the birth certificate is in PASP 149 (Personal).

12. Samuelson, Portrait of the Scholar, p. 4.

13. P. A. Samuelson, March 6, 1976, Letter to Anna Buchfuehrer, Lester Gordon, and Ethel Ruth, PASP 152 (Personal).

14. Samuelson, Autobiographical fragment. He is not completely clear on the period, saying that he was there till age five, but also that this idyllic period ran from 1916 to 1924.

15. Samuelson, Portrait of the Scholar.

16. Ibid, p. 4.

17. Samuelson, Autobiographical fragment.

18. Samuelson, Portrait of the Scholar.

19. The text says "doining." He clearly typed the letter himself and there are many handwritten corrections.

20. P. A. Samuelson, March 6, 1976, Letter to Anna Buchfuehrer, Lester Gordon, and Ethel Ruth, PASP 152 (Personal).

21. Ibid.

22. 40 might be 70. The letter is handwritten.

23. E. Ruth, March 5, 1976, Letter to Paul A. Samuelson, PASP 152 (Personal).

24. Note that Samuelson's memory of the letter may be imperfect, in that he talked of being in third grade, whereas she was clearly claiming to have taught him in first and second grades.

25. This information was provided by a family member.

26. Samuelson 2009a, p. 45.

27. The relationship is not known: he was age thirty-five. The household also included a Jenny Hopheins (age 51).

28. The source for this is a family member. Samuelson does not mention it.

29. Samuelson, Brief History of the Samuelsons.

30. E. Ruth, March 5, 1976, Letter to Paul A. Samuelson, PASP 152 (Personal).

31. Samuelson, Autobiographical fragment; see also P. A. Samuelson, December 31, 1951, Letter to Robert Summers, PASP 71 (Summers family).

32. Samuelson, Autobiographical fragment.

33. *Hyde Park Herald*, June 23, 1982, p. 11.

34. *Hyde Park Herald*, September 8, 1933.

35. *Hyde Park Herald*, November 1, 1929, p. 22.

36. *Hyde Park Herald*, November 28, 1930, p. 1.

37. *Hyde Park Herald*, December 5, 1930, p. 16.

38. This account of the Chicago school system is taken from Tyack et al. 1984:69

39. *Hyde Park Herald*, May 26, 1933, p. 1.

40. *Hyde Park Herald* April 12, 1945, p. 8.

41. *Hyde Park Herald* June 17, 1959, p. 13.

42. Hyman 2012.

43. Orear 2004, p. 64.

44. Reed and Smith 1925, p. 342, citing Shoesmith 1916.

45. Schorling 1915, p. 658, quoting an advance version of Shoesmith 1916.

46. Mathematical Association of America 1932, p. 308.

47. Schorling 1915, p. 658, quoting an advance version of Shoesmith 1916.

48. *Hyde Park Herald*, December 23, 1959, p. 12. She was later commemorated by the naming of an elementary school after her.

49. Samuelson et al. 1996, p. 970.

50. Samuelson 2009a, pp. 1103–1104.

51. P. A. Samuelson, 1992, [Answers] by Paul A. Samuelson, PASP 152 (Walker), p. 2.

52. Samuelson 1930.

53. Samuelson, Portrait of the Scholar, p. 3.

54. P. A. Samuelson, June 11, 1996, Letter to Norman Davidson, PASP 25 (D, 1991–2009, 2 of 2). This exchange is also discussed in chapter 4 this volume.

55. Samuelson 1972a; Samuelson, Autobiographical fragment.

56. For example, Samuelson, Autobiographical fragment, Ch. 1, pp. 5, 8.

57. Samuelson, Autobiographical fragment.

58. Samuelson 2009a, p. 45.

59. Samuelson, Autobiographical fragment.

60. Samuelson 2002b, p. 30.

61. Samuelson, Autobiographical fragment, Ch. 1, p. 5.

62. Ibid., Ch. 1, p. 4. A picture of Samuelson, age three, makes it clear that his account of his appearance was no exaggeration!

63. Ibid., Ch. 1, p. 5.

64. Radcliffe was Harvard's womens' college.

65. Samuelson, Autobiographical fragment, Ch 1, p. 5.

66. P. A. Samuelson, July, 1987, Roots, PASP 149 (Autobiographical).
67. Ibid. Sophie had married Fred Mendelsohn in the summer of 1914.
68. I owe this idea to Bradley Bateman.
69. This belief led him to be impatient over details about his education. This is illustrated by an exchange with Donald Walker, in which Samuelson was sent a list of thirty-six questions ranging over six pages about his mathematical and economic training (P. A. Samuelson, 1992, [Answers] by Paul A Samuelson, PASP 152 [Walker]; D. A. Walker, 1992, Paul A. Samuelson on some aspects of the origins and evolution of his economic ideas, PASP 152 [Walker]). Samuelson's response was five pages, in which he explained, essentially, that he was self-taught in mathematics. He refrained from responding to most of the detailed questions Walker had asked, even though many of them would have been easy for him to answer. There was an explanation he wanted to offer, involving a well-rehearsed account of his life, and although he did add interesting details (for example, about Beulah Shoesmith and his mathematics education at Hyde Park School), he had no interest in details that were not part of that narrative.
70. P. A. Samuelson, December 31, 1951, Letter to Robert Summers, PASP 71 (Summers family), p. 6.

Chapter 2: The University of Chicago, 1932

1. P. A. Samuelson, Undated, Autobiographical fragment, PASP 149 (Autobiographical), Ch. 2, p. 1.
2. Samuelson 2002a.
3. Ibid, p. 48.
4. Ibid., p. 48.
5. Keniston et al. 1934, p. 415.
6. Ibid., p. 282.
7. Ibid., p. 283.
8. Ibid., p. 284.
9. Ibid., p. 291.
10. Ibid., p. 361.
11. Ibid., p. 362.
12. Gideonse, Kerwin, et al. 1931, p. 30.
13. R. M. McIver, quoted in Gideonse, Kerwin, et al. 1931, p. 5.
14. Suzumura 2005, p. 332.
15. Sumner 1906, p. 99.
16. Ibid., p. 80.
17. Ibid., p. 87.
18. Gideonse, Kerwin, et al. 1931, p. 96.
19. Slichter 1931, p. 16.
20. Gideonse, Kerwin, et al. 1931, p. 101.
21. Barnett 2004, p. 529.

22. Biographical data on Director are taken from Van Horn 2010a; Van Horn 2010b.
23. Slichter 1931, p. 16.
24. Ibid., pp. 9–10.
25. Ibid.
26. Barnett 2004, p. 529. This would appear to be a reference to chapter 4, "The Mechanism of Pricing," the first section of which is titled "Arithmetical Treatment of the Problem of Equilibrium."
27. P. A. Samuelson, 1992, [Answers] by Paul A Samuelson, PASP 152 (Walker), p. 2.
28. Barnett 2004, p. 529.
29. See entry by Ronnie J. Phillips in 2006. Though relieved of the course in 1927, when he took over the course on money, he had presumably picked it up again, perhaps when Director arrived.
30. P. A. Samuelson, March 31, 2003, Letter to Roger Sandilands and David Laidler, PASP 67 (Sandilands).

Chapter 3: Natural and Social Sciences, 1932–1933

1. P. A. Samuelson, January 9, 2008, Letter to Stephen Stigler, PASP 71.
2. Coulter 1932, p. 1.
3. Ibid., p. 3.
4. Ibid., p. 163.
5. Ibid., pp. 181–189.
6. M. Crawford Samuelson, July 12, 2002, Interview with Paul A. Samuelson, Direct.
7. Coulter 1932, p. 277.
8. Ibid., p. 277.
9. P. A. Samuelson, January 9, 2008, Letter to Stephen Stigler, PASP 71.
10. Coulter 1932, p. 334.
11. Ibid., p. 339.
12. East 1927, p. 175.
13. Ibid., p. 176.
14. Ibid., p. 179.
15. Lemon and Schlesinger 1932, chapter 41. Quotation taken from Lemon and Schlesinger 1934, p. 186.
16. Lemon and Schlesinger 1934, p. 187.
17. P. A. Samuelson, June 24, 1996, Letter to Norman Davidson, PASP 25 (D, 1991–2009, 2 of 2). Samuelson noted that in economics it was known as the Le Chatelier-Samuelson Principle.
18. Gideonse, Johnson, et al. 1932, p. xi.
19. Thouless 1936.
20. Ibid., pp. 250–251.
21. Ibid., p. 237.

22. Ibid., p. 240.
23. Ibid., pp. 244–245.
24. Angell 1932, p. 187.
25. Salter 1932, p. xiv.
26. Ibid., p. 13.
27. Bonar 1911, Ch. 3.
28. Ibid., p. 59.
29. Ibid., p. 61.
30. Gideonse, Johnson, et al. 1932, p. 4.
31. Ibid., pp. 4–5. A third quotation has been omitted because of its length.
32. Ibid., p. 15.
33. Ibid., p. 21.
34. Ibid., p. 38.
35. Ibid., p. 50.
36. Ibid., p. 55.
37. Clark 1936, p. 268. Paragraph italicized in original.
38. See chapter 5 this volume.
39. Samuelson 1972b.
40. Samuelson 1951a, p. 14.
41. Gideonse, Johnson, et al. 1932, p. 129.
42. Ibid., p. 155.
43. Ibid., p. 160.
44. Ibid., p. 200.
45. Ibid., p. 215.
46. Ibid., p. 218.
47. Ibid., p. 220.
48. Ibid., p. 205.
49. Ibid, p. 205.
50. Ibid., pp. 244–245.
51. P. A. Samuelson, May 1933, Diary, PASP 149 (Autobiographical), p. 1.
52. Ibid.
53. Ibid., p. 2.
54. Samuelson 1972a.
55. P. A. Samuelson, Undated, Autobiographical fragment, PASP 149 (Autobiographical), p. 7.
56. Ibid., p. 3.
57. On February 9, 1933, the resolution "This house will under no circumstances fight for King and country" was passed with a large majority.

Chapter 4: Social Scientist to Mathematical Economist, 1933–1934

1. Biographical details are taken from Eggan 1963.
2. Eggan 1962.
3. Cole 1931.

4. This information is taken from http://www.asanet.org/about/presidents/ Leonard_Cottrell.cfm. Cottrell became president of the American Statistical Association in 1950.

5. University of Chicago 1932, p. 108.

6. Schuman 1932a, 1932b, 1932c.

7. Schuman 1934b, 1934a, 1934c.

8. Schuman 1934c, p. 42.

9. P. A. Samuelson, May 1933, Diary, PASP 149 (Autobiographical), pp. 11–12.

10. Ibid., p. 9.

11. Samuelson 1992, p. 239.

12. P. A. Samuelson, Undated, Autobiographical fragment, PASP 149 (Autobiographical), p. 8.

13. University of Chicago 1932, p. 31.

14. P. A. Samuelson, 1934, The Limitations of Collective Bargaining (Economics 240), PASP, Box 152. Other student essays are not included in the publications list.

15. Ibid., p. 1. "its own self" is in the original.

16. http://www.spring-valley.il.us/history/john_mitchell.htm.

17. P. A. Samuelson, Limitations of Collective Bargaining, p. 2.

18. Ibid., p. 4.

19. Ibid., p. 5.

20. Ibid., p. 9.

21. P. A. Samuelson, June 11, 1996, Letter to Norman Davidson, PASP 25 (D, 1991–2009, 2 of 2).

22. N. Davidson, June 18, 1996, Letter to Paul A. Samuelson, PASP 25 (D, 1991–2009, 2 of 2).

23. P. A. Samuelson, June 24, 1996, Letter to Norman Davidson, PASP 25 (D 1991–2009, 2 of 2).

24. P. A. Samuelson, 1992, [Answers] by Paul A Samuelson, PASP 152 (Walker), p. 2.

25. This is based on the course description from Econ 209 in the announcements for 1933–34.

26. P. A. Samuelson, 1934, The Relationship Between Changes in Exchange Rates and General Prices, PASP 135.

27. Ibid., p. 5.

28. The only Chicago economist cited is Theodore Yntema, but he is someone whom Paul never mentioned in his recollections.

29. See chapter 5 this volume.

30. Samuelson, Relationship Between Changes in Exchange Rates.

31. Ibid., p. 8.

32. Ibid., p. 9.

33. P. A. Samuelson, Undated, Autobiographical fragment, PASP 149 (Autobiographical), p. 6.

34. Ibid, p. 11.
35. Stigler 1988, p. 25.
36. Samuelson 2003, p. 463.
37. Ibid., p. 463.
38. Ibid., pp. 463–464.
39. P. A. Samuelson, May 1933, Diary, PASP 149 (Autobiographical), p. 12.
40. Ibid., p. 14.
41. Ibid., p. 20.
42. Ibid., p. 22.

Chapter 5: Economics at Chicago, 1932–1935

1. Barnett 2004, p. 531.
2. Ibid., p. 526. Though he remembered his class notes, there is no evidence that he had them and had consulted them.
3. P. A. Samuelson, Undated, Money at the University of Chicago, PASP 133.
4. Samuelson 1968, p. 2.
5. Ibid., p. 1.
6. Barnett 2004, p. 530.
7. Ibid., p. 527.
8. See Laidler 1999, Ch. 9.
9. Hart 1935.
10. See the discussion in Laidler 1999, chapter 9, especially pp. 231ff.
11. Wright 1932.
12. Douglas 1932, p. 8.
13. Ibid., p. 21.
14. Douglas 1934, p. xv.
15. Ibid.
16. The preface is dated January 31, 1935.
17. Douglas 1935, p. 79. The tense of the verb has been changed.
18. Ibid., pp. 80–82.
19. Ibid., p. 85.
20. Samuelson 1991a, p. 542.
21. Samuelson 1972c, pp. 5–6.
22. Ibid., p. 11.
23. Viner 2013.
24. Samuelson 1972c, p. 7.
25. Ibid., p. 7.
26. Ibid., p. 8.
27. Viner 1931.
28. Samuelson 1972c, p. 9.
29. This was circulated as the first essay in Knight 1933.
30. Knight 1933, p. 8.
31. Ibid, p. 14.

32. Ibid., p. 15.
33. P. A. Samuelson, September 14, 1994, Letter to Donald Dewey, PASP 25.
34. Knight 1982, p. 30.
35. Knight 1922.
36. Ibid., p. 459.
37. Ibid., pp. 472–473.
38. Ibid., p. 475, italics in original.
39. Ibid., p. 477.
40. Knight 1923, p. 580.
41. Ibid., pp. 580, 584.
42. Ibid., p. 582.
43. Ibid., p. 587.
44. Ibid., p. 598.
45. Ibid., p. 600.
46. Ibid., p. 583.
47. Ibid., p. 601.
48. Knight 1997.
49. Ibid., p. 71.
50. Ibid., p. 73.
51. Ibid., p. 74.
52. Ibid., p. 92.
53. Ibid., p. 97.
54. Ibid., p 97.
55. Ibid., p. 133.
56. P. A. Samuelson, Undated, Autobiographical fragment, PASP 149 (Autobiographical).
57. The handwriting of the word *secured* is not clear, and the omitted words include one that is hard to read. The "composition of prices notion" may refer to the theory, going back to Adam Smith and before, that prices can be explained by adding up their components, wages, profits, and rents. P. A. Samuelson, May 1933, Diary, PASP 149 (Autobiographical), pp. 27–28.
58. P. A. Samuelson, 1992, [Answers] by Paul A Samuelson, PASP 152 (Walker), p. 4.
59. Samuelson, Autobiographical fragment, p. 7.
60. Ibid., p. 7.
61. P. A. Samuelson, January 8, 1997, Letter to Donald Dewey, PASP 25; Samuelson 1991a, p. 537; P. A. Samuelson, February 8, 2000, Letter to Marc Nerlove, PASP 55 (N, 1991–2009).
62. Samuelson 1951a, p. 14, n1.

Chapter 6: First Term at Harvard, Autumn 1935

1. J. Viner, April 15, 1935, Reference for PAS for SSRC, PASP 74.
2. Samuelson 2003, p. 464.

3. P. A. Samuelson, Undated, Autobiographical fragment, PASP 149 (Autobiographical), p. 12.
4. Ibid., p. 14.
5. Ibid., p. 12.
6. The catalog lists both Crum and Frickey as teaching this. However, Tsuru (2001, p. 118) and Samuelson (P. A. Samuelson, January 26, 1999, Letter to Stephen Stigler, PASP 71) remember Crum as teaching it. He probably taught the first term and Frickey the second.
7. Most likely Yule 1911. Samuelson identifies the author but not the text.
8. P. A. Samuelson, January 26, 1999, Letter to Stephen Stigler, PASP 71.
9. Keller and Keller 2001, pp. 22–26.
10. They are discussed in detail below.
11. Frickey 1942; Burns 1944.
12. Bullock et al. 1927.
13. Bullock and Crum 1932, pp. 136–137.
14. Ibid., p. 138.
15. Mason 1982.
16. Crum 1932.
17. Crum 1938.
18. P. A. Samuelson, January 26, 1999, Letter to Stephen Stigler, PASP 71.
19. Mason 1982, p. 413, The exception was Chamberlin, who became chairman in 1938 for three years.
20. This is discussed further elsewhere.
21. Samuelson 2011b, p. 1.
22. Morgan 1990 assigns Persons and his A, B, C curves a prominent place in the history of econometrics.
23. See Chamberlin 1961.
24. Samuelson 2004b, p. 4.
25. P. A. Samuelson, September 26, 1989, Letter to Henry Rosovsky, PASP 63. This is discussed further in chapter 15 this volume.
26. Samuelson 2004b, p. 5. Names that Samuelson mentioned as being on the reading list were John Stuart Mill, Alfred Marshall, Chamberlin, and Robinson.
27. The typeface and style of the paper suggest it is early, and the reference, without giving details of the source, to one of Chamberlin's chapters suggests it was written for him. A footnote in which Samuelson accuses Chamberlin of misintepreting Pareto (Section III, note 2) contains the marginal remark, "Where do I suggest this?," clearly written by Chamberlin. Further evidence is provided in that P. A. Samuelson, February 1936, A fragmentary note on the equilibrium of the firm, PASP 151, dated Winter 1935/36 refers to an earlier paper on the indeterminacy of duopoly, which is presumably this paper or a variation of it. The paper is not complete, though what is labeled "Section III" seems fairly self-contained. It is possible that the title quoted may be the

title of a note attached to the main paper. The pages are, unfortunately, not all numbered and there is some uncertainty about their order.

28. P. A. Samuelson, Undated, Notes on the similarity between duopoly and bilateral monopoly, PASP 152, Section III, p. 5.

29. Ibid., p. 9.

30. Ibid., p. 9.

31. Ibid., p. 4; emphasis in Samuelson's original.

32. A footnote cited Bowley and Hicks.

33. Samuelson, Notes on the similarity, p. 1.

34. The reference is to Chamberlin 1933, p. 52, n2.

35. Samuelson, Notes on the similarity.

36. Unless Samuelson revised the paper later, and the copy in the archive bears the date of the revision, this could not be the paper that Kaldor heard Samuelson present.

37. He also noted, in a footnote, second-order conditions.

38. P. A. Samuelson, February 1936, A fragmentary note on the equilibrium of the firm, PASP 151, p. 7, n3. The italic (originally underlining) is clearly Chamberlin's.

39. Ibid., p. 24. The parenthesis is Samuelson's. The implication, as his previous paper had made clear, was that he was doubtful about whether there were non-arbitrary restrictions that could result in a determinate solution.

40. Though he did not cite him, this must have been an allusion to Hotelling's paper on spatial competition.

41. Samuelson, Fragmentary note, pp. 28–29.

42. Ibid., pp. 29–30. He notes how little work there was on this, citing Ramsey 1928 and Leontief 1934c.

43. Samuelson, Fragmentary note, p. 29.

44. Ibid., p. 30.

45. Ibid., p. 1.

46. Leontief (1925), translated as Leontief 1977, chapter 1, pp. 3–9.

47. Leontief 1936c.

48. Ibid., p. 105.

49. This point is noted by Dorfman 1973, p. 432.

50. Leontief 1935.

51. Samuelson 2004b, p. 5.

52. Tsuru 2001, p. 116.

53. The classic example is someone who eats a lot of potatoes because he cannot afford bread. If the price of potatoes rises, the person becomes even poorer and has to eat even less bread and hence more potatoes.

54. Samuelson 2004b, p. 6.

55. Tsuru 2001, p. 122.

56. The following discussion of the course is based on L. A. Metzler, 1938, Notes on Leontief's Econ. 116, Session 1937-8, LAMP Box 7 (Econ 116).

57. Ibid.

58. The reading list is written on completely different paper and does not necessarily date from the beginning of the course: given what Samuelson said about Leontief's course, it might not even have been dictated by Leontief. However the observation in the notes that theory cannot be used both to derive results and to check them suggests that Leontief was thinking in terms of estimating demand functions.

59. Samuelson 2004b, p. 6.

60. Samuelson 1972a, p. 163.

61. Tsuru 2000, p. 7.

62. Samuelson 1990a, p. 312.

63. Tsuru 2000, p. 7.

64. Tsuru 2001, chapter 7.

65. S. Tsuru, September 17, 2000, Letter to Paul A. Samuelson, PASP 73, p. 5.

66. Suzumura 2006.

67. P. A. Samuelson, Undated, Marion Crawford's Life, Direct, p. 6.

68. R. Bishop, February 16, 1978, Marion Crawford Samuelson, Direct, p. 4; R. M. Bergson, February 16, 1978, Marion Crawford Samuelson, Direct, p. 1; E. C. Brown, February 16, 1978, Marion Crawford Samuelson, Direct, p. 1; R. M. Solow, February 16, 1978, Marion Crawford Samuelson, Direct, p. 1.

69. M. Crawford Samuelson, July 12, 2002, Interview with Paul A. Samuelson, Direct.

70. P. A. Samuelson, Undated, Marion Crawford's Life, Direct, p. 1. See also Crawford Samuelson, Interview with Paul A. Samuelson, p. 1.

71. R. Bishop, February 16, 1978, Marion Crawford Samuelson, Direct, p. 2.

72. Crawford 1937.

73. Ibid., p. 28.

74. Ibid., pp. 29–30.

75. Ibid., p. 30.

76. E. B. Wilson, March 22, 1939, Letter to Griffith Evans, EBWP HUG4878.203 Box 32 (E).

77. Harris 1941, p. viii.

78. P. A. Samuelson, Undated, Marion Crawford's Life, Direct, p. 3.

79. Tsuru 2001, p. 118.

80. Crawford Samuelson, Interview with Paul A. Samuelson.

81. Ibid.

82. R. Bishop, February 16, 1978, Marion Crawford Samuelson, Direct, p. 3.

Chapter 7: Joseph Alois Schumpeter

1. This account of Schumpeter's life before he moved permanently to Harvard draws heavily on McCraw 2007.

2. P. A. Samuelson, 1991, Afterthoughts on Schumpeter, PASP 68 (Schumpeter), p. 635.

3. *Das Wesen und Hauptinhalt der theoretischen Nationalökonomie* (1908), translated as *The Nature and Essence of Economic Theory* (Schumpeter 2010).

4. Leontief 1950, p. 105.

5. Translated into English by Frank Taussig's son-in-law, Redvers Opie, just before Samuelson arrived at Harvard.

6. McCraw 2007, p. 98.

7. Ibid., pp. 130–131.

8. Discussed elsewhere. American Economic Association 1935.

9. Samuelson 1951b, p. 101.

10. Ibid., p. 100.

11. Triffin 1950, p. 413.

12. Ibid.

13. Samuelson 1951b, p. 101.

14. Ibid., p. 102.

15. W. Stolper, 1935, Notes on Ec. 11, 1934-5 (Schumpeter), WSP 2002-0207 Box 19 (Theory).

16. Hicks 1932; Robinson 1933a; Chamberlin 1933.

17. Triffin 1950, p. 413,

18. Quoted in Swedberg 1991, p. 117.

19. Schumpeter 1939, p. 31.

20. Ibid., p. 32.

21. Ibid., p. 33.

22. McCraw 2007, pp. 220–221.

23. Schumpeter 1939, p. v.

24. This incident is discussed in McCraw 2007, p. 271. One of the students present was Richard Musgrave, who said of it, "Anyway, he gave an evening seminar on Business Cycles—and then in the discussion everyone talked about Keynes, and not about his own work. So at the end he said 'whether you agree or disagree is up to you, but I wish you would at least have read it.' We felt ashamed after that that, and we wrote a letter to Schumpeter about it." (R. Hett, September 30, 2000, Transcript of Interview with Richard Musgrave, Direct.)

25. Leontief 1950, p. 105.

26. See Shionoya 1997, pp. 99–104.

27. Schumpeter 1908, pp. 340–341; translated in Shionoya 1997, pp. 107–108.

28. Ibid., pp. 106, 112, 101.

29. Ibid., pp. 115–118.

30. Morgenstern 1951, p. 198.

31. See McCraw 2007, chapter 26.

32. Backhouse 1998b compares Schumpeter's perspective with that of Thomas Kuhn (1962), another product of Harvard's concern with scientific method (see Isaac 2012).

33. Schumpeter 1954, p. 7.

34. Ibid., p. 15.

35. Ibid., p. 16; emphasis in original.

36. Hayek 1942, 1943, 1944a.

37. Schumpeter 1954, p. 18.

38. Schumpeter to Haberler, March 20, 1933, quoted in McCraw 2007, p. 220.

39. Samuelson 2003, p. 465.

40. Schumpeter 1933, p. 5.

41. Ibid., p. 5.

42. McCraw 2007, pp. 116–117.

43. Haberler 1950, p. 333.

44. McCraw 2007, pp. 155–157.

45. Swedberg 1991, p. 13.

46. McCraw 2007, p. 271.

47. Tinbergen 1951, p. 109.

48. J. A. Schumpeter, May 19, 1937, Letter to Edwin Bidwell Wilson, EBWP HUG4878.203 Box 29 (S 1937).

49. Samuelson et al. 1996, p. 163.

50. Haberler 1950, p. 342.

51. Schumpeter 1954, pp. 133–134.

52. J. A. Schumpeter, June 5, 1936, Letter to Edwin Bidwell Wilson, EBWP HUG4878.203 Box 27 (S 1936).

53. McCraw 2007, p. 222.

54. J. A. Schumpeter, January 19, 1939, Letter to Paul A. Samuelson, PASP 68.

55. J. A. Schumpeter, March 15, 1943, Letter to Paul A. Samuelson, PASP 68. See also his comment on Samuelson 1943f in J. A. Schumpeter, October 30, 1943, Letter to Paul A. Samuelson, PASP 68.

56. J. A. Schumpeter, October 30, 1943, Letter to Paul A. Samuelson, PASP 68.

57. J. A. Schumpeter, August 6, 1948, Letter to Marion Samuelson, PASP 68.

58. See McCraw 2007, pp. 403–405.

59. The incident is recounted in McCraw 2007, chapter 17.

60. P. A. Samuelson, June 3, 1940, Letter to Joseph A. Schumpeter, PASP 68.

Chapter 8: Edwin Bidwell Wilson

1. P. A. Samuelson, Undated, Autobiographical fragment, PASP 149 (Autobiographical), p. 18. See also Samuelson 1989a.

2. The main source for most of the biographical information on Wilson is Hunsaker and Lane 1973. Important discussions of Wilson are also to be found in Carvajalino 2016.

3. Wilson 1912.

4. Hunsaker and Lane 1973, p. 287.

5. Samuelson 1989a, p. 259; Samuelson 1991b, p. 337.

6. See Carvajalino 2016.

7. Samuelson 1982, p. 861.

8. Samuelson 1989a, p. 259.

9. E. B. Wilson, July 14, 1936, Letter to John D. Black, EBWP HUG4878.203 Box 27 (B 1935–36).

10. Wilson 1935, p. 717. A footnote gives the source of the quotation as Bowley 1924, p. 12.

11. J. A. Schumpeter, April 24, 1936, Letter to Edwin Bidwell Wilson, EBWP HUG4878.203 Box 27 (S 1936).

12. E. B. Wilson, April 30, 1936, Letter to Joseph A. Schumpeter, EBWP HUG4878.203 Box 27 (S 1936).

13. Ibid. The awkwardness of the second sentence is no doubt the result of Wilson having dictated the letter to a secretary, composing as he spoke.

14. Wilson 1926, p. 290–291.

15. E. B. Wilson, April 15, 1936, Letter to John D. Black, EBWP HUG4878.203 Box 26. The project is identified more fully in J. D. Black, July 7, 1936, Letter to Edwin Bidwell Wilson, EBWP HUG4878.203 Box 27 (B 1935-6), and was to be supervised by Wilson and Crum.

16. Samuelson 1991b, pp. 334–335.

17. E. B. Wilson, December 11, 1939, Letter to Lloyd A. Metzler, EBWP HUG4878.203 Box 35 (M).

18. E. B. Wilson, June 6, 1936, Letter to Joseph A. Schumpeter, EBWP HUG4878.203 Box 27 (S 1936).

19. Ibid.

20. E. B. Wilson, January 13, 1937, Letter to Lawrence J. Henderson, EBWP HUG4878.203 Box 29 (H 1937).

21. Ibid.

22. E. B. Wilson, June 6, 1936, Letter to Joseph A. Schumpeter, EBWP HUG4878.203 Box 27 (S 1936).

23. J. A. Schumpeter, May 19, 1937, Letter to Edwin Bidwell Wilson, EBWP HUG4878.203 Box 29 (S 1937).

24. Ibid.

25. I owe this point to Juan Carvajalino.

26. Samuelson 1971, p. 994.

27. E. B. Wilson, March 10, 1938, Letter to Dickson H. Leavens, EBWP HUG4878.203 Box 31 (L 1938).

28. There is nothing here to suggest that this is the case. There is nothing in them that Wilson could not have taught in 1935–36.

29. L. A. Metzler, Undated, Notes on E. B. Wilson's lectures, LAMP Box 7 (Wilson), p. 6; italics indicate Metzler's underlining.

30. Ibid., p. 10; italics indicate Metzler's underlining.

31. Leacock 1936, p. 94, discussing Pigou 1935.

32. Ibid., p. 95.

33. E. B. Wilson, July 14, 1936, Letter to John D. Black, EBWP HUG4878.203 Box 27 (B 1935-6).

34. E. B. Wilson, January 3, 1940, Letter to Lloyd Metzler, EBWP HUG4878.203 Box 35 (M).

35. E. B. Wilson, January 5, 1938, Letter to Wesley C. Mitchell, EBWP HUG4878.203 Box 31 (M 1938).

36. W. C. Mitchell, October 17, 1938, Letter to Edwin Bidwell Wilson, EBWP HUG4878.203 Box 31 (M 1938).

37. E. B. Wilson, December 11, 1938, Letter to Wesley C. Mitchell, EBWP HUG4878.203 Box 31 (M 1938).

38. E. B. Wilson, December 30, 1938, Letter to A. P. Usher, EBWP HUG4878.203 Box 31 (T, U 1938).

39. Keynes 1973[1921]; Wilson 1923.

40. Wilson 1926, p. 292.

41. Keynes 1971; E. B. Wilson, December 7, 1939, Letter to C. J. Bullock, EBWP HUG4878.203 Box 32 (B).

42. E. B. Wilson, February 12, 1937, Letter to Alvin H. Hansen, EBWP HUG4878.203 Box 29 (H 1937). The reference has to be to this review because Hansen's other review had no footnotes.

43. Hansen 1936a, p. 667, n3.

44. E. B. Wilson, February 12, 1937, Letter to Alvin H. Hansen.

45. This emphasis on establishing facts rather than debating theories is also present in the exchange between Wilson and Milton Friedman, reported in Stigler 1994.

46. E. B. Wilson, December 7, 1939, Letter to C. J. Bullock, EBWP HUG4878.203 Box 32 (B).

47. P. A. Samuelson, October 9, 1940, Letter to Edwin Bidwell Wilson, EBWP HUG4878.203 Box 35 (S). His misspelling of Gibbs has been corrected.

48. Samuelson 1982, p. 861.

49. Samuelson 1991b, pp. 334–335.

50. This is argued in detail by Carvajalino. See note 2 above.

Chapter 9: Making Connections

1. P. A. Samuelson, Undated, Autobiographical fragment, PASP 149 (Autobiographical), pp. 20–21.

2. P. A. Samuelson, 1992, [Answers] by Paul A Samuelson, PASP 152 (Walker), p. 3.

3. P. A. Samuelson, 2005, Answers to written questions, PASP 149, pp. 1–2.

4. P. A. Samuelson, Undated, Minimization, Teleology, and Causality in the Calculus of Variations and in Mechanics, PASP 138. The article is Birkhoff and Hestenes 1935.

5. P. A. Samuelson, Undated, Marion Crawford's Life, Direct. University of Wisconsin 1936 gives the address of Paul's residence as 615 N. Henry.

6. Wolf and Wolf 1938.

7. Samuelson 1937a.

8. Ibid., p. 159.

9. Ibid., p. 159.

10. Ibid., p. 160.

11. Wilson 1935.

12. Samuelson 1937a, p. 161.

13. Samuelson 1990a, p. 311.

14. Haberler 1936.

15. Samuelson 1990a, p. 311.

16. Ibid., p. 312.

17. L. A. Metzler, 1938, Notes on Haberler's lectures, LAMP Box 7 (Haberler).

18. Haberler 1936, pp. 3–4.

19. Ibid., p. v.

20. Leontief 1933; Lerner 1932, 1934; Marshall 1923 and Marshall's early unpublished essay on the pure theory of trade.

21. L. A. Metzler, 1938, Notes on Haberler's lectures, LAMP Box 7 (Haberler), p. 31. Given that, a week or so later, he recommended the paper, it is possible that this remark, which does not appear to be developed in Metzler's notes, may reflect Haberler's reading of Samuelson 1938f.

22. Ibid., p. 32.

23. Presumably Schultz 1927.

24. Of course, as cloth production rose, wheat production would fall.

25. L. A. Metzler, 1938, Notes on Haberler's lectures, LAMP Box 7 (Haberler), p. 56. Haberler had reached similar conclusions in Haberler 1936, pp. 194–195.

26. Haberler 1936, p. 250.

27. Ibid., pp. 250–251.

28. Ibid., pp. 251.

29. Stolper and Samuelson 1941. See chapter 11 this volume.

30. Haberler 1936, p. 273.

31. See Boianovsky and Trautwein 2006; Howson 2011, pp. 295–298.

32. Boianovsky and Trautwein 2006, p. 74; De Marchi 1991, p. 149.

33. Samuelson 1996a, p. 1683.

34. Haberler 1946, p. 257.

35. Boianovsky and Trautwein 2006, p. 73.

36. Ibid., p. 54.

37. Harrod 1936, p. 98; Haberler 1937b, p. 217.

38. Haberler 1937a, p. 691.

39. Later Harrod 1939 recognized the importance of lags, though arguing for a division of labor between those problems for which lags were important and those for which they were not.

40. Ohlin 1929.

41. P. A. Samuelson, April, 1937, The Effect of a Unilateral Payment Upon the Terms of International Trade, PASP 134, p. 2. He attributed the claim merely to "continental writers," which would cover Ohlin, a Swede.

42. Ibid., p. 3.

43. On June 7, Viner apologized for his excessive delay in replying, suggesting Samuelson probably sent the paper in April, as soon as it had been written.

44. J. Viner, June 7, 1937, Letter to Paul A. Samuelson, PASP 74.

45. While Viner was considering his paper, Ohlin visited Harvard, but it is not known whether he and Samuelson met on that occasion. See B. Ohlin, May, 1937, Letter to John H. Williams, JHWP Miscellaneous Correspondence and Other Papers, 1929–71; J. H. Williams, May 7, 1937, Letter to Bertil Ohlin, JHWP Miscellaneous Correspondence and Other Papers, 1929–71.

46. Samuelson 1950, pp. 369–370.

47. If all prices rise by the same proportion, the problem is trivial.

48. For useful surveys, see Staehle 1935 and Frisch 1936.

49. This result is discussed in Haberler 1928, where he referred readers to his book for a more detailed discussion of the problem.

50. Allen 1933.

51. Samuelson 2004b, p. 6.

52. Samuelson 1937b.

53. Hayek 1931.

54. Fontaine 2010, p. 233.

55. Samuelson 1937b, p. 482.

56. Wilson 1912; G. Robinson 1926.

57. See Knight 1935; Boulding 1936.

58. Samuelson 2004a tells this story.

59. Bergson 1936; Samuelson 1937a.

60. Bergson 1936, p. 33, n1; Frisch 1936.

61. Bergson 1936, p. 39.

62. These papers were discussed earlier.

63. Samuelson 1938b, p. 71.

64. Samuelson 1981, p. 224.

65. Suzumura 2005, p. 334.

66. There is no inconsistency between his reference to Italian here and his reference to French in the remark quoted earlier, for they refer to different works. It is likely that they read Pareto's books, translated into French, in the language they had been required to study as a condition for passing their generals, but that with journal articles they had no choice but to struggle with the Italian.

Care should be taken in attaching weight to Samuelson's memory of detecting Pareto's sociology in this article at this time, for when he became a junior fellow, he was to be exposed, through Lawrence Henderson, to Pareto's sociology, and this may have colored his memory of his initial reactions to Pareto.

67. Samuelson 2004a, p. 24.
68. Ibid., p. 25.
69. Samuelson 1981, p. 223.
70. Suzumura 2005, p. 334.
71. G. D. Birkhoff, January 24, 1940, Letter to Paul A. Samuelson, PASP 14 (B, 1939-51).
72. Birkhoff 1941, p. 3, n6.
73. The problem arises because the number of representatives for each state has to be an integer and cannot be a fraction.
74. Birkhoff 1941, p. 18.

Chapter 10: *Simplifying Economic Theory*

1. E. B. Wilson, January 13, 1937, Letter to Lawrence J. Henderson, EBWP HUG4878.203 Box 29 (H 1937).
2. Brinton 1959, p. 4.
3. Ibid., p. 3.
4. Wilson, Letter to Henderson.
5. See chapter 15 this volume.
6. Wilson, Letter to Henderson. The original contains the word *outs* but this was presumably his secretary's mistake and has been corrected to *doubts*.
7. The significance of Sociology 23 is discussed in Isaac 2012, pp. 70–71.
8. J. A. Schumpeter, February 1, 1937, Letter to George Birkhoff, PASP 68.
9. Ibid.
10. Samuelson 1972a, p. 164.
11. Samuelson 1946a, p. 187; Samuelson 1972a, p. 166.
12. Samuelson 1990b, p. 66.
13. Ibid.
14. Samuelson 1939d, 1940b.
15. Paul's involvement with another such cross-disciplinary institution, the Graduate School of Public Administration, is discussed in chapter 12 this volume.
16. This account of Henderson's ideas draws on Isaac 2012, pp. 66–69.
17. Henderson, quoted in Isaac 2012, p. 68.
18. Samuelson 1998c, p. 1383.
19. Isaac 2012, p. 72.
20. P. A. Samuelson, October 9, 1940, Letter to Edwin Bidwell Wilson, EBWP HUG4878.203 Box 35 (S).
21. Samuelson et al. 1996, p. 163.
22. Discussed in detail in Isaac 2012.
23. Ibid., p. 93.
24. Bridgman 1927, pp. x–xi.
25. Ibid., p. 5; Bridgman's emphasis.
26. Ibid., p. 30.

27. Ibid., p. 31.
28. Isaac 2012, p. 108.
29. Bridgman 1938, p. 114.
30. Isaac 2012, pp. 102–107.
31. Walter 1990, chapter 7.
32. Samuelson 1938a.
33. P. A. Samuelson, January 25, 1938, Letter to Edwin Bidwell Wilson, EBWP HUG4878.203 Box 33.
34. E. B. Wilson, March 10, 1938, Letter to Dickson H. Leavens, EBWP HUG4878.203 Box 31 (L 1938).
35. Epstein 1937; P. A. Samuelson, November 29, 1938, Letter to Edwin Bidwell Wilson, EBWP HUG4878.203 Box 31 (S 1938).
36. E. B. Wilson, December 21, 1938, Letter to Paul A. Samuelson, EBWP HUG4878.203 Box 31 (S 1938).
37. P. A. Samuelson, Undated, The Le Chatelier Principle of Displaced Equilibrium, PASP 147.
38. See Hicks and Allen 1934a, 1934b.
39. Samuelson 1938b, p. 64.
40. P. A. Samuelson, 1937, New Foundations for the Pure Theory of Consumer's Behavior, PASP 152. The typescript is undated but is assumed to be 1937, on the grounds that the revised version was published in February 1938. The discussion in terms of differentials is on "Insert page 20b." Even with this and another less significant insert, the paper does not represent the final version, for the history of consumer theory, summarized in a single short paragraph in the published paper, takes almost two pages in the draft.
41. Samuelson 1938b, p. 70. The spelling of Gibbs has been corrected.
42. Ibid., p. 71.
43. P. A. Samuelson, 1937, New Foundations for the Pure Theory of Consumer's Behavior, PASP 152.
44. Robbins 1932.
45. Samuelson 1938c.
46. Samuelson 1938b, p. 62.
47. Samuelson 1938e, p. 344.
48. Sweezy 1934, p. 182, quoting Kaufmann 1933, p. 392.
49. Kaufmann 1933, p. 381, n1.
50. See Hutchison 2009.
51. Samuelson 1938d; Lange 1934.
52. Samuelson 1938d, p. 65.
53. O. Lange, May 10, 1938, Letter to Paul A. Samuelson, PASP 48.
54. Samuelson 1938d, p. 70.
55. Wilson 1939.
56. E. B. Wilson, December 21, 1939, Letter to Paul A. Samuelson, EBWP HUG4878.203 Box 33.

57. References to equation numbers in Wilson's letter correspond to the same equations in the published version. Correspondence with Lange (O. Lange, September 10, 1940, Letter to Paul A. Samuelson, PASP 48; P. A. Samuelson, September 13, 1940, Letter to Oskar Lange, PASP 48) suggests that aside from some minor changes to clarify points that Lange did not think clear, the 1939 draft was substantially the same as the published version.

58. Samuelson 1942b, p. 75.

59. Schumpeter et al. 1939, p. 120.

60. P. A. Samuelson, December 12, 1937, Letter to Frank Knight, PASP 45.

61. F. H. Knight, February 10, 1938, Letter to Paul A. Samuelson, PASP 45.

62. Samuelson 1939c. The number of sections was reduced from seven to five, and an addendum to which Knight refers was removed or incorporated into the main text. Beyond that, it is not known how far Samuelson responded to Knight's criticisms.

63. Ibid., p. 297.

64. Ibid., p. 290.

65. Ibid., p. 289.

66. Ibid., p. 290.

67. Ibid., p. 292.

68. Ibid., p. 291.

69. Ibid., p. 292.

70. Ibid., pp. 295–296; emphasis in original.

71. Samuelson 1958.

72. Samuelson 1939c, p. 294.

73. Tsuru 2001, chapter 7.

74. Samuelson 1939c, p. 291, n1.

Chapter 11: Collaboration

1. W. F. Stolper, 1940, Notes on Samuelson lectures 1939–40, Parts I and II, WSP 2002-0207, Box 14 (Samuelson course notes).

2. The paper has not yet been identified. It is possibly P. A. Samuelson and M. C. Samuelson, 1938, A Fundamental Function in Population Analysis, PASP 140. However, as is pointed out below, there are problems dating that paper.

3. A. J. Lotka, May 26, 1937, Letter to Edwin Bidwell Wilson, EBWP HUG4878.203 Box 29 (L 1937).

4. A. J. Lotka, February 20, 1939, Letter to Paul A. Samuelson, PASP 46 (L, 1946-60); Lotka 1939a.

5. Samuelson and Samuelson, A Fundamental Function in Population Analysis.

6. Ibid., p. 3. There is no indication of when this sentence was deleted.

7. A. J. Lotka, March 14, 1939, Letter to Paul A. Samuelson, PASP 46 (L, 1946-60).

8. P. A. Samuelson, Undated, A Note on the Net Reproductive Ratio and the Intrinsic Rate of Population Growth, PASP 140. This paper is undated, but the typing and type of paper suggest it is of similar age. It is filed in the same folder as the paper written with Marion, suggesting that it dates from a similar time.

9. P. A. Samuelson, 1939, The Structure of a Population Growing According to Any Prescribed Law, PASP 48 (Lotka).

10. Ibid., p. 5.

11. Lotka 1939b.

12. A. J. Lotka, October 19, 1939, Letter to Paul A. Samuelson, PASP 46 (L, 1946–60).

13. P. A. Samuelson, November 7, 1939, Letter to Alfred J. Lotka, PASP 46 (L, 1946–60).

14. Samuelson wrote, "in the case of strictly periodic functions such as are met in business cycles, all moments are infinite," Samuelson, Letter to Alfred J. Lotka.

15. A. J. Lotka, November 9, 1939, Letter to Paul A. Samuelson, PASP 46 (L, 1946–60).

16. A. J. Lotka, September 12, 1944, Letter to Paul A. Samuelson, PASP 46 (L, 1946–60); P. A. Samuelson, September 18, 1944, Letter to Alfred J. Lotka, PASP 46 (L, 1946–60).

17. United Electrical, Radio and Machine Workers (CIO), Undated, Biographical sketch—Russ Nixon, Russ Nixon Papers, University of Pittsburgh.

18. Halpern 2003, p. 96.

19. Samuelson 2002a, p. 52.

20. Samuelson 1996b, p. 16.

21. Nixon and Samuelson 1940; Samuelson 1996b, p. 16.

22. Nixon and Samuelson 1940, p. 102.

23. Ibid., p. 102.

24. Ibid., p. 103.

25. Robinson 1937.

26. Nixon and Samuelson 1940, p. 103.

27. Ibid., pp. 103–104; emphasis in original.

28. Ibid., p. 104.

29. Ibid., p. 104.

30. Samuelson 1938f, p. 261.

31. Samuelson 1939a, p. 200.

32. Ibid., p. 195.

33. This was, following Viner (1937), called "Graham's paradox."

34. Samuelson 1939a, p. 205; emphasis in original.

35. Ibid., p. 205.

36. Anderson 1938, p. 104.

37. M. Samuelson 1939, p. 147.

38. Anderson 1939, p. 150; emphasis in original.

39. F. D. Graham, February 7, 1940, Letter to Paul A. Samuelson, PASP 32 (G, 1940–1952).

40. Bergson 1938.

41. Samuelson 1987, p. 240.

42. Ibid., p. 240.

43. Deardorff and Stern 1994, p. 339.

44. Samuelson 1994, p. 346.

45. Stolper and Samuelson 1941, p. 66.

46. P. T. Homan, May 2, 1941, Letter to Paul A. Samuelson, PASP 71 (Stolper, 1). The letter is reproduced in Deardorff and Stern 1994, p. xi.

47. U. K. Hicks, October 16, 1941, Letter to Wolfgang Stolper, PASP 71 (Stolper, 1). The letter is reproduced in Deardorff and Stern 1994, p. x.

48. Deardorff and Stern 1994, p. 4.

49. E.g., the Introduction to Heckscher and Ohlin 1991.

Chapter 12: Alvin Harvey Hansen

1. Samuelson 1946a, p. 187.

2. Ibid., p. 189.

3. Ibid., pp. 187–188.

4. Samuelson 1976a, p. 29.

5. Samuelson 1975a.

6. Samuelson 1976b.

7. Samuelson 1975a.

8. Samuelson 1972a; P. A. Samuelson, 1972, Dedication to Alvin Hansen, AHP Box 1. Note that this memoir included a quotation, almost two pages long, that included the account of the Keynesian revolution quoted here.

9. Samuelson 1976a, p. 28.

10. Ibid., p. 28.

11. Mehrling 1997, p. 131. He cited Samuelson 1976a as exemplifying the accepted view.

12. Schumpeter et al. 1934.

13. Ibid., p. viii.

14. Haberler 1937b, p. 281.

15. Ibid., p. 299.

16. Leontief 1936b.

17. Schumpeter 1936.

18. Ibid.

19. Leontief 1937.

20. Tobin 1988, p. 36.

21. Bryce 1988, p. 147.

22. This paragraph draws on the conversation with Bryce in Colander and Landreth 1996, pp. 43–45. See also Hamouda and Price 1998, pp. xvii–xviii.

23. Keynes 1972.

24. Galbraith 1981, p. 49.

25. Moggridge 1998 has shown, on the basis of a sample of articles covering the period 1936 to 1948, that 109 of the 147 authors for whom he had biographical data were under 35 in 1936. His statistics also confirm the dominance of Harvard.

26. Samuelson 1995b, p. 159.

27. Gilbert et al. 1938. Tobin (1998, p. 46) provides a succinct account of Tarshis's co-authors and the four who worked with them on the volume, but could not put their names to it on account of their posts in government.

28. Samuelson 1995b, p. 167.

29. Gilbert et al. 1938, pp. 88–91.

30. Samuelson 1995b, p. 167.

31. Much of this account of Hansen is drawn from Mehrling 1997, chapters 5–8.

32. In 1966, it was renamed the Kennedy School of Government.

33. J. H. Williams, May 4, 1937, Letter to Professor Wymer (?), JHWP miscellaneous correspondence and other papers, 1929–71; J. H. Williams, May 25, 1937, Letter to Alvin Hansen, AHP Hansen 3.10 Correspondence (Box 1 [1928–67]).

34. J. H. Williams, May 25, 1937, Letter to Alvin Hansen, AHP Hansen 3.10 Correspondence (Box 1 [1928–67]).

35. A. H. Hansen, June 2, 1937, Letter to John H. Williams, JHWP miscellaneous correspondence and other papers, 1929–71 (Hansen).

36. Samuelson 1976a, p. 27.

37. It should be noted that Samuelson used this phrase to describe Mitchell.

38. Given his use of the word *seems*, it is not clear that Samuelson had read Hansen's thesis, though this would probably not have affected his judgment of it.

39. Hansen 1921, pp. 7, 110.

40. Ibid., p. 88.

41. See Mehrling 1997, pp. 96–101.

42. Samuelson 1976a, p. 28.

43. Hansen 1927.

44. Clark 1926.

45. See Mehrling 1997, pp. 107–110.

46. Hansen and Tout 1933, p. 121; emphasis in original.

47. Ibid., p. 121.

48. Ibid., p. 132.

49. Hansen 1934, p. 211.

50. Ibid., p. 236.

51. Ibid., p. 236; emphasis in original.

52. Hansen et al. 1936, p. 59.

53. Ibid., p. 61.

54. E. B. Wilson, May 14, 1937, Letter to Harold H. Burbank, EBWP HUG4878.203, Box 28 (B 1937).

55. E. B. Wilson, May 12, 1937, Letter to John H. Williams, JHWP miscellaneous correspondence and other papers, 1929–71.

56. Wilson, Letter to Harold H. Burbank.

57. Harvard University 1937, p. 6.

58. Under normal circumstances one would have expected output to have increased substantially over eight years. For example, productivity growth of 2 percent a year would have caused output to be 17 percent higher; 2.5 percent a year would have caused growth of 22 percent over eight years. Salant 1976, p. 15.

59. P. A. Samuelson, June 21, 1999, Walter Salant [obituary], PASP 67, p. 1.

60. Salant 1976, p. 21.

61. Ibid., p. 22.

62. The program is in Williams 1939.

63. Samuelson 1995b, p. 165.

64. The program is in Williams 1940.

Chapter 13: Hansen's Disciple

1. The discussion of Hansen in this section draws extensively on Mehrling 1997, chapter 7.

2. Hansen 1936b, p. 830.

3. Hansen 1936a, p. 686.

4. Ibid., p. 683.

5. Ibid., p. 685.

6. Mehrling 1997, p. 133.

7. Hansen 1938, p. 72.

8. J. Tobin, April 5, 1938, Lecture by Alvin H Hansen on Keynes's General Theory, PASP 36 (Hansen).

9. Ibid., p. 3.

10. Ibid., p. 4.

11. Hansen 1939.

12. Ibid., p. 10.

13. Ibid., p. 12.

14. Ibid., p. 13.

15. Ellsworth et al. 1939, pp. 225–226.

16. Ibid., p. 226.

17. Samuelson 1939b.

18. Ibid., p. 75; emphasis in original.
19. Samuelson 1959.
20. Samuelson 1939b, p. 78.
21. Ibid., p. 75.
22. Ibid., p. 76.
23. Samuelson 1939e.
24. Ibid., p. 786, quoting John Maurice Clark.
25. Ibid., p. 787. He noted that Clark had also made "substantial contributions" to this theory.
26. Ibid., p. 791.
27. Ibid., p. 795.
28. Ibid., p. 797.
29. Samuelson 1940c.
30. This came out in September 1940. Had he submitted the same version as presented in December 1938, it would have been published much sooner, implying he had been working on it throughout 1939.
31. Samuelson 1940d, p. 493.
32. Ibid., p. 498; emphasis in original.
33. Ibid., p. 498.
34. Ibid., p. 496.
35. Ibid., p. 504.
36. Ibid., p. 497; emphasis added.
37. Ibid., p. 506.
38. Ibid., p. 496.
39. He was aware of Michal Kalecki's work on the business cycle, though if his view echoed that of his friend Leonid Hurwicz, he would not have held a high opinion of it (L. Hurwicz, August 29, 1944, Letter to Paul A. Samuelson, PASP 39).
40. P. A. Samuelson and E. Roll, August 8, 1940, Agreement with Prentice-Hall for a book on business cycles, PASP 57 (P, 1940–59).
41. This paragraph is drawn from Roll 1985.
42. Roll 1995, p. 51.
43. Ibid., p. 54.
44. Roll 1985, p. 35.
45. P. A. Samuelson, June 28, 1946, Letter to Howard Warrington, PASP 60 (Publishers, 1944–49). He did not tell Roll of this until April 1, 1947, when Prentice-Hall said that they could cancel the contract only with Roll's agreement.
46. Given that this book appeared only when they were contracted to deliver their manuscript, its appearance does not explain why they did not begin to work on the book.
47. Roll 1941, p. 363.
48. Ibid.

1. Samuelson 1997b, p. 3; Samuelson 1998c, p. 1377.
2. Samuelson 1940a, preface.
3. Samuelson 1997b, p. 1039; Samuelson 1998c, p. 1375.
4. Samuelson 1998c, p. 1375.
5. Samuelson 1940a, p. 1. All emphases in original.
6. Ibid.
7. Ibid., pp. 2, 3.
8. Robbins 1932.
9. Samuelson 1938b, p. 71.
10. Samuelson 1938a.
11. Popper's *Logik der Forschung* (1933, translated as *The Logic of Scientific Discovery*, 1959).
12. Samuelson, 1940a, p. 4.
13. Ibid., pp. 4–5.
14. Ibid., pp. 5–6.
15. Ibid., p. 8.
16. Ibid., p. 10.
17. Ibid., p. 11.
18. Ibid., p. 13; emphasis added.
19. Ibid., p. 14.
20. Ibid., pp. 30–31.
21. Ibid., pp. 35–39.
22. Ibid., p. 98.
23. See chapter 10 this volume.
24. Samuelson 1940a, p. 68.
25. Ibid., p. 92.
26. Ibid., p. 110.
27. Ibid., p. 113.
28. Ibid., p. 192.
29. E. B. Wilson, December 30, 1938, Letter to Paul A. Samuelson, EBWP HUG4878.203 Box 31 (S 1938).
30. Samuelson, 1940a, p. 196.
31. Ibid., p. 207.
32. Ibid., p. 236.
33. It should be noted that this section deals solely with the PhD thesis, and should not be read as statements about the subsequent book. As will be explained in chapter 22, the book, though it included most of the thesis, was significantly different.
34. Samuelson 1947a, pp. 5, 312.

35. There is no evidence of their discussions before Samuelson's thesis, but they kept in touch, and later correspondence in which they did discuss such problems makes it highly probable that their discussions began when they were in the Society of Fellows.

Chapter 15: Leaving Harvard

1. This chapter overlaps considerably with Backhouse 2014.
2. E. B. Wilson, March 22, 1939, Letter to Griffith Evans, EBWP HUG4878.203 Box 32 (E).
3. G. C. Evans, April 5, 1939, Letter to E. B. Wilson, EBWP personal correspondence, Box 32 (Folder E, F).
4. H. A. Freeman, December 1939, Letter to Paul A. Samuelson, PASP 31.
5. Samuelson 1996b, p. 16.
6. This is inferred from Wilson's correspondence with Paul and Compton (E. B. Wilson, October 3, 1940, Letter to Paul A. Samuelson, EBWP HUG4878.203 Box 35 (S); E. B. Wilson, November 13, 1940, Letter to Karl T. Compton, MIT-AC04 Box 239 (10).
7. K. T. Compton, October 10, 1940, Letter to Paul A. Samuelson, PASP 53 (MIT).
8. Letter to the author, February 28, 2013.
9. E. B. Wilson, October 3, 1940, Letter to Paul A. Samuelson, EBWP HUG4878.203 Box 35 (S).
10. E. B. Wilson, October 14, 1940, Letter to Paul A. Samuelson, EBWP HUG4878.203 Box 35 (S).
11. P. A. Samuelson, October 9, 1940, Letter to Edwin Bidwell Wilson, EBWP HUG4878.203 Box 35 (S).
12. See Karabel 2005; Keller and Keller 2001.
13. Harvard University, Committee to Investigate the Cases of Drs. Walsh and Sweezy 1939, p. 151. This was the "Committee of Eight," discussed later.
14. Ibid., p. 152. This was even though the committee's questions were not designed to elicit views on the subject.
15. Keller and Keller 2001, pp. 33, 36.
16. Ibid., p. 36.
17. Karabel 2005, p. 168.
18. Ibid., p. 170.
19. Samuelson 2002a, p. 53.
20. E. Leontief 1987.
21. P. A. Samuelson, November 22, 1994, Letter to Perry Mehrling, PASP 36 (Hansen).
22. Reprinted as Perlman 1996.
23. Samuelson 2002a, p. 51.

24. E. B. Wilson, May 22, 1939, Letter to Harold H. Burbank, EBWP HUG4878.203 Box 32 (B).

25. H. H. Burbank, May 31, 1939, Letter to Edwin Bidwell Wilson, EBWP HUG4878.203 Box 32 (B).

26. Keller and Keller 2001, p. 81.

27. Samuelson 2002a, p. 54.

28. McCraw (2007, pp. 229–232) documents Schumpeter's activities in this regard.

29. Extract of correspondence between Ragnar Frisch and Joseph A. Schumpeter as written down by Olav Bjerkholt, PASP 71 (Summers family) contains extracts from this series of letters, deposited at the National Library of Norway.

30. J. A. Schumpeter, December 3, 1932, Letter to Ragnar Frisch, Ragnar Frisch Papers, National Library of Norway; emphasis added.

31. Presumably this was Samuelson 2003.

32. W. Stolper, February 12, 2002, Letter to Paul A. Samuelson, PASP 71 (Stolper, 1). Paul replied that he was well aware of these efforts; P. A. Samuelson, March 11, 2002, Letter to Wolfgang Stolper, PASP 71 (Stolper, 1).

33. Tsuru 2001, p. 124.

34. E. B. Wilson, May 12, 1939, Letter to Talcott Parsons, PASP 72 (Swedberg).

35. K. T. Compton, November 12, 1940, Letter to Edwin Bidwell Wilson, MIT-AC04 Box 239 (10). Quoted in Backhouse 2014, p. 68.

36. E. B. Wilson, November 13, 1940, Letter to Karl T. Compton, MIT-AC04 Box 239 (10). Quoted in Backhouse 2014, p. 68.

37. E. B. Wilson, April 16, 1941, Letter to Edward H. Chamberlin, EBWP HUG4878.203 Box 36.

38. E. B. Wilson, November 5, 1940, Letter to Karl T. Compton, MIT-AC04 Box 239 (10). Quoted in Backhouse 2014, pp. 68–69.

39. Backhouse 1998a, p. 93.

40. E. B. Wilson, January 14, 1941, Letter to Paul A. Samuelson, EBWP HUG4878.203 Box 37 (S 1941).

41. Schumpeter 1954, p. 23.

42. E. B. Wilson, January 31, 1940, Letter to Lawrence J. Henderson, EBWP HUG4878.203 Box 34 (H).

43. Letter to the author, February 28, 2013.

44. See Keller and Keller 2001, pp. 66–68.

45. Conant's view was that their views were not particularly radical. Keller and Keller 2001, p. 67.

46. See Goodwin 2014, pp. 67–70.

47. J. D. Black, October 3, 1940, Memorandum to Professor Chamberlin, HUESR UAV349.282 Box 19 (PAS concentration folder).

48. E. B. Wilson, October 3, 1940, Letter to Paul A. Samuelson, EBWP HUG4878.203 Box 35 (S).

49. Wilson continued to be concerned about the imbalance of expertise in the department after Samuelson left, demonstrating that it was perceived as a long-term problem.

50. P. A. Samuelson, Undated, The Hurwicz 1940-41 year when MIT launched its graduate degree rocket, PASP 39 (Hurwicz).

51. This is based on a conversation with one of Samuelson's daughters.

Chapter 16: The Massachusetts Institute of Technology

1. Lécuyer 2010, p. 70.
2. Ibid., p. 70.
3. Ibid., p. 71.
4. MIT 1940a, p. 86.
5. Ibid., p. 18. See Cherrier 2014 for an overview of the history of economics at MIT.
6. This account is based on various editions of the annual MIT Report to the President, and course catalogues. It differs slightly from the account given in Killian (1985).
7. The catalogue also lists two emeritus professors.
8. MIT 1940a, p. 5.
9. MIT Report of President 1939, p. 137.
10. Samuelson 1995a, p. 964.
11. Samuelson 1998b.
12. W. R. Maclaurin, December 4, 1940, Synopsis of training and experience of staff members, Rockefeller Box 6 (MIT Institute of Industrial Relations 1939–41).
13. Samuelson 1991b, p. 332. Samuelson appears to have misremembered the name of the Walker Cafeteria.
14. H. A. Freeman, October 22, 1948, Letter to Paul A. Samuelson, PASP 31; H. A. Freeman, January 5, 1949, Letter to Paul A. Samuelson, PASP 31. Another letter is discussed later.
15. One of the few sources of biographical information is Godin 2008.
16. P. A. Samuelson, May 23, 1949, Letter to Joan Robinson, PASP 63.
17. Samuelson 2000.
18. MIT Report of President 1937, pp 17–18.
19. MIT Report of President 1938, p. 18; 1939, p. 138; 1940, p. 135.
20. W. R. Maclaurin, April 8, 1939, Letter to Joseph H. Willits, Rockefeller Box 6 (MIT Institute of Industrial Relations 1939–41). The discussion of Maclaurin's research project draws extensively on Backhouse and Maas 2016.
21. K. T. Compton, April 8, 1939, Letter to Joseph H. Willits, Rockefeller Box 6 (MIT Institute of Industrial Relations 1939–41).

22. J. H. Willits and A. Bezanson, November 27, 1940, Memorandum on interview with W. Rupert Maclaurin, Rockefeller Box 6 (MIT Institute of Industrial Relations 1939–41).

23. Ibid.

24. W. R. Maclaurin, 1940, Memorandum on proposal for advanced study in industrial economics at MIT, Rockefeller Box 6 (MIT Institute of Industrial Relations 1942–43), p. 2.

25. Godin 2008 has explored the Maclaurin-Schumpeter connection in some detail.

26. Maclaurin, Memorandum on proposal for advanced study, p. 3.

27. W. R. Maclaurin, April 3, 1941, Letter to Joseph H. Willits, Rockefeller Box 6 (MIT Institute of Industrial Relations 1939–41).

28. W. R. Maclaurin, April 1, 1941, Technological change studies: projected annual expenses, Rockefeller Box 6 (MIT Institute of Industrial Relations 1939–41).

29. Anonymous, May 5, 1941, Memorandum to Joseph H. Willits, Rockefeller Box 6 (MIT Institute of Industrial Relations 1939–41); Rockefeller Foundation, May 16, 1941, Resolution RF41042—Research grant to MIT, Rockefeller Box 6 (MIT Institute of Industrial Relations 1939–41).

30. Rockefeller Foundation, Resolution RF41042.

31. J. H. Willits, June 12, 1941, Letter to W. Rupert Maclaurin, Rockefeller Box 6 (MIT Institute of Industrial Relations 1939–41).

32. MIT 1942a, p. 21.

33. MIT 1941, p. 83.

34. Unfortunately, as his appointment was not made until after MIT's course catalogue for the following year had been published, no record remains of what he taught in his first year other than his memory that he taught mathematical statistics. It is likely he was assisting Harold Freeman, listed in the course catalogue as teaching four statistics courses in 1940–41. Given MIT's need for someone to teach these subjects, it likely that he also taught Economic Theory (Ec.17) and Business Cycles (Ec. 28), even though he was not listed in the catalogue as teaching them until the following year. Most of his courses were electives, available to those who entered either as graduate students or as undergraduates taking a five-year program that led to a master's degree.

35. P. A. Samuelson, Undated, The Hurwicz 1940-41 year when MIT launched its graduate degree rocket, PASP 39 (Hurwicz), p. 3.

36. Ibid.

37. This material draws on various editions of *Bulletin of Tufts College: Complete Catalogue*, Tufts University, Medford, MA, from which all quotations are taken.

38. P. A. Samuelson, April 13, 1942, Letter to Abram Bergson, PASP 16.

39. S. Tsuru, June 6, 1942, Letter to Paul A. Samuelson, STP B1-1-9.

40. This account is based on S. Tsuru, September 17, 2000, Letter to Paul A. Samuelson, PASP 73, 2001; and Suzumura 2006.

41. S. Tsuru, June 6, 1942, Letter to whom it may concern, STP B1-1-9.

42. P. A. Samuelson, June 10, 1942, Telegram to Shigeto Tsuru, STP B1-1-9.

43. Samuelson 1942a.

44. Ibid., p. 16.

45. See Leonard 2010. Carvajalino 2016 draws attention to Wilson's fundamental philosophical objections to the type of mathematics pursued by von Neumann.

46. Haberler to Samuelson, January 26, 1942, GHP 2(S). Samuelson (1971, p. 997) describes it as "Sometime around 1945." However, the correspondence with Haberler dates it to March 1942, and Samuelson has said explicitly that he encountered von Neumann only once.

47. Samuelson 1989b, p. 112.

48. Samuelson 1971, p. 997.

49. Samuelson 1989b, p. 112.

50. MIT 1940b, p. 175.

51. The omitted chapters were 1–3 and 5.

52. E. R. Braider, 1943, Notes on Samuelson Ec. 17 (1942–3), JTP 2003-M-005, Box 18 (Ec. 17 Ringo). The date 1941–42 has been crossed out and replaced with 1943.

53. Nelson and Keim 1941, pp. 305–323.

54. The others were Robbins 1932 and Hutchison 1938.

55. Clark 1940. It is also possible that this may be Braider's mistake.

56. Ringo's notes contain remarks such as "Seems to think disinvestment for system as a whole is impossible," suggesting she was not completely clear about what Samuelson was saying.

Chapter 17: Statistics

1. See Friedman 2014, on which this account is based.

2. He may deserve less credit than he received, in that he had been forecasting an end to prosperity since 1926, tending to forecast decline when times were good and recovery when they were bad.

3. P. A. Samuelson, December 23, 1940, Memorandum concerning Babson Trust Fund, MIT-AC04 Box 89 (Babson Trust Fund); R. E. Freeman, December 23, 1940, Letter to Horace S. Ford, MIT-AC04 Box 89 (Babson Trust Fund).

4. The others were Tibor Scitovsky, Grace Dunn, and Rutledge Vining.

5. O. Lange, December 17, 1940, Letter to Paul A. Samuelson, PASP 48.

6. This is based on an interview with Hurwicz conducted by Amy Bauer, which formed the basis for Bauer 2008. Email from Bauer to the author, November 6, 2013.

7. P. A. Samuelson, Undated, The Hurwicz 1940–41 year when MIT launched its graduate degree rocket, PASP 39 (Hurwicz), pp. 2–3; emphasis in original.

8. H. S. Ford, December 27, 1940, Letter to James R. Killian, MIT-AC04 Box 89 (Babson Trust Fund).

9. The paper was eventually published as Hurwicz 1944.

10. P. A. Samuelson, November 29, 1943, Letter to Leonid Hurwicz, PASP 39.

11. Hurwicz 1944, p. 114.

12. O. Lange, December 17, 1940, Letter to Paul A. Samuelson, PASP 48.

13. The book in which this appeared is discussed in chapter 18 this volume. Given that this was published in 1941, the work was probably undertaken by the end of 1940.

14. Samuelson 1941e, pp. 250–251.

15. Ibid., p. 253.

16. Ibid., p. 255.

17. Thomas 1989, p. 143.

18. This appeared in the January issue, so must have been written in 1941. Samuelson 1942e.

19. Ibid., p. 80.

20. Samuelson's attitude to this work is discussed in Chapter 23 below.

21. Bjerkholt 2015, p. 7.

22. This account is based on the abstracts of the papers, published in Klein 1991.

23. Samuelson 1991b, p. 337.

24. This account of the seminar is based on Bjerkholt 2007, p. 810.

25. Haavelmo 1943.

26. Klein 1943. See also Bjerkholt 2014.

27. Samuelson 1991b, p. 332.

28. Samuelson 1942d.

29. Samuelson 1943b.

30. Samuelson 1943c.

31. A. J. Lotka, November 24, 1943, Letter to Paul A. Samuelson, PASP 48.

32. Samuelson 1943i.

33. Samuelson 1943h, p. 276.

34. P. A. Samuelson, September 23, 1944, Letter to Harold Freeman, PASP 31. It refers to Harold M. Davis, but it seems likely that this was a typing error.

35. Samuelson 1942f.

36. A. J. Lotka, January 9, 1942, Letter to Paul A. Samuelson, PASP 48.

37. P. A. Samuelson, July 29, 1942, Letter to Alfred J. Lotka, PASP 48.

38. A. J. Lotka, August 3, 1942, Letter to Paul A. Samuelson, PASP 48.

39. Ibid.

40. P. A. Samuelson, August 8, 1942, Letter to Alfred J. Lotka, PASP 48. "I" has been changed to "he."

41. A. J. Lotka, August 13, 1942, Letter to Paul A. Samuelson, PASP 48.

42. Having by then read all the relevant literature, he told the story in terms of Lotka's attempting to establish his own priority (Samuelson 1976c).

43. Harris 1947. On the textbook, see chapters 25–27 this volume.

1. Samuelson 1941a, p. 177.
2. The list of conference participants and the Harvard economists who had assisted him are given in Hansen 1941a, p. viii.
3. Ibid., p. vii.
4. Ibid., chapter 9.
5. Ibid., pp. 229, 236.
6. Samuelson 1942c.
7. See Schumpeter 1954. This view has parallels with the view of science later popularized by Thomas Kuhn. See Backhouse 1998b on the parallels between Kuhn and Schumpeter, and McCraw 2007 on the writing of Schumpeter's history.
8. Samuelson 1942c, p. 575.
9. Ibid., p. 576.
10. So much so that for a modern economist, used to algebra being used in the main text, the paper makes for slow reading.
11. Samuelson 1942c, p. 584.
12. Ibid., p. 585; emphasis in original.
13. He also had a section on the "tertiary" effects of government spending, operating through affecting "confidence" in the private sector. However, he admitted that he had nothing new to say on the subject.
14. Samuelson 1942c, p. 601.
15. Ibid., p. 604.
16. Ibid., p. 604.
17. Samuelson 1968.
18. Samuelson 1941c, p. 546.
19. Ibid., p. 552.
20. He added the qualification that appropriate account needed to be taken of depreciation allowances, a problem discussed in his earlier work.
21. Samuelson 1941c, p. 547; emphasis added.
22. See chapter 10 this volume.
23. P. A. Samuelson, 1942, Regarding Pigou's 1941 review of Keynes's *General Theory*, PASP 135 (Pigou's theory of employment).
24. Bergson 1942.
25. P. A. Samuelson, April 13, 1942, Letter to Abram Bergson, PASP 16.
26. Bergson 1942, p. 286, n27; Samuelson 1941d.
27. P. A. Samuelson, May 9, 1942, Letter to Dickson Leavens, PASP 16 (Bergson).
28. The copy in the file is undated. He received comments from Lange on March 2, 1942, so must have been written by February.
29. P. A. Samuelson, February, 1942, The Modern Theory of Income, PASP 135, p. 1; emphasis in original.

30. Ibid., p. 26.

31. Ibid., p. 12h.

32. Samuelson has "F" in the diagram and "Z" in the text. The diagram has been amended to make it consistent with the text and with the second diagram.

33. Samuelson, The Modern Theory of Income, p. 12.

34. Ibid., p. 39.

35. Ibid., p. 43.

36. Ibid., p. 43. The quotation is from Keynes.

37. Ibid., p. 47.

38. O. Lange, March 2, 1942, Letter to Paul A. Samuelson, PASP 135 (re Modern Theory of Income).

39. P. A. Samuelson, March 11, 1942, Letter to Oskar Lange, PASP 48.

40. Ibid.

41. He noted that in making his remarks he was paying much attention to Haberler in the third edition of *Prosperity and Depression* (as the third edition was not published until 1943, it is not clear whether Paul meant the second edition, published in 1939, or was referring to a draft of the forthcoming third edition); Means (1939), a report for the National Resources Committee; and Scitovsky (1941).

42. P. T. Homan, April 27, 1942, Letter to Paul A. Samuelson, PASP 135 (re Modern Theory of Income).

43. Ibid.

44. A. Ashbrook, October 13, 1942, Letter to Paul A. Samuelson, PASP 12.

45. P. A. Samuelson, October 17, 1942, Letter to Art Ashbrook, PASP 12.

46. A. Ashbrook, December 15, 1942, Letter to Paul A. Samuelson, PASP 12.

47. See De Vroey 2016, 2004.

48. H. P. Neisser, July 10, 1942, Letter to Paul A. Samuelson, PASP 55.

49. H. P. Neisser, November 7, 1942, Letter to Paul A. Samuelson, PASP 55.

50. P. A. Samuelson, November 10, 1942, Letter to Hans P. Neisser, PASP 55.

51. H. P. Neisser, November 17, 1942, Letter to Paul A. Samuelson, PASP 55.

52. P. A. Samuelson, November 27, 1942, Letter to Hans P. Neisser, PASP 55.

53. Ibid.

54. H. P. Neisser, December 2, 1942, Letter to Paul A. Samuelson, PASP 55.

55. H. P. Neisser, July 10, 1942, Letter to Paul A. Samuelson, PASP 55, raised perceptive question about the mathematics used in Samuelson 1941d.

56. A. P. Lerner, November 16, 1942, Letter to Paul A. Samuelson, PASP 48, referring to an earlier conversation.

57. P. A. Samuelson, November 23, 1942, Letter to Abba Lerner, PASP 48.

58. Ibid.

59. Samuelson 1943g.

60. This could be the mistake discovered in the Gilbert-Perlo paper discussed earlier.

61. Samuelson 1943e, p. 222.

62. Ibid., p. 226, n7, cites Karman and Biot 1940, a textbook aimed at engineers.

63. Lange 1943.

64. P. A. Samuelson, April 10, 1944, Letter to Oskar Lange, PASP 48.

65. Ibid.

66. J. A. Schumpeter, March 15, 1943, Letter to Paul A. Samuelson, PASP 68.

67. This section of the paper became a part of *Foundations of Economic Analysis* and is discussed further in chapter 22 this volume.

68. Samuelson 1943a, p. 58.

69. Ramsey 1928.

70. Sauelson 1943a, p. 68; the earlier paper is Samuelson 1939c.

71. J. A. Schumpeter, March 15, 1943, Letter to Paul A. Samuelson, PASP 68.

Chapter 19: Hansen and the National Resources Planning Board, 1941–1943

1. On Currie, see Sandilands 1990 and 2004.

2. Currie in Keyserling et al. 1972, p. 141. See Backhouse 2014.

3. D. Robertson, August 12, 1939, Letter to Alvin Hansen, AHP Hansen 3.10 Correspondence (Box 2 [L-Z]).

4. A. H. Hansen, September 29, 1939, Letter to Dennis Robertson, AHP Hansen 3.10 Correspondence (Box 2 [L-Z]).

5. Stein 1969, p. 168.

6. Tobin 1976, p. 34.

7. Hansen 1940.

8. Ibid., pp. 18–19.

9. Ibid., p. 56.

10. Hansen 1941b.

11. Ibid., p. 1.

12. Ibid., p. 12.

13. For histories of the NRPB, see Reagan 1999; Clawson 1981; Warken 1979; Merriam 1944.

14. Clawson 1981, p. 149.

15. Ibid., p. 151.

16. A. H. Hansen, July 10, 1941, Letter to Paul A. Samuelson, PASP 55 (NRPB).

17. P. A. Samuelson, August 5, 1941, Personal history statement and application, PASP 55 (NRPB); U.S. Civil Service Commission, August 11, 1941, Appointment letter, PASP 55 (NRPB). To put it in perspective, this was the equivalent of around $4,600 a year. His annual salary at MIT was $3,100.

18. P. A. Samuelson, 2006, Notes written in reply to letter from S. Nasar, January 14, 2006, PASP 55.

19. P. A. Samuelson, October 20, 1945, Letter to Mr. Edgerly, PASP 73 (Treasury Department).

20. Harro Maas has provided a helpful discussion of Samuelson's activity. I am grateful for his help in locating some documents.

21. P. A. Samuelson, August 25, 1941, Suggestions for a research unit to study implications of a full employment economy, PASP 55 (NRPB). This refers to an accompanying memorandum, which is presumably Samuelson 1941b.

22. Ibid.

23. Samuelson 1941b.

24. Ibid., pp. 18–19.

25. Ibid., appendix A, pp. 22–24. These were the major headings, under which more detailed tasks were listed.

26. P. A. Samuelson, August 25, 1941, Comments on Hansen Memorandum— Post-Defense Full Employment, PASP 55 (NRPB).

27. It is not known whether they knew each other at this time.

28. AEA Membership Directory, 1948.

29. Altman 1941.

30. Ibid., pp. 8–9.

31. C. W. Eliot, February 20, 1942, NRPB Staff Memorandum: Wartime planning for continuing full employment, AHP.

32. J. D. Millett, October 30, 1941, Notes on conference at NRPB, October 30, 1941, PASP 55 (NRPB).

33. Ibid., p. 2.

34. Letters were sent to Abram Bergson, Walt Rostow, F. L. Kidner, Gregg Lewis, Alfred Neal, David Durand, Rutledge Vining, Max Millikan, and Ray Jastrum. P. A. Samuelson, Undated, List of letters sent by PAS, PASP 55 (NRPB).

35. The authorship of this list is not clear. It has "Samuelson" typed at the top, indicating that it might have been a list of suggestions that someone was making to him. The misspelling of the name of Jacob Mosak, a close friend from Chicago, must raise some doubt about whether it was by Samuelson (though the error, as was getting Alchian's name wrong, might have been made by a secretary). P. A. Samuelson, 1941, List of names, PASP 55 (NRPB).

36. M. Finnamore, October 11, 1941, Letter to Paul A. Samuelson, PASP 55 (NRPB).

37. H. S. Ellis, October 24, 1941, Letter to Paul A. Samuelson, PASP 55 (NRPB).

38. P. A. Samuelson, August 23, 1941, Letter to Walt Rostow, PASP 55 (NRPB); R. Vining, September 21, 1941, Letter to Paul A. Samuelson, PASP 55 (NRPB).

39. H. K. Zassenhaus, September 15, 1941, Letter to Paul A. Samuelson, PASP 79 (Z, 1941–2008); J. W. Seybold, September 24, 1941, Letter to Paul A. Samuelson, PASP 55 (NRPB).

40. P. A. Samuelson, October 1, 1941, Letter to George Jaszi, PASP 40 (J, 1940–84, folder 2). Some of the available economists were not eligible because of the requirement that Civil Service employees be U.S. citizens.

41. O. L. Altman, December 11, 1941, Memorandum to Thomas Blaisdell: Personnel for the study on full-employment stabilization-defense, PASP 55 (NRPB).

42. O. L. Altman, December 30, 1941, Memorandum to Thomas Blaisdell: Recommendation for the appointment of personnel to the staff on the full employment stabilization-defense study, PASP 55 (NRPB).

43. O. L. Altman, December 11, 1941, Memorandum to Thomas Blaisdell: Recommendation for the reclassification of Esra Glaser from Associate Statistician, Grade P-3, to Statistician, Grade P-4, PASP 55 (NRPB).

44. O. L. Altman, December 30, 1941, Memorandum to Thomas Blaisdell: Recommendation for the appointment of Joseph Phillips as Associate Economist, Grade P-3, on the Full employment study, PASP 55 (NRPB).

45. O. L. Altman, March 14, 1942, Letter to Tom Blaisdell, PASP 55 (NRPB), pp. 1, 6.

46. I. de Vegh, February 10, 1942, Extract of letter to Alvin Hansen, PASP 55 (NRPB). As an illustration of the problems they uncovered, Colm's data put average incomes for those in the $15,000 to $20,000 income bracket at over $20,000.

47. O. L. Altman, March 14, 1942, Letter to Tom Blaisdell, PASP 55 (NRPB), pp. 1–2.

48. Ibid.

49. P. A. Samuelson, March 24, 1942, Memorandum: Expansion in non-essential civilian capacity, PASP 55 (NRPB).

50. P. A. Samuelson, April 2, 1942, Personal notes—Mr. Samuelson, PASP 55 (NRPB).

51. S. M. Kwerel, May 11, 1942, Letter to PAS: Partition of the blast furnace industry, PASP 55 (NRPB).

52. O. L. Altman, April 16, 1942, Letter to Albert Hart, PASP 55 (NRPB).

53. A. G. Hart, April 19, 1942, Letter to Oscar Altman, PASP 55 (NRPB).

54. O. L. Altman, May 4, 1942, Memorandum to Thomas Blaisdell: Recommendation for the appointment of Professor Abram Bergson as Senior Economist, Grade P-5, to the staff of the full employment study for the period June 1 to September 1, 1942, PASP 55 (NRPB).

55. P. A. Samuelson, June 30, 1942, Memorandum to Charles Eliot: Contribution of wartime planning for continuing full employment unit to annual report, PASP 55 (NRPB).

56. National Resources Planning Board, May 28, 1942, An Interim Report on Wartime Planning for Continuing Full Employment, Section I, PASP, Box 93.

57. A. Bergson, July 7, 1942, Memorandum to Full Employment Stabilization Unit on Ezekiel, AER March 1942, PASP 55 (NRPB).

58. H. Goodman, July 24, 1942, Memorandum to Oscar Altman and Paul Samuelson, PASP 55 (NRPB).

59. H. Goodman, August, 1942, Memorandum to Oscar Altman and Paul Samuelson: Projects being undertaken by other sections of the NRPB in connection with postwar planning, PASP 55 (NRPB).

60. O. L. Altman, et al., August 1942, Studies in Wartime Planning for Continuing Full Employment, PASP 93.

61. Ibid., p. I-26.

62. Ibid., p. XXX, IV-6.

63. Ibid., p. IV-1.

64. Ibid., p. IV-5.

65. C. W. Eliot, February 20, 1942, NRPB Staff Memorandum: Wartime planning for continuing full employment, AHP.

66. B. Jacobs, December 14, 1942, Memorandum to Herbert Goodman, PASP 55 (NRPB); B. Jacobs, December 14, 1942, General criticism, PASP 55 (NRPB).

67. Ibid., p. 2.

68. Ibid., pp. 4–5.

69. Ibid., p. 4.

70. Ibid., p. 8.

71. Hansen 1942b.

72. NRPB 1943c. See Warken 1979, pp. 224–226; Clawson 1981, pp. 136–138. The delay is of interest because it shows that, though published after the similar report by William Beveridge (1942), it was written earlier. Eveline Burns had been a student at the London School of Economics, though she had not been a student of Beveridge.

73. NRPB 1943a, 1943b.

74. NRPB 1943c, p. 1.

75. Ibid., p. 1.

76. NRPB 1943a, p. 5.

77. Hansen's files contain a detailed comparison of a speech by the British prime minister, Winston Churchill, and the NRPB's Report for 1943. NRPB, March, 1943, Comparison of British and American domestic postwar plans, AHP Hansen 3.10 Correspondence (Box 2 [L-Z]).

78. Reagan 1999, p. 220.

79. Clawson 1981, pp. 182–183.

80. NRPB 1942. This "economic bill of rights" had a history going back to 1939, and involved both Delano and Roosevelt (Reagan 1999, pp. 218–219).

81. Reagan 1999, p. 219.

82. Clawson 1981, p. 184.

83. NRPB 1943a, p. 3.

84. A. Bergson, H. Goodman, and E. E. Hagen, August 21, 1942, Memorandum to Thomas Blaisdell: A project for the publication of pamphlets on economic problems in the postwar period, based on studies conducted by the Full Employment Stabilization Unit, PASP 55 (NRPB).

85. A separate document indicated the coverage of these pamphlets in more detail. August 1942, Suggested subjects for pamphlet studies, PASP 55 (NRPB).
86. T. C. Blaisdell, August 15, 1942, Memorandum to Bell, Altman, and Samuelson, PASP 55 (NRPB).
87. A. Bergson, August 31, 1942, Letter to Paul A. Samuelson, PASP 55 (NRPB).
88. E. E. Hagen, September 15, 1942, Outline of pamphlet, PASP 55 (NRPB); E. E. Hagen, September 15, 1942, Memorandum to Full Employment Stabilization Unit staff, PASP 55 (NRPB).
89. A. Ashbrook, December 15, 1942, Letter to Paul A. Samuelson, PASP 12. Samuelson's correspondence with Ashbrook is discussed in chapter 18 this volume.
90. Samuelson and Hagen 1943.
91. Keynes 1919.
92. Samuelson and Hagen 1943, pp. 2–3.
93. Ibid., p. 25.
94. Ibid., pp. 42–43; emphasis added.
95. Ibid., p. 45; emphasis in original.
96. Ibid., p. 45.
97. W. S. Salant, March 6, 1944, Letter to Paul A. Samuelson, PASP 67; P. A. Samuelson, March 9, 1944, Letter to Walter Salant, PASP 67.
98. P. A. Samuelson, March 9, 1944, Letter to Walter Salant, PASP 67, p. 2; a paragraph break before the last sentence has been removed and "is" has been corrected to "are."
99. Samuelson 1943j, p. 360, quoting Chase.
100. Reagan 1999, p. 228. The reference was to one of the reports the NRPB has issued earlier in the year.
101. See Reagan 1999 on the end of the NRPB.
102. This account of public debates over the NRPB draws on Warken 1979, p. 238.
103. Ickes 1943.
104. Warken 1979, p. 192.
105. Quoted in Warken 1979, pp. 192–193.
106. Fairchild, quoted in the *New York Times*, April 29, 1943, "Chamber Warned on Post-war Plans."
107. Warken 1979, p. 192.
108. Matthew Woll, quoted in the *New York Times*, April 29, 1943, "Chamber Warned on Post-war Plans."
109. Samuelson 1941b, p. 20.
110. E. E. Hagen, March 3, 1943, Letter to Paul A. Samuelson, PASP 55 (NRPB).
111. J. Viner, February 26, 1943, Letter to Everett Hagen, PASP 55 (NRPB); E. E. Hagen, March 3, 1943, Letter to Paul A. Samuelson, PASP 55 (NRPB); E. E. Hagen, March 5, 1943, Letter to Jacob Viner, PASP 55 (NRPB).

112. P. A. Samuelson, April 19, 1943, Letter to Thomas Blaisdell, PASP 78 (Wright).

113. H. Goodman, May 22, 1943, Memorandum to Paul Samuelson, PASP 55 (NRPB).

114. J. McMurray, June 30, 1943, Letter to Paul A. Samuelson, PASP 72 (T, 1938-1968); J. McMurray, July 1, 1943, Letter to Paul A. Samuelson, PASP 72 (T, 1938–1968).

115. W. S. Salant, August 6, 1943, Letter to Paul A. Samuelson, PASP 67.

116. J. McMurray, July 1, 1943, Letter to Paul A. Samuelson, PASP 72 (T, 1938–1968).

117. C. W. Eliot, August 23, 1943, Letter to Paul A. Samuelson, PASP 55 (NRPB).

118. See Maas 2014.

119. P. A. Samuelson, Undated, Post-war Planning as Seen by a Retired Post-war Planner, PASP 152. Though the paper is undated, a footnote (p. 2) states that a Dr. Pangloss had found that the center of the American economics profession in 1943 lay somewhere between 10th and 11th Avenues, near Pennsylvania Avenue.

120. Ibid., p. 1.

121. Ibid., p. 6.

122. Ibid., p. 2; emphasis in original.

123. Ibid., pp. 6–7.

Chapter 20: Developing the New Economics, II: Policy, 1942–1943

1. Samuelson 1943d. The paper refers to Lange's forthcoming pamphlet, about which Paul learned on March 2, 1942. It is, of course, possible that this reference was inserted later, but the discussion of the balanced budget multiplier makes it seem likely that it was written after his paper "The Modern Theory of Income," submitted to the *American Economic Review* in April–May 1942. The end-date is based on Samuelson's memory that he had worked out the balanced budget multiplier before he read Salant's paper of July 1942 (discussed below).

2. Samuelson 1943d, p. 31.

3. Ibid., p. 37; emphasis in original.

4. Ibid., p. 41.

5. Ibid., p. 41.

6. Ibid., p. 40.

7. Ibid., p. 44.

8. Samuelson 1975b, p. 43.

9. This was eventually published as W. A. Salant 1975.

10. Samuelson 1942c, pp. 599–600.

11. Samuelson 1975b and W. S. Salant 1975 discuss the history of the theorem, including the first published version. For contemporary accounts of the inflation gap, see Friedman 1942; Salant 1942.

12. P. A. Samuelson, October 13, 1942, Letter to William S. Salant, PASP 64 (S, 1939-56, Folder 2).

13. W. S. Salant 1975a, p. 13.

14. Gilbert and Perlo 1942.

15. P. A. Samuelson, November 27, 1942, Letter to Walter Salant, PASP 67.

16. M. Geisler, December 9, 1942, Letter to Walter Salant, PASP 67; W. Salant, December 10, 1942, Letter to Paul A. Samuelson, PASP 67.

17. P. A. Samuelson, December 12, 1942, Letter to Walter Salant, PASP 67.

18. V. Perlo, December 19, 1942, Letter to Walter Salant, PASP 67.

19. P. A. Samuelson, December 29, 1942, Letter to Walter Salant, PASP 67.

20. Salant 1975a, p. 10.

21. P. A. Samuelson, August 11, 1943, Letter to Walter Salant, PASP 67.

22. Ibid.

23. A. H. Hansen, September 11, 1943, Letter to Paul A. Samuelson, PASP 36.

24. MIT 1941.

25. We know the content of his lectures in that year through the notes kept by one of his students, Elizabeth Ringo (E. R. Braider, 1943, Notes on Samuelson Ec. 26 (1943), JTP 2003-M-005, Box 17 [Ec 49 Ringo]). Unlike in his courses on economic analysis, he did recommend two of his own papers (Samuelson 1941d; Samuelson 1942c). He classified business cycle theories according to whether cycles were exogenous, determined outside the system (as in Jevons's theory, which related the cycle to sunspot activity and the weather), or endogenous, self-generating, determined by the properties of the system. He explained the difference between damped systems, in which the cycle would fade away were it not for periodic shocks, and explosive ones, noting that forecasting was possible only in the former.

26. Galbraith and Johnson 1940; Gayer 1935; Clark et al. 1935; and Hansen 1941a.

27. See, for example, Laidler 1999; Young 1987; De Vroey and Hoover 2004. It is called the Hicks-Hansen model on account of Hicks 1937 having proposed the model which received its canonical statement in Hansen 1953.

Chapter 21: Scientists and Science Policy, 1944–1945

1. P. A. Samuelson, March 9, 1944, Letter to Walter Salant, PASP 67.

2. P. A. Samuelson, March 21, 1944, Letter to Karl Compton, PASP 19 (C, 1941–1951).

3. Samuelson 1997c.

4. See Conway and Siegelman 2005, pp. 109–122; Mindell 2002, pp. 277–283.

5. P. A. Samuelson, March 21, 1944, Letter to Local Board no 47, PASP 61 (Radiation Laboratory).

6. P. A. Samuelson, October 18, 1945, For Radiation Laboratory Who's Who, PASP 61 (Radiation Laboratory).

7. P. A. Samuelson, April 6, 1944, Letter to Abram Bergson, PASP 16.

8. See Mindell 2002, pp. 268–275.

9. Mindell 2000, p. 37; McCulloch and Pitts 1943.

10. I failed to find any reference to Samuelson in the Radiation Laboratory archives at NARA, Waltham, Massachusetts.

11. P. A. Samuelson, October 14, 1944, Letter to Arthur Smithies, PASP 64 (S, 1939–56, Folder 2).

12. P. A. Samuelson, Undated, A suggestion for a generalized fire control correction box, PASP 61 (Radiation Laboratory).

13. Ibid., pp. 4–5.

14. P. A. Samuelson, Undated, Differential corrections in anti-aircract trajectories, PASP 61 (Radiation Laboratory). It is not clear whether the paper was finished.

15. Samuelson 1944a, p. 1.

16. P. A. Samuelson, June 9, 2005, Letter to Sylvia Nasar, PASP 55.

17. P. A. Samuelson, June 10, 1944, Letter to Robert V. Roosa, PASP 63.

18. Samuelson, June 9, 2005, Letter to Sylvia Nasar.

19. This section draws on Backhouse and Maas 2017, which contains more detailed references to the literature.

20. See Cochrane 1978, pp. 43–57.

21. P. A. Samuelson, August 6, 1944, Letter to E J Coil, PASP 19 (C, 1941–1951); emphasis in original. AACA has been corrected to NACA.

22. P. A. Samuelson, October 27, 1944, Letter to Bruce Bliven, PASP 56 (New Republic).

23. B. Bliven, October 19, 1944, Letter to Paul A. Samuelson, PASP 56 (New Republic).

24. P. A. Samuelson, November 24, 1944, Letter to Bruce Bliven, PASP 56 (New Republic).

25. Furer 1944.

26. B. Bliven, November 28, 1944, Letter to Paul A. Samuelson, PASP 56 (New Republic).

27. P. A. Samuelson, November 30, 1944, Letter to Bruce Bliven, PASP 56 (New Republic).

28. B. Bliven, December 4, 1944, Letter to Paul A. Samuelson, PASP 56 (New Republic).

29. Samuelson 1945g, p. 7. It is assumed that the new introduction provided by Bliven was the same as the first paragraph of the published editorial.

30. P. A. Samuelson, December 7, 1944, Letter to Bruce Bliven, PASP 56 (New Republic).

31. Samuelson 1945g, p. 8.

32. V. Bush, December 28, 1944, Letter to L. A. DuBridge, OSRD Box 2 (Committee #3, 2 of 3).

33. F. W. Loomis, January 5, 1945, Letter to James R. Killian, OSRD Box 2 (Committee #3, 2 of 3).

34. Backhouse and Maas 2017 discusses the collaboration between Samuelson, Guerlac, other members of the secretariat, and the committee in detail.

35. P. A. Samuelson, January 1, 1945, Untitled manuscript, HGP Box 25 (Folder 6).

36. Guerlac 1941

37. Anonymous, 1945, A scientific high command, HGP Box 25 (Folder 3).

38. It was typed differently from documents by Guerlac and does not appear the work of a professional typist, consistent with the conjecture that Samuelson wrote it.

39. Anonymous, March 27, 1945, Minutes of the meeting of the Bowman committee, held on March 26 and 27, 1945, HGP Box 25 (Folder 1-2).

40. I. Bowman, April 11, 1945, Letter to Vannevar Bush, OSRD Box 2 (Committee No. 3, 1 of 3).

41. Anonymous, April 6, 1945, Draft of prologue to Bowman Committee Report, OSRD Box 2 (Committee #3 2-1-45 to 5-15-45), p. 1.

42. Ibid., p. 5.

43. Ibid., p. 7.

44. Bush 1945.

45. I. Bowman, April 11, 1945, Letter to Vannevar Bush, OSRD Box 2 (Committee #3, 1 of 3).

46. F. W. Loomis, April 4, 1945, Letter to Paul A. Samuelson, PASP 61 (Radiation Laboratory).

47. P. A. Samuelson, April 16, 1945, Letter to F Wheeler Loomis, PASP 61 (Radiation Laboratory).

48. P. A. Samuelson, April 26, 1945, Letter to F Wheeler Loomis, PASP 61 (Radiation Laboratory).

49. As is explained in chapter 25 this volume, by July 1945 he was sufficiently committed to this project to have received a draft contract from McGraw-Hill.

50. Samuelson 2009b.

51. P. A. Samuelson, April 26, 1945, Letter to F. Wheeler Loomis, PASP 61 (Radiation Laboratory).

52. L. Carmichael, August 3, 1945, Letter to Local Board No 47, PASP 61 (Radiation Laboratory).

53. W. R. Maclaurin, April 20, 1945, Letter to Vannevar Bush, OSRD Box 4 (Committee #3, 3 of 3).

54. C. L. Wilson, May 19, 1945, Letter to W. Rupert Maclaurin, OSRD Box 4 (Report to President, Committee #4).

55. W. Leontief, March 15, 1945, Letter to Paul A. Samuelson, PASP 48. Formally the invitation came from the committee running the group.

56. The information on Samuelson's attendance and the topics covered are taken from various documents in the "Inter Scientific Discussion Group 1944-7" folder in the Gerald Holton Papers, Harvard University Archive, HUM 132/63/3.

57. A few days later he reported that he had caught German measles.

Chapter 22: Foundations of Economic Analysis, 1940–1947

1. Samuelson 1998c, p. 1378.
2. Ibid., p. 1378.
3. E. B. Wilson, November 22, 1940, Letter to Edward H. Chamberlin, HUESR UAV349.282 Box 19 (PAS concentration folder).
4. E. B. Wilson et al., December 4, 1940, Report on examination for graduate degree, HUESR UAV349.282 Box 19 (PAS concentration folder).
5. E. B. Wilson, January 14, 1941, Letter to Paul A. Samuelson, EBWP HUG4878.203 Box 37 (S 1941).
6. S. E. Harris, January 7, 1941, Letter to Edwin Bidwell Wilson, EBWP HUG4878.203 Box 36 (H).
7. E. B. Wilson, January 14, 1941, Letter to Paul A. Samuelson, EBWP HUG4878.203 Box 37 (S 1941).
8. E. B. Wilson, January 14, 1941, Letter to Seymour E. Harris, EBWP HUG4878.203 Box 36 (H).
9. E. B. Wilson, November 22, 1940, Letter to Edward H. Chamberlin, HUESR UAV349.282 Box 19 (PAS concentration folder).
10. E. H. Chamberlin, February 10, 1942, Minutes of department meeting, HUA-E Box 10 (Department Meeting), p. 328.
11. H. H. Burbank, March 16, 1942, Letter to Paul A. Samuelson, PASP 62 (*Review of Economics and Statistics*, to 1968); P. A. Samuelson, February 20, 1945, Letter to Harold Burbank, PASP 14 (B, 1939–51).
12. D. J. Pottinger, May 29, 1942, Letter to Paul A. Samuelson, PASP 57 (P, 1940–59).
13. P. A. Samuelson, June 28, 1942, Letter to David T. Pottinger, PASP 34 (H, 1940–57).
14. Ibid.
15. P. A. Samuelson, July 8, 1943, Letter to A. P. Usher, PASP 85 (*Foundations of Economic Analysis*).
16. A. P. Usher, July 17, 1943, Letter to Paul A. Samuelson, PASP 85 (*Foundations of Economic Analysis*).
17. P. A. Samuelson, August 11, 1943, Letter to Walter Salant, PASP 67.
18. P. A. Samuelson, April 6, 1944, Letter to Abram Bergson, PASP 16.
19. P. A. Samuelson, February 27, 1945, Letter to Edwin Bidwell Wilson, PASP 77.
20. R. L. Scaife, February 21, 1945, Letter to Abbott P. Usher.

21. A. P. Usher, March 22, 1945, Letter to Roger L. Scaife, HUPF.
22. J. W. McFarlane, August 1, 1945, Letter to Roger L. Scaife, HUPF.
23. A. P. Usher, August 13, 1945, Letter to Roger L. Scaife, HUPF.
24. J. W. MacFarlane, August 31, 1945, Letter to Roger L. Scaife; R. L. Scaife, September 5, 1945, Letter to Abbott Payson Usher, HUPF.
25. R. L. Scaife, November 7, 1945, Letter to Abbott Payson Usher, HUPF; R. L. Scaife, April 22, 1946, Letter to Abbott Payson Usher, HUPF.
26. A. V. Jules, December 3, 1945, Letter to Mr. Rohr, HUPF.
27. R. L. Scaife, April 22, 1946, Letter to Abbott Payson Usher, HUPF.
28. C. W. Wilson, December 9, 1946, Letter to Alfred V. Jules, HUPF.
29. C. W. Wilson, December 13, 1946, Letter to Alfred V. Jules, HUPF.
30. C. W. Wilson, February 28, 1947, Letter to Mary Harney, HUPF.
31. R. L. Scaife, April 9, 1947, Letter to Abbott Payson Usher, HU; A. V. Jules, May 21, 1947, Letter to C. W. Wilson, HUPF; C. W. Wilson, June 9, 1947, Letter to Alfred V. Jules, HUPF.
32. C. W. Wilson, April 18, 1947, Letter to Alfred V. Jules, HUPF.
33. A. V. Jules, April 28, 1947, Letter to C. W. Wilson, HUPF.
34. W. W. S[mith], June 17, 1947, Letter to Abbott Payson Usher, HUPF.
35. A. V. Jules, June 18, 1947, Letter to C. W. Wilson, HUPF.
36. A. P. Usher, July 4, 1947, Letter to Mr. Smith, HUPF.
37. C. Morgan, October 10, 1947, Letter to Gottfried Haberler, GHP Box 1 (H).
38. C. W. Wilson, October 2, 1947, Letter to Alfred V. Jules, HUPF (Samuelson, *Foundations*). Email from Michael Aronson to REB, April 9, 2012.
39. R. P. Rohrer, September 30, 1947, Letter to Alfred V. Jules, HUPF.
40. P. A. Samuelson, September 29, 1946, Letter to Shigeto Tsuru, STP B1-1-9.
41. For a detailed list of the changes, see Backhouse 2015a.
42. Samuelson, 1940a, p. 4.
43. Samuelson 1947a, p. 5.
44. Ibid., p. 258.
45. The index entry for "Correspondence Principle" gives three additional pages. On one, the phrase is not used, and the remaining two are in a new chapter.
46. Samuelson 1947a, p. 23.
47. Ibid., p. 125.
48. Ibid., p. 141.
49. Ibid., p. 148.
50. Hicks 1939a, p. 698.
51. Stigler 1943, p. 355. The article on trade is Samuelson 1938f.
52. Stigler 1943, p. 356.
53. Samuelson 1943f, p. 605.
54. Samuelson 1947a, p. 203.
55. Ibid., p. 212.
56. Ibid., p. 212; emphasis in original.
57. Ibid., p. 219.

58. Robbins 1932.
59. Samuelson 1947a, p. 220.
60. Ibid., p. 221.
61. Ibid., p. 224. The importance of individual rationality as a distinction between the United States and the Soviet Union has been discussed by Amadae 2003.
62. Samuelson 1947a, p. 248.
63. Ibid., pp. 208, 215, 223, 226.
64. Samuelson 1942f, p. 1; Samuelson 1947a, p. 284.
65. Samuelson 1941d, 1942f, 1943a, 1944b.
66. Samuelson 1942f, p. 1; Samuelson 1947a, p. 284; emphasis added.
67. Samuelson 1943a, p. 58.
68. Ibid., p. 58.
69. Samuelson 1947a, p. 335.
70. Kalecki 1935.
71. L. Hurwicz, August 29, 1944, Letter to Paul A. Samuelson, PASP 39.
72. For example, Harrod 1936.
73. Samuelson 1947a, pp. 117–124.
74. For example, Boulding 1948b; Savage 1948. Samuelson had ordered copies of the appendices for teaching.
75. Reder 1948, p. 516.
76. Allen 1949, p. 111.
77. Samuelson 1998c, p. 1382.
78. Allen 1949, p. 112.
79. Baumol 1949, p. 159.
80. Baumol 1949; Allen 1949; Stigler 1948; Tintner 1948; Savage 1948.
81. Allen 1949, p. 113; Savage 1948, p. 202.
82. Metzler 1948, pp. 905, 906; emphasis added. See, for example, L. A. Metzler, December 22, 1944, Letter to Paul A. Samuelson, PASP 53; P. A. Samuelson, December 27, 1944, Letter to Lloyd A. Metzler, PASP 53; L. A. Metzler, June 16, 1945, Letter to Paul A. Samuelson, PASP 53.
83. May 1948, p. 94.
84. Baumol 1949, p. 160.
85. Von Neumann to Haberler, October 31, 1947; in Rédei 2005, p. 128.

Chapter 23: Postwar Economic Policy, 1944–1947

1. R. W. Goldsmith, October 5, 1943, Letter to Paul A. Samuelson, PASP 76 (War Production Board).
2. P. A. Samuelson, October 12, 1943, Letter to Raymond Goldsmith, PASP 76 (War Production Board).
3. See chapter 21 this volume.
4. P. A. Samuelson, October 12, 1943, Letter to Raymond Goldsmith, PASP 76 (War Production Board).

5. P.A. Samuelson, November 27, 1943, Letter to Raymond Goldsmith, PASP 76 (War Production Board).

6. P. A. Samuelson, January 19, 1944, Letter to Raymond Goldsmith, PASP 76 (War Production Board).

7. P. A. Samuelson, September 18, 1944, Letter to Jacob L. Mosak, PASP 49 (M, 1944–52).

8. The memorandum in which he made these points was "Financial Aspects of Demobilization, Part I—The Case for Liberalizing Wartime Earnings and Contract Settlements" (1944, PASP 76 [War Production Board]). It could have been the one sent in January. It tallies with the letter in being Part I of a memorandum addressed explicitly to Goldsmith. A different memorandum is filed with the letter, but this one does not fit and seems more likely an early draft of something he wrote a few months later, suggesting that documents are not filed in the correct sequence.

9. P. A. Samuelson, August 4, 1944, Letter to P. Bernard Nortman, PASP 76 (War Production Board).

10. P. B. Nortman, August 8, 1944, Letter to Paul A. Samuelson, PASP 76 (War Production Board).

11. This is filed with Paul's letter of January 19, though, as explained in an earlier footnote, it does not appear to be the document enclosed with that letter. The formula used to calculate the value of the multiplier, which distinguishes business and household saving, is the same as one used in a letter to Jacob Mosak (P. A. Samuelson, September 18, 1944, Letter to Jacob L. Mosak, PASP 49 [M, 1944–52]).

12. P. A. Samuelson, January 19, 1944, Estimating the primary and secondary effects of cutbacks in production, PASP 76 (War Production Board), p. 2.

13. Ibid., p. 6.

14. P. A. Samuelson, October 11, 1944, Letter to Raymond Goldsmith, PASP 76 (War Production Board).

15. R. W. Goldsmith, October 31, 1944, Letter to Paul A. Samuelson, PASP 76 (War Production Board); P. A. Samuelson, November 17, 1944, Letter to Raymond Goldsmith, PASP 76 (War Production Board); R. W. Goldsmith, November 23, 1944, Letter to Paul A. Samuelson, PASP 76 (War Production Board); R. W. Goldsmith, March 17, 1945, Letter to Paul A. Samuelson, PASP 76 (War Production Board); War Production Board, May 7, 1945, Advice of Personnel Action, PASP 76 (War Production Board); R. W. Goldsmith, May 10, 1945, Letter to Paul A. Samuelson, PASP 76 (War Production Board); P. A. Samuelson, May 8, 1945, Letter to Raymond Goldsmith, PASP 76 (War Production Board).

16. War Production Board, July 7, 1945, Advice of personnel action, PASP 76 (War Production Board).

17. R. W. Goldsmith, March 13, 1945, Letter to Paul A. Samuelson, PASP 76 (War Production Board).

18. R. W. Goldsmith, May 3, 1945, Memorandum from Raymond Goldsmith to PAS, PASP 76 (War Production Board).

19. Ibid., p. 2.

20. Anticipated dates for V-J day were June 30 and December 30, 1946.

21. R. W. Goldsmith, May 22, 1945, Letter to Paul A. Samuelson, PASP 76 (War Production Board).

22. P. A. Samuelson, May 27, 1945, Estimating Importance of Industrial Sector at High Post war Income, PASP 76 (War Production Board).

23. Estimated equations were of the form Capital = −0.417 + 0.029 GDP, with correlation coefficient of 0.573 for the period 1921–1940.

24. P. A. Samuelson, June, 1945, Economic Effects of Cutbacks, PASP 76 (War Production Board). The location of this paper in the folder suggests it dates from May–June 1945. The typing (typeface and many mistakes) suggests Samuelson typed it himself and that it was probably not sent to anyone.

25. R. W. Goldsmith, June 14, 1945, Letter to Paul A. Samuelson, PASP 76 (War Production Board).

26. R. W. Goldsmith, June 20, 1945, Letter to Paul A. Samuelson, PASP 76 (War Production Board).

27. P. A. Samuelson, June 28, 1945, Comments on the Wood memorandum, PASP 76 (War Production Board); P. A. Samuelson, June 28, 1945, Letter to Raymond Goldsmith, PASP 76 (War Production Board).

28. R. W. Goldsmith, June 21, 1945, Letter to Paul A. Samuelson, PASP 76 (War Production Board).

29. R. W. Goldsmith, June 26, 1945, Letter to Paul A. Samuelson, PASP 76 (War Production Board).

30. P. A. Samuelson, July 28, 1945, Letter to Raymond Goldsmith, PASP 76 (War Production Board).

31. P. A. Samuelson, July 28, 1945, Determinants of National Income and Inflation, PASP 76 (War Production Board), p. 8.

32. Ibid., p. 11.

33. R. W. Goldsmith, August 9, 1945, Letter to Paul A. Samuelson, PASP 76 (War Production Board).

34. WPB, October 10, 1945, Advice of personnel action, PASP 76 (War Production Board).

35. R. W. Goldsmith, October 15, 1945, Letter to Paul A. Samuelson, PASP 76 (War Production Board).

36. R. P. Goldsmith, October 10, 1945, A Simplified Analysis of the Process of Income Expansion and Contraction, PASP 76 (War Production Board).

37. P. A. Samuelson, July 20, 1944, Letter to *New Republic*, PASP 56 (*New Republic*).

38. P. A. Samuelson, August 11, 1944, Letter to Bruce Bliven, PASP 56 (*New Republic*).

39. P. A. Samuelson, August 11, 1944, Letter to Bruce Bliven, PASP 56 (*New Republic*). Mordecai Ezekiel was an economist at the Department of Agriculture.

40. P. A. Samuelson, August 17, 1944, Letter to Bruce Bliven, PASP 56 (*New Republic*).

41. P. A. Samuelson, August 25, 1944, Letter to Bruce Bliven, PASP 56 (*New Republic*). The chart was taken from Goldenweiser and Hagen 1944.

42. P. A. Samuelson, September 1, 1944, Letter to Bruce Bliven, PASP 56 (*New Republic*).

43. Samuelson 1944c.

44. Ibid., p. 297.

45. Ibid., p. 297.

46. Ibid., p. 298.

47. Ibid., p. 298.

48. Ibid., p. 298.

49. Ibid., p. 299.

50. J. L. Mosak, September 13, 1944, Letter to Paul A. Samuelson, PASP 49 (M, 1944–52).

51. P. A. Samuelson, September 18, 1944, Letter to Jacob L. Mosak, PASP 49 (M, 1944–52).

52. Samuelson 1944d.

53. Ibid., p. 333.

54. Ibid., p. 334.

55. Ibid., p. 335

56. P. A. Samuelson, October 10, 1944, Letter to S. Morris Livingstone, PASP 46 (L, 1946–60).

57. J. L. Mosak, October 7, 1944, Letter to Paul A. Samuelson, PASP 49 (M, 1944–52).

58. They were published as Smithies 1945; Livingston 1945; Mosak 1945; Roos et al. 1945.

59. Mosak 1945.

60. P. A. Samuelson, October 14, 1944, Letter to Jacob L. Mosak, PASP 49 (M, 1944–52).

61. Though Paul stated that this was written in the summer of 1944 (Samuelson 1945c, p. 674), revisions were made for the published version cited his debate with Sonne in *Modern Industry*, not initiated until November.

62. Samuelson 1945a, p. 26.

63. H. F. Merrill, November 13, 1944, Letter to Paul A. Samuelson, PASP 49 (M, 1944–52).

64. H. C. Sonne, November 22, 1944, Letter to Paul A. Samuelson, PASP 64 (S, 1939–56, Folder 2); P. A. Samuelson, November 24, 1944, Letter to Harwood F. Merrill, PASP 49 (M, 1944–52); P. A. Samuelson, November 24, 1944, Letter to E. Christian Sonne, PASP 64 (S, 1939–56) Folder 2;

P. A. Samuelson, December 1, 1944, Letter to Alvin Hansen, AHP Hansen 3.10 Correspondence (Box 1, 1928–67); A. H. Hansen, December 6, 1944, Letter to Paul A. Samuelson, PASP 36.

65. Samuelson 1945f, p. 113.
66. Samuelson 1945a, p. 27.
67. Harris 1945.
68. Coleman 1945, p. 671.
69. Ibid., p. 672.
70. Ibid., p. 673.
71. Ibid., p. 674
72. Ibid., p. 675.
73. Roosevelt 1945.
74. Samuelson 1945h, p. 136.
75. Samuelson 1945e.
76. Hansen 1945a.
77. Ibid., p. 178.
78. Ibid., pp. 21–22.
79. Ibid., pp. 18–20.
80. Samuelson 1945e, p. 410.
81. Ibid., p. 411.
82. Samuelson 1945d, p. 467.
83. Samuelson 1945h, p. 469.
84. This summary of the bill's history draws upon Bailey 1950. See also Hansen 1947, chap. 9.
85. Hansen 1945b.
86. Ibid., p. 2 of the attachment.
87. Samuelson 1945b.
88. On Hansen's view, see Bailey 1950, p. 48, n22.
89. Some of this literature is cited in Hagen 1947.
90. Samuelson 1946b. Samuelson wrote "By PAS" on his copy of the article.
91. Samuelson1946b, p. 8.
92. E. E. Hagen, February 2, 1945, Letter to Paul A. Samuelson, PASP 36.
93. Hagen and Kirkpatrick 1944; Goldenweiser and Hagen 1944.
94. It is possible that the article was Hagen 1945. This article contains a survey of the rapidly growing literature forecasting postwar conditions.
95. E. E. Hagen, November 20, 1944, Letter to Paul A. Samuelson, PASP 36, p. 2.
96. P. A. Samuelson, November 28, 1944, Letter to Everett Hagen, PASP 36, p. 2.
97. Ibid., p. 1.
98. Ibid., p. 2.
99. Ibid.
100. Hagen 1947.

101. Ibid., p. 100.

102. Samuelson 1946b, p. 9.

103. Koopmans 1947; Vining 1949.

104. Burns and Mitchell 1945.

105. P. A. Samuelson, August, 1948, Comments on Vining's methodological issues, PASP 37 (Harris).

106. P. A. Samuelson, October 1, 1943, Comments on the Bennion and Tintner manuscripts, PASP 37 (Harris). The paper he was reviewing would appear to be Tintner 1944.

107. Wilson 1946, p. 173.

108. Hansen and Samuelson 1947a, p. 186.

109. Hansen and Samuelson 1946.

110. P. A. Samuelson, February 5, 1946, Letter to Alvin Hansen, PASP 36; M. W. Latimer, February 19, 1946, Letter to Alvin Hansen, PASP 36 (Hansen); A. H. Hansen, February 23, 1946, Letter to Paul A. Samuelson, PASP 36; R. F. Jones, May 23, 1946, Letter to Alvin Hansen and Paul A. Samuelson, PASP 36 (Hansen).

111. P. A. Samuelson, August 5, 1946, Letter to Alvin Hansen, PASP 36. The chapters to which Paul drew Hansen's attention were 8 (on the causes of business rhythms), 18 (labor as an overhead cost), and 19 (overhead costs and the business cycle), together with sections on these topics in the introductory chapters.

112. P. A. Samuelson, August 7, 1946, Letter to Alvin Hansen, PASP 36.

113. Hansen and Samuelson 1947a, p. 464.

114. Ibid., p. 18.

115. Hansen and Samuelson 1947b.

116. Ibid., p. 38.

Chapter 24: Keynes and Keynesian Economics

1. Klein 2004, p. 18.

2. Klein 1942.

3. Klein and Mariano 1987; Mariano 2008.

4. Klein and Mariano 1987, p. 411.

5. Ibid., p. 411.

6. Ezekiel 1942a, 1942b.

7. Ezekiel 1944; Klein 1944c.

8. Klein 1944a.

9. Ibid., p. 435.

10. Ibid., p. i.

11. Ibid., p. ii.

12. Ibid., pp. 51–52.

13. Ibid., p. 53.

14. Ibid., p. iv.

15. Ibid., pp. 19, 124.
16. L. Klein, March 29, 1944, Letter to Alvin Hansen, AHP Hansen 3.10 Correspondence (Box 1 [A-K]).
17. Klein 1944a, p. 113.
18. Ibid., p. iii.
19. Ibid., pp. 183–184.
20. This is based on a computer search of OCR-generated text, and may have omitted instances. The bibliography and preliminary pages are omitted from the count.
21. See Klein 1954.
22. Lange 1943.
23. P. A. Samuelson, April 10, 1944, Letter to Oskar Lange, PASP 48.
24. Modigliani 1944.
25. Ibid., pp. 76–77.
26. D. H. Leavens, April 26, 1946, Letter to Ragnar Frisch, Ragnar Frisch Papers, National Library of Norway.
27. R. Frisch, May 16, 1946, Letter to Dickson Leavens, Ragnar Frisch Papers, National Library of Norway; Samuelson 1946a, p. 187, n1.
28. Samuelson 1946a, pp. 190–191.
29. Ibid., p. 191, n5.
30. Ibid., p. 188.
31. Ibid., p. 193, quoting Keynes.
32. Ibid., p. 195.
33. Ramsey 1928.
34. As was shown in chapter 10 this volume.
35. Samuelson 1946a, p. 195.
36. Ibid., pp. 200, 199.
37. P. A. Samuelson, February 16, 1945, Letter to Fritz Machlup, PASP 11 (AEA).
38. P. A. Samuelson, August, 1947, Letter to Alvin Hansen, PASP 36.
39. See chapter 12 this volume.
40. Letter from Clark to Keynes (Keynes 1979, p. 191).
41. Clark 1923, p. ix.
42. P. A. Samuelson, September 27, 1946, Letter to J. M. Clark, PASP 19 (C, 1941–51).
43. P. A. Samuelson, April 11, 1949, Letter to Lewis H. Haney, PASP 34 (H, 1940–57).

Chapter 25: Drafting the Textbook, 1945

1. Samuelson 1948 and subsequent editions.
2. Samuelson 1997a, 1998a; Samuelson et al. 1999.
3. Samuelson 1997a, p. 154.
4. R. E. Freeman, June 6, 1945, Letter to Karl T. Compton, MIT-AC04 Box 93 (8, R. E. Freeman).

5. MIT 1944, p. 34.
6. Compton 1944, p. 7.
7. McGraw-Hill Book Company, July 16, 1945, Unsigned memorandum of agreement, PASP 87 (Economics, 1945–2008, Folder 2).
8. P. A. Samuelson, February 18, 1946, Letter to Alan Sweezy, PASP 64 (S, 1939–56, Folder 2).
9. P. A. Samuelson, 1945, *Modern Economics: An Introductory Analysis of National Income and Policy*, PASP 91.
10. Samuelson 1997a, p. 157.
11. See R. V. Clemence, October 3, 1949, Letter to Paul A. Samuelson, PASP 19 (C, 1941–51), and Samuelson 1948, p. vii. The archival record is silent on Samuelson's relations with Doody.
12. P. A. Samuelson, August 30, 1948, Letter to Richard Clemence, PASP 19 (C, 1941–51).
13. Clemence and Doody 1942.
14. Ibid., p. 342.
15. Ibid., p. 343.
16. Ibid., p. 344.
17. Samuelson 1948, p. v; emphasis added.
18. See Giraud 2014.
19. P. A. Samuelson, March 2, 1946, Letter to Emile Despres, PASP 28 (Sub-committee on the problem of economic instability).
20. Samuelson 1948, p. v.
21. Armstrong et al. 1938a, 1938b. The MIT Library catalogue also contains two earlier versions, from 1934 and 1935.
22. Armstrong et al. 1938a, p. iii.
23. P. A. Samuelson, 1945, *Modern Economics: An Introductory Analysis of National Income and Policy*, PASP 91.
24. Ibid., p. I-2; emphasis in original.
25. Ibid., p. I-4.
26. Ibid., p. I-6.
27. Ibid., p. II-3.
28. Samuelson 1951a, p. 14, n1. Knight's text had been circulated only to Chicago students. It was later published as the first chapter of Knight 1951.
29. Samuelson, *Modern Economics*, p. IV-2.
30. Ibid., p. XI-19.
31. Ibid., p. XI-20.
32. Ibid., pp. XII-8, XII-10.
33. Ibid., pp. XII-10, XII-XIV.
34. Ibid., p. XII-11.
35. Ibid., p. XIV-1; passage underlined in the original.
36. Ibid., p. 2. Note that this unnumbered chapter has its own sequence of page numbers.

37. Ibid., p. 3.

38. National Resources Committee 1939.

39. Armstrong et al. 1938a, p. 399.

40. Ibid., p. 373.

41. Ibid., p. 371.

42. Ibid., p. 378.

43. P. A. Samuelson, March 2, 1946, Letter to Emile Despres, PASP 28 (Sub-committee on the problem of economic instability).

44. A. Sweezy, February 13, 1946, Letter to Paul A. Samuelson, PASP 64 (S, 1939–56, Folder 2).

45. P. A. Samuelson, February 18, 1946, Letter to Alan Sweezy, PASP 64 (S, 1939–56, Folder 2).

46. W. Stolper, February 4, 1946, Letter to Paul A. Samuelson, PASP 71 (Stolper, 1).

47. E. Despres, February 25, 1946, Letter to Paul A. Samuelson, PASP 28 (Sub-committee on the problem of economic instability).

48. P. A. Samuelson, February 18, 1946, Letter to Wolfgang Stolper, PASP 71 (Stolper, 1).

49. P. A. Samuelson, April 29, 1946, Letter to David McCord Wright, PASP 78 (Wright).

50. P. A. Samuelson, February 18, 1946, Letter to Alan Sweezy, PASP 64 (S, 1939–56, Folder 2).

51. P. A. Samuelson, February 18, 1946, Letter to Alan Sweezy, PASP 64 (S, 1939–56, Folder 2); P. A. Samuelson, March 2, 1946, Letter to Emile Despres, PASP 28 (Sub-committee on the problem of economic instability).

52. P. A. Samuelson, February 18, 1946, Letter to Alan Sweezy, PASP 64 (S, 1939–56, Folder 2).

53. P. A. Samuelson, March 2, 1946, Letter to Emile Despres, PASP 28 (Sub-committee on the problem of economic instability).

54. W. Stolper, February 4, 1946, Letter to Paul A. Samuelson, PASP 71 (Stolper, 1).

55. P. A. Samuelson, March 19, 1946, Letter to Alan Sweezy, PASP 64 (S, 1939–56, Folder 2). Presumably Samuelson had recently written this.

56. A. R. Sweezy, March 24, 1946, Letter to Paul A. Samuelson, PASP 64 (S, 1939–56, Folder 2).

57. P. A. Samuelson, April 2, 1946, Letter to George Stigler, PASP 70.

58. P. A. Samuelson, February 18, 1946, Letter to Alan Sweezy, PASP 64 (S, 1939–56, Folder 2).

59. P. A. Samuelson, April 10, 1946, Letter to Lawrence H. Seltzer, PASP 64 (S, 1939–56, Folder 2).

60. P. A. Samuelson, April 29, 1946, Letter to David McCord Wright, PASP 78.

61. F. Machlup, May 8, 1946, Letter to Paul A. Samuelson, PASP 51; P. A. Samuelson, May 10, 1946, Letter to Fritz Machlup, PASP 51.

62. McGraw-Hill Book Company and P. A. Samuelson, May 21, 1946, Memorandum of agreement, PASP 87 (Economics, 1945–2008, Folder 2).

63. P. A. Samuelson, 1946, *Economics: An Introductory Analysis*, PASP 91. The course timetable was printed at the front of the book, covering classes from October 1 to January 21.

64. P. A. Samuelson, February 17, 1947, Letter to Daniel Vandermeulen, PASP 74.

65. P. A. Samuelson, August 26, 1946, Letter to George Halm, PASP 34 (H, 1940–57).

66. P. A. Samuelson, September 27, 1946, Letter to Max Millikan, PASP 53.

67. P. A. Samuelson, April 8, 1947, Letter to Daniel Vandermeulen, PASP 74; P. A. Samuelson, June 27, 1947, Letter to Shigeto Tsuru, PASP 73.

68. K. T. Compton, September 30, 1947, Letter to Redfield Proctor, PASP 87 (MIT); K. T. Compton, September 30, 1947, Letter to Gordon S. Rentschler, PASP 87 (MIT); P. A. Samuelson, January 8, 1948, Letter to S. H. Nerlove, PASP 54 (N, 1942–51); P. A. Samuelson, January 12, 1948, Letter to D. S. Lichtenstein, PASP 87 (Economics, 1945–2008, Folder 2).

Chapter 26: Controversy over the Textbook, 1947–1948

1. This section covers material also covered in Giraud 2014, from which I have learned much. Note that many of the documents cited are archived in both Compton's papers at MIT and in Samuelson's papers at Duke, and sometimes twice in the latter.

2. Phillips-Fein 2009.

3. E. E. Lincoln, March 25, 1947, Letter to Harold H. Burbank, HUESR UAV349.282 Box 19 (PAS concentration folder).

4. H. H. Burbank, April 2, 1947, Letter to Edmond E. Lincoln, HUESR UAV349.282 Box 19 (PAS concentration folder).

5. W. J. Beadle, July 15, 1947, Letter to Ralph E. Freeman, PASP 80 (Criticisms of Textbook, 1).

6. W. J. Beadle, August 13, 1946, Letter to James R. Killian, MIT-AC20 Box 1 (Samuelson, 1946–49).

7. MIT, Department of Economics and Social Science, March 3, 1947, Minutes of the visiting committee meeting, MIT-AC394 (Visiting Committee, 1947–66), p. 2.

8. Ibid.

9. W. J. Beadle, July 15, 1947, Letter to Ralph E. Freeman, PASP 80 (Criticisms of Textbook, 1).

10. W. J. Beadle, July 15, 1947, Letter to Ralph E. Freeman, PASP 87 (MIT).

11. N. Peterson, June 26, 1947, Comments on Samuelson *Economics and Introductory Analysis*, PASP 87 (MIT), pp. 1–2.

12. W. J. Beadle, July 15, 1947, Letter to Karl T. Compton, PASP 87 (MIT).

13. E. W. Brewster, July 30, 1947, Letter to Walter J. Beadle, PASP 87 (MIT). See also C.E. Spencer, July 22, 1947, Letter to Ralph E. Freeman, PASP 80 (Criticisms of Textbook, 1).

14. F. J. Chesterman, July 21, 1947, Letter to Karl T. Compton, PASP 87 (MIT).

15. P. A. Samuelson, July 31, 1947, Letter to Walter J. Beadle, PASP 80 (Criticisms of Textbook, 1).

16. Some of the correspondence cited in this passage can be identified in the archive, but not all of it.

17. W. J. Beadle, August 6, 1947, Letter to Paul A. Samuelson, PASP 80 (Criticisms of Textbook, 1).

18. If he did reply, the letter appears not to have been preserved in the archives.

19. J. R. Killian, August 6, 1947, Letter to Walter J. Beadle, PASP 87 (MIT), p. 2; spelling as in the original.

20. J. R. Killian, August 6, 1947, Letter to Walter J. Beadle, PASP 87 (MIT), pp. 1–2.

21. J. R. Killian, August 6, 1947, Letter to Walter J. Beadle, PASP 87 (MIT), p. 2.

22. W. J. Beadle, August 6, 1947, Letter to Karl T. Compton, PASP 87 (MIT).

23. He does not give the date of the letter, but it would appear to be P. A. Samuelson, July 31, 1947, Letter to Walter J. Beadle, PASP 87 (MIT).

24. P. A. Samuelson, August 7, 1947, Letter to Karl T. Compton, PASP 87 (MIT).

25. P. A. Samuelson, August 7, 1947, Letter to Karl T. Compton, PASP 87 (MIT).

26. K. T. Compton, August 8, 1947, Letter to Walter J. Beadle, PASP 80 (Criticisms of Textbook, 1).

27. W. J. Beadle, August 11, 1947, Letter to Karl T. Compton, PASP 87 (MIT).

28. K. T. Compton, August 13, 1947, Letter to Walter J. Beadle, PASP 87 (MIT); C. E. Spencer, August 13, 1947, Letter to Walter J. Beadle, PASP 87 (MIT); E. W. Brewster, August 18, 1947, Letter to Walter J. Beadle, PASP 87 (MIT). Chesterman was also copied into the correspondence.

29. B. Ruml, August 20, 1947, Letter to Walter J. Beadle, PASP 87 (MIT).

30. S. S. Stratton, August 27, 1947, Letter to Walter J. Beadle, PASP 87 (MIT).

31. S. S. Stratton, September 12, 1947, Letter to Walter J. Beadle, PASP 87 (MIT).

32. J. R. Killian, August 27, 1947, Memorandum of luncheon discussion with Beadle, Spencer, and Brewster, PASP 87 (MIT).

33. J. R. Killian, August 28, 1947, Policy on teaching of economics, PASP 87 (MIT).

34. J. R. Killian, September 4, 1947, Letter to Walter J. Beadle, PASP 87 (MIT).

35. Ibid.

36. W. J. Beadle, September 10, 1947, Letter to James R. Killian, PASP 87 (MIT).

37. Ibid.; R. G. Caldwell, September 12, 1947, Letter to James R. Killian, PASP 87 (MIT).

38. Tarshis 1947.

39. Lane 1947.

40. Ibid., p. 1.

41. Ibid., p. 2.

42. Ibid., p. 5.

43. See Levy et al. 2012.

44. See Colander and Landreth 1998; Samuelson 1998d.

45. L. DuPont, September 12, 1947, Letter to Walter J. Beadle, PASP 87 (MIT).

46. W. J. Beadle, September 15, 1947, Letter to Karl T. Compton, PASP 87 (MIT).

47. K. T. Compton, September 18, 1947, Letter to Walter J. Beadle, PASP 87 (MIT).

48. J. B. Conant, May 3, 1947, Excerpt from *Education for Business Responsibility*, MIT-AC04 Box 192 (9).

49. W. J. Beadle, September 22, 1947, Letter to James R. Killian, PASP 87 (MIT); J. R. Killian, September 29, 1947, Letter to Walter J. Beadle, PASP 87 (MIT).

50. R. G. Caldwell, November 7, 1947, Letter to James R. Killian, PASP 87 (MIT); W. J. Beadle, November 5, 1947, Letter to James R. Killian, PASP 87 (MIT); J. R. Killian, October 31, 1947, Letter to Walter J. Beadle, PASP 87 (MIT); J. R. Killian, December 8, 1947, Letter to Dean Caldwell, PASP 87 (MIT); R. E. Freeman, December 12, 1947, Letter to Robert G. Caldwell, PASP 87 (MIT).

51. W. J. Beadle, October 22, 1947, Letter to James R. Killian, PASP 87 (MIT); V. W. Lanfear, October 6, 1947, Letter to Fred R. Fairchild, PASP 87 (MIT).

52. J. R. Killian, October 31, 1947, Letter to Walter J. Beadle, PASP 87 (MIT).

53. R. G. Caldwell, November 7, 1947, Letter to James R. Killian, PASP 87 (MIT).

54. W. J. Beadle, January 2, 1948, Letter to Ralph E. Freeman, MIT-AC04 Box 192 (10).

55. His letter was written from an address in Bridgeport, Connecticut, though letters written later on came from an address associated with the DuPont Company.

56. Samuelson was one of eight people listed by Klein (Klein 1947, p. 184). A footnote explained that they would not all describe themselves as Keynesians. Unfortunately, he did not make it clear whether Samuelson was one of those who would.

57. D. F. Carpenter, January 27, 1948, Letter to James R. Killian, PASP 87 (MIT).

58. Ibid., p. 2.

59. Ibid., p. 3.

60. W. J. Beadle, January 29, 1948, Letter to James R. Killian, MIT-AC04 Box 192 (10).

61. R. G. Caldwell, January 28, 1948, Letter to James R. Killian, MIT-AC20 Box 1 (Samuelson, 1946–49).

62. J. R. Killian, February 3, 1948, Letter to Donald F. Carpenter, PASP 87 (MIT), p. 2.

63. Ibid., p. 2.

64. Wright 1948, p. 150.

65. W. J. Beadle, April 2, 1948, Letter to James R. Killian, MIT-AC04 Box 192 (10), quoting Samuelson 1947b. This referred to Klein's book as forthcoming because it was a reprint of Samuelson 1946a.

66. Wright 1948, p. 152.

67. S. S. Pu, January 7, 1948, Letter to Paul A. Samuelson, PASP 57 (P, 1940–59); D. S. Lichtenstein, January 7, 1948, Letter to Paul A. Samuelson, PASP 87 (Economics, 1945–2008, Folder 2); P. A. Samuelson, January 8, 1948, Letter to S. H. Nerlove, PASP 54 (N, 1942–51); P. A. Samuelson, January 12, 1948, Letter to D. S. Lichtenstein, PASP 87 (Economics, 1945–2008, Folder 2); P. A. Samuelson, January 13, 1948, Letter to Shou Shan Pu, PASP 57 (P, 1940–59); P. A. Samuelson, April 9, 1948, Letter to Charles E. Lindblom, PASP 46 (L, 1946–60); C. E. Lindblom, April 12, 1948, Letter to Paul A. Samuelson, PASP 46 (L, 1946–60).

68. B. Ruml, March 11, 1948, Letter to Walter J. Beadle, MIT-AC20 Box 1 (Samuelson, 1946–49).

69. W. J. Beadle, March 23, 1948, Letter to James R. Killian, MIT-AC20 Box 1 (Samuelson, 1946–49).

70. W. J. Beadle, April 23, 1948, Letter to Ralph E. Freeman, MIT-AC20 Box 1 (Samuelson, 1946–49).

71. Keynes 1946, p. 185.

72. W. J. Beadle, April 23, 1948, Questions to Professor Ralph E. Freeman for discussion with Visiting Committee, 10 a.m., Monday, May 3, 1948, MIT-AC20 Box 1 (Samuelson, 1946–49), p. 3.

73. W. J. Beadle, et al., May 3, 1948, Letter to MIT, PASP 87 (MIT).

Chapter 27: Economics, the First Edition, 1948

1. P. A. Samuelson, August 31, 1948, Letter to Karl T. Compton, MIT-AC04 Box 192 (10).

2. Samuelson 1948, pp. 1, 4.

3. Garver and Hansen 1937.

4. Ibid., chap. 2.

5. It is impossible not to think that Samuelson probably had the University of Wisconsin in mind.

6. Samuelson 1948, p. 197.

7. Ibid., pp. 198–199.

8. Ibid., p. 199.

9. Ibid., p. 201.

10. P. A. Samuelson, 1946, *Economics: An Introductory Analysis*, PASP 91, p. II-2.

11. Samuelson 1948, p. 14, compared with P. A. Samuelson, 1946, *Economics: An Introductory Analysis*, PASP 91, p. II-3.

12. Samuelson 1948, p. 589.

13. Ibid., p. 590.

14. W. J. Beadle, July 15, 1947, Letter to Ralph E. Freeman, PASP 87 (MIT).

15. Samuelson 1948, p. 39, compared with P. A. Samuelson, 1946, *Economics: An Introductory Analysis*, PASP 91, p. II-4.

16. Samuelson 1948, p. 41.

17. Ibid., p. 602.

18. For example, P. A. Samuelson, August 25, 1947, Letter to R. A. Gordon, PASP 32 (G, 1940–1952); P. A. Samuelson, November 25, 1947, Letter to Stephen Enke, PASP 26 (E, 1942–59); P. A. Samuelson, November 25, 1947, Letter to J. M. Letiche, PASP 87 (Economics, 1945–2008, Folder 2).

19. P. A. Samuelson, February 18, 1946, Letter to Alan Sweezy, PASP 64 (S, 1939–56, Folder 2).

20. P. A. Samuelson, July 30, 1946, Letter to Arthur Burns, PASP 19; Burns and Mitchell 1945.

21. Hansen 1941a.

22. Samuelson 1948, p. 407.

23. Ibid., p. 411.

24. Ibid., p. 417.

25. For a history of this concept, see Backhouse and Boianovsky 2016b, 2016a.

26. P. A. Samuelson, 1946, *Economics: An Introductory Analysis*, PASP 91; W. J. Beadle, July 15, 1947, Letter to Ralph E. Freeman, PASP 87 (MIT).

27. Samuelson 1948, p. 435.

28. Ibid., p. 436.

29. Ibid., p. 367.

30. Ibid., p. 368.

31. Ibid., p. 375.

32. P. A. Samuelson, July 31, 1947, Letter to Walter J. Beadle, PASP 87 (MIT). This aspect of the book has been examined by Giraud 2014.

33. Schlesinger 1949.

34. Ibid., p. 4.

35. Ibid., p. 13.

36. Ibid., p. 74. He was quoting the first part of this sentence from another source.

37. Ibid., p. 153.

38. The first Schlesinger-Samuelson letter in the Samuelson archive is dated 1950. Schlesinger was about to embark on his study of the Roosevelt years, and asked Samuelson for a source that would explain the causes of the Great Depression. (A. Schlesinger, October 19, 1950, Letter to Paul A. Samuelson, PASP 68.)

39. Samuelson 1948, pp. 602–603.

40. W. J. Beadle, July 15, 1947, Letter to Ralph E. Freeman, PASP 87 (MIT).

41. P. A. Samuelson, July 24, 1945, Letter to Lawrence Klein, PASP 45.

42. P. A. Samuelson, March 2, 1946, Letter to Emile Despres, PASP 28 (Sub-committee on the problem of economic instability).

43. P. A. Samuelson, April 29, 1946, Letter to David McCord Wright, PASP 78.
44. P. A. Samuelson, September 27, 1946, Letter to Max Millikan, PASP 53.
45. Samuelson had used these terms in criticism of a recent book by Hicks, presumably Hicks and Hart 1945. P. A. Samuelson, March 2, 1946, Letter to Emile Despres, PASP 28 (Sub-committee on the problem of economic instability).
46. M. Bronfenbrenner, May 24, 1948, Letter to Stewart C. Dorman, PASP 80 (Criticisms of Textbook, 1).
47. S. E. Harris, May 25, 1948, Letter to Stuart C. Derman, PASP 80 (Criticisms of Textbook, 1).
48. P. A. Samuelson, August 31, 1948, Letter to Karl T. Compton, PASP 87 (Economics, 1945–2008, Folder 2).
49. P. A. Samuelson, August 31, 1948, Letter to Karl T. Compton, PASP 87 (Economics, 1945–2008, Folder 2).
50. Ashby 1948, p. 217.
51. Brekke 1948.
52. See Giraud 2014, who illuminatingly discusses Samuelson's attempt to maintain such a position.
53. Hart 1948, p. 912.
54. Haney 1948, p. 221.
55. S. S. Stratton, September 12, 1947, Letter to Walter J. Beadle, PASP 87 (MIT).
56. Haney 1948, p. 222.
57. Buckley 2002.

Chapter 28: Commitment to MIT

1. Weintraub 2014.
2. Killian 1985, p. 201.
3. P. T. Homan, February 4, 1944, Letter to Paul A. Samuelson, PASP 11 (AEA); P. A. Samuelson, February 9, 1944, Letter to Paul T. Homan, PASP 11 (AEA).
4. This is remark presumes that correspondence was correctly filed.
5. P. T. Homan, January 14, 1947, Letter to Paul A. Samuelson, PASP 11 (AEA).
6. P. A. Samuelson, November 15, 1946, Letter to Paul T. Homan, PASP 11 (AEA).
7. Ibid.
8. P. A. Samuelson, January 2, 1947, Letter to Nicholas Kaldor, PASP 62 (*Review of Economic Studies*).
9. N. Kaldor, December 3, 1946, Letter to Paul A. Samuelson, PASP 43.
10. P. A. Samuelson, January 2, 1947, Letter to Joan Robinson, PASP 63.
11. P. A. Samuelson, February 18, 1947, Letter to Ursula Hicks, PASP 62 (*Review of Economic Studies*).
12. P. A. Samuelson, July 29, 1947, Letter to Ursula K. Hicks, PASP 62 (*Review of Economic Studies*).

13. Ibid.
14. U. Hicks, April 27, 1947, Letter to Paul A. Samuelson, PASP 62 (*Review of Economic Studies*); P. A. Samuelson, June 16, 1947, Letter to Ursula K. Hicks, PASP 62 (*Review of Economic Studies*).
15. P. A. Samuelson, February 27, 1946, Letter to Paul Sweezy, PASP 72 (Sweezy).
16. P. A. Samuelson, September 29, 1946, Letter to Shigeto Tsuru, STP B1-1-9.
17. Ibid.
18. Ibid.
19. S. Tsuru, March 3, 1947, Letter to Paul A. Samuelson, STP B1-1-9.
20. P. A. Samuelson, March 11, 1947, Letter to Shigeto Tsuru, PASP 73.
21. P. A. Samuelson, April 21, 1947, Letter to Shigeto Tsuru, PASP 73.
22. P. A. Samuelson, June 27, 1947, Letter to Shigeto Tsuru, PASP 73.
23. S. Tsuru, September 29, 1947, Letter to Paul A. Samuelson, STP B1-1-9.
24. Tsuru 1949, p. 359.
25. I have benefited from reading the account of this episode by Harro Maas 2014, who has drawn my attention to points I might otherwise have overlooked.
26. J. Marschak, February 28, 1946, Letter to Robert M. Hutchins, UCOP Box 73.
27. Ibid. Parentheses around "at the National Bureau" have been removed.
28. J. Marschak, February 28, 1946, Letter to Robert M. Hutchins, UCOP Box 73, pp. 3–4.
29. J. Marschak, March 1, 1946, Letter to Paul A. Samuelson, PASP 49 (M, 1944–52); P. A. Samuelson, March 4, 1946, Letter to Jacob Marschak, PASP 49 (M, 1944–52).
30. T. W. Schultz, March 20, 1946, Letter to Paul A. Samuelson, PASP 68.
31. J. Marschak, March 20, 1946, Letter to Paul A. Samuelson, PASP 68.
32. P. A. Samuelson, March 23, 1946, Letter to Jacob Marschak, UCOP Box 73.
33. Ibid.
34. J. Marschak, March 29, 1946, Letter to Robert M. Hutchins, UCOP Box 73.
35. P. A. Samuelson, March 27, 1946, Letter to Theodore W. Schultz, PASP 68; T. W. Schultz, April 3, 1946, Letter to Paul A. Samuelson, PASP 68; P. A. Samuelson, April 6, 1946, Letter to Theodore W. Schultz, PASP 68; T. W. Schultz, April 9, 1946, Letter to Paul A. Samuelson, PASP 68.
36. P. A. Samuelson, April 23, 1946, Letter to Theodore W. Schultz, PASP 68.
37. P. A. Samuelson, April 23, 1946, Letter to Jacob Marschak, PASP 49 (M, 1944–52).
38. P. A. Samuelson, June 6, 1946, Letter to Theodore W. Schultz, PASP 68; T. W. Schultz, June 12, 1946, Letter to Paul A. Samuelson, PASP 68. The precise wording was "awaiting departmental appraisal and action."
39. P. A. Samuelson, June 24, 1946, Letter to Theodore W. Schultz, PASP 68.
40. I. F. Disney, June 26, 1946, Letter to Paul A. Samuelson, PASP 68.

41. E. C. Colwell, November 11, 1946, Letter to Robert M. Hutchins, UCOP Box 73.
42. E. C. Colwell, November 18, 1946, Letter to Robert M. Hutchins, UCOP Box 73.
43. R. Hutchins, November 22, 1946, Telegram to E. C. Colwell, UCOP Box 73.
44. T. W. Schultz, November 25, 1946, Letter to Paul A. Samuelson, PASP 68.
45. T. C. Koopmans, December 17, 1946, Letter to Paul A. Samuelson, PASP 45.
46. This word is not clear and may be incorrectly copied.
47. Friedman to Stigler, November 27, 1946; reprinted in Hammond and Hammond 2006, p. 46.
48. Ibid., p. 56.
49. P. A. Samuelson, March 23, 1946, Letter to Jacob Marschak, UCOP Box 73.
50. P. A. Samuelson, January 13, 1947, Letter to Theodore W. Schultz, PASP 68.
51. Ibid.
52. P. H. Douglas, January 29, 1947, Letter to Paul A. Samuelson, PASP 24 (D, 1942–64).
53. R. Blough, February 4, 1947, Letter to Paul A. Samuelson, PASP 17.
54. P. A. Samuelson, February 28, 1947, Letter to Theodore W. Schultz, PASP 68.
55. P. A. Samuelson, February 28, 1947, Letter to Paul H. Douglas, PASP 24 (D, 1942–64).
56. Ibid.
57. T. W. Schultz, March 4, 1947, Letter to Paul A. Samuelson, PASP 68.
58. P. H. Douglas, March 7, 1947, Letter to Paul A. Samuelson, PASP 24 (D, 1942–64).
59. P. A. Samuelson, March 11, 1947, Letter to Theodore W. Schultz, PASP 68.
60. W. R. Maclaurin, March 4, 1948, Letter to Karl T. Compton, MIT-AC04 Box 142 (11, Maclaurin).
61. T. W. Schultz, November 3, 1947, Letter to Paul A. Samuelson, PASP 68.
62. P. A. Samuelson, November 7, 1947, Letter to Theodore W. Schultz, PASP 68.
63. P. H. Douglas, November 12, 1947, Letter to Paul A. Samuelson, PASP 53 (MIT).
64. P. A. Samuelson, November 13, 1947, Letter to Paul H. Douglas, PASP 24 (D, 1942–64).
65. E. H. Schell, December 31, 1947, Letter to Ralph E. Freeman, PASP 87 (MIT).
66. P. A. Samuelson, January 12, 1948, Letter to Paul H. Douglas, PASP 24 (D, 1942–64).

Chapter 29: The Young Samuelson

1. Samuelson uses the term "quasi-foster home" (P. A. Samuelson, Undated, Autobiographical fragment, PASP 149 [Autobiographical], p. 14).
2. P. A. Samuelson, August, 1948, Comments on Vining's methodological issues, PASP 37 (Harris).

3. F. H. Knight, October 28, 1950, Letter to David McCord Wright, PASP 78.
4. Smith 1976b, 1976a.
5. Metzler 1948, p. 906.
6. Dorfman et al. 1958.
7. Cook 2009 discusses the historicist dimension of Marshall's work.

REFERENCES

Note: Works in Samuelson's *Collected Scientific Papers* are cited as "CSP n:m" where "n" is the volume and "m" the article number. In virtually all cases, the reprint in CSP contains the original pagination, and it is these page numbers that are used, except in cases where, perhaps because something was previously unpublished, the CSP page numbers are the only ones available. The date given is the date of the original publication.

Allen, R. G. D. 1933. On the Marginal Utility of Money and Its Application. *Economica* 40, pp. 186–209.

Allen, R. G. D. 1949. The Mathematical Foundations of Economic Theory. *Quarterly Journal of Economics* 63(1), pp. 111–127.

Altman, O. L. 1941. *Saving, Investment and National Income: A Study Made for the Temporary National Economic Committee, Seventy-Sixth Congress, Third Session.* Washington, DC: U.S. Government Printing Office.

Amadae, S. M. 2003. *Rationalizing Capitalist Democracy: The Cold War Origins of Rational Choice Liberalism,* 2nd ed. Chicago: University of Chicago Press.

American Economic Association. 1935. Program of the Forty-Seventh Annual Meeting. *American Economic Review* 25(1).

American Economic Association. 1935. Program of the Ninety-Sixth Annual Meeting American Statistical Association, Palmer House, Chicago. *Journal of the American Statistical Association* 30(189), pp. 351–358.

American Economic Association. 1948. Report of the Secretary for the Year 1947. *American Economic Review* 38(2), pp. 529–543.

American Economic Association. 1949. Report of the Secretary for the Year 1948. *American Economic Review* 39(3), pp. 481–495.

Anderson, K. L. 1938. Protection and the Historical Situation: Australia. *Quarterly Journal of Economics* 53(1), pp. 86–104.

Anderson, K. L. 1939. Comment. *Quarterly Journal of Economics* 54(1), pp. 149–151.

Angell, N. 1910. *The Great Illusion.* New York: G. P. Putnam's Sons.

Angell, N. 1932. *The Unseen Assassins.* London: Hamish Hamilton.

Armstrong, F. E., Fiske, W. P., Freeman, H. A., Ingraham, O., Maclaurin, W. R., Thresher, B. A., and Freeman, R. E. 1938a. *The Economic Process,* vol. 1. Cambridge, MA: MIT Press.

Armstrong, F. E., Fiske, W. P., Freeman, H. A., Ingraham, O., Maclaurin, W. R., Thresher, B. A., and Freeman, R. E. 1938b. *The Economic Process,* vol. 2. Cambridge, MA: MIT Press.

Arrow, K. J. 1951. *Social Choice and Individual Values.* Cowles Commission Monograph, No. 12. New York: John Wiley.

Ashby, L. D. 1948. Untitled article. *Southern Economic Journal* 15(2), pp. 216–217.

Backhouse, R. E. 1998a. The Transformation of U.S. Economics, 1920–1960, Viewed through a Survey of Journal Articles. *History of Political Economy* 30 (Suppl.), pp. 85–107.

Backhouse, R. E. 1998b. Vision and Progress in Economic Thought: Schumpeter after Kuhn. In *Explorations in Economic Methodology,* ed. R. E. Backhouse, pp. 176–189. London: Routledge.

Backhouse, R. E. 2009. Robbins and Welfare Economics: A Reappraisal. *Journal of the History of Economic Thought* 31(4), pp. 68–82.

Backhouse, R. E. 2010. An Abstruse and Mathematical Argument: The Use of Mathematical Reasoning in the *General Theory.* In *The Return of Keynes: Keynes and Keynesian Policies in the New Millennium,* ed. B. W. Bateman, T. Hirai, and C. Marcuzzo, pp. 133–147. Cambridge, MA: Harvard University Press.

Backhouse, R. E. 2014. Paul Samuelson's Move to MIT. In *MIT and the Transformation of American Economics*, Supplement to *History of Political Economy*, vol. 46, ed. E. R. Weintraub, pp. 60–77. Durham, NC: Duke University Press.

Backhouse, R. E. 2015a. Revisiting Samuelson's Foundations of Economic Analysis. *Journal of Economic Literature* 53(2), pp. 326–350.

Backhouse R. E. 2015b. Economic Power and the Financial Machine. In *Market Failure in Context*, Supplement to *History of Political Economy*, vol. 47, ed. A. Marciano and S. G. Medema, pp. 99–126. Durham, NC: Duke University Press.

Backhouse, R. E., and Boianovsky, M. 2016. Secular Stagnation: The History of a Macroeconomic Heresy. *European Journal of the History of Economic Thought* 23(6), pp. 946–970.

Backhouse, R. E., and Giraud, Y. 2010. Circular Flow Diagram. In *Famous Figures and Diagrams in Economics*, ed. M. Blaug and P. Lloyd, pp. 221–229. Cheltenham, UK: Edward Elgar.

Backhouse, R. E., and Maas, H. 2016. Marginalizing Maclaurin: The Attempt to Develop an Economics of Technological Progress at MIT, 1940–1950. *History of Political Economy* 48(3), pp. 423–447.

Backhouse R. E., and Maas H. 2017. A Road Not Taken: Economists, Historians of Science and the Making of the Bowman Report. *Isis* (forthcoming March 2017).

Backhouse, R. E., and Medema, S. G. 2009. Retrospectives: On the Definition of Economics. *Journal of Economic Perspectives* 23(1), pp. 221–233.

Backhouse, R. E., and Medema, S. G. 2014. Walras in the Age of Marshall: An Analysis of English-Language Journals, 1890–1939. In *Economics and Other Branches—In the Shade of the Oak Tree: Essays in Honour of Pascal Bridel*, ed. F. Allison and R. Baranzini, pp. 69–86. London: Pickering and Chatto.

Backhouse, R. E., and Nishizawa, T. 2010. *No Wealth But Life: Welfare Economics and the Welfare State in Britain, 1880–1945*. Cambridge: Cambridge University Press.

Bailey, S. K. 1950. *Congress Makes a Law: The Story Behind the Employment Act of 1946*. New York: Columbia University Press.

Barnett, W. A. 2004. An Interview with Paul A. Samuelson. *Macroeconomic Dynamics* 8, pp. 519–542.

Bauer, A. 2008. Leonard Hurwicz's game. *Twin Cities Business*, March 1; online at http://tcbmag.com/Leadership/Leaders/Leonid-Hurwicz-s-Game.aspx (accessed November 7, 2008).

Baumol, W. J. 1949. Relaying the Foundations. *Economica* 16(62), pp. 159–168.

Bergson, A. 1936. Real Income, Expenditure Proportionality, and Frisch's "New Methods of Measuring Marginal Utility." *Review of Economic Studies* 4(1), pp. 33–52.

Bergson, A. 1938. A Reformulation of Certain Aspects of Welfare Economics. *Quarterly Journal of Economics* 52(2), pp. 310–334.

Bergson, A. 1942. Prices, Wages, and Income Theory. *Econometrica* 10(3/4), pp. 275–289.

Berle, A. A., and Means, G. C. 1932. *The Modern Corporation and Private Property*. New York: Macmillan.

Beveridge, W. 1942. *Social Insurance and Allied Services*. New York: Macmillan.

Biddle, J. 2012. Retrospectives: The Introduction of the Cobb–Douglas Regression. *Journal of Economic Perspectives* 26(2), pp. 223–236.

Birkhoff, G. D. 1941. A Mathematical Approach to Ethics. *Rice Institute Pamphlets* 28(1), pp. 1–23.

Birkhoff, G. D., and Hestenes, M. R. 1935. Natural Isoperimetric Conditions in the Calculus of Variations. *Proceedings of the National Academy of Sciences of the United States of America* 21(2), pp. 99–102.

Bjerkholt, O. 2007. Writing "The Probability Approach" with Nowhere to Go: Haavelmo in the United States, 1939–1944. *Econometric Theory* 23(5), pp. 775–837.

Bjerkholt, O. 2014. Lawrence R. Klein, 1920–2013: Notes on the Early Years. *Journal of Policy Modeling* 36(5), pp. 767–784.

Bjerkholt, O. 2015. Trygve Haavelmo at the Cowles Commission. *Econometric Theory* 31(1), pp. 1–84.

Blumer, H. 1931. Science without Concepts. *American Journal of Sociology* 36(4), pp. 515–533.

Boas, F. 1911. *The Mind of Primitive Man*. New York: Macmillan.

Boianovsky, M., and Trautwein, H. 2006. Haberler, the League of Nations, and the Quest for Consensus in Business Cycle Theory in the 1930s. *History of Political Economy* 38(1), pp. 45–89.

Bonar, J. 1911. *Disturbing Elements in the Study and Teaching of Political Economy.* Baltimore: Johns Hopkins University Press.

Boulding, K. E. 1935. The Theory of a Single Investment. *Quarterly Journal of Economics* 49(3), pp. 475–494.

Boulding, K. E. 1936. Professor Knight's Capital Theory: A Reply. *Quarterly Journal of Economics* 50(3), pp. 524–531.

Boulding, K. E. 1941. *Economic Analysis.* New York: Harper & Brothers.

Boulding, K. E. 1948a. *Economic Analysis*, 2nd ed. New York: Harper.

Boulding, K. E. 1948b. Samuelson's Foundations: The Role of Mathematics in Economics. *Journal of Political Economy* 56(3), pp. 187–199.

Bowley, A. L. 1924. *Mathematical Groundwork of Economics.* Oxford: Clarendon Press.

Brekke, A. 1948. Review of Samuelson's *Economics Journal of Farm Economics* 30(4), pp. 799–802.

Bridgman, P. W. 1927. *The Logic of Modern Physics.* New York: Macmillan.

Bridgman, P. W. 1936. *The Nature of Physical Theory.* New York: Dover.

Bridgman, P. W. 1938. Operational Analysis. *Philosophy of Science* 5(2), pp. 114–131.

Brinton, C., ed. 1959. *The Society of Fellows.* Cambridge, MA: Harvard University Press.

Bryce, R. B. 1988. Keynes During the Great Depression and World War II. In *Keynes and Public Policy after Fifty Years. Volume I: Economics and Policy,* ed. O. F. Hamouda and J. N. Smithin, pp. 146–150. Aldershot, UK: Edward Elgar.

Buckley, W. F. 2002. *God and Man at Yale: The Superstitions of "Academic Freedom."* Washington, DC: Regnery.

Bullock, C. J., and Crum, W. L. 1932. The Harvard Index of Economic Conditions: Interpretation and Performance, 1919–31. *Review of Economics and Statistics* 14(3), pp. 132–148.

Bullock, C. J., Persons, W. M., and Crum, W. L. 1927. The Construction and Interpretation of the Harvard Index of Business Conditions. *Review of Economics and Statistics* 9(2), pp. 74–92.

Burns, A. F. 1944. Frickey on the Decomposition of Time Series. *Review of Economics and Statistics* 26(3), pp. 136–147.

Burns, A. F., and Mitchell, W. C. 1945. *Measuring Business Cycles.* New York: NBER.

Bush, V. 1945. *Science: The Endless Frontier.* Washington, DC: U.S. Government Printing Office.

Cartter, A. 1966. *An Assessment of Quality in Graduate Education.* Washington, DC: American Council on Education.

Carvajalino, J. 2016. *Edwin B. Wilson at the origin of Paul Samuelson's mathematical economics: essays on the interwoven history of economics, mathematics and statistics in the U.S., 1900–1940.* PhD Thesis, University of Quebec at Montreal.

Cassel, G. 1923. *Theory of Social Economy.* London: Fisher Unwin.

Chamberlin, E. H. 1933. *The Theory of Monopolistic Competition.* Cambridge, MA: Harvard University Press.

Chamberlin, E. H. 1961. The Origin and Early Development of Monopolistic Competition Theory. *Quarterly Journal of Economics* 75(4), pp. 515–543.

Cherrier, B. 2014. Toward a History of Economics at MIT, 1940–72. In *MIT and the Transformation of American Economics*, ed. E. R. Weintraub, pp. 15–44. Durham, NC: Duke University Press.

Clark, J. B. 1899. *The Distribution of Wealth.* New York: Macmillan.

Clark, J. M. 1923. *Studies in the Economics of Overhead Costs.* Chicago: University of Chicago Press.

Clark, J. M. 1926. *Social Control of Business.* Chicago: University of Chicago Press.

Clark, J. M. 1936. Long-range Planning for the Regularization of Industry. In *Preface to Social Economics: Essays on Economic Theory and Social Problems.* New York: Farrar and Rinehart.

Clark, J. M. 1940. Toward a Concept of Workable Competition. *American Economic Review* 30(2), pp. 241–256.

Clark, J. M., Sundelson, J. W., and NRPB. 1935. *Economics of Planning Public Works.* Washington, DC: U.S. Government Printing Office.

Clawson, M. 1981. *New Deal Planning: The National Resources Planning Board.* Baltimore: Johns Hopkins University Press.

Clemence, R., and Doody, F. S. 1942. Modern Economics and the Introductory Course. *American Economic Review* 32(2), pp. 334–347.

Cochrane, R. C. 1978. *The National Academy of Sciences: The First Hundred Years, 1863–1963.* Washington, DC: National Academy of Sciences.

Colander, D. C., and Landreth, H., eds. 1996. *The Coming of Keynesianism to America: Conversations with the Founders of Keynesian Economics.* Cheltenham, UK: Edward Elgar.

Colander, D., and Landreth, H. 1998. Political Influence on the Textbook Keynesian Revolution: God, Man and Lorie Tarshis at Yale. In *Keynesianism and the Keynesian Revolution in America*, ed. O. F. Hamouda and B. B. Price, pp. 59–72. Cheltenham, UK: Edward Elgar.

Cole, F. 1931. Race Problems as Seen by the Anthropologist. *Scientific Monthly* 32(1), pp. 80–82.

Coleman, G. W. 1945. The Effect of Interest Rate Increases on the Banking System. *American Economic Review* 35(4), pp. 671–673.

Compton, K. T. 1944. President's Report Issue, 1943–1944. *MIT Bulletin* 80(1).

Conway, F., and Siegelman, J. 2005. *Dark Hero of the Information Age: In Search of Norbert Wiener, the Father of Cybernetics.* New York: Basic Books.

Cook, S. J. 2009. *The Intellectual Foundations of Alfred Marshall's Economic Science: A Rounded Globe of Knowledge.* Cambridge: Cambridge University Press.

Coulter, M. C. 1932. *Introductory General Course in the Biological Sciences: Syllabus.* Second Preliminary Edition. Chicago: University of Chicago Press.

Cournot, A. 1838. *Recherches sur les Principes Mathematiques de la Theorie des Richesses.* Paris: Hachette.

Crawford, M. E. 1937. *A Mathematical Reconsideration of the Elasticity of Substitution.* Undergraduate thesis, Radcliffe College, Boston.

Crum, W. L. 1932. *The Modern Corporation and Private Property.* New York: Macmillan.

Crum, W. L. 1938. Rudimentary Mathematics for Economists and Statisticians. *Quarterly Journal of Economics* 52, pp. 1–164.

Currie, L. 2004. Public Spending as a Means to Recovery: August 6, 1936. *Journal of Economic Studies* 31(3/4), pp. 298–309.

Davis, H. T. 1941. *The Analysis of Economic Time Series.* Bloomington, IN: Principia Press.

Deardorff, A. V., and Stern, R. M., eds. 1994. *The Stolper-Samuelson Theorem: A Golden Jubilee.* Ann Arbor: University of Michigan Press.

De Marchi, N. B. 1991. League of Nations Economists and the Ideal of Peaceful Change in the Decade of the Thirties. *History of Political Economy* 23 (Suppl.), pp. 143–178.

Deutsch, K. W. 1980. A Voyage of the Mind, 1930–1980. *Government and Opposition* 15(3–4), pp. 323–345.

De Vroey, M. 2004. *Involuntary Unemployment: The Elusive Quest for a Theory.* London: Routledge.

De Vroey, M. 2016. *A History of Macroeconomics: From Keynes to Lucas and Beyond.* Cambridge: Cambridge University Press.

De Vroey, M., and Hoover, K. D., eds. 2004. *The IS-LM Model: Its Rise, Fall, and Strange Persistence.* Durham, NC: Duke University Press.

Dorfman, R. 1973. Wassily Leontief's Contribution to Economics. *Swedish Journal of Economics* 75(4), pp. 430–449.

Dorfman, R., Samuelson, P. A., and Solow, R. M. 1958. *Linear Programming and Economic Analysis.* New York: McGraw-Hill.

Douglas, P. H. 1932. *The Coming of a New Party.* New York: Whittlesey House/ McGraw-Hill.

Douglas, P. H. 1934. *The Theory of Wages.* New York: Macmillan.

Douglas, P. H. 1935. *Controlling Depressions.* New York: W. W. Norton.

Douglas, P. H., and Director, A. 1931. *The Problem of Unemployment.* New York: Macmillan.

East, E. M. 1927. *Heredity and Human Affairs.* New York: Charles Scribners.

Edgeworth, F. Y. 1881. *Mathematical Psychics.* London: Kegan Paul.

Eggan, F. 1962. Fay-Cooper Cole, Architect of Anthropology. *Science* 135(3502), pp. 412–413.

Eggan, F. 1963. Fay-Cooper Cole, 1881–1961. *American Anthropologist* 65(3), pp. 641–648.

Ellsworth, P. T., Samuelson, P. A., and Depres, E. 1939. The Workability of Compensatory Devices. *American Economic Review* 29(1), pp. 224–229.

Ely, R.T., Adams, T. S., Lorenz, M. O., and Young, A. A. 1931. *Outlines of Economics,* 5th ed. New York: Macmillan.

Emmett, R. B., ed. 2006. *The Biographical Dictionary of American Economists.* London: Thoemmes Continuum.

Epstein, P. S. 1937. *Textbook of Thermodynamics.* New York: John Wiley.

Estey, J. A. 1941. *Business Cycles: Their Nature, Cause and Control.* New York: Prentice-Hall.

Ezekiel, M. 1942a. Statistical Investigations of Saving, Consumption, and Investment. *American Economic Review* 32(1), pp. 22–49.

Ezekiel, M. 1942b. Statistical Investigations of Saving, Consumption, and Investment. *American Economic Review* 32(2), pp. 272–307.

Ezekiel, M. 1944. The Statistical Determination of the Investment Schedule. *Econometrica* 12(1), pp. 89–90.

Feuchtwanger, L. 2001. *The Oppermanns.* Translated by J. Cleugh. New York: Carroll and Graf.

Fontaine, P. 2010. Stabilizing American Society: Kenneth Boulding and the Integration of the Social Sciences, 1943–1980. *Science in Context* 23(02), pp. 221–265.

Frickey, E. 1942. *Economic Fluctuations in the United States.* Cambridge, MA: Harvard University Press.

Friedman, M. 1942. The Inflationary Gap: II. Discussion of the Inflationary Gap. *American Economic Review* 32(2), pp. 314–320.

Friedman, M., and Friedman, R. D. 1999. *Two Lucky People: Memoirs.* Chicago: University of Chicago Press.

Friedman, W. A. 2014. *Fortune Tellers: The Story of America's First Economic Forecasters.* Princeton, NJ: Princeton University Press.

Frisch, R. 1933. Propagation Problems and Impulse Problems in Dynamic Economics. In *Economic Essays in Honor of Gustav Cassel*, pp. 171–205. London: Allen and Unwin.

Frisch, R. 1936. Annual Survey of General Economic Theory: The Problem of Index Numbers. *Econometrica* 4(1), pp. 1–38.

Furer, J. A. 1944. Post-War Military Research. *Science* 100(2604), pp. 461–464.

Galbraith, J. K. 1981. How Keynes Came to America. In *A Contemporary Guide to Economics Peace and Laughter,* ed. A. D. Williams, pp. 43–59. London: Andre Deutsch.

Galbraith, J. K., and Johnson, G. G. 1940. *The Economic Effects of the Federal Public Works Expenditures, 1933–1938.* Washington, DC: U.S. Government Printing Office.

Garver, F. B., and Hansen, A. H. 1937. *Principles of Economics,* rev. ed. Boston: Ginn and Co.

Gayer, A. D. 1935. *Public Works in Prosperity and Depression: Prepared for the National Planning Board.* New York: NBER.

Gibbs, J. W., and Wilson, E. B. 1901. *Vector Analysis: A Text-book for the Use of Students of Mathematics & Physics.* New York: Charles Scribner's.

Gideonse, H. D., Kerwin, J. G., Staley, E., and Wirth, L. 1932. *Second-Year Course in the Study of Contemporary Society (Social Science II): Syllabus and Selected Readings.* Chicago: University of Chicago Press.

Gideonse, H. D., Kerwin, J. G., and Wirth, L. 1931. *Introductory General Course in the Social Sciences: Syllabus and Selected Readings.* Chicago: University of Chicago Press.

Gilbert, R. V., and Perlo, V. 1942. The Investment-Factor Method of Forecasting Business Activity. *Econometrica* 10(3/4), pp. 311–316.

Gilbert, R. V., Hildebrand, G., Stuart, A. W., Sweezy, M. Y., Sweezy, P. M., Tarshis, L., and Wilson, J. D. 1938. *An Economic Program for American Democracy.* New York: Vanguard.

Giraud, Y. 2014. Negotiating the "Middle-of-the-Road" Position: Paul Samuelson, MIT and the Politics of Textbook Writing, 1945–55. In *MIT and the Transformation of American Economics*, ed. E. R. Weintraub, pp. 134–152. Durham, NC: Duke University Press.

Godin, B. 2008. In the Shadow of Schumpeter: W. Rupert Maclaurin and the Study of Technological Innovation. *Minerva* 46(3), pp. 343–360.

Goldenweiser, E. A., and Hagen, E. E. 1944. Jobs After the War. *Federal Reserve Bulletin* 30(5), pp. 424–431.

Goodwin, C. D. W. 2014. *Walter Lippmann: Public Economist.* Cambridge, MA: Harvard University Press.

Green, J., and LaDuke, J. 2009. *Pioneering Women in American Mathematics: The Pre-1940 PhD's.* London: London Mathematical Society and Providence, RI: American Mathematical Society.

Guerlac, H. E. 1941. *Science and War in the Ancien Regime: The Development of Science in an Armed Society.* PhD thesis, Harvard University, Cambridge, MA.

Haavelmo T. 1941. On the Theory and Measurement of Economic Relations. Unpublished paper, Harvard University.

Haavelmo, T. 1943. The Statistical Implications of a System of Simultaneous Equations. *Econometrica* 11(1), pp. 1–12.

Haavelmo, T. 1944. The Probability Approach in Econometrics. *Econometrica* 12, pp. iii–vi, 1–115.

Haberler, G. 1927. *Der Sinn der Indexzahlen.* Tübingen: J. C. B. Mohr.

Haberler, G. 1928. A New Index Number and Its Meaning. *Quarterly Journal of Economics* 42(3), pp. 434–449.

Haberler, G. 1930. Die Theorie der komparativen Kosten und ihre Auswertung für die Begruendung des Friehandels. *Weltwirtschaftliches Archiv* 32, pp. 349–370.

Haberler, G. 1932. Money and the Business Cycle. In *Gold and Monetary Stabilization,* ed. Q. Wright, pp. 43–74. Chicago: Chicago University Press.

Haberler, G. 1936. *International Trade.* London: Hodge.

Haberler, G. 1937a. Review of R. F. Harrod, The Trade Cycle. *Journal of Political Economy* 45(5), pp. 690–697.

Haberler, G. 1937b. *Prosperity and Depression.* Geneva: League of Nations.

Haberler, G. 1946. *Prosperity and Depression,* 3rd ed. New York: United Nations.

Haberler, G. 1950. Joseph Alois Schumpeter, 1883–1950. *Quarterly Journal of Economics* 64(3), pp. 333–372.

Hagen, E. E. 1942. Capital Theory in a System with No Agents Fixed in Quantity. *Journal of Political Economy* 50(6), pp. 837–859.

Hagen, E. E. 1945. Postwar Output in the United States at Full Employment. *Review of Economics and Statistics* 27(2), pp. 45–59.

Hagen, E. E. 1947. The Reconversion Period: Reflections of a Forecaster. *Review of Economics and Statistics* 29(2), pp. 95–101.

Hagen, E. E., and Kirkpatrick, N. B. 1944. The National Output at Full Employment in 1950. *American Economic Review* 34(3), pp. 472–500.

Hall, R. L., and Hitch, C. J. 1939. Price Theory and Business Behaviour. *Oxford Economic Papers* 2, pp. 12–45.

Halpern, M. 2003. *Unions, Radicals, and Democratic Presidents: Seeking Social Change in the Twentieth Century.* Westport, CT: Greenwood.

Hamilton, W. H., and May, S. 1928. *The Control of Wages.* New York: Macmillan.

Hammond, J. D., and Hammond, C. H. 2006. *Making Chicago Price Theory: Friedman-Stigler Correspondence 1945–1957.* London: Routledge.

Hamouda, O. F., and Price, B. B., eds. 1998. *Keynesianism and the Keynesian Revolution in America.* Cheltenham, UK: Edward Elgar.

Hands, D. W., and Mirowski, P. 1998a. Harold Hotelling and the Neoclassical Dream. In *Economics and Methodology: Crossing Boundaries*, ed. A. Salanti, U. Maki, D. M. Hausman, and R. E. Backhouse, pp. 322–397. London: Macmillan.

Hands, D. W., and Mirowski, P. 1998b. A Paradox of Budgets: The Postwar Stabilization of American Neoclassical Demand Theory. *History of Political Economy* 30(5; Suppl.), pp. 260–292.

Haney, L. H. 1948. Untitled article. *Annals of the American Academy of Political and Social Science* 260, pp. 221–222.

Hansen, A. H. 1921. *Cycles of Prosperity and Depression in the United States, Great Britain and Germany: A Study of Monthly Data, 1902–1908.* Madison: University of Wisconsin Press.

Hansen, A. H. 1922. The Economics of Unionism. *Journal of Political Economy* 30(4), pp. 518–530.

Hansen, A. H. 1927. *Business Cycle Theory: Its Development and Present Status.* Boston: Ginn and Co.

Hansen, A. H. 1934. The Flow of Purchasing Power. In *Economic Reconstruction*, ed. Columbia University Commission. New York: Columbia University Press.

Hansen, A. H. 1936a. Mr. Keynes on Underemployment Equilibrium. *Journal of Political Economy* 44(5), pp. 667–686.

Hansen, A. H. 1936b. Under-employment Equilibrium. *Yale Review* 25, pp. 828–830.

Hansen, A. H. 1938. The Consequences of Reducing Expenditures. *Proceedings of the Academy of Political Science* 17(4), pp. 60–72.

Hansen, A. H. 1939. Economic Progress and Declining Population Growth. *American Economic Review* 29(1), pp. 1–15.

Hansen, A. H. 1940. Memorandum to Mr. Goldenweiser: introductory statement on research project, October 3. At http://fraser.stlouisfed.org/docs/historical/eccles/100_09_0001.pdf.

Hansen, A. H. 1941a. *Fiscal Policy and Business Cycles.* London: George Allen and Unwin.

Hansen, A. H. 1941b. Post-Defense Full Employment, Draft Statement, May 14. At http://fraser.stlouisfed.org/docs/historical/eccles/006_02_0002.pdf.

Hansen, A. H. 1942a. *After the War—Full Employment.* Washington, DC: Government Printing Office.

Hansen, A. H. 1942b. Memorandum to Dr. Goldenweiser, October 30. At http://fraser.stlouisfed.org/docs/historical/eccles/006_03_0005.pdf.

Hansen, A. H. 1945a. *America's Role in the World Economy.* New York: W. W. Norton.

Hansen, A. H. 1945b. Letter to Elliott Thurston. At http://fraser.stlouisfed.org/docs/historical/eccles/067_04_0005.pdf.

Hansen, A. H. 1947, *Economic Policy and Full Employment,* 4th ed. New York: Whittlesey House, McGraw-Hill.

Hansen, A. H. 1953. *A Guide to Keynes.* London: McGraw-Hill.

Hansen, A. H., Boddy, F. M., and Langum, J. K. 1936. Recent Trends in Business-Cycle Literature. *Review of Economics and Statistics* 18(2), p. 53.

Hansen, A. H., and Samuelson, P. A. 1946. *Economic Analysis of Guaranteed Wages.* Unpublished report to Office of War Mobilization, Advisory Board. PASP 93.

Hansen, A. H., and Samuelson, P. A. 1947a. Appendix F: Economic Analysis of Guaranteed Wages. In *Guaranteed Wages: Report to the President by the Advisory Board,* ed. M. W. Latimer, pp. 412–473. Washington, DC: U.S. Government Printing Office.

Hansen, A. H., and Samuelson, P. A. 1947b. Making the Annual Wage Work. *New York Times Magazine,* July 13, pp. 12, 35–38.

Hansen, A. H., and Tout, H. 1933. Annual Survey of Business Cycle Theory: Investment and Saving in Business Cycle Theory. *Econometrica* 1(2), pp. 119–147.

Harris, S. E. 1941, *Economics of Social Security: The Relation of the American Program to Consumption, Savings, Output, and Finance.* New York: McGraw-Hill.

Harris, S. E. 1945. A One Per Cent War? *American Economic Review* 35(4), pp. 667–671.

Harris, S. E., ed. 1947. *The New Economics: Keynes' Influence on Theory and Public Policy.* New York: Alfred A. Knopf.

Harrod, R. F. 1936. *The Trade Cycle.* Oxford: Clarendon Press.

Harrod, R. F. 1939. An Essay in Dynamic Theory. *Economic Journal* 49(193), pp. 14–33.

Hart, A. G. 1935. A Proposal for Making Monetary Management Effective in the United States. *Review of Economic Studies* 2(2), pp. 104–116.

Hart, A. G. 1948. Review of Samuelson's *Economics. American Economic Review* 38(5), pp. 910–915.

Harvard University. 1937. *Graduate School of Public Administration,* 1937–8. Catalogue. Cambridge, MA: Harvard University Press.

Harvard University. 1939. *Report on Some Problems of Personnel in the Faculty of Arts and Sciences.* Committee to Investigate the Cases of Drs. Walsh and Sweezy. Cambridge, MA: Harvard University Press.

Hayek, F. A. 1931. *Prices and Production.* London: Routledge.

Hayek, F. A. 1942. Scientism and the Study of Society, Part I. *Economica* 9(35), pp. 267–291.

Hayek, F. A. 1943. Scientism and the Study of Society, Part II. *Economica* 10(37), pp. 34–63.

Hayek, F. A. 1944a. Scientism and the Study of Society, Part III. *Economica* 11(41), pp. 27–39.

Hayek, F. A. 1944b. *The Road to Serfdom,* London: Routledge and Chicago: University of Chicago Press.

Heckscher, E. F., and Ohlin, B. 1991. *Heckscher-Ohlin Trade Theory.* Translated by M. J. Flanders and H. Flam. Cambridge, MA: MIT Press.

Hicks, J. R. 1932. *Theory of Wages.* London: Macmillan.

Hicks, J. R. 1937. Mr. Keynes and the "Classics"; A Suggested Interpretation. *Econometrica* 5(2), pp. 147–159.

Hicks, J. R. 1939a. The Foundations of Welfare Economics. *Economic Journal* 49(196), pp. 696–712.

Hicks, J. R. 1939b. *Value and Capital.* Oxford: Oxford University Press.

Hicks, J. R., and Allen, R. G. D. 1934a. A Reconsideration of the Theory of Value. Part I, *Economica,* 1(1), pp. 52–76.

Hicks, J. R., and Allen, R. G. D. 1934b. A Reconsideration of the Theory of Value. Part II: A Mathematical Theory of Individual Demand Functions. *Economica* 1(2), pp. 196–219.

Hicks, J. R., and Hart, A. G. 1945. *The Social Framework of the American Economy: An Introduction to Economics.* New York: Oxford University Press.

Hobson, J. A. 1914. *Work and Wealth: A Human Valuation.* London: Macmillan.

Hoover, K. D. 2006. Doctor Keynes: Economic Theory in a Diagnostic Science. In *The Cambridge Companion to Keynes,* ed. R. E. Backhouse and B. W. Bateman, pp. 78–97. Cambridge: Cambridge University Press.

Howson, S. 2011. *Lionel Robbins.* London and New York: Cambridge University Press.

Hunsaker, J., and Lane, S. M. 1973. Edwin Bidwell Wilson. Biographical Memoirs. *National Academy of Sciences* 43, p. 285.

Hurwicz, L. 1944. Stochastic Models of Economic Fluctuations. *Econometrica* 12(2), pp. 114–124.

Hutchison, T. W. 1938. *The Significance and Basic Postulates of Economic Theory.* London: Macmillan.

Hutchison, T. W. 2009. A Formative Decade: Methodological Controversy in the 1930s. *Journal of Economic Methodology* 16(3), pp. 297–314.

Hutt, W. H. 1930. *The Theory of Collective Bargaining.* London: P. S. King.

Hyman, H. 2012. Revisiting Beulah I. Shoesmith. At http://mathnexus.wwu.edu/Archive/news/detail.asp?ID=256.

Ickes, H. L. 1943, Bureaucrats v. Business Men. *New Republic,* August 2, 1943, pp. 131–133.

Isaac, J. 2012. *Working Knowledge: Making the Human Sciences from Parsons to Kuhn.* Cambridge, MA: Harvard University Press.

Kalecki, M. 1935. A Macrodynamic Theory of Business Cycles. *Econometrica* 3(3), pp. 327–344.

Karabel, J. 2005. *The Chosen: The Hidden History of Admission and Exclusion at Harvard, Yale, and Princeton.* Boston: Houghton Mifflin.

Karman, T. V., and Biot, M. A. 1940. *Mathematical Methods in Engineering: An Introduction to the Mathematical Treatment of Engineering Problems.* New York: McGraw-Hill.

Kaufmann, F. 1933. On the Subject-Matter and Method of Economic Science. *Economica* 42, pp. 381–401.

Keller, M., and Keller, P. 2001. *Making Harvard Modern: The Rise of America's University.* Cambridge, MA: Harvard University Press.

Keniston, H., Schevill, F., and Scott, A. P. 1934. *Introductory General Course in the Humanities: Syllabus.* Chicago: University of Chicago Press.

Keynes, J. M. 1919. *Economic Consequences of the Peace.* London: Macmillan.

Keynes, J. M. 1937. Some Economic Consequences of a Declining Population. *Eugenics Review* 29, pp. 13–17.

Keynes, J. M. 1946. The Balance of Payments of the United States. *Economic Journal* 56(222), pp. 172–187.

Keynes, J. M. 1971a [1923]. *A Tract on Monetary Reform.* London: Macmillan. Reprinted as *Collected Writings of John Maynard Keynes,* volume IV, 1971.

Keynes, J. M. 1971b [1930]. *A Treatise on Money.* London: Macmillan.

Keynes, J. M. 1972 [1936]. *The General Theory of Employment, Interest and Money.* London: Macmillan.

Keynes, J. M. 1973 [1921]. *A Treatise on Probability.* London: Macmillan.

Keynes, J. M. 1979. *Activities, 1940–4: External War Finance.* London: Macmillan.

Keyserling, L. H., Nathan, R. R., and Currie, L. B. 1972. Discussion. *American Economic Review* 62(1/2), pp. 134–141.

Killian, J. R. 1985. *The Education of a College President: A Memoir.* Cambridge, MA: MIT Press.

Klein, L. R. 1942. The Relationship Between Total Output and Man-Hour Output: Comment. *Quarterly Journal of Economics* 56(2), pp. 342–343.

Klein, L. R. 1943. Pitfalls in the Statistical Determination of the Investment Schedule. *Econometrica* 11(3/4), pp. 246–258.

Klein, L. R. 1944a. The Cost of a "Beveridge Plan" in the United States. *Quarterly Journal of Economics* 58(3), pp. 423–437.

Klein, L. R. 1944b. *The Keynesian Revolution.* Ph.D. thesis, MIT, Cambridge, MA.

Klein, L. R. 1944c. The Statistical Determination of the Investment Schedule: A Reply. *Econometrica* 12(1), pp. 91–92.

Klein, L. R. 1947. *The Keynesian Revolution.* New York: Macmillan.

Klein, L. R. 1954. Testimony of Lawrence R. Klein. In *Investigation of Communist Activities in the State of Michigan—Part I (Detroit—Education),* U.S. House of Representatives, Committee on Un-American Activities. April 30, May 3, and May 4, pp. 4991–5001. Washington, DC: U.S. Government Printing Office.

Klein, L. R. 1991. The Statistics Seminar, MIT, 1942–1943. *Statistical Science* 6(4), pp. 320–330.

Klein, L. R. 2004. Lawrence R. Klein. In *Lives of the Laureates,* 4th ed., ed. W. Breit and B. T. Hirsch, pp. 17–33. Cambridge, MA: MIT Press.

Klein, L. R., and Mariano, R. S. 1987. The ET Interview: Professor L. R. Klein. *Econometric Theory* 3(3), pp. 409–460.

Knight, F. H. 1921. *Risk, Uncertainty and Profit.* Boston: Houghton Mifflin.

Knight, F. H. 1922. Ethics and the Economic Interpretation. *Quarterly Journal of Economics* 36(3), pp. 454–481.

Knight, F. H. 1923. The Ethics of Competition. *Quarterly Journal of Economics* 37(4), pp. 579–624.

Knight, F. H. 1933. *The Dilemma of Liberalism.* Ann Arbor, MI: Edwards Brothers.

Knight, F. H. 1935. The Theory of Investment Once More: Mr. Boulding and the Austrians. *Quarterly Journal of Economics* 50(1), pp. 36–67.

Knight, F. H. 1951. *The Economic Organization.* New York: Harper.

Knight, F. H. 1982. Social Science and Political Trend. In *Freedom and Reform,* pp. 24–43. Indianapolis, IN: Liberty Press.

Knight, F. H. 1997[1935]. *The Ethics of Competition and Other Essays,* ed. M. Friedman, G. J. Stigler, H. Jones, and A. Wallis. With new Introduction by R. Boyd. New Brunswick, NJ: Transaction.

Koopmans, T. C. 1937. *Linear Regression Analysis of Economic Time Series.* Haarlem, Netherlands: F. Bohn.

Koopmans, T. C. 1947. Measurement Without Theory. *Review of Economics and Statistics* 29(3), pp. 161–172.

Kuhn, T. 1962. *The Structure of Scientific Revolutions.* Chicago: University of Chicago Press.

Laidler, D. E. W. 1999. *Fabricating the Keynesian Revolution: Studies of the Interwar Literature on Money, the Cycle and Unemployment.* Cambridge: Cambridge University Press.

Lane, R. W. 1947. Review of L. Tarshis, *The Elements of Economics. National Economic Council Review of Books,* August 1947, pp. 1–8.

Lange, O. 1934. The Determinateness of the Utility Function. *Review of Economic Studies* 1(3), pp. 218–225.

Lange, O. 1938. The Rate of Interest and the Optimum Propensity to Consume. *Economica* 5(17), pp. 12–32.

Lange, O. 1942. The Foundations of Welfare Economics. *Econometrica* 10(3/4), pp. 215–228.

Lange, O. 1943. The Theory of the Multiplier. *Econometrica* 11(3/4), pp. 227–245.

Leacock, S. 1936. Through a Glass Darkly. *The Atlantic,* July, pp. 94–98.

Lécuyer, C. 2010. Patrons and a Plan. In *Becoming MIT: Moments of Decision,* ed. D. Kaiser, pp. 59–80. Cambridge, MA: MIT Press.

Lemon, H. B. 1934. *From Galileo to Cosmic Rays: A New Look at Physics.* Chicago: University of Chicago Press.

Lemon, H. B., and Schlesinger, H. I. 1932. *Introductory General Course in the Physical Sciences: Syllabus,* 2nd ed. Chicago: University of Chicago Press.

Lemon, H. B., and Schlesinger, H. I. 1934. *Introductory General Course in the Physical Sciences: Syllabus.* Chicago: University of Chicago Press.

Leontief, E. 1987. *Genia and Wassily: A Russian-American Memoir.* Somerville, MA: Zephyr Press.

Leontief, W. 1925. Balans narodnogo khoziaistva SSSR. *Planovoe khoziaistvo* 12.

Leontief, W. 1929. Ein Versuch zur statistischen Analyse von Angebot und Nachfrage. *Weltwirtschaftliches Archiv* 30, pp. 1–53.

Leontief, W. 1932. Indications of Changes in the Demand for Agricultural Products: Discussion. *Journal of Farm Economics* 14(2), p. 256.

Leontief, W. 1933. The Use of Indifference Curves in the Analysis of Foreign Trade. *Quarterly Journal of Economics* 47(3), pp. 493–503.

Leontief, W. 1934a. Pitfalls in the Construction of Demand and Supply Curves: A Reply. *Quarterly Journal of Economics* 48(2), pp. 355–361.

Leontief, W. 1934b. More Pitfalls in Demand and Supply Curve Analysis: A Final Word. *Quarterly Journal of Economics* 48(4), pp. 755–759.

Leontief, W. 1934c. Interest on Capital and Distribution: A Problem in the Theory of Marginal Productivity. *Quarterly Journal of Economics* 49(1), pp. 147–161.

Leontief, W. 1935. Price-Quantity Variations in Business Cycles. *Review of Economics and Statistics* 17(4), pp. 21–27.

Leontief, W. 1936a. Composite Commodities and the Problem of Index Numbers. *Econometrica* 4(1), pp. 39–59.

Leontief, W. 1936b. The Fundamental Assumption of Mr. Keynes' Monetary Theory of Unemployment. *Quarterly Journal of Economics* 51(1), pp. 192–197.

Leontief, W. 1936c. Quantitative Input and Output Relations in the Economic Systems of the United States. *Review of Economics and Statistics* 18(3), pp. 105–125.

Leontief, W. 1936d. Stackelberg on Monopolistic Competition. *Journal of Political Economy* 44(4), pp. 554–559.

Leontief, W. 1937. Implicit Theorizing: A Methodological Criticism of the Neo-Cambridge School. *Quarterly Journal of Economics* 51(2), pp. 337–351.

Leontief, W. 1950. Joseph A. Schumpeter (1883–1950). *Econometrica* 18(2), pp. 103–110.

Leontief, W. 1977. *Essays in Economics: Theories Facts and Policies,* vol. 2. Oxford: Basil Blackwell.

Lerner, A. P. 1932. The Diagrammatical Representation of Cost Conditions in International Trade. *Economica* 37, pp. 346–356.

Lerner, A. P. 1934. The Diagrammatical Representation of Demand Conditions in International Trade. *Economica* n.s. 1(3), pp. 319–334.

Levy, D. M., Peart, S. J., and Albert, M. 2012. Economic Liberals as Quasi-Public Intellectuals: The Democratic Dimension. *Research in the History of Economic Thought and Methodology* 30-B, pp. 1–116.

Lewisohn, L. 1928. *The Island Within.* New York: Harper.

Livingston, S. M. 1945. Forecasting Postwar Demand: II. *Econometrica* 13(1), pp. 15–24.

Lotka, A. J. 1925. *Elements of Physical Biology.* Baltimore: Williams and Wilkins.

Lotka, A. J. 1939a. A Contribution to the Theory of Self-Renewing Aggregates, with Special Reference to Industrial Replacement. *Annals of Mathematical Statistics* 10(1), pp. 1–25.

Lotka, A. J. 1939b. On an Integral Equation in Population Analysis. *Annals of Mathematical Statistics* 10(2), pp. 144–161.

Lynd, R. S., and Lynd, H. M. 1929. *Middletown: A Study in Contemporary American Culture.* New York: Harcourt Brace.

Maas, H. J. B. 2014. Making Things Technical: Samuelson at MIT. In *MIT and the Transformation of American Economics*, Supplement to *History of Political Economy*, vol. 46 ed. E. R. Weintraub, pp. 272–294. Durham, NC: Duke University Press.

Mariano, R. S. 2008. Lawrence R. Klein. In *The New Palgrave Dictionary of Economics*, ed. S. N. Durlauf and L. E. Blume, pp. 739–746. Basingstoke, UK: Palgrave Macmillan. Online at http://www.dictionaryofeconomics.com.

Marshall, A. 1920. *Principles of Economics: An Introductory Volume,* 8th ed. London: Macmillan.

Marshall, A. 1923. *Money, Credit and Commerce.* London: Macmillan.

Massachusetts Institute of Technology (MIT). 1937. President's Report, 1938–9. *Bulletin* 73(1).

Massachusetts Institute of Technology (MIT). 1938. President's Report, 1938–9. *Bulletin* 74(1).

Massachusetts Institute of Technology (MIT). 1939. President's Report, 1938–9. *Bulletin* 75(1).

Massachusetts Institute of Technology (MIT). 1940. Catalogue. *Bulletin* 75(4).

Massachusetts Institute of Technology (MIT). 1941. Catalogue. *Bulletin* 76(4).

Massachusetts Institute of Technology (MIT). 1942a. President's Report, 1941–1942. *Bulletin* 78(1), pp. 1–232.

Massachusetts Institute of Technology (MIT). 1942b. Catalog. *Bulletin* 77(4).

Massachusetts Institute of Technology (MIT). 1943. Catalog. *Bulletin* 78(4).

Massachusetts Institute of Technology (MIT). 1944. Catalogue. *Bulletin* 79(4).

Mason, E. S. 1982. The Harvard Department of Economics from the Beginning to World War II. *Quarterly Journal of Economics* 97(3), pp. 383–433.

Mathematical Association of America. 1932. Notes and News. *American Mathematical Monthly* 39(5), pp. 306–308.

May, K. 1948. *Science & Society* 13(1), pp. 93–95.

McCraw, T. K. 2007. *Prophet of Innovation: Joseph Schumpeter and Creative Destruction.* Cambridge, MA: Belknap Press of Harvard University Press.

McCulloch, W., and Pitts, W. 1943. A Logical Calculus of Ideas Immanent in Nervous Activity. *Bulletin of Mathematical Biophysics* 5, pp. 115–133.

Means, G. C., ed. 1939. *The Structure of the American Economy. Part. 1: Basic Characteristics.* Washington, DC: U.S. Government Printing Office.

Mehrling, P. 1997. *The Money Interest and the Public Interest: American Monetary Thought, 1920–1970.* Cambridge, MA: Harvard University Press.

Mendershausen, H. 1939. The Relationship Between Income and Savings of American Metropolitan Families. *American Economic Review* 29(3), pp. 521–537.

Merriam, C. E. 1931. *The Making of Citizens.* Chicago: University of Chicago Press.

Merriam, C. E. 1944. The National Resources Planning Board; A Chapter in American Planning Experience. *American Political Science Review* 38(6), pp. 1075–1088.

Merton, R. K., Sills, D. L., and Stigler, S. M. 1984. The Kelvin Dictum and Social Science: An Excursion into the History of an Idea. *Journal of the History of the Behavioral Sciences* 20(4), pp. 319–331.

Metzler, L. A. 1948. Review of Samuelson's *Foundations of Economic Analysis.* *American Economic Review*, 38(5), pp. 905–910.

Mindell, D. A. 2000. Automation's Finest Hour: Radar and System Integration in World War II. In *Systems, Experts and Computers: The Systems Approach in Management and Engineering, World War II and After,* ed. A. C. Hughes and T. P. Hughes, pp. 27–56. Cambridge, MA: MIT Press.

Mindell, D. A. 2002. *Between Human and Machine: Feedback, Control and Computing before Cybernetics.* Baltimore: Johns Hopkins University Press

Mitchell, J. 1903. *Organized Labor: Its Problems, Purposes and Ideals and the Present and Future of American Wage Earners.* Philadelphia: American Book and Bible House.

Mitchell, W. C. 1927. *Business Cycles: The Problem and Its Setting.* New York: NBER.

Modigliani, F. 1944. Liquidity Preference and the Theory of Interest and Money. *Econometrica* 12(1), pp. 45–88.

Moggridge, D. E. 1998. The Diffusion of the Keynesian Revolution. In *Keynesianism and the Keynesian Revolution in America,* ed. H. Landreth and B. B. Price, pp. 18–31. Cheltenham, UK: Edward Elgar.

Moore, E. H. 1910. *Introduction to a Form of General Analysis.* New Haven, CT: Yale University Press.

Morgan, M. S. 1990. *A History of Econometric Ideas.* Cambridge: Cambridge University Press.

Morgan, M. S., and Rutherford, M. 1998. *From Interwar Pluralism to Postwar Neoclassicism.* Supplement to *History of Political Economy,* vol. 30. Durham, NC: Duke University Press.

Morgenstern, O. 1941. Professor Hicks on Value and Capital. *Journal of Political Economy* 49(3), pp. 361–393.

Morgenstern, O. 1951. Joseph A. Schumpeter. *Economic Journal* 61(241), pp. 197–202 [obituary].

Mosak, J. L. 1945. Forecasting Postwar Demand: III. *Econometrica* 13(1), pp. 25–53.

Myrdal, G. 1939. *Monetary Equilibrium.* Translated by R. B. Bryce and W. Stolper. London: Hodge.

National Resources Committee. 1939. *Consumer Expenditures in the United States.* Washington, DC: U.S. Government Printing Office.

National Resources Planning Board (NRPB). 1942. *Post-War Planning—Full Employment, Security, Building America.* Washington, DC: U.S. Government Printing Office.

National Resources Planning Board (NRPB). 1943a. *Report for 1943, Part I: Post-war Plan and Program.* Washington, DC: U.S. Government Printing Office.

National Resources Planning Board (NRPB). 1943b. *Report for 1943, Part II: Wartime Planning for War and Post War.* Washington, DC: U.S. Government Printing Office.

National Resources Planning Board (NRPB). 1943c. *Security, Work, and Relief Policies.* Washington, DC: U.S. Government Printing Office.

Nelson, S., and Keim, W. G. 1941. *Investigation of Concentration of Economic Power. Volume 1: Price Behavior and Business Policy.* Washington, DC: Temporary National Economic Committee.

Nixon, R. A., and Samuelson, P. A. 1940. Estimates of Unemployment in the United States. *Review of Economics and Statistics* 22(3), pp. 101–111.

Ohlin, B. 1929. Transfer Difficulties, Real and Imagined. *Economic Journal* 39(154), pp. 172–178.

Ohlin, B. 1933. *Interregional and International Trade,* rev. ed. Cambridge, MA: Harvard University Press.

Orear, J. 2004. Enrico Fermi—The Master Scientist. At http://hdl.handle.net/ 1813/74.

Perlman, M. 1996. Jews and Contributions to Economics: A Bicentennial Review. In *The Character of Economic Thought, Economic Characters and Economic Institutions: Selected Essays of Mark Perlman,* ed. M. Perlman, pp. 307–317. Ann Arbor: Universtiy of Michigan Press.

Phillips-Fein, K. 2009. *Invisible Hands: The Making of the Conservative Movement from the New Deal to Reagan.* New York: W. W. Norton.

Pigou, A. C. 1920. *The Economics of Welfare.* London: Macmillan.

Pigou, A. C. 1932. *The Economics of Welfare,* 4th ed. London: Macmillan.

Pigou, A. C. 1935. *The Economics of Stationary States.* London: Macmillan.

Pigou, A. C. 1941. *Employment and Equilibrium.* London: Macmillan.

Popper, K. R. 1959. *The Logic of Scientific Discovery.* London: Routledge.

Ramsey, F. P. 1927. A Contribution to the Theory of Taxation. *Economic Journal* 37(145), pp. 47–61.

Ramsey, F. P. 1928. A Mathematical Theory of Saving. *Economic Journal* 38(152), pp. 543–559.

Reagan, P. D. 1999. *Designing a New America: The Origins of New Deal Planning, 1890–1943.* Amherst: University of Massachusetts Press.

Rédei, M. (ed.) 2005. *John von Neumann: Selected Letters (History of Mathematics,* volume 27). American Mathematical Society/London Mathematical Society.

Reder, M. W. 1948. Professor Samuelson on the Foundations of Economic Analysis. *Canadian Journal of Economics and Political Science/Revue canadienne d'Economique et de Science politique* 14(4), pp. 516–530.

Reed, Z., and Smith, D. E. 1925. High School Mathematics Clubs. *Mathematics Teacher* 18(6), pp. 341–363.

Robbins, L. C. 1932. *An Essay on the Nature and Significance of Economic Science.* London: Macmillan.

Robinson, J. 1933a. *Economics of Imperfect Competition.* London: Macmillan.

Robinson, J. 1933b. The Theory of Money and the Analysis of Output. *Review of Economic Studies* 1(1), pp. 22–26.

Robinson, J. 1937. *Essays in the Theory of Employment.* London: Macmillan.

Roll, E. 1941. Review of J. A. Estey *Business Cycles. American Economic Review* 31(2), pp. 362–364.

Roll, E. 1985. *Crowded Hours: An Autobiography.* London: Faber and Faber.

Roll, E. 1995. *My Journey Through the Century.* Hull, UK: University of Hull.

Roos, C. F., Hurwicz, L., Higgins, B., Koopmans, T., Hagen, E. E., Fuller, K. G., Nienstaedt, L. R., and Marschak, J. 1945. Forecasting Postwar Demand: Discussion. *Econometrica* 13(1), pp. 54–59.

Roosevelt, F. D. 1945. Annual Budget Message, January 3, 1945. At http://www.presidency.ucsb.edu/ws/?pid=16584.

Russell, B., and Russell, D. 1923. *Prospects of Industrial Civilization.* New York: Century.

Rymes, T. K., ed. 1989. *Keynes's Lectures, 1932–35: Notes of a Representative Student.* London: Macmillan.

Salant, W. S. 1942. The Inflationary Gap: I. Meaning and Significance for Policy Making. *American Economic Review* 32(2), pp. 308–314.

Salant, W. S. 1975. I. Introduction to William A. Salant's "Taxes, the multiplier and the inflationary gap," *History of Political Economy,* 7(1), pp. 3–18.

Salant, W. A. 1975. II. Taxes, the Multiplier, and the Inflationary Gap. *History of Political Economy* 7(1), pp. 19–27.

Salant, W. S. 1976. Alvin Hansen and the Fiscal Policy Seminar. *Quarterly Journal of Economics* 90(1), pp. 14–23.

Salter, A. 1932. *Recovery: The Second Effort.* London: G. Bell and Sons.

Samuelson, M. C. 1939. The Australian Case for Protection Reexamined. *Quarterly Journal of Economics* 54(1), pp. 143–149.

Samuelson, P. A. 1930. Out of the Frying Pan. *The Scroll,* May, pp. 16–17.

Samuelson, P. A. 1937a. A Note on Measurement of Utility. *Review of Economic Studies* 4(2), pp. 155–161. CSP 1:20.

...cts of the Pure Theory of Capital. *Quarterly*
..., pp. 469–496. CSP 1:17.

... 1938a. The Empirical Implications of Utility Analysis. *Econometrica*
6(4), pp. 344–356. CSP 1:3.

Samuelson, P. A. 1938b. A Note on the Pure Theory of Consumer's Behaviour.
Economica 5(17), pp. 61–71. CSP 1:1.

Samuelson, P. A. 1938c. A Note on the Pure Theory of Consumer's Behaviour: An
Addendum. *Economica* 5(19), pp. 353–354. CSP 1:1.

Samuelson, P. A. 1938d. The Numerical Representation of Ordered Classifications
and the Concept of Utility. *Review of Economic Studies* 6(1), pp. 65–70. CSP 1:2.

Samuelson, P. A. 1938e. Report of the Atlantic City and Indianapolis Meetings,
December 27–30. *Econometrica* 6(2), pp. 180–192.

Samuelson, P. A. 1938f. Welfare Economics and International Trade. *American Economic
Review* 28(2), pp. 261–266. CSP 2:60.

Samuelson, P. A. 1939a. The Gains from International Trade. *Canadian Journal of
Economics and Political Science* 5(2), pp. 195–205. CSP 2:61.

Samuelson, P. A. 1939b. Interactions between the Multiplier Analysis and the Principle
of Acceleration. *Review of Economics and Statistics* 21(2), pp. 75–78. CSP 2:82.

Samuelson, P. A. 1939c. The Rate of Interest Under Ideal Conditions. *Quarterly
Journal of Economics* 53(2), pp. 286–297. CSP 1:18.

Samuelson, P. A. 1939d. Review of M. D. Anderson, *Dynamic Theory of Wealth
Distribution*. *American Economic Review* 29(2), pp. 358–359.

Samuelson, P. A. 1939e. A Synthesis of the Principle of Acceleration and the
Multiplier. *Journal of Political Economy* 47(6), pp. 786–797. CSP 2:83.

Samuelson, P. A. 1940a. *Foundations of Analytical Economics: The Observational Significance
of Economic Theory*. Ph.D. thesis, Harvard University. [Copy also archived in PASP
91]

Samuelson, P. A. 1940b. Review of E. Petersen, *Macro-Dynamic Aspects of the
Equation of Exchange*. *American Economic Review* 30(3), p. 641.

Samuelson, P. A. 1940c. Review of G. Myrdal, *Monetary Equilibrium*. *American Economic
Review* 30(1), pp. 129–130.

Samuelson, P. A. 1940d. The Theory of Pump-Priming Reexamined. *American Economic
Review* 30(3), pp. 492–506. CSP 2:85.

Samuelson, P. A. 1941a. Concerning Say's Law. *Econometrica* 9(2), pp. 177–178. CSP 2:88.

Samuelson, P. A. 1941b. *Consumer Demand at Full Production*. Washington, DC:
National Resources Planning Board.

Samuelson, P. A. 1941c. Professor Pigou's Employment and Equilibrium. *American
Economic Review* 31(3), pp. 545–552. CSP 2:89.

Samuelson, P. A. 1941d. The Stability of Equilibrium: Comparative Statics and
Dynamics. *Econometrica* 9(2), pp. 97–120. CSP 1:38.

Samuelson, P. A. 1941e. A Statistical Determination of the Consumption
Function. In *Fiscal Policy and Business Cycles,* ed. A. H. Hansen, pp. 250–260.
New York: W. W. Norton. CSP 2:87.

Samuelson, P. A. 1942a. The Business Cycle and Urban Development. .... of the Cities and Towns: Proceedings of Conference on Urbanism, Harvard University, March 5–6, pp. 6–17. CSP 2:97.

Samuelson, P. A. 1942b. Constancy of Marginal Utility of Income. In *Studies in Mathematical Economics and Econometrics: In Memory of Henry Schultz*, ed. O. Lange, pp. 75–91. Chicago: University of Chicago Press. CSP 1:5.

Samuelson, P. A. 1942c. Fiscal Policy and Income Determination. *Quarterly Journal of Economics* 56(4), pp. 575–605. CSP 2:86.

Samuelson, P. A. 1942d. A Method of Determining Explicitly the Coefficients of the Characteristic Equation. *Annals of Mathematical Statistics* 13(4), pp. 424–429. CSP 1:47.

Samuelson, P. A. 1942e. A Note on Alternative Regressions. *Econometrica* 10(1), pp. 80–83. CSP 1:46.

Samuelson, P. A. 1942f. The Stability of Equilibrium: Linear and Nonlinear Systems. *Econometrica* 10(1), pp. 1–25. CSP 1:40.

Samuelson, P. A. 1943a. Dynamics, Statics, and the Stationary State. *Review of Economics and Statistics* 25(1), pp. 58–68. CSP 1:19.

Samuelson, P. A. 1943b. Efficient Computation of the Latent Vectors of a Matrix. *Proceedings of the National Academy of Sciences of the United States of America* 29(11), pp. 393–397. CSP 1:50.

Samuelson, P. A. 1943c. Fitting General Gram-Charlier Series. *Annals of Mathematical Statistics* 14(2), pp. 179–187. CSP 1:48.

Samuelson, P. A. 1943d. Full Employment After the War. In *Postwar Economic Problems*, ed. S. E. Harris, pp. 27–53. New York: McGraw-Hill. CSP 2:108.

Samuelson, P. A. 1943e. A Fundamental Multiplier Identity. *Econometrica* 11(3/4), pp. 221–226. CSP 2:90.

Samuelson, P. A. 1943f. Further Commentary on Welfare Economics. *American Economic Review* 33(3), pp. 604–607. CSP 2:76.

Samuelson, P. A. 1943g. Review of Fritz Machlup, *International Trade and the National Income Multiplier. Journal of the American Statistical Association* 38(223), pp. 369–370.

Samuelson, P. A. 1943h. Review of Harold T. Davis, *The Economic Analysis of Time Series. Journal of Political Economy* 51(3), pp. 275–276.

Samuelson, P. A. 1943i. A Simple Method of Interpolation. *Proceedings of the National Academy of Sciences of the United States of America* 29(11), pp. 397–401. CSP 1:49.

Samuelson, P. A. 1943j. When the War Ends. *Mechanical Engineering* 65(5), pp. 360–363.

Samuelson, P. A. 1944a. *Analysis of Tracking Data: Description of Calculations.* Report 628, Radiation Laboratory. Cambridge, MA: Massachusetts Institute of Technology.

Samuelson, P. A. 1944b. The Relation Between Hicksian Stability and True Dynamic Stability. *Econometrica* 12(3/4), pp. 256–257. CSP 1:39.

Samuelson, P. A. 1944c. Unemployment Ahead I: Warning to Washington Experts. *The New Republic,* September 11, pp. 297–299.

Samuelson, P. A. 1944d. Unemployment Ahead II: The Coming Economic Crisis. *The New Republic,* September 18, pp. 333–335.

Samuelson, P. A. 1945a. The Effect of Interest Rate Increases on the Banking System. *American Economic Review* 35(1), pp. 16–27. CSP 2:95.

Samuelson, P. A., 1945b. Full Employment. *Washington Post*, September 2.

Samuelson, P. A. 1945c. The Turn of the Screw. *American Economic Review* 35(4), pp. 674–676. CSP 2:96.

Samuelson, P. A. 1945d. Bretton Woods, Pro and Con. *The New Republic*, April 9, pp. 467–469.

Samuelson, P. A. 1945e. Hansen on World Trade [review of Alvin H. Hansen, *America's Role in the World Economy*]. *The New Republic,* March 26, pp. 409–411.

Samuelson, P. A. 1945f. Is the "Easy Money" Policy a Sound One? *Modern Industry* January 15, pp. 113–126.

Samuelson, P. A. 1945g. Science and the National Defense. *The New Republic*, January 1, pp. 7–8.

Samuelson, P. A. 1945h. Toward a National Budget [unsigned editorial]. *The New Republic,*January 29, pp. 136–137.

Samuelson, P. A. 1946a. Lord Keynes and the General Theory. *Econometrica* 14(3), pp. 187–200. CSP 2:114.

Samuelson, P. A. 1946b. Unemployment Forecasts: A Failure. *American Economist* 1(1), pp. 7–9.

Samuelson, P. A. 1947a. *Foundations of Economic Analysis.* Cambridge, MA: Harvard University Press.

Samuelson, P. A. 1947b. The General Theory. In *The New Economics: Keynes' Influence on Theory and Public Policy,* ed. S. E. Harris, pp. 145–160. New York: Alfred A. Knopf.

Samuelson, P. A. 1948. *Economics: An Introductory Analysis*. New York: McGraw-Hill.

Samuelson, P. A. 1950. The Problem of Integrability in Utility Theory. *Economica* 17(68), pp. 355–385. CSP 1:10.

Samuelson, P. A. 1951a. *Economics: An Introductory Analysis*, 2nd ed. New York: McGraw-Hill.

Samuelson, P. A. 1951b. Schumpeter as a Teacher and Economic Theorist. *Review of Economics and Statistics* 33(2), pp. 98–103. CSP 2:116.

Samuelson, P. A. 1958. An Exact Consumption-Loan Model of Interest with or without the Social Contrivance of Money. *Journal of Political Economy* 66(6), pp. 467–482. CSP 1:21.

Samuelson, P. A. 1959. Alvin Hansen and the Interactions between the Multiplier Analysis and the Principle of Acceleration. *Review of Economics and Statistics* 41(2), pp. 183–184. CSP 2:84.

Samuelson, P. A. 1966. *The Collected Scientific Papers of Paul A. Samuelson,* volumes 1 and 2. Edited by J. E. Stiglitz. Cambridge, MA: MIT Press.

Samuelson, P. A. 1968. What Classical and Neoclassical Monetary Theory Really Was. *Canadian Journal of Economics* 1(1), pp. 1–15. CSP 3:176.

Samuelson, P. A. 1971. Maximum Principles in Analytical Economics. *Science* 173(4001), pp. 991–997. Also in *American Economic Review* 62(3), pp. 249–62. CSP 3:130.

Samuelson, P. A. 1972a. Economics in a Golden Age: A Personal Memoir. In *The Twentieth-Century Sciences: Studies in the Biography of Ideas,* ed. G. Holton, pp. 155–170. New York: W. W. Norton. CSP 4:278.

Samuelson, P. A. 1972b. Frank Knight, 1885–1972. *Newsweek,* July, p. 55. CSP 4:283.

Samuelson, P. A. 1972c. Jacob Viner, 1892–1970. *Journal of Political Economy* 80(1), pp. 5–11. CSP 4:282.

Samuelson, P. A. 1972d. *The Collected Scientific Papers of Paul A. Samuelson,* volume 3. Edited by R. C. Merton. Cambridge, MA: MIT Press.

Samuelson, P. A. 1975a. Alvin H. Hansen, 1889–1975. *Newsweek,* June 16, p. 72. CSP 4:287.

Samuelson, P. A. 1975b. VI. The Balanced-Budget Multiplier: A Case Study in the Sociology and Psychology of Scientific Discovery. *History of Political Economy* 7(1), pp. 43–55. CSP 4:274.

Samuelson, P. A. 1976a. Alvin Hansen as a Creative Economic Theorist. *Quarterly Journal of Economics* 90(1), pp. 24–31. CSP 4:285.

Samuelson, P. A. 1976b. In Search of the Elusive Elite. *New York Times,* June 26, p. 39. CSP 4:286.

Samuelson, P. A. 1976c. Resolving a Historical Confusion in Population Analysis. *Human Biology* 48(3), pp. 559–580. CSP 4:236.

Samuelson, P. A. 1977. *The Collected Scientific Papers of Paul A. Samuelson,* volume 4. Edited by K. Crowley and H. Nagatani. Cambridge, MA: MIT Press.

Samuelson, P. A. 1981. Bergsonian Welfare Economics. In *Economic Welfare and the Economics of Soviet Socialism: Essays in Honor of Abram Bergson,* ed. S. Rosefielde, pp. 223–266. Cambridge: Cambridge University Press. CSP 5:293.

Samuelson, P. A. 1982. Foreword to the Japanese Edition of *The Collected Scientific Papers of Paul A. Samuelson.* Edited by M. Shinohara and R. Sato, pp. 858–875. Tokyo: Keiso Shobo. CSP 5:367.

Samuelson, P. A. 1986. *The Collected Scientific Papers of Paul A. Samuelson,* volume 5. Edited by K. Crowley. Cambridge, MA: MIT Press.

Samuelson, P. A. 1987. Joint Authorship in Science: Serendipity with Wolfgang Stolper. *Journal of Institutional and Theoretical Economics* 143(2), pp. 235–243. CSP 7:584.

Samuelson, P. A. 1989a. Gibbs in Economics. In *Proceedings of the Gibbs Symposium, Yale University, May 15–17, 1989,* ed. D. G. Caldi and G. D. Mostow, pp. 255–267. Providence, RI: American Mathematical Society. CSP 7:539.

Samuelson, P. A. 1989b. A Revisionist View of von Neumann's Growth Model. In *John von Neumann and Modern Economics,* ed. M. Dore, S. Chakravarty and R. Goodwin, pp. 100-122. Oxford: Oxford University Press. CSP 6:406.

Samuelson, P. A. 1990a. Gottfried Haberler as Economic Sage and Trade Theory Innovator. *Wirtschafts Politische Bläetier* 37, pp. 310–317. CSP 7:550.

Samuelson, P. A. 1990b. Paul A. Samuelson. In *Lives of the Laureates: Ten Nobel Economists,* ed. W. Breit and R. W. Spencer, pp. 59–76. Cambridge, MA: MIT Press.

Samuelson, P. A. 1991a. Jacob Viner, 1892–1970. In *Remembering the University of Chicago Teachers, Scientists, and Scholars,* ed. E. Shils, pp. 533–547. Chicago: University of Chicago Press. CSP 7:531.

Samuelson, P. A. 1991b. Statistical Flowers Caught in Amber. *Statistical Science* 6(4), pp. 330–338. CSP 7:575.

Samuelson, P. A. 1992. My Life Philosophy: Policy Credos and Working Ways. In *Eminent Economists: Their Life Philosophies,* ed. M. Szenberg, pp. 236–247. Cambridge: Cambridge University Press. CSP 7:574.

Samuelson, P. A. 1994. Tribute to Wolfgand Stolper on the Fiftieth Anniversary of the Stolper-Samuelson Theorem. In *The Stolper-Samuelson Theorem: A Golden Jubilee,* ed. A. V. Deardorff and R. M. Stern, pp. 343–349. Ann Arbor: University of Michigan Press. CSP 7:544.

Samuelson, P. A. 1995a. At Eighty: MIT and I [Speech, Birthday Party, Boston, April 30]. CSP 7:580.

Samuelson, P. A. 1995b. Paul Anthony Samuelson. In *The Coming of Keynesianism to America: Conversations with the Founders of Keynesian Economics,* ed. D. C. Colander and H. Landreth, pp. 145–178. Cheltenham, UK: Edward Elgar. CSP 7:581.

Samuelson, P. A. 1996a. Gottfried Haberler (1900–1995). *Economic Journal* 106(439), pp. 1679–1687. CSP 7:538.

Samuelson, P. A. 1996b. On Collaboration. *American Economist* 40(2), pp. 16–21. CSP 7:583.

Samuelson, P. A. 1997a. Credo of a Lucky Textbook Author. *Journal of Economic Perspectives* 11(2), pp. 153–160. CSP 7:582.

Samuelson, P. A. 1997b. How Foundations Came to Be. In *Paul A. Samuelson's "Foundations of Economic Analysis,"* ed. J. Niehans, P. A. Samuelson, and C. C. V. Weizsacker, pp. 27–52. Dusseldorf: Verlag Wirtschaft und Finanzen. CSP 7:586.

Samuelson, P. A. 1997c. Some Memories of Norbert Wiener. In *Proceedings of Symposia in Pure Mathematics. Volume 60: The Legacy of Norbert Weiner: A Centennial Symposium,* ed. D. Jerison, I. M. Singer, and D. W. Stroock, pp. 37–42. Providence, RI: American Mathematical Society. CSP 7:549.

Samuelson, P. A. 1998a. A Golden Birthday. In *Economics,* ed. P. A. Samuelson and W. D. Nordhaus, pp. xxiv–xxvii. New York: McGraw-Hill. CSP 7:587.

Samuelson, P. A. 1998b. Harold Freeman (1909–1997) [memorial service tribute], Massachusetts Institute of Technology, March 10. CSP 7:552.

Samuelson, P. A. 1998c. How Foundations Came to Be. *Journal of Economic Literature* 36(3), pp. 1375–1386. CSP 7:586.

Samuelson, P. A. 1998d. Requiem for the Classic Tarshis Textbook that First Brought Keynes to Introductory Economics. In *Keynesianism and the Keynesian Revolution in America: A Memorial Volume in Honour of Lorie Tarshis,* ed. O. F.

Hamouda and B. B. Price, pp. 53–58. Cheltenham, UK: Edward Elgar. CSP 6:434.

Samuelson, P. A. 2000. Economics in MIT's Fourth School. *Soundings.* At http://web.mit.edu/shass/soundings/issue_oof/fea_lum_pas_oof.html.

Samuelson, P. A. 2002a. Pastiches from an Earlier Politically Incorrect Academic Age. In *Editing Economics: Esays in Honour of Mark Perlman,* ed. H. Lim, U. S. Park, and G. C. Harcourt, pp. 47–55. London: Routledge. CSP 7:593.

Samuelson, P. A. 2002b. Interview. In *Reflections on the Great Depression,* ed. R. E. Parker, pp. 25–40. Cheltenham, UK: Edward Elgar. CSP 6:437.

Samuelson, P. A. 2003. Reflections on the Schumpeter I Knew Well. *Journal of Evolutionary Economics* 13(5), pp. 463–467. CSP 7:561.

Samuelson, P. A. 2004a. Abram Bergson, 1914–2003. *Biographical Memoirs* 84, pp. 3–14. CSP 7:563.

Samuelson, P. A. 2004b. Portrait of the Master as a Young Man. In *Wassily Leontief and Input-Output Economics,* ed. E. Dietzenbacher and M. L. Lahr, pp. 3–8 (eds). Cambridge: Cambridge University Press. CSP 7:562.

Samuelson, P. A. 2009a. Paul A. Samuelson. In *Roads to Wisdom: Conversations with Ten Nobel Laureates in Economics,* ed. K. I. Horn, pp. 39–57. Cheltenham, UK: Edward Elgar. CSP 7:596.

Samuelson, P. A. 2009b. Three Moles. *Bulletin of the American Academy* 58(2), pp. 83–84. CSP 7:595

Samuelson, P. A. 2011a. *The Collected Scientific Papers of Paul A. Samuelson,* volumes 6 and 7. Edited by J. Murray. Cambridge, MA: MIT Press.

Samuelson, P. A. 2011b. The Harvard-Circle [The Schumpeter Circle at Harvard, 1932–1950]. *Journal of Evolutionary Economics* 25, pp. 31–36. CSP 7:572.

Samuelson, P. A., and Hagen, E. E. 1943. *After the War: 1918–1920.* Washington, DC: National Resources Planning Board.

Samuelson, P. A., McGraw, H. W. Jr., Nordhaus, W. D., Ashenfelter, O., Solow, R. M., and Fischer, S. 1999. Samuelson's "Economics" at Fifty: Remarks on the Occasion of the Anniversary of Publication. *Journal of Economic Education* 30(4), pp. 352–363. Samuelson's contribution in CSP 7:589.

Sandilands, R. 1990. *The Life and Political Economy of Lauchlin Currie: New Dealer, Presidential Adviser, and Development Economist.* Durham, NC: Duke University Press.

Sandilands, R. 2004. Lauchlin Currie: A Biographical Sketch. *Journal of Economic Studie,* 31(3/4), pp. 194–197.

Savage, L. J. 1948. Samuelson's Foundations: Its Mathematics. *Journal of Political Economy* 56(3), pp. 200–202.

Schlesinger, A. M. 1949. *The Vital Center: The Politics of Freedom.* Boston: Houghton Mifflin.

Schorling, R. 1915. The Problem of Individual Differences in the Teaching of Secondary-School Mathematics. *School Review* 23(10), pp. 649–664.

Schultz, H. 1927. Cost of Production, Supply and Demand, and the Tariff. *Journal of Farm Economics* 9(2), pp. 192–209.

Schultz, H. 1938. *The Theory and Measurement of Demand.* Chicago: University of Chicago Press.

Schuman, F. L. 1932a. American Foreign Policy. *American Journal of Sociology* 37(6), pp. 883–888.

Schuman, F. L. 1932b. The Ethics and Politics of International Peace. *International Journal of Ethics* 42(2), pp. 148–162.

Schuman, F. L. 1932c. The United States and International Morality. *International Journal of Ethics* 43(1), pp. 1–19.

Schuman, F. L. 1934a. The Conduct of German Foreign Affairs. *Annals of the American Academy of Political and Social Science* 176, pp. 187–221.

Schuman, F. L. 1934b. The Political Theory of German Fascism. *American Political Science Review* 28(2), pp. 210–232.

Schuman, F. L. 1934c. The Third Reich's Road to War. *Annals of the American Academy of Political and Social Science* 175, pp. 33–43.

Schumpeter, J. A. 1908. *Das Wesen und der Hauptinhalt der theoretischen Nationaloekonomie.* Munich: Dunker and Humblot.

Schumpeter, J. A. 1933. The Common Sense of Econometrics. *Econometrica* 1(1), pp. 5–12.

Schumpeter, J. A. 1934. *The Theory of Economic Development: An Inquiry into Profits, Capital, Credit, Interest, and the Business Cycle.* Translated by R. Opie. Cambridge, MA: Harvard University Press.

Schumpeter, J. A. 1936. Review of J. M. Keynes, *The General Theory of Employment, Interest and Money. Journal of the American Statistical Association* 31(196), pp. 791–795.

Schumpeter, J. A. 1939. *Business Cycles: A Theoretical, Historical, and Statistical Analysis of the Capitalist Process.* Mansfield Centre, CT: Martino.

Schumpeter, J. A. 1942. *Capitalism, Socialism and Democracy.* New York: Harper and Brothers.

Schumpeter, J. A. 1954. *A History of Economic Analysis.* New York: Oxford University Press.

Schumpeter, J. A. 2010. *The Nature and Essence of Economic Theory.* Translated by B. McDaniel. Rutgers, NJ: Transaction.

Schumpeter, J. A., Chamberlin, E. H., Mason, E. S., Brown, D. V., Harris, S. E., Leontief, W. A., and Taylor, O. H. 1934. *The Economics of the Recovery Program.* New York: McGraw-Hill.

Schumpeter, J. A. Fisher, I., Marschak, J., and Samuelson, P. A. 1939. The Pure Theory of Production. *American Economic Review* 29(1), pp. 118–120.

Scitovsky, T. 1941. Capital Accumulation, Employment and Price Rigidity. *Review of Economic Studies* 8(2), pp. 69–88.

Shionoya, Y. 1997. *Schumpeter and the Idea of Social Science.* Cambridge: Cambridge University Press.

Shoesmith, B. I. 1916. Mathematics Clubs in Secondary Schools. *School Science and Mathematics* 16(2), pp. 106–113.

Simons, H. C. 1934. *A Positive Program for Laissez-Faire*. Chicago: University of
 Chicago Press.

Slichter, S. H. 1931. *Modern Economic Society*. New York: Holt.

Smith, A. 1976a. *An Inquiry into the Nature and Causes of the Wealth of Nations*. Edited
 by R. H. Campbell and A. S. Skinner. Oxford: Clarendon Press.

Smith, A. 1976b. *The Theory of Moral Sentiments*. Edited by D. D. Raphael and
 A. L. Macfie. Oxford: Clarendon Press.

Smithies, A. 1945. Forecasting Postwar Demand: I. *Econometrica* 13(1), pp. 1–14.

Sraffa, P. 1926. The Laws of Returns under Competitive Conditions. *Economic
 Journal* 36(144), pp. 535–550.

Staehle, H. 1935. A Development of the Economic Theory of Price Index
 Numbers. *Review of Economic Studies* 2(3), pp. 163–188.

Steffens, L. 1931. *The Autobiography of Lincoln Steffens*. New York: Harcourt Brace.

Stein, G. 1934. *The Making of Americans*. New York: Harcourt Brace.

Stein, H. 1969. *The Fiscal Revolution in America*. Chicago: University of Chicago Press.

Stigler, G. J. 1941. *Production and Distribution Theories, 1870 to 1895*. New York:
 Macmillan.

Stigler, G. J. 1943. The New Welfare Economics. *American Economic Review* 33(2),
 pp. 355–359.

Stigler, G. J. 1946. *The Theory of Price*. New York: Macmillan.

Stigler, G. J. 1948. Untitled article. *Journal of the American Statistical Association*
 43(244), pp. 603–605.

Stigler, G. J. 1988. *Memoirs of an Unregulated Economist*. New York: Basic Books.

Stigler, S. M. 1994. Some Correspondence on Methodology Between Milton Friedman
 and Edwin B. Wilson, November–December 1946. *Journal of Economic Literature*
 32(3), pp. 1197–1203.

Stolper, W. F., and Samuelson, P. A. 1941. Protection and Real Wages. *Review of
 Economic Studies* 9(1), pp. 58–73.

Sumner, W. G. 1906. *Folkways: A Study of the Sociological Importance of Usages, Manners,
 Customs, Mores and Morals*. Boston: Ginn and Co.

Suzumura, K. 2005. An Interview with Paul Samuelson: Welfare Economics,
 "Old" and "New," and Social Choice Theory. *Social Choice and Welfare* 25(2–3),
 pp. 327–356.

Suzumura, K. 2006. Shigeto Tsuru (1912–2006): Life, Work and Legacy. *European
 Journal of the History of Economic Thought* 13(4), pp. 613–620.

Swedberg, R. 1991. *Joseph A. Schumpeter: His Life and Thought*. Oxford: Polity Press.

Sweezy, A. R. 1934. The Interpretation of Subjective Value Theory in the Writings
 of the Austrian Economists. *Review of Economic Studies* 1(3), pp. 176–185.

Tarshis, L. 1947. *Elements of Economics*. Boston: Houghton Mifflin.

Terborgh, G. 1945. *The Bogey of Economic Maturity*. Chicago: Chemical and Allied
 Products Institute.

Thomas, J. J. 1989. The Early Econometric History of the Consumption Function.
 Oxford Economic Papers 41(1), pp. 131–149.

Thouless, R. H. 1936. *Straight and Crooked Thinking.* London: English Universities Press.

Thurstone, L. L. 1925. *Fundamentals of Statistics.* New York: Macmillan.

Tinbergen, J. 1951. Schumpeter and Quantitative Research in Economics. *Review of Economics and Statistics* 33(2), p. 109.

Tintner, G. 1944. The "Simple" Theory of Business Fluctuations: A Tentative Verification. *Review of Economic Statistics* 26(196), pp. 148–157.

Tintner, G. 1948. Review of Samuelson's *Foundations of Economic Analysis. Journal of the American Statistical Association* 43(243), pp. 497–499.

Tobin, J. 1976. Hansen and Public Policy. *Quarterly Journal of Economics* 90(1), pp. 32–37.

Tobin, J. 1988. A Revolution Remembered. *Challenge* 31(4), pp. 35–41.

Tobin, J. 1998. An Early Keynesian Herald in America. In *Keynesianism and the Keynesian Revolution in America: A Memorial Volume in Honour of Lorie Tarshis,* ed. O. F. Hamouda and B. B. Price, pp. 45–52. Cheltenham, UK: Edward Elgar.

Triffin, R. 1941. *Monopolistic Competition and General Equilibrium Theory.* Cambridge, MA: Harvard University Press.

Triffin, R. 1950. Schumpeter, Souvenirs d'un etudiant. *Economie appliquee* 3(3–4), pp. 413–416.

Tsuru, S. 1949. Toward Economic Stability in Japan. *Pacific Affairs* 22(4), pp. 357–366.

Tsuru, S. 2000. Shigeto Tsuru (b. 1912). In *Exemplary Economists*: Volume II: *Europe, Asia and Australasia,* ed. R. E. Backhouse and R. Middleton, pp. 1–28. Cheltenham, UK: Edward Elgar.

Tsuru, S. 2001. *Recollections of Many Crossroads: An Autobiography* [in Japanese]. Tokyo: Iwanami-Shoten.

Tyack, D. B., Lowe, R., and Hansot, E. 1984. *Public Schools in Hard Times: The Great Depression and Recent Years.* Cambridge, MA: Harvard University Press.

University of Chicago. 1932. *Announcements: The Social Sciences Number for the Sessions of 1932–33,* vol. 32(11). Chicago: University of Chicago Press.

University of Wisconsin. 1936. *Directory of Summer Session Students.* Madison: University of Wisconsin Press.

Van Horn, R. 2010a. Aaron Director. In *The Elgar Companion to the Chicago School of Economics,* ed. R Emmett, pp. 265–269. Cheltenham, UK: Edward Elgar.

Van Horn, R. 2010b. Harry Aaron Director: The Coming of Age of a Reformer Skeptic (1914–24). *History of Political Economy* 42(4), pp. 601–630.

Villard, H. H. 1941. *Deficit Spending and the National Income.* New York: Farrar & Rinehart.

Viner, J. 1931. Cost Curves and Supply Curves. *Journal of Economics* 3(1), pp. 23–46.

Viner, J. 1937. *Studies in the Theory of International Trade.* London: George Allen and Unwin.

Viner, J. 2013. *Lectures in Economics 301.* Edited by S. G. Medema and D. A. Irwin. Rutgers, NJ: Transaction.

Vining, R. 1949. Koopmans on the Choice of Variables to be Studies and the Methods of Measurement. *Review of Economics and Statistics* 31(2), pp. 77–86.

von Neumann, J., and Morgenstern, O. 1944. *The Theory of Games and Economic Behavior*. Princeton, NJ: Princeton University Press.

Walter, M. L. 1990. *Science and Cultural Crisis: An Intellectual Biography of Percy Williams Bridgman (1882–1961)*. Stanford, CA: Stanford University Press.

Ward, H. 1926. *Thobbing: A Seat at the Circus of the Intellect*. Indianapolis, IN: Bobbs Merrill.

Warken, O. W. 1979. *A History of the National Resources Planning Board, 1933–1943*. Edited by F. Freidel. New York: Garland.

Weintraub, E. R. 2014. MIT's Openness to Jewish Economists. In *MIT and the Transformation of American Economics*, Supplement to *History of Political Economy*, vol. 46. ed. E. R. Weintraub, pp. 45–59. Durham, NC: Duke University Press.

Whittaker, E. T., and Robinson, G. 1926. *The Calculus of Observations: A Treatise on Numerical Mathematics*. London: Blackie.

Williams, J. H. 1939. Graduate School of Public Administration: Fiscal Policy Seminar, 1937–38. *Official Register of Harvard University* 36(4), pp. 307–310.

Williams, J. H. 1940. Graduate School of Public Administration: Fiscal Policy Seminar, 1938–39. *Official Register of Harvard University* 36(12), pp. 342–345.

Wilson, E. B. 1903. The So-called Foundations of Geometry. *Archiv fur Mathematik und Statistik* 6(3), pp. 104–122.

Wilson, E. B. 1912. *Advanced Calculus*. Boston: Ginn and Co.

Wilson, E. B. 1920. *Aeronautics: A Class Text*. New York: John Wiley.

Wilson, E. B. 1923. Keynes on Probability. *Bulletin of the American Mathematical Society* 29(7), pp. 319–322.

Wilson, E. B. 1926. Statistical Inference. *Science* 63(1629), pp. 289–296.

Wilson, E. B. 1935. Generalization of Pareto's Demand Theorem. *Quarterly Journal of Economics* 49(4), pp. 715–717.

Wilson, E. B. 1939. Pareto versus Marshall. *Quarterly Journal of Economics* 53(4), pp. 645–650.

Wilson, E. B. 1946. *Review of Economics and Statistics* 28(3), pp. 173–174.

Winch, D. 2013. *Malthus: A Very Short Introduction*. Oxford: Oxford University Press.

Wolf, M. C. 1936. Symmetric Functions of Non-commutative Elements. *Duke Mathematical Journal*, 2(4), pp. 626–637.

Wolf, M. C., and Wolf, L. A. 1938. The Linear Equation in Matrices with Elements in a Division Algebra. *Bulletin of the American Mathematical Society* 44(9, Part I), p. 639.

Wright, D. M. 1948. Review of L. R. Klein. *The Keynesian Revolution. American Economic Review* 38(1), pp. 145–152.

Wright, Q., ed. 1932, *Gold and Currency Stabilization*. Chicago: University of Chicago Press.

Young, W. 1987. *Interpreting Mr. Keynes: The IS-LM Enigma*. Boulder, CO: Westview.

Yule, G. U. 1911. *Introduction to the Theory of Statistics*. London: Griffin.

INDEX

Bowman Committee, 443–448
Bradley, Philip, 121, 126–127
Brewster, Ellis, 560–561, 565
Bridgman, Percy, 83–84, 124, 138, 162, 165,
 171, 199–201, 206, 276, 292, 334,
 450, 620
Bright, Arthur, 437
Brinton, Crane, 126, 197
Bronfenbrenner, Martin, 71, 86, 395, 593
Brown, Douglass, 238–239
Brüning, Heinrich, 253
Bryan, Malcolm, 383
Bryce, Robert, 241–243, 252, 266
Buchanan, James, 98
Buchanan, Norman, 41
Buckley, Oliver, 443
Buckley, William F., 596
Bullock, Charles, 107–108, 119, 161
Burbank, Harold, 105–106, 109, 135, 167,
 240, 251, 301–308, 310, 312, 438,
 452–453, 455, 533, 557–558, 601, 619
Bureau of Labor Statistics, 344, 391, 484
Bureau of the Budget, 383, 393, 489
Burk, Abram. *See* Bergson, Abram
Burk, Gus, 186
Burns, Arthur, 108, 160, 170, 510, 586, 622
Bush, Vannevar, 318, 432, 440, 443–445,
 447, 624

Cairnes, John Elliott, 46
Caldwell, Robert, 567, 570, 572
Capital theory, 137, 183–185, 215–216,
 337–338, 378, 600, 625, 629
Capitalism, 81, 85, 139, 240, 257, 355, 375,
 447, 469, 527, 559, 564, 568, 586, 591,
 502–505, 579–580, 582–583
Carlson, Dr., 57
Carnap, Rudolf, 276, 450
Carnegie, Dale, 329
Carpenter, Donald, 571–573
Carter, Charles, 475
Carver, Harry, 72
Carver, Thomas Nixon, 82, 107, 119
Casals, Pablo, 87
Cassel, Gustav, 34, 66–68, 88, 279, 336
Catchings, Waddill, 247
Chamberlin, Edward, 55, 104–106, 109–116,
 118, 121, 137, 164, 238–239, 284, 296,
 302, 306–310, 332, 335–336, 453–454,
 546, 601, 614
Chase, Stuart, 407–408, 503
Chatelier, Henri Le, 282
Chesterman, Frank, 560–564
Chicago Plan, 81
Chomsky, Noam, 619
Circular flow of income, 53, 88, 243, 577.
 See also Wheel of wealth

Clark, John Bates, 50, 64–65, 134, 332
Clark, John Maurice, 50–51, 86, 176–177, 247,
 263–264, 268, 335, 344, 362, 373, 454,
 511, 513, 525, 527, 529–531
Clemence, Ellie, 534
Clemence, Richard, 534–537, 542, 545, 577
Coase, Ronald, 98
Cobb, Charles, 83
Coffman, President, 245
Coil, John, 439–440
Cole, Fay-Cooper, 59
Coleman, George, 498–499
Colm, Gerhard, 383, 393, 508
Colwell, E. C., 604, 606
Commons, John Rogers, 244
Compton, Arthur, 51
Compton, Karl, 51, 296, 307–309, 317–318,
 321, 432–433, 440, 444–445, 533, 556,
 560, 562–5, 569–572, 594–595, 597,
 609, 611, 619
Conant, James Bryant, 106, 300–301, 311,
 444–445, 570
Conrad, Alfred, 305
Consumer theory, 98, 122–123, 145, 156, 168,
 177, 179, 182–183, 196, 201–211, 259,
 276, 284–285, 291, 332, 334, 360, 461,
 463, 476, 652. *See also* Indifference curves;
 Utility; Revealed preference; Propensity to
 consume
Consumption. *See* Consumer theory; Propensity
 to consume; Investment, and saving
Consumption-loan model, 214, 615
Convex sets, 287, 330
Cornfield, Jerome, 602
Cottrell, Leonard, 60
Coughlin, Charles, 19
Coulter, Merle, 36, 38–39, 41
Cournot, Augustin, 113, 137, 332
Cowles Commission, 146, 348, 350, 509, 603,
 605, 607, 509–511, 621–622, 628–629
Crawford, Edna, 126–127
Crawford, Marion, 126–131, 136, 146–147,
 166, 219–220, 222, 228–231, 243,
 245–246, 252, 270, 273, 294, 304,
 312–313, 326–327, 351, 457, 511,
 602–603, 609–611, 619, 627–628
Crawford, Will, 126
Crum, Leonard, 106, 108–110, 165, 246, 296,
 303, 309, 310, 621
Currie, Lauchlin, 81, 236, 253, 382–383,
 417–418
Curtis, Charles, 197

Davidson, Norman, 17, 67–68
Davis, Harold, 350–351
Delano, Frederick, 386, 399
Descartes, René, 26

Oligopoly, 68, 112, 115, 117, 335, 545
Operationalism, 83–84, 98, 122–124, 138,
    145, 148, 199–201, 205–208, 211, 216,
    275–277, 284, 292, 331, 334, 338, 340,
    363, 450–451, 476, 480, 519, 618,
    620–621, 628
Orear, Jay, 14

Pareto, Vilfredo, 114–115, 143, 146, 151,
    168–169, 187–189, 191, 196–198, 205,
    209, 285, 292, 332, 425, 465, 468
Parsons, Talcott, 306
Pearson, Karl, 150
Pechman, Joseph, 396
Pericles, 39
Perlman, Mark, 303
Perlman, Selig, 303
Perlo, Victor, 420–422
Persons, Warren, 107–108, 614
Peterson, Nicholas, 559
Pigou, Arthur Cecil, 49, 137, 157, 176, 187,
    328, 361, 362, 363, 463, 522, 535, 602
Piore, Frank, 433
Pitts, Walter, 434, 437
Planck, Max, 48–49, 51, 235
Planning,
    centralized, 52, 559, 574–575, 584
    and full employment, 494
    post-emergency, 384–387, 389, 391–413,
        428, 430, 451, 490. See also Forecasting
    of science, 439–448, 624
Poincare, Henri, 140, 142, 148
Popper, Karl, 201, 207, 276
Population, 219–222, 247, 255, 257, 259–260,
    267, 269, 323, 337, 349, 351–353, 385,
    388, 404, 528, 548, 616, 627
Population, Malthusian theory of, 23, 27–28,
    367–368, 465, 616
Positivism, 140, 171, 200, 201; see also
    Vienna Circle
Pottinger, David, 455
Proctor, Redfield, 570
Propensity to consume, 258, 262, 345,
    357–358, 367–370, 373–375, 417, 424,
    426–427, 483, 495, 527. See also
    Investment, and saving
Psychoanalysis, 73
Public finance, 50, 134, 161, 167, 251, 275,
    309–310, 326, 424, 427, 430, 533,
    561, 623
Purchasing power parity, 68–69

Quantity theory of money, 70, 78–79, 97, 177,
    261, 350, 359–360, 528, 551, 553, 596
Queeny, 503
Quesnay, François, 88, 119

Quine, Willard van Orman, 196, 201, 207, 216,
    276, 450, 618

Rabi, Isidor Isaac, 443, 445–446, 449,
    621, 624
Ramsey, Frank, 362, 379, 528
Rate of interest,
    and employment, 224, 258, 261, 362, 366,
        525
    and investment, 183–185, 249, 427, 550
    and monetary expansion, 175
    and saving, 415–416
    and stationary state, 379, 378–381
    and uncertainty, 430
    and velocity, 357
    theory of, 56, 72, 80, 121, 184–185, 196,
        211–214, 216, 256, 354, 358, 366,
        367–369
    wartime, 430, 496–499
Ratner, David, 20
Ratner, Stanley, 20
Reder, Melvin, 475–476
Reisinger, Annie, 134
Revealed preference, 94, 124, 206, 216. See also
    Consumer theory
Ricardo, David, 87, 137, 141, 529
Riley, Rod, 383
Ringo, Elizabeth, 332, 334, 425, 428
Robbins, Lionel, 29–31, 49, 171, 188–189,
    206, 276, 334, 379, 466, 470, 540
Robertson, Dennis, 78, 176, 266, 341,
    362, 383
Robinson, G., 163, 185
Robinson, Joan, 65, 82, 88, 110–111, 116, 129,
    137, 142, 224, 241, 332, 335–336, 365,
    376, 518–519, 600
Rockefeller, David, 147
Rogers, Will, 51
Roll, Erich/Eric, 124, 270–272, 388, 551
Roll, Freda, 270, 388
Roos, Charles, 495
Roosa, Robert, 437
Roosevelt, Franklin Delano, 19, 41, 50, 63,
    68, 90–91, 109, 131, 197–198, 236,
    238, 248, 387, 400–401, 408, 429,
    440–441, 443, 499–501, 504, 514, 547,
    557, 624
Rosenblueth, Arturo, 433
Rosovsky, Henry, 301–303, 305
Rostow, Walt, 392
Rothko, Mark, 31
Ruml, Beardsley, 386, 503, 566, 574
Ruskin, John, 49, 51, 95
Russell, Bertrand, 43
Russell, Dora, 43
Ruth, Ethel, 9, 11

Altman, Oscar, on, 390
Freeman, Harold, and, 320
Friedman, Milton, and, 603
Klein, Lawrence, and, 520
Lotka, Alfred, on, 219–222
Perlo, Victor, on, 420–422
produced by NRC/NRPB, 373, 542, 549
Schumpeter, Joseph, on, 132, 141, 143
statistical analysis of the cycle, 132,
    138–139, 246, 340–345
statistical laboratory at Chicago, 286
statistical studies of innovation, 320, 324
theory of, 345–351
unemployment, 371, 372, 373,
    404, 222–224
Wilson, E. B., on, 157, 159, 165, 194, 297,
    149–154, 149–154, 162–163
Steffens, Lincoln, 43
Stein, Gertrude, 75
Steine, Jacob, 5
Stephan, Frederick, 221
Stevens, Stanley Smith, 450
Stigler, George, 71–72, 87, 94, 98, 336, 379,
    398, 464–465, 469, 475, 553, 605, 608,
    612, 616–617
Stolper, Gustav, 134, 266
Stolper, Wolfgang, 137, 147, 219, 229–233,
    306, 456, 475, 551–553
Stolper-Samuelson theorem, 230–233
Stone, Richard, 426
Stratton, Julius, 433
Stratton, Samuel, 566, 596
Summers, Harold, 5, 20–21, 616
Summers, Lawrence, 588
Summers, Robert, 10, 20, 21, 616
Sumner, William Graham, 29–30
Supply and demand 34, 47, 48, 57, 80, 97,
    120–121, 172–173, 223, 229, 278, 286,
    288–289, 291, 321, 323, 366, 368, 368,
    371, 373, 376–377, 537, 543, 545, 547,
    552, 554
Swedberg, Richard, 306
Sweezy, Alan, 135, 207, 216, 276, 285, 311,
    383, 551–553, 586
Sweezy, Paul, 135, 242, 327, 335, 399, 564
Swope, Gerald, 317

Taft, Robert, 402, 408–409
Tarshis, Lorie, 242, 252, 534, 549, 567–569,
    571, 576, 579
Tate, John, 443
Taussig, Frank, 64–65, 87, 105, 107, 110, 119,
    126, 134–137, 177, 179, 180, 186, 232,
    301, 332, 537, 547, 559
Tawney, R. H., 29
Taylor, Horace, 453–454, 601
Taylor, Overton, 109

Temporary National Economic Committee
    (TNEC), 382–383, 390
Terborgh, George, 588
Theorems, operationally meaningful. *See*
    Operationalism
Thermodynamics, 119, 144, 151, 156, 162,
    165, 198–199, 202, 274, 291, 297,
    450, 472
Thinking, straight and crooked, 41–43
Thouless, Robert, 42, 56
Thresher, Alden, 318
Thurstone, Louis, 38
Time, as concept in economics, 117, 123,
    168–169, 177, 183–185, 199, 213–214,
    220–222, 287–288, 291, 333, 338, 344,
    366–367, 378–380
Tinbergen, Jan, 143, 263, 598, 599
Tintner, Gerhard, 475, 510
Tobin, James, 258–259, 422, 614, 617, 629
Treasury, United States, 245, 327, 358,
    382–383, 496–499, 610
Triffin, Robert, 124–125, 136–138, 141, 147,
    332, 601
Truman, Harry, 514, 590
Tsuru, Masako, 131, 327, 602–603
Tsuru, Shigeto, 111, 112, 121–122, 124–128,
    131, 147, 215, 223, 306, 327, 564,
    601–603
Tucker, Donald, 318, 572
Tuve, Merle, 441, 445

Ulam, Stanislaw, 196, 198, 618, 621
Ullmann, Joseph, 347–348
Unemployment. *See also* National income;
    Investment, and output
    involuntary, 526, 371–373
Unity of science movement, 450
University of Chicago
    attempt to recruit Samuelson, 603–612
    Hutchins program, 22–24
Usher, Abbott, 29, 109, 167, 456–459, 601
Utility, 49, 54, 88–89, 122–124, 137,
    156, 144–145, 151–152, 167–169,
    181–182, 187–188, 201, 203–210,
    213–214, 216, 226, 279–281, 283,
    285–286, 332, 337, 379, 461, 463,
    466, 468, 470, 630

Vandermeulen, Daniel, 437, 556
Veblen, Thorstein, 92, 93, 94, 157
Vienna Circle, 201, 207, 216, 276, 450
Villard, Henry, 428
Viner, Jacob, 24, 49, 70–71, 78, 79, 81, 86–90,
    96–97, 103, 105, 110, 126, 136, 177,
    179, 212, 230, 232, 253, 332, 336, 604,
    606–607, 614, 617–618
Vining, Rutledge, 392, 510, 622, 629

Wald, Abraham, 336, 347
Wald, George, 450
Walker, Francis, 31, 297, 613
Wallace, Henry, 501
Wallis, Allen, 71–72, 87,
    94, 104, 605
Walras, Leon, 88, 114, 210, 289, 475
Walsh, John, 311
War Production Board (WPB), 459, 479–488,
    489–490, 492, 508, 514, 621
Ward, Henshaw, 66
Weaver, Warren, 443, 446
Webb, Beatrice, 64
Webb, Sidney, 64
Welfare economics, 49–54, 94, 96, 98, 137,
    145, 169, 171, 186–192, 208–210,
    224–229, 244, 328, 335, 368, 456–457,
    461–470, 478, 625. *See also* Social Welfare
    Function
Welfare provision, 400–401, 502, 583, 587,
    400–401
Wheel of wealth, 53–54, 578, 625. *See also*
    Circular flow of income
White, Harry Dexter, 126, 327, 383, 504
Whitehead, Alfred North, 126, 193–194, 198,
    276, 351
Whittaker, E. T., 163, 185
Whyte, William, 197
Wicksell, Knut, 137
Wicksteed, Philip, 137
Wiener, Norbert, 166, 347, 433–434, 450, 474,
    619, 621
Wieser, Friedrich, 170

Wiesner, Jerome, 433
Williams, John, 106, 109–110, 126, 177, 180,
    243, 245, 250, 252–253, 258, 296, 302,
    368, 438
Willits, Joseph, 321
Wilson, E. Bright, 196, 292, 349, 618
Wilson, Charles, 439–441
Wilson, Edwin Bidwell, 67, 106–107, 110, 119,
    123–124, 130, 142, 144–146, 148–165, 168,
    177–179, 182, 185, 193–195, 198, 201–204,
    210–211, 214, 216, 219, 236, 251, 259,
    274–275, 283, 286–287, 291–292, 294–299,
    303–313, 329, 348–349, 353, 451, 453–434,
    457, 462, 470–472, 477–478, 510–511, 558,
    601, 615, 618, 620–622,
    625–627, 630
Wilson, John D., 388
Wilson, Woodrow, 385, 403
Wirth, Louis, 23, 27, 60
Wolf, Louise, 166
Wolf, Margarete, 166–167, 284
Woodward, Robert, 196, 618
Wordsworth, William, 196, 234
Working, Elmer, 120
Wright, Chester, 71
Wright, David McCord, 410, 455, 552, 573,
    593, 598
Wright, Quincy, 81
Wylie, Alexander, 126
Wylie, Rosemary, 126–127

Yntema, Theodore, 78, 88
Young, Allyn, 35, 54, 303
Yule, Udny, 379